THE
CHRISTIAN
TRADITION *in*

English Literature

THE CHRISTIAN TRADITION *in* *English Literature*

POETRY, PLAYS, AND SHORTER PROSE

PAUL CAVILL AND **HEATHER WARD**

WITH **MATTHEW BAYNHAM** AND **ANDREW SWINFORD**

AND CONTRIBUTIONS FROM **JOHN FLOOD** AND **ROGER POOLEY**

ZONDERVAN®

ZONDERVAN.com/
AUTHORTRACKER
follow your favorite authors

We want to hear from you. Please send your comments about this book to us in care of zreview@zondervan.com. Thank you.

ZONDERVAN®

The Christian Tradition in English Literature
Copyright © 2007 by Paul Cavill and Heather Ward

Requests for information should be addressed to:

Zondervan, *Grand Rapids, Michigan 49530*

Library of Congress Cataloging-in-Publication Data

Cavill, Paul, 1956–
  The Christian tradition in English literature : poetry, plays, and shorter prose / Paul Cavill and Heather Ward with Matthew Baynham and Andrew Swinford and contributions from John Flood and Roger Pooley.
     p. cm.
  Includes bibliographical references.
  ISBN-13: 978-0-310-25515-4
  ISBN-10: 0-310-25515-5
  1. English literature—History and criticism. 2. Christianity and literature—England—History. 3. Christian literature, English—History and criticism. 4. Religion and literature. 5. Bible—In literature. I. Ward, Heather, 1951– II. Baynham, Matthew. III. Swinford, Andrew. IV. Flood, John. V. Pooley, Roger. VI. Title.
  PR145.C38 2007
  820.9'3823—dc22   2006037571

This book refers to the Bible in the King James, or Authorized, Version except where otherwise noted. There are two reasons for this. First, it is the English translation that is most influential and widely known from the seventeenth century to the present day, a popularity merited by its accuracy and literary qualities. Second, the work preserves a great deal of the best English translation and scholarship from earlier generations (see the essay 'The Bible and Prayer Book' in section 2). Thus, the KJV often represents the understanding and even the language of the Bible not only of the seventeenth and later centuries, but also of the earlier centuries back into the medieval period.

Readers unfamiliar with the Bible or coming to it for the first time will perhaps find that the KJV presents difficulties: some words have changed meaning, and we no longer use the pronouns *thou* and *ye*, or the singular present-tense verb-forms *hath*, *doth*, or *saith* in everyday discourse. For this reason, we recommend that newcomers to the Bible select a modern rendering such as the New International Version (NIV), where these linguistic forms do not impair the accessibility of the Bible message.

Interior design by Nancy Wilson

Printed in the United States of America

07 08 09 10 11 12 • 15 14 13 12 11 10 9 8 7 6 5 4 3 2 1

To
Doug Gallaher
without whom …

CONTENTS

ℐECTION 1:
THE MEDIEVAL PERIOD

Section 2:

RENAISSANCE, REFORMATION, AND REPUBLIC

Section 3:

THE RESTORATION AND THE EIGHTEENTH CENTURY

ᏚECTION 4:
THE ROMANTICS AND VICTORIANS

ℰECTION 5:

THE TWENTIETH CENTURY

SECTION 6:

THE CHRISTIAN TRADITION

SECTION 7:

GLOSSARY

PREFACE

This book is about the Christian aspects of English literature, from the Anglo-Saxons to the writers of the twentieth century. The need for such a book will be obvious to many, both those with a professional interest and those who care about understanding what they read. The Christian tradition in English literature is becoming the province of a few specialists, a minority interest. The simple fact is that teachers of literature regularly find that students have little or no knowledge of the Bible and its basic story line, its concepts and images, its characters and themes. Many teachers themselves will admit to lacking this knowledge. Indeed, when it comes to some aspects of the Christian tradition — say, the points debated between Calvinism and Arminianism or the ideas associated with scholasticism — even specialists may struggle. The result is that important Christian aspects of literature are often misunderstood and sometimes even misrepresented.

This book has been written for today's students, teachers, and readers. It aims at giving a sense of the importance and continuity of the Christian tradition in English literature; a sense of a coherent belief-system being expressed in very different ways; a sense of the validity and power of the Christian worldview over the centuries. It has been written in the belief that this is not only worthwhile from a pedagogical point of view, but also that it will aid enjoyment of literature. We have felt delight and relief ourselves, and often experienced it in others, when some puzzling passage or allusion has been explained. Our aim, then, is to help readers to read in an informed and intelligent fashion, and for them to be able to discuss the Christian aspects of literature with confidence.

Another important aim for the writers of this book was to engage in and model responsive and responsible literary criticism. We believe that criticism should respond to texts in their literary, linguistic, and social context and that the critic's primary role is to understand and then to communicate understanding. This has not always been a popular view in recent years. We recognise some dangers in privileging the Christian grand narrative, and indeed the literary-critical metanarrative, but the greater danger seems to us to reside in ignoring these when they so clearly inform the texts. We are dealing with a *tradition*, understandings and assumptions about the world passed on from generation to generation, adopted, rejected, questioned, and adjusted — but not lost. Ours is perhaps the first generation in over a millennium in which the Christian tradition is for some readers of English literature *terra incognita*, uncharted territory.

The book gives brief and informative essays on the Christian background to the texts and the way the texts interact with the Christian tradition. The aim is to inform and stimulate rather than to be exhaustive or confrontational. There is no single definitive approach: the language, the allusions, the structure, the characters, the style, the moral architecture, the themes, the social issues, the biblical framework, the intellectual basis of the texts may all feature in the discussion. Although the approach is often expository, we aim to leave room for discussion, disagreement, and open-ended debate. We express our opinions and views, relating them to the texts under discussion, but recognise that other readers might respond differently.

We hope this book will enable readers to enjoy and understand English literature more fully. We acknowledge that we have barely scratched the surface of the Christian tradition or English literature, but we hope that we have given enticing glimpses of the riches and the pleasure that are to be found by those who delve more deeply.

Finally, we should observe that though the book has been written by scholars who are practising Christians from different traditions, it does not assume any confessional stance in its readers.

—PAUL CAVILL AND HEATHER WARD, 2007

INTRODUCTION:
HOW TO USE THIS BOOK

There is one dogmatic instruction for how to use this book. It is this: read the author or text first. However useful the critical introduction might be, however tempting it is to have a preview of the issues in the literary work from these essays, it is always best to read, understand, and react to the literature first.

OUTLINE

The book is divided into five literary periods: from medieval to the twentieth century. Within those divisions there are introductory essays, overviews, and sometimes essays relating to particular issues that were important at the time. Most of the essays deal with writers and texts that feature in the main anthologies of English literature. For reasons of space, we have had to be selective and have chosen those writers and texts that seem to us best to repay analysis in terms of the Christian tradition. With some regret, we have relegated some of the great Romantic poets to mention only in the overview, partly because their preoccupations are in some ways similar, and partly because the Christian tradition features relatively little. Similarly, we have only chosen to treat those plays of Shakespeare that appear in one of the major anthologies.

The sixth section of the book deals with the Christian tradition itself: the Bible, Christian history and theology, and hymnology. This section briefly outlines the main themes and motifs in the tradition with a view to enabling the reader to see how the literary and Christian traditions interact.

A final section, the glossary, gives information about some Christian words and ideas that are used in the text. These are linked by means of marked keywords in the main text to glossarial sections; the symbols preceding the keywords are as follows:

* – terms relating to the Bible narratives
† – terms relating to Christian themes
‡ – general Christian terminology

THE ESSAYS

The essays are headed by the author or the text treated.

Then there are abbreviated references to the places where the text can be found in the Blackwell, Norton, and Oxford anthologies of literature (see the bibliography and abbreviations below). There are, of course, many other anthologies from various publishers, and many more will be released during the lifetime of this book. But experience suggests that while the Blackwell, Norton, and Oxford anthologies may be revised over the years, they are unlikely to go out of print: they are in some sense standard texts, widely used in Britain and America.

The writer and the work are then introduced and discussed. Where appropriate, information, references, and asides of various kinds are given in footnotes. The main body of the essay will analyse an issue or range of issues relating to the Christian tradition as it bears on the writer or the work. As mentioned above, elements in the text that are treated further in the glossary are identified with *, †, or ‡.

Questions follow. In the context of private study, these will isolate issues that repay further investigation and thought. In the context of class or seminar groups, the questions will be useful for stimulating discussion; they may also be set as essays.

A brief bibliography completes the essay. We have deliberately aimed at providing information about works that should be available in smaller college libraries — good older works, standard texts and editions, collections of essays — as well as recent books and articles that may be harder to find. Another criterion of selection has inevitably been that we have found the books accurate and formative in our own thinking. Some brief comments are added, as appropriate, to indicate what in particular the item is or where its excellences lie.

Abbreviations and Bibliography

ANTHOLOGY ABBREVIATIONS

BABL   Robert DeMaria, ed., *British Literature 1640–1789: An Anthology*, 2nd edn, Blackwell Anthologies, Oxford 2001.

BACL   Alister E. McGrath, ed., *Christian Literature: An Anthology*, Blackwell Anthologies, Oxford 2001.

BACS   Derek Pearsall, ed., *Chaucer to Spenser: An Anthology of Writing in English, 1375–1575*, Blackwell Anthologies, Oxford 1998.

BAECP   David Fairer and Christine Gerard, ed., *Eighteenth-Century Poetry: An Annotated Anthology*, 2nd edn, Blackwell Anthologies, Oxford 2004.

BAMD   Greg Walker, ed., *Medieval Drama: An Anthology*, Blackwell Anthologies, Oxford 2000.

BAOME   Elaine Treharne, ed., *Old and Middle English c.890 – c.1400: An Anthology*, 2nd edn, Blackwell Anthologies, Oxford 2003.

BAR   Duncan Wu, ed., *Romanticism: An Anthology*, 2nd edn, Blackwell Anthologies, Oxford 1998.

BARD   Arthur F. Kinney, ed., *Renaissance Drama: An Anthology of Plays and Entertainments*, Blackwell Anthologies, Oxford 1999.

BARestD   David Womersley, ed., *Restoration Drama: An Anthology*, Blackwell Anthologies, Oxford 2000.

BARL   Michael Payne and John Hunter, ed., *Renaissance Literature: An Anthology*, Blackwell Anthologies, Oxford 2003.

BASCP   Robert Cummings, ed., *Seventeenth-Century Poetry: An Annotated Anthology*, Blackwell Anthologies, Oxford 2000.

BAV   Valentine Cunningham, ed., *The Victorians: An Anthology of Poetry and Poetics*, Blackwell Anthologies, Oxford 2000.

NA1, NA2   M.H. Abrams and Stephen Greenblatt, ed., *The Norton Anthology of English Literature*, 2 vols, 7th edn, New York and London 2000.

OA1, OA2   Frank Kermode and John Hollander, ed., *The Oxford Anthology of English Literature*, 2 vols, New York, London and Toronto 1973.

SELECT BIBLIOGRAPHY OF BOOKS RELATING TO THE BIBLE AND CHRISTIAN TRADITION

Robert Alter and Frank Kermode, ed., *The Literary Guide to the Bible*, London 1987.

Dee Dyas and Esther Hughes, *The Bible in Western Culture: The Student's Guide*, London 2005.

Northrop Frye, *The Great Code: The Bible and Literature*, London 1982.

John B. Gabel and Charles B. Wheeler, *The Bible as Literature: An Introduction*, 2nd edn, New York 1990.

David Jasper, *The New Testament and the Literary Imagination*, London 1987.

David Jasper and Stephen Prickett, ed., *The Bible and Literature: A Reader*, Oxford 1999.

David Lyle Jeffrey, ed., *A Dictionary of Biblical Tradition in English Literature*, Grand Rapids, Mich., 1992.

Stephen Prickett, *Words and 'The Word': Language, Poetics, and Biblical Interpretation*, Cambridge 1986.

Stephen Prickett, ed., *Reading the Text: Biblical Criticism and Literary Theory*, Oxford 1991.

Section 1

THE MEDIEVAL PERIOD

1

Overview: The Middle Ages

INTRODUCTION

The most important point to note about literature of this early period is that we must dismiss all prejudices about its 'primitiveness'. The poet of *Beowulf* is a master of his language and a subtle theological thinker; Chaucer is one of the most delicate and deadly accurate of English satirists; the poet of *The Dream of the Rood* makes a magnificent drama of the *crucifixion; and Mak the sheep stealer is a character who can be compared, within limits, to Shakespeare's greatest comic creations. What will not be obvious from some anthologies, the Norton and Oxford anthologies especially, is that alongside the great verse of the Old English period there was a large and varied corpus of often vibrant prose. There are delightful stories (Ælfric's *Catholic Homilies* and *Lives of Saints*, see the samples in *BAOME* pp. 116 f), powerful sermons (Wulfstan's *Homilies*, see the *Sermo Lupi*, *BAOME* pp. 226 f), vivid and fast-moving historical narratives (the Anglo-Saxon Chronicle, see extracts in *BAOME* pp. 20 f), all originally composed in Old English, as well as fine translations of the Bible and Latin works such as Bede's *Ecclesiastical History*.

CONVERSION AND HEATHENISM

Before the conversion to Christianity there was no discursive writing in Old English. Some brief runic inscriptions survive from this time, but writing, using the Roman alphabet and the technology of ink and vellum, came with Christianity and remained under the influence of the church. Before writing, and contemporary with it, poets composing their verse extempore entertained warriors in their halls with tales of past heroes and celebrations of more recent heroic exploits. The oral style of alliterative verse, with its incremental variation and its heroic focus, survives to some extent in *Beowulf* and *The Battle of Maldon*; the metre itself is preserved several hundred years longer in the *Brut* of Layamon of the twelfth century (see extracts in *BAOME* pp. 359 f) and in *Piers Plowman* and *Sir Gawain and the Green Knight* of the fourteenth century. While the setting of *Beowulf* is heathen, and it records heathen practices such as cremation of the dead, it is nevertheless Christian in its outlook and preoccupations, and in fact heathenism in its particularity is hard to find in Old English literature.

Bede's *History* tells the story of the conversion of the Anglo-Saxons to Christianity. In fact, Bede's great theme, his grand narrative, is the conversion to Christianity. He records the story of Cædmon because it marked a further development of God's plan as Cædmon converted the teaching of the church into 'delightful verse' for the people, using their own language and poetry to encourage them in their faith. Though he was closer in time to English heathenism than any other major writer, he records nothing substantial about its practice. There is greater depth of Christian learning in synergy with the prevailing culture in Bede and *The Dream of the Rood* than appears almost anywhere before the ‡Reformation in the sixteenth century. Though the theological aspects may be less prominent than in these particular examples, that concern to engage with the developing and changing culture is a persistent feature of medieval literature.

THE EARLIEST ENGLISH LITERATURE

The Norman Conquest of 1066 did not bring an end to English literature: Ælfric's ‡homilies and Bede's *History* (and more) continued to be copied and used throughout the Middle English period (c.1100–1500), and Layamon and others adapted French materials to the native verse style and English language. What might be called the 'origin myth' changed, though. The Anglo-Saxons were concerned with conquest, secular and religious, and the *discontinuities* between themselves and the Celtic people they replaced, and heathenism itself. The French conquerors were paradoxically more concerned with the *continuities* between themselves and the Celts, their pre-Christian and magical traditions. In Middle English literature the confrontation between Christianity and culture ceases to be central, and the Christian religion becomes part of the mental and spiritual furniture, both ubiquitous and unremarkable. That is not to say that Middle English lacks depth or passion with regard to Christianity: one has only to read the lyrics to feel the power of the *crucifixion story (*Ye that Pasen by the Weye, Sunset on Calvary*[1]), or to see how the theme of †love is transmuted in Christian consciousness (*I Sing of a Maiden, Adam Lay Bound*). But the issues are more 'modern': namely, how the challenge of the Christian message may be framed for those to whom it seems familiar and dull; how,

---

1. Also known as *Now goth sonne under wode*, its first line.

indeed, those whose lives are shaped by the tradition may be helped to find it fresh and vital.

Chaucer takes the path of satire, showing the contempt of his ‡Monk for the 'olde thinges' and the callousness of self-interest in his ‡Friar, ‡Summoner, and ‡Pardoner. Langland opts for seriousness, with his ‡allegorical figures pointing to eternal realities; the Gawain poet, and to some degree the author of the *Ancrene Riwle*, explore the similarities and points of contact between knightly ideals and Christianity; Julian and Margery write with the immediacy of visionary experience and combine other-worldliness with earthy detail; the medieval plays often exploit broad comedy to make their point and bring the biblical message into the experience of ordinary people.

ENGLISH, FRENCH, AND LATIN

In many ways both language and literary styles in Middle English are more flexible than in Old English. In Old English there is one verse form, the alliterative metre depending on repeated consonant or vowel sounds within a strict four- or six-stress pattern in each line. Prose tends to eschew complex time relationships because of the two-tense verbal system and sometimes echoes the alliterative patterns of verse.

The Norman Conquest brought French courtly poetry with its variety of line length and rhyme arrangement, and with it, more complex syntax and new vocabulary. There are now different registers, broadly the popular (Anglo-Saxon), the courtly (French), and the learned (Latin). In the lyrics *Ye that Pasen by the Weye* and *Sunset on Calvary* all the vocabulary is of Anglo-Saxon origin; and in *Adam Lay Bound* only 'clerkes' and 'Deo Gratias' are respectively French and Latin, obliquely indicating the French dominance of the spheres of learning and religion. Chaucer's Knight 'loved chivalrye / Trouthe and honour, freedome and curteisye' (General Prologue, 45–6), and here the French and English terms are interleaved: though the senses of the English words 'trouthe' and 'freedome' are rather different today, in Middle English they nevertheless are still less abstract than 'chivalrye', 'honour', and 'curteisye'. Chaucer's Doctor can hardly be described without the learned Latin-derived French words 'apothecaries', 'letuaries', 'mesurable', superfluitee', 'norissing', and 'digestible'; Chaucer drily notes 'his studye was but litel on the Bible' (General Prologue, 440).

It was in this linguistic context that John Wyclif advocated the translation and use of the Bible in English. Wyclif's major works were in Latin and included attacks on the authority of the church and the ‡pope. The translation project was carried through by Wyclif's followers and published in 1389, five years after

Wyclif's death. A brief illustration may serve to show some of the qualities of the work. At John 10:12, the Wyclif version reads,

> Forsoth a marchaunt, and that is not schepherde, whos ben not the scheep his owne, seeth a wolf comynge, and he leeueth the scheep, and fleeth; and the wolf rauyschith, and disparplith the scheep.[2]

Chaucer's ‡Parson:

> kepte wel his folde,
> So that the wolf ne made it nought miscarye:
> He was a shepherd and nought a mercenarye.
>
> —General Prologue 514–17

The difference between the two passages, apart from the fact that the Wyclif version intends to translate as closely as possible the Latin Vulgate (which it does, almost word for word: 'mercennarius et qui non est pastor cuius non sunt oves propriae ...'[3]), lies in the choice of vocabulary: the Wyclif version chooses two words of French origin, *marchaunt* and *disparplith*. The first of these is imprecise, the same word used for the merchant of Matthew 13:45, a trader in pearls (see the *parable of the pearl of great price): contrast Chaucer's precise and effective use of the Latin word *mercenarye*. The second, *disparplith*, is a rare and now unfamiliar word meaning 'scatters'; Chaucer's word *miscarye* has two main senses, 'destroy' and 'bring to abortive birth' (the latter sense common from the sixteenth century), both of which capture clearly what wolves do to sheep.

Although the Wyclif translation is from the Latin (not the original Hebrew and Greek), and although it is over-literal and difficult to read, so far as the authorities were concerned it was subversive. In 1428 Wyclif's bones were dug up and burned at the order of a church council (the Council of Constance, 1415) by way of executing judgement on his theological 'errors'. In many ways the ideas in Wyclif's work anticipated the great upheaval of the ‡Reformation over a hundred years later, when again the issues of authority and access to the Bible in the vernacular would divide the nations of Europe.

By the end of the Middle English period, literature in English had broken down some of the divisions that helped maintain social, political, and ecclesiastical structures of authority. Literacy was more common than at any time

---

2. The quotation is from the normalised version of Rev. Joseph Bosworth and George Waring, ed., *The Gothic and Anglo-Saxon Gospels ... with the Versions of Wycliffe and Tyndale*, 3rd edn, London 1888.

3. The quotation of the Vulgate Latin is from Robertus Weber, ed., *Biblia sacra: iuxta vulgatam versionem*, 4th edn rev. by B. Fischer *et al.*, Stuttgart 1994.

before; French and Latin vocabulary, courtly and learned literary styles, had been assimilated into the vernacular. The Bible was accessible to some people in their own language. The time was ripe for a flowering of literature, a renewal of popular Christianity; a sense of potential in its widest sense is to be found. The power of Shakespeare or Milton is not a sudden descent of genius after the barrenness of the so-called Dark Ages; it arises out of the creative resolution of tensions, linguistic, social, and theological amongst others, of the Middle English period.

QUESTIONS

1. Compare and contrast *The Dream of the Rood* and *Ye that Pasen by the Weye* and *Sunset on Calvary*. What appeals to you about each of them, and what do you think are the most striking differences between them?
2. Do you agree that 'the confrontation between Christianity and culture ceases to be central' in Middle English literature, whereas it remains the core focus for Old English literature? Choose some examples to justify your view.

BIBLIOGRAPHY

J.A. Burrow, *Medieval Writers and Their Work: Middle English Literature and Its Background, 1100–1500*, rev. edn, London 1993.

David Daniell, *The Bible in English: Its History and Influence*, London 2003, is a recent and full treatment of the origins and development of English biblical translation.

An excellent introduction to Christian themes and images in medieval literature is Dee Dyas, *Images of Faith in English Literature, 700–1550: An Introduction*, London 1997.

For an overview of Old English literature, its language, styles, and themes, see Malcolm Godden and Michael Lapidge, ed., *The Cambridge Companion to Old English Literature*, Cambridge 1991.

For Wycliffite writings, both translations and expositions, see Anne Hudson, ed., *Selections from English Wycliffite Writings*, Cambridge 1978.

David Wallace, ed., *The Cambridge History of Medieval English Literature*, Cambridge 1999.

2

BEDE AND CÆDMON'S *HYMN*

[*BACL* pp. 126 f; *BAOME* pp. 1, 4 f; *NA1* pp. 23 f; *OA1* p. 19.
The translation used here is that in *NA1*.]

Bede's whole life was shaped by the Christian tradition. At the age of seven, he was committed to the ‡monastery of Jarrow in northeast England, where he spent the rest of his life, fifty-five years or so. In the godly, disciplined, and learned environment of the monastery he flourished and became a 'candle of the church', one whose writings became standard works used and copied throughout western Europe. In his lifetime Bede was famous for his biblical commentaries, educational and scientific works, but in later times his *Ecclesiastical History of the English People* has emerged as his most significant book. Bede's entire surviving output was written in Latin.

The *Ecclesiastical History* tells the story of the settlement of Britain by the Anglo-Saxons and how these heathen invaders subsequently converted to Christianity. Bede sees the Anglo-Saxons as God's scourge on the wicked British, who, though they were Christian in name, failed to live Christian lives. Bede borrowed much of this material relating to the fifth and sixth centuries from Gildas, a Briton, but in later episodes Bede is himself dismissive of Celtic Christians, seeing them as obstinate. For example, Bede refers to the battle of Chester c. 616, in which 1,200 ‡monks from the Welsh ‡monastery of Bangor were slaughtered by the heathen Anglo-Saxon king Æthelfrith, as the fulfilment of a †prophecy; Augustine of Canterbury had predicted that if the Welsh did not help to convert the Anglo-Saxons they would suffer. And Bede makes much of the fact that at the Synod of Whitby of 664, some Celtic Christians refused to accept the discipline and authority of Rome and exiled themselves to Ireland.

Bede was a careful and accurate historian, but his work is history in the mould of the biblical Acts of the Apostles and later ecclesiastical historians such as Eusebius of Cæsarea. History is interpreted as the working out of God's purposes, with miracles and †prophecies, and signs and wonders of all kinds being performed by ‡saints. In the story of Cædmon, the underlying theme is the conversion of the English, which Cædmon assists by making the Christian message known in a new way, namely in the highly specialised form of

Anglo-Saxon poetry. According to the story, Cædmon was given the gift of poetry by an †angelic visitor, though he had never before known any poetry or songs and deliberately avoided occasions when songs were sung because he disliked them.

There are many parallels to the story of Cædmon in biblical and early Christian literature.[1] For example, St Peter's vision in Acts 10, when he is told to kill and eat animals not permitted by Jewish dietary laws, and so learns that the Christian message is for all, not just for Jews, is similar. Cædmon is told to do what he would not otherwise have chosen to do, that is to sing, and so the Christian message is more widely made known. Bede emphasises Cædmon's missionary significance not only by giving an account of the effect of his verse and the range of subjects he treated (all of which fell into the category of medieval basic instruction for Christians, the ‡catechism),[2] but also by means of the miraculous element. In addition, he makes Cædmon's gift correspond to that of St Paul, quoting Galatians 1:1: he was 'not taught … by men or by human agency', but called by God.

With such a build-up, some have found the *Hymn* that Cædmon composed, and that was subsequently passed on and recorded in manuscripts of Bede's *History*, an anticlimax. Bede remarks that the verse he records is only the first lines of Cædmon's work; and he acknowledges that the Old English version (which he did not record but clearly knew) could not be translated into Latin 'without losing some of the beauty and dignity'. The style of Old English poetry is iterative; that is, its main ornament is expansive semi-repetition. In the Old English *Hymn*, the concept 'God' is cloaked in seven different terms, one of which is repeated ('eternal Lord', *ece Drihten*), as well as the pronoun 'he'. Most often these terms use an ordinary word meaning 'lord', with an adjective (e.g. 'eternal') or a modifier (e.g. 'heaven-kingdom's') to show that God is both like and unlike human kings. He has power, but his power is over all things; he is king and lord, but he is eternal.

Though this pattern is repeated, it is not *mere* repetition. God in his very nature merits human praise as 'heaven-kingdom's Guardian' (line 1); while in his care towards humankind in *creation he is 'mankind's Guardian' (line 7). The guardianly nature of God is shown in different aspects; and in the process, the familiar Anglo-Saxon idea of a human king as a guardian to his people is given new meaning, since God is guardian not only of the †heavenly kingdom

---

1. G.A. Lester, 'The Cædmon story and its analogues', *Neophilologus* 58 (1974), 225–37. This article shows that there are analogues in non-Western literature too.

2. See V. Day, 'The influence of the catechetical *narratio* on Old English and some other medieval literature', *Anglo-Saxon England* 3 (1974), 51–61.

but of all people too. God is seen in the variety of his personal characteristics, while humankind is seen in general. Cædmon thus works with familiar ideas but expands their range enormously, creating the vocabulary of a vernacular poetic theology. For Bede, he was the finest Christian poet in English, having many imitators.

Bede specifies that Cædmon was a herdsman on the ‡monastic estate at Whitby, and that he entered the monastery there. Cædmon's name is Celtic (not Anglo-Saxon) and Bede has to specify that Cædmon's language was English, indicating that there were still speakers of Celtic in the northeast of England at this time. Whitby was a monastery reformed by Abbess Hild under the guidance of Bishop Aidan, chief missionary of the Celtic Christian party. The Synod of Whitby was held there to debate which style of Christianity, Roman or Celtic, should be adopted in Northumbria. Bede had little sympathy with the Celtic party, as we have seen, but in humble Cædmon and in the outcome of the Whitby council, he saw Celt and Saxon draw together in unity under the guidance of God for the more effective preaching of the Christian message.

QUESTIONS

1. The story of Cædmon is known only from Bede's history, and is not independently recorded elsewhere. Would you find Cædmon's *Hymn* interesting or significant without Bede's story?
2. Is there any overlap between stories of miracles in Anglo-Saxon sources and the fabulous elements in medieval romance, or 'magical realism' in contemporary literature? If so, what function do these elements have?

BIBLIOGRAPHY

Paul Cavill, *Anglo-Saxon Christianity*, London 1999, contains a chapter on Bede and Cædmon focusing on aspects of 'conversion' in the story.

Bertram Colgrave and R.A.B. Mynors, *Bede's Ecclesiastical History of the English People*, London 1969, is the standard text in Latin with facing-page English translation.

David Howlett, 'The theology of Cædmon's Hymn', *Leeds Studies in English*, New Series 7 (1974), 1–12, argues that the poem is essentially ‡Trinitarian.

P.R. Orton, 'Cædmon and Christian poetry', *Neuphilologische Mitteilungen* 84 (1983), 163–70.

A.H. Smith, ed., *Three Northumbrian Poems*, rev. edn, Exeter 1978: an edition of the earlier versions of the poem.

3

THE DREAM OF THE ROOD

[*BACL* pp. 137 f; *BAOME* pp. 108 f; *NA1* pp. 26 f; *OA1* pp. 104 f]

There are many specifically Christian poems in Old English, ranging from long heroic adventures of ‡saints to short riddles with solutions such as 'Gospel-book'. A good number of such poems were collected in the Anglo-Saxon manuscript now kept at Vercelli in Italy and known as the Vercelli Book. The book includes a selection of prose ‡homilies as well as poems and clearly was a collection of devotional material, perhaps for the use of a wealthy ‡pilgrim. A remarkable thing about the poem now known as *The Dream of the Rood* is that it combines heroic adventure, elegy, riddle, and sermon styles in an almost seamless blend to tell the story of the *crucifixion of Christ and its significance.

The poem opens with the voice of a dreamer telling us of a dream in which he saw a tree lifted up in the sky, exalted and adorned with gold and precious stones, gazed upon by †angels and everything on earth. The glory of the vision makes the dreamer feel uneasy with himself, a feeling exacerbated when the tree's gold covering changes and blood shows through. The dreamer watches in mingled awe and horror, until the tree speaks. The poem now borrows the mechanism of the riddle as the tree tells its own story; and at the same time, it demystifies the riddle with which the poem starts as it explains the disturbing mixture of glory and horror. The tree reveals that it was the instrument of death for the young hero, God himself, who willingly embraced it, and who bled and died on it.

The first part of the tree's story is at once elegiac and heroic. The tree is mistreated and made into an instrument of torture, a †cross or 'rood' (the Anglo-Saxon word for a cross). There is an elegiac tone of lament as the cross tells of its experiences, both before and after the *crucifixion. When the young hero, Christ, appears, the tree responds with loyalty and obedience to his command to stand fast, just as a warrior would do in battle for his lord. But the embrace by which that loyalty is shown is the fastening of Christ to the cross; and the cross, the loyal retainer sharing his lord's suffering, by his very loyalty becomes the slayer of his lord. Eventually the lord is taken from the cross to be buried, and it is left standing bereft, until it too is buried. But later it is discovered and covered with precious metal by the lord's friends.

The †cross then goes on to explain this strange course of events in the mode of the sermon. It explains that the cross was once thought of as the most horrible device of torture, but since Christ died on it, it has become honoured and respected: a way of life rather than a means of death. The cross goes on to expound the Christian ‡creed (very clearly using the Apostles' Creed here) and talk of its role as the sign of salvation at the †last judgement. The mingled awe and horror with which the vision began, with gold and blood, has become a visual image for the paradoxes of the *crucifixion: death as the way to life, suffering as the way to glory.

The dreamer responds by making the †cross his guide and friend and looks forward to the time when the cross will take him to the eternal banquet of †heaven, where he can enjoy the bliss of being at home, surrounded by those he loves. The poem closes with a triumphant expedition by Christ from heaven to rescue and bring home those who were languishing in †hell too.

Central to the effectiveness of this poem is the apparently effortless way in which it translates the historical and theological detail of the *crucifixion into the Anglo-Saxon cultural milieu. Christ becomes a heroic lord, the †cross a loyal retainer facing a terrible dilemma in a climactic battle. †Heaven is an Anglo-Saxon hall with feasting and fellowship, and the †harrowing of hell (the expedition at the end of the poem) is a warlike foray in which captives are res-cued and brought home. This 'translation' occurs not only at the level of struc-ture but also within the vocabulary. When Christ's retainers take him down from the cross, he is 'weary of limb' and he 'rests': these are Old English heroic euphemisms for death, used widely in poems such as *Beowulf* and elsewhere. The retainers put 'the Wielder of Triumphs' into a tomb they have made, just as Beowulf's retainers put his remains in a barrow. But the euphemisms, and the epithet 'Wielder of Triumphs' for a dead man, give the glimmer of hope that death is not the end for this hero: the language hints at a theological point.

The device of the †cross allows the poet to explore the suffering of the *crucifixion without detracting from Christ's deity or from his willingness to undergo death on the cross. These were major debating points in the early church, and the poet shows great skill in using the cross to convey the nasty reality of crucifixion while avoiding theological controversy.[1] At the same time, the cross faces the dilemma of obeying a lord who is apparently wrong, where

---

1. Rosemary Woolf, 'Doctrinal influences on *The Dream of the Rood*', *Medium Ævum* 27 (1958), 137–53, explores the theological tensions of the time in some detail.

obedience leads to defeat and humiliation. The poet thus brings the events of the crucifixion within the range of experience of the Anglo-Saxon warrior, confronting him with issues of loyalty and honour that he might have to face in his own life. At the end of the poem, as the dreamer looks forward to the great feast in †heaven, and †hell's captives are rescued by Christ, the poet also puts these mundane concerns into a perspective of final and complete triumph.

Some lines of the †cross's speech are carved on the Ruthwell Cross.[2] This is a carved stone preaching cross, marking the place where Christian instruction was given before there were church buildings. While it is unknown precisely how the *crucifixion poem was transmitted, the distance in space and time (approximately 600 miles and 300 years) between the Ruthwell Cross and the Vercelli Book poem suggest that it might have become part of the festivals of the cross at ‡Easter and other times (e.g. Holy Cross Day, 14 September).

QUESTIONS

1. How effective do you find the phases of emotion the poem presents us with: wonder, unease, pride, humiliation, confidence, hope, triumph, and so on?
2. What does the dream framework contribute to the poem?
3. Why is the †harrowing of hell at the end of the poem?
4. The poem uses different speakers and explores various paradoxes. Does it achieve unity and coherence? If so, how?

BIBLIOGRAPHY

J.A. Burrow, 'An approach to *The Dream of the Rood*', *Neophilologus* 43 (1959), 123–33: a standard essay on the topic, full of insight.

Paul Cavill, *Anglo-Saxon Christianity*, London 1999, contains a chapter setting the poem in the context of Christian poetry, and exploring how the poet uses the resources available to him.

O.D. Macrae-Gibson, 'Christ the victor-vanquished in *The Dream of the Rood*', *Neuphilologische Mitteilungen* 70 (1969), 667–72. A brief examination of one of the poem's main paradoxes.

Michael Swanton, *The Dream of the Rood*, rev. edn, Exeter 1987, is the best edition of the text, with excellent introduction, notes and glossary.

---

2. See Brendan Cassidy, *The Ruthwell Cross: Papers from the Colloquium Sponsored by the Index of Christian Art…*, Princeton 1992, for illustration and discussion of the cross.

4

BEOWULF

[*BAOME* pp. 157 f; *NA1* pp. 29 f; *OA1* pp. 20 f.
The translation used here is that of Seamus Heaney in *NA1*.]

The poem of *Beowulf* is known only from a manuscript of around the turn of the first millennium, though it shows signs of having been composed and probably written down much earlier.[1] It is not known by whom, for whom, when, or in what circumstances the poem was composed, why it was copied, or what reception it might have had in the medieval period. What is clear from the poem itself is that it was composed by someone educated in the Christian tradition and with a good knowledge of the legendary history of the Germanic races. The monster stories in the first part draw on well-known folk-tale motifs, while much of the hero's reflection in the second half tells of historical tribal conflicts in northern Europe in the sixth century.

The story focuses on the hero Beowulf. In the first part of the poem he hears of the miseries of King Hrothgar, whose hall has suffered the attacks of the man-eater Grendel, and he decides to help. He sails to Denmark from his home in south Sweden and soon faces the monster who comes to feed on human flesh. In a hand-to-hand encounter Beowulf rips off Grendel's arm, and Grendel runs away to die in his lair. Hrothgar praises Beowulf and honours him with a rich banquet. But that same night, Grendel's Mother, seeking revenge for the death of her son, attacks the hall and carries off one of Hrothgar's closest friends. Beowulf and his men are led to the frightful lair by the Danes, who follow the trail of Grendel's blood. Beowulf dives into the eerie pool to find a cave under the water, where he fights Grendel's Mother. After a hard fight, Beowulf kills Grendel's Mother, hacks off Grendel's head, and swims back up to the surface. Hrothgar gives another sumptuous banquet in honour of the hero, rewards him with many gifts, and gently warns him that his prowess cannot last forever. In due course Beowulf sails home and reports his adventures to Hygelac, his king and uncle.

---

1. Michael Lapidge, 'The archetype of *Beowulf*', *Anglo-Saxon England* 29 (2000), 5–41, argues for an eighth-century original on the basis that repeated errors in the surviving manuscript derive from copying poorly formed letters characteristic of eighth-century scribes.

The second part of the story focuses on a time fifty years after the early successes of the hero. Beowulf is now king, and a dragon, disturbed by a thief robbing its treasure hoard, begins to ravage his land with its fiery breath. Beowulf determines to fight the animal and takes eleven chosen men with him. Ten of the men run off as Beowulf fights and fails to kill the dragon. One remains, his kinsman Wiglaf, and together they destroy the dragon. Beowulf is mortally wounded, however, and dies soon after seeing the dragon's hoard of treasure. He is given a lavish funeral and is remembered by his men as 'most gracious and fair-minded, / kindest to his people and keenest to win fame' (3181–2).

The whole story is located in the days of Germanic heathenism. The death of Beowulf's uncle Hygelac, which leads to his becoming king, can be dated to the 520s AD, centuries before the Danes became Christian. Yet most of the characters are portrayed as pious and monotheistic. They refer to God frequently and in a wide variety of terms, except that no reference is made to the events of the gospel, to Christ, or to the church.[2] Some scholars interpret this overall use of Christian elements as being the result of the poet's lack of interest in theology or his ignorance; or as deriving from a pagan poem reworked by a Christian or an ‡allegorical purpose on the part of the poet.[3] Others see it as part of the poet's sympathetic and imaginative representation of what it was like to live in a world before Christianity was preached.

The framework of references to God and religion is recognisably Christian. Idolatry is specifically condemned by the poet (175–88), and in this and other passages, †heaven and †hell are presented as alternative destinies for the ‡soul after death. These references are clearly patterned: Grendel is associated with †hell (e.g. 99–114, 783–89, 849–51), whereas Beowulf and Hrothgar, among others, trust in and thank God for help (e.g. 685–7, 1626–8). God is creator (92–8), father (188), judge (441, 978), and helper (1662). This means that the poet had sufficient vocabulary and understanding to talk about more specifically Christian doctrine had he intended to; but he seems not to have intended to. Rather he let the interest of the story and the pathos of its ending stir the imagination.

There are hints of a Christian critique of the heroic world in *Beowulf*. The contrast between Beowulf's success and confidence in the first half of the story and his gloom and ultimate failure and death in the second half is marked.

---

2. See Paul Cavill, 'Christianity and theology in *Beowulf*' (Bibliography), pp. 25–6, especially footnote 32, for the variety of terms used.

3. E.B. Irving Jr, 'Christian and pagan elements' in R.E. Bjork and J.D. Niles, ed., *A Beowulf Handbook*, Exeter 1997, pp. 175–92, gives an excellent outline of the main lines of interpretation in this area.

Confidence is the province of the young man, but it does not last, as the aged Hrothgar tells the young Beowulf (1724–84), recommending that he looks to 'eternal rewards' (1760). At the end of his life, Beowulf is glad to have won treasure for his people and gives thanks to God for it (2794–2801), but his people bury it with him, 'as useless to men now as it ever was' (3168). There are dark sayings about the inevitability of feuds, the horrors of war, the endless cycle of violence and revenge from which there is no escape in the heroic world: all this might be calculated to make the Anglo-Saxons think about their values and priorities in the light of their Christian faith.

Christianity is arguably the uniting theme of the poem, but it is not applied at all simplistically. For example, the folk-tale monster Grendel is given a biblical genealogy (descended from *Cain: 107, 1261) and †demonic nature, so that in fighting him, Beowulf is fighting for what is good and right. Battles in which Beowulf fights human opponents are more in the background of the poem. And the dragon is made a natural creature despite its symbolic use in the Bible for the †devil (in the book of Revelation particularly), so that in fighting the dragon, Beowulf succumbs to nature and the limitations of his own human nature. The poet used what he knew and what he believed with delicate yet profound imagination: this is what makes *Beowulf* a great Christian poem.

QUESTIONS

1. Do you agree that Christianity is the uniting theme of the poem? What evidence would you use to support or undermine the claim?
2. How can a poem such as *Beowulf* be Christian yet omit to mention Christ? What makes a work of literature 'Christian'?

BIBLIOGRAPHY

Paul Cavill, 'Christianity and theology in *Beowulf*', in Paul Cavill, ed., *The Christian Tradition in Anglo-Saxon England: Approaches to Current Scholarship and Teaching*, Cambridge 2004, pp. 15–39. Argues that Christianity is important in the poem and that recent scholars have often misinterpreted it.

F. Klaeber, *Beowulf and the Fight at Finnsburg*, 3rd edn, Boston MA 1950, is the standard edition of the poem.

Andy Orchard, *A Critical Companion to Beowulf*, Cambridge 2002. Covers the range of interpretation of the poem with insight and good sense.

J.R.R. Tolkien, '*Beowulf*: the monsters and the critics', *Proceedings of the British Academy* 22 (1936), 245–95. A powerful interpretation of the poem as an imaginative work of art.

D. Whitelock, *The Audience of Beowulf*, Oxford 1951. A short book, which established the Christian nature of the poem securely.

5

THE OLD ENGLISH ELEGIES: *THE WANDERER* AND *THE WIFE'S LAMENT*

[*BAOME* pp. 42 f, 76 f; *NA1* pp. 99 f, 102 f; *OA1* pp. 100 f (*The Wanderer*)]

The Wanderer and *The Wife's Lament* are both found only in the Exeter Book, the most substantial surviving collection of Old English poems. They are commonly assembled with other poems in that collection such as *The Seafarer* (*BAOME* pp. 48 f) and *Deor* (*BAOME* pp. 60 f) as examples of the genre of 'elegy'. This is a serviceable term that captures something of the tone of the poems in which voices lament misfortune and loss and the condition of the world. There are many differences between the poems, however, and the two under discussion here interestingly illustrate one such, in that the eponymous Wanderer finds some sort of consolation for his pain, while the eponymous Wife does not.

For the Anglo-Saxons home was the place where the individual had importance and a role in society. To be exiled meant the loss of a sense of belonging with all that that involves: personal history, significance, and frank relationships with others. The cold, dreary, and unpleasant places on land and sea that exiles refer to thus become physical images for the sense of loss, fear, and loneliness that they inwardly experience.[1] In exile, mere survival necessitates pretence: the 'stiff upper lip', keeping his miserable thoughts to himself, that the Wanderer talks of as a 'fine custom'; and the silent longing and anxiety expressed by the Wife in her poem.

Not unnaturally, both protagonists try to find ways of getting back to normal after their initial loss: following the death of his lord for the Wanderer and the departure of her husband for the Wife. The Wanderer tries to find another lord who might take him in and befriend him but on his journeys experiences the illusory consolation of dream phantasms whose voices turn out to be the harsh cries of seagulls. The Wife tries to follow her husband but flees the hos-

---

1. This aspect of the 'pathetic fallacy' is discussed by E.G. Stanley, 'Old English poetic diction and the interpretation of *The Wanderer, The Seafarer,* and *The Penitent's Prayer*', *Anglia* 73 (1955–6), 413–66.

tility of his kinsfolk at home only to find the hostility of her husband 'hiding murderous thoughts in his heart' and all but imprisoning her in the remote and dreary cave.

It is after these attempts to redress their miserable lot that the speakers in the two poems start to express different outlooks on life. The Wanderer starts to generalise about the human condition and finds the beginnings of consolation in philosophising. The language of the last paragraph of *The Wife's Lament* is ambiguous, but here too there is a process of reflection where the Wife asks what it is that has created the situation in which she finds herself. Crucially, the Wanderer moves from one who characterises himself as an exile, a wanderer, an 'earth-walker', to one who has become 'wise in heart';[2] the Wife remains wrapped up in her (thrice-repeated) longing.

A turning point for the Wanderer is the experience of false consolation when the familiar voices of his friends turn out to be the seabirds' calls. He realises that all the apparently solid things that he has valued—the companionship of the hall, the boldness of the young—are actually as ephemeral and illusory as the seagull cries he has just heard. In view of the suddenness with which such things disappear, it becomes clear to him that restraint and moderation are proper for the wise man in participating in the human, social world. He laments with feeling the loss of horse, warrior, lord, the place of feasting, the joys of the hall. But for him, the stone wall, high and enduring, the remains of a lost culture, but cold, lifeless and subject to constant attack by the merciless elements, stands as an image of life after loss. This is how life really is when one sees it detached from the illusions created and fostered by human society. So finally the Wanderer returns to the point where his poem started: the favour of God. The grace of God, experienced unexpected and unsought by the Wanderer in the loss and misery of this life, is the place of certainty, comfort, and stability to be looked forward to and sought by everyone. This is home for the Wanderer.

The Wife's loss is both less terminal and more practical than the Wanderer's. Her husband has apparently reneged on his oath that only death would separate the two of them, and she feels the separation keenly: death would be easier to accept than the passing of their friendship and intimacy. She tries to rationalise his behaviour as conforming to that 'fine custom' that the Wanderer speaks of: her husband has to keep a 'glad countenance' because it is expected. But she knows that whatever his present situation, 'he suffers great anguish' just

---

2. See T.C. Rumble, 'From *eardstapa* to *snottor on mode*: the structural principle of *The Wanderer*', *Modern Language Quarterly* 19 (1958), 225–30.

as she does. Her own suffering, which makes her feel that each day is as long as the days of midsummer, is exacerbated by the sense that he too 'remembers a happier place', he too is in exile. She cannot give up her love, and yet neither can she resolve the impasse caused by her husband and his kinsfolk. She has simply to wait for him.

The contrast between the two poems is expressed in the last sentence of each. *The Wanderer* ends on a note of hope, *Wel bith*—literally, 'It is well with the one who seeks favor'; *The Wife's Lament* ends with *Wa bith*—literally, 'It is woe for the one who has to wait'. The Wanderer has achieved that detachment from the world and its delusions that medieval ‡monasticism and ‡pilgrimage aimed to achieve. The Wife remains embroiled in an intractably difficult relationship, which she is unwilling or unable to give up. Yet it would be unwise to see the difference between the two poems as one of Christian versus non-Christian. The Wanderer sits apart and looks to †heaven for his consolation, a path that many took; the Wife holds on to love—her love for her husband and the remembrance of his love for her—and finds no consolation. She refuses to detach herself and suffers the consequences; this too is a path of faithfulness.

QUESTIONS

1. The Old English of *The Wife's Lament* only makes clear the gender of the protagonist by grammatical endings on words (the modern title is given by editors). Do you think there is anything gender-specific about the conclusions that the Wanderer and the Wife come to?

2. There is no mention of God in *The Wife's Lament*. *The Wanderer* speaks on the one hand of 'the favor of the Lord', and on the other he attributes the devastation he sees in the world to the 'Maker of mankind' (paragraph 9). What do you think is the nature of the Christianity in these poems? If *The Wife's Lament* is not a Christian poem, how would you characterise its worldview?

BIBLIOGRAPHY

T.P. Dunning and Alan J. Bliss, *The Wanderer*, London 1969, is a full, thorough, and well-annotated edition of the poem.

Martin Green, ed., *The Old English Elegies: New Essays in Criticism and Research*, London and Toronto 1983. A collection of essays, uneven in quality and significance, but stimulating, with a useful bibliography.

Anne L. Klinck, ed., *The Old English Elegies: A Critical Edition and Genre Study*, Montreal and Kingston 1992. A comprehensive collection of the Old English texts, including similar ones from Latin, Norse, and other languages, with good notes and introduction.

6

THE ANGLO-SAXON CHRONICLE AND FRENCH LEGENDARY HISTORIES

[*BAOME* pp. 20 f (pre-Norman Conquest selections), 254 f; *NA1* pp. 110 f]

The Anglo-Saxon Chronicle is unique in European literature: a prose chronicle, recorded year after year for nearly three centuries, in the vernacular language. The core material of the early chronicle was first compiled in around 891, in the reign of King Alfred the Great, and sent out to various ‡monastic centres; later bulletins were also despatched and copied into the records kept by the monasteries. Both before and after the Norman Conquest, though, the records cease one by one, until the last known, that kept at Peterborough, finally stops at the year 1154. In the nature of the case, the chronicle had many writers, each with their individual preoccupations. Yet two threads run through the record from beginning to end: the first thread is that this record is a national history, an account of the English in their trials and triumphs; the second thread is that history, in general and in particular, has meaning in a Christian moral framework.

The chronicle extract relating to the death of William the Conqueror (1087, *NA1* pp. 110–12) in the Peterborough Chronicle exemplifies both these threads. The chronicler writes of William as wise and powerful, a patron of the church and the ‡monasteries. The description begins with William fulfilling the conventional requirements of a devout and strong king (the implications for the people of having a weak king are made plain in the entry concerning Stephen's reign, 1137). Wulfstan, Archbishop of York before the Conquest, had written that the king should promote the Christian faith and punish evildoers severely.[1] Bede had also written about the great days of King Edwin when it was possible for a woman and her newborn child to travel about without fear of molestation,[2] and William achieved that level of control in the land too: the chronicler

---

1. Karl Jost, ed., *Die 'Institutes of Polity, Civil and Ecclesiastical'*, Bern 1959, section 2.
2. Bertram Colgrave and R.A.B. Mynors, ed., *Bede's Ecclesiastical History of the English People*, London 1969, Book II, chapter 16, p. 192. This is recorded by Bede as a proverb current in his day, and is thought by Judith McClure, 'Bede's Old Testament kings' in P. Wormald, with D. Bullogh and R. Collins, ed., *Ideal and Reality in Frankish and Anglo-Saxon Society*, Oxford 1983,

notes that a man could travel 'throughout the kingdom with his purse full of gold' because of the peace of the land under the strong king. But in both the prose and the verse into which it merges, the chronicler points out those areas where William fell short of the man he should have been. He abused his power over churchmen, including his brother; he extorted money from his subjects; and he was more a 'father' to the deer than to his people. In these things he flew in the face of convention, the accepted norms for Christian kingship. He was guilty of pride and in great need of God's mercy and ‡forgiveness.

The chronicler concludes his account of William's reign and character with another convention that he borrowed from Bede. Bede (see the essay on Bede earlier) wrote in his preface to his great work, the *Ecclesiastical History*, that good examples in history encourage the good in their goodness.[3] Telling history truthfully has a moral purpose, but to fulfil that purpose the truth has to be told. The verse at the end of the entry is more artful and more emotive than the prose and overwhelmingly negative in its judgement of William's character. It is quite possible that this was a poem that circulated at the time, recording the feelings of ordinary English people about the French king. At any rate, here the chronicler cuts free of convention so that he is able to tell the truth and in the process teach his audience. And the truth for the chronicler was that William was quite good in some things and very bad in others. He gives a voice to the English in the verse and thus makes the moral of his narrative clear.

Forty years later, a (presumably) different chronicler tells the story of Henry of Poitou's trickery and deception in pursuit of the abbacy of Peterborough (*NA1* pp. 113–14). Again the moral purpose of the account is clear. The relatively restrained, cold narrative of all Henry's stratagems and achievements is summed up in the image of the drone bee and in the statement that 'he did no good there and left nothing good there'. But again, this chronicler gives voice to the people in the tale of the 'Wild Hunt', the riding out of phantom †devilish black hunters and animals. No explanation of the significance of this repeated event is given beyond that it coincided with the arrival of Henry at Peterborough. But perhaps no further explanation is needed: the forces of evil were unleashed.

---

pp. 76–98, at p. 88, to be modelled on I Kings 4:25, where it is said that under Solomon everyone lived in security, 'each man under his vine and his fig tree'.

3. 'Should history tell of good men and their good estate, the thoughtful listener is spurred on to imitate the good; should it record the evil ends of wicked men, no less effectually the devout and earnest listener or reader is kindled to eschew what is harmful and perverse, and himself with greater care pursue those things which he has learned to be good and pleasing in the sight of God' (Colgrave and Mynors, *Bede's Ecclesiastical History*, Preface, pp. 2–3).

And so they were in King Stephen's reign, as recorded in the annal for 1137 (*BAOME* pp. 256–9, *NA1* pp. 114–15). The utter and abject misery caused by the weakness of Stephen may have caused the chronicler of this reign to exaggerate in the detail of the suffering of the people. He probably turned to the ‡martyrologies to find the infliction of bizarre tortures that he attributed to the barons of his own time. 'Never', he says, 'were any martyrs so tortured as these were.' But his point is that the ‡martyrs of history were comforted, strengthened, and made invulnerable to pain, whereas in his days, 'it was openly said that Christ and his saints were asleep'. The people had nowhere to turn, and the chronicler sees this as the †judgement of God: 'we suffered nineteen winters for our sins'.

The ultimate message of this passage is that such things do not 'just happen' and their causes are not merely political. The moral framework in which the chroniclers wrote their history made it possible for them to point out flaws and ‡vices in kings and ‡abbots but also made it necessary to include themselves and God's †judgement upon their ‡sin. This is a profoundly uncomfortable exercise, and it may be among the reasons why the chronicle ceased to be written.

A different kind of history grew in popularity in the twelfth century, the 'legendary history' of Geoffrey of Monmouth, Wace, and Layamon (*NA1* pp. 115–26). This was history rewritten and romanticised for the consumption of the French aristocracy in England and subsequently for most of the populace. It traces the origins of Britain to Rome by way of Vergil's *Æneid*, and focuses on the character of King Arthur: Arthur represents and practises French ideals of chivalry and courtliness. Although these writers have no qualms about introducing sorcery and magicians, elves and giants (essentially folk-tale elements), Arthur also represents Christianity in the fight against the heathen Saxons. The 500 years or so of Anglo-Saxon Christian history, with its concern about matters of national significance and public order as expressed in the chronicles, are elided in favour of a British, pre-Saxon Christianity inherited through Anglo-French romance on the one hand and Anglo-French ecclesiastical authority on the other. Legendary history did not completely supplant 'real' history, but it was highly effective in changing the way English people thought of themselves. The sharp focus of the Anglo-Saxon chronicle on national history and moral framework is replaced by new origin myths and ideals of chivalry that legitimise Anglo-French rule and custom.

QUESTIONS

1. Is it fair to think of the Anglo-Saxon Chronicle and the legendary histories as similar kinds of writing? How do they differ, and to what purpose? What is the moral focus of legendary history?
2. Discuss how the Chronicle uses conventions (some of which are outlined above) to achieve its ends. What conventions do you see employed in the extracts of legendary history, and to what ends?
3. What differences do you perceive in the representation of Christianity between the Chronicle and the legendary histories?

BIBLIOGRAPHY

Cecily Clark, ed., *The Peterborough Chronicle, 1070–1154*, London 1958, is the standard edition of the later Peterborough Chronicle, with good introduction and notes.

Antonia Gransden, *Historical Writing in England*, 2 vols, London 1974–82. A comprehensive scholarly review of historical writing from its beginnings in England to the end of the Middle Ages.

J.S.P. Tatlock, *The Legendary History of Britain*, London 1950. An old but thorough treatment of historical and legendary writing.

7

THE MEDIEVAL BEAST FABLE:
MARIE DE FRANCE, GEOFFREY CHAUCER'S
THE NUN'S PRIEST'S TALE, AND ROBERT
HENRYSON'S *THE COCK AND THE FOX*

[*BACS* pp. 485 f (Henryson); *NA1* pp. 140 f (Marie), 296 f (Chaucer),
439 f (Henryson); *OA1* pp. 176 f (Chaucer)]

The medieval beast fable owes a good deal to Aesop, the Greek composer of the most enduringly popular examples of the genre. But throughout the medieval West there were slightly different traditions including the exemplum,[1] and the physiologus, or bestiary, which interpreted the characteristics of animals ‡allegorically[2] and invented some animals and some characteristics entirely to fit the allegory.[3] These were moralising genres, using animals to teach human beings lessons about life, character, and the way of the world, and to a greater or lesser degree, all were used in schools as teaching texts. They were not, however, innately satirical. Another tradition was the 'beast epic', which was more satirical in its bent. One of the most interesting features of *The Nun's Priest's Tale* is the way Chaucer creates tension between the moralising tendency of one part of the tradition and the sharp irony and satire of the other.

Marie composed a number of brief and longer fables; indeed one of Chaucer's sources for *The Nun's Priest's Tale* was Marie's fable *Del cok e del gupil* (*The Cock and the Fox*), which in its turn borrowed from the medieval French beast epic *Roman de Renart*.[4] Henryson, for his part, modelled his fable on Chaucer's. But there is no real linear 'progression' between Marie in the twelfth century, Chaucer in the fourteenth century, and Henryson in the fifteenth century: each of them selects different features of the tradition for emphasis. Yet all of the

---

1. For example the biblical proverb, 'Go to the ant, thou sluggard; consider her ways, and be wise', Proverbs 6:6 (KJV).

2. See *BAOME* pp. 54 f for the Old English ‡allegory *The Whale*; and *OA1* pp. 196 f for the Bestiary.

3. See *The Nun's Priest's Tale* line 451 where the mermaids of 'Physiologus' are mentioned, and *OA1* pp. 479 f for the Old English *Phoenix*.

4. Larry D. Benson, ed., *The Riverside Chaucer*, 3rd edn, Oxford 1987, p. 936.

examples we have here focus on the use of words, speech and its relative truth, and the capacity of words to deceive.

The two Marie fables broach issues that Chaucer will take up in more detail: the use of language to confuse and oppress in *The Wolf and the Lamb* (*NA1* pp. 140–1); and in *The Wolf and the Sow* (*NA1* p. 141), the cunning use of language to save oneself and others. In the latter, Marie advocates ‡equivocation, particularly by women, as a way of avoiding the murderous attentions of men (this is an issue that will be significant in the English ‡Reformation, see the essay on Robert Southwell). When those with power use deception and false words to deprive the poor of whatever they have, it may be necessary, Marie suggests, to use their own linguistic weapons against them. Certainly Chauntecleer, in both Chaucer and Henryson, is initially deceived by the fox's words and in turn finds it necessary to deceive the fox to save his own life.

Chaucer's tale has two main parts: the first is a debate about dreams between Chauntecleer and Pertelote; and the second is the action in which the fox seizes the cock and the cock escapes. The first part serves two main purposes: it serves to characterise the cock, and it focuses attention on the issue of how words and ideas can be manipulated purely for the sake of winning an argument. Chaucer's Chauntecleer proves to his own satisfaction that dreams are meaningful, using classical and biblical examples: proverbs, the idea of ‡predestination, and as a conclusive argument against Pertelote's common sense, the *fall, specifically that 'wommanes conseil broughte us first to wo / And made Adam fro Paradise to go' (437–8). Despite all this proof that dreams might contain warnings, Chauntecleer is instantly deceived by the fox's flattery, even when the fox precisely fits the description of the animal that terrified him in his dream. The whole debate has been an exercise of Chauntecleer's masculine pride: he wants to believe that his dreams are more important than a stomach complaint for which his wife prescribes a 'laxatyf' (177); but he wants most of all to win the argument.

As a consequence, the flattery of the fox, appealing (as Chauntecleer has done) to Boethius and literature and the supposed learning of the cock, has instant effect. Chauntecleer cannot see the 'traison' of the fox (503) any more than he could see the obvious meaning of the dream; indeed he closes his eyes in the effort to impress the fox with his singing. The fox snatches the cock and runs away, and pandemonium is let loose in the farmyard. In this emergency, the cock appeals to the pride of the fox and persuades him to turn and mock the pursuers, and as soon as the fox opens his mouth to do so, the cock escapes. In conclusion, the two voice the morals arising from the tale: the cock thinks the lesson is about keeping his eyes open (611–12), the fox thinks it is about keeping his mouth shut (613–15). The Nun's Priest, however, concludes with the remark of St Paul (Romans 15:4) that 'al that writen is / To oure doctrine it is ywrit' (that is, for our learning), implying that there is more to be gleaned from the tale than these simple morals. And so there is.

Henryson's version of the story is less complex than Chaucer's. He omits the disputation about dreams, and Chaucer's lavish and courtly description of the cock that sets him up for a fall. Henryson's cock is 'jolie' and 'right corageous' (19–20), but nevertheless falls for the fox's guile in offering honour and service. The effect of this is to bring the fable closer to the biblical story of the *fall of humankind in Genesis and the traditional story of the ‡fall of the angels (the latter specifically mentioned, 200–3), where pride is undoubtedly present in the tempted, but the emphasis is more upon the deception of the †tempter. In Chaucer, Chauntecleer almost argues himself into his come-uppance, whereas in Henryson he is 'unwise' (183).

Chaucer's Chauntecleer is uxorious but concerned to put the hens down. Pertelote cares about the cock but is dismissive of his posturing. Both are portrayed with good humour, and neither comes out of the tale affirmed in their views. The cock is right about the dream but stupid—he even misreads the moral direction of the story, which is hardly (for him) about keeping his eyes open; the hen is wrong about the dream but far more sensible, paying no attention to Chauntecleer's learned huffing and puffing and keeping her eyes open to danger. The tale thus becomes an exploration of marriage, gender-roles, †wisdom, authority, truth, deception. Within the context of the Canterbury Tales, many of these issues take on particular interest and resonance as the tale is told by a man subject to a woman, the Priest to the Prioress (and it is to be noted that Harry Bailey, the Host, makes lewd comment on the virility of the Nun's Priest in the epilogue to the tale).

Henryson's fable is far more direct and clear in its moralising: 'Thir twa sinnis, flatterie and vanegloir, / Are venomous' (211–12). Chauntecleer is certainly guilty of pride (78–9), though little is made of it. By contrast, Henryson not only gives space to the fox's flattery but also to the hens' fickleness and spite when Chauntecleer is captured. This is a different take on the gender issues, less forgiving than Chaucer's but reinforcing the moral. Coppok's little ‡homily on Chauntecleer's ‡sins of lechery and pride (134–47) reveals more about her than about him: the religiously self-righteous are as guilty of pride, perhaps, as the vainglorious.[5] Henryson's tale is not without its humour, but it returns to its

---

5. Stearns, *Robert Henryson*, p. 68, takes the view that this is fundamentally Henryson's opinion on the issue of marriage relationships, the 'rigidly righteous attitude of orthodox morality', and so he does not interpret Coppok as self-righteous.

origins in the urgency of its morals. Chaucer delights and entertains in order to make his audience think about a range of moral issues.

QUESTIONS

1. If it is not about keeping one's eyes open and one's mouth shut, what is the moral focus of *The Nun's Priest's Tale*?
2. Does Christianity have a particular moral role in the beast fables?
3. How and why do you respond differently to Chaucer and Henryson?

BIBLIOGRAPHY

Nevill Coghill and Christopher Tolkien, *Chaucer: The Nun's Priest's Tale*, London 1959. A good edition of the Chaucer tale, with useful background.

Douglas Gray, *Robert Henryson*, Medieval and Renaissance Authors, Leiden 1979. A biographical and literary study of Henryson: compares *The Cock and the Fox* with Henryson's *Orpheus and Euridice*.

John McQueen, *Robert Henryson: A Study of the Major Narrative Poems*, Oxford 1967, esp. pp. 135–44. McQueen's study of *The Cock and the Fox* begins, 'The subject is Nobility, with its obverse Pride' (p. 135).

Marshall W. Stearns, *Robert Henryson*, New York 1949.

8

ANCRENE RIWLE

[*BACL* pp. 201 f (from *Ancrene Wisse*, see below); *BAOME* pp. 307 f; *NA1* pp. 153 f]

One of the earliest and most highly regarded forms of dedicated Christian life was that of the solitary, the ‡hermit. The first ‡monk, St Antony, heard Jesus' words to 'deny himself … and … follow me' (Matthew 16:24 NIV) as a call to leave civilisation and live in the †desert, to meet Christ in prayer, and to engage in spiritual combat with the forces of evil within human nature and those without — the power of evil at work in the world. The first Desert ‡Fathers (as these early ‡monks were known) lived in informal groupings rather than in absolute solitude; they offered one another spiritual guidance and support but had no officially-formulated rule prescribing their lifestyle and its spiritual rationale. In the west this form of ‡monastic life (*monos* means 'single') continued alongside the more dominant communal lifestyle of the great ‡monasteries of the Benedictines and Cistercians.

The *Benedictine Rule*, the most popular and enduring rule for ‡monastic life in the Middle Ages, had some severe strictures against the abuse of solitary life by those who wandered, unable to accept obedience to a superior and stability within a single place. The *Rule* legislated for community life but embraced the ascetic discipline and spirituality of ‡eremitical (‡hermit) life. Hence in the western church it was common for solitaries, especially if they were women, to request or be given some kind of spiritual rule to which they could conform their lives in obedience. This prevented the solitary from living a self-willed, self-chosen life, contrary to the pattern of obedience established by Jesus' human life. The *Ancrene Riwle* was written as a guide for the spiritual life of ‡anchoresses, three sisters in Herefordshire, England, who had decided to withdraw from the world. The text was popular and is found in several different versions: the *Riwle* for the three sisters at the beginning of the thirteenth century, and also a later version, *Ancrene Wisse*, which was adapted for a wider audience.

As one might expect, the battle imagery found in 'The Parable of the Christ-Knight' and in the quotations from St Benedict in the preamble has a common biblical root. In the letters of the New Testament it is made clear that the human race is in constant battle with 'principalities and powers' so that Christians must gird themselves like soldiers in spiritual armour and take up the sword of the Spirit (Ephesians 6:10–18). But the writers of the New Testament also believed that this spiritual battle took the form of individual mopping-up operations after the decisive battle had been won. Christ won a decisive victory over death, the last enemy. He is the Victor, the conquering soldier in the battle against evil (Romans 6:1–11). If Christians are called to be soldiers of Christ it is because they are called upon to imitate their Lord and must make Christ's victory their own.

The ground is prepared here for the development of the idea of Christ as a knight that we find in the parable. Indeed it is a concept that had already entered the mindset of those who legislated for or advised the eleventh- and twelfth-century ‡hermits. The only officially recognised rule for a community of hermits was written for the hermits on Mount Carmel in Israel, many of them former crusaders. Their rule expresses their desire to live in allegiance to Christ, wearing the armour of salvation and bearing the sword of the Spirit. They who were once soldiers bearing allegiance to a liege-lord, a knightly figure, were now to be soldiers in a spiritual combat, in allegiance to the Lord of all. They had exchanged service of an earthly knight for service of the definitive, divine knight who bore arms against the †devil and his principalities and powers.

Within the tale are two other biblical references that the medieval reader might be expected to recognise. The image of the lady besieged in her †castle and wooed by her lover king echoes the imagery used by the Old Testament †prophets of a virgin Israel, who is besieged by the consequences of her own infidelity and human weakness, forever entering alliances with earthly powers instead of trusting in God; but who is, nevertheless, liberated by the †love and †light of God (see, for example, Isaiah 47 and Jeremiah 3:1–5). In Christian reading this became a vivid image of the human state and of each individual, besieged by ‡sinfulness and wayward natural desires, rescued by a loving, ‡self-sacrificial ‡saviour (compare, for example, Donne's use of the same imagery in Holy Sonnet 14). The pattern of the parable echoes Jesus' *parable of the wicked tenants in the vineyard in the New Testament, which itself echoes a similar image in the Old Testament. In the Old Testament, Isaiah sees Israel as God's vine, planted and nurtured by God but bearing no fruit, that is, being unfaithful, and therefore handed over and destroyed (Isaiah 5:1–7). Jesus uses this image of a vineyard to express his people's infidelity and God's constant overtures to them in a manner similar to the gifts bestowed on the besieged lady. Finally the owner's son is sent, is murdered, and the vineyard given to others (Matthew 20:1–16).

Here, of course, the †parables diverge. Whereas Jesus' parable stresses the continuing infidelity of the tenants, the Christ-Knight parable emphasises †love and the recognition of love. The mood and tone is much more that of St Paul and St John in their emphasis upon the love of God made visible in the death of Christ (see Romans 5:8–11; II Corinthians 5:19–21; I John 4:9–10). The lover-beloved framework of the story also echoes the Song of Songs, another story in which the loved lady is lower in status than her princely lover: the bride is swarthy from working in the fields yet is beloved of the king—although here the beloved does not besiege the †castle but comes knocking at the door of the loved one's †house (see Song of Songs 1:5–6). In Christian eyes, this was the story both of the †love between Christ and his bride, the church, as suggested by St Paul (for example, in Ephesians 5:24–33) and in the book of Revelation, and of the wooing of each individual ‡soul by Christ. We can see this also in St Bernard's writings on the Song of Songs, which exemplify the contemporary reading of this biblical poem.

The Lady's 'castle of clay' also evokes biblical images. Clay is human flesh, the dust or mud of the earth from which *Adam is formed (Genesis 2:7). It is also the 'earthen vessel' bearing the treasures of Christ found in St Paul (II Corinthians 4:7) and the rebellious clay resisting being formed by God the potter (Isaiah 45:9). This sums up the reality of the Lady (the ‡soul), made for the glory of God but always threatened by disobedience. The image of the body or person as the †house also has its roots in scripture. We have seen the lover knocking at the beloved's door in the Song of Songs, an image repeated in the book of Revelation (where Jesus says, 'Behold, I stand at the door and knock', Revelation 3:20). But the house is also an image much used in the †parables of Jesus, where the emphasis is upon the house as personal identity. So is each individual, for the person from whom †devils are driven out is a clean, swept house (Matthew 12:43–5), and the one who sets his heart on Christ is like someone who builds his house on rock (Matthew 7:24–7). So this whole little story is replete with biblical imagery, laying the groundwork for the image of Christ the knight, which is then developed in the rest of the parable.

QUESTIONS

1. In what ways does your awareness of the biblical background to the image of Christ the knight contribute to your understanding of this parable?
2. In what ways does your awareness of the allusions to the self as (a) bride (b) †house contribute to your understanding of the parable?

BIBLIOGRAPHY

Giles Constable, *Three Studies in Medieval Religious and Social Thought*, Cambridge 1995.

Denis Renevey and Christiana Whitehead, ed., *Writing Religious Women: Female Spiritual and Textual Practices in Late Medieval England*, Cardiff 2000.

Anne Savage and Nicholas Watson, trans., *Anchoritic Spirituality: Ancrene Wisse and Associated Works*, New York 1991: a collection of works in English translation, with good introduction.

W.J. Sheils, ed., *Monks, Hermits and the Ascetic Tradition*, Oxford 1985. A varied collection of essays.

Sir Gawain and the Green Knight

[*BAOME* pp. 628 f; *BACS* pp. 234 f (fitts 3 and 4); *NA1* pp. 156 f; *OA1* pp. 284 f.
The translation used here is that of Marie Boroff in *NA1*.]

Sir Gawain and the Green Knight was composed in the late fourteenth century by a contemporary of Chaucer and Langland. The anonymous poet wrote in the northwest Midlands of England and shows a good knowledge of the Wirral peninsula of modern Cheshire in *Sir Gawain*. Preceding the poem in the unique manuscript are three other works, possibly by the same poet: *Pearl*, *Patience*, and *Purity* (or *Cleanness*). The manuscript has a number of small illustrations, but despite this and some letter decoration, it is neat rather than impressive. Composed far from London and the royal court, accompanied by didactic work such as a verse-paraphrase of the biblical book of Jonah (*Patience*), and in an undistinguished manuscript — the reader is not led to expect quite the degree of sophistication that this poem reveals.

The verse combines the alliterative style inherited from Old English with a stanza arrangement of much more recent origin and an unusual rhyme-scheme: the stanza varies in length, but closes with five short lines (called the 'bob and wheel') that rhyme. There are 101 stanzas, and near the end, line 2525 echoes line 1. This numerical structure is not mere decoration: the action of the poem lasts a year and a day and the number 5 features prominently in Gawain's knightly emblem of the pentangle (619 f). There are four parts to the poem (called 'fitts'), three hunts and challenges to Gawain's ‡virtue, two ladies (one of whom does the challenging, the other of whom planned the whole 'game', 2445 f), and one Green Knight and one Gawain. In a sense, the poem follows this kind of numerical pattern and narrows down its focus so that the final question is whether Gawain is unique, a man of singular virtue, undivided in his knightly honour.

There are four fitts. The first fitt sets the court of King Arthur in a (pseudo-) historical context and brings the challenge of the Green Knight's beheading-game. The Green Knight swaggers into King Arthur's Christmas and New Year festivities and calls into question the valour of the king and court with his proposal that blows with the axe should be exchanged a year apart: he, the first to receive, and the knight who takes up the challenge to take a blow the following year. Gawain, with elaborate courtesy claiming to be the most dispensable of the knights, takes up the challenge and beheads the Green Knight; the latter, having picked up his head, reminds Gawain of the bargain and rides off, leaving the court in a stir.

The second fitt details Gawain's preparations and journey to find the Green Chapel where the return blow is to be given. In this part Gawain arrives at the castle of the hospitable lord (later named as Bercilak) and lady where he will face challenges to his courtesy and chastity. These are the focus of the third fitt, in which another bargain is made, that the lord and the knight should exchange whatever they gain in their respective sports—hunting for the lord and dallying with the ladies for the knight. In the three hunts, the winnings are exchanged, except that Gawain keeps the lady's sash or girdle, which she has told him has protective powers, and he wears it to the final encounter with the Green Knight. The fourth fitt brings the denouement, where the Green Knight nicks Gawain's neck in the beheading test and reveals that he is Bercilak and knows all about the green girdle. Gawain then journeys back to Camelot, wearing the girdle as a badge of shame.

The Christian time frame and detailed worldview of the poem are important elements of the background. Bercilak attends ‡mass before going out to hunt, and Gawain goes to ‡confession before making his way to the Green Chapel (1876 f). The 'endless knot' (630) of the symbolic pentangle is made up of five senses, five fingers, five wounds of Christ, five joys of †Mary, and five knightly ‡virtues, an amalgam of traditions in which Christian ideas mingle with and give shape to ideals and practices of different kinds. Christianity is part of the normality of the poem, against which is set the challenge of the Green Knight, at once a Christmas game and an enchantment of 'Morgan the Goddess' (2452). What is not quite clear, though, is whether the poet had a specifically Christian message for the audience of this poem: critics continue to debate this issue.[1]

In a superficial sense very little changes in the poem. Gawain returns to Arthur's court with the honour and reputation of the Round Table undiminished, in echo of the poem's return to its pseudo-historical beginning with Brutus. It might even be argued that Gawain is substantially unchanged. He is scrupulous throughout: scrupulously correct in his courtesy in accepting the challenge of the Green Knight at the beginning, scrupulous in allowing the single wound from the axe at the end, and scrupulous in acknowledging his

---

1. See D. Pearsall, 'Courtesy and chivalry' in Brewer and Gibbon, ed., *A Companion to the Gawain-Poet*, p. 353, for references to scholars taking this approach.

fault in the test on his return. In the middle he is scrupulous in not succumbing to the sexual †temptation of his hostess, scrupulous in not exposing her to shame, and scrupulous about not taking the way out of the challenge offered by the guide on the way to the Green Chapel (2118–25). The one failure in his scrupulosity is in not declaring and handing over the green girdle as winnings according to the bargain with Bercilak. This brings to the fore the main change in the poem: the substitution of the green girdle for the pentangle as Gawain's emblem and the symbol of the Round Table.

The pentangle is an image of mystical perfection befitting the untried Gawain:

> For ever faithful five-fold in five-fold fashion
> Was Gawain in good works, as gold unalloyed,
> Devoid of all villainy, with virtues adorned ... (632–4)

The green girdle on the other hand is 'the badge of false faith' that Gawain feels he must bear (2509) until he dies. Gawain is notably different from the Green Knight and King Arthur and his court in his understanding of the significance of the green girdle. As far as the Green Knight is concerned, Gawain 'lacked a little in loyalty' (2366), but he goes on to say,

> I hold you polished as a pearl, as pure and as bright
> As you had lived free of fault since you were born. (2393–4)

Similarly, King Arthur and the court do not take Gawain's shame very seriously, happily wearing the green girdle in honour of the knight.

The substitution of the green girdle for the pentangle might be seen, then, as an acknowledgement of Gawain's humanity. For him, with his scrupulosity, it represents a great fall; for everyone else it represents the triumph of experience over innocence, of realism over idealism. They see Gawain's response as over-scrupulous, and indeed it is. Gawain wishes to be perfect, to be able to 'undo' (2511) his fault or separate himself from it;[2] but the poet reminds us almost casually as he finishes, it is 'He that was crowned with thorn' who brings us[3] 'to His bliss', the perfection of †heaven. The muted, ambiguous message of the poem may be that the knightly way, with all its †temptations and trials, is good and valuable, Christian and honourable (this would be a welcome message to the poet's aristocratic audience); but it is not a way of perfection in itself.

---

2. 'bot vnhap ne may hit', as it is in the Middle English original. Tolkien and Gordon translate 'For a man may hide his (spiritual) harm, but cannot unfasten (get rid of) it' (p. 130).

3. Once again, as it is in the Middle English original: 'He bryng vus to his blysse!'

QUESTIONS

1. What do you think the 'moral' of the poem is? What evidence would you use to support your conclusions?
2. Do you agree that Gawain's response to his fault is over-scrupulous? How do you account for his reaction?
3. How important is Christianity in the poem: is it only part of the background to a basically secular story, or does it have a more significant role?

BIBLIOGRAPHY

D. Brewer and J. Gibbon, ed., *A Companion to the Gawain-Poet*, Cambridge 1997. A thorough, up-to-date review of the background and culture in which the poems of the Gawain manuscript were composed. A very full bibliography and indexes complete a useful reference book.

J.A. Burrow, *A Reading of Sir Gawain and the Green Knight*, London 1965, is a thoughtful, fitt by fitt, reading of the poem.

W.A. Davenport, *The Art of the Gawain-Poet*, London 1978.

Ad Putter, *Sir Gawain and the Green Knight and French Arthurian Romance*, Oxford 1995, is an examination of the poem in its context.

The standard text is J.R.R. Tolkien and E.V Gordon, ed., *Sir Gawain and the Green Knight*, 2nd edn rev. by N. Davis, Oxford 1967; Malcolm Andrew and Ronald Waldron, ed., *The Poems of the Pearl Manuscript*, rev. edn, Exeter 1987, is a good text of all the poems in the manuscript.

GEOFFREY CHAUCER,
THE CANTERBURY TALES

THE GENERAL PROLOGUE

[*BAOME* pp. 585 f; *BACS* pp. 80 f; *NA1* pp. 215 f; *OA1* pp. 130 f]

The General Prologue sets the scene for the collection of stories that Chaucer planned as his *Canterbury Tales*. In the fiction of the work, a miscellaneous group of ‡pilgrims had met at the inn called the Tabard in Southwark, outside London, and would travel from there to Canterbury to visit the shrine of Thomas Becket. The hosteller of the Tabard proposed that they all travel together and that each should entertain the company with two tales on the way there and two on the way back. Only a relatively small number of the tales were completed by Chaucer before his death in 1399, and these are found in various manuscripts, grouped together in different ways and in different combinations, with connecting links of dialogue and comment from Harry Bailey, the hosteller (or Host, as he is most often known). Most of the existing tales are in verse, the exception being *The Parson's Tale*, which is a prose sermon. It is generally thought that Chaucer wrote the Prologue early on in his project, perhaps in 1387 or so.

The Prologue sets the scene, introduces the characters and the narrator, and sets up the competition between the ‡pilgrims that will give the book its framework. One of the delights of the Prologue is the character of the narrator, presented as naive, deferential and eager to please, but whose eyes and ears — and wit — are razor sharp. He sees and hears the pilgrims without explicitly judging, yet his descriptions lay bare the characters with all their pretensions, affectation, and self-delusion. Several of the characters are described as 'worthy', and more than one is 'verray parfit' (the Knight 72, the Doctor 424), and it is the reader who has to discern the differences between them. This is achieved on the basis of the detail the narrator presents about each one, sharp observations catching the life and quality of the person in a few phrases. We instantly recognise the Prioress who orders her life around propriety, minuteness, and romantic sensibility; the Merchant who constantly mentions, in passing, his profitable deals 'souning alway th'encrees of his winning' (277); the big, loud, lewd Miller — yet these people are in no sense stereotypes.

There is a perceptible contrast between the portraits of some characters and others. There is a knowingness, and sometimes full irony, in many of the accounts. The ‡Monk's disdain for the tradition and rule of his order is encapsulated in comparisons with foodstuffs, not worth a 'pulled hen' or 'an oystre' (177, 182). The Merchant's concealed debt, the fact of the Guildsmen being driven on by the aspirations of their wives, the Doctor's special regard for gold, the Cook's cancerous leg ulcer, the Wife of Bath's facility in the 'olde daunce': all these things gently mock the characters. The contrast between these and the portraits of the Knight, the ‡Parson, and the Plowman,[1] in particular, is noticeable.

The account of the Wife of Bath begins 'A good Wif was there of biside Bathe' (447), and that of the next character, the ‡Parson, begins 'A good man was there of religioun' (479). In just one phrase we have common humanity, both characters are 'good' of their kind, but one is 'of biside Bathe' the other 'of religioun'. In the accounts, it becomes clear that the characters put the emphasis on different parts of these initial descriptions: the Wife has made a profession of marriage and wifehood, whereas the Parson has made a profession of 'religioun'. The Wife is soon 'out of alle charitee' (454) if her precedence in church is ignored, whereas the Parson practises charity in its widest sense, not claiming his tithes and giving his own income to his parishioners.

The mention of the five marriages of the Wife (462) brings to mind the *woman of Samaria in John's Gospel 4:18 who also had had five husbands; this and the various details of her appearance and manner hint at the liberal attitude towards sex that her tale articulates and defends. In contrast to this (and notably to the behaviour of the ‡Pardoner and ‡Summoner too), the ‡Parson's purity ('clennesse' 508) in behaviour and motive is emphasised. His portrait is laced with biblical references and his characteristics can be found in contemporary Christian teaching. He is a true shepherd of his sheep (515–16 cf. John 10:12), and he practises what he preaches (499, 529–30 cf. Matthew 5:19; Acts 1:1). The Host remarks 'I smelle a Lollere in the wynd' when the Parson objects to his oaths: ‡Lollards were sectarians despised and persecuted by the establishment for taking the Bible and Christian standards of behaviour seriously.

It would be a mistake to imagine that Chaucer had deeply-held sympathy for ‡Lollards or any other religious persuasion. Yet the issue of religion is one frequently used to discriminate between characters; it is a ubiquitous moral standard, the more powerful for being undefined. It is easy to forget that the

---

1. See *Piers Plowman*, and the essay below on that work, for the ploughman as an exemplary religious figure.

framework of the whole *Canterbury Tales* is a religious ‡pilgrimage to the shrine of St Thomas of Canterbury. Thomas Becket was notable in that his life exemplified precisely a distinction between the secular and the spiritual. Before he became Archbishop of Canterbury he was worldly, politically effective, and businesslike as Lord Chancellor. Upon his elevation to the archbishopric, he became personally ascetic, wearing a hair shirt, and persistently opposed the king on matters of principle. He was famously the 'turbulent priest' the king, Henry II, wanted to be rid of. He was murdered in 1170 by the king's barons.[2] This hardly surfaces in the *Canterbury Tales*, where the pilgrimage is initially presented as a kind of natural springtime migration (1–18), but it is there as a subtext, a persistent subliminal reminder that religion is important, even a matter of life and death. There are those who think it matters, like the Knight and the ‡Parson, and those who use its status, privileges, and rituals for their own purposes like the ‡Pardoner, the ‡Friar, the ‡Summoner, and (in her own way), the Wife of Bath.

QUESTIONS

1. What do you think Chaucer's attitude to Christianity was, and how does he reveal it in the Prologue?
2. Does Chaucer have a moral focus, or is he simply enjoying a joke at the ‡pilgrims' expense?
3. Why is it difficult to make 'good' characters interesting? (You might like to consider the ‡Parson alongside Fanny Price in Jane Austen's *Mansfield Park*.)

BIBLIOGRAPHY

Larry D. Benson, ed., *The Riverside Chaucer*, 3rd edn, Oxford 1988: the standard edition of Chaucer's works.

Muriel Bowden, *A Commentary on the General Prologue to The Canterbury Tales*, New York 1960. Still the best and most accessible introduction to the characters and their roles.

B.F. Huppé, *A Reading of the Canterbury Tales*, New York 1964.

Jill Mann, *Chaucer and Medieval Estates Satire: The Literature of Social Classes and the General Prologue to the Canterbury Tales*, Cambridge 1973.

---

2. See D.H. Farmer, *The Oxford Dictionary of Saints*, 3rd edn, London 1992, under Thomas of Canterbury.

THE PARDONER'S PROLOGUE AND TALE

[*BACL* pp. 240 f; *BACS* pp. 164 f; *NA1* pp. 281 f; *OA1* pp. 257 f. The line numbering differs in the various texts: the numbering (and spelling) below is from *NA1*; *OA1* has two lines extra, so 133 in *NA1* is 135 in *OA1*.]

The character of the ‡Pardoner has raised critical questions, many in recent years focusing on his sexual orientation and its significance. Attention has also turned to the degree of condemnation Chaucer intends the reader to accord him. It is to this second issue that we turn here.

There are implications in some of the ‡Pardoner's statements in his Prologue, to which Chaucer's contemporaries may have been alert, that make him a picture of complete ‡sinfulness. For example, 'I bekke / As dooth a douve' (108–9) echoes Jesus' command to his followers to be 'wise as serpents and harmless as doves' (Matthew 10:16). It is clear that the Pardoner's imitation of a dove in this context hides the worldly wisdom of the serpent who is the great deceiver and the father of lies (see Genesis 3 and John 8:44 and the Pardoner's reference to spitting venom, 133, one of the things the cobra was reputed to do in the medieval bestiaries). This is precisely the behaviour of which the Pardoner boasts: it becomes clear that he can be seen as a partner in the †devil's work.

This idea of the ‡Pardoner as the serpent in dove's clothing is developed in his description of his treatment of enemies. His account of his own behaviour then proceeds to establish the truth of his own text for preaching. His love of money is the root of his own evil as St Paul taught (I Timothy 6:10, and that verse in Latin, *Radix malorum est cupiditas*, the Pardoner's sermon text, 46, 138). For love of wealth he breaks the *commandments against bearing false witness and coveting his neighbour's property. Such envy and covetousness are two of the ‡seven deadly sins and they lead him habitually to commit the remaining five. He is wrathful in his denunciation of others, proud in his boasting about his own preaching, gluttonous in his love of food and drink, lustful in his desire for a jolly wench in every town (165), and slothful in his refusal to do honest work.

Indeed he sets himself against the apostle Paul, who earned his own living while preaching the gospel and teaching that whoever refused to work should not eat (II Thessalonians 3:10). The ‡Pardoner's refusal to do any work with his hands (156) is another reflection of his pride. He refuses to share the common lot of humans who must gain their food from their labour as the consequence of the *fall (Genesis 3:19). To crown it all, his avarice leads him to the ‡sin decried in Old and New Testaments, cheating the poor, the widow, and the fatherless children (162–3). His behaviour is the reverse of that pure and undefiled religion which the letter of St James describes as concern for widows and orphans and keeping oneself uncontaminated by the world (James 1:27).

Chaucer uses his biblical knowledge and the Christian tradition of the ‡seven deadly sins to make the ‡Pardoner here a true exemplum of his own text.

The ‡Pardoner's tale itself is set in the perspective of coming †judgement, a popular subject for preaching at the time. There is an irony in this tale that purports to prove that avarice is the root of all evil, following St Paul's teaching that the love of money is the root of all evil (I Timothy 6:10). If it is read carefully, one can see that, in this tale, love of money does not actually lead to other ‡sins; the rioters are already established sinners. They are introduced as habitually committing the sins of gluttony and lust. Indeed the ‡Pardoner's denunciation of gluttony in the light of the *fall of *Adam and Eve (215–24) is closer to St Augustine than to St Paul, locating the root of sin in concupiscence, that is, in the uncontrolled lusts of the flesh. Furthermore, in their habitual cursing the rioters are breaking the third *commandment against taking God's name in vain. They do not yet provide an illustration of the Pardoner's text; rather they offer an image of humankind made forgetful by concupiscence that they must face death and †judgement.

Later in the story their vainglory and pride is shown in their belief that they can defeat death, when, according to the Christian teaching they purport to uphold, only Christ can do that. Their attitude to the old man also suggests their lack of regard for the wider implications of the fourth *commandment to honour parents, a commandment generally taken in the church of the period to imply a reverence for old age.

Furthermore, as the old man says, they break the golden rule given by Jesus to treat others as you would wish them to treat you (Matthew 7:12). So in fact the men are deep into all kinds of evil before they find the gold. In the understanding of the time, it is their lack of training and practice in ‡virtue, and their forgetfulness of death and †judgement, that makes them so readily succumb to the †temptation of the gold. Since it is their companions in ‡sin whose demise they wish to revenge on Death it is clear that they are already on the way to encountering him, if not in the way that they imagine. Covetousness is the last step leading to death, but other evils have paved the way to it. Ultimately, the ‡Pardoner's story reflects the text 'the wages of sin is death' (Romans 6:23) rather than his chosen target of avarice.

Close attention to the Christian allusions clarifies Chaucer's irony for us here. The ‡Pardoner is proud of his preaching, falsely thinking it preaches a message against avarice. His tale remains a lie, an untruth. His conversation, however, in which he speaks truthfully, if unwittingly, about his own behaviour provides a true illustration of the relationship between avarice and the other ‡vices. He is the exemplum for his own text. And perhaps we may discern here another irony: just as the Pardoner cannot recognise the application of his chosen text to himself, so too he cannot discern the true text for his tale in its relation to himself. He is as unaware as his revellers that ‡sin leads to death, and he is as unprepared as they were for death and †judgement.

QUESTIONS

1. Examine carefully the ironies within the ‡Pardoner's self-presentation.
2. What does the figure of the old man add to this tale?
3. What other evidence can you find in the tale for the ‡Pardoner's lack of awareness of its true message?

BIBLIOGRAPHY

Robert Boenig, 'The Pardoner's hypocrisy and his subjectivity', *American Notes and Queries* 13 (2000), 9–16.

Mary Flowers Braswell, 'Chaucer's palimpsest: Judas Iscariot and the *Pardoner's Tale*', *Chaucer Review* 29 (1995), 301–10.

Jane Dillon, 'Chaucer's game in the *Pardoner's Tale*', *Essays in Criticism* 41 (1999), 208–14.

Elizabeth R. Hatcher, 'Life without death: the Old Man in Chaucer's *Pardoner's Tale*', *Chaucer Review* 9 (1975), 246–52.

Lee W. Patterson, 'Chaucerian confession: penitential literature and the Pardoner', *Medievalia et Humanistica* 7 (1976), 15–68.

Paul Sheneman, 'The tongue as sword: Psalms 56 and 63 and the Pardoner', *Chaucer Review* 27 (1993), 396–400.

William Langland, *Piers Plowman*

OVERVIEW

[*BACL* pp. 229 f; *BAOME* pp. 547 f; *BACS* pp. 182 f; *NA1* pp. 317 f; *OA1* pp. 348 f.
The text used below is that of *NA1*.]

Langland wrote his 'dream poem' at a time when England was demoralised in the aftermath of the Black Death, which had decimated the population and undermined its social fabric. Social disorder and unease was accompanied by equal ferment in the church: traditional beliefs and practices were beginning to be questioned and the disciplines of Christian life relaxed, particularly among some religious communities and clerics, so that the populace were left without adequate moral and spiritual guidance. This, at least, is Langland's view of his times. Consequently the world he presents to us is one sorely in need of a renewed moral and spiritual vision that will also restore the common good of the people.

In his vision of the field of folk (17), the dreamer dresses himself like a sheep in wolf's clothing, 'in the habit of a hermit unholy of works' (2), and instantly raises in the Christian's mind phrases and warnings from the gospels about that other †wolf in sheep's clothing as well as warnings about the *hireling shepherd and the danger for his sheep (John 10:1–15). The dreamer is a sheep, someone needing a shepherd and guide, but, in his abandoned state, dressed to move among the wicked as one of them. He tells us that he is travelling in a world where values are reversed. The shepherds of God's flock are all hirelings, intent on their own benefit in neglect of their sheep; to survive, one must appear as one of them. That he is a *wandering* sheep (7) immediately alerts us to the fact that he is a ‡sinner, a lost sheep, in need of ‡salvation, recalling Luke's *parable of the lost sheep whom the *good shepherd, Jesus, goes out to seek (Luke 15:4–7). In this topsy-turvy world it is the dreamer-sheep who must go out in search of salvation, looking for the true good shepherd among all the hirelings. It alerts us to a *fallen world, a world at a distance from its maker. We are also reminded, however, that it is the finding of the *lost sheep in the parable which brings great joy in †heaven.

In this way we are immediately introduced to the two levels on which the dream-vision works. We are to be taken into the reality of contemporary English life, but simultaneously into a story of a †journey of ‡repentance and reconciliation, which the nation and each individual must undergo, the journey out of ‡sin and 'back to the true shepherd of their souls' (I Peter 2:25). For Langland, this journey is back not only to Christ but also to fidelity to the ‡pope as the voice of Christ on earth, in rejection of the contemporary questioning of ‡papal authority. This is why, when the dreamer experiences his final ‡revelation about ‡salvation, he sees Christ fighting the battle of salvation wearing the colours and arms of Piers Plowman. The name Piers is a variant of Peter; Peter, and his successors, the popes, represent Christ on earth just as the ploughman represents the sons of *Adam, the sons of earth whose humanity Christ assumes in becoming a man and restores to friendship with God in his *crucifixion and *resurrection.

This notion of a †wolf in sheep's clothing extends to the attack on false ‡hermits and ‡mendicants pretending a piety they do not possess. Langland here shows the ambivalence Christians traditionally felt to the idea of the wanderer. The ‡monastic ideal valued stability, that is, commitment to the one place, the one community, the one pattern of life. The ideal for the hermit, whether living alone or in a loose cluster of hermits, was stability in his own cell. Stability led to a loss of self-will through obedience to the demands of the unchanging situation; it also involved hard work to maintain life.

The necessity of work was seen as the result of the inherited †original sin of *Adam and Eve, an acceptance of the common lot of humanity. 'In the sweat of thy face shalt thou eat bread' (Genesis 3:19) was a result of losing that relationship between man and earth that made it easy and pleasant to get a living from the land. This view was enhanced by the teaching of St Paul against those who refuse to work and go around creating trouble for others (II Thessalonians 3:6–12). So the strictures against a wandering beggar are not only a condemnation of the hypocrisy and moral breakdown of Langland's own times particularly associated with the new ‡mendicant (begging) orders, they reflect the tensions in the church of his time over this wandering form of life.

What Langland focuses on here is a breakdown of the common weal, the common good, in the satisfaction of natural appetites for sex, food, possessions, which leads people to live a life based on fundamental untruths. The lies of the preacher, the contradictions between what is said and the actual fact, are symbolic of the untruthfulness of the total situation Langland describes. People live as though the satisfaction of their desires and the acquisition of superfluity is all; they live like beasts, forgetful of their relationship to God and to one another; love of themselves has replaced a †love of God and neighbour for which they are made.

They are forgetful also of the truth of death and †judgement. 'Sleep and sloth' (45) recalls the foolish virgins in the *parable of the wise and foolish virgins who slept while waiting for the bridegroom, and, having no oil for their lamps, miss his return at the end of time (Matthew 25:1–13 and St Paul's injunctions to stay awake in I Thessalonians 5:1–11). They are forgetful of the human condition where they had been called upon to work. They need to be recalled to a way of living that is true to their human condition. The dreamer's need to search for Holy Truth is the deepest need of the field of folk, for in St John's Gospel Jesus is 'the way, *the truth,* and the life' (John 14:6, my italics).

With the emphasis on work it is therefore no surprise that it is Piers, the ploughman—an image of the faithful worker—who can guide ‡pilgrims to truth. Piers fulfils the ‡monastic ideal of stability: for forty years he has worked, living according to truth's requirements. Work here acquires a double significance. He has been faithful to the reality of his *fallen nature, but he has also worked to follow truth, to serve truth and not himself. The contrast between the ‡pilgrim, who has all the badges to prove his devotion, and Piers, who has remained faithful and attentive to conscience, is a contrast in the saying of Jesus 'Not every one that saith unto me, Lord, Lord, shall enter into the kingdom of heaven; but he that doeth the will of my Father which is in heaven' (Matthew 7:21).

Piers shows that the way to truth is not in the external act of ‡pilgrimage but in following a way of life according to the *commandments. He describes an inward pilgrimage to the heart, the spiritual centre of the human being, bringing about the completion of the promise given by Jesus, the way, the truth and the life, that those who †love him will keep his commandments and become one with him (John 14:15–21).

QUESTIONS

1. Compare and contrast this example of a dream poem with any other you have already read or studied. Identify common elements and what is distinctive here.

2. Follow up the biblical references to sheep and shepherd and see how they apply in detail to this passus.

3. In what ways are your understanding of the presentation of (a) wandering (b) work in *Piers Plowman* affected by your knowledge of the biblical and historical background?

BIBLIOGRAPHY

John A. Alford, ed., *A Companion to Piers Plowman*, Berkeley CA 1988.
Giles Constable, *Three Studies in Medieval Religious and Social Thought*, Cambridge 1995.
Britton J. Harwood, *Piers Plowman and the Problem of Belief*, Toronto 1992.

PIERS PLOWMAN, PASSUS 18:
THE HARROWING OF HELL

[*BACL* pp. 231 f; *NA1* pp. 336 f]

Two connected issues that troubled Christians in the earlier centuries of the Christian era were the fate of the 'just', such as the Old Testament patriarchs Abraham and Isaac, who died before Christ's saving *crucifixion and *resurrection, and the final fate of ‡sinners. At the last day would †hell be emptied or would some be truly ‡damned for all eternity? One doctrine that soon developed to explain the way in which Christ's ‡salvation was able to apply retrospectively was the belief that in the period between his death and resurrection, Christ descended into hell to raise *Adam, Eve, and the 'just'. This belief developed from I Peter 3:19, where Jesus is said to have 'preached to the spirits in prison', and was reinforced by St Paul's teaching that all things, including those in the underworld, will bend the knee at the name of Jesus (Philippians 2:10). This suggests that the domain of the dead too is now under the sway of Christ. This doctrine was universally accepted and was incorporated into the church's ‡creeds.

The second issue was much more controversial. A minority of the church ‡Fathers, like St Gregory of Nyssa in the fourth century, held that at the end of time everyone, whether †baptised or not, whether believers or not, would be restored to God whilst the majority adhered to the primacy of scripture's depiction of †judgement and eternal †hell fire. The two-stage †harrowing that the dreamer envisions reflects this theological debate which Langland finds in the ‡apocryphal Gospel of Nicodemus. He is very careful to restrict himself to the fate of Christians, the baptised, thus avoiding the accusation of ‡heresy, while the thrust of his writing suggests his agreement with the minority view.

That Langland's Jesus should resemble Piers and the good Samaritan (10) is no surprise. According to St Augustine's reading of the *parable of the good Samaritan (Luke 10:29–36, in which a Jewish traveller is set upon, left for dead by the wayside, and rescued by a Samaritan, a traditional enemy), we can see Christ as the good Samaritan. The traveller is poor humanity waylaid and beaten by ‡sin and rescued by Christ, yet appearing as one who would be despised and rejected. It was human beings, *Adam and Eve, who rejected God in the Garden of *Eden. It is only God, sharing that human nature, who can reunite them and destroy the power of death over them.

In early Christianity there were many attempts to explain how ‡salvation was brought about through the †cross. One approach was the notion of battle, the cosmic battle between life and death, God and the †devil, taking up lines in the story of the expulsion of *Adam and Eve from the Garden of *Eden in which the offspring of the serpent and of Eve were established as enemies (Genesis 3:15). This was interpreted as the enmity between the devil and humanity brought to its climax in the clash between the devil and Christ in the *crucifixion, a battle in which *Adam and Eve's, and therefore humanity's, defeat by the devil is definitively reversed. It was important that this battle was fought in a human being, so that what was lost in the flesh could be regained in the flesh (see I Corinthians 15:20–26 — 'all die in Adam, all are alive in Christ; through one man, Adam, we die, through one man, Christ, all shall be made alive').

For some of the church ‡Fathers there is another reason why Christ 'be not disclosed ...' It is Jesus' flesh, his humanity, which tricks the †devil into conflict. Knowingly, he would not have entered the battle for he would know he could not win against God. Deceived by Jesus' humanity into believing him only another human being to be destroyed, he enters battle. This is why, later in the passus, the *crucifixion is called 'a trick by which to trick trickery' (168). Sometimes this is also presented in the imagery of fishing. Christ's human flesh is the bait; the †devil, seeing only the outside, takes it only to find *he* has been taken by God.

It was common, too, in theories about how the death and *resurrection of Christ worked to save human beings, to suggest that justice as well as mercy must be satisfied. This is so here: it is not mercy that adopts this trick but justice. Their argument here, and over the need to know well-being by losing it, echoes the teaching of one of the earliest ‡Fathers of the church, St Irenaeus. For Irenaeus, *Adam and Eve were beguiled because the serpent took advantage of Eve's immaturity and inexperience. Adam and Eve were only young; they needed to learn through their experience and therefore could not be held fully culpable.

The logic of lines 210–40 likewise follows the ancient understanding of the *fall into †original sin that is enshrined in the hymn, the ‡Exsultet, which Catholics sing at the ‡Easter vigil (the ‡mass that celebrates the *resurrection): 'O happy fault, O necessary sin of Adam that won for us so great a redeemer'. The fall out of relationship with God was a calamity for humanity, but it brought about the greater blessing of the †incarnation of Christ. Through his death and *resurrection, it was believed, human beings were raised to an even higher state than they had had before the fall, as adopted children of God. When we read this alongside the promise that †hell will ultimately be emptied, we see how much Langland is stressing the total victory of God over all evil; nothing at all can defeat the designs of God to bring life and ‡salvation to those he has created. However demoralised are the people he depicts, Langland's final viewpoint is optimistic because the victory belongs to God.

Much more could be said of this passus. What is to be stressed here is Langland's use and appreciation of traditions and arguments, not only within the Christianity of his own day, but within the Christian millennium that preceded it.

QUESTIONS

1. How is your understanding of the identity of Piers affected by your understanding of the biblical and doctrinal background to this passus?
2. To what extent do you consider an understanding of the doctrinal issues about ‡salvation and †judgement necessary to an appreciation of this passus?
3. Would you agree that this passus offers an optimistic vision?

BIBLIOGRAPHY

John A. Alford, ed., *A Companion to Piers Plowman*, Berkeley CA 1988.

Helen Barr, ed., *The Piers Plowman Tradition: A Critical Edition of Pierce the Ploughman's Crede, Richard the Redeless, Mum and the Sothsegger, and The Crowned King,* London 1993. A useful annotated edition of texts in the *Piers Plowman* mould.

Giles Constable, *Three Studies in Medieval Religious and Social Thought*, Cambridge 1995.

Britton J. Harwood, *Piers Plowman and the Problem of Belief,* Toronto 1992.

Middle English Lyrics

[*BACS* pp. 387 f; *NA1* pp. 349 f; *OA1* pp. 411 f]

'Four thousand winter thoughte he not too long.' It takes a huge effort for us to imagine a worldview in which time is as telescoped as this. The four thousand years of the Adamic bondage, calculated from genealogies in the Old Testament, run from the *fall of *Adam until the time of Christ, and the writer of *Adam Lay Bound* knows that he is writing only fifteen hundred years or so after that. Such a time-frame makes it much easier to imagine the Christ-event as a unique saving action in the middle of human time. The religious lyrics, like the ‡mystery plays of the same period, are to some extent a means of making knowledge of this ‡salvation available in English rather than in Latin or Norman French. In song, at least, this tradition probably owes much to the Franciscan ‡friars, whose deliberate policy it was to use song as a means of communication.

The choice of 'winter' as the measure of passing time, while conventional, is also thematic. Humanity passes four thousand dark winters in bondage to ‡sin and subject to death. By contrast, Christ who saves humanity from this plight is 'As dewe in Aprille / That falleth on the flowr' (*I Sing of a Maiden*). This sense that *Adam is to winter as the Christ-event is to spring is very English—or at least northern European—for it is just coincidence that ‡Easter falls in the English springtime. These lyrics are full of the sense of season, often as a conventional literary opening: 'Sumer is ycomen in ...'; 'Bitweene Merch and Averil ...' In terms of the imagination of time, this reliance on the symbols of the changing seasons, though conventional, still reinforces the sense of the unity of time. We can only look back to the world of the Middle English lyrics past the great changes of early modernity and the Industrial Revolution; but when the writers of the lyrics looked back to the Christ-event and beyond, they looked into an agrarian world much more like their own, in which the unchanging rhythm of the seasons marks the greater similarity of time present to time past.

A good number of religious lyrics are about the †cross. *What is he, this lordling, that cometh from the fight* is reminiscent of *The Dream of the Rood* in its emphasis on the courage of Christ the warrior knight and 'champioun'. This motif obviously owes much to warrior legends, but it is important to note here that Herebert is able to find a biblical passage, Isaiah 63, which resonates with that tradition. From at least as early as the Acts of the Apostles in the New Testament, chapters 40–66 of the Old Testament book of Isaiah were interpreted by Christians as predicting the *crucifixion and ‡redemptive suffering of Jesus of Nazareth as the Messiah.[1] *What is he* ... reflects the startling juxtaposition of God's angry †judgement and tender mercy, which is so frequent a theme in the Old Testament †prophets. The poem makes the †cross the locus of both. Here Christ the brave and lonely warrior both enacts and bears ('Adreint all with shennesse, ydrawe down with shame') the severe judgement of God so that he can 'helen mankinde in fight'. These images resonate with what is sometimes called the 'classical' view of the ‡atonement of Christ, in which the theme of Christ the Victor predominates over the idea of Christ the Victim, the †sacrifice made for human ‡sin: but both ideas owe much to Isaiah.

Two short lyrics reflect the tradition of meditation on the †cross and wounds of Christ. In *Ye That Pasen by the Way*, the key source text is again from Old Testament †prophecy, Lamentations 1:12: 'Is it nothing to you, all ye that pass by? behold, and see if there be any sorrow like unto my sorrow, which is done unto me, wherewith the LORD hath afflicted me in the day of his fierce anger.'

The injunction to 'behold and see' the †cross was taken particularly seriously in Christian spirituality and persisted well into the modern period.[2] Thomas à Kempis's *Meditation on the Wounds of Christ* is a spiritual classic; but the genre also invades secular literature, notably, perhaps, when Shakespeare's Macbeth describes the wounds of the holy Duncan, 'his silver side laced with his golden blood'. The literalness of such imagery later becomes somewhat too strong for Christian taste, so Christians still sing Isaac Watts's 'When I survey the wondrous cross', but tend to omit the verse 'His dying crimson, like a robe, / hangs from his body on the tree ...'

Roman Catholic expression within this genre places particular emphasis on the presence at the †cross of †Mary the mother of Christ. In *Sunset on Calvary*, the artist uses the eyes of Mary as a way into understanding and expressing the sorrow of the cross. This interpolation of Mary between the Christian observer and the suffering Christ is a crucial imaginative step in many aspects

---

1. The question, thus, is not about the name of the knight, but his identity—Messiah, Judge, the one who treads the winepress in anger (Isaiah 63:3).

2. It was a key passage in the liturgy of ‡Good Friday in the medieval church, and appears in several other lyrics: see Woolf, *Religious Lyric*, pp. 42–5, 321–3.

of Roman Catholic spirituality. Notice again the link to a particular time: in this case, sunset. In the biblical account, the sky is darkened at the time of the *crucifixion; but here the *tristesse* of dusk is simply likened to the grief of Mary, as the shadow of the cross falls across her face. Just as the Adamic bondage is appropriately symbolised by winter, so Calvary is appropriately symbolised by nightfall.

In *I Sing of a Maiden*, the emphasis on †Mary and the new life of spring are again brought together. There is a strong contrast here with the warrior Christ of *What is he …*, as the gentleness of Mary softens his †incarnation, making it like the stillness of falling dew in April. In this lyric, the incarnation is both natural in itself and is likened to natural processes. But while there is emphasis on the natural in *Sunset on Calvary* — and we notice the elemental vocabulary of *sonne, wode, tree*, pity (*me reweth*), and the simple human relationship of mother and her son (*sone*) — there is also theological beauty in the tableau: the *faire rode* is certainly Mary's face,[3] but it is also the *rood*, the †cross, that paradox of beauty and horror so well explored by the Anglo-Saxon poet of *The Dream of the Rood*. The happy ability of the medieval mind to find theological beauty in horror, and theological consolation in the *fall, is also at the core of *Adam Lay Bound*: none of the benefits of Christianity would have come about, and †Mary would not have become *hevene Queen*, were it not for the *felix culpa*, the 'happy fault' of mankind's first ‡sin. This idea expressed in the ‡Easter ‡Exsultet is once more given joyful voice here. Sad or exuberant, Christian doctrine allows expression to a delight in paradox: nature is both enjoyed for itself and turned on its head.

QUESTIONS

1. The lyrics exploit traditions of chivalry and romance in approaching the Christian story. Do you think these traditions help you to see the Christian story in a fresh light? What aspects are particularly effective?
2. The lyrics, the religious ones included, were undoubtedly popular: why were they, do you think?

---

3. See Duncan, *Medieval English Lyrics*, p. 224, for the tradition that †Mary's face became black with grief at the *crucifixion. Ambiguity is brilliantly exploited by this poet: in *sonne* and *sone*, sun merges into son; the *wode* is both wood/forest and †cross; the *rode* is both face and cross; the *tre* is both tree and cross.

BIBLIOGRAPHY

Thomas G. Duncan, ed., *Medieval English Lyrics 1200–1400*, Harmondsworth 1995. A useful collection of some of the best texts, with brief textual comment.

Rosemary Greentree, *The Middle English Lyric and Short Poem*, Annotated bibliographies of Old and Middle English Literature 7, Cambridge 2001. A full, critical bibliography detailing a huge range of work, with helpful annotations.

Siegfried Wenzel, *Preachers, Poets and the Early English Lyric*, Princeton 1986. Argues that the lyrics were used in preaching and teaching.

Rosemary Woolf, *The English Religious Lyric in the Middle Ages*, Oxford 1968. A brilliant study.

13

JULIAN OF NORWICH

[*BACL* pp. 246 f; *BACS* pp.297 f; *NA1* pp. 355 f]

Julian was one of a later generation of those ‡anchoresses whom we have previously encountered in the discussion of the *Ancrene Riwle*. Her calling was not only to be a ‡hermit but to be one whose cell signified both the Christian's death to self and to the world and represented their hiddenness in God (see Colossians 3:3).

Frequently ‡anchorites and ‡anchoresses had spent some time in a ‡monastic community where they received their formation in the life of a consecrated person. It has been speculated that this had been Julian's experience and that this had offered her the opportunity to acquire her knowledge of Latin as well as laying the foundations for her later thinking. Whatever the case may be, Julian had certainly had the opportunity to become a learned woman, her teaching reflecting many of the spiritual currents of her age. Living in Norfolk with its close contacts with Holland, Julian was also in a religious environment that welcomed contemporary Flemish ‡mystical writings and the teaching of European mystics such as the lay Dominican, Catherine of Sienna.

Julian's teaching on the all-sufficiency of God and the inability of lesser things to satisfy human longings stems from Jesus' saying in the gospels that a person profits nothing by gaining the whole world at the loss of their ‡soul (Matthew 16:26) and from his imagery of himself as the long-awaited bridegroom (Matthew 9:15–16). In the Old Testament only God the bridegroom is able to rescue and restore his bride, Israel (see, for example, Isaiah 47; Jeremiah 3:1–5).

This teaching of Jesus is developed by St Paul as death to self (i.e., to self-interest and self-concern) in order for Christ to become the centre of one's life (see Galatians 2:20). It lies behind Julian's references to being 'noughted' for †love (chapter 5). To be 'nothing' in this sense is not a state of psychological self-demeaning; rather it is an acceptance that only God is self-sufficient and uncreated, so the human being has no possibility of existence without him. This theme is developed at length in *The Scale of Perfection*, a treatise on spiritual life by Walter Hilton, Julian's contemporary.

Julian's meditations on the 'homeliness' of God in the †incarnation also has biblical roots (chapter 7). The image of the great lord's homeliness with his poor servant echoes Jesus' comparison of himself with the lord who makes his servant sit down to eat (Luke 12:36–40). In this image Julian is expressing the 'courtesy' of God in the incarnation: God stoops to raise his beloved creatures, enhancing their dignity without compromising his. This note, too, we have found in that basic guide to the ‡hermit life the *Ancrene Riwle*.

Julian's teaching that ‡sin is necessary, found in chapter 27, may appear startling. It reflects, however, the optimism for the cosmos central to the New Testament. Ultimately, all things will be reconciled to God in Christ and will be brought under his rule (see, for example, II Corinthians 6:16–18; Colossians 1:16–20) and there will be 'a new heaven and a new earth' (Revelation 21:1–8). Within this framework the sin that seems devastating from a human viewpoint will not have final power. In this reading of the New Testament hope, Julian is also fortified by the teaching of St Thomas Aquinas, the dominant theological voice in the medieval church, that sin is 'nothing' or 'insubstantial'; evil has no separate existence but is only distortion of the good.

Since Julian's meditations on ‡sin are in relation to the suffering and death of Jesus, which is God's answer to sin, they are also linked to the approach to †original sin in the great hymn, the ‡Exsultet, sung in the celebration of ‡Easter: 'O happy fault, O necessary sin of Adam that won for us so great a redeemer'. In accordance with the spirit of liturgical worship she sees sin as a mystery to be celebrated as part of God's design for the ‡salvation of the world, rather than as an intellectual problem to be analysed. In this she shows her affinity with an older tradition of ‡monastic theology that was giving place to the more discursive, analytical approach of the ‡scholastic theology rapidly developing in her day.

Like her other images, Julian's vision of Christ our Mother (chapter 58) is rooted in the New Testament and its traditional interpretation. In the gospels Jesus likens himself to a mother hen, brooding over Jerusalem like a mother bird over her chicks (Matthew 23:37). Similarly in his approaching ‡passion and death Jesus is likened to a pregnant woman waiting to give birth (John 16:20–1). In John's Gospel water and blood flow from the pierced side of Christ, comparable to the water and blood associated with childbirth: Jesus gives birth to the new man, the human being restored in Christ (John 19:34). In this sense he is mother.

Developing John's theology, the early church saw this water from Christ's side as the water involved in †baptism, which enables the Christian to appropriate ‡salvation and become Christ-like. In the blood, similarly, they saw the body and blood of Christ in the ‡eucharist, the ‡sacrament that feeds the life of the Christian. Jesus is therefore mother in giving birth and in sustaining his offspring. The widespread acceptance of this perception of Christ is evident in the use of the mother pelican as his symbol: she was believed to feed her young with blood pecked from her own breast.[1]

We find this imagery in chapter 61 where we also find Julian's meditations on two other gospel pictures: Jesus calling the children to him (Matthew 19:13–15) and the prodigal son returning to his father (see the *parable of the prodigal son Luke 15:11–32).

In this first scene Jesus is 'motherly', drawing the children to him when his disciples wish to send them away. He asserts that the kingdom of †heaven is the province of those who become like little children. In the second scene, from the *parable of the prodigal son, the wastrel son returns to his father, prepared to be treated no longer as a son but as a servant. He discovers that the father has never felt anything but †love for him. The feelings and thoughts about his loss of entitlement to be called a son, with their expectations of paternal rejection and anger, reveal the estrangement as residing in the son's mind and as totally absent from the father's. The latter's sole emotion is that of love for a son now restored to his proper state.

Julian combines these two images. Rather than being like the adult son, with wrong ideas about the nature of God, people must be like the little child running back lovingly to the mother, knowing there is nothing in her but †love and welcome.

The certainty with which Julian concludes her meditations on her ‡revelations is equally rooted in the optimism of the New Testament. Jesus *has* overcome the world (John 16:33); no temporal trial can separate the Christian from the †love of God (Romans 8:31–9). After the turmoil and pain there is no more weeping, no more death, no more †darkness (see once more Revelation 21). Julian's 'revelations' add nothing new to the revelation of God in the Christian gospel; rather they cast new light on that gospel, enabling her readers to return to it with new insights and awareness.

QUESTIONS

1. To what extent can one respond to Julian's writing without knowledge of her biblical and theological background?

---

1. An illustration of this is to be found in the Mappa Mundi of Hereford Cathedral, drawn c.1300. A caption to the bird in Latin reads in translation 'for my young I rend my heart' and the picture shows the bird pecking at its breast.

2. How effective are Julian's images in conveying her meaning?
3. What themes in Julian's writings seem familiar to you from reading other medieval works?

BIBLIOGRAPHY

Frances Beer, *Women and Mystical Experience in the Middle Ages*, Woodbridge 1992.

Elizabeth A. Clark and Herbert Richardson, ed., *Women and Religion: The Original Source-book of Women in Christian Thought*, New York 1977, new edn 1996.

Carolyn Dinshaw and David Wallace, ed., *The Cambridge Companion to Medieval Women's Writing*, Cambridge 2003.

Carol M. Meale, *Women and Literature in Britain 1150–1500*, Cambridge Studies in Medieval Literature, 2nd edn, Cambridge 1996.

Joan Nuth, *Wisdom's Daughter: The Theology of Julian of Norwich*, New York 1991.

Denis Renevey and Christiana Whitehead, ed., *Writing Religious Women: Female Spiritual and Textual Practices in Late Medieval England*, Cardiff 2000.

14

Margery Kempe

[*BACS* pp. 369 f; *NA1* pp. 366 f]

Margery Kempe was a Norfolk woman, a contemporary of Julian of Norwich, although of a very different background and education. Julian's religious life, however, was clearly nurtured in some kind of literate, educated environment that emphasised interiority; whilst Margery's formation was that of the majority of devoted, illiterate laypeople, dependent upon popular preaching, iconography, and devotional practices.

Margery's first crisis after childbirth arose out of the church's teaching about the ‡confession of ‡sin in the process of reconciliation (Margery's 'being shriven'). Margery would have been taught that ‡absolution (that is, release from sin) depended upon the full confession of all known sins. A ‡penitent might be unaware of, or forget, a particular offence; this was no barrier to absolution but the sin was to be mentioned as soon as it came into the penitent's awareness. Deliberate concealment of sin, on the other hand, rendered absolution invalid because the confession was in bad faith. Margery's †temptations veer between persuasion that the unconfessed sin can be dealt with without the ‡sacrament (an idea potentially ‡heretical) and that she is ‡damned on account of the invalidity of previous confessions.

Today one might consider that Margery was suffering from post-natal depression, which enabled her spiritual torment to overwhelm her reason. However that may be, it is clear from Margery's account that her salvation came from the realisation, akin to that of Julian of Norwich, of the gospel message that God does not forsake his people, however much they believe this is so: the estrangement belongs to their misunderstanding of God and the subsequent image of the divine that they develop.

This new understanding of God marks the beginning of Margery's unconventional Christian life which made Margery in her day a rather controversial figure. Other women in Europe, like the Béguines, lived lives dedicated to God but without religious vows. Those who lived in communities were generally tolerated because they were following a settled way of life. Those who lived outside a community, like Marguerite Porete, might travel, as did Margery, and share their ‡mystical experiences. They attracted both followers and persecutors, the latter frequently equating the freedom of their lives with sexual licentiousness. Margery's lifestyle can be understood within this context to some extent; what makes her exceptional is her marital status, a problem to her contemporaries as to herself.

For Margery's age, complete dedication to God seemed to require the single-mindedness and purity that was only possible through celibacy. Although Christians valued marriage as an image of the relation between God and humanity, there remained a deep ambivalence regarding sexual intercourse even in marriage. This had roots in Jesus' teaching and in later theological developments.

Unlike most of his Jewish contemporaries, Jesus commended celibacy in his comment that some men become eunuchs for the sake of the kingdom (Matthew 19:10–12). Similarly St Paul favoured celibacy as a means of giving total attention to God, especially in his expectation of Jesus' imminent return (I Corinthians 7:1–9, 17–31). Thus, though marriage was accorded high status by St Paul (Ephesians 5:25–33), celibacy for the sake of the kingdom was accorded the higher value.

This positive approach to sexuality became combined in later thought with a more negative approach to sexuality. For St Augustine, the central authority in the western church, †original sin was intrinsically related to disordered sexuality. For St Augustine, like his contemporaries, †love was not a matter of uncontrollable emotion but of the will. To love is to will the good of another rather than to seek personal gratification. Original sin had led to desire perverting the sexual impulse, displacing the centrality of love-as-will; this meant that any act of intercourse involved an element of ‡sin. For those who followed St Augustine's teaching, therefore, a sexually active marriage could not lead to the same heights of holiness as a life of celibacy.

We can see both of these elements in Margery's characteristic way of describing her desire for a celibate relationship with her husband. She desires to be 'free', that is free to direct all her energies, including the sexual, to God, like a eunuch for the kingdom. She also desires to be 'clean', suggesting the lack of purity which she sees within married love.

If Margery's status was one source of concern to her contemporaries, so was the nature and expression of her spirituality. Like her male counterpart Richard Rolle, Margery was influenced by the growing emphasis on 'affective' spirituality and devotion. This concentrated upon evoking an emotional response of ‡penitence and devotion to Christ through engaging in imaginative meditation on his suffering and death and on the griefs of his mother, †Mary. The question arising out of this kind of meditation was of the validity of any resulting experience: was it the product of imagination, of ‡demonic suggestion, or a genuine contact with God? Margery seems aware of this problem in her seeking advice from Julian of Norwich. Her counsel is learned and measured, drawing on the teaching of St Paul (Romans 8:26) and on the teaching of the ‡Fathers of the church like St Jerome, regarding 'the gift of tears'. Julian describes these tears as tears 'of contrition, devotion or compassion'. One difficulty for Margery, for her contemporaries, and for us, lay in determining the part personality played in her response to this gift and which of these three characteristics was uppermost.

As Margery herself describes it, it is not the presence of tears that causes disquiet but the noisy display involved that appears to invite attention. Her description of her attempts to restrain her weeping seem to bear comparison with those of other ‡mystics who describe phenomena such as levitation (being raised from the ground). Most scholars regard such phenomena in mystical experience as peripheral to the person's encounter with God. Their nature and extent are the consequence of spiritual immaturity and the individual's psychology. They are the reverberations, as it were, in the mind and body, of a spiritual experience beyond the person's capacity for sustaining it. Generally, dramatic phenomena lessen or cease as the mystic matures spiritually.

This appears to be the case with Margery. Her closing years are not characterised by any extravagant displays of religious emotions but by †loving and ‡penitent care for her husband. The compassion she had felt in the imaginative contemplation of the suffering of Christ is now experienced in practical care and compassion for a human being. Her contemplation of the suffering of God-made-human ends in contemplation of that same God in the flesh of those he came to save. This relationship between contemplation and compassion is a litmus test for the validity of Christian ‡mystical experience. Ultimately, therefore, it is not to Margery's psychology that we should look in a valuation of her spirituality: we must focus on the love and compassion to which such spirituality gives rise.

QUESTIONS

1. What were your first responses upon reading Margery's account?
2. In what ways have these responses been modified or challenged by your understanding of Margery's religious context?
3. In what ways does Margery's experience compare and contrast with that of Julian of Norwich?

BIBLIOGRAPHY

Frances Beer, *Women and Mystical Experience in the Middle Ages*, Woodbridge 1992.

Elizabeth A. Clark and Herbert Richardson, ed., *Women and Religion: The Original Source-book of Women in Christian Thought*, New York 1977, new edn 1996.

Carolyn Dinshaw and David Wallace, ed., *The Cambridge Companion to Medieval Women's Writing*, Cambridge 2003.

Karma Lochrie, *Margery Kempe and Translations of the Flesh*, Philadelphia 1991.

Carol M. Meale, *Women and Literature in Britain 1150–1500*, Cambridge Studies in Medieval Literature, 2nd edn, Cambridge 1996.

Denis Renevey and Christiana Whitehead, ed., *Writing Religious Women: Female Spiritual and Textual Practices in Late Medieval England*, Cardiff 2000.

15

ALLEGORY IN THE MORALITY PLAY
AND ITS LITERARY LEGACY

[*BAMD* pp. 1 f; *NA1* pp. 379 f]

‡Morality plays developed in the later Middle Ages when the capacity for ‡allegory was very highly developed. In medieval allegory every character or play represents a character trait or aspect of human life. For its effectiveness, allegory asks us to focus on an abstract quality that has been given a physical reality as a person or place. For example, when we see Avarice we are asked to see this ‡vice in action, not to endow the character with human emotions and motives. Allegory is difficult for modern readers as we are so accustomed to analysing individual characters and finding the springs of their behaviour in terms of psychology. Allegory tends to break down human character or activity into component parts and thus to generalise about human motivation. Merely because these aspects or parts are presented as individual personages in the play, we should not fall into the habit of responding to them as complete characters.

What is interesting for us in medieval ‡morality plays is the psychological realism within the depiction of ‡allegorical characters at the service of an older, Christian view of the human being. As in any Freudian or post-Freudian analysis, the human being is under attack from powerful, instinctual forces, but these do not add up to his or her identity. At the heart of the person lies the ability to withstand the attacks of the ‡vices and to choose the development of ‡virtues. What constitutes a person, therefore, is not the shaping force of any genetic inheritance, psychological makeup, or family life, but possession of ‡free will exercised in the choice of vices or virtues. These shape character. We must remember of course that in Christian thought the just use of free will was damaged by the †original sin of *Adam and Eve. So, like Adam and Eve, human beings are now inclined to use their free will to choose in ways that damage their human integrity, rather than further it. And, like Adam and Eve, they are also subject to the wiles of an external force of evil.

Let us look now at three typical features of ‡allegory which influence much of our literature.

1. The ‡allegorical †journey. This has its origins in the biblical journey of the *Exodus of the Israelites, when freed from slavery in Egypt, through the †desert to the promised land. It readily becomes allegorised as a Christian's journey through life. The rescue from the waters of the Red Sea is the beginning of new Christian life in, for example, receiving †baptism. To this is added the journey in the New Testament *parable of the prodigal son. The prodigal son makes a journey into a far-off land, that is into estrangement from God, and must make the journey of ‡repentance back to his father's house. Both these ideas of journey feature in *Everyman*, where Everyman must die, and make his ultimate journey to his father's house; and of course we see this later in such popular works as *Pilgrim's Progress*.

2. The second image is one of the †house, or the †castle, representing sometimes the complete person and sometimes his or her state of mind or ‡soul. For example, we speak of people living in fear or in hope as if the latter were houses or places. In the ‡morality play, such figurative language is made concrete. The soul dwells in the house of fear. The concreteness of the image is seen to come from the gospels (see discussion of the †castle in the essay on *Ancrene Riwle*). So we find in *The Castle of Perseverance* that the soul resisting †temptation dwells in this castle, and later, in Robert Browning's poem 'Childe Roland to the Dark Tower Came', we find another understanding of the mystery of the human person as the dwelling within the innermost citadel of a castle.

An awareness of the significance of these two images will prove vital to understanding later literature which makes use of these ‡allegorical devices. One can think not only of the directly allegorical †journey in *Pilgrim's Progress* but also its function, for example, in Fielding's *Joseph Andrews* and of Charlotte Brontë's *Jane Eyre* where the journey is combined with the use of the allegorical †house. In *Joseph Andrews*, for example, Joseph must leave the house in which he has served and set out on a journey, which becomes a journey of self-discovery about his origins and his nature. And in *Jane Eyre*, from childhood to mature womanhood, Jane journeys between different houses that represent different states both of †temptation and of self-realisation.

3. Perhaps most important for the understanding of Shakespeare and the Jacobean drama is the late ‡morality figure, the ‡Vice. The Vice, not surprisingly, is the enemy of the human, with an implacable hatred of the good. His goal in life is to destroy such goodness in human beings. To do so, the Vice takes lessons from the serpent in Genesis 3:1–5, claiming friendship and concern for his target so that he can misdirect his or her will. So the serpent who speaks so alluringly to *Eve to persuade her that God has ill intent behind his prohibition of the fruit of the tree of the knowledge of good and evil is the archetypal Vice

figure. The Vice is the plotter, the string-puller, the manipulator, responsible for most of the action in the morality play. This makes the Vice the dramatic source of apparent creativity and energy. (We might regard *Judas as a Vice, too, in his false friendship and *betrayal of Jesus. It is Judas who causes the crisis of Jesus' arrest and trial whilst Jesus is the victim of human activity, a contrast strongly heightened in the ‡passion plays of the Towneley Cycle of ‡mystery plays.)

The ‡Vice is also the shape-changer, the one who will take on various guises in order to deceive and lure his victim, just as the medieval church understood the †devil to have assumed the shape of the serpent in Genesis 3. All this is in contrast to the simple truthfulness of God who cannot deceive, is unchanging, and whose activity is also known as rest rather than manic energy. The kind of energy and shape-shifting that the Vice represents would be understood by a medieval audience to suggest the uncentred, unanchored energy of evil, rather than the stillness which is appropriate to God.

The ‡Vice figure also makes it clear that the human struggle against evil is made difficult because evil so often appears in the guise of goodness. People do not choose evil knowing it is evil but are drawn into it by the gloss of apparent good that may come with it. A good example of the development of the Vice figure in slightly later literature is Falstaff in *Henry IV, Part I* and *Part II*. From his original choice of name for Falstaff (Oldcastle, the name of a traditional Vice) it is clear that Shakespeare intended this character to be understood as a Vice figure and in fact he is referred to as this in the actual text. The Vice, like Falstaff, seems superficially attractive and jolly, but we can see that to follow his way would lead not only to Hal's moral downfall but also to the downfall of political goodness. Hal has a destiny to fulfil that will bring about a good within the country. Falstaff's designs are not only against Hal individually but against the building of the kingdom which he represents.

Another obvious Shakespearean ‡Vice figure is Iago in *Othello*, who again feigns friendship in order to destroy Othello and who seems to have no rational reason for his hatred for the Moor except for the latter's innocence and good-ness. And in fact, in much popular literature to this day, a common plot feature is 'the false friend' who manages to bring about the defeat or the defrauding of his victim, a figure we frequently find in the novels of Charles Dickens and in a character like Fainall in Congreve's *The Way of the World* (see the essay on this play). This is a legacy from the ‡morality play.

QUESTIONS

1. How would you explain the difference between metaphor and ‡allegory?

2. Consider any pre-twentieth-century piece of fiction (including fable and fairy tale). See if you can recognise any of the features of the ‡morality play at work in them and explore how they are used.

3. Follow up some of the biblical references and consider how they relate to what you have discovered in your answer to question 2.

BIBLIOGRAPHY

Dorothy H. Brown, *Christian Humanism in the Late English Morality Plays*, Gainesville FL 1999.

John D. Cox and David Scott Kastan, ed., *A New History of Early English Drama*, New York 1997.

Robert A. Potter, *The English Morality Play: Origins, History and Influence of a Dramatic Tradition*, London 1975.

16

MYSTERY PLAYS: *THE WAKEFIELD SECOND SHEPHERDS' PLAY*

[*BAMD* pp. 42 f; *NA1* pp. 391 f; *OA1* pp. 368 f]

The English ‡mystery plays are concerned with the mystery of ‡redemption, which encompasses the whole of human history, from the ‡fall of the angels before the *creation to the *second coming of Christ in †judgement. In this sense, the history of the world is understood as the history of ‡salvation. Traditionally, these cycles of plays were called 'Corpus Christi' cycles. They were performed around the time of this Catholic feast that celebrates the gift of Christ's presence in the ‡eucharist. This is important because the eucharist is understood to make the past present, but also to anticipate the end of time. To celebrate the eucharist is to make present now the *last supper, the *crucifixion, and the *resurrection of Christ, but it is also to anticipate the †wedding feast of the Lamb.

This is exactly the approach to time in the plays, nowhere seen more clearly than in *The Second Shepherds' Play*. In this play, anachronism is used deliberately. The shepherds are decidedly shepherds of their own age as well as representers of the past. They stand for all, past and present, who are waiting for ‡salvation and groaning under the weight of earthly oppression and difficulty. The birth of the child who is to be revealed to them is not only an event in the past; it is also a spiritual reality now. Christians cannot simply recall the past; they must make it a present experience, as contemporary preachers and ‡mystics affirmed.

The presence of Mak the sheep stealer reminds us that Christ is the *good shepherd. But Christ also warned against the thieves who break into the fold to steal the sheep, and the *hireling shepherds who leave the sheep when the wolf attacks (John 10:1–15); and in another place he warned against †wolves in sheep's clothing (Matthew 7:15). Quite quickly the audience is alerted to the human potential for mimicking or parodying the divine, to the necessity of exercising discernment to avoid being fooled by the †devil, the father of lies, and to the need to recognise the presence of the divine.

In the comedy exposing Mak's theft, these parodies take on full force. The ‡sinful Mak hides his sin by pretending that the lamb is a child. The shepherds, prepared to express their natural tenderness for a child, need to exercise discernment. They must look at the swaddled lamb-child and recognise what it really is. After experiencing this human trickery, the shepherds are then led to experience God's use of concealment and ‡revelation. They are led to this true newborn child-lamb who is the *Lamb of God. Just as they exercise discernment in unmasking the false lamb-child, here they discern the true child-lamb and adore.

Jesus says that the *good shepherd knows his own sheep (John 10:1–15). These shepherds, like him, are good shepherds who can recognise true lambs and the *Lamb of God. The child's humanity does not offer any obstacle to their perception. That the child is the lamb reminds us of the theological meaning of this feast of Christmas: God has taken on humanity; he conceals and reveals himself in human flesh so that he might become the †Lamb of sacrifice, the *Lamb who takes away the ‡sin of the world. Every time the audience of this play attended ‡mass, they would hear the words 'Ecce agnus dei qui tollis peccata mundi'— 'Behold the Lamb of God, which taketh away the sin of the world!', from St John's Gospel (John 1:29). Even unlettered mass-goers, unable to understand the Latin, would have known from stained-glass windows, from preaching, from popular glosses on the mass, what this text meant. They would see in this child-lamb not only the wonder of the †incarnation but also the mystery of ‡redemption, since this lamb is the Lamb of sacrifice. Further, they would be called back to the ‡eucharist, the *feast of the Lamb, where there is a similar masking of the divine in the material appearance of bread and wine and a similar challenge to faith. The shepherds look with the eye of faith and so see the divine reality in the stable. Just as they could not be fooled by the false lamb-child in Mak's cottage, they are not deceived here. Similarly the worshipper at mass, looking with the eye of faith, is not deceived by appearances but discerns the divine reality.

The child-lamb reminds us also of the vulnerability that God takes to himself in the †incarnation: he makes himself open to parody and to human contempt and violence. Coming as a †Lamb of sacrifice, we are reminded that the baby is vulnerable to the good and bad intentions of human beings, just as the stolen lamb was to those of Mak. The child can be recognised and adored, or go unrecognised and be destroyed. We see this clearly in one of the gifts that the shepherds present. The bob of cherries is not simply a nice idea, a rustic touch: the cherry with the hard, permanent stone at the middle suggests the immutable, eternal divinity of Christ surrounded by the soft, vulnerable and easily corruptible flesh. The shepherds are signalling to the audience that they are not just simple men who are easily roused to tenderness by the presence of a new-born baby (as we saw in their initial response to Mak's lamb-child), but witnesses to the dawning of ‡salvation.

They are also the first to meet the challenge of recognition and worship or rejection and destruction that this child-lamb presents to characters throughout the New Testament plays in the ‡mystery cycles. These culminate in the Last Judgement play based on the *parable of the sheep and the goats, in which the ability to see Christ's existence hidden within human poverty and vulnerability is the entrance to eternal life for the sheep while the undiscerning behaviour of the goats leads to ‡damnation when Christ comes again (Matthew 25:31–46). This play puts the imagery of this *Second Shepherds' Play* into its fullest perspective. The shepherds' task of seeing the *Lamb in the child is not a single action only here in the stable; rather it is the challenge of all Christian life. Furthermore, it is this capacity for recognition that makes of the Christian a sheep, of the same kind with the Lamb, rather than a goat, which (since goats and sheep in this area are superficially similar) is an imposter, just like Mak's lamb-child. We appreciate this play most fully when we place this first coming of Christ as a baby within the context of his *second coming in the lives of his followers and of his final coming in †judgement.

QUESTIONS

1. Explore the ways in which the shepherds are presented as contemporary characters as well as characters in the past. What effects would you expect this to have on an audience when you consider the play as a challenge to recognition?
2. Compare and contrast the shepherds' approach to Mak's lamb-child and to the Christ-child in the light of the theme of recognition.
3. Follow up the biblical references here and trace the ways in which they inform the imagery and meaning of the play.

BIBLIOGRAPHY

David Fowler, *The Bible in Middle English Literature*, Seattle 1984.

Jeffrey Helterman, *Symbolic Action in the Plays of the Wakefield Master*, Athens GA 1981.

V.A. Kolve, *The Play Called Corpus Christi*, London 1966. An essential discussion of time in the ‡mystery cycles.

Linda E. Marshall, 'Sacral parody in the Secunda Pastorum', *Speculum* 47 (1972), 720–36. A useful discussion of parody in this play.

Lynette Muir, *The Biblical Drama of Medieval Europe*, Cambridge 1995.

Miceal F. Vaughan, 'The three advents in the Secunda Pastorum', *Speculum* 55 (1980), 484–504.

Rosemary Woolf, *The English Mystery Plays*, Berkeley and Los Angeles 1972. A standard text which takes a different approach (from Kolve, above) to the link to the Corpus Christi feast.

17

EVERYMAN

[*BAMD* pp. 42 f; *NA1* pp. 445 f; *OA1* pp. 388 f]

The fifteenth century was a time in which popular preaching and art reflected a concern with the imminence of death and †judgement. An awareness of human mortality was stimulated by the experience of the plague, the Black Death. Images of death in art like the 'Death and the Gallant' church frescoes at Old St Paul's, for example, showed young courtiers in their prime fingering the robes of beauty and passion but confronted with the stark image of death, either in the shape of a reaper figure with a sickle or with the sight of the skull, the *memento mori* 'remember your death'. Building on the injunction to keep death and dissolution before one's eyes in Ecclesiasticus 28:6, these images evoke the atmosphere of the Psalms and biblical †wisdom literature, with their continual reminder not to forget God the creator, or put trust in passing wealth (see Psalms 49; 99; 103:15 – 16; 104:29 – 30; Ecclesiastes 12). In the New Testament, a *parable of Jesus similarly reminds his hearers of mortality and judgement: the rich man who stores all his wealth in barns and sets himself to enjoy himself does not know that he will die that very night (Luke 12:16 – 21).

The opening lines of *Everyman* echo the Psalms in the condemnation of the man who loses himself in pleasure, forgetful of the God who made him, and remind us that 'all flesh is grass' (Isaiah 40:6). The account book mentioned by Death (103 – 10), in which deeds good and bad are recorded, was a popular image at a time when †judgement was conceived in terms of the merits a person had attained through their virtuous acts, both towards God and their neighbour. The idea probably derives from Daniel 7:10 and Revelation 20:12, where the books are opened and the dead are judged 'according to their works'. When Everyman is called to account for the way he has led his life, the only accounts of any worth to him will be his good actions. All other 'treasures' will be of no use, and these include not only the obvious treasures of earthly wealth but all those other things that people value such as friendship and reputation.

Everyman has been storing up treasures on earth, not in †heaven (427 – 8), serving Mammon instead of God (Matthew 6:24). His love of money has blinded him to the needs of the poor (430 – 1). He has clearly taken his own way rather than heeding Christian teaching about the dangers of love of money and possessions (I Timothy 6:10). If Everyman is to be saved he must learn to see Christ in the poor and lose his attachment to every passing worldly treasure. This is the work of ‡repentance that, in the medieval church, usually involved acts of ‡penance, that is, of expressions of sorrow for ‡sin. It is in order to repent that Everyman needs the friendship of Knowledge. This Knowledge, which comes to Everyman's aid, in association with Good Deeds, is not rational or worldly knowledge, but knowledge of the ways of God; this can lead Everyman to knowledge of himself and his sinfulness and thus bring him to repentance, ‡confession, and amendment — and ultimately to ‡salvation.

The idea behind physical ‡penance in the medieval church was to curb the desires of the flesh, which lead to ‡sin, and to amend forgetfulness of God. In physical suffering, penitents recall all the physical pain endured by Christ in his ‡passion and death. They recall all that Christ suffered for †love of them and in order to ‡redeem them. The response of Good Deeds to Everyman's ‡repentance alerts us to the different meaning of that phrase here. Good deeds are not simply the good actions done for others. Good deeds are all those actions that turn the person towards God, the source of goodness and so include praying, Bible reading, and performing acts of penance.

As well as acts of ‡penitence, good deeds include the reception of any ‡sacrament, such as the ‡eucharist or the sacrament of ‡penance (popularly called ‡confession, but frequently referred to in medieval texts as 'being shriven'). The garment given to Everyman when he ‡repents and which he needs when he comes before God (638–41), suggests the wedding garment in the *parable of the wedding feast (Matthew 22:1–14). To be a fit guest at the †wedding feast of the Lamb, Everyman needs the garment of ‡salvation, to avoid the fate of the hapless guest in this parable. The medieval church saw this garment as signifying the innocence that was restored to the Christian in †baptism. Everyman has now re-appropriated his lost baptismal innocence through his repentance. Like the *prodigal son in the famous parable, Everyman has returned to his father and has been given new clothing (Luke 15:11–32).

Like the *memento mori*, *Everyman* is intended to warn its audience of the importance of using life well, in awareness of the brevity of life and the imminence of †judgement. Its message is stark but ultimately hopeful. Everyman can and does ‡repent; although his worldly treasures betray him, he is not left without means of return to the father's house. At his death, in his last speech, he can use the very words of Jesus on the †cross (Luke 23:46), 'Into thy hands, Lord, my soul I commend' (880), and repeat it, to close, in Latin, 'In manus tuas ... commendo spiritum meum' (886–7). Everyman is thus sure of his ‡salvation, and the †angel declares the 'reckoning ... crystal clear' (898). The positive note of the play (it is, after all, intended as entertainment) is reinforced by the Doctor (theologian) closing with a vision of the glories of †heaven; but not before he has reminded the audience that if the 'reckoning be not clear' (914), a dire fate awaits: the cursed will be sent to the everlasting fire, 'ignem eternum' (915; Matthew 25:41). This time the Latin is not translated.

QUESTIONS

1. Compare *Everyman* and the *parable of the prodigal son (Luke 15:11–32). What do the differences reveal about the distinction between metaphorical and ‡allegorical story?
2. Follow up some of the biblical references and consider how they are related to the tone and meaning of the play.
3. To what extent do you consider an appreciation of this play is attainable without some awareness of this background?

BIBLIOGRAPHY

David C. Fowler, *The Bible in Middle English Literature*, Seattle 1984.

Donald Gilman, ed., *Everyman and Company: Essays on the Theme and Structure of the European Moral Play*, New York 1989.

Lynette R. Muir, *The Biblical Drama of Medieval Europe*, Cambridge 1995.

Rosemary Woolf, *The English Mystery Plays*, Berkeley and Los Angeles 1972.

18

SIR THOMAS MALORY, *MORTE DARTHUR*

[*BACS* pp. 431 f; *NA1* pp. 419 f; *OA1* pp. 444 f]

The life and literary work of Sir Thomas Malory are extraordinary in many ways. He was a military adventurer and contrived to be on the wrong side in the Wars of the Roses more than once, spending time in prison and dying in disgrace in March 1471, excluded from a general pardon issued to his former opponents by the restored King Edward IV. Among the crimes attributed to him were rape, robbery, and extortion.[1] It was while he was in prison that he composed the *Morte Darthur*. Although the material has been plundered by children's writers and storytellers with Malory's own sense of its narrative power, poets as different as Spenser (*Faerie Queene*) and Tennyson (*Idylls of the King*) have responded to its imaginative power.

Malory's compendium of Arthurian tales was to have huge literary influence, not least because it was edited and published by William Caxton in 1485, soon after Malory's death. Malory repeatedly refers to 'the French book' as his source, but he gathered the stories from a number of French romances, including the *Suite du Merlin*, and also English poems and prose legends. In his own prose, he makes self-contained stories with strong plots, complex characters, and terse dialogue. Part of a source Malory used was called *La Mort le Roi Artu*,[2] and the death of the king was a focus for a number of writers: but for Malory, and Caxton who gave it the title, the whole epic builds towards the sense of an ending, the death not only of Arthur but of chivalry and the knightly ideal. Though only a small proportion of *Morte Darthur* is directly concerned with the death of the king, and despite the episodic nature of the stories it tells, the title of the work and its plangent ending give it a sense of elegiac completeness.

---

1. But see the discussion of these crimes in a legal context in C.S. Lewis's essay, 'The English Prose *Morte*', in J.A.W. Bennett, ed., *Essays on Malory*, pp. 7–28, at pp. 8–11. Lewis argues that the accusations might not have been proved and that the proceedings were often 'moves in family quarrels'; and especially that rape 'need mean no more than abduction; from a legal point of view Lancelot committed rape when he saved Guinevere from the fire' (p. 10).

2. E. Vinaver, ed., *Malory: Works*, p. vii.

Several critics see a contradiction between Malory the writer, an alleged robber and rapist, and the ideals of which he writes, the honour and 'worship' of the knights and their elaborate system of courtesy. But the real contradictions lie within the knightly ideal itself: how can gentleness, grace, piety, courtesy, and purity co-exist with blood-letting on a grand scale? How can the claims of honour and loyalty be served when they conflict with each other? And indeed, how can those knightly ‡virtues co-exist with fallible human nature? In the character of Sir Lancelot, Malory shows how ideal and reality clash. Malory tries to draw a veil over the adultery of Lancelot and Guinevere with his coy comment that 'love that time was not as love is nowadays' (424), but it is that forbidden love that gives opportunity to Sir Agravain and Sir Mordred in their conspiracy against the pair. The end of the Round Table is precipitated by disloyal love on the part of Lancelot and Guinevere, and loyal hatred on the part of Sir Agravain and Sir Mordred: flawed human nature cannot maintain or be contained within the ideals of courtly love and brotherly fellowship.

For much of the book, Malory is concerned to allow the knightly ideal to be foregrounded and avoids a direct confrontation with Christianity.[3] All the trappings of Christianity are present in the tales: oaths, references to ‡martyrs and ‡saints, to †Mary and God; there are †prophecy and prayer, visions and Christian rites. It is only after the final battle, however, that the Christian elements are allowed to impinge more on the knightly ideal. The threefold testing of Sir Bedivere when he is repeatedly told to throw the sword Excalibur into the lake, reflects Peter's denial of Christ in John's Gospel (as Arthur says, 'now hast thou betrayed me twice' 433, cf. John 13:38; 18:18–27); and Lancelot's threefold vision telling him to go and bury Guinevere reflects Peter's vision in Acts (435, cf. Acts 10:9–17). And whatever the mythical trappings of the death (or departure, at least) of Arthur, the return of the King takes some resonance from the *second coming of Christ predicted throughout the New Testament.

Malory was particularly interested in the character of Lancelot, and in many ways the knight is a believable character. His knightly prowess is un-

---

3. F. Whitehead, 'Lancelot's penance', in J.A.W. Bennett, ed., *Essays on Malory*, pp. 104–113, argues that treating Malory's book as if it were 'an improving religious work' (p. 112) is a mistake, and this is generally agreed. Indeed he suggests that Lancelot's behaviour is 'not in keeping with the monastic way of life he has adopted' (p. 113); but the essay above sees the ‡hagiographical features of this part of the story as indicating how Malory shaped his work, and interprets those things which Whitehead sees as 'worldly affections' as aspects of the ‡monastic and ‡saintly habits Lancelot has adopted. We can see Lancelot as pining or as ‡fasting; as grieving the loss of Guinevere or as ‡repenting his part in it: the text generally places more emphasis on the saintly aspects. See further C. David Benson's essay, 'The ending of the *Morte Darthur*' in Archibald and Edwards, ed., *A Companion to Malory*, pp. 221–38.

matched, but his human failings cause the destruction of the very institution he seeks to uphold. The story captures the fantasy world in which the lovers live and contrasts it with the harsh reality they have to face afterwards. When Lancelot and Guinevere are caught together by the conspirators, they freely use the vocabulary of Christianity ('Jesus Christ, be Thou my shield and mine armor!' 425), but they scarcely take the moral requirements of Christianity to heart. With that may be contrasted the ‡penitence expressed by Guinevere in praying never to see Lancelot again before her death (435), and in Lancelot's mourning for the queen, 'not … for any rejoicing of sin' but in remembrance of his 'unkindness', a word meaning 'unnaturalness' or 'ill-nature'.

King Arthur allows that Lancelot is 'the best knight among us all' (422). But Malory also wants him to be the most Christian, and to that end he uses the conventions of medieval ‡hagiography (stories of the ‡saints). Lancelot keeps vigils at the tombs of the king and queen, living in prayer and ‡fasting like a ‡monk or ‡hermit; he knows when he will die, despite the confidence of his companions that he is healthy; the Bishop has a dream of Lancelot entering †heaven to the celebration of †angels; and when Lancelot dies, he dies smiling and a sweet smell exudes from his body; he is much mourned. These are all motifs which attach to great saints as found in their Lives, those legends that were possibly the most popular, widespread, and enduring of medieval literary genres: Malory consciously uses these motifs to make his audience aware of the particular saintliness of Lancelot.

The book ends conventionally too, with Malory's wish that his readers pray for his 'good deliverance' while he is alive, and for his ‡soul when he is dead. Malory, the alleged robber and rapist, signs himself as 'the servant of Jesu both day and night' (439). Having made mistakes, been loyal to the wrong person, fought in a war that had a devastating outcome, and had time to reflect, Malory the 'knight presoner' may have found in Lancelot the reflection of himself, and in the telling of Lancelot's story, the resolution of his own contradictions.

QUESTIONS

1. Do you find the character of Sir Lancelot believable? Why, or why not?
2. Is there any contradiction between what we believe to have been Malory's moral history and his sympathetic depiction of the ideals of knightly chivalry? Is it reasonable to make connections between the man and his writing?

BIBLIOGRAPHY

Elizabeth Archibald and A.S.G. Edwards, ed., *A Companion to Malory*, Cambridge 1996. Covers a range of issues, from sources to style, from literary studies to modern reception; the book has a select bibliography.

J.A.W. Bennett, ed., *Essays on Malory*, Oxford 1963. A rewarding collection of essays.

P.J.C. Field, *Romance and Chronicle: A Study of Malory's Prose Style*, London 1971.

F. Riddy, *Sir Thomas Malory*, Medieval and Renaissance Authors, Leiden 1987. An authoritative review of the man and his work.

E. Vinaver, *Malory: Works*, 2nd edn, Oxford 1971. The standard edition of the *Morte Darthur*.

Section 2

RENAISSANCE, REFORMATION, AND REPUBLIC

1

Overview: The Sixteenth and Early Seventeenth Centuries

In the Europe of the early modern period, Christianity, politics, and literature are inextricably linked. The attack on the hegemony of the Roman Catholic church, from the earlier proto-Protestantism of Wyclif and Hus, through the searching questioning of early ‡humanists like Erasmus, to the full ‡Reformation assault of Luther and ‡Calvin, depended to a large degree on the new possibilities of the propagation of ideas by literature: literature that was political, as well as religious, dynamite—not too strong a term for its explosive and violent effects on the whole of European polity in the period. The seminal works of the early sixteenth century are in prose; and it is important to note that English ideas at this period depend to a great extent on continental authors like Erasmus, Machiavelli, and Castiglione. The break-up of the Roman Catholic hegemony and the rapid proliferation of religious and other texts in the vernacular languages rather than in Latin was in a real sense a break-up of Europe as a relatively stable political entity, so that the early part of this period marks the last flowering of one mode of England's intellectual dependence on Europe.

We now associate the early modern period in English literature overwhelmingly with drama. For good or ill (mostly for good) Shakespeare's persistent influence dwarfs that of any other writer; but it is also true that he was just the outstanding example of the coming together of new possibilities of theatricality with a language that was developing with remarkable rapidity. This theatre depended, without doubt, on the earlier religious traditions of the ‡mystery and ‡morality plays, but it was increasingly patronised and fostered by the wealthy and aristocratic, giving rise to England's first professional theatre companies working in purpose-built auditoria. This development happened mostly towards the end of the sixteenth and the beginning of the seventeenth centuries.

Yet Shakespeare was a poet before he was a dramatist, and his poetry is part of a vibrant tradition, again patronised, and often practised, by members of the aristocracy. The anthologies rightly give particular weight to Spenser, whose poetry undoubtedly influenced Shakespeare. Spenser's work, of course, has strong Protestant religious undertones. The ‡Jesuit Robert Southwell, from the other side of the English ‡Reformation controversy, brings a particularly continental, as well as a Roman Catholic, sensibility to his work. It is very possible that Southwell criticised the early poetry of Shakespeare, to whom he was distantly related, for its failure to deal with religious themes. Shakespeare's *Venus and Adonis* dealt with erotic love, in the classical sense of that term, whereas Southwell's poetry dealt exclusively with religious themes. Whether this was at first by necessity or choice, it is clear that the later Shakespeare had no option but to be a secular writer, if he was to write for the stage. The roots of English theatre in the ‡moralities and ‡mysteries may have been religious, but those plays were a genre for a time when religion was relatively undivisive. In the Reformation period, the map of Europe was being torn up and redrawn according to its rulers' opinions about religion, and theatre was to become too public and potentially powerful a medium, especially in London, for the authorities to permit religious drama. The theatre was subjected to increasing religious censorship. For example, the themes of religious interest and controversy that dominate the plays of Christopher Marlowe, who died in 1593, are almost entirely absent from the work of Shakespeare, who died only twenty-three years later.

The primacy of the theatre was, however, to be short-lived; though, again, we have to be careful not to underestimate the importance of post-Shakespearean theatre in its own time, just because its products are not popular now. Nevertheless, as the seventeenth century progresses through the troubled Stuart period into the Civil War and the ‡Puritan republic, the influence of the theatre rapidly diminishes. Ultimately, it is almost completely destroyed until the Restoration of the monarchy in 1660, though a few authors like Davenant are still producing dramatic texts in the Republican period. In this period, it is poetry that again dominates the conventional canon: and much of the very best poetry is religious in nature, and in several cases written by clergymen. If there is a golden age of English religious poetry, this is surely it: the work is full of deep religious feeling, vibrant variety, and artistic and technical ingenuity, in the different styles — and different religious personalities and insights — of Herbert, Donne, Milton, and many more.

As the introduction to the seventeenth century in *NA1* observes, the difference in genre and aesthetic sensibility between, for example, Shakespeare and Donne, tends to make us think of them as non-contemporary, whereas Donne's early poems are in circulation well within Shakespeare's creative lifetime; yet the introduction in *NA1* also rightly questions the attribution to Donne of the invention of 'Metaphysical' poetry. This is in part also related to a re-evaluation of the distinctive importance of George Herbert and his ultimate influence on his successors. The clear differences thus identified between Donne and Herbert in terms of artistic sensibility and poetics are accompanied by similar differences in religious sensibility and its mode of expression. Both poets can make us feel that their faith is deep and personal; but their religious questions are differently framed and one senses in Herbert's work a didacticism that is not quite so present in Donne's: but Herbert's didacticism has an undeniable integrity and authenticity. Donne and Herbert both start work within the period of the increasingly uneasy late Tudor and early Stuart religious compromise. Milton, by contrast, is firmly a poet of the Commonwealth court after the Civil War. Again his poetry is religious and doctrinal, but less personal and more formal and, of course, most famously in the form of epic religious narrative. Indeed in this respect he seems to look forward more to the secular Restoration poetry of Pope and Dryden than back to the religious work of Donne, Herbert, and their contemporaries and immediate successors.

Perhaps, also, Milton's work looks forward to the emergence of imagined narrative in prose, which will become the dominant form of literature in the eighteenth century—and indeed remain so until the present. Imagined prose texts are just beginning to emerge importantly among Milton's contemporaries in the second quarter of the seventeenth century, but production really starts to increase after the Restoration. In religious terms, the work of Milton's fellow-‡Puritan John Bunyan is clearly the outstanding example.

QUESTIONS

1. In what ways can we trace the influence of the medieval ‡mystery and ‡morality plays in the drama of the sixteenth and early seventeenth centuries?
2. How does Shakespeare's stature affect our assessment of other authors and other genres in the late sixteenth and early seventeenth centuries?

BIBLIOGRAPHY

Patrick Collinson, *The Sixteenth Century 1485–1603*, The Short Oxford History of the British Isles, Oxford 2001, and *The Birthpangs of Protestant England: Religious and Cultural Change in the Sixteenth and Seventeenth Centuries*, Basingstoke 1988. Collinson's works here focus particularly on religious and cultural change, while giving a general overview of England and Britain in the period. Students should look also at the bibliography for the ‡Reformation in general.

David Daniell, *The Bible in English*, New Haven and London 2003.

Christopher Hill, *The English Bible and the Seventeenth Century Revolution*, London 1994. Hill's consideration of the importance of the English Bible should be read in conjunction with David Daniell's work on the explosion of publication of the Bible in this period.

Roger Pooley, *English Prose of the Seventeenth Century, 1590–1700*, London 1992.

Murray Roston, *Sixteenth-Century English Literature*, London 1982. Roston provides a useful overview of the literature of the sixteenth century, while Roger Pooley's focus on seventeenth-century prose avoids over-concentration on poetry and drama.

2

SIR THOMAS MORE,
UTOPIA

[*BACS* pp. 573 f; *BARL* pp. 21 f; *NA1* pp. 503 f; *OA1* pp. 552 f]

Thomas More is one of the most enigmatic, perhaps even contradictory, figures of the Tudor period. A hugely successful statesman, lawyer, and ambassador, it had seemed that he would become one of the key figures in the emergence of ‡humanism, corresponding as an equal with Erasmus and other leading humanist scholars and contributing to the new learning that sought to soften the excesses of the ‡scholastic theological speculation that had dominated university faculties. He was also a very rich man, a very married man, and a deeply committed father; yet there was a time when he was deeply attracted by the celibate and wealth-denying life of a ‡monk, and for many years he wore a hair shirt for ‡penitence, under the robes of law and state.

Two of the passages from *Utopia* reproduced in the anthologies ('Their Gold and Silver' and 'Marriage Customs' *NA1*, 'Utopian Contempt for Gold' and 'Utopian Marriage Customs' *OA1*) are strongly reminiscent of this sense of what lies concealed under clothing. Ambassadors come to the nowhere state, gorgeously dressed in robes dripping with gold. More was often an ambassador and probably accompanied Henry VIII to the Field of the Cloth of Gold. But the hair shirt would have been ever-present to remind him of his fallen and mortal state, with much the same effect that the Utopians' scorn of gold has on the visiting ambassadors. The same concern for what lies underneath the surface is shown in the startling Utopian practice of bride and groom being shown naked to each other, albeit under supervision, before committing themselves to wedlock. These scenes were written long before More's later master would be disgusted by the prospect of marriage to Anne of Cleves, claiming to have been misled by pictorial misrepresentation of his bride.

Stephen Greenblatt has written of More's suspicion of the dramatic spectacles of state in which he nevertheless played a seemingly enthusiastic part. Greenblatt suggests that Utopia's ambiguities and ambivalences reflect More's sense that his participation was always superficial—always a matter of surface representation.[1] In this context, what has come to be the defining act of More's life, his defiance of Henry over his divorce from Catherine of Aragon, might seem to be an assertion of the conscience of the private individual over the superficial public persona of the civil servant. At some level, this description of More's courageous stand must be true; but at another level, as Peter Ackroyd has persuasively written in his biography of More, Protestantism appeared to More, especially in his controversy with William Tyndale, to be a deeply misguided assertion of private religious conscience over the influence of the *consensus fidelium* — the opinion of the Catholic church given authority by the unity of the church and by the apostolic commission to the ‡papacy.[2] It remains the case that Protestantism appears to Catholic thought as perennially divisive in tendency; a view that seems to be borne out by the continuing divisions of Protestantism from the ‡Reformation onwards.

There seems little doubt that this is how emergent Protestantism appeared to More and that his stance on the royal divorce stemmed from this fundamental feeling. It shows a key difference between More and the ‡humanists on the one hand and ‡Reformers like Luther on the other. The institutions of the Catholic church were for More the bedrock that permitted questioning, originality, and freedom of thought, in the confidence that nothing could be brought down by or destroyed by them. For men like Luther, the institution itself was corrupt at every level and, crucially, could not be allowed to claim unique authority over the interpretation of scripture to justify its own positions.

More's complex and sometimes contradictory personal history makes it more difficult to judge his literary achievement. *Utopia* is an interesting piece of work, but it is hardly as interesting as the life of the man who wrote it. Thomas More stands as a man who lived in the very middle of the turbulence of the early English ‡Reformation, then tried to stand against the flow and was inevitably, but rather gloriously, swept away.

QUESTIONS

1. Does *Utopia* tell us anything about More's view of the contemporary Roman Catholic church?

2. What do you find of literary interest or value in *Utopia*?

---

1. Stephen Greenblatt, *Renaissance Self-Fashioning*, Chicago 1983, pp. 11–73.
2. Ackroyd, *Life, passim.*

BIBLIOGRAPHY

Sorting reliable material about More from the mountain of ‡hagiography can be difficult. The two following biographies make for interesting comparison. Ackroyd's is remarkable as much for its evocation of More's London as of the man himself.

Peter Ackroyd, *The Life of Thomas More*, London 1998.

Anthony Kenny, *Thomas More*, Oxford 1983.

E.E. Reynolds, *Thomas More and Erasmus*, London 1965: traces a relationship which locates More firmly within Catholic ‡humanism.

Gerard B. Wegemer and Stephen W. Smith, ed., *A Thomas More Source Book*, Washington DC 2004. An excellent resource for those beginning study of More.

3

THE BIBLE AND PRAYER BOOK

BIBLE TRANSLATIONS

[*BACL* pp. 356 f (King James Version); *BACS* pp. 588 f (Tyndale); *BARL* pp. 54 f (Tyndale), 181 f (Book of Common Prayer); *NA1* pp. 538 f; *OA1* pp. 528 f]

The comparison of the different Bible translations generated by the ‡Reformation and ‡Counter-Reformation is a very specialist area, requiring, as it does, some knowledge of Latin, Hebrew, Aramaic, and Greek. In English literary tradition, the clear winner has been the version commissioned and authorised by James I of England and IV of Scotland, known alternatively as the Authorized Version or the King James Version. Most of the biblical phrases embedded in English-speaking culture come from this version. It was compiled by select committees of scholars working independently, but it nevertheless retains a very significant proportion of the translation of Tyndale.[1] Tyndale is probably the originator of the word 'scapegoat', widely used today, though not in quite the technical sense for which it was coined (see Leviticus 16:8, 10, 26). The exception to the rule that the King James Version is the one most widely known is perhaps the book of Psalms. The Church of England's Book of Common Prayer (of which much more later) includes all 150 Psalms for use in liturgy, and uses the translation of Miles Coverdale for them, so that the Psalms became much better known in that version. Yet there are other claimants: insofar as early modern translations have influenced Shakespeare, for example, it is commonly believed that the Geneva Bible in English would be the version with which he was most familiar. The Bishops' Bible was also widely known and used by King James's translators. The extraordinary explosion not only of versions of the Bible but of the numbers of copies of them produced in the ‡Reformation period has recently been described by David Daniell in his *The Bible in English*, surely destined to remain the authoritative work on the subject for some time.

Both *NA1* and *OA1* give parallel versions of I Corinthians 13, so it will be useful briefly to consider this passage. This inevitably draws attention to †love.

---

1. Daniell, *The Bible in English*, p. 448, reports recent studies suggesting that the Authorized Version retained about 83% of Tyndale's translation of the New Testament, and about 76% of his version of the Old Testament.

The choice of the Latinate word 'charity' (so Douai-Rheims and the KJV) as against the Germanic 'love' (so Tyndale and Geneva) to translate the Greek word *agape* is regarded by *NA1* as reflecting a more Catholic emphasis on the idea of good works, and thus as a reflection of the middle ground which King James's translators attempted to hold. This may be so; but it is also the reflection of a genuine difficulty of translation, for while the English word 'love' must do duty for romantic and erotic love, familial love, and the †love of God, the Greek word *agape* is much more restricted in the New Testament to divine love and its reflection in the love that Christians should have for each other and for their neighbours. In assessing this translation, therefore, the suggestion that 'charity' carries an implication of good works must also be balanced against the fact that its etymological root is another Greek word *charis*, normally translated 'grace' and referring specifically to divine love and mercy.

At any rate, the influence of the KJV has meant that the triad of I Corinthians 13 has come down to us as 'faith, hope and charity'. Elsewhere in this book it is suggested that this passage (presumably from the Geneva) may lie behind Shakespeare's conception of †love in *King Lear*. The text is still popular for weddings and sometimes for funerals — most famously, recently, the funeral of Diana, Princess of Wales. It is also a specific reminder that the apostle Paul, who is regularly accused, amongst other things, of harshness, arrogance, misogyny, and the deeper sin of just being difficult to read and understand, wrote arguably the most beautiful passage in the New Testament. The hymnic quality of these verses (though they are not part of a hymn) is a reminder, too, of the centrality and freshness of the idea of *agape* in the new religion of Christianity, about which Paul was writing to these early converts at Corinth. Love is the absolute centre of Christianity: the love of God expressed in the person and work of Christ and the love for each other and for their neighbours that Christians are supposed to live out. Whatever the merits of the individual translations given here and the others that could have been added to the list, together they mean that many Christians to whom these ideas were the absolute bedrock of the faith could, for the first time, read them in their own language and take them into their thinking and imagination in an entirely new and much more direct way.

WILLIAM TYNDALE

Tyndale's importance as an early Bible translator has already been touched upon. The passage here on scriptural interpretation is representative of the kind of thinking that brought him into such direct conflict with Thomas More. That such a passage should be written at all was for More an encouragement to the theologically unlearned to make their own interpretation of scripture, which was very likely to lead them astray. There is no sense, reading More's bitter polemic against Tyndale, that he was writing merely out of a sense of duty: his passionate defence of the authority of the Catholic church, expressing its mind through the tradition of the church ‡Fathers and the leadership of the ‡papacy, is entirely consistent with the path of resistance to Henry VIII, which led to his death. Tyndale also, of course, was executed for his faith; and the tragedy of the religious divide of the ‡Reformation could hardly be better illustrated than by the violent deaths of these excellent and godly men, bitter opponents in the controversy.

By a similar irony, Tyndale's insistence upon and defence of the plain or literal sense of scripture was in part undoubtedly an attack on the same ‡scholastic theologians who had previously been the targets of More's ‡humanist writings. There was a pervasive tendency to ‡allegorise, for example, the †parables of Jesus, removing their power as simple and direct teaching narratives. Tyndale's insistence that if one sticks to the literal meaning one can 'never err or go out of the way' is a statement of supreme faith in the Bible as the trustworthy word of God. And herein, precisely, lies the ongoing controversy between Protestants and Roman Catholics: the former tending to believe that the Bible can defend itself from misinterpretation; the latter tending to believe that the tradition of the church's interpretation is an essential safeguard against error.

Tyndale's passage on the ‡forgiveness of ‡sins, from *The Obedience of the Christian Man*, may at first sight seem a relatively eirenic reflection on the forgiveness of God; but like all ‡Reformation texts, it has a polemical tinge. Christ the everlasting and ever-sufficient satisfaction for sins is strongly reminiscent of the most obviously anti-Catholic section of the Communion liturgy of the Book of Common Prayer, denying the need for the repeated sacrifice of the ‡mass: 'who made there [that is, on the cross], by his one oblation of himself once offered, a full, perfect and sufficient sacrifice, oblation and satisfaction for the sins of the whole world …'[2] Similarly, there again seems no need here for the intermediary ministry of the Roman Catholic priest in the ‡confessional; and, especially, no need for good works or any kind of ‡penance to compensate for wrongdoing. Appeal is directly made to Christ, the advocate with the Father, and it is instantly successful if accompanied by returning to right living.

---

2. This, of course, hinged upon the misinterpretation of a poorly articulated doctrine of the ‡eucharist among Roman Catholics. The belief was not that each ‡mass repeated the sacrifice of Calvary but that it made the one past sacrifice available in the present.

JOHN CALVIN

[*BACL* pp. 326 f; *NA1* pp. 544–7]

The doctrines of ‡Calvinism have had a lasting explicit presence in the Christianity of the English-speaking world. The ‡Puritan tradition of Cromwell, Milton, and Bunyan, feeding into the nonconformist tradition after the Restoration of the monarchy, and ultimately into many strands of the ‡Evangelical tradition from the Clapham Sect and early ‡Methodism onwards, still figures largely in English Protestantism and as an increasing, and increasingly vocal, minority in the Church of England itself. Whereas in America, of course, Calvinism has had an assured and pre-eminent place in Christianity from the Pilgrim Fathers onwards. In continental Europe also, arguably the greatest Protestant theologians of the twentieth century, above all Karl Barth, have applied and adapted Calvinism for current thought.

The extract in *NA1* deals with Calvin's most controversial doctrines, ‡predestination and the related doctrine of election: the idea, simply put, that God decides in advance and chooses those who will go to †heaven irrespective of human choice. Alongside these doctrines goes a third, the total depravity of the human condition: the idea that human nature is so distanced from God by its ‡sinfulness that it has nothing to recommend it for ‡salvation; which is why only God's choice and God's grace can be of any effect to save human beings.

It is perhaps worth reciting some of the biblical passages on which these doctrines depend. The doctrine of election begins from one simple sentence of Jesus in John's Gospel. 'Ye have not chosen me,' he says to his disciples, 'but I have chosen you' (John 15:16). These words recall a simple fact on which the gospels in large measure agree: that Jesus commandingly chose his closest followers rather than appealing to them to join him. It is in the writing of Paul, however, that the doctrine of ‡predestination finds fuller expression; for example in Romans 8:29–30: 'For whom he did foreknow, he also did predestinate to be conformed to the image of his Son, that he might be the firstborn among many brethren. Moreover whom he did predestinate, them he also called: and whom he called, them he also justified: and whom he justified, them he also glorified.'

To the same letter of Paul is owed the doctrine of total depravity: 'For all have sinned, and come short of the glory of God; being justified freely by his grace through the redemption that is in Christ Jesus' (Romans 3:23–4). The last three words are vital to the understanding of these thinkers: for Paul, Calvin, and subsequent ‡Calvinism, the election of believers is somehow encompassed in the election of Christ, classically expressed in Ephesians 1:3–4: 'Blessed be the God and Father of our Lord Jesus Christ, who hath blessed us with all spiritual blessings in heavenly places in Christ: according as he *hath chosen us in him before the foundation of the world*, that we should be holy and without blame before him in love' (my emphasis).

The obvious problem with these doctrines is that they seem unjust, which Paul knew just as well as ‡Calvin, giving the objection voice in Romans 9:19: 'Thou wilt say then unto me, "Why doth he yet find fault? For who hath resisted his will?"' But for Paul, as for Calvin, it is inadmissible for the clay to argue with the potter. Above all, they are both concerned to preserve the idea that ‡salvation is the free gift of God and cannot be earned. Both would have denied that God chooses unjustly or capriciously; but both deny more fundamentally any human claim to merit. And for both of them this makes God's †love, in saving the entirely undeserving, greater.

At the time of the ‡Reformation, and in the English Commonwealth, one particular aspect of ‡Calvinism demands further mention: its attempt to order civil society according to the strict doctrines of the church. Calvin argued for some separation between the powers of church and state, but in his own work in Geneva, there was great interpenetration of church discipline with the regulation of the ruling councils. The Reformation, in England as elsewhere, always involved the problem of the relationship between secular power and the power that the church, Catholic or latterly Protestant, claimed or was permitted. The Commonwealth attempt to run the government on Protestant Christian grounds was deemed a failure; but forms of church government in the nonconformist tradition are an enduring part of the Calvinist legacy. The emphasis on the relative importance of the ordained pastor (Presbyterianism), or the gathered local church (Congregationalism) became matters on which Protestant churches divided; but in all shades of nonconformity the emphasis on the empowerment of the lay congregation and their responsibility for their own organisation, and indeed for all aspects of their Christian living, is an enduring and valuable part of Calvinism's legacy.

ANNE ASKEW, LADY JANE GREY

[*NA1* pp. 547–53]

The scaffold speeches of Anne Askew and Lady Jane Grey are from this Protestant tradition of all believers acquainting themselves with the Bible as the Word of God and understanding it for themselves. The availability of the Bible to laypeople, in their own language, and the education of Christian women were both goals of pre-‡Reformation Catholic ‡humanism. Now, however, the alliance of this new-found independence with the new doctrines of the ‡Reformation, themselves essentially new interpretations of scripture, seems to give rise to a new confidence, as the set-piece confrontations of Anne Askew, as well as the poetry of Aemilia Lanyer elsewhere in the anthology, bear witness.

SOLEMNISATION OF MATRIMONY FROM THE BOOK OF COMMON PRAYER

[BACL pp. 473–6; NA1 pp. 553–6]

When Jane Austen's Emma, before the doubtless envious Mr Elton, finally calls Mr Knightley 'George', and when Richard Mason's solicitor objects to the marriage of Rochester and Jane Eyre, we are referred to specific moments in the service of Solemnisation of Matrimony from the Book of Common Prayer. This is the point where, as Emma, puts it, 'I will promise to call you once by your Christian name. I do not say when, but perhaps you may guess where; — in the building in which N. takes M. for better, for worse'; and the point where the clergyman is to ask whether anyone knows 'any just cause or impediment why these persons may not be joined in holy matrimony'. The phrase 'to hold one's peace', meaning to keep silent, has its enduring presence in the language precisely because it is what objectors, if they do not speak at that point, must do for ever after. The version in NA1 is not, of course, from the Book of Common Prayer authorised in 1662 and still current in the Church of England more than three hundred years later; but from one of the prototypes of a hundred years before; but the service is essentially the same, so that its life is more than four hundred years.

The Book of Common Prayer is now much less used in the Church of England than it was; but the pressure to change English liturgy arose only at the beginning of the twentieth century and it did not at first arise principally from the fact that the language of the BCP was antiquated but rather from the fact that the success of the Anglo-Catholic ‡Oxford Movement at the end of the nineteenth century led to strong pressure for reintroduction of aspects of the Roman Catholic ‡mass, which the BCP did not permit. As the editor of NA1 correctly points out, the service of Holy Communion or Lord's Supper devised by Cranmer for the BCP had been a direct attack upon the liturgy of the Roman Catholic ‡mass. First, the name was changed: this would be called the mass no longer. Second, it was in English, not Latin. Third, it did not always translate the Latin but often radically changed aspects of the wording, to make clear in particular that the service was not a repetition of Christ's †sacrifice and to downplay, if not completely obliterate, the idea of transubstantiation. Perhaps most importantly, however, the structure of the ‡mass was deliberately torn apart: the *Gloria in excelsis Deo*, for example, being moved right to the end of the service as a general hymn of praise; and the great consecration prayer itself being split in two, with the two parts separated by the reception of the bread and wine. The priestly ‡absolution was discontinued: instead of the priest saying that he ‡forgave the ‡sins of the people, he merely announced that God forgave all those who were truly ‡penitent — and they had not had to attend ‡confession to achieve this state.

Moreover, the BCP envisaged relatively infrequent communion, providing long speeches for the priest to give the week before he intended to hold such a service, so that the people might be prepared for what is clearly expected to be an event made special partly by its infrequency. For Roman Catholicism, then as now, the ‡mass was the staple of worship every Sunday and was to be celebrated every Sunday. The Protestant churches, including the Church of England, devised Sunday services without communion, at the heart of which were many extracts from the Bible: some, including the Psalms, for the people to say each week as part of the liturgy; different passages to be read each week from Old and New Testament; and a sermon to be preached morning and evening.

In England, therefore, the staple diet of worship for three hundred years was BCP Morning Prayer, more commonly known as Mattins (see *BARL* pp. 182 f), and later when evening worship became more possible and popular, BCP Evening Prayer. Often, the latter service is known as Evensong, because over time these services became unimaginable without music: psalms and canticles were chanted, and other parts of the liturgy were often intoned by the priest. Some of the most lasting impact of the words of the BCP has been because of this sung form, particularly championed by English cathedrals and copied in local parish churches. The use of music in liturgy was (and is) hotly debated — for example as one of the many issues that divides the clergymen Mr Slope and Mr Harding in Trollope's *The Warden*. In particular, the *Magnificat* and *Nunc Dimittis*, both extracts from Luke 3 and the canticles most commonly used in Evensong, retain some hold in popular culture. Individual prayers from the Book of Common Prayer, including the weekly collects, have given many phrases that lived for a long time in English culture. Not unnaturally, the BCP service that had the widest attendance of all over several centuries has given a number of memorable phrases to the language: 'Ashes to ashes, dust to dust; if Lillee don't get yer, Thommo must', sang Australian cricket fans in the 1970s, quoting in part from the BCP service for the Burial of the Dead (*BACL* pp. 476–7).

THE BOOK OF HOMILIES AND
THE LAWS OF ECCLESIASTICAL POLITY

[*NA1* pp. 556–63; *OA1* pp. 1424–9]

The Book of Common Prayer is widely regarded as a fine literary creation. With only occasional exceptions, Cranmer's prose style still too easily wins out in comparison with the Anglican liturgies that have now more or less fully replaced it. There is every reason to believe, also, that Cranmer was sincere in his Protestant theological stance and in perceiving the need for a Protestant liturgy for a Protestant Church of England. Yet the Book of Common Prayer was also, like the King's Bible and the Book of ‡Homilies, a means of imposing uniformity on the nation at a time when internal division and external enemies were a real threat to stability and the state. The 'Homily Against Disobedience and Willful Rebellion' is a very obvious example. We have already seen, also, in our discussion of ‡Calvin, the pressing need, in all the newly Protestant states, for new structures of church government and organisation and a new understanding of the church's relation to the state. On these and other theological issues of the ‡Reformation, Hooker's *Of the Laws of Ecclesiastical Polity* remains the principal Anglican text. The English Reformation rather glaringly lacks a theologian of the stature of Luther, Calvin, Melanchthon, or Zwingli. If there is any claimant, it must be Hooker; yet his work has remained a specialist interest: for example, it would be rare for him to figure in the theological modules even of Anglican priests in training. Hooker's relative obscurity probably reflects, in part, the extent to which the English Reformation was more politically and less theologically driven than the Reformation in continental Europe. Moreover, the very close relationship between the Church of England and the state, created by the Reformation and persisting in England ever since, seems to have tended to a kind of theological and ecclesiastical middle way (or to some critics, both Catholic and Protestant, a muddled way). To some extent, however, this is also Hooker's achievement. Traditional Anglicans claim that the Church of England rests on a triple foundation of scripture, church tradition, and reason: Hooker's argument in the *Laws*, relying on reasoning from natural law, is on this understanding the founding example of the third strand.

THE LORD'S PRAYER

The most pervasive and most resilient of the BCP's texts must be its version of the Lord's Prayer. In any gathering of English Christians, and even more so in any gathering of English unchurched people, the default version of the Lord's

Prayer is still that of 1662. Various changes have been attempted. Perhaps the most successful is 'those' for 'them' in 'as we forgive those who' instead of 'as we forgive them that', yet even in the modernised version now more commonly used in English Anglican worship, no satisfactory alternative has been found for 'hallowed' or for 'Lead us not into temptation.' And, to the despair of their Catholic friends, English Protestant Christians still insist on the Lord's Prayer's ending on all occasions with a doxology, which is some version of 'For thine is the kingdom …'[3]

QUESTIONS

1. What difference did it make to have the Bible widely available in English?
2. To what extent does its literary merit contribute to the enduring influence of the Book of Common Prayer?
3. To what extent does its literary merit contribute to the enduring influence of the King James Bible?

BIBLIOGRAPHY

David Daniell, *The Bible in English*, New Haven and London 2003.

David Daniell, *William Tyndale: A Biography*, New Haven 1994.

Lewis Frederick Lupton, *A History of the Geneva Bible*, London 1966.

Judith D. Maltby, *Prayer Book and People in Elizabethan and Early Stuart England*, Cambridge 1998.

Martyn Percy, *Introducing Richard Hooker and the Laws of Ecclesiastical Polity*, London 1999.

Gerard B. Wegemer and Stephen W. Smith, ed., *A Thomas More Source Book*, Washington DC 2004.

---

3. It should be noted, however, that in this respect the Church of England has been probably the most conservative of the churches in the international Anglican Communion. Other churches have settled on alternatives more easily. It is somewhat beyond our remit, but perhaps worth mentioning, that the Church of England's missionary role across the British Empire means that Cranmer's text has had a cultural influence in many parts of the world.

4

EDMUND SPENSER

SPENSER AND CHRISTIANITY

[*BACL* pp. 345 f ('The Hymn of Heavenly Beauty'); *BACS* pp. 663 f (*Shepheardes Calendar*); *BARL* pp. 197 f; *NA1* pp. 614 f; *OA1* pp. 652 f]

Spenser (1552? – 1599) lived and wrote at a time when vying versions of Christianity were locked in frequently deadly conflict. That he was a Protestant poet and utterly opposed to Roman Catholicism is evident from his earliest work (translating anti-Catholic poems), through the *Shepheardes Calendar* (in which the September eclogue warns against the dangers to England of Catholic missionaries), and in *The Faerie Queene* with its depiction of Duessa in Book I.

'Protestant' at Spenser's time, however, embraced a considerable spectrum of beliefs, from Elizabeth's Anglican settlement with its relative tolerance of Catholicism, to a ‡Puritanism that felt further reform of the Church of England was needed to purify it of ‡papist elements. Where in this spectrum Spenser's sympathies lay has been a source of much debate, and doubtless like many in that turbulent era his thought on religious matters evolved as time went on.

Spenser's religious views cannot wholly be defined in terms of any of the prevailing Protestant orthodoxies. His work displays significant elements of ‡neoplatonism, which, for example, can be seen in his discussion of poetic inspiration in the October eclogue and its sharp distinction between mundane and purer love. This neoplatonism was supplemented with a syncretism of elements of the esoteric Christian ‡Kabbalism to be found in the writings of European scholars such as Johannes Reuchlin (1455–1522) and Heinrich Cornelius Agrippa (1486–1535).[1]

AMORETTI AND *EPITHALAMION*

The remainder of this essay will focus on the Christian elements of the *Amoretti* and *Epithalamion* as religious issues are not to the fore in the October

---

1. Frances Yates, *The Occult Philosophy in the Elizabethan Age*, London and New York 1979, rpt 2001, pp. 111–27. The ‡Kabbala was a Jewish ‡mystical tradition which began in the twelfth century AD.

eclogue and the dense religious reference in *The Faerie Queene* will be the subject of a separate essay.

When Spenser turned to the production of a sonnet sequence he was participating in a (by then) well established literary genre that traced its roots in England back to the Italian love poetry of Francesco Petrarch (1304–74) in his *Rime Sparse*, through its adaptation by authors such as Wyatt, Surrey, and Sidney (selections of whose sonnets are generously represented in *NA1*).

The reader who gives some time to the consideration of the sonnets of Spenser's precursors will see that the genre was a highly conventional one. Traditionally, the sequence was addressed by a male lover to an unattainable beloved. The pain and simultaneous exaltation of the experience was expressed by the sonneteer in the use of paradoxes and stock imagery such as his being represented as a vessel caught up in a storm (see *Amoretti* 34) and the use of the blazon, an enumeration of the beloved's physical beauties (*Amoretti* 64; *Epithalamion* 170–8). Despite his integration of these traditional elements, Spenser departs radically from previous writers. The first word of the first sonnet, 'Happy' already alerts us to this, as in this sequence, the beloved does not remain unobtainable, in fact she weds the poet (the subject of the celebration of *Epithalamion*). Spenser's is not a celebration of profane love; rather it is a love whose goal is an orthodox Christian one, that is marriage.

The *Amoretti* display a carefully thought-out structure, which combines the number symbolism beloved of Christian ‡Kabbalism with the Protestant liturgical calendar to be found in the Book of Common Prayer. For example, *Amoretti* 62 clearly refers to Lady Day, March 25th, the day on which the world was said to have been created and on which Christ was conceived. If each of the following sonnets represents a day, *Amoretti* 68 with its ‡Easter imagery is associated with March 31st, the date of Easter Sunday in 1594 when the sequence was written.[2]

The *Amoretti* thus employ Christian reference in a manner that is atypical of lovers' sonnet sequences. When, therefore, in *Amoretti* 67 we read of the huntsman chasing the deer, we do not just bring to mind the similar imagery employed in Petrarch's *Rima* 190 and Wyatt's sonnet 'Whoso list to hunt' (*BARL* p. 106; *NA1* p. 527; *OA1* p. 621); we also think of Psalm 42, 'As the hart brayeth for rivers of water, so panteth my soul after thee, O God',[3] a psalm sung by converts before their †baptism on ‡Easter eve, and thus a fitting one

---

2. Germaine Warkentin, '*Amoretti, Epithalamion*', in A.C. Hamilton, *et al.* ed., *The Spenser Encyclopedia*, Toronto, 1990, pp. 30–8, at p. 33. For a further instance of carefully plotted number systems see the note on *Epithalamion* in *NA1* p. 864.

3. In the Geneva Bible, the version Spenser would have used.

to emphasise water (the stream) and to precede the celebration of Easter in *Amoretti* 68.[4]

Sonnet 68 is the most overtly religious of the sequence. It celebrates Jesus' †love of humankind manifested in the sufferings he underwent to ‡redeem people from ‡sin. The love that Spenser speaks of here is not the burning erotic fires of Petrarchan love but the sacred love of God for those whom he created: 'So let us love, deare love, like as we ought, / Love is the lesson which the Lord us taught.'[5]

The source for some of the imagery of *Amoretti* 64 shows that the Christian poet did not have to look only to secular sources for imagery which celebrates the sexual. The biblical Song of Songs (or Song of Solomon) opens, 'Let him kiss me with the kisses of his mouth', and goes on to celebrate what was in Spenser's day considered to be an ‡allegory of the union of Christ with his church, with a profusion of erotic and fecund imagery (so, for example, the poem's columbines and lilies are to be found *inter alia* in Song of Songs 4:1 and 2:1 respectively). The Song of Songs was, after the Psalms, one of the most translated and annotated books of the Old Testament in the English Renaissance, fascinating Protestant readers with its heady mix of the sexual and the religious.

The epithalamium is a Latin literary form. As such, it is hardly surprising to see it begin with an evocation of the Muses and go on to invoke Hymen and Bacchus. In the same manner as in the *Amoretti* however, Spenser adapts the form to fit in with his Protestant beliefs. While it preserves much mythological imagery, at the poem's centre is a Christian marriage service before an altar attended by 'the holy priest' (224) and choirs of †angels singing alleluia (240). The poem's music is not just that of Orpheus (16); it is also the roaring organ 'playing the praises of the Lord in lively notes' (219). Similarly, although there is the celebration of the nuptial bed common to epithalamia, this one is focussed on producing children rather than on the joys of sex itself. Paradoxically, it invokes the pagan 'high heavens, the temple of the gods' (409) for a worthy Christian end, namely that they 'may raise a large posterity' (417), not just that Spenser will have heirs to the family name and fortunes, but to increase the number of the godly Protestants on earth (420–23).

Although the intertextuality of the poem is principally bound up with Latin sources, Christian images and allusions are sprinkled throughout. The

---

4. Brooks-Davies, ed., *Shorter Poems*, p. 267. The ideal wife is represented as a deer in Proverbs 5:19.

5. See John 15:12: 'This is my commandment, that ye love one another, as I have loved you', a verse used on Spenser's own wedding day. For this and a list of the dense web of scriptural allusions in this sonnet see Brooks-Davies pp. 268–9.

'Doe you awake' of line 23 onwards recalls once more the Song of Songs, this time 2:10, 12: 'Arise, my love ... the time of the singing of birds is come, and the voice of the turtle [i.e. turtledove] is heard in our land.' Or again, Psalm 91:12 ('They shall bear thee in their hands, that thou shalt not hurt thy foot against a stone') is called to mind by lines 47–8: 'And let the ground whereas her foot shall tread, / For feare the stones her tender foot should wrong' / Be strewed with fragrant flowers all along.'

QUESTIONS

1. What are the different kinds of love to be found in *Amoretti* and *Epithalamion*?
2. Do the references to pagan mythology threaten to overwhelm the Christian imagery in Spenser's poetry?
3. Compare Spenser's use of the love sonnet with that of one of his predecessors represented in *NA1* or another anthology.

BIBLIOGRAPHY

Douglas Brooks-Davies, ed., *Edmund Spenser: Selected Shorter Poems*, London and New York 1995. Contains all of the *Amoretti* and *The Shepheardes Calendar* along with *Epithalamion* in a well-annotated, modern spelling edition.

Anthea Hume, *Edmund Spenser: Protestant Poet*, Cambridge 1984.

Carol V. Kaske, 'Spenser's *Amoretti* and *Epithalamion* of 1595: structure, genre, and numerology', *English Literary Renaissance* 8 (1978), 271–95. Deals with some of the numerological issues in Spenser's *Amoretti* in detail.

John H. King, *Spenser's Poetry and the Reformation Tradition*, Princeton NJ 1990.

THE FAERIE QUEENE, BOOK I

[*BARL* pp. 244 f; *NA1* pp. 628 f; *OA1* pp. 662 f]

The first book of *The Faerie Queene* is an excellent introduction to the work as a whole, not simply because it is the opening of the epic, but also because it is relatively focused (on the spiritual †quest of Redcrosse Knight) and works towards an ordered and clear ending. It is also generally considered to be the one most focused on religious ‡virtue. Its hero is 'the Knight of the Red Crosse, or of Holiness' and his appearance in the company of—amongst others—Knights

4 | Edmund Spenser

of Temperance, Chastity, and Justice is a reminder of how interconnected are the sacred and the secular in Spenser's work.

One summary of the action of Book 1 of *The Faerie Queene* is provided by Alexander Globe: 'The narrative of FQ 1 refers to Adam's Fall and Christ's redemption at the same time as it anticipates final salvation in a heavenly Eden.'[6] Reading its ‡allegory in this manner, Book 1 tells of the spiritual †quest of an Everyman, who, by virtue of his humanity, is at once both *Adam and Christ. This warrior is pledged to the assistance of a 'lovely Ladie', the fair Una, whose royal parents, the rulers of *Eden, have been imprisoned by a dragon.

This brief schema does not do justice to the complexity of Spenser's art. *The Faerie Queene* is a polyvalent ‡allegory. Redcrosse is at once the Christian knight on whose breast is 'a bloudie Crosse … The deare remembrance of his dying Lord' (Canto 2, 10–11), while he is *also* that very dying Lord, *in addition to* being the man whose ‡sin brought about the necessity of such bloody ‡redemption. In this way, Spenser's poem can be read from multiple and simultaneous perspectives. The allegorical significance of Redcrosse shifts depending on the narrative. In doing so, it denies its reader any rigid imposition of signification. There is not even an elaborate system of concentric layers to be brought to the interpretation of the story, as this separation would deny the rich simultaneity of a worldview that connects the prehistoric *Adam, the extra-historical Christ, and the historical Christian.

Redcrosse is called 'Georgos'. The first syllable, *gé*, translates the Greek for 'earth'. This recalls Redcrosse's identity as *adamah*.[7] The red of the knight's †cross may not merely recall the blood of Christ; it may also remind the reader of the red earth that God used to form *Adam (see the account of the creation of Adam in Flavius Josephus's *Jewish Antiquities*).[8] The figure of the knight is an archetypal figure of the masculine. At the end of his †quest, as Redcrosse battles the dragon, one is reminded once more of his identity as Adam/Christ. Collapsing in the face of the dragon's 'Huge flames, that dimmed all the heavens light' (Canto 11, 390), he falls down at the foot of the Tree of Life. This locates the combat in *Eden as 'Great God it [the tree] planted in that blessed sted' (Canto 11, 412). The Tree of Life, which stands near the Tree of the Knowledge of Good and Evil, is at once both the Tree of Life from Genesis and the †cross. Because of this latter identity, its balm, the blood of Christ, has restorative powers and Redcrosse falls into a deep healing sleep.

6. Alexander Globe, 'Eden', in A.C. Hamilton *et al.*, ed., *The Spenser Encyclopedia*, p. 233.
7. Globe, 'Eden', p. 233.
8. H.St J. Thackeray, ed. and trans., *Josephus, Jewish Antiquities*, Books 1–3, Cambridge MA 1998, p. 16. Flavius Josephus (38–100 AD) was a Jewish priest, theologian, and historian.

The identity of Una is as involved as that of Redcrosse. Una is, *inter alia*, the type of the ideal church. Her name is a clue to her identity. As Una, 'one', she is the one true church, a fitting heroine for Book One of the poem. Her unity also alludes to her perfection and her holiness/wholeness. Her face, like the multiplicity of meanings of the text, is hidden by a 'vele, that wimpled was full low' and she rides on 'a lowly Asse more white then snow' (Canto 1, 31, 29). The image of the woman on the ass recalls †Mary and the flight into Egypt, just as the animal's colour reminds one of Una's purity. This feature is emphasised by the fact that the reader first meets her accompanied by 'a milke white lambe' (Canto 1, 36) with which she is identified in ‡virtue: 'So pure and innocent, as that same lambe, / She was in life and every vertuous lore' (Canto 1, 38–8). Una, the daughter of *Eve, is therefore also a representation of Mary, the second Eve.

Una 'by descent from Royall lynage came' (Canto 1, 39). An orthodox Protestant image of the national church and its head Elizabeth, she is defined in terms of the succession of the throne of England rather than the apostolic succession of the ‡popes of Rome. As befits her role, she urges the power of faith when Redcrosse is confronted by Errour (Canto 1, 165), and when she falls amongst the rude and pagan satyrs she tries to teach them holy truth (Canto 6, 168). Una is also recognised as an ‡allegory of the church because of her relationship to Redcrosse/Christ. The two are to be joined together in the ‡eschatological †marriage of the Lamb of Revelation 19:7.[9] In fact, the identities of the couple are reciprocal in that the two are defined in the light of one another, as it is equally true that Redcrosse figures Christ because of his relationship to Una. In a narrative formed on symmetries, the identities of the couple are mutually reinforcing.

Redcrosse and Una first encounter ‡sin early on in the proceedings of Canto 1. They are happy to relieve their immediate distress in sheltering in a wood, 'Whose loftie trees yclad with sommers pride, / Did spred so broad, that heavens light did hide' (Canto 1, 58–9). Proverbs 16:18 warns that pride comes before destruction. Just as the road to †hell is broad and paved with good intentions (see Matthew 7:13), the well-meaning adventurers in the wood with its 'pathes and alleies wide' (Canto 1, 61) are soon caught up in the delight of the variety of its trees and the beguilement of its birdsong. They have thus entered the 'wandring wood … Errours den' (of course, Errour derives her name from *errare*, 'to stray', Canto 1, 114). This is the beginning of Redcrosse's romantic and spiritual combat—in which the reader can join him.

---

9. It is worth noting that Book 1 ends in the couple's betrothal and not in their marriage. The marriage of Redcrosse and Una would not just finish Book 1; in some sense it would finish the whole epic.

QUESTIONS

1. What is Redcrosse's greatest spiritual struggle?
2. Do Redcrosse's gravest dangers come from within or without?
3. Where does the poem make reference to the Roman Catholic church and what stance does it take towards it?

BIBLIOGRAPHY

Douglas Brooks-Davies, *Spenser's 'Faerie Queene': A Critical Commentary on Books I and II*, Manchester 1977. An accessible introduction to Book I.

A.C. Hamilton *et al.*, ed., *The Faerie Queene*, Harlow 2001. A thoroughly annotated edition of the complete poem.

Graham Goulder Hough, *A Preface to The Faerie Queene*, London 1962. A straightforward introduction to reading *The Faerie Queene*.

James Nohrnberg, *The Analogy of the Faerie Queene*, Princeton NJ 1976. A more challenging and detailed work on Spenser's writing.

5

ROBERT SOUTHWELL,
'THE BURNING BABE'

[*BARL* p. 647; *NA1* p. 956; *OA1* p. 612]

The date for 'The Burning Babe' is 1602, whereas the date of Robert Southwell's death is 1595. Because of the secrecy of Southwell's ‡Jesuit mission, his poetry was not published until after his death, although it may have had some circulation in Roman Catholic ‡recusant circles before that time. In fact, the undoubted later popularity of Southwell's work almost certainly owed a great deal to the nature of his death and the manner in which he bore it. For similar reasons, he is now a ‡saint of the Roman Catholic church. Southwell was executed for treason; yet he had written passionately and cogently of the recusants' loyalty to England and Elizabeth I in his 'An Humble Supplication to Her Majestie'. At the latter end of Elizabeth's reign, however, amidst the insecurity aroused by the problem of the succession, there was no tolerance of the Jesuit mission. The priest-hunter Topcliffe suborned a woman in one of the houses that hid Southwell, and he was thereafter mercilessly tortured and ultimately executed. The accounts of his death all agree that he bore it bravely and humbly, that he evoked great sympathy, and that this contributed to the subsequent vogue for his poetry.

One particular theme of Southwell's trial has important implications in the work of a more famous contemporary. The ‡Jesuits had developed a doctrine of ‡equivocation — essentially saying something that appeared to mean one thing but might also mean the opposite — so that those who hid the Jesuit priests might lie to the authorities with a clear conscience. We must bear in mind that these people must have been devoutly religious to run the risk of hiding Southwell and his Jesuit superior Henry Garnet, so that it is probable that this doctrine was genuinely pastoral and not merely tactical, as Topcliffe and the authorities argued. There is a folk story of a hostess with a priest hiding under the floorboards beneath her who responds to the question, 'Is there a priest in the house?' with the bold 'Not unless I'm standing on him.' The story can hardly be true; but this is an exact example of equivocation and the use to which it was put. Southwell's argument at the trial, and Garnet's later treatise on the subject, inevitably had to be more subtle, to justify less transparent deceptions of the authorities, but the allegation at the trial largely was that he had encouraged treason by encouraging ‡recusants to lie to the officers of the Crown.

In literature, the doctrine of ‡equivocation is most familiar to us as the theme of the Porter's scabrous satire in Shakespeare's *Macbeth*. The Porter uses the word 'equivocator' to describe one of those he is admitting to 'the everlasting bonfire'. But equivocation is woven into the whole thematic structure of the play in its use by the Witches: 'th'equivocation of the fiend that lies like truth' and in its relation to the pervasive imagery of doubling and multiplication: 'Double, double, toil and trouble ...', 'Yet I'll make assurance double sure', and so on. There is not much doubt that the equivocator in question is Garnet, who was executed for his alleged complicity in the Gunpowder Plot and who had written a well-known treatise on equivocation, composed, or at least published, after Southwell's death, to justify the doctrine for which Southwell had been executed.

Garry Wills has argued further that the imagery of Southwell's 'Burning Babe' can be traced in Macbeth's 'naked babe' soliloquy: and it has been suggested that imagery from another similar Southwell poem, 'New Heaven, New Warre', is also an influence at this point. If so, its inclusion complicates the pattern of allusion to ‡equivocation in *Macbeth*, not least because it is prefaced by Lady Macbeth's echoing of equivocation in the preceding scene, in which she says that all her duty to Duncan 'done twice and then done double / Were poor and single business'. Here the hostess, emphatically so described in the text, uses the language of doubling to emphasise her complicity with the Witches; but in the next scene, her husband uses the poetry of one of the proponents of equivocation to give voice to the resistance of his conscience to the evil he is contemplating. And in using Southwell's poetry in this way, it may well be that Macbeth evokes the image of the ‡saintly poet himself, of whom it might truly be said, as Macbeth says of King Duncan, that he had borne his faculties so meek that his ‡virtues pleaded like †angels, trumpet-tongued, against the deep ‡damnation of his taking off.

In 'The Burning Babe', for all the apparent simplicity and near sentimentality of the baby and its suffering, the range of imagery is complex. Southwell makes allusion to several different biblical and traditional ideas. Perhaps most obviously, the baby is the Christ-child of Christmas, bringing warmth in the English winter with which the poem begins. But the child is also the innocent suffering victim of Calvary, the fire burning him fed by 'wounding thorns' (a reference to the crown of thorns), and his blood made into a bath for washing.

The fire is also fed by the justice and mercy of God:[1] one of the earliest (and continuing) debates of Christianity was how God's justice and mercy could both be satisfied in the ‡atonement brought about by Christ. And the reference to the furnace and 'defiled souls' may perhaps be to ‡purgatory, but certainly to the biblical idea of God coming in †judgement in Malachi 3:2, 'But who may abide the day of his coming? and who shall stand when he appeareth? for he is like a refiner's fire.'

Southwell uses the simple device of relating a strange and perplexing vision without detailed explanation. Many would have recognised his allusions to the Christian and biblical traditions and thus have the context to understand the poem, but even those who did not might find their 'heart burn within' them (Luke 24:32) when they made the connection between the suffering of the child and 'Christmas day'.

QUESTIONS

1. Do you think Southwell's imagery works? Follow up the imagery of fire in a biblical dictionary and discuss Southwell's allusions.
2. Assess the relationship between Southwell and Shakespeare.

BIBLIOGRAPHY

There is still not much material on Southwell, who now commands interest as much for his possible relation to Shakespeare as for his own.

Christopher Devlin, The Life of Robert Southwell, Poet and Martyr, London 1956. Devlin's Life has a ‡hagiographical quality which sometimes leaves it unpersuasive.

James H. Macdonald and Nancy Pollard Brown, ed., The Poems of Robert Southwell, S.J., Oxford 1967: has a reliable introduction.

Scott R. Pilarz, Robert Southwell and the Mission of Literature 1561–1595: Writing Reconciliation, Aldershot 2004.

---

1. God is not mentioned in the poem, of course.

6

CHRISTOPHER MARLOWE,
DOCTOR FAUSTUS

[*BARD* pp. 155 f; *NA1* pp. 970 f; *OA1* pp. 845 f]

Christopher Marlowe was accused of being an atheist. The matter was never brought to trial because he was killed shortly before he was to appear before the Elizabethan Council. The official verdict of the inquest into his death was that he died in a dispute about 'the reckoning'—the bill—in a private party in a hired room, and that he was killed in legitimate self-defence. Scholars have always questioned this, and, most recently, Charles Nicholl has traced some of the complicated relationships of the English espionage service of which there is little doubt that Marlowe and the other guests that day were members. The implication is that Marlowe might have known too much about the service to come to trial before the whole Council and was therefore deliberately silenced by his erstwhile colleagues.[1]

Marlowe's alleged atheism, then, is a matter of some doubt, because it is clear that there was a general search for grounds on which to convict and silence him. Something similar may be said about his alleged homosexuality. A recent biographer, David Riggs, has written:

> The question of whether or not Marlowe was a homosexual is misleading ... [In] the final weeks of his life ... he was accused of atheism, coining and crypto-Catholicism. In the course of producing this moral monster, his accusers further denounced him for supposedly saying that 'all they that love not Tobacco and Boys were fools' and proclaiming 'that St John the Evangelist was bedfellow to Christ' ... these sensational utterances lead us away from the flesh-and-blood Christopher Marlowe ... into the symbolic

---

1. Charles Nicholl, *The Reckoning: The Murder of Christopher Marlowe*, London 1992. For our present purpose, it is important to note that the targets of espionage were Roman Catholics, at home and abroad.

universe of Elizabethan morality ... the search for Marlowe's innate sexual identity leads nowhere.[2]

The last sentence is somewhat overstated, but Riggs is certainly correct in pointing out the acute difficulty we have in getting reliable information about any aspect of Marlowe's adult life, because of the overlay of misdirection and propaganda that inevitably surrounds a spy who is subsequently viewed as a traitor. To take another religious example, it is worth remembering that, as well as atheism, Marlowe was also accused of crypto-Catholicism. This may be simply untrue; or it may reflect a pose that he adopted for his anti-Catholic espionage activities; or it may be that real Catholic sympathies gave him useful cover: or it may be that any combination of the above was true to differing degrees at different times!

For our present purpose, Marlowe's alleged homosexuality is of interest only as it bears on his alleged atheism and the attitude that both these factors might engender with regard to the peril of one's ‡soul. Marlowe's concern with religion is inescapably a major theme of his plays. And religion is, moreover, explicitly and repeatedly linked to violence and cruelty: both the violence of God as †judge and avenger; and the violence and cruelty of religious people against those whose faith is different from their own. In addition, in *Edward II*, Marlowe chooses as his theme a homosexual king of England, whose viciously cruel murder was universally held to be a parody of the sodomy that was regarded as the reason for his failure as a king.[3] The extent to which Marlowe was personally convinced that homosexual practice was morally allowable or that atheism was philosophically coherent cannot be ascertained, but it remains the case that he would have had to hold both those views in extreme tension with the culture in which he had been rigorously educated, which taught him that both rendered him liable to eternal ‡damnation and punishment. In his plays, that punishment is vividly, often cruelly, displayed.

It is notable, however, that the comments attributed to Marlowe with regard to religion all have a sense of play—perhaps a sense of irony—and it is important to bear this is mind when judging his treatment of religious themes. Irony is one of the distinctive notes of Marlowe's voice, and it is hard not to feel that his choice of topics, and indeed of central characters, for his plays is

---

2. David Riggs, *The World of Christopher Marlowe*, London 2004, p. 76. The first three words of the title are important. Riggs attempts a new historicist biography, reflected in the paradoxical attack on traditional ‡humanist concerns in the passage cited.

3. Edward was allegedly murdered by the insertion of a red hot spit into his anus. McAlindon importantly notes, however, that in *Edward II*, 'Remarkably for the period, there is no suggestion that homosexual love is in itself wicked or unnatural' (*English Renaissance Tragedy*, p. 111).

to some extent ironically determined by a quizzical eye turned upon religion. Tamburlaine is the Christian God's chosen instrument of †judgement on Islam and Babylon, and Marlowe's Christian audience would have understood him as such; but he is himself a non-Christian barbarian. Marlowe's *The Massacre of Paris* has not fully survived, but its theme is a brutal act of inter-Christian violence. *The Jew of Malta* is another story of vicious inter-religious strife, in which adherents of Judaism, Christianity, and Islam are all implicated, to the not very great credit of any. Of the death of Edward II, McAlindon writes, 'the burning spit may seem too monstrous to be associated with any conception of justice; but comparable horrors were commonplace in pictorial and written descriptions of Hell, Lightborn's name is an obvious Anglicisation of Lucifer, and Christians did believe that Hell was part of eternal law.'[4] Finally, in *Doctor Faustus*, Marlowe makes a full dramatic exposition of the Christian doctrine of †hell, ending with the apostate Faustus's horrifying screams as he enters it.

Faustus would clearly not be an atheist in the modern sense of that term: there is no evidence in the text that he does not believe in God; rather he chooses to ignore the *commandments of God for the sake, above all, of knowledge. In terms of the Christian tradition, he would therefore be first an apostate—one who having been a Christian renounces his Christian allegiance—and a Satanist. But it must be noted that, from the first, he does not essentially want power in order to live the traditionally conceived immoral life of luxury and lust. Indeed, in *Doctor Faustus*, the scenes that tend to grate on a modern sensibility are those where, given the power he has been seeking, Faustus can only seem to use it like a cut-price party entertainer, making illusions that may have fascinated the theatrical audiences of time but seem trivial and stale now.[5] McAlindon argues, though, that the triviality of Faustus's 'shows' bears real theological significance. †Tempted, like *Eve, to become like God (Genesis 3:5), Faustus in fact only becomes a man who is allowed to play at being God:

> Fundamental to the meaning and method of the play is the old theological argument that magic, drama, and pagan mythology are all closely related instruments in Satan's endeavour to pervert mankind from the contemplation of the unchanging truths as embodied in the Christian faith and in the Bible.... Faustus's

4. McAlindon, *English Renaissance Tragedy*, p. 112.
5. It can be difficult, though, for us to imagine the kinds of necessity imposed on the playwright by the taste of the time. For example, it is almost certain that at some point the Hecate scenes and the Witches' dances were added by Thomas Middleton to Shakespeare's *Macbeth*, possibly at the expense of some Shakespearean material now permanently lost to us; but few directors would now consider the Hecate scenes worth staging.

addiction to show,... from a biblical standpoint ... simply confirms his essential humanity, his weakness for what is 'pleasant to the eyes' [Genesis 3:6].[6]

The Christian tradition did not deny the possibilities of magic, but consistently disapproved the practice of it as potentially involving the power of †Satan. The point is essentially a simple one: if there is only one true good God who alone can work miracles, then any other miraculous and magical phenomenon must come from a source of evil power. The key New Testament narrative about this is the story of Simon Magus in Acts 8:9–24. Simon Magus was a sorcerer in Samaria, who became a Christian but then tried to buy from the Christian apostles the spiritual power that he saw them demonstrate. His wanting to buy it is roundly condemned by Peter as showing an entirely ‡sinful attitude to spiritual power. Part of the point is that Christians should seek not spiritual power (and, one might add, any other kind of power) for its own sake, or for their own aggrandisement. It is against this firm tradition that Faustus's pact with Mephistophilis is judged and condemned.

In the final act, however, Marlowe does succeed in evoking the audience's compassion for Faustus and, perhaps, our reflection on our own humanity. The brilliantly effective use of time and the clock imports a universal dimension. As Donne's bell tolls for every man, so Faustus's clock chimes for every man, recalling the earlier Everyman of the ‡morality play (see the essay on *Everyman*), just as Mephistophilis recalls the ‡Vice; but it also chimes, in particular, for this man who might have become master of any proper discipline he chose, mourned by the final Chorus in a single monosyllabic image as full of pathos and power as anything in early modern tragedy: 'Cut is the branch that might have grown full straight.'

QUESTIONS

1. Consider the Epilogue to *Doctor Faustus*. Some modern directors and interpreters read it as ironical, and Faustus's last words as something approaching relief. Do you think this is possible, or is it anachronistic? Justify your answer from the rest of the play.

2. Is Faustus ultimately unrealised? Give your reasons for your answer.

---

6. McAlindon, *English Renaissance Tragedy*, pp. 125–7.

BIBLIOGRAPHY

Douglas Cole, *Suffering and Evil in the Plays of Christopher Marlowe*, Princeton NJ 1962.

T. McAlindon, *English Renaissance Tragedy*, London 1986.

Paul Whitfield White, ed., *Marlowe, History, and Sexuality: New Critical Essays on Christopher Marlowe*, New York 1998.

7

WILLIAM SHAKESPEARE

SHAKESPEARE AND CHRISTIANITY

The industry of Shakespeare criticism really begins in earnest in the early twentieth century; and the ideology of that period created a paradigm for criticism that was still in place well into the second half of the century. Part of that ideology was the sense that religion was less and less important as a cultural phenomenon and, in particular, was seen as playing less and less an important part in the understanding of human behaviour, compared to the emerging insights of human psychology. So, for example, A.C. Bradley, interpreting Banquo's struggle with his conscience in this light, feels able to do so without reference to the Christian doctrine of †temptation as it would have been understood in Shakespeare's time.[1] Alongside this secularising of the categories of interpretation went a view that Shakespeare's personal religion was not an important thing to understand, and an assumption that it was in any case probably the same as everybody else's: which came to mean the kind of relatively quietist Anglicanism that was normal amongst the English critics, and that also fitted with what was the standard view of the English ‡Reformation — that after the religious upheavals of the reigns of Henry VIII, Edward VI, and Mary, everything settled down peaceably under good Queen Bess.

At the end of the twentieth century, as is well known, this comfortable critical paradigm had been broken down in all its aspects, its timeless verities exposed as heavily conditioned by its own time and culture. And one important aspect of Shakespearean criticism in this later period has been a much more serious concern with the religion of Shakespeare's time and of Shakespeare himself. The first and most obvious thing to be said is that Shakespeare was a Christian, living in a Christian culture and society. It is difficult now for us to grasp the extent of the hegemony of Christianity in Shakespeare's world.

In the west, even those of us who are religious believers are now educated in a thoroughly secular mindset: faith tends to be removed to the private sphere,

---

1. A.C. Bradley, *Shakespearean Tragedy*, first published in 1904 and the subject of numerous reprints. In the London 1966 edition, the well-known excursus on Banquo in *Macbeth* is on pp. 319–27: eight pages which might be summed up in the single sentence — Banquo, like Macbeth, is really †tempted; but unlike Macbeth, he consistently resists.

in part as a defence against the difficult questions posed by modernity and postmodernity. In Shakespeare's time, almost the exact opposite was true. Even the very few who affirmed themselves as non-believers had been educated in a thoroughly religious mindset, which was both the public and private ideology. In this period, the assumptions one made about one's personhood and one's personal, social, political, and cultural relationships were inescapably religious. Of course, the Protestant ‡Reformation was the beginning of a process that increasingly emphasised the personal and individual over the corporate and communal in Christianity; and it undoubtedly created a climate in which intelligent people had to think carefully about their religious belief and practice, since the wrong belief and the wrong practice could be fatal for some. But the Catholic/Protestant divide did not at this time offer a secular option outside Christianity.[2] It is in this sense that Shakespeare's work must be considered as religious and indeed Christian, simply as a function of the time and place in which it was written.

The personal faith of Shakespeare himself is now similarly the subject of a great deal of critical scrutiny and debate. The main question has become to what extent Shakespeare and his family were adherents of the old Catholic faith. As with a number of aspects of his life, there is a specifically tantalising amount of information: just enough to make possible a valid, reasoned, critical debate, but almost certainly not enough, in the present state of our knowledge, to reach a firm conclusion. There is undoubtedly a possibility, however, that Shakespeare was, at some points in his life, a secret Catholic: as secret as all Catholics were increasingly forced to be in the increasingly unquiet reign of Elizabeth. All Elizabeth's foreign enemies were Catholics, and to be aligned with them came to be a treasonable offence. In *Macbeth*, for example, Shakespeare shows an ambivalence about the Catholic ‡recusant cause, behind the public surface of the Porter's scabrous criticism of the ‡Jesuit ‡equivocators (see further the essay on Robert Southwell).

Shakespeare's Catholicism cannot be taken as a firm critical conclusion in the state of current knowledge. It is important to say, however, that in measure as we think the possibility increases, we must also think in similar measure of the importance of religion to him. To be a Catholic was a difficult and dangerous commitment. Perhaps it is true that Shakespeare was not a sufficiently important political figure to risk the ultimate penalty. But if we take seriously

---

2. The main moderation of the Christian hegemony was not, at this point, secularism, but the recovered Graeco-Roman classical worldview: not its polytheism, of course, but its principles of interpretation in medicine, human psychology, gender, family life, society, politics, and cosmology. See, for example, T. McAlindon, *Shakespeare's Tragic Cosmos*, Cambridge 1990, *passim*.

the possibility of his adherence to the old faith, we must take seriously also the depth of his faith, and its likely influence upon his writing.[3]

In conclusion, then, the explicitness, personal depth, and church allegiance of Shakespeare's faith will probably always evade us—apart from anything else, they probably varied over time, like most people's—but what is important is that we take seriously the facts that Shakespeare himself, and his body of work, were participant in a thoroughly religious and thoroughly Christian culture, which we need to try to understand, both in general and in detail.

QUESTIONS

1. Can any evidence of Shakespeare's personal religious inclination be gleaned from his plays?
2. Discuss the significance of religion in any of Shakespeare's plays.

BIBLIOGRAPHY

Two reliable lives in differing styles are Anthony Holden, *William Shakespeare*, London 1999; and Park Honan, *Shakespeare: A Life*, Oxford 1998.

E.A.J. Honigmann, *Shakespeare: The Lost Years*, 2nd edn, Manchester 1998. From the plethora of Shakespeare biographies, E.A.J. Honigmann's treatment remains seminal for the new consideration of Shakespeare's faith and possible Catholicism.

Samuel Schoenbaum, *William Shakespeare: A Documentary Life*, Oxford 1975: essential for discovering the details of evidence on which the ever-growing edifice of Shakespeare biography is allegedly based.

An excellent initial bibliography of the important instigators of the present debate about Shakespeare's possible Catholicism, notably Eamonn Duffy, Gary Taylor, and Peter Milward SJ, can be found at <http://www.bc.edu/ bc_org/avp/cas/relarts/shakespeare/Shakesbibl.html>.

TWELFTH NIGHT

[*NA1* pp. 1043 f]

Written around 1601, *Twelfth Night* comes last in the line of Shakespeare's romantic comedies. The twelve days following Christmas were a time of feasting and revelry sometimes known as the 'Feast of Fools' and the interplay of folly

---

3. See especially Richard Wilson, *Secret Shakespeare*, Manchester 2004, and also Richard Dutton, Alison Findlay, and Richard Wilson, ed., *Theatre and Religion*, Manchester 2003.

and †wisdom is a primary theme throughout the play. This binary opposition may easily be traced to its many occurrences in Old Testament and ‡apocryphal wisdom literature where wisdom is intimately related to moral ‡virtue and folly to moral deficiency. The true fool is one who misuses his abilities, above all one who rejects the wisdom of God. At the time of the Renaissance wisdom was a high ideal to aspire to—a far cry from the modern concept of wisdom as mere prudential behaviour. According to Eugene Rice, it 'defined man's dignity and described the highest degree of perfection of which human nature is capable'.

Some proverbs of the Old Testament seem tailor-made for Sir Toby, one of several characters lacking in human dignity: 'It is as sport to a fool to do mischief: but a man of understanding hath wisdom' (Proverbs 10:23); and 'The heart of the wise is in the house of mourning; but the heart of fools is in the house of mirth' (Ecclesiastes 7:4). These aptly describe the situation below stairs in Olivia's household. The 'caterwauling' of Act 2 scene 3 provides one of the heights of misrule, to which we might apply the proverb that 'the tongue of the wise useth knowledge aright: but the mouth of fools poureth out foolishness' (Proverbs 15:2). Where shame is predicted for the foolish—'The wise shall inherit glory: but shame shall be the promotion of fools' (Proverbs 3:35)—it is hard not to think of the ‡purgatorial humiliation of Malvolio and the discomfiture of Sir Andrew.

The Fool, Feste, is introduced in Act 1 scene 5 and the folly-wisdom pairing is immediately established. Feste himself asserts in proverb-like fashion 'Better a witty fool than a foolish wit.' He is a Fool, but not foolish. That other kind of folly, he tells Viola, 'does walk about the orb like the sun; it shines everywhere'. Feste might have studied, in Solomon's phrase, everything that is done 'under the sun' (Ecclesiastes 1:14 and frequently), and observed along with that wise monarch of the Old Testament that there is also a connection between †wisdom, folly, and madness: 'I gave my heart to know wisdom, and to know madness and folly' (Ecclesiastes 1:17). In the wisdom literature of the Bible the binary pair, folly and wisdom, frequently becomes a ‡trinity incorporating madness.

This motif of madness runs throughout the play—the word occurs more often in *Twelfth Night* than any other of Shakespeare's plays—and is found most noticeably in connection with the taunting of Malvolio. In Act 3 he is mercilessly accused of madness, as he is of †devil-possession. When Olivia interrupts Feste at the end of the play with 'How now, art thou mad?', it reasserts a running question of just who is mad, alongside the corollary of just who is truly foolish. It is not only the killjoy ‡Puritan culture that comes under attack in *Twelfth Night* but the behaviour of many of the characters: 'Are all the people mad?' cries Sebastian when set upon by Sir Andrew.

Though Feste himself is not without his failings, Viola observes of him:

This fellow is wise enough to play the fool…
For folly that he wisely shows is fit;
But wise men, folly-fall'n, quite taint their wit. (Act 3 scene 1, 61–9)

With dramatic irony it is at this moment that Sir Andrew enters, though the 'folly-fall'n' in *Twelfth Night* might include a number of characters at various points besides him. The motif of tainting recurs through Acts 3 and 5 with moral connotations. Keep away from the fool, we are told in Ecclesiasticus, 'and thou shalt never be defiled with his fooleries … never be disquieted with madness' (22:13).

Sir Andrew Aguecheek is the most foolish person in the play and is characterised by Maria in Act 1 scene 3 before we meet him as such: 'a fool', 'a foolish knight', 'a very fool'. Moral charges are coupled with her indictment: Sir Andrew is 'a prodigal', 'a great quarreller', 'a coward', and is 'drunk nightly'. Sir Toby's use of his supposed friend for financial gain, as well as his own sport, foreshadows Iago's gulling of the foolish Roderigo who aspires to Desdemona's hand in *Othello* with that play's strong opposition of ‡vice and ‡virtue.

Olivia's penultimate speech refers to Malvolio as 'poor fool'. His folly is also closely allied with his moral shortcomings, especially his self-love. Malvolio's conceit is played upon in Maria's plan to gull him — 'on that vice in him will my revenge find notable cause to work', she cries.

The moral framework for *Twelfth Night* is established early on. In the play's second scene, that between Viola and the Captain, Sebastian's courage and hope in extremity are commended, the loyalty and commitment of the Captain to Viola is unquestionable, and perhaps most importantly, Viola's judgement that the Captain has no duplicity — 'I will believe thou hast a mind that suits / With this thy fair and outward character' (Act 1 scene 2, 50–1) — sets him as a foil against all those in the play who embrace disguise, doubleness, and inconstancy. Similarly constant and devoted is Antonio to Sebastian, a further representative of open, decent behaviour in the play. Viola's reply to Antonio in Act 3 scene 4 is a catalogue of ‡vices displayed by other characters:

I hate ingratitude more in a man
Than lying, vainness, babbling drunkenness,
Or any taint of vice whose strong corruption
Inhabits our frail blood. (Act 3 scene 4, 363–6)

That final clause is an iteration of the Christian position on *fallen humankind, the doctrine of †original sin. In the closing scene, Antonio's selfless

†love for Sebastian is one of the lasting ‡virtues espoused by the play. His major speech gives him certain Christ-like connotations, telling how he exposed himself to danger 'pure for his love', describing his 'redemption' of Sebastian from the sea when 'a wrack past hope he was', giving him life.

QUESTIONS

1. What evidence can you find for the triadic theme of †wisdom—folly—madness in the character of Olivia?
2. For Aristotle, †wisdom was necessary for the acquisition of self-control, patience, and generosity among other moral ‡virtues. Patience and self-control are perhaps best exemplified in Viola. Trace the development also through *Twelfth Night* of the theme of giving/selfishness.

BIBLIOGRAPHY

J.M. Lothian and T.W. Craik, ed., *Twelfth Night*, The Arden Shakespeare, London and New York 1975. A very full commentary and introduction, with an emphasis on theatrical qualities.

Eugene Rice, *The Renaissance Idea of Wisdom*, Cambridge MA 1958. A comprehensive study of the history of †wisdom in the fourteenth and fifteenth centuries in Europe, including a number of strains of Christian thought and the relationship between the Christian tradition and secular notions of wisdom.

Camille Slights, 'The principle of recompense in *Twelfth Night*', *Modern Language Review* 77 (1982), 537–46. Reprinted in Harold Bloom, ed., *William Shakespeare's Twelfth Night*, New York 1987. This essay traces the path from disorder to harmony, both social and personal, in *Twelfth Night*.

KING LEAR

[*NA1* pp. 1106 f]

Lear's place in real history is very uncertain, but in Shakespeare's sources the Britain of Lear's time is a Christian land. Shakespeare has removed any reference to Christianity that he found in his sources and included a number of references to pagan deities and several to Nature as a goddess. It is instructive to compare *Macbeth*, where he includes a great deal of Christian imagery, both of good and evil, that was not in his sources. In *Macbeth* the kingdom, Scotland, is run by an ageing king. It is not clear that Duncan is as old as Lear, but he is clearly delineated as the godly *pater patrias*, whose key function, in nearly all his speeches, is to bless: to speak well of people, to confer honorific titles on them, and to bless them with prosperity. Lear is, of course, even more clearly a father than Duncan but, from the first, his attempt to confer prosperity on his daughters and his kingdom goes astray. Lear's first mistake becomes a curse to his kingdom; and his vicious set-piece curses of his daughters are some of his most memorable language. It is only near the end of the play, in his reconciliation with Cordelia, that the proper relationship and language of paternal blessing is restored: together with reciprocal ‡forgiveness from Cordelia to her parent.

At one level *King Lear* is an extraordinary language game in which Shakespeare exuberantly deploys the language of blessings, curses, repartee (the Fool), raving madness (Edgar), chilling sanity (Cornwall, Goneril, Regan), delusion (Lear), †wisdom (the Fool, the later Lear and Gloucester), folly (Lear), bluntness (Kent), flattery (the early Goneril and Regan, Oswald), and, of course, in the first instance, Cordelia's silence. 'What shall Cordelia speak? Love and be silent' (Act 1 scene 1, 62).[4] There are many set-piece encounters of different languages in *Lear*, even, strikingly, down to the level of Kent and Oswald, where the latter's essential smallness of personality is linguistically satirised: 'Thou whoreson Z. Thou unnecessary letter' (Act 2 scene 2, 63). But it is this language encounter, or non-encounter, between Lear and Cordelia that is most essential to the play's discourse. It sets the tragedy in motion:

> Lear: What can you say
>   To gain a third more opulent than your sisters?
> Cord: Nothing, my Lord.
> Lear: Nothing?
> Cord: Nothing.
> Lear: Nothing will come of nothing. Speak again.
>   (Act 1 scene 1, 85–90)

The heavy emphasis on 'nothing', appearing five times in the space of ten words, is obvious, and to the early modern mind, the equivalence of nothing with chaos is also inevitably present.[5] It is in the context of this silence that we should also understand Cordelia's quietness, first mentioned by Kent in this scene: 'Nor are those empty-hearted whose low sound / Reverbs no hollowness'

---

4. References to *King Lear* are to the Folio text, ed. primarily by Gary Taylor and printed as *The Tragedy of King Lear*, in Stanley Wells and Gary Taylor, ed., *The Oxford Complete Works of Shakespeare*, Oxford 1988.

5. *Creation is *ex nihilo* 'out of nothing', and the pre-existing nothingness is chaos: 'the earth was without form and void and darkness covered the surface of the deep' (Genesis 1:2).

(Act 1 scene 1, 153–4), and returning heart-breakingly in the final scene as the grieving Lear again desperately looks for his daughter to speak:

Lear: What is't thou say'st? — Her voice was ever soft,
Gentle and low, an excellent thing in woman …
(Act 5 scene 3, 247–8)

Do you see this? Look on her. Look, her lips.
Look there, look there. (Act 5 scene 3, 287)

Interpreters have tended to suggest that at the end Lear is looking for movement of Cordelia's lips as evidence of her breathing, but it may not be so: it is her speaking that still he wants to hear and, at the end as at the beginning, she answers nothing.

Similarly, at the very end of the play, the importance of what we speak and say, and its relation to what we truly feel, is a crucial part of Edgar's summary, in which the first person plural pronouns reach out to embrace the audience as well as the characters, in a truly Aristotelian way:

The weight of this sad time we must obey
Speak what we feel, not what we ought to say.
The oldest have borne most. We that are young
Shall never see so much, nor live so long. (Act 5 scene 3, 299–302)[6]

A number of the play's central themes are reprised in these two couplets. *Lear* is about both the quantity and the quality of suffering that a human being can bear. Lear himself, stripped to nakedness, driven from his sanity, at the mercy of the elements in the storm, is a figure of humanity's utter helplessness. He is mirrored, in the subplot that is entirely Shakespeare's addition to the narrative, by Edgar's assumption of the persona of the naked madman whom his father Gloucester sees in the storm before he is blinded, discovering, at the same time, that Edgar has not betrayed him. Their subsequent encounter in Act 4 scene 1 includes some of the play's most direct reflection on the nature of suffering. Note again, though, that Edgar, for reasons that really remain obscure to the end of the play, does not speak to his father as himself, just as Cordelia was not able, at first, to open her heart to the father she clearly †loves. Indeed we never see or hear Edgar, as Edgar, address Gloucester throughout the play: we only hear Edgar's report that, on the verge of the uncertain conflict against Edmund, he asked his father's blessing and explained 'from first

---

6. I prefer the Folio's attribution of these lines to Edgar, to the attribution of them to Albany in the Quarto.

to last ... our pilgrimage' (Act 5 scene 3, 187–8). Here is the encounter in Act 4 scene 1:

Glo: I stumbled when I saw ...

    ... O dear son Edgar,
The food of thy abused father's wrath —
Might I but live to see thee in my touch
I'd say I had eyes again...

Edg: O gods! Who is't can say, 'I am at the worst'?
I am worse than e'er I was...
And worse I may be yet. The worst is not
So long as we can say, 'This is the worst'.

Glo: I'th' last night's storm I such a fellow saw
Which made me think a man a worm. My son
Came then into my mind...
As flies to wanton boys are we to th' gods;
They kill us for their sport...

Edg: Bless thee, master...

Glo: Heavens deal so still. Let the superfluous and lust-dieted man
That slaves your ordinance, that will not see
Because he does not feel, feel your power quickly ...
(Act 4 scene 1, 19–63)

It is important that Edgar's first word to his father is a blessing. I have included in these excerpts all the scene's directly religious imagery. Stephen Marx has suggested that the complex of imagery of human suffering in *Lear* relates it at some level to the biblical book of Job, the great text on human suffering from the Hebrew †wisdom tradition; but whereas Job is an explicitly religious text, the religious dimension of the question of human suffering is not strongly stated in *King Lear*. In Job, the set question really is why a good God would allow good men to suffer. In *Lear*, as Edgar's summary at the end and his language here in Act 4 scene 1 indicate, the question is more how much a man can bear: and what one might be left with when one has borne more than any human being could reasonably be expected to take.

If there is any Christian dimension to *King Lear*, it is that the answer to that question is †love. Suffering in *Lear* is only partially ‡redemptive: both Gloucester and Lear (and, indeed, Edgar and Cordelia) achieve a clearer understanding after they have suffered, but it could not seriously be argued that what they learn is a matching recompense for the suffering they have to undergo to learn it. What we are left with, in each case, however, is the qualitative possibility of the depth of human love, which has somehow been distilled to its essence by the pain they have suffered. And the essence to which it is distilled is the Christian dyad of blessing and ‡forgiveness, especially in the explicitly religious scene of Lear's imagining:

> Lear: No, no, no, no. Come let's away to prison.
> We two alone will sing like birds i'th' cage.
> When thou dost ask me blessing, I'll kneel down
> And ask of thee forgiveness; so we'll live,
> And pray, and sing...
> As if we were God's spies...
> Upon such sacrifices, my Cordelia,
> The gods themselves throw incense. (Act 5 scene 3, 8–21)

It is important, in each case, that this †love can be expressed in the direst circumstances: by Edgar and Gloucester as beggar and blind man; by Cordelia and Lear as prisoners in danger of imminent death. When death does come to both Gloucester and Lear, it is the heart, the seat of love, that breaks—in each case, perhaps, 'smilingly', if Lear thinks that Cordelia's lips are really moving.

Which brings us back to the different kinds of speaking and language in the play. It is very possible that Kent's implied rebuke to Goneril and Regan as 'empty-hearted' vessels that 'reverb[s] ... hollowness' bears some reference to I Corinthians 13:1 — a chapter that notably brings together themes similar to Edgar's final summary: the tension between †love and language; the perseverance and ‡forgiveness of love; its ultimately enduring quality, when all the noise of language has come to an end. This is indeed a play in which love has, ultimately, borne all things and forgiven all things; where the multi-faceted languages of tongues and †prophecies, with all their capacity for madness, folly, and deception, have passed away; where even hope has vanished; but where, even for the dying Edmund, love alone remains.

QUESTIONS

1. Is Cordelia's silence entirely justified?
2. Do Lear and Gloucester lack proper parental affection for Goneril and Regan and Edmund respectively?
3. Read I Corinthians 13 and discuss its relevance to the play.
4. What is the relation between the personal, the familial, the social, and the universal in *King Lear*?

BIBLIOGRAPHY

Steven Marx, *Shakespeare and the Bible*, Oxford 2000, esp. '"Within a foot of the extreme verge": the Book of Job and *King Lear*', pp. 59–78.

T. McAlindon, *Shakespeare's Tragic Cosmos*, Cambridge 1991.

Kenneth Muir, ed., *King Lear*, The Arden Shakespeare, London and New York 1972. A thorough annotated edition of the play.

8

John Donne

SONGS AND SONNETS

[*BARL* pp. 896 f; *BASCP* pp. 35 f; *NA1* pp. 1233 f; *OA1* pp. 1015 f]

Like his contemporaries Philip Sydney and Edmund Spenser, Donne was affected by the tradition of the Petrarchan sonnet, which centred so much on the trials of love and especially the trials of unfaithful love. Donne takes the tradition in a different way. His love lyrics are essentially concerned with the problem of establishing constancy and stability in a world of change. For Donne, love is perilous when it involves two human beings who can die, who can experience self-deception and mutability, who are subject to external forces. He therefore searches in his love lyrics for a vision of love that transcends time and chance by participating in the eternal, a love in which mutability and loss are impossible.

In order to achieve this vision, Donne frequently ascribes to the experiences of earthly lovers what might normally be ascribed to the nature or †love of God. In that sense, we cannot fully appreciate Donne's love lyrics until we appreciate the Christian culture from which he comes, and in saying this we must remember that Donne's upbringing was Catholic and that it is those first religious impressions to which he returns in so many of his poems.

In 'The Good-Morrow' he implicitly parallels the ultimate ‡revelation of Christianity to the world and the lovers' discovery of true love, thereby imputing to the latter a spiritual and eternal nature. This is achieved primarily by his use of allusions in lines 6–7: 'If ever any beauty I did see, / Which I desired, and got, 'twas but a dream of thee.' To a Christian of his period and particularly to a Catholic Christian as Donne once was, these lines would have a special relevance at two levels. At a more general level, this comparison with dream and reality was a customary way of understanding the relationship both of the Old Testament to the New Testament, and of Greco-Roman mythology to Christianity. Past experiences and ways of understanding God were not destroyed by the coming of Christ, but fulfilled by them. Dreams, or concepts of goodness, truth, and †love, were understood as foreshadowings of a supreme reality now revealed in Christ.

Previous loves, therefore, are not experiences of falling in and out of love, of change and inconstancy, but preparation by means of foreshadowing for initiation into an eternal, unchanging †love. All encounters with beauty are but preparation for the fulness of the beautiful, just as, for the Christian, all experiences in religion are preparations for the fullness of the ‡revelation of God in Christ. Further, these lines more directly echo the ‡eucharistic hymns with which Donne would have been acquainted as a Catholic. For the Catholic, the eucharist is the fulfilment of all the other forms of covenant relationship between God and humanity, of all other forms of †sacrificial meal sealing such a relationship, and of all other ways in which God fed his people in the Old Testament, such as manna in the †desert. As the hymn for the eucharistic festival of Corpus Christi, 'Pange lingua', expresses it, in its nineteenth-century translation, 'Types and shadows have their ending / For the newer light is here.'

The ‡eucharist is the seal of an unbreakable †love relationship; it is the †marriage feast of the Lamb. Donne puts fulfilled human love into this eucharistic context to suggest just such an eternal and undying covenant in the flesh, a covenant that therefore defies time and change. The eucharist seals a relationship between God and humanity in the †sacrificed and glorified risen body of Christ offered as food for the ‡soul. It is a covenant, a pledged relationship in the flesh of Christ, that fulfils the earlier covenant of the flesh represented by circumcision for Jews. It also fulfils and makes tangible the understanding of the relationship between God and humanity as husband and bride seen in the †prophets Isaiah and Hosea (see, for example, Isaiah 54:5–8; Hosea 2). In the †incarnation, God and humanity become 'one flesh' and the marriage is consummated on the †cross.

All this is signified by the ‡eucharist as understood by Catholics and is well represented in the famous painting by Jan van Eyck of 'The Adoration of the Mystic Lamb'. This image of perfection is then sealed in line 9 in the allusion to I John 4:18, 'perfect love casteth out fear'. The closing lines suggest an underlying anxiety about the effects of mutability and the possibility of loss, but this is set against Donne's utmost efforts to establish the eternal, immutable quality of mutual love.

This concern to establish eternal, divine value in human love celebrated in and by human bodies is evident in several other poems. In 'The Ecstasy', whether one reads it as a poem of seduction or a meditation on the relation of ‡soul and body, Donne makes use of the theology of St Thomas Aquinas. In this theology, human beings are embodied spirits, or 'ensouled' bodies. The body is the means whereby a person exists, that is, the person 'is' through his or her body. The soul receives external impressions, that is, comes to know reality, through the senses, but it is also the body that expresses the soul's unique identity to the world. As Gerard Manley Hopkins later declares, 'man's spirit is flesh-bound when found at best' ('The Caged Skylark'). This is important for Donne. If love is a matter for bodies only, then it is doomed. It can know only the fate of everything else mortal. If, however, the body is the means by which spirit reveals and expresses itself, then this mortal flesh participates in, and provides a vehicle for, the eternal.

In poems such as 'The Canonization', 'The Relic', and 'The Funeral', Donne again takes up the Catholic idea that the body is expressive of ‡soul and participates in its holiness. Hence lovers whose souls have loved immortally can convey through the remains of their bodies something of the holiness of this love. It is because of this relationship between soul and body that the true, eternal lovers in 'A Valediction: Forbidding Mourning' care *less* to lose physical contact rather than care not at all. Donne uses his Catholic inheritance to deny the Platonic claim that love is not a matter of the body but also to avoid the claim that all love is carnal and therefore transient. True †love transcends time but participates in the world of time and therefore of 'enfleshment'.

QUESTIONS

1. To what extent is your reading of 'The Good-Morrow' modified by your appreciation of Donne's approach to time and eternity in this poem?
2. 'The Ecstasy' can be read as a poem of seduction or as a meditation on the relationship of ‡soul and body. To what extent does your understanding of Donne's attitude to the body enable you to establish your reading of the poem?
3. In the light of your awareness of Donne's approach to time and to the body, explore these themes in either 'The Canonization' or 'The Relic' or 'The Funeral'.

BIBLIOGRAPHY

Anne Barbeau, 'Donne and the real presence of the absent lover', *John Donne Journal* 9 (1990), 113–24.

A.B. Chambers, 'Glorified bodies and the "Valediction Forbidding Mourning"', *John Donne Journal* 1 (1982), 1–20.

Rodney Stenning Edgecombe, 'Eschatological elements in Donne's "Anniversarie"', *John Donne Journal* 15 (1996), 63–74.

Achsah Guibbory, ed., *The Cambridge Companion to John Donne*, Cambridge 2006.

Albert C. Labriola, 'Sacerdotalism and sainthood in the poetry and life of John Donne: "The Canonization" and canonization', *John Donne Journal* 14 (1995), 113–26.

R.E. Pritchard, 'Donne's image and dream', *John Donne Journal* 13 (1994), 13–28.

HOLY SONNETS

[*BARL* pp. 942 f; *BASCP* pp. 51 f; *NA1* pp. 1268 f; *OA1* pp. 1050 f]

At the time of composition of the *Holy Sonnets*, formalised methods of meditation upon the Bible were popular in the Catholic church and critics now accept their influence upon Donne's *Holy Sonnets*. The purpose of the meditative process was to stir the ‡soul to religious emotion leading to some appropriate response in changed attitude or behaviour. A scene from the gospels was imagined, or a truth of Christian faith set before the mind's eye. The scene or concept was explored imaginatively in order to produce a personal response rather than intellectual understanding. The four subjects traditionally suggested for meditation of any kind were death, †judgement, †heaven, and †hell, as these were most likely to stimulate desire for God in the individual and an awareness of ‡sin leading to ‡repentance. These four subjects preoccupy Donne in the sonnet sequence.

†Judgement referred not simply to the judgement of the individual upon their death but to the †last judgement when all the dead would rise from their graves and be judged. The supreme image for this was the biblical *parable of the sheep and the goats, in which those who recognised Christ in the poor are recognised by him and enter †heaven, whilst those who failed to do so find no recognition and enter †hell (Matthew 25:31–46). While this promoted some fear of judgement, some assurance was offered by the *parable of the workers in the vineyard in which the last workers to be employed received as much as the first because of their master's generosity. This was interpreted in the Catholic tradition as emphasising the importance of deathbed conversion and hence the importance of the moment of death for one's eternal ‡salvation. It was important to remember death, and likewise instructive was the fate of the rich fool in another *parable who stored his wealth in barns, ready to enjoy life, unaware that his death was imminent (Luke 12:15–21). Donne was raised in this tradition, acquiring an instinctive awareness of the necessity of preparation for death and the horror of sudden death; its influence pervades this sequence.

In Sonnet 14, for example, this awareness of death leads to consideration of the dangers to the ‡soul presented by 'the world, the flesh and the devil', which have beset humankind since the *fall of *Adam and Eve. 'The world' implies all the attractions of the fallen state, 'the lust of the flesh, and the lust of the eyes and the pride of life' condemned by John (I John 2:16, and see also the essay on Congreve's *The Way of the World*). 'The devil' is here the rebel against God and the 'serpent envious' who led Adam and Eve to disobedience (Genesis 3) and continues to †tempt their offspring; whilst 'the flesh' is not the body but the unbridled lusts to which it is subject. We can read this sonnet as a meditation on the effects of this †original sin, for it was understood to open the way to 'the world, the flesh and the devil' by weakening the will and darkening the understanding. Here it does just that. Donne feels that his will is captive while his understanding fails to provide that clear grasp of truth he so greatly needs.

His situation echoes that of St Paul when he complains of his condition in that he cannot do the good he wishes to do and does the evil he wishes to avoid (Romans 7:18–20). Donne's dramatic language conveys the intensity of his experience of enslavement but also his awareness, again like St Paul, that deliverance can only come through God's grace. The image of the heart being 'battered' by the holy ‡Trinity, the 'three-person'd God', recalls the related usage in *The Castle of Perseveraunce* and the medieval idea of Christ the knight fighting for the human ‡soul. The demand to be burnt reminds the audience that fire, representing the Holy Spirit, must first appear to destroy before it can complete its work of purification and transformation. The plea for ravishment recalls humankind's bridal identity in relation to God: Donne's soul is an intended bride who must be snatched from the clutches of the usurping world, flesh, and †devil, much as the virgin Israel, the spouse of God, must be rescued from its enslavement to ‡sin and foreign powers in the †prophecies of Isaiah and Jeremiah.

Another traditional theme for meditation was the blood of Christ. In biblical thinking blood signified the life principle so that the blood of Christ represented his †sacrificial giving of his life in death. The 'new covenant', the new relationship between God and humanity, was made in the blood of Christ. The flowing of his blood from his side (understood as his heart) was readily identified as the flow of God's mercy and †love. Being washed in Christ's blood was therefore being cleansed from ‡sin by the mercy of God. So in Sonnet 9 Donne prays for the blood of Christ and his loving mercy, and for his own tears, sign of his ‡repentance and love, to cleanse him from sin by destroying the memory of it. The language evokes the mood of Psalm 51, the traditional ‡penitential psalm recalling King David's sin in having Uriah the Hittite killed so that he,

David, would be able to marry Uriah's wife Bathsheba. This psalm, like Donne's sonnet, prays God to blot out his sin and wash him from guilt. Donne sets his own experience of penitence within the context of all Christian failure and ‡forgiveness.

Just as Donne finds himself torn between †love of God and love of the world, he also finds himself divided in this experience of ‡penitence. He moves between love of God and fear of ‡damnation, confidence in a God of mercy and terror before a God of justice. Meditation on the suffering and death of Jesus was urged, to stimulate sorrow for ‡sin and love of God. In Sonnet 19, Donne's awareness of his dividedness lets him settle for fear of punishment, while in Sonnet 13 this inner division is implicit. The description of Christ is intended to arouse love and pity but the note of fear persists. 'Blood fills his frowns' is an ambiguous description while the rhetorical question in lines 7 and 8 could invite an affirmative answer, despite the uneasy response, 'No, no' of line 9: 'And can that tongue adjudge thee unto hell / which prayed forgivenss for his foes' fierce spite?' Fear of the wrath of God for the sins that *crucified Christ, which Donne knows to include his own, lingers. This raises the issue about the status of his penitence: is he motivated by pure love of God or fear of punishment? This was important for Donne the Anglican because his new ‡creed asserted that perfect contrition out of love alone was necessary for ‡salvation whilst his former Catholicism accepted the possibility of imperfect contrition arising out of fear.

Donne's language and thought are expressive of his individual conflicts and spiritual longings, but for it to be appreciated fully we must set his work within the Christian tradition that has fed his imagination and his intellect.

QUESTIONS

1. Take one sonnet not examined here and consider its use of traditional meditative themes.
2. Donne is often accused of being more concerned in these sonnets with his ego than with God. To what extent would you agree with this view?
3. To what extent do you consider that sympathy with the Christian content of these sonnets is necessary for a full response to them?

BIBLIOGRAPHY

Donald Friedman, 'Christ's image and likeness in Donne', *John Donne Journal* 15 (1996), 75–94.

Achsah Guibbory, ed., *The Cambridge Companion to John Donne*, Cambridge 2006.

Louis L. Martz, 'Donne and Herbert: vehement grief and silent tears', *John Donne Journal* 7 (1988), 21–34.

J.T. Rhodes, 'Continuities: the ongoing English Catholic tradition from the 1570s to the 1630s', *John Donne Journal* 12 (1993), 139–52.

A.J. Smith, ed., *John Donne: Essays in Celebration*, London 1972.

9

AEMILIA LANYER

[*BARL* pp. 824 f; *BASCP* pp. 29 f; *NA1* pp. 1281 f]

The studiedly ambiguous judgement on Lanyer in *NA1* p. 1282—that her poetry 'at times invites some comparison with Donne and Crashaw'— accurately reflects the difficult question of her critical status: whether the intrinsic merit of her poetry is as great as her importance as a published early modern woman, writing explicitly with a woman's voice, for women, on women's themes, and on behalf of women. The postscript to *Salve Deus Rex Judaeorum* is headed 'To the Doubtful Reader'—'doubtful' about the title itself (see *NA1* p. 1282). The modern reader is likely to be more doubtful, though, about the quality of Lanyer's poetry. A second question concerns the sincerity of her work. Because it is explicitly and lengthily addressed to patrons, and in fact to different patrons in different editions, and because the praise of those patrons is so closely related to the poems' central themes, it has been suggested, by female critics as well as male, that the quality of her work is sometimes compromised by its self-interestedness.

Lanyer's attitude to religion has been questioned under the latter heading. On the one hand, Elaine V. Beilin argues at length that Lanyer's patrons are principally praised as exemplars of a sincerely argued reclamation of the importance of women in the Christian tradition.[1] Lanyer attributes her own religious conversion to the Protestant faith to the time that she spent with the Countess of Cumberland, and quite naturally associates the Christian ‡virtues with the Countess, her family, and the estate at Cooke-ham (pp. 1287 f). Barbara Lewalski, on the other hand, suggests that Lanyer's Christianity may be primarily the vehicle for her feminist agenda.[2] But the Countess's piety is attested from other contemporary sources, and if Lanyer was converted there, there is similarly no reason to doubt that her praise of Cooke-ham is a sincere reflection of the joy of that experience.

It is clear, too, that Lanyer's knowledge of the Bible was personal and internalised through her own religious reading. This is clear in some of the dedica-

---

1. Beilin, *Redeeming Eve*, passim.
2. Lewalski, 'Of God and good women', especially p. 207.

tory passages, of which, besides those to the Countess, to Queen Anne, and to the virtuous reader (pp. 1282 f) there are others to aristocratic patrons with whom Lanyer could claim some relationship, as well as one addressed 'To all vertuous Ladies in generall'. Taking this last as an example of Lanyer's use of biblical motifs, the images of the wedding garments (8) and the oil-lamps (12) are in fact taken from similar but different †parables (in Matthew 22:11 and 25:4 respectively). Lanyer connects them naturally, as she also connects the 'purple scarlet white' of 'The robes that Christ wore before his death'—colours that are again drawn from different accounts in different gospels (Mark 15:17; Matthew 27:28; and Luke 23:11 respectively) and the move from these colours to Solomon's robes and their comparison to the lilies of the field (17, 19, 21) is to Christ's teaching in Luke 12. Again the move is thematically coherent and unforcedly made, in contrast to some later passages in 'The Passion of Christ' where Lanyer inevitably moves more mechanically through the sequence of the events in the ‡passion text. In the same lines 'To all virtuous Ladies in generall', a reference to Psalm 133 'Aaron's precious oil' (36) is linked to an image from Revelation 7 'palms of vict'ry'; the 'myrrh, gum, aloes, frankincense' of line 41 are similarly not found together in one list, but are a mixture of different lists in which two or three of them are found. These passages suggest an author who knew these biblical themes well enough to handle them with confidence and security: and this goes some distance towards suggesting a sincerity of personal belief.

Beilin argues that our doubting of Lanyer's sincerity is to some extent a matter of poetics. Because the presence of women in early modern poetry is usually women as they interest, and are seen by, the male poet, our understanding of what is sincere in poetry has been specifically conditioned by the tendency of male authors, including Shakespeare, to suggest a tension between the appearance of a woman, which the male finds attractive, and the more complex and problematic reality of relating to a real woman as a person. Lorna Hutson more specifically argues that the mutually authenticating relationship between male poet and male patron in Shakespeare's early sonnets claims a naturalness in which the authority of the male patron is seen as intrinsic. The contrast between the 'fair youth' and then the 'dark lady' of the later sonnets suggests that this authority cannot be natural to the female patron: 'For a female author cannot mirror a female patron if the space of the gilding mutually authentic gaze ... [is] ... a space of discursive and political opportunity conceivable only between men.' For Hutson, the attempt to create a feminine community of author and readers is central to Lanyer's poetic ambition.[3]

---

3. Hutson, 'Why the lady's eyes are nothing like the sun'.

In the rest of the ‡passion narrative in 'Salve Rex', the most striking passages are certainly those in which Lanyer enters imaginatively into the experience and feelings of the women to whom the passion text relates. *NA1* specifically excerpts 'Eve's Apology in Defense of Women' in which Lanyer uses the motif of Pilate's wife to argue on behalf of *Eve and all her daughters and to plead with Pilate for the life of Christ. Later, in passages perhaps more movingly written, Lanyer speaks on behalf of the women of Jerusalem weeping for Jesus and his address to them; again the women become representative — here of female opposition to the tyranny which is usually the work of men and under which Christ is suffering (968–1008). Similarly the grief of Christ's 'woeful mother' (1008) is movingly described, though again the subsequent set-piece reminiscence of the *annunciation is perhaps less effective.

The feminist thrust of this writing is clear, but also its participation in a fairly orthodox tradition, though perhaps it now reads as more orthodox than it did in Lanyer's time. Her reading of the ‡atonement which is achieved by the ‡passion of Christ is orthodox at all points, though it is interesting to speculate whether her very strong account of human ‡sinfulness is influenced by ‡Calvinist ideas of total depravity:

> Our ragged clothing scorns he not to wear,
> Though foul, rent, torn, disgraceful, rough and gross,
> Spun by that monster sin, and weaved by shame,
> Which grace itself disgraced with impure blame. (1124–7)

At moments like this, the claim by some feminist critics that Lanyer's Christ is a feminised portrayal looks perhaps less likely: which is not to deny that it is immensely valuable to have this picture of the ‡passion through the eyes of a distinctively female and feminist early modern poet.

QUESTIONS

1. Can Hutson's view of the relationships of early modern patronage fully account for modern suspicions of Lanyer's sincerity?
2. To what extent is Lanyer's Christ a feminised figure?
3. In what ways does Lanyer 'invite some comparison with Donne'?

BIBLIOGRAPHY

Elaine V. Beilin, *Redeeming Eve: Women Writers of the English Renaissance*, Princeton NJ 1987.

Margaret Patterson Hannay, ed., *Silent but for the Word: Tudor Women as Patrons, Translators, and Writers of Religious Works*, Kent OH 1985.

Lorna Hutson, 'Why the lady's eyes are nothing like the sun', in Clare Brant and Diane Purkiss, ed., *Women, Texts, and Histories 1575–1760*, London 1992, pp. 13–38.

Barbara Lewalski, 'Of God and good women: the poems of Aemilia Lanyer', in Margaret Patterson Hannay, ed., *Silent but for the Word*.

Randall Martin, ed., *Women Writers in Renaissance England*, London and New York 1997.

10

BEN JONSON, *POEMS*

[*BARL* pp. 867 f; *BASCP* pp. 79 f; *NA1* pp. 1292 f; *OA1* pp. 1064 f]

Unlike many writers of his age, Jonson does not appear to be a poet or playwright deeply inspired by the Bible or by the Christian tradition. This does not mean that there is no such inspiration, rather it suggests that we must seek it in the overall pattern of his work and in the overall implications of his subject matter and its treatment, especially in a study of his plays. A few of Jonson's poems, however, make this underlying Christian approach to life more evident.

'To Heaven' is one of the few poems in which he meditates on his inner life. Lines 5–6 echo the strictures in the *sermon on the mount against the hypocrisy of the Pharisees in displaying their piety in public prayer (Matthew 6:5–6). They gained their reward on earth in the praise given them by men and women. Jonson disclaims such pharisaical ends in this public expression of ‡penitence and devotion. In asking that God be 'all in all' to him, his faith, hope, and †love, Jonson is echoing both St Paul in his 'hymn to love' in I Corinthians 13, but also his Catholic teaching that these three theological ‡virtues are the gifts that alone enable people to respond to God. They are gifts from the blessed ‡Trinity that make the person able to share the life of the Trinity, and are given in †baptism, the ‡sacrament that initiates a person into Christian life.

Jonson's play with the idea of three, in relation to the three gifts, first, midst, and last, converted one and three, and identifying the gifts with his †judge, witness, and advocate, imply the presence and work of the ‡Trinity within him: the Father as judge, the Son as witness, the Spirit as advocate. What is happening within him, his desire for God, is a gift of the Trinitarian God who dwells within him through his †baptism, rather than a state he has engendered himself. It is not God who has left him, but he who has departed from God or been exiled. He has let himself be carried away by other desires. When God 'stooped' (14), it was to make him aware that he has never departed, for Jonson realises he is 'everywhere'. Consequently 'dwell' (15) can be addressed as much to himself as to God. He desires that God should never leave, having just discovered his ever-presence. But he has also discovered his own desire to dwell here and no longer to be exiled from him.

Jonson has found himself in the central Christian situation, aware of the great, unmerited gift of God's †love and indwelling presence, and of his own frail humanity. The humanity he owns is not simply his own ‡sinfulness, for which he faces the fear of death and †judgement, but is primarily the *fallen state for which he has no responsibility. '[U]nto labour born' (18) alludes to Genesis 3:19 where *Adam, separated from God, must eat bread in the sweat of his brow, from daily labour. 'Conceived in sin' (18) reminds the audience both of this inherited state, but also, in the allusion to Psalm 51:5, of the personal ‡sin to which it leads: this psalm is associated with the ‡penitence of David for causing the death of Uriah the Hittite so that David could marry Uriah's wife, Bathsheba. So Jonson sets his own desire for God within this framework of a more universal experience.

Human frailty is not only moral, but also physical. In the presence of God, Jonson also feels the weight of mortality with its accumulated griefs and sufferings echoing psalms such as Psalms 22 and 38, which were traditionally used by Catholics as expressions of ‡penitence. But he is also painfully aware of the possibility of self-delusion that besets the spiritual person in this state. Acute awareness of the frailty and mortality of the human condition can make people long for 'easeful death' in the belief that they long for God. He is not so much alluding to Romans 7:24 (as suggested in the notes in *NA1* p. 1403) but to Philippians 1:18–26 (see also II Corinthians 5:1–5). Here Paul says that he wishes to die and be with the Lord, but also wishes to stay alive for the sake of those he serves. Paul is holy here (24) because it is quite clear that his desire for death has no selfish motive. Jonson fears his prayers will not be judged to have such clarity.

In this poem Jonson shows a familiarity with scripture and with doctrine that is not immediately apparent in his longer works. It alerts us to the need to be aware of a biblical and Christian mentality undergirding his use of classical models and allusions. For example, the praise of a natural beauty and fertility of the estate in 'To Penshurst' owes much to the beliefs about *Eden current in the Renaissance. All in Penshurst is fruitful and generous. There is no toil involved in fishing for the aged carp that 'run into' the net and for the 'bright eels that leap on land before the fisher or into his hand' (33–8). The house is built without excessive toil or distress to the labourer, its walls reared with 'no man's ruin, no man's groan' (46). This is a †Garden of *Eden before the *fall of *Adam and Eve, where the earth yields its fruit in harmony with its human gardeners, in abundance and without need for human toil: as Genesis 3:17–19 expresses it, toil and battle with nature are consequences of the rupture in the relationship between humanity and God.

It is a place, too, of harmony between people who are not used or exploited in heavy labour. Jonson is suggesting a total innocence in the inhabitants of Penshurst that makes it an experience of life before the disharmony between God and humankind, between individual humans and between humankind and the earth, blighted life.

Jonson is not content, however, to make Penshurst only another *Eden, a †garden. He is also concerned to set the cultured, civilised life of its inhabitants within a Christian context. The parents are chaste and faithful, models not only for their children of prayer, but 'of manners, arms and arts' (98). At first reading this combination of education in piety and in the cultured behaviour of the nobility may seem arbitrary or an attempt to gild aristocracy. It takes on a fuller resonance, however, when we read it in the light of the tradition of Christ the knight which we have seen in the *Ancrene Riwle* and *Piers Plowman*.

In Jonson's era the figure of the knight had become that of the gentleman, schooled in the discipline of arms, of courtesy, and of study. As Christ was a model of the true knight, so he became the model of the true gentleman. When Jonson praises the inhabitants of Penshurst, he is setting before his readers a Christian ideal of human existence and of human relationship with the earth and with fellow men and women.

QUESTIONS

1. Look up the references to the Psalms mentioned above and consider how these relate to the content, mood, and tone of 'To Heaven'.
2. Read Genesis 1 and 3, and consider how these chapters relate to the mood and tone of 'To Penshurst'.
3. To what extent do you consider a full reading of 'To Penshurst' is possible without awareness of its Christian background?

BIBLIOGRAPHY

Martin Elsky, 'The mixed genre of "To Penshurst" and the perilous spring of Netherlandish landscape', *Ben Jonson Journal* 9 (2002), 1–36.

Harris Friedberg, 'Ben Jonson's "To Penshurst": pastoral, georgic, epic', *English Literary Renaissance* 4 (1974), 111–36.

Richard Harp, 'Jonson's "To Penshurst": the country house as church', *John Donne Journal* 7 (1988), 73–90.

Michael McCanles, *Jonsonian Discriminations: The Humanist Poet and the Praise of True Nobility*, Toronto and London 1992.

11

JOHN WEBSTER,
THE DUCHESS OF MALFI

[*BARD* pp. 557 f; *NA1* pp. 1432 f]

The Duchess of Malfi is a critical riddle. Some critics regard it as a fully-achieved Jacobean tragedy, others as a high melodrama; some acclaim the Duchess as a model of the Christian heroine, triumphing over persecution to achieve dignity in resignation. Others regard it as a nihilistic drama, offering no positive vision of the human condition. This essay will try to elucidate some of the claims for this play as a drama expressing Christian values.

The opening speeches suggest a Christian context in which to view the play. Antonio's speech not only identifies him as a ‡virtuous man but it also suggests his participation in a model of virtuous government. The background to the allusions to Christ expelling the moneychangers, *cleansing the Temple (Matthew 21:12–16) is a contemporary, French, political treatise on the divine right of kings. The king is the chosen one of God, like King David in the Old Testament. His court is therefore like the Temple, intended to be pure of all corruption and mercenary dealings. The cleansing of corruption from court is therefore a Christ-like action and betokens future Christ-like leadership.

Against this is set the reality of the political world, not only of corruption, but especially of spying and manipulation. This introduces another worldview in which the world and its people are not controlled ultimately by God and his vice-regents, nature and the king, but by the plotting and devices of human beings. The world no longer has an underlying order and plan, but is totally malleable to the choices and machinations of people. In some other Elizabethan and Jacobean plays that operate in this framework, this vision of the world is destroyed in the overthrow of the principal plotter/avenger who overreaches himself and brings about his undoing. In this way human pretensions to control are denied. The audience for *The Duchess of Malfi* must ask itself whether this is the case in this play.

The plotter in other Jacobean tragedies is clearly linked to the ‡Vice figure of the ‡morality play (see the essay on the morality play). We see this too in the character of Bosola. He is a character who, like the Vice, is antagonistic to goodness and is set to bring about the downfall of the ‡virtuous character by pretending friendship. Here the Vice is the spy, the agent, not of a malevolent †devil, but of malevolent humans, the duchess's brothers. These assume god-like powers of control and use Bosola as a tool against the Duchess. Their evil is evident in their embracing of Machiavelli's dictum that 'the end justifies the means', a belief condemned in the Catholic morality the characters are supposed to embrace. It is evident too in the use of human beings as tools, objects, rather than as beings with their own wills and integrity.

In a ‡morality play, such evil would be unmotivated, clearly the product of a super- or sub-human force. Here it emanates entirely from the lusts and greed of its human characters. Does Webster wish his audience to see evil as issuing from the 'pride of life' of his characters, identified as one of the three †temptations of *fallen humanity (I John 2:16–17), or purely from the animal nature of humanity with all its potential for perversion? Ambiguity also surrounds Bosola. His spur to action is thwarted ambition and betrayed trust; so, too, his 'repentance' for the death of the Duchess comes more from the Duke's rejection of him than from true ‡repentance for his deed.

Whatever its source and nature, such ‡repentance cannot produce 'good fruit', only death. By accident, he kills Antonio. The plotter is defeated by chance, but defeated in trying to do good rather than ill. This chance is not one that rebukes human pretension and speaks of an underlying order, since it destroys the one indisputably good character, Antonio. Randomness, rather than Providence (that is, God's watchful oversight of the world) dominates.

And what of the character of the Duchess? Can we see her as a Christian heroine, purified by suffering and an ultimate model of ‡virtue? Clearly the text would seem to point us in this direction. Many assertions are made of her nobility, and she is the incessant, innocent object of her brother's greed, lust, and malice. There was, however, in some Christian thinking of the period, an ambiguity about the widow. St Paul's writings seemed to suggest that Christian widows should remain so and that second marriages were simply a yielding to the desires of the flesh (I Corinthians 7:8–9). Paradoxically, in our eyes, this would be seen as more so were the marriage purely a love match rather than a political expediency. Clearly, in the Duchess of Malfi's case, this theological issue is the excuse for purely human considerations: inheritance rights, family pride, as well as incestuous desires.

Does this in itself warrant a judgement of the Duchess as a model of moral innocence? The argument pivots around her behaviour in persecution. Critics who argue for her true elevation as a model of Christian nobility, and the moral centre of the play, must measure her characteristics against the yardstick of the teachings of Christ. The Duchess does suffer persecution in the cause of right but certainly does not bless those who curse her and ill-use her (Matthew 5:10), nor does she offer any ‡forgiveness to those who offend her, but only contempt (see Matthew 5:43–5; 18:21–2).

In the biblical tradition and the spirituality issuing from it, innocent affliction was seen to issue in self-knowledge, especially in an awareness of human frailty and ‡sin. Is this seen in the Duchess? Although she remains assured throughout of her dignity and value (Act 3 scene 5, 120 to the end), she fails to see in her afflictions the guiding castigation of †heaven (see Revelation 3:19). Her resignation to death issues not from any desire for God in another world but from contempt for the life imposed on her. The attempt by Bosola to make her consider the reality of human mortality, that is, to meditate on his rather gruesome version of the *memento mori* (see the discussion in the essay on *Everyman*) evokes no response. Nothing makes her examine her own conscience, nor seek to question her identity as anything other than her inherited aristocratic status: 'I am the Duchess of Malfi still' (Act 4 scene 2, 128).

It could be argued, therefore, that far from offering a model of a Christian heroine, Webster is presenting a nobility that stands not on a dignity issuing from God irrespective of status in the world, but from a proud refusal to surrender before the randomness and malice of a godless world.

QUESTIONS

1. Examine closely the Duchess's statements regarding ‡forgiveness, renunciation, and her need for divine guidance together with those regarding her contempt for her captors and for her life. To what extent do these make a coherent attitude to her situation?
2. Examine closely the scenes in which Bosola changes allegiance and analyse the causes.
3. To what extent would you consider randomness a guiding principle of the action of the play?

BIBLIOGRAPHY

Charles R. Forker, *The Skull Beneath the Skin: The Achievement of John Webster*, Carbondale IL 1986.
John C. Kerrigan, 'Action and confession, fate and despair in the violent conclusion of *The Duchess of Malfi*', *Ben Jonson Journal* 8 (2001), 249–58.

Michael Neill, *Issues of Death: Mortality and Identity in English Renaissance Tragedy*, Oxford 1997.

Kimberly A. Turner, 'The complexity of Webster's Duchess', *Ben Jonson Journal* 7 (2000), 379–402.

12

FRANCIS BACON

[*BARL* pp. 592 f; *NA1* pp. 1528 f; *OA1* pp. 1434 f]

Francis Bacon was a lawyer before he was a scientist, though his reputation lies in the latter sphere. Like many eminent lawyers, he also became a politician. His career was stellar in the law under James I, as he successively was knighted (1603), became Attorney General (1613), and then Lord Chancellor (1618). His legal and political career was effectively ended in 1621 when he was found guilty of corruption and imprisoned, but he continued his literary efforts, completing the third and fullest edition of his *Essays* in 1625, and revising others of his works. Some have attributed the works of Shakespeare (the details of whose career are shadowy by comparison with those of his contemporary) to Bacon, but the habitual styles and preoccupations of the two are notably distinct. Shakespeare is a writer of passion and almost infinite range, whereas Bacon aims at compression and precision usually combined with an element of scientific detachment.

He wrote widely and his works were remarkably popular in his own time and for centuries after. He wrote fluently in Latin, the language of learning, as well as in English. His major scientific work in Latin, the *Novum Organum*, attempted to set out a completely new inductive method of research;[1] and his *Advancement of Learning*, written in English and later translated into Latin, has features in common with this but ranges widely over human knowledge, including the arts and theology. His *Essays*, in English, are sharply focussed discourses, dealing with practical, moral, and religious issues in a condensed style: the (accurate) impression of breadth the *Essays* leave the reader with derives more from their collective subject range than from the expansiveness of treatment. This in turn is a result of the addition of essays to the original collection of ten in the first edition of 1597, building to fifty-eight in the edition of 1625, and the filling out of some individual essays with a more discursive style (see the two versions of 'Of Studies' in *NA1* pp. 1541–2).

Bacon was a pioneer of Enlightenment thinking, a committed advocate of the empirical method of science. His works proposed a new approach to

---

1. Urbach and Gibson, *Novum Organum*, p. 7. It should perhaps be noted that though a good deal of science enters into the work, it is not a work of pure science; it is, rather, a philosophical work.

understanding the world: it was to be studied in two aspects, 'the book of God's word', that is through the revealed truths of the Christian religion; and 'the book of God's works', that is through scientific exploration (*The Advancement of Learning*, Book I, 1). Although this schema may seem to imply a necessary difference between the two aspects, one accepting authority and the other proceeding purely by experiment and induction; and although Bacon is very severe in demonstrating the irrationality of certain religious (particularly Roman Catholic) practices, Bacon was too much the politician and scholar to reject what most people accepted as true in either sphere. His advice in the essay 'Of Great Place' is to 'ask counsel of both times: of the ancient time what is best, and of the latter time what is fittest', and this very neatly reflects his own practice. His scientific works as much as his literary ones are peppered with quotations and aphorisms that he regards as authoritative and true.

Bacon was honoured by the Royal Society at its inception in 1662 as a founding father of science. It would, however, be mistaken to think of him as working in a laboratory as a practising scientist. He did not even take much notice of important discoveries of the time, such as the astronomical work of Copernicus and Kepler, and the work of Harvey on the circulation of the blood.[2] In the essay 'Of Superstition' he remarks 'wholesome meat corrupteth to little worms', and it may be that he believed that to be literally true; at any rate, he died of bronchitis caught while collecting snow 'in order to observe the effect of cold on the preservation of [the] flesh of [a chicken]'.[3] Corruption both physical and moral was a matter of interest to him: he writes about lies ('Of Truth'), bribery ('Of Great Place'), and the tendency of institutions to corrupt into 'petty observances' ('Of Superstition'), and although he writes with detachment, he also writes with familiarity as a self-confessedly corrupt and disgraced politician. In this, the scientific and religious aspects of his personal philosophy are merged: he knows that one does not have to be honest to tell the truth—science deals with precise observation; and he knows that evil ministers can still do good[4]—religion deals with human imperfection. The 'segregation' of theology and science into 'two truths'[5] is more a development

---

2. Vickers, *Francis Bacon and Renaissance Prose*, p. 2. Bacon makes some rather dismissive comments on Copernicus in *The Advancement of Learning*.

3. Sir Leslie Stephen and Sir Sidney Lee, ed., *The Dictionary of National Biography*, London 1917 – , vol. I, p. 280.

4. Article XXVI of the 'Thirty-Nine Articles of Religion', one of the foundation documents of the Church of England, is entitled 'Of the Unworthiness of the Ministers which hinders not the effect of the Sacrament', and specifically addresses the issue that the wickedness of those in authority in the Church might be thought to invalidate their ministry.

5. A view advanced in the introductory section of *NA1* p. 1530.

of the Enlightenment than Bacon's own approach: Bacon's scientific utopia includes worship of God as a natural response to the wonder of the world (*The New Atlantis*, *NA1* p. 1552).

The essay 'On Truth' illustrates Bacon's learning and approach. Footnotes show the range of reference he makes: to the Bible, Greek philosophy, church ‡Fathers, Latin natural philosophy, and the French essayist Montaigne. The structure of the essay, simply expressed, is that it begins with a question of truth directed in judgement against Christ, and ends with a question of truth directed in †judgement by Christ. The power of the first line, with its biblical quotation 'What is truth?' (John 18:38) — a serious question shattered by 'jesting Pilate' who 'would not stay for an answer' — is undeniable. Bacon follows this line of enquiry: what is truth and what is the attraction of lies? He passes on to the importance of the search for and possession of truth as 'the sovereign good of human nature', he sees the source of truth as God, and the practice of truth as 'the honour of man's nature'. In closing, he comes back to the biblical understanding that truth will be judged 'when Christ cometh'.

The significance of biblical and theological understanding is clear here. But under the appearance of detachment (there is, for example, no first-person reference), Bacon deals with matters familiar and personal. What is the attraction of lies? The insight of Bacon, the man of the world, is that it is variety: 'A mixture of a lie doth ever add pleasure.' And the biblical quotations at the beginning and end are not only emphatic but also arise in specifically *legal* contexts: Pilate is sitting in judgement on Christ, but not concerned to understand the case in hand; the quotation from Luke at the end of the essay comes at the close of the *parable of the unjust judge, a man who decides cases for his own convenience. It is these matters that show Bacon, lawyer and man of the world, in a more self-reflective light than his style would otherwise indicate.

Bacon was a man of his time. As a Protestant, he rails against the Roman Catholic church for its 'superstition' in inventing processes to support a preconceived theology ('Of Superstition', *Novum Organum* 62) and he does not think highly of public entertainment ('Of Masques and Triumphs'). As a man of the age of expansion, he theorises about colonies ('Of Plantations'[6]) and

---

6. The footnote in *NA1* pp. 1536–7, in which it is asserted that 'Bacon's essay completely avoids the most acute moral issues English colonization was posing: English participation in the brutal African slave trade; and the stocking of "plantations" in Ireland with Scottish Presbyterian settlers', is strangely inaccurate. Bacon specifically mentions his aversion to 'displanting' or 'extirpation' in lands already occupied; and he also demands that settlers treat any indigenous peoples 'justly and graciously'. Interestingly Bacon uses here the first-person pronoun, 'I like a plantation in pure soil', and so on; in the context of Bacon's general detachment, this marks the view as both emphatic and personal.

invents utopian societies (*The New Atlantis*). But his breadth of knowledge and application of †wisdom, biblical, classical, and scientific, is unique: this is what marks him out as a Christian writer of lasting importance.

QUESTIONS

1. Bacon uses the aphorism—an emphatic, authoritative statement (see the opening sentences of many of his *Essays* for examples)—extensively. Select some examples and discuss how they are used.
2. How would you characterise Bacon's theology?
3. Do you think Bacon is much concerned with ethics?

BIBLIOGRAPHY

Michael Kiernan, ed., *The Oxford Francis Bacon XV: The Essayes or Counsels, Civill and Morall*, Oxford 1985. The Oxford Francis Bacon, in progress, is the standard text of Bacon's works. This is a carefully annotated original-spelling edition of the *Essays*; see also Kiernan, ed., *The Oxford Francis Bacon IV: The Advancement of Learning*, Oxford 2000.

Peter Urbach and John Gibson, trans. and ed., *Francis Bacon: Novum Organum with Other Parts of The Great Instauration*, Chicago and La Salle 1994.

Brian Vickers, *Francis Bacon and Renaissance Prose*, Cambridge 1968. A good analysis of Bacon's style.

B.H.G. Wormald, *Francis Bacon: History, Politics and Science, 1561 – 1626*, Cambridge 1993. Gives attention to Bacon's background and scientific work.

13

GEORGE HERBERT

HERBERT AND *THE TEMPLE*

[*BARL* pp. 1015 f; *BASCP* pp. 177 f; *NA1* pp. 1595 f; *OA1* pp. 1165 f]

Herbert was born towards the end of the Elizabethan age. His mature poetry was written during the reign of Charles I when the Church of England was once more seeing itself as a purified, reformed Catholic church rather than as one adhering exclusively to Protestant theology and practice. This was the period of the 'Caroline Divines', men such as Lancelot Andrewes and Mark Frank, who sought to root doctrine and practice in the teachings of the major bishop-theologians of the church of the first ten centuries, before the schism between the Catholic and Orthodox churches. That Herbert was in accord with their principles is evident in such poems as 'To all angels and saints' and 'Ana(Mary)gram' (*OA1* p. 1174). In line with their approach, Herbert's inspiration is primarily from the Bible read in the context of the church's life of worship and celebration of the two ‡sacraments, †baptism and the ‡eucharist. We will see this throughout this exploration of Herbert's poetry.

The *NA1* introduction to Herbert rightly states that the key to this collection of poems lies in the title he gave to the whole work, *The Temple*. According to St Paul, the ‡soul or heart of a human being is a living temple, a place which was made holy for the worship of God (I Corinthians 3:16–17). But Paul, in this same letter, makes it clear that together, individual temples also constitute a greater temple, the whole worshipping body of Christ (I Corinthians 12:12–17). What happens in the inner temple of the individual, therefore, is not simply a private matter: it contributes to the life of the whole and in some sense echoes it. By calling his sequence *The Temple* Herbert is not simply expressing his own spiritual struggles, but is illuminating aspects of every Christian's struggle to make the inner self a place for the true worship of God.

He expresses this more universal experience by interconnecting two patterns: the first is the necessity for the individual to struggle towards acceptance of ‡salvation as an undeserved gift even while subject to ageing and death; the other, the pattern of the church's year. The connecting factor between these two patterns is the experiential meaning of Christ's †cross, death, and *resurrection for the Christian and the whole church.

Opening with 'The Altar', this sequence of poems reminds us forcibly that the self-offering of the Christian to Christ begins in acceptance of Christ's self-offering for and to the Christian. It establishes both themes. It begins with meditations on the ‡salvation brought by the death and *resurrection of Christ and the ‡soul's desire to respond adequately in ‡repentance and †love, making Christ's †sacrifice its own, and not attempting to earn salvation. But these opening poems also set the struggle within the church's liturgical year. What the individual Christian experiences catches the mood of the wider body in celebrations of key events in the life of Christ and the life of the church.

Thus we find cycles from ‡Easter to *Ascension (when Christ returns to the Father after his *resurrection), to *Pentecost (the coming of the Holy Spirit on the twelve apostles of Christ and the beginning of the church), to All ‡Saints, November 1st, ‡Advent (the time of awaiting the coming of Christ), to Christmas. That these cycles repeat themselves is part of the design; the Christian yearly cycle repeats its immersion in the main moods and in the remembrance of key events. Alongside poems that explicitly refer to such seasons are the personal poems that nevertheless link to the season: the recurrent poems of ‡penitence, struggles, and affliction are allied to Lent; those of abandonment and waiting, like 'Denial', to Advent; those of fulfilment to Easter and Christmas. Just as the liturgical pattern has recurrent marked changes of mood, Lent into Easter, Advent into Christmas, so too has the personal experience. Growth is not in a continuous upward climb, but like the liturgical year it circles round in a sequence of troughs and heights which deepen the ‡soul's experience of self-surrender to God. But it is also an experience of ageing, as we see in 'The Forerunners'. So for example, the period before Advent is a time of waiting for the coming of the ‡saviour, so that 'Come, come, my God, O come!' in 'Denial' (14) is both a personal plea and an echo of the Advent liturgy and hymnody. It echoes, too, the closing lines of the book of Revelation that undergirds the Advent season: 'Even so, come, Lord Jesus' (Revelation 22:20).

This notion of the inner †journey being paralleled with an external cycle and journey is clear in 'The Bunch of Grapes'. Herbert sees the contradictory nature of his own and each Christian's response to God, typified in the Israelites' pattern of obedience, rebellion, and ‡repentance during their forty years of wandering in the †desert after their liberation from slavery in Egypt (the *Exodus), when their physical regression back to the Red Sea stimulates repentance and deeper obedience. The Exodus and the liberation from slavery in Egypt is seen by Christians as foreshadowing the liberation from ‡sin effected by Christ. In this way, the Israelite wandering in the desert evokes each Christian's experience of rebellion against God and obedience in response to ‡salvation. Herbert sets all individual vicissitudes within this framework.

Rebellion and obedience are key themes for Herbert because they take us to the heart of his understanding of ‡salvation. In the Garden of *Eden, *Adam rebels and disobeys God, losing intimacy with God for himself and his descendants (Genesis 3). As St Paul says 'in Adam all die' but Christ's obedience to God, as far as 'even the death of the cross' cancels out the disobedience, restores relationship and life so that 'in Christ all will be made alive' (I Corinthians 15:21–2; Philippians 2:8). So for Herbert the conflict in each Christian is between Adam, the old man, and Christ, the new man. Each Christian must learn obedience to God, an obedience that brings him to the †cross, in imitation of Jesus (Hebrews 5:7–10 and Jesus' prayer in *Gethsemane in which his agony at the prospect of death is surrendered to the will of his Father, Luke 22:42).

For Herbert the †cross in human daily life is not some terrible experience of suffering; rather it is the crossing or contradiction of all that human nature expects. This operates at all kinds of levels. In 'Redemption', human nature seeks God among the magnificent of the earth, but finds him dying a criminal's death. In 'Easter', it must accept that returning to dust in death, dying with Christ, is a necessary prelude to rising with him. In 'Easter Wings', he explores this paradox further. It is only the acceptance of frailty, of ‡sinfulness, of inadequacy that can enable him to rise with Christ. It is only acceptance of being dust that enables him to transcend his own earthliness and fly. If we remember that *Adam is made from the dust of the earth, then we can see again that Herbert is insisting that the ‡soul must accept what is of Adam, and rely on the obedience of Christ.

QUESTIONS

1. In what ways does it enrich your understanding of the poems to read them both as personal experience and as the pattern of Christian life?
2. In what ways do the concepts of human rebellion and Christ's obedience illumine the meaning of Herbert's poems?
3. How important is an awareness of Herbert's broader scheme to an appreciation of individual poems?

'AFFLICTION (I)' AND 'THE COLLAR'

[*BARL* pp. 1027, 1055; *BASCP* pp. 178, 199; *NA1* pp. 1599, 1609;
OA1 p. 1173 ('The Collar')]

'Affliction (I)' is central to Herbert's tracing of the pattern of contradiction, of the †cross in his experience, the pattern identified by most Christian ‡mystics in the ‡soul's †journey to God. This begins in early delight in God, a delight in the consolations found in belief and devotion—'milk and sweetnesses' (19)—and is a form of self-seeking. God is loved for what he gives. Faith and †love are then purified by withdrawal of these consolations, the cross is known in the crossing of expectations, of self-will, and of the desire for self-justification (55–60). The roots of ‡sin are exposed as rebellion, but love is also exposed as a deeper force, a love for God in himself and not for his gifts or from fear of ‡damnation. Rebellion reminds him that the only other master to serve is the †devil; to ask 'let me not ...' is to say 'I deserve to lose you if I do not love you'.

We find here, as in other poems of rebellion like 'The Collar', that it is at the height of the rebellion that the contrary voice of †love is heard. This is because in this state the ‡soul is truly at the centre of the †cross, at that tension between human will and God's will: where one is most intense, so will the other be. The cross resulted in ultimate victory for Jesus, for God's will. And so for the faithful souls who trust in Jesus' victory and not in their own strength, there is victory. 'Affliction (I)' and 'The Collar' both end with words expressive of relationship, 'my dear Lorde', 'my Lorde'. The conflict is resolved by Herbert admitting that he belongs not to himself but to Christ, the Lord to whom he is vassal and, in 'The Collar', heir, 'childe'.

So let us look at 'The Collar'. The link to a clergyman's collar is historically uncertain, but what I think we can say is that Herbert intends us to see how 'choler', anger at the crossing of human nature, required by his search for God, has turned the service of God, which is perfect freedom, into an experience of slavery, the slave's collar. His rebellion and anger at the ways of God, which have not given him the human satisfaction of success, fulfilled ambition, and sensory pleasures, have led him into a spirit of slavery. At the height of rebellion, awareness of the true nature of Christ's claim on him reasserts itself: he is child, son, heir. His life is not the service of an enslaving tyrant but of a †loving friend and Father: as St Paul writes to the Romans (8:15–18), 'ye have not received the spirit of bondage ... but the Spirit of adoption, whereby we cry, Abba, Father.... we are children of God: And if children, then heirs: heirs of God and joint-heirs with Christ; if so be that we suffer with him, that we may also be glorified together.' In these words of St Paul we find Herbert's answer to his rebellion.

Anyone who has this relationship must expect to experience what Christ experienced. By implication Herbert has brought us back to the †cross, the cross implicit in the ‡eucharistic symbolism of the poem, for the board he strikes is the eucharistic table or altar; the wine and the blood are reminders of the cross and of the self-gift of Christ to humanity. It reminds us of the contradictory logic of God that deals with ‡sin and disobedience by †sacrificing himself.

Herbert's rebellion is a refusal to accept that this is the way it should be for the Christian. He is met by the fidelity of a God who is obedient to his relationship with humanity. Herbert is still 'child', even when his humanity wants to reject this. Furthermore, of course, 'child' is a reminder that, although Herbert experiences his life as service and as the service of an independent adult free to take his service elsewhere, he is not in fact the giver in this relationship: he is the child in receipt of his needs and in a relationship of derivation and dependence.

This is a †wisdom he finally accepts in 'The Flower'. Here there is acceptance of human frailty and contingency, of being cast down into dust, of having no independent ground of worthiness on which to stand before God but also of being a thing of beauty, made by its nature to share in the rhythm of death and *resurrection. Here he acknowledges that all the contradictions, the crossings he has rebelled against or suffered, are not indeed external impositions but experiences integral to human nature as †loved and ‡redeemed by Christ and shaped by being conformed to the pattern of Christ's death and resurrection. Struggle and pain has now become the tranquil acceptance of death and resurrection.

QUESTIONS

1. Compare and contrast the mood and tone of 'Affliction (I)' and 'The Collar'. What does this add to our understanding of Herbert's attitude to suffering, rebellion, and obedience?
2. To what extent is your appreciation of these two poems enriched by awareness of Herbert's understanding of the †cross in human life?
3. To what extent does a knowledge of Herbert's Christianity add to an appreciation of these poems?

'LOVE (III)'

[*BACL* p. 426; *BARL* p. 1065; *BASCP* pp. 206–7; *NA1* p. 1614; *OA1* p. 1178]

All that we have seen in Herbert's poetry is exemplified in this final poem in the sequence, 'The Church'. Here, all that was hitherto distorted is seen clearly, all that was cock-eyed is seen plain. This conclusion to the sequence is also the conclusion to life. It follows poems centred on ageing and death. At the end of a life of service it becomes clear that it was, in fact, a life of being served. The Christian understands at the end that his life has been about struggling to accept, rather than to give, †love.

The image of God the waiter/servant picks up on many biblical images of God, primarily Luke's picture of Jesus returning to serve at the table the faithful servants found waiting for him (Luke 12:36–40). This also recalls, for example, God feeding the Israelites manna in their †desert wanderings and the miracle of the feeding of the 5,000 by Jesus, and Herbert weaves these into this picture of intimacy. It takes up, too, Jesus saying 'I am among you as one who serves' (Luke 22:27) and puts it into the context of the *last supper and the ‡eucharist, to which both these biblical feedings were understood as pointing. By doing so it sets the whole poem in a eucharistic context so that the meal to which he is invited is a sharing in the life of Christ, being nourished by the fruits of his self-gift on the †cross. Because the eucharist was also associated with the †wedding feast of the Lamb at the end of the world, we see that the meal to which Herbert is invited is eternal life, a life which starts well before death in the acceptance of Love's invitation.

This understanding is deepened by the allusions to Jesus' use in the gospels of the imagery of the †wedding feast and the great banquet as images of final union between God and human beings at the end of the world (see, for example, Luke 14:15–24). These allusions widen the perspective beyond the fate of the individual Christian and help us to maintain a dual vision. What is true for humankind is nevertheless an ultimate reality, an intimate reality for the individual person in Christ. Calling Christ 'Love' directs us also towards the letters of St John, which repeatedly insist that God is †love (but also insist that the love that saves humanity is God's love for them, not theirs for him). God's love for humanity, shown in the †sacrifice of Christ, must be received by people if they are to return love for him and for others. In this way, they must be served by Love before they can serve him. John's writings continue to hover in the background but are seen more specifically in the allusion to his image of Jesus knocking at the door and coming to eat with whoever opens to him in Revelation 3:20–21. The image here is not of Christ's service but is clearly an acceptance of the invitation. Love knocks, bids a welcome, that is, invites a response to share not simply in the feast of eternal life, but in the intimacy of table fellowship, which seals friendship and affinity. Furthermore, the servant image recalls Jesus as servant washing the feet of his disciples, a similar invitation to intimate identification that Peter, like the persona of the poem, initially rejects (see John 13:1–20).

A further layer is added by the association with the Song of Songs, where the bride proclaims 'He brought me to the banqueting house, and his banner over me was love' (Song of Songs 2:4). Since the Song of Songs was read by Herbert's age as the ‡mystical union between God and the individual ‡soul, as well as a relationship between God and the church, we can see how Herbert knits his personal and universal Christian experience into one fabric by combining these three biblical ideas: ‡eucharist, the end of time, and mystical union. Herbert ensures that we do not narrow the scope or meaning of the poem to one dimension or perspective.

The opening of the poem puts in a nutshell the major cause of the previous struggle. 'Guilty of dust and sin' is an interesting conjunction. Guilty of ‡sin implies knowledge of actual and potential wrongdoing. Guilty of dust suggests shame at the nature of one's own existence (see Genesis 3:19). It implies a kind of hurt pride—'I will not accept an invitation which reveals my own unworthiness'—that makes the acceptance of †love, freely offered regardless of merit, not simply humbling but humiliating. Throughout the sequence we have seen Herbert's struggle with his desire to deserve ‡salvation and to meet God on equal terms. He now undermines all of this pretension to equality through the very structure of the poem.

It is †Love who bids welcome, who draws near, who questions. The initiative is always with God. Herbert, or the ‡soul, is always the recipient, the responsive one. We see, too, how this humility exposed as pride also serves as a means to evade the demands of love. Drawing back through unworthiness keeps Herbert free of what love might ask of him. It is interesting to note the use of tenses. Love says 'you shall be the worthy guest'. Worth comes from accepting the invitation, not as a prerequisite, while Herbert ignores this to focus on his own qualities, or lack of them. Herbert/the soul looks at what he can or cannot offer; love looks at what he will become by accepting this free gift.

In the final stanza, once more the ‡soul wants to hide from God in shame, just as *Adam did after the *fall when he realised he was naked (Genesis 3:10, 'I heard thy voice in the garden, and I was afraid, because I was naked; and I hid myself'). Disobedience reinforces itself through shame and will not allow such an unequal meeting. †Love continually reminds us that, as Herbert says elsewhere, 'Adam took the fruit, but it is Christ must climb the tree', that is, the †cross ('The Sacrifice', 202–3). Adam's shame is nullified by Christ's shameful death on the cross.

†Love bids Herbert specifically, 'taste my meat'. Now in St John's Gospel Jesus declares, 'My meat is to do the will of him that sent me' (John 4:34). This invitation to eternal life, to intimacy with Christ, is an invitation to share in the obedience of Christ to the Father, an obedience that 'crosses' his own will and leads to †sacrificial death. By accepting the invitation to table, the ‡soul is accepting the way of the †cross, not as a sacrifice to Christ, but as a sacrifice with him. The battle of the soul against the radical inequality of the relationship is resolved once Herbert yields. In eating Love's meat the two share the same life, the same way, the same end.

It is interesting to note the change in tense of this final stanza. Herbert sets his words and deeds in the past tense, but †Love speaks in the present. We are left to reflect that, though Herbert's acceptance marks his particular history as past or completed events, Love speaks in an eternal 'now and ever' open invitation.

QUESTIONS

1. What picture of love does Herbert create here?
2. Follow up the reference to the Song of Songs and its context. In what ways does acquaintance with this biblical poem affect your understanding of the love Herbert depicts?
3. Follow up some of the other biblical references. In what ways does acquaintance with these extracts add to your developing understanding of Herbert's depiction of love, and of the meaning of the poem?

BIBLIOGRAPHY

Terry G. Sherwood, *Herbert's Prayerful Art*, Toronto 1989.

Harold E. Toliver, *George Herbert's Christian Narrative*, Pennsylvania 1993.

R.V. Young, *Doctrine and Devotion in Seventeenth-Century Poetry: Studies in Donne, Herbert, Crashaw and Vaughan*, Cambridge 2000.

14

HENRY VAUGHAN

VAUGHAN AND CHRISTIANITY

[*BASCP* pp. 442 f; *NA1* pp. 1615 f; *OA1* pp. 1189 f]

Vaughan has often been regarded by scholars as an unorthodox Christian, more influenced by the study of hermetic philosophy than the Christian scriptures. Alternatively he has been seen as the most biblical of all English poets. Indeed, a careful reading of his poetry reveals a strong biblical and orthodox Christianity. What distinguishes him from his great inspiration and older contemporary, George Herbert, is his stronger belief, lost in the Protestant world he inhabited, that the book of scripture was accompanied by the book of nature. This is the belief that God the creator has left his imprint on his handiwork.

This view is quite consonant with St Paul's view in Romans 1:18–23 that knowledge of the existence of God is available through nature. Humanity's likeness to God, however, is corrupted by the *fall, and this has damaged its capacity to read this evidence of God, though it still exists. †Original sin creates an environment in which man's spiritual senses are increasingly dimmed. Just as each individual grows more and more accustomed to ‡sin (see 'The Retreat'), so too the whole race sinks deeper into ignorance of God.

So for Vaughan, *salvation is envisaged in terms of a return to origins rather than as a totally new and future event. The goal is the innocence of *Eden, giving intimacy with God in a *creation that reflects his glory. For the individual this implies a return to infancy. Like the Greek ‡Fathers of the church, by whom he was greatly influenced, Vaughan understood †original sin differently from his ‡Calvinist contemporaries. Rather than a radical corruption rendering each person totally degenerate from birth, they saw the 'curse of Adam' as the birth of a child, created by God, into an environment in which it was easy to do evil and very difficult to do good.

Growing up, therefore, meant growing into being increasingly accustomed to evil and increasingly losing familiarity with goodness. This is clear in a poem like 'The Retreat'. The young child has not yet learnt corruption and therefore can retain intuitions about God and respond to his presence in his *creation.

His desire to travel back echoes not only Mark 10:15 in which Jesus asserts that one must be as a child to enter the kingdom of †heaven, but is also reminiscent of the insistence in John's Gospel on being 'born again', which can be read as requiring the return to an earlier state of innocence and dependence (see John 3:1–8).

In 'Corruption', the process of growing used to ‡sin is shown to affect the whole human race. We begin with *Adam, fresh out of *Eden. He is not so far from it in time and in experience as not to remember and long for it. Despite the consequence of his sin for his relationships with earth that we find in Genesis 3:19, he is kept aware of what he has lost. But we can see the logic of Paul's thought in Romans 1: the older the race grows, the further it moves from God. It loves †darkness because its deeds are evil (John 3:19–21). The rainbow of God's promise to Noah that he would never again destroy the world by *flood is hard to discern, so it seems that the world is headed for destruction (see Genesis 9:1–17). But the lines 'All's in deep sleep …' (37–8) is a call to hope, a reminder that God is working to bring *salvation, for it recalls the words of Isaiah 9:2 (and echoes Isaiah 60:1–2) that the †light is coming for those who wait in the darkness of death.

These words are associated with the season of ‡Advent. This season traditionally looked not only to the coming of *salvation in the birth of Christ, the †light to the nations, but also to the coming of Christ at the end of the world. The end, therefore, was envisaged not as a destruction of the earth, but as its coming to fulfilment, being replaced by a new †heaven and a new earth, as Vaughan suggests in the allusion to Revelation 14:15 regarding the reaping †angel. Corruption seems to *fallen humanity to be only bad news. The poem seems to see it as such, were it not for this last Advent note. The sickle and the angel will deal with all the weeds, but will also gather in a harvest. When the earth has run its course, it does not fall into nothingness, but will return, as Vaughan longs for it to, to the one who created it.

The biblical image of the harvest in the gospels and New Testament writings like the book of Revelation, takes up the Old Testament image of humanity as like the grass or the flower of the field (Psalm 90:5–6). This emphasises the transience of humankind and their place within *creation. Within the *sermon on the mount, Jesus adapts this imagery to one much more positive about human value: humanity is more valuable to God than the passing flower (Matthew 6:28–31). To be a plant, then, is to be something of beauty and value. This is one layer of biblical allusion within 'Unprofitableness', working in conjunction with an allusion to Luke 17:7–10 about eschewing any desire for reward in serving God, which lends the poem a different perspective. Read as it stands, both the title and the poem present a rather negative view of the persona's spiritual state. Read in the light of the gospel passage, it becomes also a meditation on acceptance of God's grace without personal merit. The servant, after doing his duty, is to call himself unprofitable, because he is not offering anything extra beyond his nature and duty as a servant. He is simply being and returning what he is. He provides nothing extra, no interest, no profit.

Now, unlike the servant, the plant in the poem exercises its nature by receiving rather than giving. If it were a beautiful flower, its beauty would still be unprofitable because its beauty would be simply an expression of itself. We might, however, be misled by the natural beauty into believing that this was some return for the care lavished upon it. We cannot be so misled here for the plant is a weed; the only return it can make is to be itself, a stench, or fog. It is thankless, not because it fails to make a return, but because it can do no more than be what it is. All that we have, Vaughan seems to be saying, is given us by God in *creation and in ‡salvation. We cannot give him back his gifts with profit. We can only accept what we are, whether that be the beauty of the flower, or the apparent ugliness and uselessness of the weed.

If we read the poem taking the two meanings together, we can see Vaughan illuminating the experience. Read outside the gospel message, we see the human experience only as one of failure, weakness, and barrenness in relation to God. Read within it, we see God's perspective, a lavishing of †love and care on his *creation unconditionally, without the expectation of return. If the persona is by nature a weed, then it does its duty by being a weed: it can do no more. Its merit lies in this acceptance. Employing biblical allusion here allows Vaughan to give an understanding of the human experience of living by grace rather than works, but also to set that experience within a wider understanding of the nature of God.

QUESTIONS

1. Some critics regard the attitude to childhood in 'The Retreat' as sentimentality. In the light of the biblical background to the poem, would you agree with this judgement?
2. To what extent do you think it is possible to read 'Corruption' as an optimistic poem?
3. How positive do you think Vaughan's attitude is to his humanity in 'Unprofitableness'?

'THE WORLD' AND 'THE NIGHT'

[*BABL* pp. 152–3 ('The Night'); *BASCP* pp. 449, 455; *NA1* pp. 1622, 1626;
OA1 pp. 1194, 1197]

Vaughan's total opus needs to be read with the nature imagery used in the Old Testament Psalms, the Song of Songs, the †parables of Jesus, and the †light and †darkness imagery of John's Gospel in mind. This complex of uses can be seen in 'The World' and 'The Night', possibly two of his most complete and satisfying poems.

The starting point of 'The World' is, as Vaughan himself tells us, John 2:16–17, the origin of the Christian concept of the battle with the world, the flesh, and the †devil. 'The world' here does not mean the *created earth, but the human creation, *fallen into concern with itself, with the transience of erotic love, with power, and with wealth. One reads behind it the words of Jesus, 'What is a man profited, if he shall gain the whole world, and lose his own soul?' (Matthew 16:26), so often read in relation to the contemplation of death in the midst of worldly pleasure.

We can see here also the influence of many traditional medieval images that illustrate the teaching, for example the paintings of 'Death and the Gallant', the young lover holding to his nose a rose, the symbol of erotic, romantic love, confronted with the image of death. The image of worldly goods in *Everyman* and of the corruption of wealth in Chaucer's ‡*Pardoner's Tale* also resonates here. Vaughan is possibly consciously working in a tradition that his readers would recognise from popular preaching, from popular iconography, and from literature relating it to the strictures in the gospel and epistles of St John on *fallen humanity's preference of night to day. In John 3:19–21, Jesus says that people prefer night because their deeds are evil, and the daylight exposes this, making them face it. Vaughan develops this: people prefer to remain in †darkness, attached to their evil, rather than come into the †light and be obliged to recognise their evil for what it is and face a changed life without it.

But this allusion to John's Gospel draws in two other echoes for Vaughan that bring his meditation to a conclusion. His pondering on eternity as a ring employs another tradition. Eternity, or the God of eternity, was traditionally seen as a circle because it has no beginning and no end. It provides, therefore, the perfect contrast with our earth-bound understanding of time as linear. Seeing the circle as a ring, however, also draws to it the nuptial imagery used especially in John, but throughout the New Testament, for the relationship between †heaven and earth, Christ and the church, and throughout the Christian ‡mystical tradition for the union between Christ and the ‡soul (see, for example, Matthew 9:14–17; 25:1–3; Ephesians 5:25–33).

Vaughan alludes directly to the nuptial imagery of John's Revelation. This combination of nuptial union with the imagery of †darkness and †light leads Vaughan back to the prologue of John's Gospel. Here light shines in darkness and only the few, as in the poem, welcomed it. And it is those who do so welcome it that receive power to become children of God, children of the light (John 1:1–10). Hence what appears in the poem as a sudden ‡mystical intuition is in fact a distillation of his meditation on these Johannine themes.

In 'The Night', Vaughan asks that we be agile readers, alert to all the different meanings and nuances of his use of biblical imagery. In the story of Nicodemus to which he alludes (John 3:1–21), †light represents the world and †darkness represents the eternal. It is fear of the world's reaction that makes Nicodemus come to Jesus by night. This coming to Christ by night then reminds Vaughan of the gospel accounts of Jesus spending nights alone in prayer. Night then evokes something positive, the solitude and stillness of this time of communion between Father and Son; night is the time of meeting.

We have two thoughts leading from this. The beauty of stillness means that God can be apprehended in the calm of the natural world, but more, meeting by night evokes the bride's waiting for the coming of the beloved in the Song of Songs (see, for example, 3:1–2). In the Christian ‡mystical tradition this is an image of the ‡soul waiting in inner solitude and silence for the coming of Christ, which leads to the mystical union of the soul with him. Night therefore becomes the image for the state of the contemplative soul which is in †darkness, that is, no longer aware of any other desires but the desire for God. It is this state that Vaughan longs for, in contrast to his life in the world, where he is led by its light towards ephemeral pleasures.

This contrast between the false light of the world and the true †light of the world that is Jesus according to John (John 9:5) leads to the resolution of the poem that is informed by Vaughan's knowledge of the Christian ‡mystical tradition. The †darkness of God is caused by his excess of light to our eyes; we are, as it were, blinded by the light and so dwell in what appears to us as the darkness of God. Only the purified ‡soul after death will be able to endure the light. In this context, the longing for union with God implies immersion in the darkness of God. When read in this perspective, the shifts and turns of Vaughan's thought are seen as integral to its development and to the shape of his poem.

QUESTIONS

1. In the light of Vaughan's use of the Bible and Christian tradition do you consider it more fruitful to read 'The World' as an account of a personal vision or as a meditation on Christian truths?
2. Trace the shifts in tone and meaning of Vaughan's use of the imagery of night in 'The Night'.
3. To what extent do you consider it possible to read Vaughan fruitfully without an appreciation of his use of the Bible?

BIBLIOGRAPHY

Philip West, *Henry Vaughan's Silex Scintillans: Scripture Uses*, Oxford 2001.

R.V. Young, *Doctrine and Devotion in Seventeenth-Century Poetry: Studiers in Donne, Herbert, Crashaw and Vaughan*, Cambridge 2000.

RICHARD CRASHAW

'ON THE WOUNDS OF OUR CRUCIFIED LORD'

[*BASCP* pp. 322 f; *NA1* p. 1629; *OA1* pp. 1178 f]

Crashaw was a younger contemporary of Herbert and is commonly grouped with him and their elder, Donne, as a Metaphysical poet. Where he differs from them is in his Catholicism: he draws both themes and images from Roman Catholic liturgical and devotional traditions. To our twenty-first-century ears, this little poem may seem bizarre, even distasteful. It would not always have been so. In the early church, emphasis was upon the wounded side of Christ, from which blood and water, symbols of †baptism and of the ‡eucharist, flowed. It was a restrained devotion, pointing believers to the ‡sacraments of baptism (water) and eucharist (blood), deriving from the description of the piercing of Jesus' side on the †cross given in John's Gospel (John 19:34). In the eleventh and twelfth centuries, the western church developed an emphasis upon the wounds of Christ, which was more affective, that is, concerned not to stimulate reflections on doctrine, but emotions of love, sorrow, and ‡repentance. Crashaw writes in this tradition of emotive imagery.

In this tradition it was not only the death and *resurrection of Christ that were seen as ‡redemptive, but also all the subjection to human suffering that led up to it. We can see the beginning of this understanding in the teaching of Gregory Nazianzen, the great theologian of the eastern church in the fourth century: 'what he has not assumed, he has not healed'. Christ has taken on our full humanity, which includes our human vulnerability and subjection to the cruelty of others. Whatever Christ suffers in the flesh brings healing, because such suffering is now shared by God.

Crashaw also uses a long tradition of gem imagery, issuing from Old Testament and New Testament sources. For example, from the *parable of the pearl of great price develops the image of Christ, the Pearl, for whom all else must be given (Matthew 13:45–6). The imagery of the book of Revelation, in which each gate of the eternal †city is set with different stones, led to a whole system of gem symbolism (see Revelation 21:9–27). We see this in the iconography of the late Middle Ages and early Renaissance. For example, Grunewald's Isenheim altarpiece has a vividly realistic painting of the *crucifixion in which blood flows from wounds in hands and feet. In the panel beneath this, of the *resurrection, these wounds are no longer wounds, but rubies. Because of Christ's resurrection, the blood of his suffering is now a thing of beauty and great price.

Crashaw is working in this tradition, using the language of gems but outside the medieval system of symbolism. He does, though, use all this traditional iconography within a more explicit New Testament allusion. The 'thou' whom he addresses in line 9 is firstly the woman of ill repute who kisses Jesus' feet and weeps over them, while anointing them with nard. Traditionally identified as Mary Magdalene, she became the church's symbol of the ‡repentant ‡sinner weeping for her sins (John 12:1–8). So we can see that this 'thou' is every Christian who has wept in love and contrition. †Love is expressed in the pearls of sorrow, of teardrops, costly to the ‡penitent but in reality water. This love is more than amply repaid in the truly precious blood of Christ, his life poured out for the sinner in the *crucifixion. And so what might appear as a rather forced metaphysical conceit can be understood as a way of meditating on this gospel scene, putting it into the context of the †cross and evoking from the reader yet more love and penitence.

'IN THE HOLY NATIVITY OF OUR LORD GOD: A HYMN AS SUNG BY THE SHEPHERDS'

[*BASCP* pp. 327 f; *NA1* pp. 1635 f]

In this poem, too, within an explicitly gospel scene, Crashaw uses two implicit related gospel images. The *Benedictus*, the song of Zechariah at the naming of John the Baptist, heralds a ‡saviour who 'breaks on us like the dawn from on high', therefore 'bringing eternal day' (Luke 1:46, 55). And this child, in the prologue to John's Gospel, is 'the light shining in the darkness' that cannot be overcome (John 1:5). We are left in no doubt that this very human scene is also the ‡revelation of divinity.

Crashaw may seem to be enjoying the contrast beloved of metaphysical poetry, but here it is the contrast within the biblical message that he is elaborating. His treatment of the Blessed Virgin †Mary is traditional and reflects early liturgical texts. Because she is chosen to be mother of God, Mary is 'higher than the seraphim', the highest rank of †angel. To be a worthy place for the Son, she must be total purity, unaffected by the burning of the fire of lust and inappropriate desires. The purity of God requires a place where this kind of warmth is absent, the humanity of the child needs the warmth of self-forgetful mother-love, those found in a 'maid' mother; this is 'cold' only in contrast with the burning of disordered human lust.

Lines 59–64 reflect again the earliest liturgical texts, which themselves echo the book of Revelation in heralding the coming of a new †heaven and a new earth (Revelation 21); in this birth a new heaven and new earth have already come, the foundations, as it were, are laid. Christians rejoice now at this birth on earth but also look to a greater, further rejoicing when time ends.

This sense of anticipation is also present in the hints Crashaw gives about the future of the child, which makes the celebration of Christmas inseparable from ‡Easter. He exploits the latent ambiguity of the word 'east'. Eyes breaking 'from their East' (33) alerts us to the Magi coming from the east, but more than this, it reminds us that this child is the Risen One who rises like the sun from the east. The latency of death and *resurrection within this feast is also hinted at by the phoenix imagery. Traditionally we would expect this image in the reflection on death and resurrection. The phoenix dies and rises from its own ashes: it is symbolic of the risen Christ. This child is *born* as ‡saviour.

Here, in the reminder that the †incarnate Son is the Word, we are also reminded that we cannot celebrate the birth of Christ in isolation from the mysteries of *creation and ‡redemption. This babe is the ‡saviour; the *Lamb to whom the shepherds bring a lamb, is himself the †Lamb of sacrifice. Himself consumed by the fire of †love, like the phoenix, Christ's burning love for humanity, which gives them light, will transform them so that they too become burnt offerings to his love.

This poem once more works as a meditation on a gospel scene, exploring the theological implications, but moving us emotionally by the sensuousness of the imagery. The Chorus then involves the readers, not only in praise, but in recognition that a response is also invited. Crashaw is thus more subtle and far deeper than we may have credited. What might appear merely pretty or artful conceits in fact carry with them a wealth of biblical and traditional, and especially liturgical, allusions.

QUESTIONS

1. Do you think it is possible to appreciate 'On the Wounds of Christ' without knowing the gospel story on which it is based?
2. In what ways is your appreciation of 'On the Wounds of Christ' affected by your awareness of the biblical roots of Crashaw's imagery?

3. To what extent is an understanding of the references to †cross, *resurrection, and the new †heaven in 'On the Holy Nativity' necessary for an appreciation of this poem?

BIBLIOGRAPHY

A.D. Cousins, *The Catholic Religious Poets from Southwell to Crashaw: A Critical History*, London 1991.

John R. Roberts, ed., *New Perspectives on the Life and Art of Richard Crashaw*, Columbia 1990.

George Walton Williams, *Image and Symbol in the Sacred Poetry of Richard Crashaw*, 2nd edn, Columbia 1967.

R.V. Young, *Doctrine and Devotion in Seventeenth-Century Poetry: Studies in Donne, Herbert, Crashaw and Vaughan*, Cambridge 2000.

Andrew Marvell, 'Upon Appleton House'

[*BASCP* pp. 399 f, esp. 410 f; *NA1* pp. 1684 f, esp. 1704 f; *OA1* pp. 1141 f, esp. 1157 f]

In 'Upon Appleton House' (1651) Marvell draws on the country house tradition. The classical pastoral impulse combines here with concepts of devotion to God and rejection of worldly †temptations. It is part political ‡allegory and part Protestant meditation, with strong recurrent motifs of *fall, ‡purgation, and regeneration, incorporating a *crucifixion image at its heart. It is these ideas which give this long, discursive poem its unity.

The moral context is established in the initial stanzas where humility is extolled through discussion of Appleton's architecture: in essence it is not overblown; it is done without pretension. It is contrasted with the Tower of Babel, built in overweening pride to reach to †heaven (Genesis 11). Everything at Appleton House correlates with the modesty of the owner Thomas Fairfax, all is orderly and becoming, recorded in verses informed by the Protestant ethic: wealth is given by God, and his creatures are responsible for its stewardship. The religious context is also soon established utilising biblical types, as often throughout the poem. As 'an Inn to entertain / Its Lord a while, but not remain', it recalls the *nativity story as well as the passage in Hebrews that indicates that Christians are just passing through this life en route to 'a better country' (13:14). The image suggests also that each incumbent reenacts the life of Christ on earth.

After these introductory stanzas the story of Isabel Thwaites a century before is told. The house was built originally as a priory and here a prioress is shown enticing Isabel to take the veil, promising a paradise of innocence, protection from men, chastity, devotion, prayer, beauty, and delight. She is very much cast in the role of †tempter by phrases such as 'The nun's smooth tongue has sucked her in' (200). Sensuality is presented as the great enemy, with a clear attack on Catholicism, which was seen as relying inordinately on the senses to inculcate its dogmas.

Cognisant of the prioress's desire to procure Isabel's estate, Fairfax's ances-
tor comes to the rescue. 'I know what fruit their gardens yield', he claims (219),
referring to the fruit with which *Eve was †tempted. Though he condemns
the priory, he voices regret for good corrupted—an essential motif in 'Upon
Appleton House'. The virginal Isabel is rescued and delivered into the holy state
of matrimony in an imitation of Christ's ‡redemptive act.

Fairfax's daughter Maria is now placed in a †garden idyll, virginal and pure,
conjuring up parallels with the Virgin †Mary, or with *Eve before the *fall. England itself is described as a †garden, equated with *Eden, complete with †angels
guarding its gate and 'luckless apple', representing the state of Britain before
the Civil War. In a typically elaborate conceit, Marvell uses the garden image
to lament the passing of an age without war and the loss of good conscience; we
are to understand that the perfection of the garden, as of Britain and the human
‡soul, is constantly under threat from outside forces.

The scene moves now beyond the flower garden to the hay meadow. The
passage of mowers through the tall grass is likened to the Israelites entering the
Promised Land 'as grasshoppers' in the book of Numbers 13:32–3. Further references to the children of Israel encompass the provision of quails (corncrakes
killed during the mowing process), and manna (the dew), and the parting of
the Red Sea—in this case the 'green sea' divided by the mowers. Such imagery
taken from the biblical Israelite journeys and battles was common currency to
the ‡Puritan revolutionaries, easily applied to their struggle.

In stanza 59 the creation of lakes is likened to the Old Testament *flood,
from which the poet takes refuge in ancient woodland, which in turn is compared to Noah's ark. Here he engages in near ‡mystical contemplation. This
forest-ark is a 'temple green', complete with †angelic choirs—the native birds.
The poet meditates on how the great oak (symbol, of course, of monarchy) is
easily felled since it has already been eaten away within by the 'Traitor-worm'.
The allusion to the †Satan-serpent of Genesis is followed by explicit reference
to the inward corrupting nature of †original sin: '(As first our Flesh corrupt
within / Tempts impotent and bashful Sin)' (555–6).

The poet sees himself as 'some great Prelate' wandering under the trees
wearing a cope of leaves and tendrils. In stanza 76, Marvell considers how his
mind is made safe and strengthened by this place and by this manner of contemplation, safe from the world and its charms, and from the beauty which so
easily seduces the human heart. He longs therefore to be all the more enveloped
by protective nature, invoking a ‡mystical *crucifixion image with its connotations of death to the flesh and the world, as a key to spiritual life: 'Do you, O
Brambles, chain me too, / And courteous Briars, nail me through' (615–16).

He wishes to be 'staked' in the place where the cleansing waters of the *flood have been. In the succeeding stanza the now retreated flood has left the meadow 'as green silks but newly washed', encouraging associations of †baptism and ‡purgation. No serpent remains. It is a picture of regeneration, of re-creation. The implication is that church, state, individual, and *fallen nature itself must all undergo similar purgation to achieve renewal.

The river now is 'harmless', its curves protective. Here is a scene of pastoral rest and plenty, a renewed *Eden, into which walks Maria in perfect harmony with the land. The environment now reflects Maria's purity, sweetness, and beauty. She who speaks with 'Heaven's Dialect' is presented as a girl of high ‡virtue: she has escaped the ambushes of young love and the ‡vice of vanity. A 'sacred bud' on the family tree, she enhances the Fairfax line. Marvell lists and rejects superlatives from classical literature: Maria's environment, Appleton House, revolves instead around she who is 'Heaven's Center, Nature's Lap, / And Paradise's only Map' (767–8). While the world at large is in a *fallen state ("Tis not, what once it was, the World', 761), her Appleton is an ordered †heaven.

QUESTIONS

1. How are the themes of regeneration apparent in Marvell's other poems?
2. How is the battle against the senses depicted in the rest of his work?

BIBLIOGRAPHY

John Carey, ed., *Andrew Marvell*, Harmondsworth 1969. Contains a useful short essay on the biblical and theological contexts of 'Upon Appleton House' from Maren-Sofie Røstvig, *The Happy Man: Studies in the Metamorphoses of a Classical Idea, Vol. 1, 1600–1700*, 2nd edn, Oslo 1962.

Donald Malvin Friedman, *Marvell's Pastoral Art*, London 1970. Contains an extensive chapter on the country house and pastoral poems—a thorough and detailed study.

George DeForest Lord, ed., *Andrew Marvell: Complete Poetry*, New York 1969, rpt London 1984. A standard edition of the poems.

17

JOHN MILTON

MILTON AND CHRISTIANITY

[*BABL* pp. 24 f; *NA1* pp. 1771 f; *OA1* pp. 1205 f, 1367 f, 1412 f]

Milton's poetic career was driven by a consistent, even systematic attempt to convert each of the major poetic genres to ‡Reformed Christianity. For example, the early drafts of a tragedy to be called 'Adam Unparadised' became the epic *Paradise Lost*. Towards the end of his life Milton returned to the model of Greek tragedy to tell the story of Samson from the Old Testament. In his earliest published pieces, he took up the lesser genres of pastoral elegy (in *Lycidas*) and the courtly masque (*A Mask*, commonly known as *Comus*) and turned them towards a more overtly Christian, even ‡Puritan ideology. During the 1640s and 1650s, when Milton was more involved with pamphleteering and, for a while, the business of government, he turned the sonnet, a form more often associated with love or personal religious devotion, into a public form — or rather, one that linked public events with personal feeling in a new way. So 'Captain or Colonel, or Knight in Arms' (*BASCP* p. 310), sometimes called 'When the Assault was Intended to the City' (*OA1* p. 1220), was a plea for mercy intended to be attached to Milton's door when it was feared that the king's army might invade London in 1642 (and published in 1645). 'On the Late Massacre in Piedmont', although not published until 1673, calls for God's vengeance on those who had killed the Protestant Vaudois in the Italian Alps, a sign of Milton's sympathies with international Protestantism.

This conversion of the genres is also a way of assessing another key part of Milton's cultural formation, which is, like that of many of his contemporaries, classical ‡humanism. Pastoral, ode, epic, and tragedy, even the persuasive oration that is *Areopagitica*, all derive from classical models. Milton had a reverence for them; they were what he was educated to admire. In his prose essay 'Of Education' he recommends that school students read a great variety of classical authors, even if they might occasionally have to read modern authors for subjects like geography. To that extent, Milton was like any number of Christian ‡humanists of the period. However, just as in *Areopagitica* he argues the need for the reformation of ‡Reformation, so, in his ambitious long poetic works, he enacts the reformation of the best classical (and later) poetic models. The early ode 'On the Morning of Christ's Nativity' celebrates the end of the pagan gods, biblical and Egyptian; but classical antiquity still has a place, because of its (retrospectively apparent) †prophecy of Jesus. There was a time when Milton's poetic voice was criticised for being too Latinate. It is not strictly true, but his vocabulary and syntax allude to Latin (and the other languages he knew) more consistently than those of most of his contemporaries.

What of Milton and the Bible? His three major works, *Paradise Lost*, *Paradise Regained*, and *Samson Agonistes*, are reworkings of biblical material. To use a term that would not have meant much in his own day, Milton read the Bible as literature. He read it as a source of doctrine and history as well, but he was interested in its language (he read Hebrew as well as Greek), its style, its genres, its local stories, and its larger, over-arching narratives. Most of all, he followed the stories through. Where the Bible is laconic, he filled in the detail and pursued the implications. He invented dialogue for *Adam and Eve, God and the Son, Jesus, and †Satan.

Milton's Christianity, then, is unquestionably central to his work, even if it is more often the politics, or the questions of gender, that animate much recent discussion. We have his *De Doctrina Christiana*, a systematic theology compiled in Latin but not discovered until 1823. There has been some discussion of Milton's responsibility for this, but it seems, from recent research, that it is his. Since then, Milton has been accused of ‡heresy. Everyone has accepted his ‡Arminianism, a position not popular in earlier, largely ‡Calvinistic ‡Puritanism, but hardly a heresy. It asserts the importance of human ‡free will, a position crucial to Milton's defence of God's justice and goodness in *Paradise Lost*. Milton's description of the relationship between the Father and the Son in Book 3 of the poem, and more explicitly in *De Doctrina*, has clear Arian tendencies (an early church heresy), but it is debatable how far that is visible in his poetic descriptions. There are moments where he seems to be mortalist (the heresy that holds that the ‡soul dies with the body until the general *resurrection). On top of that, his advocacy of divorce in a series of tracts in the 1640s led to accusations of libertinism.

Milton is not an easy Christian writer, for this and other reasons. He does not lend himself to 'devotional reading', as Herbert might, or for ‡Evangelical purposes, as Bunyan often has. He has always appealed to rebels, however, inside and outside Christianity. This is partly to do with his close association with the Commonwealth and his enthusiastic defence of the execution of Charles I. The English Romantics, especially Blake and Shelley, were particularly keen, and Blake's dictum in *The Marriage of Heaven and Hell*, 'he was a true Poet and of the Devil's party without knowing it', has haunted Milton criticism ever since (for more on this, see the essay on *Paradise Lost*). He is very good at investigating the big questions, however, and readers (and teachers) of Milton find themselves debating them.

For example, in *Lycidas*, Milton asks what is the point of studying, or rather:

> Alas! What boots it with uncessant care
> To tend the homely slighted shepherd's trade,
> And strictly meditate the thankless Muse? (64–6)

Isn't it better to seize the day, enjoy yourself? Fame is no answer, if you're going to die early like Milton's friend Edward King, to whose memory the poem was dedicated. The following lines make a provisional answer, but the way the whole poem develops, as an emotional complex as well as a theological one, is important.

Or take the problem of Samson's death at the end of *Samson Agonistes*. Are the 'rousing motions' he feels at the end an indication that God's Spirit has returned to him? Or a return to the fruitless violence of his early career? *Samson* is also a key example for the historical approach to literature. As a nonconformist text published in the Restoration, it problematises the link between individual regeneration and political liberation. Milton was as strongly affected by the experience of defeat as he was by being a part of England's most successful revolutionary movement.

QUESTIONS

1. What answers to his questions and doubts does Milton find in the course of *Lycidas*? Are they intellectual, theological, emotional, or some combination of these?

2. Can we use the ending of *Samson Agonistes* to think about the problem of violence from a Christian perspective? Or is the play a resolutely Old Testament rendition of the story? Compare Milton's treatment with the biblical story in Judges 13–16. Do you agree with Neil Keeble that 'What is remarkable about *Samson Agonistes* is not Milton's fidelity to the facts of his biblical story but his subordination of them to his theme of personal regeneration' (*The Literary Culture of Nonconformity*, p. 197)?

3. What are the links between Milton's political commitment and his Christian convictions?

JOHN MILTON, *PARADISE LOST*

[*BABL* pp. 42 f; *BACL* pp. 436 f; *NA1* pp. 1815 f; *OA1* pp. 1258 f]

If a classic is a piece of literature that lasts because different readers, from periods and cultures sometimes far removed from its original readership, find it still speaks to them, then *Paradise Lost* is a great classic. It is a difficult poem, but, in teaching and in discussion, draws out a high level of thinking. It asks the big questions — do we have ‡free will? Is the existence of an omnipotent, good God compatible with the existence of evil? And it raises other major issues, for example about the nature of marriage and whether the role of *Eve in the *fall is indicative of a misogynistic strain in Christianity.

Paradise Lost was published in ten books in 1667, and a revised version in twelve books in 1674, to which were added the prose ‘arguments’ or summaries of each book, and two defences of its unrhymed character, one by Milton, and one in a (rhymed) verse commendation by Andrew Marvell. It is an epic, self-consciously in the tradition of the classical epic (particularly Virgil) and the English epic (particularly Spenser).

Book I, after a magnificent invocation of the ‘heavenly muse’, begins in †hell, where †Satan and the other fallen †angels have just been thrown. In starting thus, Milton obeys the epic tradition of beginning in the middle of the story, like Dante and Spenser before him. It may also be the only place where the audience, the fallen readers of the story of the *fall, can start. The question is, can the poem recover? The history of western literature is full of seductive evil, and Milton’s Satan is one of the most impressive of those creations; but where are the figures of seductive good? The criticism of the poem has been haunted, since the Romantic period, by the fascination of Satan and the relative woodenness of God the Father and Christ. Blake put it most eloquently, as the voice of the Devil in *The Marriage of Heaven and Hell* (1790) claims, ‘The reason Milton wrote in fetters when he wrote of Angels & God, and at liberty when of Devils and Hell, is because he was a true Poet and of the Devil’s party without knowing it.’

One way of reframing this problem is to see Milton’s poem as an exemplary critique of epic heroism; and thus †Satan becomes a kind of parody of the epic hero. For example, he journeys from †hell to earth on a mission of destruction, as opposed to Virgil’s Aeneas, journeying from the destruction of Troy to the foundation of Rome. The speeches in Pandemonium are full of specious logic and bravado — ‘Better to reign in Hell, than serve in Heaven.’ The grisly, incestuous ‡trinity of Satan, ‡sin, and death prefaces his rather bumpy ride through Chaos to *Eden. In between, in Book III, is the vision of †heaven, with the harmonious rapport between Father and Son. By a perspective device, Satan appears like a tiny irritant making his way to earth. Milton has to navigate the difference between ‡predestination (still a dominant feature of British Christianity in the seventeenth century) and God's omniscience. Says the Father to the Son:

> ... they themselves decreed
> Their own revolt, not I: if I foreknew,
> Foreknowledge had no influence on their fault. (III:116–18)

The poem covers the story of *creation, *fall, and ‡redemption, what Leopold Damrosch has nicknamed 'God's Plot',[1] but not in that order. The fall of man and Christ's redemption is all mapped out in Book III. Milton could hardly have made use of suspense: everyone knows that *Adam and Eve will fall. The questions about it are more interesting—How? Why? Who is to blame? In the picture of Adam and Eve in prelapsarian bliss, Milton remarkably portrays sex and work as fulfilling and, in cunning use of sensual language, precisely paradisal. Even so, there is an uneasy sense that the audience, like the Protean figure of †Satan, are voyeurs. The consequences of the fall—embarrassment, marital arguments, each blaming the other, and lustful sex before being ejected from *Eden—have to be set against the success of Milton's portrayal of a state merely hinted at in Genesis.

*Eve is a problem for modern readers. She is clearly below *Adam in the intellectual and spiritual hierarchy, and yet their marriage is described as 'one flesh, one heart, one soul' (VIII:499). Milton can be described as a misogynistic theologian—so much so that one feminist critic suggested he be removed from the canon. Yet many of Milton's most sympathetic contemporary critics have been women, and there is something in Milton that subverts conventional associations of gendering the ‡virtues. Adam, at the end of the poem, resolves to follow the new way 'by things deemed weak / Subverting worldly strong' (XII:567–8 and echoing I Corinthians 1:25–7). In his divorce tracts, as well as this poem and *Samson Agonistes*, Milton voices both what we might see as progress towards equal human dignity for women and men, and also a tendency to blame women. His, or his characters', misogyny? Or should we recognise that Milton was an idealist (sometimes a disappointed idealist) about the harmony that men and women should make?

Milton's poem is not a philosophical theodicy (i.e. a philosophical defence of God's justice). It is aware of the usual arguments, and it is unusual, and intel-

---

1. Leopold Damrosch Jr, *God's Plot and Man's Stories: Studies in the Fictional Imagination from Milton to Fielding*, Chicago 1985.

lectually ambitious, in its attempt to understand the steps that led to the *fall, and the precise thoughts and feelings of each of the major players. Its ambition 'to justify the ways of God to man' is vast. Its success is in the rigorous debates it has inspired in critics and students; and in the undoubted emotional engagement that goes with the decision to aim for the highest note in epic, Christian poetry.

For much of his writing career, Milton was politically engaged, not only as an apologist for the execution of Charles I, but also, from 1649, as Secretary for Foreign Tongues. After the Restoration, though, this had to end. Is it possible to see in *Paradise Lost* a conscious rejection of that, a retreat into the purely theological? Or is this a coded message about the experience of defeated idealism? The danger of a simply ‡allegorical approach, that †Satan is code for Charles I, or Cromwell, or other military and political leaders of the 1650s, is that it reduces a complex discussion of the relationship between power, religion, and deviousness to something less, a propaganda piece. One clue might be in the figure of Abdiel, who exposes Satan's revolutionary rhetoric in Book V; another in the distinction between wilful rebellion and just resistance in the War in †Heaven episode.

At the end, *Adam is given a sight of the future, of the ‡salvation of his descendants through Christ, which causes him to rejoice that from his fault 'much more good thereof shall spring' (XII:476), and so the *fall will, in a way, be regarded as fortunate. Adam and *Eve are still ejected from *Eden in a brilliantly balanced coda. They have each other, they have Providence and God's umpire conscience; but they are, profoundly, 'solitary'.

QUESTIONS

1. What are Milton's principal ways of defending God's justice? Where are they most successful? Where are they most vulnerable?
2. Do you think Milton gets into more trouble by elaborating on Genesis, or does it give him important opportunities?
3. How might one defend Milton from the accusation that he has made †Satan more sympathetic than God?
4. What can be gained from historicised and political readings of the text? To what extent do you find that contemporary political concerns inform the critical battles over Milton's politics?
5. Is Milton's portrayal of *Eve misogynistic? To what extent is his portrayal of 'our general mother' more, or less, sympathetic than that of the Bible?

BIBLIOGRAPHY

Sharon Achinstein, *Milton and the Revolutionary Reader*, Princeton NJ 1994, and her more recent *Literature and Dissent in Milton's England*, Cambridge 2003: the politics and background of the poet and poem.

Two older books on *Paradise Lost*, available in many college libraries, are worth attending to: Dennis Harry Burden, *The Logical Epic: A Study of the Argument of Paradise Lost*, London 1967; and Dennis Richard Danielson, *Milton's Good God: A Study in Literary Theodicy*, Cambridge 1982.

Of the many readers' guides, look at Thomas N. Corns, *Regaining Paradise Lost*, London 1994; and David Loewenstein, *Paradise Lost*, 2nd edn, Cambridge 2004. Loewenstein's more detailed *Representing Revolution in Milton and his Contemporaries: Religion, Politics, and Polemics in Radical Puritanism*, Cambridge 2001, is probably the best guide to the politics of the poem.

Dennis Danielson, ed., *The Cambridge Companion to Milton*, 2nd edn, Cambridge 1999, is a good general starting point. The essay on Milton's women in this volume, by Diane K. McColley, is a sympathetic view; see also her book *Milton's Eve*, Urbana IL 1983.

Stanley Fish, *Surprised by Sin: The Reader in Paradise Lost*, 2nd edn, Basingstoke 1997: an influential book whose central thesis is still persuasive (and see his more recent, more elaborate, and more eccentric *How Milton Works*, Cambridge MA and London 2001).

There are numerous studies of Milton and the Bible: see especially David Gay, *The Endless Kingdom: Milton's Scriptural Society*, Newark DE 2002; Dayton Haskin, *Milton's Burden of Interpretation*, Philadelphia 1994; and James H. Sims and Leland Ryken, ed., *Milton and Scriptural Tradition: The Bible into Poetry*, Columbia 1984.

N.H. Keeble, *The Literary Culture of Nonconformity in Later Seventeenth-Century England*, Leicester 1987.

James Grantham Turner, *One Flesh: Paradisal Marriage and Sexual Relations in the Age of Milton*, Oxford 1987, discusses the issues in a helpfully wide context.

Section 3

THE RESTORATION AND THE EIGHTEENTH CENTURY

1

Overview: The Restoration and the Eighteenth Century

The period of the Restoration until the end of the eighteenth century is one of immense change and intellectual enquiry. There is growing confidence in the human capacity to know about and control the world following on from major discoveries in the field of science, such as Harvey's discovery of the circulation of the blood. At this time we find, for example, the development of the first encyclopaedia in France and in England the composition of the first philologically informed dictionary. This confidence in human powers together with the growing freedom of expression in religion made for an age that produced literature embracing widely divergent worldviews.

The restoration of the monarchy in 1660, and, as a consequence, the reestablishment of the Church of England, gave influence once more to the thought of the Anglican bishops commonly called the Caroline Divines. These were theologians, such as Mark Frank, who looked to the ‡patristic period for their theology and sought to affirm the Church of England as a purified Catholic rather than a Catholic/Protestant church. They were the theologians of what was to become the Non-juring Movement after 1688. Non-jurors were the clerics who refused to swear the oath of allegiance to William and Mary after the Glorious Revolution of 1688. They rejected both the establishment of the church as Protestant and Parliament's right to determine the monarchy and its powers. They were consequently the religious leaders of what came to be called the High Church within the Church of England (because they held a high doctrine of the church and its ‡sacraments) and they were also identified with the developing Tory party in their commitment to the monarchy. They laid the foundations for the thinking of the ‡Tractarians in the nineteenth century.

It was to this Non-juring tradition that the eighteenth-century Englishman and writer William Law belonged. His chief work, *A Serious Call to a Devout and Holy Life*, was very influential among nineteenth-century and early twentieth-century Anglo-Catholics. His later, more ‡mystical work, which drew on the thought of Jacob Boehme, was an important influence on the theology and stories of the Scottish fantasy writer George MacDonald.

The burgeoning confidence we have noted can be related to the development of ‡Deism in the eighteenth century. As the word suggests, Deism is concerned with the existence of a deity or supreme being about whom little can be said beyond his identity as the first cause of the world, its originator and designer. For Deists, the world was a highly complex, interacting mechanism, like an intricately made watch, and so the absence of a designer or cause of such a mechanism was unthinkable. As Voltaire said, he could not imagine the existence of so great a clock apart from the existence of a clock maker.

Beyond this, however, the ‡Deist would not go. Just as a watchmaker does not interfere with the running of the mechanism he has created, so too the deity does not intervene with the world he has set in motion. Once created, it operates according to its own laws and leaves human beings free to operate as they will within it. There is in this no place for the providence of God, interfering on behalf of his *creation, nor for any prayer beyond acknowledgement of the creator. Swift takes issue with these ideas in *Tale of a Tub* and *Gulliver's Travels*, and Pope, equally, in his *Essay on Man*.

At the opposite pole to ‡Deism lies a steady development of all kinds of Dissenting Christianity. By Dissenters we mean those who dissented from the beliefs of the established Anglican Church. They belonged usually to Baptist sects, as did John Bunyan, or to ‡Evangelical communities, which emphasised personal experience and the attainment of ‡salvation by faith alone. Following the Restoration, Dissenters were free to worship and were able to become established members of the respectable working class and growing middle class, although still excluded from the universities and government.

Their continued exclusion from the world of politics led them to use their talents and belief in personal industry in the world of trade. Following a ‡creed that eschewed vanity, show, and conspicuous consumption, and which emphasised prosperity as a sign of God's favour and therefore of ‡salvation, many Dissenters achieved positions of wealth and importance among the growing merchant class. We find this world vividly portrayed in such novels as *Moll Flanders* and *Roxana* by Defoe and *Pamela* and *Clarissa* by Samuel Richardson.

Indeed, the rise of the novel in the eighteenth century is often related to the Dissenters' habit of self-scrutiny in order to discern the marks of election (that is, of being among those saved by the arbitrary will of God), as well as to root out ‡sin. Such concern led to the production of journals and accounts of individuals' lives in which God's actions and their responses could be traced. These journals, therefore, became more than stories, a sequence of unconnected life events: they became plot, since the activity of God and response to grace were seen as the causative connecting features behind all events. In this habit we see one aspect of the novelist's craft.

The majority of Dissenters tended to hold to the belief that †original sin totally destroyed the image of God in humanity, leaving human nature totally depraved and without any natural capacity for goodness. Such extreme ‡Calvinists held that ‡salvation came to individuals purely by arbitrary divine election. One could in no way merit such salvation, but only seek to discover, within oneself, signs of it. It was believing this and finding no such signs in himself which led the poet William Cowper to mental illness.

Such a position was strongly opposed by Benevolism and the resulting concept of 'the good heart'. This was developed by Lord Anthony Ashley Cooper, third Earl of Shaftesbury, under the influence of the seventeenth-century Cambridge Platonists. The Cambridge Platonists adhered to the philosophy and theology of the eastern ‡Fathers of the church, the bishop-theologians who articulated many basic Christian doctrines in the first ten centuries of the church's life. Like these Fathers, the Christian Platonists did not deny †original sin, but they did deny the extent of its destruction of the image of God in humanity.

For the Cambridge Platonists there remained in every human something of the 'original innocence', derived from their likeness to God. Goodness was therefore natural to human beings; evil was an aberration. ‡Salvation by Christ was necessary to restore the image to its full brightness within the humanity Christ shared. Shaftesbury, as the nineteenth-century Anglican Bishop Westcott suggested, took the hope and glory of this vision of humanity but ignored the Cambridge Platonists' acceptance of the effects of †original sin and therefore of the human capacity for evil. His Benevolism therefore asserted the essential goodness of human beings and their innate capacity for discerning and choosing moral goodness. The essential disposition of human beings to others was that of benevolence, or kindness.

This was developed popularly as belief in 'the good heart' and was often used as a means of excusing or explaining away bad behaviour. A character may be essentially 'good-hearted' and their lapses a consequence of weakness rather than a conscious rejection of their basic nature. We find this approach in Richardson's last novel *Sir Charles Grandison* and especially in the novels of Henry Fielding.

In Fielding, Benevolism is linked to what is known as Latitudinarianism within the Church of England in the eighteenth century. Latitudinarians were more concerned with Christian living than with adherence to doctrines and practices. For them, faith was to be identified within a person's life and behaviour, more than in their profession of the ‡creeds. So we find in Fielding characters like ‡Parson Trulliber in *Joseph Andrews*, whose concern for orthodox profession of the doctrine of ‡salvation by faith is not matched by his capacity for hospitality and kindness. And throughout Fielding's novels we find young women whose sexual laxity is simply the negative aspect of a kind and loving nature that frequently contrasts sharply with the correctly believing, but cold, people around them.

In *Tom Jones*, Fielding's approach to Benevolism comes closer to that of the Cambridge Platonists themselves. Tom's 'good nature' has to be realised through the disciplining of his wayward tendencies. As in a medieval tale, he must endure captivity and ‡purgation before he can fully exercise his intrinsic capacity for goodness.

This emphasis on the 'good heart' developed also into the cultivation of sensibility. The 'good heart' became the 'man of sentiment'; goodness became equated with the capacity for emotional response. One might say that Descartes's 'I think, therefore I am' was replaced by 'I weep, therefore I am' as we find in Sterne's *A Sentimental Journey*. It is this equation of goodness with extreme feeling that Jane Austen questions in *Sense and Sensibility*.

Mainstream Anglicanism held aloof from such an emphasis on feeling, holding to the primacy of a 'reasonable' faith. Whilst this was a motivating force for such churchmen as Jonathan Swift, for many it seemed to lead to an acceptance of forms and practices with little outward fervour. The establishment of the Church of England meant that all too often the church's ministry was not a vocation, a calling, but a gentleman's profession alongside the army and the law.

Among those who maintained a life of fervent devotion were the High Church followers of the Non-jurors whom we have already met. It was from such a background of a High Church disciplined life that John Wesley, the founder of the ‡Methodists, emerged. After his experience of 'the heart strangely warmed' during a service with the Moravians (followers of the ‡Reformer John Hus), Wesley began his preaching. Banned from doing so in churches, Wesley preached in churchyards and fields. He ultimately broke from the Church of England when he ordained a minister without reference to the bishops who had refused their cooperation. The negative response of the established church and of those who feared the impact of Methodism on the settled social fabric can be seen in nineteenth-century novels such as Charlotte Brontë's *Shirley* and George Eliot's *Adam Bede*. Nevertheless, Methodism became a potent social force towards the end of our period and the hymns produced by Charles and John Wesley became an important part of popular culture.

Towards the end of the century, the ferment of republicanism, especially in France, had its effect in questioning the order of society previously held to be divinely ordained. This gave further impetus to the relationship between ‡Methodism and the growing movement for labourers' rights in the nineteenth century, while the reception of members of Catholic religious orders fleeing persecution in France countered to some degree the anti-Catholic feeling fomented by the Gordon Riots of 1780 (the background for Dickens's novel *Barnaby Rudge*). This paved the way for the gradual re-introduction of a publicly acknowledged Catholicism into England.

From such a brief overview of the religious currents of this century we may see how misleading and inappropriate was the old title for the eighteenth century — 'the Age of Reason'.

BIBLIOGRAPHY

Marshall Brown, *Preromanticism*, Stanford 1991.

Clement Hawes, *Mania and Literary Style: The Rhetoric of Enthusiasm from the Ranters to Christopher Smart*, Cambridge 1996.

Jonathan Lamb, *The Rhetoric of Suffering: Reading the Book of Job in the Eighteenth Century*, Oxford 1995.

Marcus Walsh, 'Profession and authority: the interpretation of the Bible in the seventeenth and eighteenth centuries', *Literature and Theology* 9 (1995), 383–98.

2

JOHN BUNYAN

[*BACL* pp. 467 f; *BABL* pp. 163 f (*Grace Abounding*); *NA1* pp. 2132 f; *OA1* pp. 1573 f]

Look at any Christmas card that depicts the Magi—the wise men who, according to the New Testament, brought gold, frankincense, and myrrh to the infant Jesus. If the card is modern, it is overwhelmingly likely that it will be a picture of their journey, at night time, following a distant star. If the card is a reproduction of a work of art from a previous century, on the other hand, it is much more probable that it will depict the adoration of the Magi, showing them presenting their gifts at the manger: not the journey, in other words, but the arrival. The difference is more philosophical than artistic. Our age is much more comfortable with the journey than arrival, with the open-ended question than the answer. For us, it is better to travel hopefully than to arrive.

‡Pilgrimage—holy †journey—is a part of all major religions, and has always been part of Christian spirituality. In the existing Roman Catholic tradition of John Bunyan's time and earlier, for example in Walter Hilton's *Scale of Perfection*, there was some ‡allegorisation of the notion of journey in the spiritual life. Perhaps, however, Bunyan wrote in conscious opposition to the Roman Catholic idea of pilgrimage, which focuses on journeying to a site in this world: for the first thing we need to notice about the book we usually call *The Pilgrim's Progress* is that this title is a shorthand. The full title is *The Pilgrim's Progress from This World to That Which is to Come*. In this pilgrimage, which is life itself, the ultimate destination is all-important from the outset, and it is specifically not in 'This World' but beyond it.

Readers and critics enjoy the adventures Christian experiences on the road, from the †City of Destruction to the †Cross and ultimately to the Celestial City. In Part 2 of the *Pilgrim's Progress*, Bunyan abates the unease that the reader may feel at Christian running away from the city leaving his wife and children to their fate, as they too embark on the ‡pilgrimage to the Celestial City. But critics have found the end of Part 1 of *Pilgrim's Progress* difficult to forgive, as Ignorance gets easily across the great river of Death to the gates of the Celestial City, only to find that, having no 'certificate', he is bound and carried to the side of the hill, and 'put in there'. And Bunyan concludes, 'Then I saw that there was a way to Hell, even from the Gates of Heaven, as well as from the City of Destruction. So I awoke, and behold it was a Dream.'[1] A paragraph earlier, looking in at the Celestial †City, as Christian and his fellow ‡pilgrims enter, the dreamer comments, 'When I had seen, I wished my self among them.'

This ending, despite the horror of critics, is essential to Bunyan's message and method. Bunyan is scathing about the worldly, secular, overwhelmingly polite and moral Christianity of his bourgeois characters such as Worldly Wiseman and By-Ends. It is not too difficult to see Restoration Anglicanism in Bunyan's sights here. But in these last paragraphs he also shows his fundamental rejection of ‡Calvinist ideas of ‡predestination. The dreamer has no certainty that he will be one of those he sees in the †city, and he yearns not only for the state of beatitude he sees, but also for the security of knowing. There is no knowing, though: even at the very gates of †heaven, there is a way to †hell; and even the whole heroic †journey, through trials and terrors to the final destination, has the uneasy uncertainty of a dream. There is a good deal of Bunyan's personal experience here, as elsewhere in the book. The spiritual struggles recorded in *Grace Abounding* show a man with a vivid imagination snatching comfort from biblical words and images that flash upon his mind, but only feeling the comfort momentarily. Bunyan preaches often in *Pilgrim's Progress*, but he is never complacent: he sees the 'way to Hell' not just for others, but potentially for himself.

One of the reasons for the response of critics to the ending of the book possibly lies in the way Bunyan describes Ignorance's approach:

> When he [Ignorance] was come up to the Gate, he looked up to the writing that was above; and then began to knock, supposing that entrance should have been quickly administred to him: But he was asked by the men that lookt over the top of the Gate, Whence came you? and what would you have? He answered, I have eat and drank in the presence of the King, and he has taught in our Streets. Then they asked him for his Certificate, that they might go in and show it to the King. So he fumbled in his bosom for one, and found none.

Bunyan's depiction of the thoughtless optimism of Ignorance generates sympathy for the character: he meets little trouble crossing the river and simply

---

1. Quotations are taken from Roger Sharrock, ed., *John Bunyan: Grace Abounding ... and The Pilgrim's Progress*, London 1966: this edition in the Oxford Standard Authors series preserves the text of the first edition of 1678, distinguishing later additions.

expects none as he asks for entrance. But Bunyan's real genius here lies in the use of the verb 'fumbled'. The whole nature and predicament of the man (for he has become precisely that) is encapsulated in that word: he doesn't know, he tries to find, and finally realises he hasn't got, what he needs above everything else. Ignorance escapes from, and expands beyond, his ‡allegorical character; he becomes someone we might meet any day of the week. Yet he is truly ignorant. Bunyan's characters and landscapes become real, believable, individual, and almost tangible in his hands, despite the twin structural devices of unreality, namely allegory and dream. The offence lies in the way, having made such people real, he then allows them to be condemned. But that is Bunyan's conviction and without it, *Pilgrim's Progress* would be only a †journey and not an arrival.

Pilgrim's Progress has only one rival as the major English work of Protestant literary art, Milton's *Paradise Lost*, and comparison between the two is instructive. Milton was a writer of the London court, albeit of the Protestant parliamentary court of the Commonwealth: and the †heaven he imagines in *Paradise Lost*, with its †angels in carefully ranked hierarchy, and its fallen angel †Satan as a figure of political intrigue, is recognisable as a court. Milton's genre and style are similarly courtly: the magnificent sweep of the epic poem. But to see Bunyan's Christian bowling boldly along the King's Highway in the open country, singing as he goes, is to wonder if Milton had ever done anything quite so ordinary or vulgar. Even if we did not know that Bunyan's father was a tinker, travelling about mending pots, we would somehow know that Bunyan had walked the country: and an entirely different England from Milton's is illuminated by his direct and forceful style.

It was an England in which Bunyan suffered great danger and hardship. He knew and had accompanied his father to the fairs and markets he describes in *Pilgrim's Progress*. He had later been recruited to fight in the Parliamentary army in the English Civil War. We do not know whether Bunyan experienced military action (he was stationed at the garrison of Newport Pagnell), but *Pilgrim's Progress* was written in Bedford Gaol, as Protestant leaders like him found themselves imprisoned for their refusal to conform to the re-established religion of the state. These two aspects of Bunyan's experience, fairs and persecution, combine in the depiction of the ‡pilgrims' attempt to pass through Vanity-Fair. The pilgrims attract attention to themselves because of their different dress, their 'Language of Canaan', or different speech, and their indifference to the goods offered by the market. These reflect the habit of ‡Puritans who dressed plainly, spoke as much as possible in the words of the Bible, and (during the Commonwealth) tried to close down fairs and entertainments and despised the goods the fairs offered for sale. For this, the pilgrims are 'put into the Cage', tried by a biased jury, tortured, and finally Faithful is burnt at the stake. Bunyan knew at first hand the ways of the fairs and the mob violence that lay beneath the surface. The religious ferment of the Civil War years was not resolved by the restoration of the monarchy and the Anglican church: as far as Bunyan was concerned, the Christian gospel was merely repressed by unjust laws.

Bunyan is not at all neutral in his story. He is a man of conviction and principle, and he writes with the bias of his party and the forcefulness of his age: some features of these are undoubtedly unpalatable to other ages. The simplicity of the ‡allegorical †journey story line of *Pilgrim's Progress* has made it one of the most widely read of English stories, in particular one widely read by the young. But simplicity and allegory are not uncommonly sneered at in the modern age, as they were in the eighteenth century. So why is the book still read? The popularity and enduring appeal of the book derive in part from Bunyan's use of language, that precise ordinariness that was remarked on earlier; and in part from the imaginative engagement of the writer. In *Pilgrim's Progress* we read a book that was lived before it was written, and we recognise the reality of that life even as we read of allegorical abstractions.

QUESTIONS

1. Can we trace earlier literature that influenced Bunyan?
2. Assess the access which Bunyan's writing gives to the thought and experience of contemporary nonconformity.
3. How does *Pilgrim's Progress* achieve its effects?

BIBLIOGRAPHY

Monica Furlong, *Puritan's Progress: A Study of John Bunyan*, London 1975.

Richard Greaves, *John Bunyan and English Nonconformity*, London 1992.

Anne Lawrence, W.R. Owens, and Stuart Sims, ed., *John Bunyan and his England, 1628–88*, London 1990.

Roger Ian Sharrock, *John Bunyan*, rev. edn, London 1968. A biographical study by one of the foremost Bunyan scholars.

3

Aphra Behn

[*BABL* pp. 225 f (*Oroonoko* pp. 245 f); *NA1* pp. 2165 f]

Aphra Behn was a prolific writer best known today for such Restoration dramas as *The Rover* (see *BARestD* pp. 337 f). Her novella *Oroonoko: Or The Royal Slave* represents a departure from her earlier forms and subject matter. Written in 1688, though set in the early 1660s, *Oroonoko* may be seen in the context of the antislavery writings of the 1660s.

Critics have noted how the narrator of *Oroonoko* is torn by contradictions — she is allied to the white imperialist powers and yet as a woman she is powerless; she is part rebel, standing up for the unjustly oppressed, and part complicit in their oppression; she criticises, but also benefits from the slave system. This ambivalence is evident also in her attitude to Christianity, which is associated inexorably with the white colonising male.

The story opens with a vivid comparison of the colony of Surinam in the West Indies to *Eden. The native Indians are compared to 'our first parents before the Fall'. The narrator declares: 'these people represented to me an absolute idea of the first state of innocence, before man knew how to sin'. An ambivalence is soon apparent however: these Indians are as much noble savage as they are *Adam; Surinam is as much earthly paradise as it is Eden.

The contradiction is made explicit when Behn states that 'Religion would here but destroy that tranquillity they possess by ignorance, and laws would but teach 'em to know offense, of which now they have no notion'. Further ambivalence may be deconstructed here as the terms Behn uses to eschew Christianity are themselves drawn from the Christian Bible. She employs the language of the Pauline doctrine that declares that 'the law entered, that the offence might abound' (Romans 5:20) and 'I had not known sin, but by the law' (Romans 7:7).

The Indians are shown to be without duplicity or guile. They have no concept of what it is to be a 'liar' until the white man comes: breaking one's word is an alien concept. They are contrasted with the 'vice or cunning' which Behn claims taints the white man.

The scene soon moves to Africa: here Prince Oroonoko, though he is not given the same natural innocence as the Indians, is credited several times with 'greatness of soul', and with 'true honour' that may be simply defined as keeping one's word. He appears in every way the perfect man. Behn indicates these qualities come very naturally to him and, pointedly, without the need for Christianity. We might note at this point also that Oroonoko's childhood governor was banished 'for some heretical notions he held, and though he was a man of very little religion, he had admirable morals and a brave soul': that is, Behn suggests again, without the need for Christianity. The charge against Christianity is then made explicit: 'Such ill morals are only practised in Christian countries, where they prefer the bare name of religion, and, without virtue or morality, think that's sufficient.'

The central moral issue of integrity or honour is brought into sharp focus by the slave-ship captain's betrayal of Oroonoko. *Betrayal becomes a recurring motif thereafter. Oroonoko is betrayed a second time when sold off on arrival at the colony of Surinam. Ironically, we are told the captain 'could not resolve to trust a heathen, he said, upon his parole, a man that had no sense or notion of the God that he worshipped'. It is but one of the frequent swipes at Christianity throughout the novella. At every turn Oroonoko is set as a noble contrast to the perfidious Christian coloniser, particularly the deputy governor William Byam who is characterised as a dissembler. Cries the honourable Prince, ''Tis worth my suffering, to gain so true a knowledge both of you and of your gods by whom you swear.'

Nevertheless there remains an ambivalence in Behn's stance. Though it is clear Oroonoko dislikes what he hears, the narrator is shown telling Imoinda 'stories of nuns, and endeavouring to bring her to the knowledge of the true God'. The narrator is herself the coloniser, western, white, and also Christian, despite the anti-Christian tenor of her narration.

Oroonoko, though he condemns the duplicitous Christians, telling Byam 'there was no faith in the white men or the gods they adored', is clearly shown in Christ-like terms later in the story, his sufferings akin to Christ's ‡passion. He is Christ-like in integrity and guilelessness, standing noble in the face of *betrayal, his rich attire replaced with coarse brown linen. His fellow slaves 'cast themselves at his feet', and 'paid him even divine homage'. He enters a land of captivity, where he finds his lost bride, in a manner reminiscent of the principle of †incarnation. The concept of the royal slave itself has strong biblical antecedents: the Son of God is also the suffering servant, Christ is the Shepherd-King.

Oroonoko is deserted by the other slaves when their insurrection fails — as Christ was abandoned by his disciples. He is betrayed again — by Trefry, his most trustworthy white ally. Multiple instances of *betrayal recall *Judas. We think of the fickle Palm Sunday crowd who were soon baying for Christ's *cru-cifixion when we read that those slaves 'who but a few days before adored him as something more than mortal, now had a whip to give him some lashes'. He is whipped with the other slaves, 'rending the very flesh from their bones; especially [Oroonoko], who was not perceived to make any moan or to alter his face, only to roll his eyes on the faithless governor', and we are reminded of Christ, silent before the Roman governor, Pilate.

We may make the comparison with Christ carrying his †cross and being of-fered vinegar to quench his thirst when they led Oroonoko, 'bleeding and naked as he was, and loaded him all over with irons; and then rubbed his wounds, to complete their cruelty, with Indian pepper'. Finally, we are told 'he gave up the ghost', the very words used in the gospels to describe the moment of Christ's death (John 19:30).

QUESTIONS

1. What ‡virtues and customs do you find mentioned in *Oroonoko: Or The Royal Slave* that you would consider specifically Christian?
2. Oroonoko tells the slaves 'they had lost the divine quality of men and were become insensible asses'. How does Behn's novella treat the topic of human dignity, defining what it means to be truly human?

BIBLIOGRAPHY

Margaret Ferguson, 'Juggling the categories of race, class and gender: Aphra Behn's *Oroonoko*', in Janet Todd, ed., *Aphra Behn*, Basingstoke 1999. This essay considers in particular being black, the character of the black woman Imoinda, and the ambivalent status of the narrator.

Derek Hughes and Janet Todd, ed., *The Cambridge Companion to Aphra Behn*, Cambridge 2004. Wide-ranging essays on the writer and her background. The essays by Laura J. Rosenthal, '*Oroonoko*: reception, ideology, and nar-rative strategy', pp. 151–65, and Joanna Lipking, '"Others", slaves, and colonists in *Oroonoko*', pp. 166–87, are of particular interest.

Jacqueline Pearson, 'Gender and narrative in the fiction of Aphra Behn', in Janet Todd, ed., *Aphra Behn*. An analysis of narrative technique correlated to issues of gender and power.

Janet Todd, ed., *The Works of Aphra Behn*, 7 vols, London 1992–6. The standard edition of all the available works.

4

WILLIAM CONGREVE,
THE WAY OF THE WORLD

[*BABL* pp. 440 f; *BARestD* pp. 647 f; *NA1* pp. 2215 f; *OA1* pp. 1669 f]

Congreve was writing after the restoration of the monarchy in 1660, in a society enjoying a relaxation of the ‡Puritan restrictions on entertainments and festivities imposed during the Protectorate under Oliver Cromwell. On first reading, then, it may seem that this witty play, set in this milieu, has no point of contact with the Christian or biblical tradition. Closer attention, however, may make the form of the play more familiar. The approach to the characterisation recalls that of the ‡morality play (see the essays on this genre and on *Everyman*). Fainall, for example, is comparable to the ‡Vice figure, pretending friendship in order to bring about the downfall of 'friends': his name suggests him as a personification of greed and of the hypocrisy typical of the Vice. He would 'fain have all' and 'feigns all'. So too the name of his accomplice, Mrs Marwood, suggests a propensity for doing evil, a will for evil. Set against these are characters whose traits are less damaging and more ambiguous. Petulant implies a child whose candour stems from unconscious egotism devoid of the deliberate malice of Fainall and Marwood. Likewise, Witwoud epitomises the vanity of the person who moulds his personality according to current fashion. In similar manner, Sir Wilful's name indicates his nature as the impetuous child whose desires have not yet fixed on their object. His counterpart is Lady Wishfort whose strong wishes lead her to crave gratification but do not lead to the conscious acts of will of Marwoud. We have here characters who have lost a common moral compass and can only act according to their impulses. They highlight the true candour, wit, and integrity of Millamant and Mirabell.

The difficulty of discerning true worth in this society is suggested by the names of these two protagonists. Millamant has ambiguous implications of either being greatly loving or loving many; in this environment the possibility of such a distinction is threatened. Similarly, Mirabell, lover of the beautiful, may be admirer either of superficial allure or of true beauty. We see here an embattled goodness and integrity besieged by its parodies and superficial and immature craving, which easily falls victim to the designs of determined evil. We are in the world of the ‡morality play, reinterpreted for the age.

The title of the play, *The Way of the World*, furthermore, points us towards the Christian habits of thought that inform it. The term 'world' has specific meaning in the writings of St John in the Bible. It does not denote the created earth. What the word means here is what *fallen humanity has made of this earth, that is, societies dominated by 'lust of the flesh, lust of the eyes and the pride of life' (I John 2:16). This is the 'world' of Congreve's play, ruled as it is by lust for power, money, and sensual gratification, which are regarded as ends in themselves. It is a society in which 'love' is understood only in terms of such lust, unmindful of any greater †love or any higher destiny. It is therefore also unmindful of any other reason for relationship between human beings beyond that of self-gratification. The 'way of the world' is to make human beings wolves to one another, transforming social life into a deadly and predatory game in which it is essential to be one step ahead.

Congreve deepens his analysis of this society in the penultimate scene in which the 'way of the world' is described by Mirabell as the 'way of the widows of the world'. Biblically widows are representative figures of vulnerability and social need; they have a special call on their fellow human beings for protection. This is a deeply ambiguous comment. It implies that the way of his world leads to the insecurity and poverty of the widow. In this context it also suggests that in Congreve's society widows must learn to look after themselves; innocence must not mean ignorance, but being 'wise as serpents' as Jesus counselled (Matthew 10:16). Caring for the widow is the biblical touchstone of ‡virtuous living; their neglect and their need to defend themselves provide clear evidence of a disordered society.

We must remember, however, that this is a comedy and that, true to its genre, *The Way of the World* has a happy ending in which goodness triumphs over evil and human folly. This is consonant with the Christian worldview Congreve adopts here. The 'world' is based upon the transience and insubstantiality of the *creation when it is alienated from its creator. It cannot have ultimate power over the goodness coming from God; as Jesus told his followers, he has overcome 'the world' (John 16:33). The audience can both deplore and scoff at the 'world' represented to it because its downfall is assured.

In addition to offering this implicit overall Christian vision, Congreve also satirises some aspects of the religious life of his day, particularly with regard to the theatre, in a way which deepens his analysis of the sickness of his society. Many Christians supported the ‡Puritan outlook, dominant during the period of the Protectorate, that led to the closure of theatres. They believed that drama was based upon lies: actors dissembled unreal situations and feigned emotions. Furthermore, theatres encouraged the sexes to mix in viewing scenes of heightened passions, a situation likely to lead to sexual immorality. This is the attitude Congreve satirises in Act 5 scene 5 in which Lady Wishfort describes her daughter's upbringing. By putting these opinions in the mouth of the character whose own sexual desires have led to the situation she abhors, Congreve exposes the hypocrisy and absence of true morality behind this attack on the theatre. Not only were such detractors frequently in denial concerning their own sexual desires, like Lady Wishfort, but they were also, like her, unable to see the ‡sins against charity that abounded in their behaviour and in the society they upheld. Their form of Christianity has ignored the many instances in the gospels in which sins against chastity are put in a wider context by Jesus. It was, for example, a 'woman of ill repute' who anointed Jesus' feet and was told that her sins were ‡forgiven because she had loved much, while he rebuked his hosts for their lack of †love (Luke 7:36–50). Similarly, it was the woman accused of adultery who was spared stoning when Jesus ruled that only the person without sin should throw the first stone (John 8:2–11). Lady Wishfort represents her 'world' in deploring the theatre and shrinking from the prospect of sexual scandal while leaving without condemnation both deception and the exploitation of the vulnerable.

We can see in *The Way of the World* the way in which, within a Christian worldview, ideals and biblical lessons can be embodied in a dramatic work that operates entirely in the language and style of its own age and setting.

QUESTIONS

1. Read the essay on the ‡morality play. In what ways do you find it helpful to read *The Way of the World* in the light of the morality play?
2. Elucidate the various ideas suggested by the title of this play in the light of its ending.
3. To what extent do you agree that this is a Christian play?

BIBLIOGRAPHY

Arthur W. Hoffman, *Congreve's Comedies*, Victoria BC 1993.

Kathleen Martha Lynch, *The Social Mode of Restoration Comedy*, New York 1926.

Anita Sieber, *Character Portrayal in Congreve's Comedies The Old Bachelour, Love for Love, and the Way of the World*, Lampeter 1996.

David Thomas, *William Congreve*, Basingstoke 1992.

5

Jonathan Swift

SWIFT'S THOUGHT

[*NA1* pp. 2298 f; *OA1* pp. 1733 f]

The nub of Swift's thought is his statement that mankind is not 'a reasonable animal' but one 'capable of reason'. For Swift, with his theological education, this would have had a Christian, theological significance. Swift lived in an age when reason was seen as a godlike endowment. ‡Deism, the belief that God the creator was like a watchmaker devising his machine and leaving it to work according to its own mechanism without intervention, was popular (see the overview essay above). This implied a God who is mind alone, a God of plan and calculation, but one unconcerned with the lives and sufferings of his *creation. He is the mathematician God we see in Blake's drawing of Jehovah, using his compass in the act of creation.

Saying that man is a reasonable animal implies that such a dominance by the mind is perfection for humankind. Altering this statement to 'capable of reason' allows for three vital changes. Firstly, being reasonable suggests, in this context, being godlike. Being capable of reason implies the *possibility* of being like God, a state that can be attained, rather than one that exists. It ensures that human beings are not seen to be naturally godlike or 'little gods' in themselves. This militates against the movement in Swift's period that elevated human beings above any need for a god beyond themselves. Secondly, it emphasises that human beings are animals, they have bodily lives and functions that make them mortal and frail, subject to all the drives and instincts of the animal world. This too cuts across pretensions to godlike status. Thirdly, and conversely, capacity for reason makes it clear that reason is not the sole attribute of the human being as indeed it is not of God. Human identity and life is distorted if capacities for other godlike attributes are not also included, especially the capacity for †love and friendship.

GULLIVER'S TRAVELS

[*NA1* pp. 2329 f; *OA1* pp. 1782 f]

In *Gulliver's Travels* these themes are pursued in various ways. In Parts 1 and 2, Swift centres on the embodied nature of the human being and the consequences of this. Through both adventures Gulliver and his readers are led to encounter and accept the inescapable 'bodiliness' of human beings. Gulliver cannot live purely by reason. All his activities are conditioned by his being embodied, and his judgements are based initially on reactions to bodies, to those of the Lilliputians and the Brobdignagians, and to his own in relationship to them.

Gulliver's own reactions expose a captivity of the reason to the judgements of irrational bodily senses. In Lilliput, Gulliver is seduced by the attractiveness of the miniature bodies which minimise awareness of the embodied nature of humanity. As a result, Gulliver expects more of them, morally, and is disillusioned by the depravity he finds. Humanity cannot improve its moral condition by trying to reduce or deny its embodied, animal state. Prettifying, making toylike, or reducing attention to embodiedness contribute to the myth of godlikeness.

Conversely, in Part 2, the giants of Brobdignag reveal Gulliver's rejection or disgust at humanity's embodiment. Gulliver is repelled by the grossness of the flesh of the Brobdignagians and is †tempted to judge their moral character in accordance with it. Gulliver has to learn that embodiment brings with it the capacity for warmth and affection, that this gross body is also the means for communication, care, and concern. It is, after all, a nursing mother who first arouses nausea in Gulliver. In short, he experiences a Christian truth that humankind is neither godlike, on account of its mind or reason, nor wholly bestial, on account of its body and instincts, but a meeting-place for the two, combining capacity for godlikeness and capacity for bestiality. This was the doctrine of the church ‡Fathers which formed the backbone of Swift's Anglican, but non-‡Calvinist, anthropology, an anthropology that links him with the worldview of Shakespeare and Donne as well as of his contemporaries, Addison and Steele.

Parts 3 and 4 probe further the contemporary equation of reason with rationalist philosophising and mathematical logic, and the equation of this reason with godlike human perfection. One aspect of Laputa is Swift's rejection of ‡Deism and its view of reality. In Laputa, everything is defined and designed according to mathematical principles and figures. The complexity of beauty is, for example, reduced to geometry; applying this to a woman or an animal reduces the sentient, living beings to mathematical concepts (Part 4, ch. 6).

This equation of mathematical logic with reason has two consequences. Firstly, the people despise the body and its activities. They abjure physical means of measurement like the tape-measure, for example. They cannot embody their concepts in the material world. Their reason detaches them from the common sense that derives from experience of the physical world. Furthermore, their understanding of the human excludes all possibility of imagination and creativity. The creating God and the creature are reduced to numbers. The materiality of the *creation is despised and this leads to an ugly and unaccommodating world. This is far from the picture of God and of creation in Genesis 1 where creation springs from the word, with all the consequent associations of dialogue and relationship, and the physical creation itself being in God's eyes 'very good'.

In his treatment of the Struldbruggs, Swift deals with the diametrically opposed tendency to imagine eternal life as human immortality, rather than as a new state brought about through sharing in the life of God. In the Christian view, eternal life is a state in which the flesh is ultimately a participant: as Christ was raised from the dead and appeared in bodily form, so at the end of time all will be included in this *resurrection. Swift contrasts the neglect of the flesh in the Laputan world with his society's tendency to ignore the reality of man's *fallen state and the contrasting original goodness of the material world. In traditional Christian doctrine immortality without subjection to decline and decay was a birthright of *Adam and Eve. The *fall into disobedience and ‡sin entailed the loss of such immortality. Man and the world were thenceforth subject to death and decay. Consequently death would be simultaneously a curse and a blessing: a curse because people were not made for death; a blessing because of the reality of decay. Gulliver is in thrall to the human dream of immortality as endless life: Laputans show the reality. Through the Struldbruggs Swift points us to the distinction between our version of eternal life and the Christian doctrine of *resurrection.

In Part 4, Swift polarises two possible views of human beings so that we can come to an understanding of a mediating position. The Houyhnhnms, all mind and reason, show the limitations of this ideal of perfection. There is no room in their lives for the illogical ways of friendship and †love. They reveal the unattractiveness of this as a model of humanity and as an implicit model of the divine. The Yahoos represent the opposite vision of humanity as purely animal. The human midway position is indicated in Gulliver's discussion with the Houyhnhnms about his clothing (Part 4, ch. 3). Being a clothed animal, in Gulliver's *fallen world, distinguishes humans from animals: having eaten the fruit and fallen into ‡sin, *Adam and Eve cover themselves and later God himself provides animal skin clothing (Genesis 3:7, 21).

Unlike other animals, *Adam and Eve in Genesis become self-aware as part of their *fall. That they are conscious of their sexuality denotes a wider consciousness regarding other aspects of instinctual life. They are not automata, driven solely by instinct. Their consciousness implies capacity for responsibility as we see in Genesis 3. Adam and Eve's consciousness of ‡sin results in awareness of their nakedness and leads them to find covering, to make positive choices regarding their state. Although they share physical attributes and a capacity for Yahoo-like bestiality, this self-aware capacity for choice differentiates human beings from them. To Swift's contemporaries this point would be emphasised by Gulliver's echo of St Paul's language about clothing the body (I Corinthians 12:23–4).

Gulliver's Houyhnhnms masters' reflections on Yahoo brutality approach this point from the other direction. If man is midway between Yahoo and Houyhnhnms, then human capacity for bestiality exceeds that of the animal driven only by instinct; human beings are capable of choosing, and refraining from, bestiality. A corrupted, that is, *fallen, capacity for reason appears the source of all his ills. The Houyhnhnms' rationality, however, also reveals a dark side — eugenics; an inability to love individuals with passion and commitment; an inability to temper the rigour of reason to the individual circumstances.

It is noteworthy that the Houyhnhnm with whom Gulliver has most in common is the inferior ‡soul, Nag, who 'has some tenderness' for him. What is missing in the perfection of the Houyhnhnms is a capacity for mercy and for love, which involves passionate commitment — a commitment, Swift's Anglicanism taught, that is essential to a God who is †love (see, for example, Ezekiel 34:12–16; Hosea 11:1–9; John 15:9–17; I John 4:7–10). Gulliver's idolising of the Houyhnhnms renders him incapable of loving his wife and fellows because he utterly rejects *fallen, embodied human nature. He is the mirror image of the proud Yahoo human who is incapable of acknowledging such fallenness. Swift draws no conclusions but leaves his readers to exercise the discernment of which Gulliver has always proved himself incapable.

QUESTIONS

1. Read the first three chapters of Genesis and consider the contrast between the view of the created world in these chapters and in this text.
2. In what ways has your personal reading of *Gulliver's Travels* developed in the light of your knowledge of its religious background?

3. Follow up some of the biblical references in the last paragraph and consider Gulliver's response to the Houyhnhnms in the light of these. What is the importance of Gulliver's being deranged and alienated from his family at the close of your conclusions?

BIBLIOGRAPHY

Christopher Fox, ed., *The Cambridge Companion to Jonathan Swift*, Cambridge 2003. This includes useful essays on Swift's religion and on other related aspects of his life and times.

Claude Rawson, ed., *Jonathan Swift: A Collection of Critical Essays*, New York 1995.

Marcus Walsh, 'Swift and religion', in Fox, ed., *The Cambridge Companion to Jonathan Swift*, pp. 161–76.

6

JOSEPH ADDISON AND
SIR RICHARD STEELE

[*BABL* pp. 501 f; *NA1* pp. 2479 f; *OA1* pp. 2027 f, 2178 f]

Addison and Steele were born in the same year, 1672, and both went to school in London and to university at Oxford, though Addison took a degree while Steele did not. Their collaboration on the periodicals *The Tatler* and *The Spectator* was a productive one, in which they could deal with similar topics and characters from slightly different points of view yet with a unity of intention to instruct and entertain. These essays combined the wit of the later periodical *Punch*, the literary-critical emphasis of modern bookish papers such as *The Times Literary Supplement*, the opinion-piece topical analysis of newspaper leaders, and, in a very decorous fashion, the stereotypical character-interaction of the modern soap-opera. Their appeal was wide, and it took the breadth of Addison and Steele, the depth of Samuel Johnson, and the versatility of Oliver Goldsmith (all notable periodical essayists of the eighteenth century) to sustain it.

The eighteenth-century periodical aimed to meet the needs of the wealthy middle class, people with time on their hands through success in the professions, business, and trade, yet without the heritage of social rank and breeding that would give them some instinctive knowledge of how best to use their time and wealth. Addison's essay on the aims of *The Spectator* makes clear that such people — 'all contemplative tradesmen, titular physicians, fellows of the Royal Society, Templars that are not given to be contentious, and statesmen that are out of business', the 'blanks of society', that is, the idle, and 'the fair ones', that is, women — needed something to occupy their minds, to stimulate their conversation, and to entertain them in the triviality of their daily occupations. The titles of the periodicals suggest something of the preoccupations of their readers and writers: *The Tatler* connotes gossip or conversation, *The Spectator* connotes close observation; both imply moral evaluation at some level.

The characters Addison and Steele use in *The Spectator* are types: Sir Roger de Coverley is a baronet and hereditary landowner, Sir Andrew Freeport a merchant, Captain Sentry a retired soldier, and Will Honeycomb a gentleman of fashion with independent means ('The Spectator's Club'). These interact with each other, and the writers entertainingly narrate stories about them, especially Sir Roger. The habits, manners, and adventures of these characters are emblematic of those of the upper and middle classes at large. But Steele, in outlining his *dramatis personae*, mentions respectfully, without naming, the clergyman who occasionally joins the others at the club. He is 'a very philosophic man, of general learning, great sanctity of life, and the most exact good breeding' (*NA1* p. 2487); he is reticent, but speaks 'with much authority' on 'some divine topic'; he is 'one who has no interest[1] in this world,... one who is hastening to the object of all his wishes and conceives hope from his decays and infirmities'.

This description of the clergyman perfectly outlines the role of Christianity in this society: it is to be, as he is, concerned with matters of religion, on which it can speak forcefully, but it is to be detached from the pastimes and occupations of the world. Just so, in the *Spectator* essays, Christianity appears from time to time, speaks with 'much authority', but is assumed to have limited involvement in the public world. The discontinuity of the two spheres is amusingly brought out in the essay 'Sir Roger at Church'. Church attendance is a good thing because it keeps people from savagery and makes them appear to best advantage, clean and in nice clothes. Sir Roger happily and incongruously interprets the service as he wishes, accepts the acknowledgement of the congregation, his tenants, but enjoys good relationships with the vicar. The church and the world have different preoccupations but usually work in harmony.

In the essay in this book on Samuel Johnson, the difference between the public and private discourses of faith is noted. Johnson's personal prayers are directly addressed to 'Jesus' and to God as Father. But in his public works he uses the same kind of circumlocution for God we find in Addison and Steele, 'Infinite Goodness', 'the Supreme Being', and 'the Divine Being', for example. This is a kind of politeness or courtesy, but it also illustrates a reaction against the 'enthusiasm' of some sects in the previous century and the progress of Enlightenment thinking. These two factors are evident in Addison's essay 'On the Scale of Being'.

The essay starts from the evidence of the world to deduce the character of the Being who made it: 'Infinite Goodness is of so communicative a nature that it seems to delight in the conferring of existence upon every degree of perceptive being.' The logic of the essay is that since there is a scale or order of creatures

---

1. This does not mean that the clergyman is indifferent to the world, but rather 'interest' means 'concern, material or emotional investment'. The ‡parson in the neighbouring parish to Sir Roger de Coverley's, who has fallen out with the squire, has failed to be detached from the concerns of the world, and consequently fails in his calling.

that rises from insect or shellfish through a linked diversity to man, then it is reasonable to suppose there are higher beings between man and God. Man occupies 'the middle space between the animal and intellectual nature': he is 'associated with angels and archangels' but subject to corruption and dissolution. Addison is clearly assimilating the Christian doctrines of *creation and a spiritual world of †angels and other powers with the Enlightenment scheme of enquiry and evidence. But unlike the ‡Puritans, he works from the visible world to argue towards a spiritual world (though he does not call it that: for him it is 'intellectual'[2]); and he starts from observation and works towards doctrine and finally scripture (ending with his quotation from Job).

The Christianity of the eighteenth-century periodical essay is generally concerned with manners, courtesy, order, and decency. It is restrained and dignified, of an Anglican and non-‡Calvinist cast. It is not much concerned with spirituality in the modern sense of personal faith and self-actualisation, but rather is concerned with the outward, public practice of Christian belief. Its teaching is moral rather than doctrinal.

QUESTIONS

1. Addison 'despised dullness, which he believed to be a social sin as unforgivable as a breach of hospitality' (Bloom, Bloom, and Leites, *Educating the Audience*, p. 16). Do you think Addison and Steele managed to make their writing both morally instructive and entertaining?
2. How, and how effectively, is Christianity presented in Addison and Steele?

BIBLIOGRAPHY

Robert J. Allen, ed., *Addison and Steele: Selections from The Tatler and The Spectator*, 2nd edn, London 1970. A usefully annotated edition.

Edward A. and Lillian D. Bloom, Edmund Leites, *Educating the Audience: Addison, Steele, and Eighteenth-Century Culture*, Los Angeles 1984.

---

2. In this he echoes ‡patristic Christian categories of thought, in which God as pure spirit is also pure knowing or 'intellect', so that spiritual beings are similarly 'intellectual'.

7

ALEXANDER POPE, *ESSAY ON MAN*

[*NA1* pp. 2554 f; *OA1* pp. 1891 f]

Writing in what is popularly called 'The Age of Reason' or 'The Enlightenment', Alexander Pope's thought was influenced by his Catholicism and by the philosophy of Leibniz and Christian Wolff. The popular expressions of this philosophy were satirised by Voltaire in *Candide* and summarised as 'all things are for the best in the best of all possible worlds'. Pope interprets Leibniz in a way that attempts to set limits to the claims for human reason being made by his contemporaries.

Leibniz was addressing the problem of evil and suffering from within belief in a benevolent, omnipotent, and omniscient God. His response was a reinterpretation of Christian doctrine about ‡free will, arguing that the possibility of moral evil and its subsequent suffering was necessary in a world with moral freedom, but that this evil was realised within a world predisposed towards goodness. This became popularised as a belief that particular evils were employed by Providence for a greater good, however difficult it might be for human beings to see the greater good. This is the force of Pope's 'All partial evil, universal good.'

Pope accepted the Leibniz-Wolff philosophy because he was anxious to curb the pride in the mind that afflicted many thinkers and scientists in this age of Enlightenment and because of his Catholic conviction that all evil is ultimately brought to good through the death and *resurrection of Christ. Against the belief that the mind of man can ultimately know all about the universe and control it, Pope set a vision of a being whose perfection, that is, completeness, implies limitation. Thus man is imperfect, not because he lacks godlike knowledge and power, but because he is true to his nature as a creature placed midway between earth and †heaven, who will not be complete until he is united with God (see I John 3:2–3).

Like Swift and Addison, Pope adheres to the medieval concept of the chain of being, extending downward from God and his ranks of †angels to nature (his vicegerent) to humanity and down through the various ranks of animate and inanimate nature. Man is midway, the vital link between the spiritual and the material, an understanding we can see from the earlier stages of Christian theology as in, for example, St Gregory of Nazianzen and St Maximus the ‡Confessor, whose writings emphasised humanity's place as mediator between God and earth.[1] Participating in both the spiritual and the material, man's perfection is to maintain this position, neither to be immersed in the physical, nor to claim to know all the mysteries of the spiritual. He is so placed as to intuit and dimly perceive aspects of the 'higher' world but not to know and understand them fully. His questioning of the ways of God, his complaints about evil and suffering, for example, issue from his rebellion against his place in the scheme of things.[2]

Such thoughts are set within an implicitly biblical framework in the reference to the Garden of *Eden in line 8. Man's origin and his *fall all lie within the providence of God. *Adam's †original sin was a desire to surpass his created status and 'be as God' with full knowledge of good and evil (Genesis 3:5). Pope then puts his treatment of pride within the context of the ‡fall of the angels: in the traditional story Lucifer cannot bear to be subservient and so attempts to usurp God's place and as a result brings †hell into existence.

Pope is not praising ignorance but objecting to the contemporary trend of making the human mind the touchstone of everything, and human beings the ultimate masters of their own lives. He founds his view of human beings implicitly on Jesus' teaching in the *sermon on the mount (Matthew 5–7). The 'sparrow fall' refers to Jesus' teaching not only about God's providence but also about humanity's inability to improve itself (Matthew 6:25–34). Humanity perfects itself by accepting its dependence on a providence it does not fully fathom and accepting its inability to go beyond the limits of its created nature. Pope supports his argument, too, by implicit reference to Paul's concept of the Body of Christ in which each person has a particular role (I Corinthians 12:12–30) and extending it to a cosmic scale. Chaos issues from humanity's refusal to be one particular function in a larger reality.

He also bases his view of man on the Christian ‡virtue of hope (see, for example, Romans 8:18–25). The perfection of humanity lies in its being content

---

1. For further discussion of this theology, see St Gregory's 'Orations' in Edward Gifford, H. Browne, E. Charles, and James Edward Swallow, trans., *Gregory Nazianzen and Cyril of Jerusalem, Catechetical Lectures; Orations; Select Letters*, Select Library of Nicene and Post-Nicene Fathers, 2nd series, vol. 7, Grand Rapids MI, rpt 1893. And the standard study of St Maximus is Lars Thunberg, *Microcosm and Mediator: The Theological Anthropology of Maximus the Confessor*, 2nd edn, Chicago 1995.

2. It is precisely this area of concern, with its focus on the questions raised by evil and suffering, that informs the debates in the biblical book of Job.

with present imperfection, knowing that completeness, that is, blessedness, comes with the full vision of God. 'Hope springs eternal' because humans are made for this future perfection. Human misery comes from believing that it can and should be here and now, the ‡sin of *Adam making humans act as though they were the god of God (122). Hence when Pope declares 'whatever is, is right', he is not speaking in social terms, defending the existing order, but in ontological terms: that is, he is talking about the disposition of the universe and the way it is made. In his opening lines, he refers to the world as a 'mighty maze' but not without a plan, and he does so within the context of the Garden of *Eden and the *fall of humanity in *Adam and Eve.

This, for the mind of a Catholic and a reader of Milton like Pope, would inevitably point to the conclusion that all partial evil is universal good. This is because the *fall of *Adam is traditionally seen as 'the happy fault' that won for the world 'so great a Redeemer', a belief celebrated in the hymn the ‡Exsultet sung each year at the Catholic ‡Easter Vigil celebrating the *resurrection of Christ. The apparent disaster of the fall of humankind becomes, in God's providence, part of a larger intention to raise human nature to a new status in Christ. Pope articulates in this poem a universalised concept of human nature, but he employs the language and the concepts offered by the biblical and Christian doctrine about humanity that underpin his Leibnizian framework because this, he is convinced, is the truth about humanity and God.

QUESTIONS

1. How would you summarise Pope's argument in this poem?
2. How persuasive do you find it?
3. To what extent is your answer to the previous question affected by your knowledge of the biblical and Christian sources of Pope's thought?

BIBLIOGRAPHY

Pat Rogers, *Essays on Pope*, Cambridge 1993.
Geoffrey Tillotson, *Pope and Human Nature*, Oxford 1958. A classic study.

8

SAMUEL JOHNSON

[*BABL* pp. 638 f; *NA1* pp. 2660 f; *OA1* pp. 2077 f]

Johnson (1709–84) was the son of a bookseller of Lichfield, an old cathedral town in the English Midlands. Books gave him his education, and in due course his writing both made him a living and brought him a pension. The breadth and depth of his reading is clear in almost everything he wrote but perhaps is most evident in the *Dictionary* of 1755: here he shows a knowledge of the range of languages that have contributed to the word-stock of English, and gives brief literary quotations to illustrate the senses of the words. He did the 'harmless drudgery' of lexicography uniquely well; it gave expression not only to his breadth but also to his habitual precision.

Boswell's *Life* deals mainly with Johnson's later period, when his fame was established and he had been granted the pension that relieved him of some of the pressure of writing for his living. Boswell gives us a man of contradictions: Johnson is both brilliant and boorish, he is moralistic and deeply fallible. Boswell's Johnson is one of those 'teachers of morality' who 'discourse like angels, but ... live like men' (*Rasselas*, ch. 18), who are not to be hastily trusted. Inevitably this impinges on the way we read his work, and it is indeed useful to know something of the man's personal life, especially of his recurrent ill-health and poor sleeping. But the sense of contradiction in Boswell rarely appears in Johnson's own writing. In Johnson's major works, we see principally the brilliance and the moralism.

Johnson was not unaware of his own imperfections. But even in the *Prayers and Meditations*, Johnson's personal reflections published posthumously (1785), where there is an overwhelming sense of his own inadequacy and need of God's mercy, there is still the same brilliant sharpness of observation, with himself as the subject observed:

> When I look back on the resolutions of improvement and amendment, which have year after year been made and broken, either by negligence, forgetfulness, vicious idleness, casual interruption or morbid infirmity; when I find that so much of my life

has stolen unprofitably away, and that I can descry by retrospec-
tion scarcely a few single days properly and vigorously employed;
why do I yet try to resolve again? I try, because reformation is
necessary, and despair is criminal. I try, in humble hope of the
help of God.

As my life has, from my earliest years, been wasted in a morning bed, my purpose is from Easter-day to rise early, not later than
eight. (Meditation, ‡Good Friday, April 14, 1775.)

There is here in the first paragraph, the full, precise and honest diagnosis of
his condition in his balanced rhetorical style; and in the second paragraph, the
earnest resolve to change, in direct, plain language. The fact that he has already
indicated that he has repeatedly failed in his resolutions before, and by his own
later testimony failed in this one, illustrates two features of his work: he deals,
however rhetorically and moralistically, with real human questions; and he is
seldom or never cynical, being one of those who 'pursue with eagerness the
phantoms of hope' (*Rasselas*, ch. 1).

Johnson wrote many of his works in imitation of classical models: his 'Vanity of Human Wishes' (see also *BAECP* pp. 289 f) is in imitation of Juvenal, and
Rasselas is something like a dramatised Socratic dialogue. Both, however, owe
something to biblical models, particularly the biblical †wisdom literature of
Ecclesiastes. *Rasselas* combines an oriental tale with the search for happiness,
wisdom, and the experimental 'choice of life' of Ecclesiastes. Ideas, new and old,
are discussed, places are visited, and experiences are tried by the characters in
the exploration of what makes for happiness. As in Ecclesiastes, the particular
doctrines of religion are excluded so that the purely empirical evidence may
be investigated, but the existence of God, 'the Creator', 'the Being who made
the soul' is not doubted (ch. 48). But in contrast to Ecclesiastes, the conclusion
concludes nothing: the characters return to Abyssinia, from where they started.
Johnson does not proclaim the meaninglessness ('vanity' in Ecclesiastes) of
everything, but he does acknowledge the elusiveness, the vanity, of the 'wishes
that [the characters] had formed'.

That 'vanity' did not exclude the possibility of improvement. Just as Johnson embraces the necessity of personal reformation (above), so he repeatedly
expresses the need for social and moral improvement more generally. The end
of 'The Vanity of Human Wishes' urges honesty in prayer, obedience to the
will of God, faith, and †love as the way to happiness, which is granted by 'celestial Wisdom'. Shakespeare, despite his many excellences, is not morally serious
enough for Johnson, for 'it is always a writer's duty to make the world better'.

Johnson's criticism of Shakespeare is morally perceptive when he sees that the playwright fails to 'produce the proper instruction required' in *Twelfth Night*; and his moral objection to the death of Cordelia in *King Lear* is again just, and deeply felt. In both these cases the modern critic or theatre-goer might object that he has missed the overall point of the plays, plumbing the depths of despair in the one, and celebrating unrestrained joy in the other; but Johnson's view that Shakespeare was the poet of 'nature' had the necessary corollary that such things go beyond nature, are indeed morally unnatural.[1]

Johnson has the ability to surprise and delight simply by the precision of his expression. Nearly every paragraph has some insight, and it is difficult to select particular examples. Johnson always seems to know what is right and expresses it with epigrammatic force, most frequently in two balanced phrases: for example, 'The life of a solitary man will be certainly miserable, but not certainly devout' (*Rasselas* ch. 21), or 'Marriage has many pains, but celibacy has no pleasures' (ch. 26). The point of these maxims is not to capture absolute and invariable truth but to summarise †wisdom and experience: the very balance of his style indicates the habit of mind of someone who sees life from more than one angle; who, if he tends to generalise, generalises judiciously and as comprehensively as possible.

The incidental aspects of his style and matter (the rhetorical balance, the end-stopped couplets of 'The Vanity', the lack of psychological realism in the characters of *Rasselas*) may make his work seem dated. But the quality of his thought makes connections across the centuries: Shelley borrowed the idea of the poet as 'the legislator of mankind' from *Rasselas* (ch. 10); substantial parts of Wordsworth's *Preface to the Lyrical Ballads* might be summarised in Johnson's dictum that 'Poetry is the art of uniting pleasure with truth, by calling imagination to the help of reason' ('Milton'); and all critics could benefit from taking to heart his criticism of the wit of the Metaphysicals — 'Their thoughts are often new, but seldom natural; they are not obvious, but neither are they just; and the reader, far from wondering that he missed them, wonders more frequently by what perverseness of industry they were ever found' ('Cowley').

QUESTIONS

1. Do you find Johnson's assurance enjoyable? Why or why not?
2. Do you agree with Johnson that 'it is always a writer's duty to make the world better'? How would you define a writer's duty today?

---

1. A theme of *King Lear*, cf. John F. Danby, *Shakespeare's Doctrine of Nature: A Study of King Lear*, London 1949.

3. Why do you think Johnson maintained such a clear distinction between private and public in his writing and his expressions of faith?

BIBLIOGRAPHY

Greg Clingham, ed., *The Cambridge Companion to Samuel Johnson*, Cambridge 1997. Essays about Johnson and his work.

Robert DeMaria Jr, *The Life of Samuel Johnson: A Critical Biography*, Oxford 1993.

Donald Greene, *Samuel Johnson: The Major Works*, rev. edn, Oxford 2000. A compact collection of the best of Johnson's writing.

Donald J. Greene, *Samuel Johnson: A Collection of Critical Essays*, Englewood Cliffs NJ 1965.

Joseph Wood Krutch, *Samuel Johnson*, London 1948. An older literary and biographical study.

9

JAMES BOSWELL, *LIFE OF JOHNSON*

[*BABL* pp. 851 f; *NA1* pp. 2749 f; *OA1* pp. 2044 f]

There can be little doubt that Boswell's most significant work is his *Life of Johnson*, published in 1791, seven years after the death of his subject. While almost any selection from the book will show the assiduity, liveliness, and freshness of Boswell's account of the great man, illustrating many of Johnson's quirks and insights, no selection from it can quite capture the scale of the work. It is a great biography of a great man, with the size and scope of the book commensurate with the greatness of Johnson's mind and character. More than that, it is the biography of an age, thronged with people, teeming with ideas and places vividly drawn from life. Boswell's achievement is to give the impression that this is how it actually was; and while much discussion has ensued about how much Boswell has shaped and manipulated his material (as indeed he shows himself manipulating circumstances in, for example, the meeting of Johnson and Wilkes, *NA1* pp. 2772–7, *OA1* pp. 2064–8), we can be sure that much of what Boswell records is accurate. As he demonstrates, he has gone to extreme lengths to recover documents and reminiscences from others as well as to preserve Johnson's casual writings and to record his own memories.

Boswell's *Life* is rather a novelty. By Boswell's time, the Christian tradition already had a very long pedigree of biographical work, from the *Lives* of the ‡martyrs, ‡saints, and ‡popes of early Christianity, right through to Foxe's *Book of Martyrs*, and the less sanguinary autobiographical accounts of godly lives such as those of Richard Baxter or Martha Moulsworth, and Izaac Walton's biographies.[1] But while it is perfectly clear that Boswell's Johnson is profoundly devout, the *Life* is a biography of a Christian, not a Christian biography. The latter is concerned with God's action in the world on and through the individual; the former is concerned with the action (and in this case, most especially), thought, and conversation of the individual in the world.

---

1. Johnson's own *Lives of the Poets* are of a different kind again, though sharing similarities with Walton: they are more literary-critical than biographical.

This point can be illustrated by those passages that relate to Johnson's fear of death. Boswell was deeply interested in this matter and it brings from him the remarkable image of Johnson's fears being like the wild animals set to attack the gladiator in the arena (1769, *NA1* p. 2769). There is a detachment about the question in Boswell that would be impossible, or at least unnatural, in a Christian biography. Indeed, the reader might suspect that in broaching 'the subject of death', Boswell was using a technique that he used to illuminating effect with Voltaire, eliciting from the latter a quite unexpected ‡confession of faith (*NA1* pp. 2751–2). But with Johnson it elicits extreme agitation, which Boswell is content to record but declines to analyse or account for. It is Boswell's excellence as a biographer that he shows us Johnson in 'minute particulars', but he leaves it to others to explain Johnson's faith.

Johnson, as his sermons and prayers show, was well-read in scripture, the church ‡Fathers, and in Anglican spirituality. In his *Prayers and Meditations* he frequently resolves to read his Bible more, to read more in 'speculative theology'. But speculation in this area was neither his inclination nor his habit. Christianity was axiomatic for him, and to question this was to question everything on which his life was based. Boswell shows us how his faith worked itself out: his habitual generosity to the unfortunate;[2] his self-criticism; his principled egalitarianism;[3] his disdain for deception and flattery;[4] his piety and orthodoxy. He does not, however, get to the root of this important aspect of Johnson's life. Johnson was an ‡Arminian by conviction, and rejected ‡Calvinist ideas of ‡predestination; it seems most likely that his 'dread of death, or rather, "of something after death"' (*NA1* p. 2770) — Boswell's inverted commas suggest that either Johnson, or perhaps Boswell himself, could not be brought to specify the nameless dread — was a fear of God's †judgement informed by an awareness of his imperfections.[5]

Boswell notes more than once that Johnson 'appeared to have a pleasure in contradiction', though he steered clear of disputes on the 'great truths of religion and morality' (*NA1* p. 2772). This does not mean that his views on these topics were merely private, but rather that he did not choose to argue about

---

2. He gave lodging to the blind (and somewhat cantankerous) Mrs Williams (*NA1* p. 2773) as well as to Dr Levet, whose clientele was of the poorest (see his poem on the doctor's death, *BAECP* pp. 298–9, *NA1* p. 2672, *OA1* p. 2088).

3. See the anecdote about Mrs Macaulay (1763, *NA1* p. 2767), and his general dislike of American slave-holding.

4. The letter to Lord Chesterfield is magnificent (1754, *NA1* pp. 2759–62, *OA1* pp. 2057–9).

5. See the excellent article, 'Johnson's Christian thought', by Michael Suarez, SJ, in *The Cambridge Companion to Samuel Johnson*, pp. 192–208.

them. His comments on his friend Christopher Smart, recorded by Boswell early in his acquaintance with Johnson, are remarkable for their humanity, wit, and clear-sighted piety:

> Now although, rationally speaking, it is greater madness not to pray at all than to pray as Smart did [in the street], I am afraid there are so many who do not pray, that their understanding is not called in question.... He insisted on people praying with him: and I'd as lief pray with Kit Smart as anyone else. Another charge [of madness against Smart] was that he did not love clean linen; and I have no passion for it. [1763, *NA1* p. 2765]

Here is Johnson expressing in his clear and authoritative fashion things that are close to his heart. If it is rational to pray, then Smart was merely unusual for praying in the street, and it is merely convention that justifies not praying on the street. And Johnson, as a friend, would willingly agree to a friend's insistence that they pray together. And in addition he shares with his friend no fondness for clean clothes. Johnson is not arguing that his friend is sane, but exercising his 'pleasure in contradiction' by showing rationally that on several grounds he is as mad as Smart; and this is to be seen in the context of Johnson's morbid fear of insanity (1729, *NA1* p. 2756). In many cases Johnson's intellect and argument, directed against the thoughtless, proud, or shallow, is scathing; here it is warm and personal.

Boswell set out to write 'not his panegyric, which must be all praise, but his Life; which great and good as he was, must not be supposed to be entirely perfect' (Plan, *NA1* p. 2753). Johnson appears great and good, but it is a greatness and goodness that coexists with personal ugliness, 'morbid melancholy', ill-temper, prejudice, indolence, and untidiness. Boswell has captured both the stature and the humanity of Johnson: in Boswell, we not only hear the brilliance of Johnson's conversation, we see through the eyes of a friend into his being. We can be grateful that Boswell, rake as he was, wrote the biography of this Christian man, unimpaired by the need to justify Johnson's opinions or his faith.

QUESTIONS

1. Discuss the difference between Christian biography and biography. Compare Boswell's *Life of Johnson* with Bede's story of Cædmon (*NA1* p. 24), or Foxe's 'Death of Anne Askew' or 'Lady Jane Grey' (*NA1* p. 551) or Walton's *Life of Donne* (*NA1* p. 1583).

2. Compare the Johnson you read about in Boswell with the man writing *Rasselas* and other pieces. What are the similarities and differences?

3. Find out more about ‡Arminianism. How much of Johnson's fear of death do you think was theological and how much personal or psychological?

BIBLIOGRAPHY

Harold Bloom, ed., *James Boswell's Life of Samuel Johnson*, New York 1986. A useful collection of essays.

Greg Clingham, ed., *The Cambridge Companion to Samuel Johnson*, Cambridge 1997. Essays about Johnson and his work, rather than Boswell, but good background material for understanding Boswell.

George Birkbeck Hill, ed., rev and enlarged by L.F. Powell, *Boswell's Life of Johnson . . .*, 2nd edn, 6 vols, London 1964. The standard text.

10

Slavery and Freedom

[*NA1* pp. 2806 f]

The British slave trade was a major factor in the country's economy for nearly a hundred years, from at least the time of the Treaty of Utrecht (1713), a key clause of which (the *Asentio*) gave Britain Spanish permission to trade with South America and the Caribbean. By this means, the Tory administration of Robert Harley (later first Earl of Oxford and Mortimer) intended to relieve the Government's huge financial deficit, selling shares in the slave trade to private investors in the South Sea Company. Apologists for Harley's ministry included key literary figures like Pope, Gay, and Swift, of whom he was an important patron. From the first, they display some unease about the slave trade, but usually express no outright opposition to it, despite the fact that by at least as early as 1740, it must have been clear that the trade, in addition to depriving people of their liberty and transporting them from everything they knew, was killing them in very substantial numbers, both in the horrors of the Middle Passage and on the Caribbean plantations.[1] John Richardson argues that there is a pervasive sense of a 'managed discomfort' about slavery in the writings of Pope, Gay, and Swift especially. For example, in relation especially to Swift's 'Modest Proposal' (*BABL* pp. 425 f; *NA1* pp. 2473 f; *OA1* pp. 1767 f), he suggests that the economic calculus and cruelty of rearing human babies for food is too grimly resonant of the economics and savagery of the contemporary slave trade to be coincidental.

A contemporary exception to imaginative literature's comparative silence on the slave trade may be Daniel Defoe, if he was indeed the author of the following passage, first published in 1724, in which the French pirate or privateer captain Misson tells his men that, 'The trading for those of our own species, could never be agreeable to the eyes of divine justice: that no man had power over the liberty of another, and while those who professed a more enlightened

---

1. See especially John A. Richardson, *Slavery and Augustan Literature.*

knowledge of the Deity sold men like beasts, they proved that their religion was no more than grimace.'[2]

Richardson writes: 'Religion and natural liberty were familiar topics, and the writer uses them to confront the involvement of Christian and supposedly freedom-loving peoples in slavery.' These and other writings show, then, that even quite early in the first half of the eighteenth century, slavery in the British colonies was, in some detail, an uncomfortable part of educated consciousness; and that some of that discomfort, at least, was based on religious principle. Nevertheless the trade was not abolished in the British Empire until 1807, and slavery itself not until 1833. Millions of Africans died while the pressure for abolition, from devout Christians and others, gained ground only slowly over the next seventy years.

During that period, very significant changes of course occurred in literary aesthetics and Christian piety, as well as in politics. As an instrument of economic policy and a staple of the British economy, the slave trade effectively began in the Augustan period, and thus at a time when the Church of England and its feeder universities were, in religious terms, dominated by a complacent nominal assent to Christian doctrine and practice. Abolition happened after the rapid rise of ‡Methodism, the Clapham Sect, the French Revolution, and the emergence of Romanticism. Somewhere between the two is the important literary work, for example, of the fervent ‡Evangelical William Cowper, who, urged on by his friend Rev. John Newton, wrote a number of antislavery poems as the Abolitionist Movement began to gather strength.[3] Newton, an Anglican clergyman, is now most familiar to us as the author of the hymn 'Amazing Grace', but his extraordinary personal history included time as a slave in Africa and three journeys as the master—and thus chief trader—of ships in the triangular trade.[4]

Cowper's relationship to the slightly later Romantic movement is a subject of some disagreement—indeed the Romantic poets themselves disagreed on the merits of his poetry—but there can be little doubt that Romanticism was always certain to be inimical to slavery. In a well-regarded study, Debbie Lee has suggested that the Romantic insistence on imagination as consisting especially

---

2. Arthur L. Hayward, ed., *A General History of the Robberies and Murders of the Most Notorious: from their First Rise and Settlement in the Island of Providence to the Present Year. By Captain Charles Johnson*, London 1955, p. 38. 'Captain Charles Johnson' was possibly a pseudonym of Daniel Defoe.

3. For example the satirical *Sweet Meat has Sour Sauce*, published in 1788.

4. See Bernard Martin and Mark Spurrell, ed., John Newton, *The Journal of a Slave Trader … 1750–1754. With Newton's Thoughts Upon the Slave Trade*, London 1962.

of fellow-feeling[5] inevitably gave rise to an empathy with the African slaves which is reflected, for example, in the illustrative work of Blake's engravings for John Gabriel Stedman's *Narrative of a Five Years' Expedition against the Revolted Negroes of Surinam*.[6] For Lee, a key aspect of the great Romantic concern with selfhood, self-understanding, and self-expression is the concomitant understanding of alterity: the relationship to selves other than one's own. In some cases, this kind of view might be theologised: thus Coleridge, for example, who was an active Abolitionist in Bristol for some years, 'attributes alterity to the Trinity and, therefore, to transcendental being';[7] but, whatever their theological position, Blake, Wordsworth, and other Romantics all contributed antislavery literature to the cause, as did a number of less well-known ‡Evangelical writers like Hannah More.

The key Christian figure in the Abolition movement, however, is the Parliamentarian William Wilberforce, whose name is indelibly linked to Abolition. A devout ‡Evangelical, with a reputation for deep personal piety, he had been converted in 1784 in his twenty-fifth year, and was Member of Parliament for Hull (1780–1824). Newton, with whom he was friendly, was important in influencing him to take his Evangelical faith into the practice of politics. He devoted himself from 1788 onwards to the Parliamentary campaign for abolition of the slave trade.

Wilberforce was not, on the whole, a theologian. He and his fellow ‡Evangelicals took the simple line that the slave trade was ‡sinful, that the nation needed to ‡repent of it, and that the nation would not prosper if it continued in it. His address to the House of Commons had even a ‡confessional tone. To the modern Christian reader, used to the emphases of late twentieth-century Liberation Theology, the Abolitionists do not seem to use some of the Christian theological concepts at their disposal. We should remember that Wilberforce's was a Parliamentary political campaign, which required some degree of pragmatism: nevertheless, we saw in the passage from Defoe/Johnson that some level of theological discomfort with slavery appears as early as 1724; so some reflection on the relationship between Christian theology and slavery is the final concern of this essay.

---

5. Lee cites especially Adam Smith's *Theory of Moral Sentiments:* Debbie Lee, *Slavery and the Romantic Imagination*, p. 34.

6. Lee, *Slavery and the Romantic Imagination*, pp. 66–119.

7. Lee, *Slavery and the Romantic Imagination*, p. 36. It is interesting that at this point Lee lays particular theoretical emphasis on the philosopher Emmanuel Levinas, as do a number of contemporary Christian theologians—see, for example, David Ford, *Self and Salvation*, Cambridge 1999. I do not always find Lee's reading of individual texts convincing, but the thrust of her argument is surely correct.

Western thinking about slavery is inescapably theological because early Christianity, especially in the writing of St Paul, expressed its ‡salvation as being freed by Christ from slavery to ‡sin and death. There was a clear analogy to the real freeing of slaves in Roman culture, in which freedom was thus not an abstract concept, but a real experience, the undoubted joy of which gave particular power to the analogy. Olaudah Equiano's description of his own experience of being freed from Caribbean slavery (in *BABL* pp. 871 f; *NA1* pp. 2821 f) is surely an accurate reflection of that feeling in many times and cultures.[8] Paul's conception of freedom was essentially spiritual, however, and its complete fulfilment was ultimately the promise of †heaven hereafter. He wrote that 'in Christ there is neither Jew nor Greek, there is neither bond nor free, there is neither male nor female: for ye are all one in Christ Jesus' (Galatians 3:28), but we know that in the business of organising his churches, he did not, and probably could not, give this rhetoric full practical expression. We have, of course, the intriguing New Testament letter Philemon, in which Paul commends a runaway slave Onesimus, whom he clearly values highly, back to his master Philemon. It is a fascinating snapshot of the way in which the dominating relationship of slave to master was genuinely relativised by the fact that both were now brothers in Christ and both under the authority of the apostle, but Paul does not question Philemon's legal right over his slave; and there is no sense that Philemon ought to free him.

Christians are inclined to say that the seeds of the abolition of slavery are sown in Galatians but, as we have seen, it took several hundred years in many Christian cultures for the seeds to grow, and abolition was as much brought about by the forces of secular liberalism as by the belated recognition by Christians of what had always been implicit in their heritage. In Britain, at least, it appears that Christian complicity in the slave trade was, as Cowper alleged, part of a failure of the church, especially the Church of England, to take its broader moral responsibilities seriously, in a time when it was dominated by complacency in relation to emergent social issues both abroad and at home as a result of the mainly nominal Christianity practised by its adherents.[9] ‡Methodism and the related ‡Evangelical revival were necessary correctives that came to play leading roles in a more energetic response to the need for change.

---

8. See especially Orlando Patterson, 'Slavery: the underside of freedom', in Jack Hayward, ed., *Out of Slavery*, pp. 7–29. Patterson goes on to an exegesis of a suggested difference between the concepts of freedom between Galatians and Romans, which is more doubtful, though not uninteresting.

9. Consider also, for example, the Church of England's general failure to support Wesley's vital ministry to the new working class.

QUESTIONS

1. Why, from this distance of time, are we justified in condemning those involved in the Atlantic slave trade?
2. What is the relationship between the Atlantic slave trade and racism in the twenty-first century?
3. What has post-colonial criticism added to our understanding of English literature?

BIBLIOGRAPHY

Jack Hayward, ed., *Out of Slavery: Abolition and After*, London 1985.

Debbie Lee, *Slavery and the Romantic Imagination*, Philadelphia 2001.

John Richardson, *Slavery and Augustan Literature: Swift, Pope, Gay*, London 2004.

11

JAMES THOMSON

[*BABL* pp. 624 f (Winter); *BAECP* pp. 211 f (Spring); *NA1* pp. 2822 f (Autumn); *OA1* pp. 2183 f (Summer and Winter)]

Thomson may be thought of as the father of English nature poetry. His seminal work, *The Seasons*, was written over a period of five years and published complete in 1730. Although 'Spring' was third to be written, Thomson placed it first in the final collection. Consequently it sets the contexts in which the rest of the work must be read: springtime is presented as the season most akin to God's original *creation and his intention for the *fallen world.

In 'Spring' we are presented with a natural world 'full of life and vivifying Soul', where 'Man superior walks / Amid the glad Creation, musing Praise, / And looking lively Gratitude'. The plenitude and *Edenic qualities of an idealised spring are celebrated, at a time when humankind was 'uncorrupted' and nature harmonious, with †love pervading all. Since the *fall however,

> joyless Inhumanity pervades,
> And petrifies the Heart. Nature disturb'd
> Is deemed, vindictive, to have changed her Course.

In consequence the seasons, in their more inimical aspects, oppress 'a broken World'.

A Christian understanding of the natural world is thus established: nature displays structure, order, and sometimes harmony; it is reminiscent at times of *Eden; it is *fallen, however, from its original splendour, often appearing disordered; it is the context where human beings live out spiritual and moral lives; it is sustained by God, a God who is present in nature, as 'every purer Eye' may discern, and who is to be praised; it attests his bounty; and it has a beneficial spiritual and moral influence upon humankind. Whether Thomson writes passages of pure description, moral didacticism, philosophy, scientific enquiry, or interjections of praise, which recur like Pauline doxologies, these are the contexts in which the poem must be understood.

Thus in 'Autumn' the water cycle evidences the 'full-adjusted Harmony of Things' and yet the autumnal fogs are explicitly compared to the †darkness and disorder before *creation:

> mingling thick,
> A formless grey Confusion covers all
> As when of old (so sung the HEBREW BARD)
> Light, uncollected, through the Chaos urg'd
> Its Infant Way; nor Order yet had drawn
> His lovely Train from out the dubious Gloom.

In the section on late evening and night Thomson first describes fog and then moonlight and the aurora borealis in finely observed detail and great beauty. He dismisses superstitious reactions to the northern lights, elevating scientific reason in their place. The section concludes by describing a rustic figure wandering through the night.

This passage exemplifies much of Thomson's technique in its interplay of imagination, science, natural description, and spiritual allusiveness, shifting constantly between the literal and the metaphoric or analogical. The description of the fog foreshadows the chaotic powers of night and the confusion of the crowd, but this is subsumed for now under the exquisite brilliance of the moon. This latter description indicates Thomson's awareness, as often in his delineation of an unconfined prospect, of that which is beyond, of that which is 'other'. The moon's 'breaking through' is for him an indication of the impingement of God's realm upon this world, sometimes with grace and humility — 'she seems to stoop', and sometimes sublimity — 'up the pure cerulean rides'. The constant shifting of the night scene in this passage indicates the variety and plenitude of nature, the beauty that is to be discovered even in nature's most dangerous habit, and for Thomson inculcates an awe of God's might.

The imagery of †light is heightened further in the aurora borealis, which overtakes the moon in its vastness and complexity of movement. The passage on the panic evinced by the superstitious crowd is a parody of ‡apocalypse — armies in the sky, blood-like colour, the plains of Armageddon, earthquake, consuming fire, plague (famine, flood, and pestilence), empires overthrown, and nature itself about to be destroyed. To the enlightened eye, however, the 'purer Eye' acclaimed in 'Spring', it is but 'beautiful and new'.

A description of night follows. Its †darkness is 'quenching', 'black and deep'. Order, beauty, gaiety, variety, and the distinctiveness of things are lost. Yet at the same time 'Magnificent and vast, are heaven and earth'. Contrasting with the crowd, running wildly in panic, is the lone individual, representative of each human being making his or her way through this life. The ‡soul that wanders seems to be in a spiritual night or †wilderness: 'benighted' and 'bewildered' — his physical circumstances analogous to his spiritual state. Like Christian in *Pilgrim's Progress* he must circumnavigate the mire, the 'pits of death', the 'dangerous ford', without light from any window to guide. He may all too easily sink, 'Rider and horse, amid the miry gulf': the biblical language here alludes to the death of the Egyptians when the Red Sea closed over them, 'the horse and his rider hath he thrown into the sea' (Exodus 15:1). Two lights are described, representing alternative possibilities of ‡salvation or deception. The 'wildfire' *ignis fatuus*, 'deceitful', leads astray; but the 'meteor' *ignis lambens*, shows the 'narrow path' to safety, recalling Christ's asseveration 'narrow is the way, which leadeth unto life' (Matthew 7:13).

The later digression on the smoking out of the beehive with fumes of sulphur continues the moral overtones, comparing the treatment of the bees with the overthrow of a city hit by earthquake and descending into a †hellish 'Gulph of blue sulphureous Flame', with the interjected lament:

O Man! tyrannic Lord! how long, how long,
Shall prostrate Nature groan beneath your Rage,
Awaiting Renovation?

Here Thomson alludes to St Paul who looks forward to the ‡redemption of the *fallen *creation: 'the creature itself also shall be delivered from the bondage of corruption ... the whole creation groaneth and travaileth in pain ... even we ourselves groan within ourselves, waiting for ... the redemption of our body' (Romans 8:21–3).

The Seasons ends on a triumphant, ‡redemptive note. 'Winter' concludes:

And see!
'Tis come, the glorious Morn! the second Birth
Of Heaven, and Earth! Awakening Nature hears
The *new-creating Word*, and starts to Life,
In every heighten'd Form, from Pain and Death
For ever free.

The original work of *creation is reenacted and the perfection of 'Spring' is reasserted for eternity.

QUESTIONS

1. How do ideas of God's power, †wisdom, and †love create a unifying underpinning for the poem?
2. How far do the motifs of the first three chapters of Genesis inform *The
   Seasons*?

BIBLIOGRAPHY

Ralph Cohen, *The Unfolding of The Seasons*, London 1970. A detailed and systematic study of the poem—a seminal critical text.
James Sambrook, ed., *The Seasons*, Oxford 1981. This edition contains an extensive introduction and notes.

12

THOMAS GRAY

[*BABL* pp. 747 f; *BAECP* pp. 347 f; *NA1* pp. 2825 f; *OA1* pp. 2202 f]

Gray published very few poems. The 'Elegy Written in a Country Churchyard' is incomparably his best known work and, probably, his best. It was written intermittently over several years, and we have a number of surviving manuscripts from different stages of its composition. The combination of these factors has meant that the great preponderance of critical work on Gray is consideration of the 'Elegy'. This is in fact particularly true of the discussion of Gray's religious faith, because the 'Epitaph' with which the 'Elegy' concludes, with its apparently conventional religious sentiment, is one of the later additions to the work of which we know. The earlier version, 'Stanzas Wrote in a Churchyard', still extant in a manuscript at Eton College, is much shorter and concludes as follows:

> And thou, who mindful of the unhonoured dead
> Dost in these notes their artless tale relate
> By night and lonely contemplation led
> To linger in the gloomy walks of fate
>
> Hark how the sacred calm, that broods around
> Bids every fierce tumultuous passion cease
> In still small accents whispering from the ground
> A grateful earnest of eternal peace
>
> No more with reason and thyself at strife
> Give anxious cares and endless wishes room
> But through the cool sequestered vale of life
> Pursue the silent tenor of thy doom.[1]

It might appear that this ending is less religious than the 'Epitaph', since it contains less overtly religious language, but on the whole scholars have regarded these lines as expressing an orthodox Christian-Stoic attitude to death, in which the inevitability of death is to be accepted, and death's aftermath,

---

1. H.W. Starr and J.R. Hendrickson, ed., *Poems of Thomas Gray*, p. 40.

the calm of 'eternal peace' becomes also the state of mind to which humanity should aspire, giving way neither to the frenzy of 'tumultuous passions' nor to the anxiety of 'endless wishes'. For though there is no explicit mention of God here, we should note that the calm is 'sacred', that the 'still small' accents are a direct allusion to I Kings 19:12,[2] and that the 'eternal peace' is, at least potentially, a Christian reference. The question thus becomes whether the ending we now have is in some respects less orthodoxly religious, or more ambivalent in its attitude to death. Or at least these questions are part of the obviously prior question of what the changed ending generally achieves in contrast to the ending of the Eton version.

Despite the constraints of recent theory, scholarship that deals with the complex of questions about the ending of the 'Elegy' makes extensive reference both to Gray's intention and to his life. In fact, the question of the relationship of Gray to the persona of the 'Elegy's' narrator has been the most insistent question even of recent scholarship. On the subject of religion, B. Eugene McCarthy has written: 'Gray said relatively little about religion ... so that we have at best a cloudy view of his faith.... His was a rational faith, close to what was called natural religion, close even to Deism but without its sense of an impersonal God.' McCarthy cites part of Gray's 'Essay on the Philosophy of Lord Bolingbroke', in which Gray quotes with approval from William Wollaston: 'Have I been set so far above [animals and plants] in life, only to be levelled with them in death?'[3] McCarthy calls Gray's faith 'teleological': essentially meaning that he believed that human life showed clear signs of having been designed by a maker and that to understand how to live one should seek to understand the purpose or end (Greek *telos*) to which the maker's design tended. This view is borne out by Gray's letters, in which the infrequent references to religion are typically offered in comfort to a friend who has experienced bereavement, and draw consolation from the notion of God's having made humanity for a purpose. Thus to Norton Nicholls: 'He who best knows our nature (for he made us what we are) by such afflictions recalls us ... to our duty and to himself.' Or to Dr Mason, 'May He who made us, the Master of our pleasures and of our pains, preserve and support you ...'[4]

From this perspective, it is probable that the 'Elegy' brought into relationship themes that were deeply connected in Gray's thought: his understanding of his own nature and the relationship of that understanding to the notion of

---

2. 'And after the earthquake a fire; but the Lord was not in the fire; and after the fire a still small voice.'

3. McCarthy, *Thomas Gray*, pp. 147–8 and note p. 248.

4. John Beresford, ed., *Letters of Thomas Gray*, London 1925, 1951, 23 September 1766 (p. 302), and 28 March 1767 (p. 308), respectively.

death. It is worth noting that two other of his important poems were occasioned by bereavement: the 'Ode on the Death of a Favourite Cat' (*BABL* p. 749; *BAECP* p. 352; *NA1* p. 2829; *OA1* p. 2206) and the posthumously published and deeply felt 'Sonnet' on the death of his friend Richard West (*BABL* p. 748; *BAECP* p. 349).[5] Gray understood his nature to be melancholic. He writes to West, 'Mine, you are to know, is a white Melancholy … for the most part; which, though it seldom laughs or dances … yet is a good easy sort of a state.… Its only fault is insipidity.… But there is another sort, black indeed, which I have now and then felt.'[6] The 'Elegy' clearly and consciously stands in the melancholic tradition and thus in the tradition which Gray thought was intrinsic to the nature that his maker had given him. Insofar as there is a move away from Christian stoicism in the 'Epitaph', it probably is indeed towards a more individuated expression of what Gray perceived to be his real persona; but his understanding of the givenness of that persona was still theological. And in reflecting, as in the 'Epitaph' he appears to do, on the end of his own life, he brought into consideration the teleological aspect of that understanding. In terms of Christian doctrine, this is entirely orthodox, but it is much more a *creational than a ‡redemptive theology. There is little sense, either in the 'Elegy' or in any of Gray's writing, of the need of a ‡saviour. Together with perhaps a sense of melancholic longing for the friend he had lost in West, there may indeed be some real unorthodox weight behind the parenthesis in 'He gain'd from heaven ('twas all he wish'd) a friend' (124).

In one other specific change that Gray made to the 'Elegy' over time, Hampden, Milton, and Cromwell in lines 57–60 were replacements for Cato, Tully, and Caesar. Quite clearly, the English names are much more appropriate to the poem's sense of place than the Roman ones they replace: it is hard, even though we know it, to believe that the Englishness of these lines is a second thought.[7] From our perspective, though, we should at least note that this is a very Protestant list of English figures, all associated with the ‡Puritan side in the English Civil War. There is a balance, or perhaps an ambiguity, in how Gray treats these figures. Charles I appears as a 'tyrant' (58), yet Cromwell is not 'guiltless of his country's blood' (60). On the whole, however, the idea that there were faults on both sides in the English Civil War, which we must recall had ended only a hundred years before, was an important part of the settlement that followed it. We should perhaps not read too much into this list of Protestant figures. Rather,

---

5. H.W. Starr and J.R. Hendrickson, ed., *Poems of Thomas Gray*, London 1966, p. 92.

6. Amy Louise Reed, *The Background of Gray's Elegy*, p. 243.

7. In fact, classical allusions were second nature to Gray, who was also a very competent poet in Latin.

their Englishness contributes a great deal to the sense of English history in this most English of poems: and their author's religion, in its embrace of a natural theology which avoids most of the controversies of the ‡Reformation, is perhaps very English too.

QUESTIONS

1. Assess the relationship of Gray's religious thought to ‡Deism.
2. What makes Gray's 'Elegy Written in a Country Churchyard' so popular?
3. Is the popularity of Gray's 'Elegy Written in a Country Churchyard' suspicious?

BIBLIOGRAPHY

B. Eugene McCarthy, *Thomas Gray: The Progress of a Poet*, London 1997.

Amy Louise Reed, *The Background of Gray's Elegy: A Study in the Taste for Melancholy Poetry 1700–1751*, New York 1962. An extensive study of the melancholic tradition in the 'Elegy'.

H.W. Starr and J.R. Hendrickson, ed., *The Complete Poems of Thomas Gray: English, Latin and Greek*, Oxford 1966. The standard edition of the poems.

13

WILLIAM COLLINS

[*BABL* pp. 767 f; *BAECP* pp. 369 f; *NA1* pp. 2833 f; *OA1* pp. 2189 f]

William Collins was one of the so-called 'Nature poets' writing in the mid-to late eighteenth century. His *Odes on Several Descriptive and Allegoric Subjects* were published in 1747 at a time of great activity among this group: the previous year had seen the publication of James Thomson's complete version of *The Seasons* and Joseph Warton's *Odes on Various Subjects*. In 1747 Gray's *An Ode on a Distant Prospect of Eton College* came out, as did Thomas Warton's *The Pleasures of Melancholy*.

Collins's 'Ode on the Poetical Character' is, like much of his poetry, pre-Romantic, and as such has a particular place in the development of notions of imagination and creativity. The concept that a poem is imitation, holding its mirror up to nature, is being replaced at this time by an understanding of the poem as a second creation, formed by the poet in an act comparable to God's *creation of the world.

M.H. Abrams traces this trend, showing how the notion of the poet's invention as analogous to God's *creative act goes back to fifteenth-century Italy. The idea of the poet as maker was introduced in England by Sir Philip Sidney, who alludes for instance to 'the heavenly Maker of that maker'. Later the term 'creation' was frequently used of poetry by such writers as Donne and Pope. In the 1740s critics were often engaged in discussing these matters; for instance in 1741 Bodmer declared that Milton possessed 'an unfathomable power comparable to that of God himself' — a concept important for Collins in his burning desire to emulate Milton. Reason is being dethroned in the second half of the eighteenth century and increasingly replaced by what Collins's friend Joseph Warton, referring to Shakespeare, called a 'lively creative imagination'. This all anticipates Coleridge's treatment of the Imagination as a high principle of Romanticism.

Collins's 'Ode on the Poetical Character' focuses on the day of *creation, exploring the analogy with the imaginative creation of poetry. In the strophe, Collins exalts Fancy (before Coleridge the term was interchangeable with

Imagination)—that 'Divinest Name'—to whom the 'God-like Gift' of poetry is given in order for her to pass it on to the fortunate few.

In the epode Fancy is called the 'Enthusiast', meaning literally 'one possessed by a god', and is depicted as a key agent in the *creation of the world. God has 'call'd with Thought to Birth' the cosmos and places Fancy 'on his Saphire Throne'—an image both of the skies and of the sapphire throne of God himself, as depicted in Ezekiel: 'And above the firmament that was over their heads was the likeness of a throne, as the appearance of a sapphire stone' (1:26). The sky is termed a 'vaulted Shrine' in an extension of the religious imagery and the music of 'Seraphic Wires' is to be heard extolling the †love and mercy of God, perhaps a precursor of Shelley's image of the wind playing upon an Aeolian harp, a common Romantic analogy of the creative act.

Fancy remains in 'veiling Cloud', as God himself is often depicted in the Old Testament (as in Exodus 13:22; 24:15; Isaiah 4:5), while she 'Breath'd her magic Notes aloud'. This is parallel to the creative fiat 'Let there be light'. At the sound of her voice Apollo, god of poetry as well as the sun, is born.

Creating poetry is designated 'hallow'd Work' at the end of this stanza, and those who seek after it are deemed to verge on the presumptuous. Their 'presuming Hopes' recall the 'hopeless Fair' who in the strophe reached out 'unblest' to claim the prize of Florimel's girdle (which represents for Collins the poetic gift), and were denied. Hope is mentioned again at the end of the poem where Collins himself aspires to the divine gift—and is denied.

With further religious and ‡mystical connotations a personified 'Ecstatic Wonder' sits nearby, carefully distinguished from 'dang'rous passions' since Collins is, after all, still in the eighteenth century. Wonder sits listening to 'the deep applauding Thunder', alluding perhaps to the sound of the voice of God as it is described a number of times in the Bible (for example, Exodus 19:19; Psalms 29:3; 68:32; Job 37:5). The inclusion of Truth as a partner to Wonder reveals Collins's concern that emotion should be balanced by something more objective and also treats the perennial question of whether poets are liars. Personified Truth is in 'sunny Vest array'd', intimating a link with the poetic god Apollo with his shining hair.

Finally, in the antistrophe, Collins presents a pastoral, Miltonic passage that depicts his hero in an *Eden very close to †heaven with the poet's ear closely attuned to the higher realm. Collins would like to follow in Milton's poetic footsteps but ends pessimistically, knowing he is inadequate for the task and convinced that English poetry is in decline. For Collins, true poetic power is rare: 'The Cest of amplest Pow'r' is given to few.

One of Collins's great strengths lies in his use of personification. This is apt since figurative language was being viewed at the time — for instance by Cowley and Addison — as an instance of the godlike 'second creation' of the poet. According to Joseph Warton in 1753, 'Prosopopoeia, therefore, or personification, conducted with dignity and propriety, may be justly esteemed one of the greatest efforts of the creative power of a warm and lively imagination.'

Thus in 'Ode on the Poetical Character', Fancy is not just a rhetorical figure with a capital letter to mark it out as such, but a product of the creative imagination active in a manner analogous to God's own work in shaping the universe. Collins's depiction of Fancy displays a highly visual imagination at work in the vibrant descriptions. By adding to the personification many attendant details, however, and some less developed personae such as Wonder and Truth, which serve to support the main focus, Collins creates a cumulative effect that is not merely visual but symbolic and visionary, fitting for a poem which elevates Fancy alongside God: 'Heav'n, and *Fancy*, kindred Pow'rs'.

QUESTIONS

1. How is the personification in 'Ode to Evening' developed into visionary symbol?
2. What evidence of Collins's pre-Romantic qualities can you discover in his other poems?

BIBLIOGRAPHY

M.H. Abrams, *The Mirror and the Lamp*, Oxford 1953. An important study of the development of Romantic theory.

R. Wendorf and C. Ryskamp, ed., *Collins: The Works*, Oxford 1979. The standard complete edition.

A.S.P. Woodhouse, 'Collins: Neoclassical and Pre-Romantic' (1965), in J.R. Watson, ed., *Pre-Romanticism in English Poetry of the Eighteenth Century: The Poetic Art and Significance of Thomson, Gray, Collins, Goldsmith, Cowper & Crabbe*, Basingstoke 1989. A short essay setting the poet in the literary tradition.

14

CHRISTOPHER SMART

[*BABL* pp. 785 f; *BAECP* pp. 426 f; *NA1* pp. 2839 f; *OA1* pp. 2217 f]

Smart was a contemporary of Samuel Johnson. Unlike Johnson, who adhered to the 'middle way' of Anglicanism, Smart was a fervent ‡Evangelical Christian, apt to be carried away by spiritual 'enthusiasm', which was poorly tolerated by those Christians who expected decorum and rationality to guide religious behaviour. As the introduction to his work in *NA1* suggests, his later body of poetry is unique in its time, and yet it does have links both with his literary forebears and with the Romantic movement. More than this, it is deeply rooted in a theological appreciation of the Bible, as we see in his poem 'Jubilate Agno'. This poem is not only a hymn of praise for *creation; it is the creation's praise for its ‡redemption in the †sacrifice of Christ, the *Lamb of God (see John 1:29). It takes its inspiration from the book of Revelation in which all the company of †heaven falls prostrate in praise and adoration of the Lamb upon his throne (Revelation 7:9–17).

Smart combines this New Testament portrayal of the praise of the †heavenly kingdom with Old Testament songs of praise. Smart's sense of a living world, praising its creator and ‡redeemer by being itself, echoes the *Benedicite*, the hymn of praise in The Book of Common Prayer and originally from Catholic versions of the †prophecy of Daniel. This hymn, like 'Jubilate Agno', is praise by *creation for creation, but also implicitly, for ‡salvation. The hymn is sung by the three young men cast into the fiery furnace by Nebuchadnezzar because of their refusal to worship a golden image. They survive and are seen in the furnace accompanied by a fourth, the presence of God as an †angel (Daniel 3).

Both the *Benedicite* and 'Jubilate Agno' are songs of praise for the gift of life and for the renewal of that life. The language of 'Jubilate Agno' echoes Nebuchadnezzar's instructions to worship the golden image he has erected: 'Praise the Lord, O you just, give the glory to our God and to the Lamb: nations and languages and every creature in which is the breath of life' (compare Daniel 3:4, 7). The *Benedicite* calls upon all creatures to bless and highly exalt the Lord. They can do this in no other way than by expressing the nature given to them.

And so, for Smart, his consideration of his cat, Jeoffry, is a particular expression of that praise. Smart simply explores the ways in which Jeoffry expresses praise in the varied aspects of his behaviour.

The combination of Jeoffry's praise for *creation and ‡redemption is emphasised by his response to 'the glory of God in the east'. Sunrise is for Christians a sign of the *resurrection of Christ, that is why their churches are always built facing the east. In this way, a response of worship at sunrise is praise and thanksgiving both for the creation of the new day, but also for the day of resurrection. Furthermore, this hallowing of the day of resurrection looks toward the last day and the final resurrection of the dead, when the *Lamb appears in glory. Jeoffry fully shares, then, in the worship of the Lamb on his throne, which is the binding theme of the whole poem.

This same combination of praise for the inextricably linked gifts of *creation and ‡salvation are evident in 'A Song to David'. Stanza 30 provides the key to this in 'His Word accomplishes the design'. 'Word' here does not simply indicate that God spoke. His Word is Christ; the Word in the prologue of John's Gospel (John 1:1 – 15) and the letters of St John (I John 1:1). In the New Testament and in later Christian doctrine, the world is created by God through Christ, the Word of God. Salvation, then, is implicit in creation; the ‡saviour is also the creator, so that it is entirely within the theological logic of the poem that this celebration of creation should end in praise 'of Him that brought salvation down'.

If we look at stanzas 41 – 70, we see that they emphasise the adoration yielded by *creation in and through its own being. Smart links this praise of creation for creation with Christ, the Word who created it; as we see in Stanza 71 'in the dome of Christ, the sparrows find a home'. This is an allusion to Psalm 84:3 where the sparrow and the swallow find their home in the Temple. Now Christ in his *resurrection is the new, eternal Temple in which creatures find their haven.

This poem is remarkable for the way in which Smart links *creation and ‡salvation through the *ten commandments (see Deuteronomy 5:6 – 21). With great theological acuity, Smart sees these commandments as protective of creation: the words of the Law are in tune with the Word of creation. Hence it also becomes logical to understand Jesus' claim to fulfil rather than destroy the Law. He, the creating and saving God, is already implicit in the commandments given to protect what was formed by him, as we see in stanzas 42 and 45. We can see, therefore, that though the poem is a song to David, it points us throughout beyond David to Christ whom David foreshadows and foretells. David, the builder of the Temple, the temporal king, points towards the King who is to come, the King of the universe, the creating Word, the new Temple, Christ, the fulfilment of the Law, Christ the ‡saviour.

David's role as poet is to be the †prophet, the one whose life and creativity focuses attention not on himself, but on Christ, the Truth (compare stanza 14). This high conception of the role of the poet, as speaker of and witness to truth, connects Smart's work to pre-Romantic theorising about the status and role of the poet as inspired seer found in a fuller development, for example, in Keats's 'Hyperion'. In Smart's poetry we find a theological vision, deeply rooted in the scriptures and in Christian doctrine, but also able to point us towards the ways in which Romantic poets employed this tradition to express their own vision.

QUESTIONS

1. Read the *Benedicite* in The Book of Common Prayer (Morning Prayer) and compare the mood and tone with those of 'Jubilate Agno'.
2. Read the *ten commandments in Deuteronomy 5:6–21 and examine how these are employed in stanzas 42–5 of 'A Song to David'. Consider the extent to which knowledge of this source illuminates the meaning of the poem.
3. To what extent do you think it is possible to appreciate Smart's poetry without an understanding of their religious impulse?

BIBLIOGRAPHY

Clement Hawes, ed., *Christopher Smart and the Enlightenment*, New York 1999.

Clement Hawes, *Mania and Literary Style: The Rhetoric of Enthusiasm From the Ranters to Christopher Smart*, Cambridge 1996.

Marcus Walsh, 'Profession and authority: the interpretation of the Bible in the seventeenth and eighteenth centuries', *Literature and Theology* 9 (1995), 383–98.

15

OLIVER GOLDSMITH, 'THE DESERTED VILLAGE'

[*BABL* pp. 814 f; *BAECP* pp. 459 f; *NA1* pp. 2857 f; *OA1* pp. 2235 f]

Goldsmith lived at a time of great change and poverty in rural England. It was a time when Enclosures were being enacted, and the small fields of minor landowners and farmers were being forcibly consolidated by the larger land-owners for their own convenience.[1] He has been widely criticised, not least by his contemporary Crabbe, for his idealisation of country living, his portrayal of it as abounding in joys and benevolence. In one sense, we can see him as partici-pating in the debate between the values of the countryside and the †city, which had been a literary theme from the times at least of the Roman poet Horace. But we can see in 'The Deserted Village' a specifically Christian angle on this debate. His strictures are largely an attack on the power of 'the world', that is, human life focused on material and sensory satisfaction, against the innocent life God ordained for human beings.

Rural life is idealised because it is understood as a life closer to that in-tended by the God who made *Adam and Eve to inhabit and cultivate a †garden. It is their succumbing to pride, to lust, to greed—that is, to the values of the town and the 'development' of the country—that leads to the loss of *Eden and the loss of harmony. The values of the town are those of Bunyan's 'Vanity Fair' in *Pilgrim's Progress*, and rather than the Christian being †tempted by Vanity Fair, it is as though Vanity Fair has overtaken the countryside and all are obliged to inhabit it (see the essay on John Bunyan).

This triumph of Vanity Fair is evident in lines such as 'ill fares the land' (lines 51–68). Money triumphs over human values; princes and lords are made

---

1. The first main changes in land ownership and distribution took place in the years 1755–70, when 38% of Parliamentary Enclosures took place. To pass through parliament an Enclosure Act needed only the support of the owners of about three-quarters of the land in the parish and in many cases this might be a very few men. These landowners were then empowered legally to enclose the common land (which, as its name implies, was for the use of all the people and belonged to all) and the old arable open fields, and use them as their own. See further David Hey, ed., *The Oxford Companion to Local and Family History*, Oxford 1996.

'by breath' because it is by the word and whim of humans that they are elevated. But breath also suggests flimsiness, a trifling state, an empty state, that is, vanity. The lines also evoke echoes of such Psalms as Psalm 146, warning against reliance on princes; Psalm 37, emphasising the vanity of the wicked and exploiters of the poor; and Psalms 90, 103, and 144, reminding readers of the brevity of life and hence the vanity of human pretensions. Goldsmith suggests that the land is possessed by those who ignore this advice, so that it is literally overtaken by the vanities of wealth and pomp, evidence of the triumph of greed and pride.

'Pomp' is an important term in this context since Christians were frequently adjured to reject the 'pomp and show' of †Satan. This connotation is highlighted when we meet the term again in lines 259–64, 'the long pomp, the midnight masquerade'. Here the word 'pomp' evokes only the pandering to sensual pleasures, which are revealed as empty and deluding promises, echoing again the mood of the Psalms. Furthermore, the picture of rural poverty and of inhospitality in the towns is not only a portrait of the triumph of 'the world'; it is also a portrait of the neglect of the poor and of the worker roundly condemned in the Old and New Testaments (see, for example, Isaiah 1:10–17; 10:1–3; Amos 5:10–13; 8:4–7; Micah 2:7–11).

Line 105, 'no surly porter stands in guilty state', echoes the *parable in Luke's Gospel of the rich man unaware of the beggar, Lazarus, at his gate (Luke 16:19–31). It recalls many traditional stories of the spurning of Christ in the appearance of a beggar, derived in part from the great *parable of the sheep and the goats, in which Christ identifies himself with the hungry and the homeless. Those who spurn the needy and hungry find themselves spurned by Christ when he returns at the end of time (Matthew 25:31–46).

The picture of the aged widow left in penury and of the peasant's eviction from grazing on common land, evokes many Old Testament strictures against abandonment of the aged and the widow and recalls the command in Deuteronomy that fields should not be harvested to the very edges so that the poor can glean; the fruits of the earth should always be regarded as gifts equally for the poor and the widow (see Deuteronomy 24:19–22; 26:12–15). In England, the picking of such 'scanty blade' by the peasants' animals is now denied. The basic biblical understanding is that the land belongs to God. The earth is his gift to sustain all people, making all possession of it provisional and subject to his primary purpose. This understanding of the land, Goldsmith is saying, is being fundamentally flouted by the Enclosure movement.

The portrait of the village preacher has much in common with the Christian ideal outlined four centuries earlier by Chaucer in his depiction of the ‡parson of the town. Goldsmith's preacher is marked by all the characteristics of the Christ-like minister. He is a mature Christian, not blown about by every wind of doctrine, as St Paul says (see Ephesians 4:14–16), nor with an eye to obtaining favour and advancement, like the *hireling shepherd (see John 10:11–13), as we see in lines 145–6. He is selfless in putting the ‡sinner's needs before his own, like a *good shepherd who disregards his own safety in going after his own sheep (compare Jesus' *parable of the lost sheep in Luke 15:4–7). As a good father in God, he admonishes people to avoid the sin, but forbears to pass †judgement. Unlike the rich man in the *parable of the rich man and Lazarus, he knows and welcomes the beggar at his gate. The prodigal son finds welcome and acceptance (see the *parable of the prodigal son, the welcome of the ‡repentant wastrel in Luke 15:11–32). Like God, he is no respecter of persons but gives himself for all (see Matthew 5:43–6) and inspires not only by his teaching but by his own example (lines 166–70). Most of all, he is a man who 'seeks first the kingdom of heaven' as Jesus taught in the *sermon on the mount (Matthew 6:33). His †love for his flock is without self-interest, but comes from his centredness on God.

Goldsmith's idealisation of rustic life enables him to reiterate the Christian values that he understood to have pervaded English life and that he now sees as disappearing under the onslaught of the values of 'the world', a world of conspicuous consumption and neglect of the poor, a world in which people may gain everything material and yet lose their ‡soul.

QUESTIONS

1. Compare and contrast this treatment of rural life with any other that you have studied. What do the similarities and differences suggest about Goldsmith's vision?
2. Look up some of the references to the Psalms and examine how their content and tone influence the content and tone of this poem.
3. In what ways does your knowledge of the biblical background of the poem inform your appreciation of its meaning and artistry?

BIBLIOGRAPHY

William Black, *Goldsmith*, London 1878.

Harold Bloom, ed., *Oliver Goldsmith: Modern Critical Views*, New York 1987.

James Hall Pitman, *Goldsmith's Animated Nature: A Study of Goldsmith*, London 1924.

16

WILLIAM COWPER

[*BABL* pp. 825 f; *BAECP* pp. 526 f; *NA1* pp. 2875 f; *OA1* pp. 2245 f]

In the case of William Cowper, as the introduction in *NA1* makes clear, the circumstances of the poet's life are an inescapable part of any critical discussion of his poetry. For our purposes, this particularly involves an examination of his experience of Christian faith. There has been some controversy about the relationship between this aspect of his life, his mental state, and his poetry. It was after the first severe episode of his mental illness that Cowper experienced an ‡Evangelical conversion. It is clear that his episodes of mental illness happened both before and after his conversion but that after his second serious episode of illness he formed the apparently unshakeable conviction that he had committed an unforgivable ‡sin. The notion of 'unforgivable sin' in Christianity arises from a literal interpretation of a combination of two passages in the New Testament:

> I say unto you … he that shall blaspheme against the Holy Ghost hath never forgiveness, but is in danger of eternal damnation. (Mark 3:28–9)

> For it is impossible for those who were once enlightened … and were made partakers of the Holy Ghost, And have tasted the good word of God … If they shall fall away, to renew them again unto repentance. (Hebrews 6:4–6)

Cowper's logic was that his conversion was the time when he had been 'enlightened, and … made partaker … of the Holy Ghost' and that his subsequent attempted suicide was to 'fall away' and thus 'blaspheme against the Holy Ghost'. Thus he had 'no forgiveness' and was 'in danger of eternal damnation', which could not be escaped by fresh ‡repentance. It was probably the finality of the consequences of attempted suicide that made him think of this act as an irreversible apostasy.

The logic of this literal interpretation has always persuaded a small number of ‡Evangelical Christians to feel like this about themselves; yet reading

Cowper's letters, one feels, first of all, that in his relatively sane periods, this belief was partly used to avoid the publicity of attending church — a publicity that Cowper perhaps rightly thought might be dangerous to his mental equilibrium; and secondly that in the severer episodes of his illness, logic was hardly a factor.

This is not to deny that this is what Cowper believed about himself, as he repeatedly asserts, but what then remains startling is that he could write so tenderly of his ‡Evangelical conversion and so lyrically of other Christian themes. 'The Stricken Deer' (*NA1* pp. 2877 f) speaks of Christ, bearing the wounds of the *crucifixion, healing Cowper's own wounds and bidding him live. Cowper, the stricken and now healed deer, removes himself from the herd and observes them from afar (for example in those passages in *The Task* which speak of London society). There are obvious Old Testament resonances here: 'All we like sheep have gone astray; we have turned every one to his own way; and the LORD hath laid on him the iniquity of us all' (Isaiah 53:6).

Cowper claimed that in *The Task* his descriptions of rural landscape and domestic interior and exterior scenes (*NA1* pp. 2875 f) have a naturalness both of observation and of language. This impression is heightened by an intrusion of the poet as personal observer, which can sometimes sound strange to modern ears but which is another of the reasons why this poetry always draws our attention to the life of its author.

The theology of *The Task* is increasingly orthodox and ‡Evangelical. In Book 1, nature and landscape are hardly theologised at first. It is only after Cowper has introduced the theme of the †city, and its corruption, that he moves to the famous assertion 'God made the country, and man made the town' (749). The title of Book 2, 'The Time-Piece', is at first confusing because we expect a reference, as in 'The Sofa', to the domestic item of the title, and there is none. But Book 2 is Cowper's explicit reading of the signs of the times (see Matthew 16:3), in which phenomena, from natural disasters to corruption in the church and the universities, are explained in theological terms. In Books 3 and 4, the ethical and religious notes are more quietly pervasive, as in 'The Garden' and 'The Winter Evening' Cowper moves from the very domestic to wider concerns then back again. Books 5 and 6, 'The Winter Morning Walk' and 'The Winter Walk at Noon', are more overtly religious. Here nature is viewed in Pauline terms as testimony to the greatness and goodness of God, touched by the hand of Christ. A surprisingly modern, though not vegetarian, sensibility to animal welfare is expressed here — just as elsewhere Cowper's typically Whig and ‡Evangelical views on slavery and monarchy would not seem entirely out of place today. In the theological conclusions of Book 6, Cowper paints strong pictures drawn from Christian ‡eschatology: Isaiah's vision of an entirely ‡re-deemed nature where 'The lion and the libbard and the bear / Graze with the fearless flocks' (6:773 f, cf. Isaiah 11:7); and the new Jerusalem of Revelation 21, 'Bright as a sun the sacred city shines!' (6:800).

The 'Landscape Described' and 'Crazy Kate' (*NA1* pp. 2875 f), both re-flect the motif of the sea, which Cowper persistently finds threatening. It is the sea that kills Kate's lover. In the landscape the noise of the floods is safe because 'distant' (191); only the 'softer voice of … [the] fountain' is allowed to be 'neighb'ring' (192). Whether Cowper's fear of the sea owed anything to his long relationship with John Newton, who had been a sea captain, and indeed a slaver, and in whose preaching the sea was a key theme, must remain conjec-tural; but in *The Castaway* (*BABL* pp. 839 f; *BAECP* pp. 552 f; *NA1* pp. 2880 f; *OA1* pp. 2248 f), Cowper's last original extant English poem, the image of the sea is given full and terrifying scope and again linked very directly to the poet's own condition.

This poem, based on a true story that Cowper had read (see lines 49–52), was written after Mary Unwin's death in Norfolk, to where his well-meaning relative Rev. Johnny Johnson had removed the couple at the onset of Cowper's last and longest bout of illness in July 1795. He never recovered to the level of health he had known at Olney, and later at Weston, and died in April 1800. The manuscript of *The Castaway* is dated March 1799. There can be few more bit-terly beautiful expressions of the despair of mental illness than this. Cowper enters fully into the feelings of both the castaway and his shipmates but also shows that he has graphically imagined the dreadful moment of drowning, 'he drank / The stifling wave, and then he sank' (46–7). The style of *The Castaway* is in general more lyrical than, for example, *The Task*, which only serves to heighten the brutal simplicity of those last four monosyllables of this line, 'and then he sank'. The analogy of the drowning man is explicitly religious: 'No voice divine the storm allayed; / No light propitious shone' (61–2) and the end-ing captures the deep loneliness that Cowper felt in his despair: 'We perished, each, alone.' How much emphasis is added by the commas.

Cowper clearly consistently believed that this was his ending and, in his moments of deepest illness, believed it with a painful destructiveness. The pres-ent writer hopes for him what he wrote of himself in happier times: 'The Lord shall be my righteousness / The Lord for ever mine' (William Cowper, *Olney Hymns*, 'Jehovah our Righteousness', 19–20).

QUESTIONS

1. What, if any, was the effect of Cowper's ‡Evangelical conversion on his poetry?
2. What did Coleridge mean by describing Cowper's poetry (approvingly) as 'religious chit-chat'?
3. From your reading of his poetry, what views about personal ‡salvation and ‡damnation do you consider Cowper held?

BIBLIOGRAPHY

James King, *William Cowper: A Biography*, Durham 1986.

J. Sambrook, ed., *William Cowper: The Task and Selected Other Poems*, London and New York 1994.

W.T. Webb, ed., *Selections from Cowper's Letters*, London and New York 1895.

Section 4

THE ROMANTICS
AND VICTORIANS

1

OVERVIEW: ROMANTICISM

The English Romantics are often connected with the biblical and Christian tradition in English literature only in so far as they are seen to react against it. We see them exploring a world of sensation or adopting an approach to nature that seems, in some ways, to reject Christian views. Percy Bysshe Shelley, for example, consciously rejected the Christianity of his time, and neither Keats nor Wordsworth proposed an approach to nature that would have happily been adopted in the pulpit during the early years of the nineteenth century.

This situation, however, issues partly from the rather dry, rationalistic approach to religion with which our poets were acquainted. Mainstream Anglicanism had adopted a rationalist approach to questions of faith. Works like William Paley's *Natural Theology*, attempting to provide evidence of the existence and attributes of the deity, made of religion a dry exercise of reason in which the living universe was reduced to a set of proofs for the existence of God. The establishment of the church seemed equally to reduce Christianity to a system for maintaining the social and political hierarchy, which the rise in republican thinking and action was questioning.

Indeed, Shelley's early rejection of Christianity in his pamphlet *A Case for the Abolition of Christianity* was in fact a criticism of the imposition of compulsory Christianity on the people. He was concerned with the injustice ensuing for those who did not share orthodox Christian beliefs and for the way in which Christian beliefs were used to justify inhumane treatment of working people. It is Shelley the idealist who is disappointed by the lack of idealism that he finds in his contemporary Christianity.

What the English Romantics found, however, in the German Romantics and in the pre-Romantic English writers of the eighteenth century was in fact a reflection of an alternative theological vision derived ultimately from the ‡patristic (that is, belonging to the church ‡Fathers) and ‡mystical tradition in Christianity. It is for this reason that a later generation of Anglicans like the ‡Tractarians and F.D. Maurice, Christian poets like Robert Browning, and fantasy writers like George MacDonald, were able to integrate insights from Romantic poetry into their own theological views. This earlier theology was developed in an intellectual environment in which Platonism was the dominant philosophy, so that its expressions and modes of thought are frequently Platonic in form.

The two aspects of Platonism that most affect our discussion are Plato's theory of forms and his understanding of the mind. Plato taught that, behind all forms in the world, there exists the eternal 'idea' of that form. Love, for example, exists as idea. All experiences of love are a participation in this idea, so that the many experiences are but manifestations of the one. This was contradictory to the later Aristotelian idea that it is from our experiences of the many, e.g., our various experiences of love, that we form the idea or the concept of the one, of love. This has important consequences for our understanding of intellectual activity. As F.D. Maurice says, the Platonist-inspired thinker is a digger, not a creator; his thinking digs to expose pre-existing, if not previously recognised, realities.

The second aspect of importance here is the understanding of the mind, or *nous* (the Greek word for mind). Mind here is not discursive thought, but pure knowing or insight. *Nous* in the human being is a fragment of the eternal *nous* that must be released from illusion so that it can ascend to the Godhead. This notion gave the early ‡Fathers a language in which to express the †incarnation as the ultimate ‡revelation of the unseen and of the relationship between the creator and his created images.

The human being was made as an image of God to share in the life of the Godhead, just as forms participate in the reality of the idea which they manifest. And, similarly, if *nous* is 'the spark of God within', which must ascend to union with eternal Mind, so the image of God within human beings could be brought to fulness by the ‡salvation won through Christ in his †incarnation, death, and *resurrection so that they are again free to share in the life of God. Although the ‡Fathers used some existing thought forms, they nevertheless eschewed the Platonic view of the body and created matter since God had ennobled *creation in taking it upon himself in the †incarnation.

It was this Platonised Christianity that the English Romantics imbibed through the German Romantics such as Novalis and through voices in eighteenth-century literature such as Shaftesbury's 'School of Sensibility'. Through these, they encountered elements of the ‡patristic doctrine of the Cambridge Platonists (if not always directly as was the case with Coleridge). The poet Gray's letters and Thompson's 'Hymn to the Supreme Being' reintroduced in different terms the earlier Christian concept of 'the book of nature'. God was revealed and made accessible in the created world, which was a living entity rather than the mechanism envisaged by ‡Deism and reinforced by such works as Paley's *Natural Theology*.

Alongside this came a renewed interest in Hebraic poetry. This brought the Romantics into contact with the panentheism of the Old Testament world-view. Whilst pantheism identifies the world with God, panentheism believes all things dwell *in* God: they express him, but are not identical with him. So, for example, 'The heavens declare the glory of God' (Psalm 19:1) but are not *the same thing as* him. The earth or the heavens may belong to God and enthrone him, but they are not equated with him. This panentheism opened the way for the Romantics to make a new response to nature and to rediscover, in their own way, what medieval Christians had conceived of as 'Dame Natura', Lady Nature, the vicegerent of God.

If Hebraic poetry contributed to the Romantics' reawakening to nature, it also profoundly influenced their understanding of the human person, especially their understanding of the poet, in ways that chimed with platonically inspired works such as Akenside's 'The Pleasures of Imagination'. Here the poet is the seer or †prophet, the genius divinely inspired to see and speak the truth. Hence the exploration of the poet's own inner life was seen not as a flight into egocentric subjectivity, but as a means of gaining access to truth. What the poet is given in this inner †journey is not understood as the expression of individual views or experiences, but as a universally valid statement about humanity. The poet is to make the journey to the centre of the self where the truth about human life can be known. The poet expresses a reality common to all those 'mute inglorious Miltons' who have no poetic genius or daemon.

This conception of the poet clearly links him with the Hebraic †prophet. Prophets speak not from their own volition but because they are chosen to speak, and to speak not their own thoughts but those of God. The Hebraic prophet, furthermore, was generally the outsider who suffered for the gift of vision and who underwent some kind of purification for being able to undertake the prophetic task. So Elijah was forty days in the †desert (I Kings 19:1–8) and Isaiah's lips were purified by burning coals (Isaiah 6:1–9). This was one element in the Romantics' concept of the poet as the visionary outsider, but also as one who must lose his own individuality in order to be able to see and speak as a representative person, as we find in Keats's 'The Fall of Hyperion'.

Another related aspect of the Old Testament †prophet was his suffering on behalf of the people and his denunciation of the injustice within his society. This spoke to a generation that had witnessed the French Revolution and saw no alleviation of the human suffering in the developing industrialisation within their society. The ensuing intellectual atmosphere freed Romantics like Wordsworth, Shelley, and Keats to explore the fringes of the platonised Judeo-Christian tradition in, for example, the writings from ‡heretical philosophy and from the Jewish ‡mystical writings, the ‡Kabbala, in order to develop their understanding of the spiritual basis for human interrelationship.

In such ways the 'Romantic vision' owed much to the biblical and Christian tradition in western culture, a tradition more openly embraced by Coleridge, whose development of Kantian thought regarding reason and understanding is directly related to that of the Cambridge Platonists and whose definition of imagination as 'the representation of the eternal act of creation in the infinite "I am"', sets him squarely within a Christian Platonic tradition. 'I am' is the name of God given to Moses from the burning bush (Exodus 3:1–6). For Coleridge, the act of imagination is a participation in the infinite creativity of God; the human mind produces manifestations of the mind of God.

It is the Romantics' renewal, albeit frequently in heterodox guise, of an older theological understanding of nature, selfhood, and creativity that enabled the ‡Tractarians, the revivers of Catholicism within Anglicanism, who were never 'liberal' in their theological thinking, to incorporate Romantic insights into their work. Keble, one of the leaders of the Movement and Oxford Professor of Poetry, taught that Plato was 'the gospel to the Greeks', that is, God's way of preparing them for the full ‡revelation of Christianity. They were capable of finding in the Romantics a similar echo of that revelation.

QUESTIONS

1. How would you characterise Keats's approach to the role of the poet in 'The Fall of Hyperion'? How would you relate this to the role of the †prophet?
2. Do you find a similar vision in Shelley's 'Hymn to Intellectual Beauty'?
3. What aspects of these two poems would you consider to have a potential attractiveness to Victorian Christians who were concerned about an excessive emphasis on individualism and the breakdown of awareness of human interrelationship?

BIBLIOGRAPHY

David Jasper, *The Sacred and Secular Canon in Romanticism: Preserving the Sacred Truths*, Basingstoke 1999.

Stephen Prickett, *Origins of Narrative: The Romantic Appropriation of the Bible*, 2nd edn, Cambridge 2005. This is an essential work for appreciating the Romantics' approach to the Bible.

David Pym, *The Religious Thought of Samuel Taylor Coleridge*, New York 1979.

2

APOCALYPTIC AND THE
IDEA OF JERUSALEM

[*NA2* pp. 117 f]

The Greek word *apokaluptein* means 'to reveal': hence the last book of the New Testament, usually called Revelation, is sometimes called the ‡Apocalypse. The adjective 'apocalyptic' has come to refer specifically to the kind of imagery and symbolism found in Revelation, and also in the second half of the book of Daniel, to some extent in Ezekiel, and in some of the inter-testamental literature. In English literature, Revelation becomes especially important in connection with Romanticism in the immediate aftermath of the French Revolution. Revelation predicts the end-time: a time of great upheaval and violence, after which God will establish a thousand years — a millennium — of peace. Put simply, there was a tendency for English writers and artists to think that the French Revolution was part of the upheaval that would usher in the end time.

It is important to point out that, although many of these thinkers, artists, and political actors undoubtedly regarded themselves as seeing and implementing the start of a new era, nevertheless the impulse to analyse great and disturbing political events in terms of predictions of the end time is exactly what created Jewish ‡apocalyptic literature in the first place, more than two and a half thousand years earlier. And always at the heart of that ‡revelation, really or symbolically — usually both — is the †city of Jerusalem. Apocalyptic in Ezekiel, and the apocalyptic traces in Isaiah 40 onwards (known as Deutero-Isaiah) and other †prophets, were a response to the fall of Jerusalem to the Babylonians in the seventh century before Christ; and there is an astonishingly direct artistic line from that event to Blake's *Jerusalem*.[1]

In the first millennium BC, King David establishes a national capital at Jerusalem and, crucially, establishes the religious cult of the Lord there, though it is his son Solomon who first builds a temple in Jerusalem. This temple is the

---

1. And even, of course, a similarly direct political line to the founding of the modern state of Israel.

place where the Lord is thought especially to dwell. When Jerusalem falls to foreign invaders, it is religiously, as well as politically, a cataclysmic event. Almost immediately, the †prophets prophesy that after a period of chastisement in exile, 'a remnant will return' (Jeremiah), and a new Jerusalem will rise from the ruins, to be reached by a new highway through the †desert (Isaiah). This is the beginning of the ‡apocalyptic, and specifically of the idea of a new Jerusalem, in the Hebrew scriptures. A remnant did return across the †desert and the new Jerusalem did indeed rise from the ruins: and we have the story in the books of Ezra, Nehemiah, Haggai, and Zechariah.[2] It rose to fall again, however, first coming under the post-Alexander Ptolemaic and Seleucid dynasties and, later, under the Roman empire, which succeeded them. It is the Ptolemaic and Seleucid period, and especially the Seleucid desecration of the temple in Jerusalem, that is the background of the apocalyptic imagery in the second half of the book of Daniel, which is probably the first extended passage of ‡apocalyptic Jewish literature that we know of.[3]

A key figure in the establishment of the expected new Jerusalem is the Messiah, 'one like the Son of man' to whom is given 'everlasting dominion' in Daniel 7:13. Under Roman rule expectation of his coming continues, so that, 150 years or so after the book of Daniel, the pressing question about figures like John the Baptist and Jesus of Nazareth is whether they are the fulfilments of that expectation. This is exactly the question that John sends his disciples to ask of Jesus in the New Testament: 'Art thou he that should come, or do we look for another?' (Matthew 11:3). The New Testament's answer is, of course, that Jesus is the expected Messiah, the new king, but his death poses problems that, in the earliest Christian texts like I and II Thessalonians, are resolved by the expectation of his imminent return, or *second coming.

Meanwhile, expectation that the Romans will leave or be driven out of Jerusalem eventually leads to an uprising of which the result is the second destruction of Jerusalem in AD 70. By that time, indeed some time earlier, the expectation of Jesus' imminent return has been disappointed, but his reappearance on earth is regarded as deferred rather than cancelled. The book of Revelation unites these strands of ‡apocalyptic expectation from a Christian perspective. The middle chapters of Revelation depict a cosmic warfare waged between †Satan and forces of †darkness against the †angels of †light, with ter-

---

2. Again, the resonances of this can be very modern: compare the repair and rebuilding of Berlin in the reunited Germany and the huge new road-building programme designed to carry prosperity to former East Germany.

3. One could argue that some parts of Ezekiel might make this claim; but it is clear, at least, that Daniel has more similarities to later ‡apocalyptic literature than Ezekiel.

rible consequences for the earth. Rome is also still part of the enemy of the Christians in Revelation, not least because by this time (around AD 100) direct persecution of Christians by the emperors Nero and Domitian has already occurred. The apocalyptic expectation is still expressed in terms of a new Jerusalem, to replace the one that has been destroyed. This one, however, is not to be built up from the ruins, but to come down, ready-made, from †heaven: it might be an ideal †city on earth, but it can also be easily understood as a symbol rather than a reality.

At the centre of the new Jerusalem is the figure of the returned Christ, the †sacrificial *Lamb of God. This is vital for the reinterpretation of the ‡apocalyptic that becomes the millenarianism of the early Romantic period, because it means that at the centre of the new ideal †city will be a figure who is human. The apocalyptic figure of the Son of Man is originally found in Daniel, and the title 'Son of Man' becomes Jesus' favourite self-designation in the synoptic gospels. Since millenarian expectation arises in the context in which the Rights of Man are the key theme of the new political thought, it is easier than one might think to transfer the millenarian expectation to the emerging secularism of modernity.

Crucially, too, the new Jerusalem does not have a temple. This is a specifically Christian (i.e., non-Jewish) motif, making the usual New Testament claim that the old Jewish covenant is superseded by Christ, but the absence of a religious shrine, as such, at the centre of the †city undoubtedly also facilitated the appropriation of millenarian ideas by secular thinkers.

In Christian religious terms, millenarianism resonates with Protestantism. At one level this might seem obvious: at the ‡Reformation, Protestantism emerges not only as theological, but also as social, protest; the one Republican period in British history was thoroughly, if not extremely, Protestant. Perhaps more tellingly, Protestantism had, and still has, the tendency to elevate individual religious interpretation at the expense of ecclesiastical tradition. So Protestant and post-Protestant thinkers tend to assert the right to interpret the symbolism of the ‡apocalyptic for themselves and to apply it to their own reading of the signs of the times. Sometimes, as in the case of the Irvingites or the Plymouth Brethren, this leads to small sects who retain their ‡Trinitarian Christian orthodoxy but take on very specific views of the imminence of the *second coming of Christ. In other cases, as for example the ‡Deist and ‡Unitarian movement, new unorthodox doctrines of God arise from the freedom to think one's own religious thoughts which Protestantism offers. The proliferation of new Christian and para-Christian sects at this period is matched by the proliferation of different views of the new millennium, which in the end contributes much to the rapid decline of this kind of thought.

The revolutionary theme, especially from France, has already been mentioned. It is important to note that, although English thinkers were repulsed by the increasing bloodiness of the Revolution, this aspect of change was in some ways consonant with the violence that pervades the middle chapters of the book of Revelation and might be considered as to be expected at the dawn of the new millennium. Even Napoleon, Britain's enemy, could be reconfigured into some of the more negative roles of Revelation, as he swept across Europe, often leaving devastation in his wake. Thus the millenarian hope survived for some time after the French Revolution but seemed to offer no very realistic hope of ushering in a universally peaceful era.

Industrialisation was developing at this time too. Its particular association with the element of fire, and thus with †hell, was certainly another factor in the rise in millenarianism. Industrialisation offered new, often desperately ugly, landscapes of which fire and smoke were key constituents, as well as the increasingly common sight of human beings living and working in filthily overcrowded conditions. Tim Fulford writes:

> De Loutherborg, looking at the furnaces in Coalbrookdale, imagined 'the Industrial Revolution as Hell, foreshadowing John Martin's perception of the Black Country as an image of the final conflagration'. Contemporary Britain's 'dark, Satanic mills' were, for others as for Blake, symbols of an apocalypse, and it was the mission of artists to supersede these symbols with prophecies of a millennium in which humanity would be renewed.[4]

This image, like all the others we have considered, makes clear how deeply embedded was the book of Revelation, and indeed the whole Bible, in the culture of Britain at this time. If the French Revolution was an explicitly secular and antireligious phenomenon, it nonetheless remains the case that British thinkers mostly took the categories already at their disposal to analyse it and to predict its effects, and that those categories were derived from the Christian culture that remained, for some time, the dominant cultural narrative of Britain.

---

4. Tim Fulford, 'Millenarianism and the study of Romanticism', in Fulford, ed., *Romanticism and Millenarianism*, p. 15. Growing up in the Black Country of the English Midlands, the present writer knew a local rhyme, 'The Devil stood on Brierley Hill and far around him gazed / And said, "I nevermore shall be at Hell's fierce flames amazed"'.

QUESTIONS

1. Blake and Priestley (among others) supported the French and American Revolutions. Why?
2. Wordsworth and others initially supported the French Revolution, but were ultimately repelled. What did they hope for, and how did their hopes change?
3. How important was the imagery of ‡apocalyptic in determining responses to change at this time?

BIBLIOGRAPHY

Tim Fulford, ed., *Romanticism and Millenarianism*, New York 2002. Fulford's introduction to these essays is probably the best short introduction to this topic in its relation to literature.

Jon Mee, *Dangerous Enthusiasm: William Blake and the Culture of Radicalism in the 1790s*, Oxford 1992.

3

WILLIAM BLAKE,
SONGS OF INNOCENCE AND EXPERIENCE

[*BABL* pp. 911 f; *BAR* pp. 60 f; *NA2* pp. 43 f; *OA2* pp. 17 f]

The subtitle of Blake's *Songs* in their later printings was 'the two Contrary States of the Human Soul'. Although *Songs of Innocence* was published separately, from 1789 onwards, *Experience* was always published with *Innocence*, first in 1794. In discussing the *Songs*, it is customary to make reference to the lines from Blake's *The Marriage of Heaven and Hell*, 'Without Contraries is no progression. Attraction and Repulsion, Reason and Energy, Love and Hate, are necessary to Human existence.'[1] This is a useful perspective, because although *Innocence* and *Experience* are obviously contrary to each other, with poems exploring contrary states in the two parts, the emphasis should perhaps be placed on the *progression*: Innocence and Experience are in themselves inadequate for the goal that Blake envisages. Thus the pessimistic feel of the collection, moving from the tripping rhythms and pastoral images of *Innocence*, to the darker and more complex themes and images of *Experience*, may well give way to a sense of optimism, in that neither state is adequate for human progression.

Blake was never quite orthodox, yet his works are full of biblical references and theological arguments. The *Songs of Innocence and Experience* are filled with images and expressions that slightly skew Christian ideas. For example, the 'Introduction' to *Innocence* portrays 'The Holy Word' (one of St John's images for Christ in John 1) wandering weeping in the evening in what appears to be the Garden of *Eden and 'Calling the lapsèd Soul', a quite new vision of the *fall and its aftermath.[2] There is also direct and explicit criticism of the church's involvement in exploitation and oppression: in 'London', the call of the boy-sweep 'Every blackning Church appalls' (10); and in 'The Little Vagabond', the speaker says, 'the Church is cold, / But the Ale-house is healthy & pleasant & warm' (1–2).

---

1. Erdman, *Poetry and Prose of William Blake*, p. 34.
2. Though the syntax of the poem is ambiguous, as the footnote in *NA2* p. 49 observes, the reference to Genesis 3:9, 'And the LORD God called unto Adam', directly following the verse that refers to 'the LORD God walking ... amongst the trees of the garden', Genesis 3:8, surely makes the nature of the caller clear.

The two 'Holy Thursday' poems illustrate as well as any the contrasts of the contrary states of Innocence and Experience. In *Innocence* there is a strong narrative thread: the children walk to St Paul's, sit, raise their hands, and sing. The picture is rich with primary colours, 'red & blue & green', and natural similes and metaphors, 'white as snow' 'like Thames' waters', 'flowers', 'lambs', 'like a mighty wind'. There is repetition of 'innocent' and 'multitudes'. The poem ends with a simple moral: 'Then cherish pity, lest you drive an angel from your door' (12), a reference to Hebrews 13:2 as noted in most editions. The connection of the moral with the rest of the song is tenuous, but it perhaps suggests that the innocent children are †angels.[3]

'Holy Thursday' in *Experience* is tense and questioning, uncertain. The natural images of *Innocence* are transformed into conditions of hardship and difficulty, here the 'babes' live sunless, with bare fields, thorns, and eternal winter. The poem is built on contradiction, both superficially in that the land is 'rich and fruitful' while being 'a land of poverty', but especially in the last stanza. This in some ways answers to the moral of 'Holy Thursday' in *Innocence*: that gave instruction to generosity and hospitality, but this simply asserts that the sun and rain make hunger and poverty unimaginable, when clearly they are not so. There is possibly a reference to Matthew 5:45 here: 'your Father which is in heaven ... maketh his sun to rise on the evil and on the good, and sendeth rain on the just and on the unjust'. God provides for the world, and there is no reason for hunger and poverty. But the assertion does not make it so. The point is perhaps that people fail to make social issues personal, leaving matters as they are rather than doing something. Abstract generalisation substitutes for earnest personal involvement. Here, then, the two poems clearly exemplify contrary points of view.

'The Clod and the Pebble' in *Songs of Experience* is a poem without a counterpart in *Innocence*, at least partly because it contains contraries within it. The poem begins with reference to I Corinthians 13, St Paul's characterisation of Christian †love: 'Charity', says the apostle, 'seeketh not her own' (I Corinthians 13:5). In the poem, the clod 'trodden with the cattle's feet', sings,

> Love seeketh not itself to please,
> Nor for itself hath any care
> But for another gives its ease
> And builds a Heaven in Hell's despair.

---

3. The ironic reading of this poem, as exemplified in the footnotes of *OA2* but often found elsewhere, is perhaps oversubtle, or at least not the point of view of *Innocence*.

The pebble 'warbles' the exact opposite, 'Love seeketh only self to please ... / And builds a Hell in Heaven's despite.'

Despite the utter simplicity of expression in the poem, the difficulty here is to grasp a perspective from which the verses might be interpreted. Is the voice referring to the roles of the sexes, with the clod representing the female and pebble the male? Is the whole view that of Experience, hence purely cynical? Is the voice of the clod the voice of Innocence heard by the ear of Experience? Superficially, the clod's way is better than the pebble's, but it is joyless, whereas the pebble does at least experience joy and delight. But perhaps the most disturbing word in the poem is the one that begins the songs of each of the voices, 'Love'.

'Love' in 'The Clod and the Pebble' is deeply ambiguous. It can be self-denying and joyless, or self-assertive and abusive. The voice of this poem will neither simply accept the biblical definition of †love (and perhaps the fact that it does not use the biblical term 'charity' is significant here), nor deny the humanity of even the most abusive versions of 'love'.

This is at least partly because Blake had radical ideas about divine and human nature. He reacted very strongly against the ‡Deism of his time, seeing it as mechanistic and rationalistic. The poem 'The Divine Image' in *Songs of Innocence*, for example, refuses to distinguish the divine and the human:

> For Mercy, Pity, Peace and Love
> Is God, our father dear;
> and Mercy, Pity, Peace and Love,
> Is Man, his child and care. (5–8)

Further, the voice of Innocence refuses to distinguish people on the grounds of religion:

> And all must love the human form,
> In heathen, Turk, or Jew,
> Where Mercy, Love, & Pity dwell,
> There God is dwelling too. (17–20)

There is a passing reference to the Book of Common Prayer here: one of the collects (set prayers) for ‡Good Friday prays to God, 'Have mercy upon all Jews, Turks, Infidels, and Hereticks, and take from them all ignorance, hardness of heart, and contempt of thy word.' Once again, the voice sets itself against the authority of orthodox belief.

Blake's radical and visionary theology is presented and explored in the later works. What we have seen in examining the *Songs of Innocence and Experience* is that the poet's work needs to be read with care: the simplicity of the verse belies the demanding, questioning, and radical nature of the ideas it contains.

QUESTIONS

1. Is Blake's work Christian? What evidence have you found in support of your answer?
2. How important to the whole collection of *Songs of Innocence and Experience* is the idea of progression? How do you see it being worked out?
3. How convincingly are the 'two contrary states of the human soul' portrayed in the *Songs of Innocence and Experience*?

BIBLIOGRAPHY

G.E. Bentley, Jr, *The Stranger from Paradise: A Biography of William Blake*, New Haven CT and London 2001. A biography of the poet by one of the foremost Blake scholars.

Margaret Bottrall, ed., *William Blake, Songs of Innocence and Experience: A Casebook*, London 1970. A good collection of essays.

David V. Erdman, ed., *The Complete Poetry and Prose of William Blake*, newly rev. edn, New York 1988. A standard edition of the works.

Northrop Frye, ed., *Blake: A Collection of Critical Essays*, Englewood Cliffs NJ 1966: an older selection of essays, several on *Songs of Innocence and Experience*, but also some exploring wider issues in relation to this author.

4

WILLIAM WORDSWORTH

[*BACL* pp. 551 f ('Tintern Abbey' and the 'Immortality' ode);
BAR pp. 385 f (the 13-book *Prelude* of 1804–6);
NA2 pp. 219 f, esp. 303 f; *OA2* pp. 124 f, esp. 187 f]

It is generally held that Wordsworth wrote his best poetry in the years between *Lyrical Ballads* (1798) and about 1805.[1] In the *Lyrical Ballads* he was finding a poetic voice and exploring ideas about poetry, its nature, focus, and language. By 1805 the poet had written drafts of *The Prelude* but also most of the poems included in *NA2* and *OA2*: the 'Immortality' ode, 'Resolution and Independence' and other often-quoted pieces such as 'I Wandered Lonely as a Cloud' and the sonnet 'Composed upon Westminster Bridge'. In these poems, with a few false notes, Wordsworth has achieved what readers most value: the immediacy and power of experience realised in a language that is at once elevated and direct. The poet captures that 'emotion recollected in tranquillity' of which he writes in the Preface to *Lyrical Ballads*.

A great deal of Wordsworth's best poetry is concerned with looking back, feeling again and re-creating the vivid and impressive scenes of his earlier years. He is at his best when he brings to his verse the sense of wonder and excitement, the overwhelming and numinous power of sights, sounds, and feelings. In 'Tintern Abbey' he speaks of the 'glad animal movements' of his 'boyish days' (73–4), and he similarly speaks (in a passage later erased) of his 'consciousness of animal delight' in *The Prelude* (1805–6 version, IV:397). These references to the 'animal' concern the unreflective, passionate, focused sense of involvement in the world. When the poet responds to nature around him and in him, he sees the grandeur and majesty both of the great and awesome and of the minute, ordinary, and insignificant. But it is not forced or calculated or particularly rational. The art is in the expression and not the thought or philosophical system.

---

1. Helen Darbishire, 'Wordsworth's *Prelude*' in McMaster, ed., *William Wordsworth: A Critical Anthology*, pp. 271–87, at p. 271, for example.

Wordsworth does not think theologically, or if he does, the thought is not usually biblical or doctrinal or particularly orthodox. A poetic fragment dwells on 'the one interior life / That lives in all things' and

> In which all beings live with God, themselves
> Are God, existing in one mighty whole,
> As indistinguishable as the cloudless East
> At noon is from the cloudless West ...[2]

The faculty that Wordsworth calls the 'false secondary power by which / In weakness we create distinctions' (lines between those just quoted above) cannot help but note the slide from panentheism (that all things live in God) to pantheism (that all things are God) in these lines. But for Wordsworth such rationalising observations and distinctions are unimportant. His enthusiasm is for the thoughtless innocence of such people as the young Mary Hutchinson, later his wife:

> God delights
> In such a being; for her common thoughts
> Are piety, her life is gratitude. (*Prelude* XII:171 – 3)

With this may be compared the very modulated praise reserved to

> the best of those who live
> Not unexalted by religious faith,
> Nor uninformed by Books, good books, though few ... (XIII:241 – 3)

The Bible or theology were not unimportant to Wordsworth, though. In his later years he was a staunch Anglican. But he could not fully or poetically embrace the hidebound, severe, and constraining side of the Christianity of his time. The 'Ode to Duty' makes the attempt to understand the value of one of the principles embraced by Christianity. The tension, however, is clear: there are those who need the rod (3), as well as those who do Duty's work 'and know it not' (12); Duty herself is stern (1, 41), yet 'benignant' (42). Although the flowers laugh before Duty (45), they are not the dancing, gleeful flowers of 'I Wandered Lonely as a Cloud' — they are not real but abstract, added to lighten the mood of a severe and dutiful poem. And this is pretty generally true of Wordsworth's view of religion as it appears in his poetry: Christianity was true, but true in an abstract sense demanding dutiful obedience; not a life of joyful freedom

---

2. Quoted from Darbishire, 'Wordsworth's *Prelude*' in McMaster, ed., *William Wordsworth: A Critical Anthology*, p. 278.

immediately and deeply felt. Helen Darbishire, in particular, has shown how Wordsworth's editing of *The Prelude* to include more overtly Christian statements has not, in general, improved the verse.[3] The changes and additions are of a generalising nature, not obviously personal.

In his letter to Isabella Fenwick about the 'Immortality' ode (*NA2* p. 286), he mentions the appeal to him of the biblical stories of Enoch (who 'was not; for God took him', Genesis 5:24) and Elijah (who 'went up by a whirlwind into heaven', II Kings 2:11), because the idea of death as a 'state applicable to [his] own being' was hard for him to accept. In the 'Immortality' ode itself, he prefers the idea that the ‡soul is and always has been immortal, to the more orthodox view that the soul is created, regretting only the offence that such a view might cause to others. The fundamental ideas of the poem, the appeal of lines like 'trailing clouds of glory', could be reconciled with Christian theology: there is no difficulty with the notion that human beings come from God 'who is our home', and that children are uniquely close to God's heart. Jesus' teaching that the kingdom of †heaven belongs to the childlike (Matthew 18:1–5; Mark 10:15; Luke 18:17) might have been a point of departure. But Wordsworth's own sense — and experience, as he saw it — of the sanctity of childhood led him to his views as expressed in the poem.

The Prelude faces the implications of this optimistic view of human nature. The subtitle, 'Growth of a Poet's Mind', outlines the poem's intended subject, but what is noticeable is that a sense of growth as significant change and development is largely lacking. The poem evokes all the nostalgia and longing for timelessness, uses all the rich images of nature and spiritual harmony that we find throughout Wordsworth's poetry. These are the guides and teachers Wordsworth chooses to acknowledge, and we have to read closely to notice the contribution to his understanding of biblical allusions and explicitly religious teaching.[4]

It is possible to argue that Wordsworth's Christian additions to the poem in later years actually represent the 'growth' of the poem's subtitle, and that they are in some sense a response to the profound moral shock that the savagery of

---

3. Darbishire writes of these passages, 'They generally mar the poetry; they always disguise the truth', 'Wordsworth's *Prelude*' in McMaster, ed., *William Wordsworth: A Critical Anthology*, p. 274. So also the footnotes in *NA2*.

4. We might note 'Like a false Steward who hath much received, / And renders nothing back' (I:268–9) — correctly identified by the note in *NA2* as from Matthew 25:14–30; and 'Of first and last, and midst, and without end' (VI:641) incorrectly identified in the same source as from Revelation 1:8, but actually from Revelation 2:8; and '... relinquishing the scrip and staff ...' (IX:36) — a reference to Matthew 10:10 and parallels, which mentions those travellers' aids that the apostles of Jesus had to do without when they went about preaching.

the Revolution in France gave him. Book XI recalls the joyous optimism of the Revolution's inception:

> Bliss was it in that dawn to be alive,
> But to be young was very Heaven! (XI:108–9)

But as the Revolution turned into a blood-bath, the poet's mind, unable to resolve what it had 'learned … of truth' (286) with events as they happened, broke down:

> … I lost
> All feeling of conviction, and, in fine,
> Sick, wearied out with contrarieties,
> Yielded up moral questions in despair. (XI:302–5)

In telling phrases, Wordsworth uses the Bible to describe the crowning of Napoleon:

> This last opprobrium, when we see a people
> That once looked up in faith, as if to Heaven
> For manna, take a lesson from the Dog
> Returning to his vomit. (XI:360–3)

The people of France sought liberty, equality, and fraternity, which Wordsworth equates with spiritual food, the manna from †heaven mentioned in John 6:31, 58. But in accepting Napoleon as emperor, he sees them restoring the very institution from which they wanted to be free, namely despotic rule: the earthiness of the biblical proverb of the dog returning to its vomit, from Proverbs 26:11 and II Peter 2:22, captures the disgust the poet felt.

Wordsworth faced the implications of his view of human nature and suffered a breakdown. He nevertheless remained an optimist, one of those 'Prophets of Nature' for whom he looks at the end of *The Prelude*; his life and his poetry exemplify his view that hope for the future lies not in political revolutions but in human goodness and love. He lacked Christian doctrine but saw clearly the fundamental importance of the principle of †love, a principle that made St Paul almost a poet (see I Corinthians 13).

QUESTIONS

1. Do you agree that Wordsworth was not a theological thinker? Does it matter whether he was or not?

2. Look up I Corinthians 13 and compare it with your favourite passages of Wordsworth's poetry. What points of overlap and contrast are there?

BIBLIOGRAPHY

Stephen Gill, *Wordsworth: A Life*, Oxford 1989, and ed., *The Cambridge Companion to Wordsworth*, Cambridge 2003, are two valuable works on Wordsworth's life and work.

Graham McMaster, ed., *William Wordsworth: A Critical Anthology*, Harmondsworth 1972, in the Penguin Critical Anthologies series, contains an excellent range of studies.

E. de Selincourt and H. Darbishire, *The Poetical Works of William Wordsworth*, 5 vols, Oxford 1959, is the standard text of Wordsworth's poetry.

5

WILLIAM WORDSWORTH AND SAMUEL TAYLOR COLERIDGE, *LYRICAL BALLADS*

[*BAR* pp. 198 f and 324 f; *NA2* pp. 222 f; *OA2* pp. 124 f]

Lyrical Ballads was a collection of poems that significantly influenced the development of poetry in the nineteenth century. The first edition was published anonymously in a single volume in 1798, with a brief prefatory advertisement that referred to the experimental naturalistic style and diction. It contained four poems by Coleridge ('The Rime of the Ancyent Marinere', 'The Foster Mother's Tale', 'The Nightingale', and 'The Dungeon'), and the remaining twenty-three were by Wordsworth. The editions of 1800 and later changed the order of several poems in the collection and were much enlarged by the addition of a second volume of poems mostly by Wordsworth. The 'Advertisement' was also replaced by Wordsworth's 'Preface', a long essay on the nature, purpose, and style of poetry.

Perhaps the main thrust of Wordsworth's Preface is to argue that poetry is about passion, feeling, and emotion 'recollected in tranquillity' and transmuted by the operation of the poetic imagination into verse that communicates truth about humanity and gives pleasure to the reader. The emphasis here is on emotion and imagination, and Wordsworth deliberately eschews artificial 'poetic diction' in his verse: this diction is explicitly both the language of the Classical tradition with its 'reddening Phoebus' (p. 245) and 'celestial ichor' (p. 246), and that of the Christian tradition with its tears 'such as Angels weep' (p. 246) — a quotation from Milton's *Paradise Lost*. For Wordsworth, it is imagination and passion that elevate the subjects treated, not poetic style or formal language. He therefore treats 'low and rustic' topics using what he calls 'the very language of men'.

Not everyone has been convinced by Wordsworth's ideas concerning poetry and language. Coleridge argued that while 'low and rustic life' is given dignity by Wordsworth's imagination, rustic language is by no means always to be identified as the best medium for poetry.[1] Byron's famous quip in 'English Bards and Scotch Reviewers' that Wordsworth 'both by precept and example

---

1. *Biographia Literaria*, chapter 17, *NA2* pp. 483–4; *OA2* pp. 650–4.

shows / That prose is verse and verse is merely prose' — illustrates something of the passion of Wordsworth's Preface and a sense of the oddity of his verse. The banality, cliché, and predictable rhymes of 'Simon Lee' have been cited as clear evidence that Wordsworth had not found a mature style when this poem was composed; but against that must be cited 'Tintern Abbey', a powerful, personal poem in stylistically mature blank verse. What may rescue the more ballad-like and occasional poems of the collection from absurdity is the depth of feeling — many focus on loss and death — and sometimes the weight of a thought: for example, the last two lines of 'Simon Lee', the poet's lament for 'what man has made of man' ('Lines Written in Early Spring' 8, 24), and 'We murder to dissect' ('The Tables Turned' 28).

Wordsworth's Preface highlights some changes in his conception of the collection, changes that are also reflected in the order of the contents. In chapter 14 of *Biographia Literaria*, Coleridge noted that one of the original objects of *Lyrical Ballads* was in fact that he, Coleridge, should treat 'persons or characters supernatural, or at least romantic' (*NA2* p. 478; *OA2* p. 645): this makes the inclusion of the 'Ancyent Marinere' (as it was then) more readily explicable. In the first edition of *Lyrical Ballads*, 1798, 'The Ancyent Marinere' was printed first in the collection, and Wordsworth, at least, attributed some of the unfavourable reviews the collection attracted to the archaisms of the poem.[2] Coleridge revised the poem for the second (1800) and later editions; he removed some of the more garish horrors and archaic linguistic peculiarities, typified by the substitution of 'Ancient Mariner' for 'Ancyent Marinere'. Wordsworth rearranged the poems and wrote the 'Preface' to make clear his change of focus away from the supernatural and towards ordinary life and language.

The placement in the 1800 and later editions of the collection of 'The Ancient Mariner', second from last in the first volume, before Wordsworth's 'Tintern Abbey', invites comment. Both are in some sense personal poems: Coleridge's dreams and reading sparked the story of ‡sin and ‡repentance in the 'Ancient Mariner', and 'Tintern Abbey' is Wordsworth's reflections on the influence of natural beauty on his personal development. Both are deeply religious poems, though very different in their focus. 'The Ancient Mariner' is set within the old tradition of Christianity, using its rich vocabulary (see the essay below), but exploring the distinction between those for whom prayer and †love and respect for the natural world is the framework of life, and the one who lives with guilt and continual ‡penance. 'Tintern Abbey' uses the vocabulary

---

2. See the letter from Wordsworth to his publisher, Cottle, June 1799: 'It seems that The Ancyent Marinere has upon the whole been an injury to the volume, I mean that the old words and the strangeness of it have deterred readers from going on.'

of religion about nature (or Nature): Wordsworth writes of the ‡sacramental 'presence' (94) in nature, the 'spirit' (100) in all things, the 'soul' and guide of 'moral being' (110–11); and he makes a 'prayer' for his sister (121), finding their 'cheerful faith' (133) that what they see is 'full of blessings' (134) reinforced; and finally, Wordsworth talks of himself as 'a worshipper of Nature', dedicated to her 'service' with love, zeal, and 'holier love' (151–5). Coleridge wrote with apparent surprise that Wordsworth evoked 'admiration ... distinguished by its intensity, I might almost say, by its *religious* fervour';[3] but this poem in particular transfers the language of Christian theology and experience to nature and clearly expresses Wordsworth's own, at times pantheistic, religious fervour.

What is true in 'Tintern Abbey' is true to a lesser extent in other poems. God is hardly mentioned except in the little girl's voice in 'We are Seven' (51) and the old man, Matthew's, voice in 'The Two April Mornings' (4) in the 1800 edition. In both of these examples God is the one whose will it is that people should die.[4] By contrast, it is Nature that inspires the ‡soul ('Early Spring'), impresses the mind with 'wise passiveness' ('Expostulation and Reply' 24), teaches morality ('Tables Turned'), and is generally beneficent and creative. In his later poetry, particularly in *The Prelude*, Wordsworth was to articulate a more unified and more nearly Christian understanding of the world of God, Man, and Nature,[5] but in *Lyrical Ballads* he seems to be reacting against rationalism and claiming for nature, human and scenic, that purity, goodness, and regenerative power that Christians attributed to the nature and action of God.

QUESTIONS

1. What would you characterise as the main themes of the *Lyrical Ballads*? What religious significance do you think the writers gave to them?
2. Is there a difference of approach to issues of religion or faith between Wordsworth and Coleridge in the collection?
3. What do you think the poets were trying to achieve by their use of religious language?

---

3. *Biographia Literaria*, chapter 14, *NA2* p. 479; *OA2* p. 646, Coleridge's emphasis.

4. Other poems in *Lyrical Ballads* not included in *NA2* or *OA2* include mentions of God. The impression that God is generally punitive is confirmed, however: see for example 'Goody Blake and Harry Gill', where God answers Goody Blake's prayer that Harry Blake be punished (99–102), and 'The Female Vagrant' where the speaker is urged to trust God and pray (but is unable to) as she and her father are being evicted from their cottage (34–6).

5. Helen Darbishire, 'Wordsworth's *Prelude*', *The Nineteenth Century*, 1926, rpt in Graham McMaster, ed., *William Wordsworth: A Critical Anthology*, Harmondsworth 1972, pp. 271–87, writes, 'Wordsworth's creed may be said in three words: God, Man, Nature' (p. 280).

BIBLIOGRAPHY

Editions of the texts include those of R.L. Brett and A.R. Jones, *Lyrical Ballads, Wordsworth and Coleridge: The Text of the 1798 Edition with the Additional 1800 Poems and the Preface*, 2nd edn, London 1991; and Derek Roper, ed., *Lyrical Ballads 1805*, 3rd edn, Plymouth 1987 (the 1805 text with extensive notes).

Patrick Campbell, ed., *Wordsworth and Coleridge Lyrical Ballads: Critical Perspectives*, London 1991, gives attention to the history of criticism and modern views in an accessible style.

Stephen Gill, *Wordsworth: A Life*, Oxford 1989, and ed., *The Cambridge Companion to Wordsworth*, Cambridge 2003, are two valuable works on Wordsworth's life and work.

Stephen Prickett, *Wordsworth and Coleridge: The Lyrical Ballads*, London 1975, is a good and very short introduction.

6

SAMUEL TAYLOR COLERIDGE, 'THE RIME OF THE ANCIENT MARINER'

[*BAR* pp. 528 f; *NA2* pp. 422 f; *OA2* pp. 238 f]

Coleridge composed the 'Ancient Mariner' at a time of relative peace and productivity in 1797–8. It was originally conceived as a collaborative venture with Wordsworth, planned to pay the expenses of a walking holiday, and Wordsworth contributed a few lines before withdrawing from the project when he saw that he was holding Coleridge back. But more significantly, the idea for the crime of the Mariner, the shooting of the albatross, for which he undergoes such extraordinary ‡penance, was Wordsworth's. The naturalistic detail of the poem (the polar ice, the effect of being becalmed, for example) had been assimilated by Coleridge from his reading the accounts of early voyages collected by such writers as Samuel Purchas. He had also been reading Bishop Percy's *Reliques of Ancient English Poetry*, a collection of early poems and ballads, which not only gave him some of the archaic diction he used in the 'Ancient Mariner' but also something of the worldview of medieval folk poetry: a vision of a world populated by spirits, daemons and †angels, ‡saints, ‡hermits, and ‡sinners; a world where the supernatural impinges unpredictably on the ordinary. Coleridge revised the poem to remove some of the archaisms, and he added the gloss in the edition of 1817.

The poem deals with fundamentally Christian concerns, ‡sin and its consequences, and its basic worldview is Christian. The Mariner commits a wanton sin in killing the albatross, and that violation of the moral order brings into being an extraordinary chain of horror and reprisal until, as the gloss puts it, 'the curse is finally expiated'. But while the casual vocabulary of the characters and the glosses, the notions of sin and ‡penance, and particularly the moral, are all recognisably Christian, the drama of the poem presents a worldview not easily identifiable with that of any of the versions of Christianity current in Coleridge's time. It is the world of medieval romance and wonder story, in which Coleridge was attempting to imitate 'the *style*, as well as the spirit of the elder poets'[1] on the one hand; and on the other, it is the world of dream and

---

1. From the 'Advertisement' to the first edition of *Lyrical Ballads*, 1798; emphasis as there.

nightmare, where events have little logic or rationale. Coleridge lived for much of his life unable to sleep without terrifying dreams, dependent on opium and tormented by feelings of guilt. The skeleton ship of the story derives from a dream related by Coleridge's friend, John Cruikshank, and in one of the editions of the poem (1800) it was subtitled 'a Poet's Reverie'.

The notion that the poem in some respects resembles a dream may help us to understand it.[2] There are perhaps four main turning points in the story, once the Mariner has the wedding guest's attention: the killing of the albatross, and how the bird 'begins to be avenged'; the dicing-game of Death and Life-in-Death, in which Death wins the crew and Life-in-Death the Mariner; the Mariner's blessing of the water snakes; and the return to the everyday world as the Mariner asks the ‡Hermit for ‡absolution and 'the penance of life falls on him'. In this way the poem goes from the ordinary world of weddings, into the dream realm of the sea voyage with its supernatural events, and back again to the ordinary world.

Once the Mariner has killed the albatross in wanton cruelty, his nightmare begins with the physical torment of thirst, and emotional loneliness and despair. But the two central turning points both focus on spiritual events and are both unexpected. The dicing-game opens up a terrifying vision of a world depending on pure chance, the possibility that the world is governed by a power as cruel and wanton as the Mariner was himself.[3] The Mariner faces this prospect utterly alone, with no human or spiritual companionship, beyond even the compassion of Christ (the lines 'And never a saint took pity / On my soul in agony', 234–5, in the editions of 1798–1805 read, 'And Christ would take no pity …'). The 'spell begins to break' when the Mariner is distracted by the water snakes and 'a spring of love' gushes from his heart and he blesses them 'unaware'. The unconscious human, moral, and aesthetic response of the Mariner to creatures not in themselves pleasant (282–91),[4] reactivates his spiritual capacity and he finds he can pray. The 'gentle sleep' which †Mary grants him 'from Heaven' follows. The point here, though, is that the two central movements of the poem spring from the workings of capricious chance, nightmarish

---

2. R.L. Brett, ed., *S.T. Coleridge*, Writers and their Background, London 1971, prefers to minimise the dream element and sees the poem as representing the experience of Christian conversion.

3. See E.E. Bostetter, 'The nightmare world of *The Ancient Mariner*', *Studies in Romanticism* 1 (1962), 341–54. Bostetter usefully assesses the dream-nightmare qualities of the poem in the light of the theological implications and Coleridge's fears and experiences.

4. This love approximates (only approximates, because it is directed towards the non-human creation) to the Christian notion of *agape*, the †love that God has for undeserving humankind, and which he asks Christians to practise: see John 15:12, where Jesus says, 'love one another, as I have loved you'. With the Mariner's blessing of the water snakes compare the way Coleridge blesses the rook in 'This Lime-Tree Bower My Prison', 70.

in inception and unpredictable and unbidden in resolution. From here on, the curse and the nightmare begin to fade and the power of †love takes over: the Polar Spirit who 'loved the bird that loved the man' (404) moves the ship until eventually it returns to port.

The final movement of the story is when the Mariner returns home and sees his 'own countree' (467) again. The departing nightmare, the 'frightful fiend' (450) behind him, disperses as the seraphs animating the bodies of the crew wave their farewells (a companionable gesture that soothes the Mariner, 496–9). And, as the ‡Hermit approaches, the ship sinks 'like lead' (549 — as had the albatross, 291). The Mariner's cry, 'O shrieve me, shrieve me, holy man!' (574) returns the drama to where it began, with the Mariner's shooting of the albatross. This is the ‡sin he wishes to ‡confess and gain ‡absolution for, and it is very ambiguously passed over: the ‡penance that Mariner has to endure is to wander the earth and tell his tale — the compulsion returns periodically — and he apparently cannot die.[5]

Coleridge was uneasy with what he called 'the obtrusion of the moral sentiment so openly' (*NA2* p. 438 note) in the poem. He saw it as 'a principle or cause of action', and in a limited sense it is: the action is sparked by the shooting of the albatross. But the core of the poem is precisely the 'work of pure imagination', a fantastic tale of the Arabian Nights kind that he describes it as in his reply to Anna Barbauld (*NA2* p. 438 note). The 'moral' in its more usual sense of the lesson to be drawn from the story, is found in the frame setting of the wedding feast, and taking their cue from the poet, some scholars have found the lack of connection between the story and this moral disconcerting.[6] If, however, we see the action of the poem as taking place in a dreamworld full of capricious spiritual powers, and from which the Mariner emerges carrying a burden of guilty experience, the return to the moral order and spiritual regularity of the waking life is bound to seem disjunctive and uneasy.

But the moral is not irrelevant to the story. Its very simplicity is designed to comfort and soothe, while the supernatural story is designed to disturb and challenge the wedding guest and the reader.

---

5. Coleridge was interested in the biblical story of *Cain, who was a 'wanderer and fugitive' marked by God so that he should not be killed (Genesis 4), and the somewhat similar legend of the Wandering Jew: see J.L. Lowes, *The Road to Xanadu: A Study in the Ways of the Imagination*, London 1927, rpt 1978, especially pp. 227–38. It is noteworthy that Coleridge frames the Mariner's compulsion to tell his tale in the words of Jeremiah: the Mariner says 'till my ghastly tale is told / My heart within me burns' (584–5), as Jeremiah also reports, 'his word was in mine heart as a burning fire ... and I could not stay' (20:9).

6. For a good summary, see P. Campbell, *Wordsworth and Coleridge Lyrical Ballads: Critical Perspectives*, London 1991, pp. 66–76.

He prayeth best, who loveth best
All things both great and small;
For the dear God who loveth us,
He made and loveth all. (614–17)

This is a return to the regularity, the predictability, the certainties of everyday life. The moral sums up the assumptions on which normal, Christian life is based, but it comes with the greater power from one whose disordered and terrifying experience has called into question and made him doubt those assumptions.[7] Moreover, the repeated emphasis on †love and prayer links the moral closely with the positive force of love in the nightmare phase of the story, where it was the Mariner's 'spring of love' (284) that began to break the spell and allowed him to pray. The Mariner's experiences are not to be generalised or replicated: they did not take place in the 'real' world. But the force of love and the power of prayer, beneficially operative in the Mariner's nightmare world, can indeed be generalised and replicated in the real world of the wedding guest and the reader.

QUESTIONS

1. Wordsworth criticised the Ancient Mariner for having 'no distinct character, either in his profession as Mariner, or as a human being'. What is your view of the Mariner?
2. What do you think the moral message of the poem is? Do you think a moral is necessary for such a poem? Does the moral 'obtrude' as Coleridge thought, or is the poem lacking a moral as Barbauld suggested?

BIBLIOGRAPHY

'The Rime of the Ancient Mariner' will be found in editions of *Lyrical Ballads* such as those of R.L. Brett and A.R. Jones, 2nd edn, London 1991, and Derek Roper, 3rd edn, Plymouth 1987.

P.H. Fry, ed., *Samuel Taylor Coleridge, The Rime of the Ancient Mariner*, Case Studies in Contemporary Criticism, Basingstoke 1999, includes texts of 1798 and 1817 and an array of new critical essays from Reader-response, Marxist, New Historicist, Psychoanalytical and Deconstruction perspectives.

---

7. A point made by H. House, *Coleridge*, London 1953, p. 92, who remarks that it is 'a moral which has its meaning *because it has been lived*' (House's emphasis).

Richard Holmes, *Coleridge: Early Visions*, London 1989, and *Coleridge: Darker Reflections*, London 1998, a large-scale biography of the poet.

A.R. Jones and W. Tydeman, ed., *Coleridge, The Ancient Mariner and Other Poems: A Casebook*, London 1973, contains a useful collection of contemporary sources and reviews and two modern essays on 'The Ancient Mariner'.

J. L. Lowes, *The Road to Xanadu: A Study in the Ways of the Imagination*, London 1927, rpt 1978, while not always easy to assimilate, is an important study.

Robert Penn Warren, *Selected Essays*, rpt London 1964, contains his justly celebrated and important article, 'A poem of pure imagination: an experiment in reading'.

7

MARY SHELLEY, *FRANKENSTEIN*

[*NA2* pp. 903 f]

Mary Shelley's *Frankenstein* (1818) is a novel of the Romantic period. It treats the theological themes of *creation, *fall, and †hellish isolation, drawing particularly upon Milton's *Paradise Lost.*

In the initial framework narrative of the seafarer Walton, Frankenstein's story is presented as a moral fable told to discourage vainglory and overreaching ambition. Such was the ‡sin of *Adam: 'ye shall be as gods' was the serpent's lure in Genesis. †Satan's 'Ye shall not surely die' (Genesis 3:4), also resonates with Frankenstein's obsessive desire to conquer the degenerative processes of the human body.

Walton's history parallels Frankenstein's, for his ambition incorporates the overcoming of the natural world in his attempt to reach the Pole. 'What can stop the determined heart and resolved will of man?', he asks. Against the background of advances in science around the turn of the eighteenth to nineteenth century this may be seen as Mary Shelley's warning to an entire generation in danger of overreaching itself.

The moral ambiguity of Walton's expedition is evident first in his defiance of his father's injunction against it — similar to *Adam's defiance of God's command — and then in his assertion that the death of a sailor is 'a small price to pay for the acquirement of the knowledge which I sought; for the dominion I should acquire ...' Here Shelley brings together the Genesis notions of seeking forbidden knowledge, of going far beyond the commission given to Adam to 'have dominion ... over every living thing' (Genesis 1:26), and of the consequent punishment of death. Frankenstein's stark warning to Walton explicitly uses the serpent image of Genesis: 'You seek for knowledge and wisdom, as I once did; and I ardently hope that the gratification of your wishes may not be a serpent to sting you, as mine has been.'

As Frankenstein's own story gets under way it is constantly qualified in the same terms as Walton's. When he leaves for Ingolstadt University at the age of seventeen he 'ardently desired the acquisition of knowledge'; once there, he finds his professor acclaiming modern scientists in hyperbolic and resonantly biblical terms — 'They ascend into the heavens', just as the †prophet Isaiah had written of †Lucifer, 'thou hast said in thine heart, I will ascend into heaven … I will be like the most High' (Isaiah 14:13–14). In the final section of the novel Frankenstein sums up his condition by referring again to Lucifer's rebellion: 'like the archangel who aspired to omnipotence, I am chained in an eternal hell'. Fittingly, the frozen northern wastes where the novel begins and ends are akin to Milton's †hell where †Satan and his cohort found themselves:

> Beyond this flood a frozen Continent
> Lies dark and wild…
> Thither … all the damn'd
> Are brought…
> From Beds of raging Fire to starve in Ice …
> (*Paradise Lost* II:587–600)

Frankenstein enacts an inversion of the *creation story. The creature that Frankenstein describes in its first moments of life is grotesque beyond comprehension, unlike the Genesis story in which everything God had made 'was very good'. The creator Frankenstein flees in horror and disgust from the room. Frankenstein is both like God, as creator, and like †Satan, as tormented overreacher. He is like *Adam in the prelapsarian innocence of his childhood, but *falls from that state, also like Adam.

The monster considers how God made *Adam 'beautiful and alluring, after his own image', but that by contrast he is 'a filthy type' of Frankenstein. In a further twist on the biblical story the monster says to Frankenstein, 'I ought to be thy Adam; but I am rather the fallen angel.' Much is made of the comparison of his lot, and his resulting nature, with †Satan's.

Mary Shelley has much of the monster's education depend upon overhearing *Paradise Lost* read aloud. It excites in him 'every feeling of wonder and of awe'. He acknowledges an affinity with *Adam who was also alone in *Eden, though his creator took 'especial care' with him. But it is in †Satan that he eventually sees himself: he becomes envious, he curses his maker, he discovers within himself destructive impulses and inward disintegration — 'I, like the arch-fiend, bore hell within me', he claims. The monster's softer feelings give place to 'hellish rage and gnashing of teeth' in a phrase familiar to the †parables of the gospels that also describes †hell (see, for example, Matthew 8:12; 13:42; 22:13). 'Evil thenceforth became my good', he says in a reversal of the spiritual and moral order, almost directly a quotation of Satan's 'Evil, be thou my good' in *Paradise Lost* IV:110. The monster's own explanation of his fall owes more to Rousseau and Godwin than Milton; if he had been treated well, he would have behaved well. Nevertheless in his final speech to Walton he terms his own behaviour 'sin' and reflects upon his fall: 'I cannot believe that I am the same creature whose thoughts were once filled with sublime and transcendent visions of the beauty and majesty of goodness. But it is even so; the fallen angel becomes a malignant devil.'

What the monster termed 'the beauty and majesty of goodness' he learned not just from *Paradise Lost*, but from observing the De Lacey family. If there is an opposition to the destructive aspects of the novel it is to be found in Shelley's depictions of family life and friendships. Frankenstein's parents are the first model for this; devout, humble, tender, benevolent — for instance in their visiting of the poor and their adoption of Elizabeth. Elizabeth is herself a ‡saintly moral example, possessing 'the living spirit of love'. Frankenstein's mother †sacrifices her life in her care of Elizabeth. In turn, the De Lacey family are characterised by their selflessness as they give up food for their father and in their kindness to each other.

Frankenstein conversely neglects family, friends, and all fellow creatures, ending his days wandering, *Cain-like, alone. The monster too is alone, an *Adam without his Eve. We are returned therefore to Genesis where God says, 'It is not good that the man should be alone' (Genesis 2:18). Even †Satan, the monster points out, 'had friends and associates in his desolation; I am alone'.

QUESTIONS

1. How does Mary Shelley juggle potentially conflicting ideas from Rousseau and from Milton?
2. To what extent does the author try, subconsciously or otherwise, to subvert the *Paradise Lost* story?

BIBLIOGRAPHY

Marilyn Baker, ed., *Mary Wollstonecraft Shelley, Frankenstein or, The Modern Prometheus (The 1818 Text)*, Oxford and New York 1998. Includes an excellent, scholarly introduction.

Sandra M. Gilbert and Susan Gubar, 'Horror's twin: Mary Shelley's monstrous Eve', in *The Madwoman in the Attic: The Woman Writer and the Nineteenth-Century Literary Imagination*, New Haven CT and London 1979. This is a seminal feminist text, tracing a female literary tradition through several nineteenth-century women writers.

Martin Tropp, *Mary Shelley's Monster*, Boston 1977. Considers Frankenstein from a mythic and cinematic angle, and looks at the personality of the writer.

8

OVERVIEW: THE VICTORIAN PERIOD

'Crisis of faith' and 'the age of doubt' are phrases you might often hear in describing the Victorian age. The 'melancholy withdrawing roar' of faith in Matthew Arnold's poem 'Dover Beach' has sometimes been taken as a guiding image regarding Christianity in the Victorian era. Like many generalisations, this carries some truth but also much distortion. Faith, especially if understood as religious practice, might be said to have progressed rather than declined throughout Victoria's reign. Certainly, figures for church attendance were higher at the end of the nineteenth century than at the beginning, and similarly, the Christian faith and Christian activists were equally involved in social and political life in the closing decades as in the earlier.

So, first of all, why are 'doubt' and 'crisis' so frequently associated with the religious life of the Victorian era? We might consider three main causes: developments in biblical studies; the beginnings of sociological thought; and the impact of scientific thinking, especially regarding evolution, this last being considered in its own essay.

First, biblical studies. From the time of the ‡Reformation, the ancient idea that the scriptures were open to different readings had been lost among some Christians, so that they read the whole of the Old Testament as historical fact, rather than as truth expressed through myth, history, story, and poetry, as it is commonly read today. By such Christians, Moses was held to be the author of the first five books of the Bible, for example. New ways of studying the Old Testament in the mainly German 'Higher Criticism' began to challenge its reading as a purely historical document and thus to undermine faith in its truth among such churchmen.[1] Great attention was given, for example, to the resignation

---

1. Thomas Hardy's poem 'The Respectable Burgher: On "The Higher Criticism"' (published 1901) wittily summarises the impact of the new theories:

Since Reverend Doctors now declare	That David was no giant-slayer,
That clerks and people must prepare	Nor one to call a God-obeyer
To doubt if Adam ever were;	In certain details we could spare
To hold the flood a local scare;	– Since thus they hint, nor turn a hair,
To argue, though he stolid stare,	All churchgoing will I forswear,
That everything had happened ere	And sit on Sundays in my chair,
The prophets to its happening sware;	And read that moderate man Voltaire.

of Bishop Colenso of Natal, when his study of the Pentateuch especially, and the book of Judges, suggested that for Moses to have authored it, he would have needed to have lived until he was 4,000 years old. This was, however, not a universal response to such discovery. The comment of the great Anglican theologian, Frederick Denison Maurice, suggests the existence at the time of other ways of reading the Bible: 'The poor Bishop of Natal labours under the misapprehension that theology is a branch of mathematics.' In other words, the Old Testament is to be read as theological truth, truth about God and his ways as revealed in history; it should not, and could not, be reduced to a succession of literal facts.

We must beware, furthermore, of identifying this challenge to biblical interpretation with the reception of Darwinian evolution in relation to contemporary readings of the first two books of Genesis. During this period no academic theologian espoused an entirely literal reading of the *creation story, although we cannot know what view was adopted by the ordinary reader (see further the essay on Evolution).

In the study of the New Testament a more historical approach led, for example, to the questioning of the miraculous elements in the gospels and to an emphasis on the humanity of Christ, as we find in such works as *Das Leben Jesu* (*The Life of Christ*) by David Strauss and a similar *Life* produced by Ernst Renan, towards the end of the period.

The more 'scientific' historical approach of Higher Criticism was allied intellectually to our second strand in the causes for doubt and crisis in belief. This is the rise of sociological thinking. This led to religion being studied as a human and social phenomenon rather than as a divine reality and ‡revelation; emphasis was upon the human experiences to which religion gave expression and the social structures to which it gave rise. George Eliot, for example, was persuaded from her ‡Calvinist, ‡Evangelical beliefs by the writings of Feuerbach on the religion of Man. Feuerbach asserted that 'God' was a way of speaking about our ideal of humankind; in this line of thought Jesus becomes an example of fulfilled human potential rather than a divine figure. This was emphasised too in her reading of Comte, seen as the forefather of sociology. For Comte, all religion was a way of speaking about man and his capacity for progress.

A purely human Jesus fits well with a view of God as simply the ideal of perfect humanity. Eliot's translation of *Das Leben Jesu* (combined with her study of Feuerbach and Comte) shows how the interplay between biblical studies and new sociological and philosophical theorising could produce radical doubt and a re-interpretation of traditional religion. An example of the effect of this kind of speculation on Christians of the time can be seen in the portrayal of Mr Hale in Elizabeth Gaskell's novel *North and South*. A Church of England clergyman, Mr Hale is worried by these new aspects of intellectual life and feels he can no longer continue in his ministry.

These two strands also weave into our third, probably best-known, claimed cause for doubt in the Victorian era, that is, the impact of scientific thinking and especially the development of evolutionary theories, which is the subject of a separate essay.

The reason why we may be more aware of the negative impact of these new ways of thinking on Christian faith lies possibly in its greater dramatic quality compared with assimilation and development. Crisis is more newsworthy than continuity. Similarly, change and conflict are more readily the stuff of dramatic plotting than the intellectual labour of interpreting new ideas. We might therefore expect to find these provide more attractive themes for literature. We turn now, therefore, to other aspects of the role of Christian faith and biblical tradition within Victorian culture and its literature.

Perhaps the first thing to note is the continuing immense importance in literature and art of biblical ‡typology. We said that new ways of reading the Bible were growing in the Victorian period, but still there endured an older way of reading the Old Testament for the way it pointed to Christ. It was common to read the Old Testament figures like Joseph, David, and Elijah, for example, as in some way types of Christ, that is, figures who point to, who foreshadow, what is to come. These types, as we have seen in the discussion of the ‡mystery plays and John Donne, are images or preparations for the coming of final truth. This habit of thinking persists in the Victorian period. It means that characters are considered in their relation to Christ as images, or shadows, of him. For example, in Dickens's great novel *Bleak House*, Nemo, the despised destitute character who becomes a central figure of compassion and reconciliation in his death, is given many of the attributes of Christ. We are able to see in Nemo (his name means 'no man') a figure of Christ the Everyman, Christ who was, in the words of Isaiah, 'despised and rejected of men' (Isaiah 53:3), Christ whose universal brotherhood is rejected by those who crucify him.

Secondly, if progress had been a concept to challenge faith in the Romantic period, in Queen Victoria's reign it had begun to be assimilated into that faith. The nineteenth century as a whole witnessed a revival in the study of the ‡Fathers of the church. These were theologians and bishops from the second to the eighth centuries AD, who worked out the major doctrines of Christian faith, accepted by all the churches until the ‡Reformation. ‡Unitarians (who deny the ‡Trinity, that is, three persons but one God), for example, began a study of the ‡Fathers in the hope of proving their non-Trinitarian position, that Christ was a created intermediary. One notion they found there, especially in the theologian Gregory of Nyssa was *epektasis*, the dynamic progress of the ‡soul into God. God is infinite, without end; the soul, even in union with God, can never stop moving or progressing, because there is no end to be reached. This was a doctrine that the young Robert Browning imbibed from the ‡Unitarian William Johnson Fox, and it inspired his poetry, together with his own reading of the same Fathers. This is a doctrine about the individual soul and its spiritual progress as the process of self-actualisation and participation in God's glory. Such a vision, shared by other students of the Fathers, permeated the century.

Now this idea of progress is essentially optimistic. The tendency throughout the Victorian period was for religious optimism about the future glory of man to develop into a belief in his gradual perfectibility. By the end of the Victorian period, classical Anglican theology thus participated in the general cultural optimism about human betterment through scientific and technical progress.

The early nineteenth-century interest in the ‡Fathers was also fuel for another important change in the face of English Christianity: the rise of Anglo-Catholicism from the ‡Oxford Movement, sometimes called ‡Tractarianism because of the production of their 'Tracts for the Times'. Spearheaded by four Anglican clerics, Pusey, Keble, Froude, and Newman, the Oxford Movement claimed the inheritance of the church ‡Fathers and of the foundational Anglican theologians of the seventeenth century, often called the Caroline Divines. This inheritance, they claimed, was evidence that the Church of England was not Protestant, but a purified, true Catholicism. This was claimed especially in Tract 90, where its author, John Henry Newman, proposed a reading of the Thirty-Nine Articles of the Anglican Church in a Catholic manner. The Oxford Movement challenged ‡Evangelicals on their understanding of the church and liberals on their understanding of †baptism, the priesthood, and the nature of human ‡salvation; but their emphasis was on the meaning and implications of the doctrine of the †incarnation, close to the view we find in Robert Browning.

For the beginnings of ‡Tractarianism, this emphasis gave a strong social dimension to its theology and practice. If each human being was made in the image of God and this image could be fully restored in †baptism, then each had great dignity and value regardless of birth. And since each person was made according to the same image, each shared a common identity. Such awareness made the Tractarians responsive to the social impact of industrialisation and to the needs of the new city dwellers. It gave impetus to the development of religious communities in the Church of England that could directly combat ignorance, neglect, and want.[2] We find its literary influence in the poetry of Christina Rossetti and in the novels of Charlotte Yonge, which also depict the impact of Tractarianism on the conduct of middle-class Christian life.

‡Tractarianism as it developed later in the century in Cambridge had a more liturgical and aesthetic dimension. Vestments were worn, statues erected, flowers and candles appeared on altars, and the bread and wine consecrated at the ‡eucharist was reserved in the tabernacle to be venerated. This occasionally caused celebrated conflicts between Tractarian vicar and non-Tractarian bishop, leading even to court cases and imprisonment. A bitterly satirical look at this later Tractarianism and at other aspects of Victorian religion can be found in Samuel Butler's *The Way of All Flesh*.

At the same time as this revival of Catholicism was taking place within the Church of England, another significant aspect of Victorian religious life was the lifting of most legal restrictions against Roman Catholics and the restoration of the Roman Catholic hierarchy in 1850. This allowed a wider spread of education for Catholics at all levels and the establishment of ‡monastic boarding schools; it enabled wealthy Catholics to re-enter mainstream society and influence it. The work of religious communities, opening parish schools and welfare centres, raised the literacy levels and health of poor Catholics, especially of the Irish immigrants who had hitherto been neglected in the major industrialised centres. Not only were material and spiritual well-being improved, but at all levels of society a Catholic sensibility was able to influence both popular and 'high' art and literature. Without this we would not have, for example, the poetry of Gerard Manley Hopkins, Coventry Patmore, Francis Thompson, or, later, Elgar's *Dream of Gerontius* — both the musician and the librettist, John Henry Newman, being Catholics. Both the return of Roman Catholicism and the rise of liturgical Anglo-Catholicism influenced the Aesthetic Movement, evident in the life and works of Walter Pater, arguably its founding father, and Oscar Wilde, his disciple. Both of these ended their lives as Catholics.

‡Evangelical Christianity was equally a force in society. The social awareness that had led to the overthrow of slavery in the early years of the century was consolidated in the Victorian period. The Evangelical Lord Shaftesbury led the fight against child labour. We can see the impact of his work in, for example, Elizabeth Barrett Browning's poem 'The Cry of the Children'. This was the great era of the Sunday school, offering not only Christian doctrine but basic literacy to children and adults alike, and of the Evangelically-founded children's

---

2. For further discussion, see the essay on The Woman Question below.

societies such as Dr Barnardo's, concerned with the plight of orphaned and abandoned city children.[3]

Commonly understood as arising from the broad school of Anglicanism, neither ‡Tractarian nor ‡Evangelical, Christian Socialism also kept Christianity to the fore in social and political life. Founded by the theologian, F.D. Maurice, and Charles Kingsley, author of 'social novels' *The Water Babies* and *Alton Locke*, Christian Socialists worked and agitated for justice and education for working men and women, based on the same implications of the †incarnation that impelled the Tractarians to action.

We find, therefore, in Victorian religion, vibrancy and social activism as well as crisis and challenge. What also arises is an interest in Spiritualism as a developed religious system, satirised in Robert Browning's poem 'Mr Sludge the Medium', possibly because of his wife Elizabeth's interest in it. In literature, this interest seems to integrate with the influence of the earlier Gothic tale to develop the genre of the ghostly tale, often associated with M.R. James, but also with mainstream writers like Dickens, Mrs Gaskell, and, later, Thomas Hardy. Despite the progress of scientific thinking and the challenge offered to a religious understanding of life, the Victorian period seems as convinced as any other that life cannot be explained simply by scientific data.

QUESTIONS

1. To what extent have you previously understood the Victorian period as an age of doubt and of the waning of Christianity?
2. Take any piece of Victorian writing and see if you can identify the use of ‡typology within it.
3. Take any piece of Victorian writing and see if you can identify its approach to progress. To what extent is it concerned with spiritual development? To what extent is this linked with capacity for material progress?

BIBLIOGRAPHY

Leon Chai, *Aestheticism: The Religion of Art in Post-Romantic Literature*, New York 1990.

Raymond Chapman, *Faith and Revolt: Studies in the Literary Influence of the Oxford Movement*, London 1970.

---

3. See further the essay on Industrialism below.

Daniel Cottom, *Abyss of Reason: Cultural Movements, Revelations, and Betrayal*, Oxford 1991.

Peter Allan Dale, *In Pursuit of a Scientific Culture: Science, Art, and Society in the Victorian Age*, Madison 1989.

Elisabeth Jay, ed., *The Evangelical and Oxford Movements*, Cambridge 1983.

Alan Kreider and Jane Shaw, ed., *Culture and the Nonconformist Tradition*, Cardiff 1999.

George P. Landow, *Victorian Types, Victorian Shadows: Biblical Typology in Victorian Literature, Art and Thought*, London 1980. An essential work for an appreciation of the influence of the Bible in this period.

Edward Norman, *The Victorian Christian Socialists*, Cambridge 1987.

Stephen Prickett, *Romanticism and Religion: the Tradition of Wordsworth and Coleridge in the Victorian Church*, Cambridge 1976. Important for reaching an appreciation of the way Romanticism was assimilated into Victorian Christianity.

Geoffrey Rowell, ed., *Tradition Renewed: The Oxford Movement Conference Papers*, London 1986.

9

THOMAS CARLYLE

CARLYLE'S VIEW OF CHRISTIANITY

[*BAV* pp. 43 f; *NA2* pp. 1066 f; *OA2* pp. 799 f]

Carlyle was known by his fellow mid-Victorians as 'the sage of Chelsea'. Although he eschewed formal philosophy, it was the power of his independence of mind and his idiosyncratic yet powerful literary style that made him an intellectual force in the Victorian age. Carlyle rejected the formalism he saw in the Christianity of his day, which he called in *Sartor Resartus* the 'old clothes' of a perennially valid vision of the world. He rejected the reduction of a transcendent reality to a system of beliefs and forms of worship: this we find in his little verse denouncing both Pusey, the leader of the ‡Tractarians, and Frederick Denison Maurice, the leader of the Christian Socialist Movement. In *Past and Present*, he complains

> The builder of this Universe was wise,
> He plann'd all souls, all systems, planets, particles:
> The Plan He shaped all Worlds and Æons by,
>   Was — Heavens! — thy small Nine-and-thirty Articles?[1]

And he adapts his little rhyme against Maurice:

> Thirty-nine English Articles,
>   Ye wondrous little particles,
> Did God shape His universe really by you?
> In that case I swear it,
>   And solemnly declare it,
> This logic of Maurice's is true.[2]

It was not so much the Christian vision of life that Carlyle denounced, but the distortion of that vision into a self-contained religious system and the

---

1. Traill, ed., *Works of Carlyle*, vol. 10, *Past and Present*, p. 117.
2. James Anthony Froude, *Thomas Carlyle: A History of his Life in London, 1834–1881*, 2 vols, London 1884, I:40.

self-conscious pride behind rationalistic definitions of reality. As he advised his friend, Sterling, 'man must be content with the agnosticism of "the all" and "the immensities", eschewing the reduction of infinitude to rational categories'.[3]

Carlyle had been much affected by his reading of German philosophers like Kant and Fichte and the German Romantics. From the latter, he absorbed ideas inherited from the spirituality of Jacob Boehme and the Rhineland ‡Mystics, who were much preoccupied with the indwelling of God within the self. His reading of Kant was prepared for by his previous acquaintance with the English philosophers, the seventeenth-century Cambridge Platonists, whose teaching he would have encountered as a student at Edinburgh University. The Cambridge Platonists were Anglican theologians who rejected the ‡Calvinism of the time and enabled the theology and philosophy of the eastern church to retain some influence in Anglican thought and in British philosophy.

Carlyle's thought depends upon the implicit distinction made by the Cambridge Platonists between reason and understanding. What the Platonists regarded as reason was the human capacity to correspond with the 'reason' of the world, the way the world is, as it were intuiting the numinal reality within or beneath phenomena. Reason, for the Cambridge Platonists, means what the earlier ‡Fathers had called 'intellect', that is, pure intuitive knowing, a participation by the intellectual creature in the pure intellect of God who has no need of discursive reasoning.

Reason, or 'understanding' in the Cambridge Platonists' terms, is specific to man and is the capacity of the created being for logical, deductive thought-processes. Varying levels of capacity for reasoning, that is, for the possession of understanding, do not therefore affect each person's identity as an intellectual being. Since ‡patristic intellect is the 'reason' of the Cambridge Platonists, their use of mind denotes the spiritual centre of man, the basis of his selfhood as an image of God. Carlyle adopted such a distinction between spiritual capacity and human stupidity in his early thought.

Carlyle wanted to reject, as the Cambridge Platonists had done before him, a view of humanity that reduced him and set a gulf between humanity and God. They sought to establish the dignity of man as the image of God in their belief that the good person is the dwelling place of God, and insisted that human beings should reverence God within themselves as beings made in the image of God. It is this conviction that also inspires the call for reverence for humanity as 'the true Shekinah' that Carlyle makes in *On Heroes and Hero Worship*.[4]

---

3. Traill, ed., *Works of Carlyle*, vol. 11, *Life of Sterling*, pp. 55–6.
4. Traill, ed., *Works of Carlyle*, vol. 1, *Sartor Resartus*, p. 52, vol. 5, *On Heroes ...* p. 10.

'Mind' is here the capacity that Carlyle saw in man for becoming spiritual, being 'that faculty whereby man is made capable of God'.[5] This mind, through its reason, receives what is supernatural so that man can be seen to be made capable of receiving what is beyond him. This is the beginning of the natural supernaturalism or 'Descendental Transcendentalism' that we find in Carlyle. In this belief about the nature of the mind lies the basis for human equality in the thought of the young Carlyle, as in the Cambridge Platonists. As suggested earlier, mind is the common basis of humanity and reason is a universal capacity. Carlyle avers in *Chartism*: 'All men, we must repeat, were made by God, and have immortal souls in them. The Sanspotato is the selfsame stuff as the superfinest Lord Lieutenant.'[6]

But this is not to reject the concept of †original sin. The Cambridge Platonists were aware of man's capacity for evil. But they see that evil-doing is also doing violence to the self. Benjamin Whichcote, one of the prime leaders of the Cambridge Platonists, affirmed 'it should be one man a god to another, but we, through our degeneracy, make it to be every man a wolf to another'.[7] And so we find Carlyle affirming in his work, *Boswell's 'Life of Johnson'*: 'What, indeed, is man's life generally, but a kind of beast-godhood; the god in him triumphing more and more over the beast ...?'[8]

Carlyle insists that the human being is at once 'a pitiful, hungry biped' and 'a reflex and image of God's whole universe'. The beast, he affirms, begins to triumph when the poor biped aspires to independent godhood, claiming godlike knowledge, ignoring earthiness, but judging of the eternal by the earthly senses. In order to know their greatness as temples of the Shekinah, human beings must also know themselves as the writer knows himself, as a 'dust-making, patent Rag-grinder'.[9] They must be deflated from their pretensions to an independent and †angelic status in order to know their creatureliness as their means of becoming truly godlike. For Carlyle, then, true human †wisdom comes with acceptance of the world and the human situation within it, as it does for Teufelsdroeckh in *Sartor Resartus*.

5. Ernest Trafford Campagnac, ed., *The Cambridge Platonists. Being Selections from the Writings of Benjamin Whichcote, John Smith and Nathaniel Culverwel*, Oxford 1901, p. 51.

6. Traill, ed., *Works of Carlyle*, vol. 29, *Critical and Miscellaneous Essays*, p. 136.

7. William Cecil de Pauley, *The Candle of the Lord: Studies in the Cambridge Platonists*, London 1937, p.16.

8. Traill, ed., *Works of Carlyle*, vol. 28, *Critical and Miscellaneous Essays*, p. 75.

9. Traill, ed., *Works of Carlyle*, vol. 1, *Sartor Resartus*, p. 44.

QUESTIONS

1. What did Carlyle mean by 'mind' and 'reason'? How does this usage differ from our present-day use of these terms?
2. What do you understand by Carlyle's expression 'beast-godhood'?
3. How would you summarise Carlyle's understanding of the human person and of the human situation in the world?

SARTOR RESARTUS

[*BAV* pp. 47 f; *NA2* pp. 1077 f; *OA2* pp. 802 f]

As we have seen, *Sartor Resartus* is a rejection of the formulae of religion employed in Carlyle's day. Central to this work is the necessity of accepting the human situation, and the experience of its protagonist, Teufelsdroeckh, that this acceptance is also a ‡revelation that the power behind the universe is eternal †love, a revelation bringing about awareness of the bonds of love between people. Teufelsdroeckh has realised, in his own experience, what St John had declared, that God is love and that this love is known in fellow human beings (I John 4:1–16).

Hence, in *Sartor Resartus* he rebukes the scientists who claim knowledge and control over the universe in terms that echo God's words to Job about human pretensions to have been present at the beginnings of *creation (Job 38–9): 'Was Man with his Experience present at the Creation, then, to see how it all went on? Have any deepest scientific individuals yet dived down to the foundations of the Universe, and gauged everything there?'[10]

In *Sartor Resartus* Carlyle is also re-expressing ancient Christian belief through the clothing motif. Clothing represents the attributes of personality, status, and self-image upon which human beings base their claim to individuality and self-worth. This desire for self-made individualism, for a value based on individual gifts, obscures the true worth of the human being that lies in being an embodied image of God. The uniqueness of each human embodiment is sufficient distinction from one another and, therefore, need no longer preoccupy human beings. This embodied nature links each to each, both in its nature as a gift of the creator and in the vulnerability and capacity for suffering that it entails. This was also the teaching of the church ‡Fathers, a teaching obscured by the popular ‡Calvinism of Carlyle's day and the growth of individual laissez-faire capitalism. We see it, in its fully Christian context, in the preaching of F.D. Maurice whose consistent message was of the abiding relationships of

---

10. Traill, ed., *Works of Carlyle*, vol. 1, *Sartor Resartus*, p. 204.

human brotherhood/sisterhood existing between all human beings because of their sharing of the same Elder Brother, Christ.

It is in the light of Carlyle's sharing this Christian belief that human value and identity are gifts of God, his image, and thus that human beings are brothers and sisters, that one must understand self-denial as it is found in *Sartor Resartus*. Self-denial is the rejection of an individualistic approach to life that sets the isolated personality at the centre. It is only by rejecting this individualistic view of the self that true self-unfolding as an image of God can occur. Here too Carlyle's voice chimes with that of the Cambridge Platonists and the eastern ‡Fathers as they insist 'all self-seeking and self-love do but imprison the soul and confine it to its own home'.[11] To come to true felicity is to universalise oneself, becoming a microcosm whose 'I am' is an image of the 'I Am' of God. When this occurs, the Platonists affirm, 'to enjoy a man's self is the greatest good in the world'.[12]

And so we have Carlyle affirming similar apparent paradoxes. On the one hand he affirms 'that law of Self-Denial, by which alone man's narrow destiny may become an infinitude within itself'.[13] But on the other hand, 'The meaning of life here on earth might be defined as consisting in this: To unfold your *self*, to work what thing you have the faculty for. It is a necessity for the human being, the first law of our existence.'[14] What Carlyle saw and expressed through his imagery of clothing in *Sartor Resartus* was that increasingly in his age, people were denying the self that could become an infinitude and insisting upon individual distinctiveness and isolation. This was to be one of his major lessons for his age: he felt it was being led by the dominance of an economic model of humanity that esteemed individuality and independence, separating men and women one from another; and he wished people to see their value as lying elsewhere. So he says in his early Journal and later in *Sartor Resartus*, '*The Fraction of Life can be increased in value not so much by increasing your Numerator, as by lessening your Denominator. Nay, unless my Algebra deceive me, Unity itself divided by Zero, will give Infinity.*'[15]

Carlyle uses the clothing image in *Sartor Resartus* to develop this thought: exaggerated individualism is blinding society to the deeper bonds that unite each to each: 'Clothes gave us individuality, distinctions, social polity; Clothes have

---

11. John Smith, 'The excellence and nobleness of true religion', in de Pauley, *The Candle of the Lord*.

12. Benjamin Whichcote, in de Pauley, *The Candle of the Lord*, p. 15.

13. Traill, ed., *Works of Carlyle*, vol. 26, *Critical and Miscellaneous Essays*, p. 161.

14. Traill, ed., *Works of Carlyle*, vol. 5, *On Heroes …*, p. 225, Carlyle's italics.

15. Traill, ed., *Works of Carlyle*, vol. 1, *Sartor Resartus*, pp. 152–3, Carlyle's italics.

made Men of us; they are threatening to make Clothes-screens of us.'[16] This happens when individuality is given priority over common beast/godhood.

Carlyle's views on work must be set in this same context. We must beware of interpreting this in the light of the so-called 'Protestant work ethic' in which work is prized and success in work is seen as evidence of God's justification. If we look at young Carlyle's use of the word 'work', we shall see that it is primarily another term for 'self-actualisation'. To 'unfold yourself' is to 'work what thing you have a faculty for',[17] while the aim of work is not material but spiritual productivity: 'The man is the spirit he worked in: not what he did, but what he became.' When Carlyle insists 'Up and be doing! Hast thou not the strangest, grandest of all talents committed to thee, namely, LIFE itself? O Heaven! And it is momentarily rusting and wasting, if thou use it not. Up and be doing!'[18] — he is not advocating material productivity; rather he is invoking the *parable of the talents (Matthew 25:14–30).

In this *parable, the master goes away, leaving each of three servants with a number of talents, that is, money to be put to use during his absence. Two servants do this, while the third simply buries his in the ground. When the master returns, two servants have made a profit on their money and the one who has buried it in the ground can only return it to his master. Carlyle sees this in its original meaning: humanity is given the gift of life, or possibly, in this parable, the gift of faith, which has to be used so that human beings can become everything that they are created to be. People must be 'up and doing' so that they avoid the cardinal ‡sin of sloth, the failure to live up to the glory of human nature.

Carlyle castigated his age for looking in the wrong places for its sense of human worth and for putting its energies into economic and religious endeavours that could not express the true destiny of human beings and the true nature of their societies.

QUESTIONS

1. Look up Job 38–9 and consider its relationship to *Sartor Resartus* in terms of mood and tone.
2. What is your understanding of Carlyle's approach to self-denial and self-actualisation?

---

16. Traill, ed., *Works of Carlyle*, vol. 1, *Sartor Resartus*, p. 31.

17. Traill, ed., *Works of Carlyle*, vol. 5, *On Heroes...*, p. 225.

18. James Anthony Froude, *Thomas Carlyle: A History of the First Forty Years of His Life, 1795–1835*, 2 vols, London 1882, II:87, Carlyle's capitals.

3. How effective is Carlyle's clothes imagery in conveying his understanding of the dilemma of his society?

BIBLIOGRAPHY

G.K. Chesterton, *Thomas Carlyle*, London 1902 and rpt frequently. A stimulating review of Carlyle's work, from a perspective close to Carlyle's own.

Charles Frederick Harrold, *Carlyle and German Thought: 1819–1834*, New Haven CO 1934.

Fred Kaplan, *Thomas Carlyle: A Biography*, Cambridge 1993. Makes extensive use of Carlyle's letters to explicate his thought and set him in his contemporary context.

Carlisle Moore, '*Sartor Resartus* and the problem of Carlyle's conversion', *Publications of the Modern Language Association* 70 (1955), 662–80.

John Nichol, *Thomas Carlyle*, London 1892 and rpt frequently. Includes a chapter on Carlyle's religion.

Augustus Ralli, *A Guide to Carlyle*, 2 vols, London 1920.

Henry Duff Traill, ed., *The Works of Thomas Carlyle (Centenary Edition)*, 30 vols, London 1896–99.

10

Elizabeth Barrett Browning

[*BAV* pp. 148 f; *NA2* pp. 1173 f]

That Elizabeth Barrett Browning spent much of her early life as an invalid, restricted by her possessive father until her marriage to a fellow poet, Robert Browning, is widely known. That she also had an extremely sound classical education, making of her a formidable Greek scholar, is less well known. Less known still is the fact that this scholarship introduced her to the theological writings of the Cappadocian ‡Fathers, the seminal minds within the developing Christian church of the fourth and fifth centuries. From this study she gained a very high view of the dignity and destiny of all humanity, a view that underlines her passionate defence of exploited freedom in 'The Cry of the Children' and of the creative freedom of human beings, female as well as male, that we see in 'Aurora Lee'. 'The Cry of the Children' is based upon the Christian doctrine of the fatherhood of God in whose image all are created, making everyone brothers and sisters. Her constant refrain 'my brothers' recalls her readers to this fact of human relationship in God, and her question about all actions is, Is this how brothers should treat one another? This fundamental relationship with God is made explicit in lines 113–24:

> Two words, indeed, of praying we remember,
> And at midnight's hour of harm,
> 'Our Father', looking upward in the chamber,
> We say softly for a charm.
> We know no other words except 'Our Father'. (113–17)

If humanity is in the image of God, then conversely humanity gains some of its own understanding of God from the way in which humanity behaves. Humanity can reflect back a true picture of a God of †love through loving behaviour, or present a false image distorted by human greed and callousness. This thought lies behind lines 125–36, reinforced by Jesus' reminders in the gospels that love and ‡virtue are proved by actions and not by words (Matthew 7:21–3). The exploiters of the children are condemned not only for their destruction of a natural joy, which is the children's birthright, but also because they have deprived the children of the supernatural joy of knowing themselves the loved children of God 'the glory / Which is brighter than the sun' (139–40).

In this context, the reference to their †angels in high places is not a piece of sentimentality but an evocation of Jesus' defence of children in Matthew 18:1–10. The angels bear witness against the exploiters before the children of God. This element of †judgement continues in the image of the gold-hoarder (157), which recalls Jesus' warnings that you cannot serve God and mammon (Matthew 6:24) and his *parable of the hoarder of wealth called unexpectedly to account for his life (Luke 12:16–21). This emphasis is maintained until the last stanza; the last four lines remind us of Abel's blood crying out for vengeance to †heaven for his murder by his brother, *Cain (Genesis 4:1–16).

In 'Aurora Lee' the same doctrine of the dignity and destiny of the human being underpins the picture of Aurora's development. Aurora asserts the integrity and responsibility of all human beings for their individual lives. Women too are made in the image of God and bear the responsibility for its development to the full, and face †judgement for failure so to do. The Protestantism in which Elizabeth Barrett Browning was reared stressed such individual responsibility in its rejection of the Catholic notion that the merits, that is, the accumulation of goodness and ‡virtue of one person, could be applied to another. It was reinforced in a more positive way by her immersion in the works of the Cappadocian ‡Fathers. In their anthropology, the identity of the human being is given by God but each individual person has a task of actualising that identity. One has to 'become' a person: it is a work given to individuals and their special responsibility.

In this sense, the person made to be a poet falls short of the mark if that identity is not fulfilled. Although women are created to be complementary, this does not allow the woman to merge her identity and abandon her responsibility in the identity of her husband. The two becoming 'one flesh', the biblical statement regarding marriage (Mark 10:8, among other references) does not eradicate this individual responsibility. This is indicated by Jesus' response to a testing question about a widow, married successively by seven brothers and successively widowed: in †heaven they 'neither marry, nor are given in marriage' (Luke 20:35). Jesus' response makes it clear that the marriage union does not affect this fundamental singleness before God.

This orthodox Christian concept of 'becoming a person' being a task, being work, also lies behind Aurora's rejection of her aunt's pallid virtue. Lines 270–312, describing Aurora's aunt's life and character, present a life half-lived so that the full dimensions of the human being in the image of God cannot be fulfilled. In Christian thought, ‡virtues are moral strength or capacities and as such require practice and development. A life that avoids any situation of challenge or test cannot therefore be truly virtuous since it evades any possible exercise of these gifts. The aunt's virtuous life is in fact an un-virtuous life of moral cowardice. Her frigidity and control come not from the taming of passions encountered, struggled with and overcome, but from a refusal to enter battle with them at all.

This is not the model of Christian ‡virtue offered in Christ who underwent †temptations in the †desert (Matthew 4:1–11; Mark 1:12–13; Luke 4:1–13); was anguished at the prospect of death to the point of sweating blood in the Garden of *Gethsemane (Luke 22:39–44); and is presented to us in the letter to the Hebrews as one 'in all points tempted like as we are, yet without sin', to become perfect through suffering (Hebrews 4:15; 5:7–10). Elsewhere in the New Testament, Christian life is presented in terms of interior warfare, suggesting an engagement with passions, impulses, and temptations, rather than a withdrawal into a spiritually semi-comatose state such as that of Aurora's aunt (Ephesians 6:10–20).

The egalitarianism to which Elizabeth Barrett Browning's interpretation of the Cappadocians gave rise is also evident in her criticism of Aurora's aunt's philanthropy. Not only is it limited to sewing, thus evading human contact, but it also reduces the gospel message of common brotherhood with the poor to a safer adaptation to prevailing class distinctions. We may be 'one flesh', but the flesh of the poor neither requires nor deserves what is appropriate to the more gently bred (297–301). What the doctrine of shared identity and brotherhood would make an act of justice is implicitly reduced to an act of charity towards a lesser, alien class who require less.

Elizabeth Barrett Browning interprets the Greek ‡Fathers' teaching on human identity in the light of the Romantic understanding of poetry as a vocation akin to that of the †prophet (see 'Overview: Romanticism'). The true Old Testament prophet did not choose to be such but was chosen by God and would be condemned by him if he refused to fulfil his given task. We see this in the stories of prophets Isaiah, Amos, and Jeremiah (see Isaiah 6:1–13; Jeremiah 20:9; Amos 7:14–16), and especially in the humorous story of Jonah who did everything possible to evade the prophetic task assigned to him but was eventually out-manoeuvred by God. Aurora is conceived in the same light: her future as poet is a choice of personal life over death. Her speech is not her own, but what is given her by God to speak, just like the prophets.

†Prophecy, in Christian terms, witnesses to the dual nature of the human being who is made in God's image, made for participation in his life, for the

'unseen', but is yet also a created being sharing in animal life and forever †tempted to make this physical, fleshly life the limit of its perspective and destiny. Aurora's remark 'a starved man exceeds a fat beast' recalls Jesus' repetition of an Old Testament assertion 'man shall not live by bread alone, but by every word that proceedeth out of the mouth of God' (Matthew 4:4; Deuteronomy 8:3). It is not enough to raise the status of the human being as a material creature: the true elevation comes when human beings can recognise their spiritual status, their *creation in the image of God, and their destiny to fulfil that identity. As Elizabeth Barrett Browning conceives it, the duty of the poet, such as Aurora Lee, is to alert society to this fact.

QUESTIONS

1. Look up some of the references for 'The Cry of the Children' and explore the ways in which they influence the tone and content of the poem.
2. Look up some of the references for 'Aurora Lee' and consider the role of the poet in the light of their stories.
3. To what extent is your reading of 'Aurora Lee' developed or altered in the light of your knowledge of the biblical and Christian background?

BIBLIOGRAPHY

Deborah Byrd, 'Combating an alien tyranny: Elizabeth Barrett Browning's evolution as a feminist poet', *Browning Institute Studies* 15 (1987), 23–41. Examines Barrett Browning's place in the history of women writers, looking at her reading and influences as well as the development of her social thought.

Helen Cooper, *Elizabeth Barrett Browning: Woman and Artist*, Chapel Hill Carolina 1988.

Deirdre David, *Intellectual Women and Victorian Patriarchy: Harriet Martineau, Elizabeth Barrett Browning, George Eliot*, London 1987. In chapter 8, 'Woman's art as servant of patriarchy: the vision of *Aurora Leigh*', pp. 143–58, David argues that 'Aurora Leigh' is a traditional and conservative endorsement of patriarchal politics.

Barbara Charlesworth Gelpi, '"Aurora Leigh": the vocation of the woman poet', *Victorian Poetry* 19 (1981), 35–48. Sees 'Aurora Leigh' as an exploration of Barrett Browning's changing attitudes toward herself, her profession, and womanhood.

Linda M. Lewis, *Elizabeth Barrett Browning's Spiritual Progress: Face to Face with God*, London 1998.

Susan Walsh, "'Doing the Afra Behn": Barrett Browning's portrait of the artist', *Victorian Poetry* 36 (1998), 163–86.

11

ALFRED LORD TENNYSON, *IN MEMORIAM*

[*BAV* pp. 198 f, esp. 218 f; *NA2* pp. 1198 f, esp. 1230 f; *OA2* pp. 1180 f, esp. 1226 f]

Tennyson (1809–92) was extraordinarily successful as a poet: his books sold in their thousands and were avidly read by all kinds of people from Queen Victoria through to the working classes. In his later life, he was Poet Laureate, he held a state pension, and his income from his books was very considerable. A turning point in his career was the year 1850, in which year he married Emily Sellwood, published *In Memoriam*, and accepted the Poet Laureateship after the death of Wordsworth. Prior to this, and despite the relatively well-received publication of his poems of 1842, which established his reputation, Tennyson's affairs had been in a state of flux, and the poet himself suffered from self-doubt and fears about his health. The year 1850 saw Tennyson established: *In Memoriam* sold well, and other mature poetry followed — *Maud* in 1855, *Idylls of the King* in 1859 (later augmented), and *Enoch Arden* in 1864.

In Memoriam is central to Tennyson's career, both in terms of time (he was forty-one in the year it was published, and he lived to eighty-three) and in terms of poetic achievement. The poem (or poems, since the links in the structure between the sections are slight) captured the imagination of generations and expressed many of the characteristic concerns of the Victorian age. Expressions from the poem have become emblematic of Victorian issues and are still used in ongoing debates. ''Tis better to have loved and lost / Than never to have loved at all' (XXVII:15–16) is quoted to justify the pursuit of romance; 'Nature, red in tooth and claw' (LVI:15) is frequently used to represent the argument that the repugnant savagery of the natural world disproves a benevolent creator; 'There lives more faith in honest doubt, / Believe me, than in half the creeds' (XCVI:11–12) is still quoted in defence of approaches to Christianity that stress openness above doctrine; and 'Ring out the old, ring in the new' (CVI:5) has become a catchphrase for those who believe in progress and 'moving on'.

There is no question that these are serious issues in the poem as well as for Victorian and later readers. But it may be worth backtracking a little to understand the genesis of the poem. Tennyson joined his brothers at Trinity College Cambridge in 1827. Arthur Hallam, brilliant, wealthy, and well-connected, went up to Trinity the following year. By the end of 1829, Tennyson and Hallam were friends and had planned a joint volume of poems; a year later Hallam had visited the Tennysons and become engaged to Alfred's sister Emily. As a cure for persistent ill-health Hallam went abroad but suddenly died of a brain haemorrhage in Vienna in September 1833 at the age of twenty-two. The impact of his death on Tennyson was immediate and lasting. In the short term, Tennyson composed poetry rapidly and well; in the longer term he reflected on Hallam's death and its significance for himself and his view of the world. *In Memoriam* is the fruit of that longer reflection.

In Memoriam is essentially a poem about grief and loss. The structure and metre express the way these turn people in on themselves. The metre, with its rhyme-scheme a-b-b-a, predominantly end-stopped lines, and complete stanza sense-units, is ideal for the encapsulation of single thoughts or images. The self-contained nature of the stanza sometimes makes it difficult to carry thoughts through a whole section and the poet often uses repetition or parallelism[1] for the purpose of creating a sense of continuity and coherence (see, for example, CVI); sometimes, however, repetition gives a profound sense of helplessness (see, for example, the intricate and varied repetitions in LIV; note also the repeated Christmas sections, XXVIII, LXXVIII, and CIV).

The depth of Tennyson's grief for Hallam, and the unrestrained terms in which he expresses his love for the man, have led some scholars to believe that his passion was homoerotic.[2] It is curious that Tennyson published *In Memoriam*, anonymously, the same year that he rather hurriedly married Emily Sellwood; it may be that although Arthur continued to exercise an influence on the poet (*Idylls of the King* is of course about King Arthur), 1850 was the year in which Hallam's hold over his imagination and emotions relaxed somewhat.

T.S. Eliot held the view that '*In Memoriam* can ... justly be called a religious poem, but for another reason than that which made it seem religious to his contemporaries. It is not religious because of the quality of its faith, but because of the quality of its doubt. Its faith is a poor thing, but its doubt is a very intense experience.'[3] Eliot was largely right about the technical achievement of

---

1. See Sinfield, *The Language of Tennyson's In Memoriam*, p. 91, where he writes, 'the syntax is distinctly reminiscent of the Bible, for Hebraic verse was based on the principle of parallel constructions'.

2. For mild surmise on this subject see Page, *Tennyson*, pp. 59–60.

3. T.S. Eliot, *Selected Prose*, Harmondsworth 1953, p. 172.

the poem, '132 passages, each of several quatrains in the same form, and never monotony or repetition', but whether he was right about the religious quality of the poem largely depends on what we interpret 'faith' and 'doubt' to mean. Eliot probably believed that the Christian pieties of the opening stanzas and the Victorian faith in progress expressed in the Epilogue were sufficient to satisfy the poet's contemporaries — these are the poet's overt expressions of 'faith', and are perhaps not the most attractive or profound verses of the poem to the modern or post-Victorian reader. But that the poet expresses 'doubt' in a religious sense is open to question.

What in fact Tennyson is uniquely good at is expressing the questions that bereavement and loss batter the mind with. The famous passage in LVI —

> ... shall he,
>
> Man, her last work, who seemed so fair,
> Such splendid purpose in his eyes,
> Who rolled the psalm to wintry skies,
> Who built him fanes of fruitless prayer,
>
> Who trusted God was love indeed
> And love Creation's final law —
> Though Nature, red in tooth and claw
> With ravine, shrieked against his creed —
>
> Who loved, who suffered countless ills,
> Who battled for the True, the Just,
> Be blown about the desert dust
> Or sealed within the iron hills? (8–20)

— is a question, or rather a series of questions. And the questions are important. What is the purpose of life if there is no God? What kind of God is it whose †love and law are violated so savagely by Nature? And what kind of justice is served upon those who love and suffer and struggle by the random dissolution of death? These are questions that Christians must face, questions that are asked by writers from the book of Job through to C.S. Lewis. The section concludes,

> O life as futile, then, as frail!
> O for thy voice to soothe and bless!
> What hope of answer, or redress?
> Behind the veil, behind the veil. (27–8)

Tennyson has no certainty to offer. It is not even clear *whose* voice is desired. Though the repeated phrase at the end gives some sort of closure, it is categorically not the disclosure that the poet longs for.[4]

Victorians found faith in *In Memoriam*; Eliot found doubt; a modern reader will probably find questions. But all of these are in some ways secondary to the overwhelming sense of personal pain at the loss of his friend that Tennyson expressed in the poem. The poet faced that pain and its implications with honesty: honesty about himself (perhaps the anonymous publication of the poem was due to a fear that he had revealed too much of himself) and honesty about his faith. It is because we have seen the man like an 'infant crying in the night' (LIV:18) that we accept that at times he felt consolation:

> Then was I as a child that cries,
> But, crying, knows his father near. (CXXIV:19–20)

There is little certainty or dogma here, but a fitful sense of the presence of God.

QUESTIONS

1. Read as much of the book of Job as you can, and then C.S. Lewis's short book, *A Grief Observed*, London 1964 (interestingly in view of the anonymous publication of *In Memoriam*, this book was published first in 1961 under the pseudonym N.W. Clerk). Discuss the way grief and the theological questions it raises are treated in these and *In Memoriam*.
2. How do you respond to the opening and closing sections of the poem? Do they accurately reflect what is to come in the poem and what has been said by the end?
3. Do you get any significant sense of Hallam as a person?

BIBLIOGRAPHY

A.C. Bradley, *A Commentary on Tennyson's In Memoriam*, 3rd edn, Hamden CT 1966. A classic study of Tennyson's poem.

Norman Page, *Tennyson: An Illustrated Life*, London 1992. An accessible and well-illustrated short biography.

---

4. For a discussion of the possible meanings of the veil here, see Shatto and Shaw, *In Memoriam*, pp. 221–2. 'Behind the veil' probably means something like 'beyond death', but whatever it is, it remains hidden.

Christopher Ricks, *Tennyson*, London 1972. A fine critical biography.

Susan Shatto and Marion Shaw, ed., *Tennyson: In Memoriam*, Oxford 1982. A full edition with detailed commentary.

Alan Sinfield, *The Language of Tennyson's In Memoriam*, Oxford 1971. A thorough study of the rhetoric and language of the poem.

Robert Browning

BROWNING AND CHRISTIANITY

[*BAV* pp. 332 f; *NA2* pp. 1345 f; *OA2* pp. 1278 f]

Browning was reared in a nonconformist household that encouraged the young man's wide reading and his poetic endeavours. His early poetry was greatly influenced by Shelley, but he also owed a debt to the early preaching of the ‡Unitarian, William Johnson Fox, from whom he imbibed a vision of humanity's *creation for continual growth towards the infinite God.

Browning's poetry only makes its fullest sense when we read it in the light of his belief in the †incarnation, that is, of God taking on human flesh, the whole of human nature, while losing nothing of his Godhead. It is the belief that, in the person of Jesus of Nazareth, the unseen, spiritual, unchanging, and eternal God became also a human being, sharing human involvement in pain, change, and a time-bound outlook on experience. God stooped to share human life so that human beings could aspire to share in God's life. An exchange has taken place: what belongs to humanity is now also in God: what belongs to God can now also be humanity's destiny.

This means that, in Browning's poetry, people are always pushing at the limits set by their state as created, embodied beings. People's vision and re-sources are limited by their physicality and mortality. But these limits must be transcended if the destiny offered by the †incarnation is going to be fulfilled. In order to be fully human people must aspire to reach beyond the limitations set by their human nature to attempt to reveal a glimpse of God in their lives.

If this were all Browning wished to express in his poetry, we would scarcely know it by the title 'Christian'. Many thinkers have suggested that there is a 'divine spark' in every human being. What makes his poetry distinctively Chris-tian is that he takes the other side of the belief in †incarnation equally seriously. God has joined himself inseparably with human beings in their physical lives; he is 'hidden' there. To fulfil their destiny, people must aspire beyond their mortal lives, but also accept them in all their messiness and uncertainty. Hu-mans can only develop their spiritual nature if they simultaneously accept the limitations of their own embodied nature. God-like humanity will not be found by flying off into the ether, but in aspiring towards a higher vision within all the compromises and misunderstandings that result from time-bound, earth-bound lives.

As Browning saw it, the messiness and limitedness of the earth-bound side of human lives is the way in which God protects their freedom. The direct vision of God would leave humans with no option but to worship. Making them to be spirit-bearing and, simultaneously, spirit-hiding flesh, gives them their own ground to stand on and helps them to make their own decisions for or against God. These ideas are most evident in 'Rabbi Ben Ezra' and 'Andrea Del Sarto', while 'Caliban upon Setebos' explores Browning's understanding of the human need for a religion based on the †incarnation.

In this last poem, Caliban has a belief in two gods; Setebos is a cruel, unpredictable force, a projection of all Caliban's most primitive, vicious instincts. The power Setebos wields is the power of human selfishness and lust. The second god is 'The Quiet', a benevolent, transcendent reality that has no contact with humanity. This, Browning says, is natural man's idea of religion: it is either a writing large of his own instincts onto another entity, or the apprehension of an eternal, entirely spiritual goodness that has no contact with his own earthly life. What he needs, Browning implies, is the entry of this eternal benevolence into the world of human instinct. Humankind needs the ‡revelation of God's radical engagement with his *creation. In the †incarnation, no longer are the worlds of benevolent godhood and depraved bestiality kept apart.

Browning studied some of the major thinkers in the early Christian church. He agreed wholeheartedly with their belief in human beings being responsible for their own development. This we find, for example, in the teachings of Gregory of Nyssa: humanity is not the architect, but the craftsman, of its own being. Human makeup, all that we are as human beings, is given by God. We are not responsible for our birth and death, or for the particular gifts and limitations of our individual personalities. We are, however, responsible for what we make of these raw materials.

As Browning understood this tradition, one way of exercising our duties and responsibilities to become fully human is to engage wholeheartedly with the process of time and change. He explores this in 'Rabbi Ben Ezra' using two images for the shaping effect of time and history: firstly, 'the dance of plastic circumstance', and secondly the image of God as a potter, first used in the Old Testament book of the †prophet Isaiah (Isaiah 64:8). In the poem, humanity is still the clay, but the wheel, rather than God himself, is time and change, history working as the agent of God. This clay too differs from the clay of Isaiah because it is responsive and responsible. It is clay that can refuse to give itself to the movement of the wheel, that can refuse to accept all the shaping effects of time and change. In so doing it is clay that fails to become the person it is capable of becoming. Such failure leads to dead ends, to wasted lives and talents, as we see, for example, in the early poem 'Pictor Ignotus' and 'Andrea Del Sarto'.

In 'Andrea Del Sarto' the focus is not so much on time as on creative vision, the capacity for self-transcendence. Andrea longs for perfection: he achieves this at the technical level, but the masterpiece eludes him — why? Because his vision is earth-bound, tied to whatever gives him present pleasure and satisfaction. He cannot, for example, let go of his immediate pleasure in his beautiful but straying wife, in order to strive to convey a beauty lying at the edge of his imagination beyond his present reach.

Although he acknowledges that 'man's reach must exceed his grasp / Or what's a heaven for?' (97–8), he ratifies his choice of earth-bound perfection, his wife, and so misses his fulfilment both as artist and as human being. He refuses to take ultimate responsibility for what he is making or not making of his life and talent by blaming God, choosing to see himself as destined by God rather than as a free moral agent: 'How strange now, looks the life he makes us lead; / So free we seem, so fettered fast we are!' (50–1).

Andrea's idea of perfection is static and so his understanding of life — his own and that of all humans, is static too.

QUESTIONS

1. Elucidate Caliban's understanding of 'The Quiet' and of Setebos.
2. Look up Isaiah 64:8; compare Browning's use of the image and the tone he adopts in 'Rabbi Ben Ezra'.
3. How persuasive do you find Andrea's blaming of God for his relative failure?

'CHILDE ROLAND TO THE DARK TOWER CAME'
[BAV pp. 354 f; NA2 pp. 1367 f; OA2 pp. 1314 f]

Browning's Christian faith and his assimilation of biblical imagery to provide material for his poetry is evident in 'Childe Roland to the Dark Tower Came', a poem that, Browning says, seemed to have been given him like a dream. It can be said to be a depiction of the Christian's task to make the inner †journey to 'the heart', the place of truth about the self, the place where both God and individual godlessness are encountered. This journey is perilous because it entails challenging the existence of that God and all beliefs about oneself.

Browning's epigraph from *King Lear* is a vital clue to the meaning of this poem. In this play Edgar, in escaping from the false accusations against him, is hiding on a heath, pretending to be Poor Tom the lunatic. King Lear arrives and, in seeing Edgar, has a vision of elemental man as nothing but an animal, which precipitates his descent into madness. Tom proves, however, not to be the whole truth about human beings. Lear travels through his land possessed by his conviction about the total depravity of man, only to be reclothed when he is finally reunited with his loving daughter, Cordelia (this echoes the Catholic rite of †baptism in which new Christians are clothed in a white garment to indicate their new life). He learns in his gracious reception and ‡forgiveness by her that there is a grace-full state for man as well as a bestial state, but he can only know this through the confrontation on the heath. Such a confrontation is also made by Childe Roland.

Browning's image of the keep of the †castle is a familiar usage in medieval and ‡mystical literature for the self (see *The Castle of Perseverance* or Donne's Holy Sonnet 'Batter My Heart, Three-person'd God'). Here, its identity as the self is confirmed by the suggestions of uniqueness and impenetrability, being 'blind' (182) and 'without a counterpart / In the whole world' (183–4). But the tower is also ambiguous, for to Roland the turret is also 'blind as a fool's heart' (182). The fool's heart, according to the psalmist, is one in which it is said 'there is no God' (Psalms 14:1 and 53:1). The inner nature of man offers no †light upon itself, suggesting, in this obscurity, the absence of any goodness, that is, of any ultimate Being within it. Like the fool's heart, it witnesses only to non-being. But it is precisely the fool who denies God. The mad Lear who faced human nakedness was restored on receiving the grace-full †love of Cordelia. The enigmatic tower may also enclose a giant of love. To search for the heart, for the innermost self, Browning is telling us, is a perilous undertaking, for it offers no prior assurance about the nature of that self so found, and the dust of man's earthly being may be encountered before the glory of his participation in eternal being.

The †quest for the tower involves painful knowledge of the earthiness of earth-bound man. The seeker is predisposed to anticipate evil and not good from the tower, because the †journey lies through the desolation, maliciousness, and infidelity of man's earthiness. Before the spiritual reality of man can be finally challenged he must experience his involvement with a *fallen, suffering world. The nightmare terrain through which Roland passes is withered *creation awaiting ‡redemption along with man, and which man encompasses:

> I cannot help my case;
> 'Tis the Last Judgment's fire must cure this place,
> Calcine its clods and set my prisoners free. (64–6)

It is therefore also the world of man's own fallen nature in which desire for vengeance is dominant, a world of rigorous, even malicious justice:

> Seldom went such grotesqueness with such woe;
> I never saw a brute I hated so;
>   He must be wicked to deserve such pain. (82–4)

This is the paranoid world of the psalmist, anticipating not †love and brotherhood, but snares and deceits of the enemy:

> My first thought was, he lied in every word,
>   That hairy cripple, with malicious eye. (1–2)

Suspicion, hatred, antagonism and inability to ‡forgive are warring passions encouraged by memory of infidelity:

> … I fancied Cuthbert's reddening face
>   Beneath its garniture of curly gold,
>   Dear fellow, till I almost felt him fold
> An arm in mine to fix me to the place
> That way he used. Alas, one night's disgrace!
>   Out went my heart's new fire and left it cold. (91–6)

All these lines have multiple echoes from numerous psalms. We might look, for example, at Psalms 14, 35, 38, 55, and 129, but we will also find evocations of Psalms 56, 57, 86, and 88. Browning is setting Childe Roland's †journey in the context of the experiences of the psalmists, the psalmists who know God but are not yet saved, have not yet had the ‡revelation of the †incarnation, and therefore do not know the true glory of human life lying within this experience of pain, rejection, and *betrayal.

The paradox of the †quest is the nature of the attainment of its end; the valour of the challenge is rewarded with, rather than fulfilled by, the perception of the end and it is given when Childe Roland's own resources are exhausted. The Tower is not discovered by Roland, but revealed *to* him. The innermost self is present but eludes the mind as long as it clings to its own expectations and preconceptions. Those who confront the mysterious reality of being are both responsible for themselves but finally dependent upon the grace of God. The moment of epiphany is the moment of despair in the natural powers necessary for reaching this point.

It is therefore also a moment of loss: Roland dies to his sense of self-sufficiency and prepares to abandon life in facing unknown reality. In making his challenge, Roland is exploring the condition of all human beings rather than his own personality, and, in his solitary †quest for his own self, he has discovered his involvement with a *fallen world and with the lives of others. Browning presents us with a Christian vision of the human being as made for relationship, a vision that is common to many other Christians of his age who shared in different ways in the same theological and biblical tradition.

QUESTIONS

1. Look up in the Themes section the image of the †quest/journey and consider the way in which Browning employs this tradition.
2. Follow up some of the references to the Psalms and explore the influence of their content and tone on this poem.
3. To what extent do you consider a satisfying reading of this poem is attainable without reference to Browning's allusions to the Bible and to Christian imagery?

BIBLIOGRAPHY

Martin Garrett, *Elizabeth Barrett Browning and Robert Browning*, London 2001.

Stefan Hawlin, *The Complete Critical Guide to Robert Browning*, London 2001. An extremely useful introduction to the Browning oeuvre.

Henry Jones, *Browning as a Philosophical and Religious Teacher*, Glasgow 1891.

John Maynard, *Browning Re-Viewed: Review Essays 1980–1995*, New York 1998. An essential collection of essays, looking at changes of approach in Browning criticism.

J. Hillis Miller, *The Disappearance of God: Five Nineteenth-Century Writers*, Cambridge MA 1963. Also deals with Arnold, De Quincey, Emily Brontë, and Hopkins.

Mary Sanders Pollock, *Elizabeth Barrett and Robert Browning: A Creative Partnership*, Aldershot 2003.

William Whitla, *The Central Truth: The Incarnation in the Poetry of Robert Browning*, Toronto 1963. An essential work for gaining an appreciation of Browning's theology.

Sarah Wood, *Robert Browning: A Literary Life*, Basingstoke 2001.

13

EMILY BRONTË

[*BAV* pp. 429 f; *NA2* pp. 1418 f]

Written at the start of the Victorian era, Brontë's novel *Wuthering Heights*, and her collection of poems, are strongly influenced by the Romantic movement. A clergyman's daughter, she had a fairly rigorous Protestant upbringing, and one might expect this too to show itself in her work. The reality, however, is more ambiguous.

A conflation of Romantic and religious imagery can be found in many of her poems. 'I'm Happiest When Most Away' uses the motif of the spirit riding free of the human body, the 'house of clay' (2) representing material flesh, taken from the earth and destined to return to it. It is a familiar religious image of body and spirit, but it is combined in Brontë with a Romantic concern for the powers of the imagination. On a wild but brightly moonlit night she imagines her ‡soul liberated from the body and all material things, and transported through great expanses of space, encountering the infinite in an image of pure spirit wandering through the immensity. The phrase 'I am not and none beside' (5) has the intensity and jubilant note of transcendent experience. The poem indicates the absence of fear of death and a sense that the poet is not at home in the body. There is a strong sense of religious ‡mysticism.

'The Prisoner. A Fragment' describes a similar 'out of the body' experience. A Christian interpretation of the poem might identify its 'messenger of Hope' (35) with Christ, bringing 'release to the captives ... liberty [for] those who are oppressed' (Luke 4:18), equating 'eternal liberty' (36) with the 'eternal life' of scripture — particularly in the light of the later assertion that the captor's wiles are 'overruled by Heaven' (64). The liberty accorded is again one of ‡mystical transport.

A sense of peace and harmony sustains the captive girl as she encounters 'the Invisible, the Unseen' (49) but, as in 'I'm Happiest When Most Away', it is only temporary in this world — her ‡soul must return for now to the body. The material world is indicated by dark granite vaults, 'triple walls', flagstoned floors, iron gates, and chains whereby the girl is incarcerated, herself compared to a sculptured marble effigy. To this contrasts the image of flight beyond the body and its senses — the soul 'stoops' like a hawk at the edge of a great gulf, its wings 'almost free', and then it 'dares the final bound' (52): bound in the sense of rapid forward movement, but also indicating the crossing of a boundary, the breaching of material confinement. This *'final* bound' indicates, too, a foreshadowing of death. In this ecstatic experience the soul finds its 'home', a traditional Christian metaphor for †heaven, and in this state the girl discovers a perfect, consoling calm.

Her visionary ecstasy is presaged by the wind: as 'I'm Happiest When Most Away' began on a windy night, so the liberating messenger of 'The Prisoner' comes by night and 'with western winds' (37). It represents a conflation in this quasi-Christian context of Romantic and biblical imagery: it has the force of the *pneuma* of the New Testament, which is the wind of God's Spirit, combined with a more Shelleyan symbolism of ‡mystical presence.

The girl declares that her visions 'kill [her] with desire' (40). They provoke an intensity of longing such as many Christian ‡mystics describe. In 'The Interior Castle', for instance, St Teresa of Avila describes much that we find in Brontë: detachment from all things of this life, the 'flight' of the ‡soul in total self-forgetfulness, moments of union with the divine that strengthen the soul, profound silence (Brontë's 'soundless calm' 45), sublime joy, the encounter with transcendent mysteries beyond both body and mind. St Teresa describes how the venomous creatures in the †castle's precincts, representing the †temptations and enemies of the soul, are deprived of their power in the higher reaches of prayer, and in the same manner Brontë's persona asserts that through her mystical experience her captors are stripped of their power over her.

The late poem 'No Coward Soul is Mine' has often been taken as representative of Emily Brontë's faith with its abjuration of fear and doubt and its affirmation of Faith, Life, Immortality, †love, the infinite God, and defeat of the final enemy Death. The language with which the life-giving spirit is described in the fifth stanza is heavily biblical — in Genesis the Spirit of God is said to 'brood' over the waters at *creation (Genesis 1:1) — as also in the final verse where 'Breath' is also a common biblical expression for the Holy Spirit. The image of the anchor that holds the poet firm in her faith recalls the Epistle to the Hebrews where hope based on the promise of God is termed an 'anchor of the soul, both sure and stedfast' (Hebrews 6:19).

'No Coward Soul is Mine' seems then to contain traditional Christian thought and imagery more obviously than the other poems. In its first half Brontë directly addresses God, using the personalised 'thou' and the 'Almighty' of both Bible and Prayer Book, and the God she addresses is within (5–6), drawing perhaps on the Pauline doctrine of the body as the temple of the Holy Spirit, rather than encountering 'the Invisible, the Unseen' in the remote expanses of ‡mystical space above and beyond the body. Though it draws on the Genesis picture of pre-creation, however, the idea of God's Spirit hovering over the chaotic wastes is akin to the earlier visions of immense space where her spirit wanders free. This subsequently gives place to the notion of total absence of the material, 'Though Earth and moon were gone / And suns and universes ceased to be' (21–2), and the stanza elevates the idea of pure Existence, subsumed in God. There seems to be no room here for the doctrine of the *resurrection of the body. The poem does nevertheless conclude, triumphantly and in relatively orthodox Christian terms, with the denial of Death. Death is rendered as powerless as the jailer of 'The Prisoner'.

QUESTIONS

1. To what extent do Emily Brontë's poems incorporate, or go beyond, both Christianity and Romanticism?
2. Is death a positive or negative force in Brontë's work?

BIBLIOGRAPHY

Stevie Davies, *Emily Brontë: Heretic*, London 1994. Although largely conjecture, this feminist study explodes the myth of Emily Brontë's sheltered innocence.

Lyn Pykett, *Emily Brontë*, Basingstoke 1989. Incisive and wide-ranging discussion of the oeuvre, drawing on issues of gender and genre.

Derek Roper with Edward Chitham, ed., *The Poems of Emily Brontë*, Oxford 1995. A thorough, scholarly edition.

14

MATTHEW ARNOLD

[*BACL* pp. 636 f; *BAV* pp. 522 f; *NA2* pp. 1471 f; *OA2* pp. 1365 f]

The Victorian critic and poet Matthew Arnold produced most of his work in the period 1850–80. As well as setting criteria and standards for literary criticism that are still influential, and identifying Shakespeare and Virgil as touchstones for judging literature, he wrote of loss of faith, the discrediting of religion, and was strident in his criticism of ‡Puritan institutions.

In the essay 'Culture and Anarchy' for instance, he sets Greek Hellenism against middle class ‡Puritan organisations, whose informing 'idea of human perfection is narrow and inadequate'. Arnold's own ideal is famously defined as 'sweetness and light'. In 'The Study of Poetry' he envisages poetry as replacing traditional religion since it is able 'to interpret life for us, to console us, to sustain us' — all of which are of course standard functions of religion. Religion and philosophy, he claims, are 'but the shadows and dreams and false shows of knowledge', whereas 'strength and joy' may be drawn from poetry. These ideas of truth, consolation, spiritual sustenance, strength, and joy are all concepts familiar to the Christian.

This turning from traditional religion is reflected by Arnold's exploration of lost faith, hope and †love, the ‡trinity of ‡virtues written about in I Corinthians, in a number of his poems written in the early 1850s.

'Dover Beach', probably Arnold's best known poem, deals specifically with loss of faith. There is nothing triumphant in Arnold's treatment of the subject, however, quite the reverse. He is rendered melancholy by his reflection on a faith that he believes has been discredited and rendered obsolete — he hears in the ebb and flow of the waves an 'eternal note of sadness' (14). The image of the ebbing tide symbolises the retreating power of faith in western civilisation. Once encompassing us 'like the folds of a bright girdle furled' (23) with its connotations of comfort and protection, the 'Sea of Faith' is withdrawn, its †light replaced by night, with only the faintest of glimmerings to relieve its †darkness. Though to Arnold and his beloved the night seascape appears beautiful and dreamlike, the reality is that there is 'neither joy, nor love, nor light,

/ Nor certitude, nor peace, nor help for pain' (33–4). The surface calm of the first stanza belies a reality of chaos and struggle. The final two stanzas each conclude with a Hardyesque image of humankind isolated and vulnerable in a vast, uncaring universe.

'Stanzas from the Grande Chartreuse', written at approximately the same time, conveys a similar sorrow at loss of faith: Arnold's visit to a Carthusian ‡monastery high in the mountains causes the poet to reflect on his personal loss of faith. Chided in his mind by the teachers who have led him away from faith, he views the Carthusians with a 'mournful awe' (82). He feels isolated between two worlds: that of faith, and that of the 'sciolists' (99) who ridicule his melancholy and with whom he feels no affinity either. Life without faith brings no rest and the poem becomes lament, ending with a picture of the Carthusians holding out against the enticements of the world, gazing upon the candles, which are their 'emblems of hope' (201).

If these poems treat the loss of faith, 'The Scholar Gypsy' may be said to depict a loss of hope, for this is a recurring motif. The poet is envious of the outlandish character, so single-minded in his pursuit of strange gypsy arts. By contrast he sees himself fraught with 'the sick fatigue, the languid doubt', not knowing 'for what he strives', and without hope: 'Who wait like thee, but not, like thee, in hope' (161–70). The picture he goes on to paint of the contemporary scholar is of a person without conviction, with casual beliefs, whose understanding does not help him to live any better, a person with vague, unfulfilled resolves, ever disappointed, full of hesitations, never making true progress. Like the scholar-gypsy he awaits 'the spark from heaven' (171), but in vain. Those who are honoured by academia pass on to him only how they have managed their own wretchedness: they try to endure 'this strange disease of modern life' with patience, but none has the qualities of 'unclouded joy' or confidence for the future that the scholar-gypsy evinces: 'none has hope like thine!' (196). He will retain this hope however only by shunning contact with the modern world, for he would soon become infected by 'our mental strife' (222) and then would his 'hopes grow timorous' (227) and be lost.

To Arnold's reflections on the absence of faith and hope in his times can easily be added the third of St Paul's ‡trinity: charity. 'Isolation. To Marguerite' and 'To Marguerite. Continued' each depict a state of isolation and loss of love. In the first of these the poet's lover has rejected him after a period of absence, and he returns to his former solitude. The poem assumes a more universal import in its later stanzas, commenting on the vanity of mortal love and the essential aloneness of the human condition. It suggests that there can be no union with another; we cannot escape our isolation — the nearest some get is merely to dream of it, 'through faith' escaping their loneliness. It is a mode of faith that Arnold cannot sustain. In the subsequent poem of the sequence, 'To Marguerite. Continued', the theme of alienation persists. The conceit of mortals as islands lost in a vast sea is developed at length. The bird of love, the nightingale, sings 'divinely' (10) — an adverb judiciously chosen — but this becomes a torment to the hearer, creating a longing resembling despair, provoking a feeling that all islands were once joined in one but nevermore. It is 'a God' (22), the poet bitterly claims, that decreed this estrangement of humankind from one another. 'A Buried Life' treats similar themes, meditating on the difficulty of communicating to any other person one's inner life, for most men remain 'alien to the rest / Of men, and alien to themselves' (21–2).

The loss of the Pauline ‡trinity of faith, hope, and †love haunts all Arnold's poetry of this period, reflecting his melancholy farewell to Christian belief.

QUESTIONS

1. How does Arnold attempt to maintain a spiritual dignity in the face of a world which appears to have discredited Christian belief?
2. How is the image of the sea developed stanza by stanza in 'Dover Beach', to express the passage from optimism to hopeless realism?

BIBLIOGRAPHY

Kenneth Allott, ed., *The Poems of Matthew Arnold*, 2nd edn, London 1979. Includes detailed annotation and commentary.

Vincent Thomas Buckley, *Poetry and Morality: Studies on the Criticism of Matthew Arnold, T.S. Eliot and F.R. Leavis*, London 1959. A detailed study of the effect of Arnold's moralism and view of religion on his criticism, with particular focus on his essay 'The Study of Poetry'.

J. Hillis Miller, *The Disappearance of God: Five Nineteenth-Century Writers*, Cambridge MA 1963. A fresh interpretation of Arnold, examining his acceptance of the 'withdrawal' of God and the nineteenth-century developments which led to this. Other writers treated are De Quincey, Robert Browning, Emily Brontë, and Hopkins.

15

CHRISTINA ROSSETTI

[*BAV* pp. 662 f; *NA2* pp. 1583 f; *OA2* pp. 1426 f]

Christina Rossetti was a ‡Tractarian Anglican (see 'Overview: The Victo-rian Period'). Tractarians emphasised the value of the 'devout life', a structured daily life of devotion that eschewed the pursuit of pleasure. Tractarian spiri-tuality stressed humility, lowliness, self-effacement, and self-denial, holding duty in high esteem. Even its most brilliant adherents like the Oxford poetry professor and theologian John Keble sought a life out of the public eye and the allure of the 'world'.

In common with Catholics of the time, a common spiritual exercise among ‡Tractarians was meditation on the shortness of life and the inevitability of death and †judgement. This lent a seriousness to every day as potentially one's last. It was also intended to set the necessity of daily self-denial in the light of eternal joy. Thus, though Christina Rossetti's concern with death may owe much to her own temperament, it was lent a more positive note by her convic-tion about eternal life.

That meditation on death reveals the seriousness of life and the necessity of engaging with it is evident in 'Dead Before Death'. If Jesus said 'by their fruits ye shall know them' (Matthew 7:20) then the subject of this poem is indeed known as one who has rejected living in truth and self-knowledge, gaining no profit in †wisdom from experience of life. Facing the reality of physical death challenges people to recognise that eternal life does not begin after death, but in the way that they employ the life given to them.

This same note is struck in the late sonnet to Cardinal Newman. New-man is one who, unlike the subject of 'Dead Before Death', has lived and loved and is therefore fitted for the feast of eternal life. This poem shows us another theme in Rossetti's poetry, the impossibility of sensual or earthly pleasures to provide satisfaction. Line 4 is ambiguous. 'Thy fast was long' suggests first and foremost Newman's long life (he died aged 90), which kept him from the face to face vision of God for which he longed. In this sense his life was a ‡fast from direct vision. This linking of fast and the absence of direct contact with God is suggested in Jesus' comment that his disciples do not fast while he is with them (Matthew 9:15). Now he may feast: that is, take full pleasure in the vision of God. But fast also implies the fasting from lesser distracting pleasures that such desire to feast on the presence of God entails. She wishes him the fulness of love because he had chosen the 'deep' of divine †love over the 'shallows' of human affection. That this may have a price for his feelings is suggested by the theologically precise expression 'thy will / Chose love' (5–6). Rossetti stressed that Newman was guided by his will and not by his feelings, that he understood true love to be a matter of choices and of the use of the will rather than a state of feelings.

The seriousness of moral choices in daily life and the assault on the Christian's ‡virtue from the desire for sensual pleasure is seen in 'Goblin Market'. Goblins, in popular Christianity, are images of enemies to the ‡soul. We see this, for example, in Bunyan's hymn 'Who Would True Valour See': 'Hobgoblin, nor foul fiend, shall daunt his spirit'. We can think of goblins as powers in nature and therefore in the earthiness of human nature that are opposed to goodness. Rossetti's contemporary, the fantasy writer, George MacDonald, uses the goblin as the image of human sensual passions — greed, lust, power, and so on — in such fantasy stories as *The Princess and the Goblin*. They live underground, that is, in sensual human nature, and they seek to take over the whole person. The goblin is a figure essentially linked to sensuality and to the ephemerality of sensual pleasure, but also to the defeat of the rational, choosing self by the desire for pleasure.

The goblin's fruit is called 'orchard fruit' (3). As such it should remind us of the forbidden fruit of that first orchard in the Garden of *Eden: fruit that is pleasing to the eye and pleasant to the taste, but also fruit that brings mortality to *Adam and Eve when they eat it (Genesis 3:1–7). The fruit that the goblins offer is the satisfaction of sensuality that leads to death.

The market also reminds us of Vanity Fair in Bunyan's *Pilgrim's Progress*. Both are markets where sensuality and material pleasures beguile the Christian en route to †heaven. That Lizzie and Laura are young suggests the vulnerability to sensual †temptations of the adolescent. Lines 129–30 support this reading. Both lines are quotations from Psalms. What is claimed in Psalm 19:10 to be 'sweeter than honey from the rock' is the law of the Lord, while in Psalm 104:15 wine is given by God to make 'glad the heart of man'. These fruits, then, are parodies of the divine, seeming to offer more satisfaction than God can give. They seem to offer a pleasure of lasting value. That this is an illusion is suggested by Laura flinging away their empty rinds: once devoured so greedily, nothing of worth remains.

The character of Lizzie shows that ‡virtue does not lie in the absence of †temptation, but in the determination not to heed it. Lizzie is not dead before death: she is alive to the lure of forbidden fruits, but also to their destructiveness. Her action on behalf of her sister is †sacrificial. Just as Jesus was tested by the †devil in the †desert (Matthew 4:1–11), in being besieged by the goblins Lizzie is tempted like her sister, but does not succumb. Experienced through Lizzie's love, the true nature of the sensual pleasures they represent is revealed to Laura (510–12). She metaphorically dies to ‡sin and then is restored to fulness of life both physically and morally, following the pattern of spiritual renewal Christians undergo in †baptism or in any experience of ‡repentance. In this poem, therefore, Rossetti is offering us an entirely Christian moral vision within the framework of fable.

QUESTIONS

1. To what extent does your awareness of Rossetti's religious views affect your understanding of her view of life and death?
2. Read the †temptation story in Genesis 3 and consider the ways in which this can be said to determine Rossetti's presentation of the goblins and their fruit.
3. To what extent do you think this poem can be seen primarily as a Christian moral tale?

BIBLIOGRAPHY

Joseph Bristow, 'The culture of Christina Rossetti: female poetics and Victorian contexts', *Victorian Studies* 44 (2002), 501–3. A helpful overview of responses to Rossetti.

David Kent, ed., *The Achievement of Christina Rossetti*, Ithaca and London 1987. A very useful collection of essays, setting Rossetti within her ‡Tractarian milieu.

Scott Rogers, 'The edge of sisterhood in Christina Rossetti's "The Convent Threshold"', *Journal of Pre-Raphaelite Studies*, new series 14 (2005), 30–42. This is a good source of articles on all aspects of Rossetti.

Dolores Rosenblum, 'Christina Rossetti's religious poetry: watching, waiting and keeping vigil', *Victorian Poetry* 20 (1982), 33–50.

G.B. Tennyson, *Victorian Devotional Poetry: The Tractarian Mode*, Cambridge MA and London 1981. Helpful in appreciating Rossetti within her religious and poetic setting.

16

GERARD MANLEY HOPKINS

[*BACL* pp. 656 f; *BAV* pp. 853 f; *NA2* pp. 1648 f; *OA2* pp. 1465 f]

The ‡Oxford Movement, which began with Keble's sermon 'On the National Apostasy' in 1833 (*BACL* pp. 570–9), culminated in the poetry of one of our profoundest Christian poets, Gerard Manley Hopkins (1844–89). A great admirer of George Herbert and, from his own age, Christina Rossetti, he celebrates God's ‡sacramental presence in the world as well as exploring his own intensely personal struggles in verse. The poems were not published until nearly thirty years after his death, in 1918, when they were highly influential on the development of modern poetry, especially in terms of their technique.

Those written in 1877 are generally recognised to be a self-contained group taking nature as their focus. They were written while Hopkins was at the ‡Jesuit College of St Beuno in North Wales. They draw greatly upon the surrounding countryside and are greatly concerned with Hopkins' ‡sacramental view of nature.

'God's Grandeur' demonstrates the method of these poems. A biblical analogue for its first line, 'The world is charged with the grandeur of God', might be Psalm 19:1, 'the heavens declare the glory of God', but Hopkins replaces 'declare' by 'charged', for God is not only reflected by nature but is ‡sacramentally present within it. 'Charged' has overtones of a fulness that is ready to burst out. Hopkins used a similar image in one of his sermons: 'All things therefore are charged with love, are charged with God and, if we know how to touch them, give off sparks and take fire, yield drops and flow, ring and tell of him.' 'God's Grandeur' has two images to illustrate the principle of sacramentalism and to show how God's presence breaks forth: flaming out and oozing out, one sudden and the other gradual. The images of flame and shining anticipate the way in which morning 'springs' forth in the sestet.

A biblical source for the metaphor, 'It gathers to a greatness, like the ooze of oil / Crushed' (3–4), lies in favour of oil oozing from olives as they are crushed and then used for the Tabernacle lamps of the Old Testament. There are also associations of *Gethsemane, which name means 'oil-press', and to the sweat and blood of Christ. Biblical commentators conventionally interpret oil as a type of the Holy Spirit. There are at least three biblical images of the Holy Spirit in this poem: oil, fire, and the dove.

The line 'Why do men then now not reck his rod?' (4) suggests mankind's rejection of Christ's authority and his †cross, and it resonates with the exploration in the second quatrain of the rejection of Christ in nature where men are seen to be out of touch with the natural world. That everything 'wears man's smudge and shares man's smell' (7) is reminiscent of the *fall and the curse — 'in the sweat of thy face shalt thou eat bread' (Genesis 3:19). The concept that the foot cannot feel, 'being shod' (8), takes up the Old Testament tradition of holy ground, such as that upon which Moses stood at the burning bush when, as in the second line of 'God's Grandeur', God's presence was revealed through flame (Exodus 3).

The sestet is concerned with the ‡redemption of the *fallen world — there is a latent freshness beneath the bare soil waiting to be drawn up. Such redemption includes the ‡salvation of humankind and is represented by images of the rising sun and the brooding of the †heavenly dove over a new *creation. The Holy Spirit broods over the world each morning as in Genesis: 'the spirit of God moved upon the face of the waters. And God said, Let there be light …' (Genesis 1:2–3).

Hopkins is assimilating well-established biblical symbols and archetypes in this period of his poetry. Later that year, 1877, he left the seclusion and beauty of St Beuno's for a period of ministry in Oxford, Bedford Leigh, Liverpool, London, and Glasgow. In the poems of this more priestly period the focus shifts from nature to man. The poems often include such folk as he would have encountered in each parish and express his compassion for them and a concern for the ‡salvation of ‡souls. In 'Felix Randal', based on an actual event in Hopkins' ministry, he refers to doctrinal concepts through the theological word 'ransom', and to the ‡sacraments of the church, but there is somewhat less focus than previously on broader symbolic images.

In the so-called 'terrible sonnets' of 1885, which depict Hopkins' desolation at this time, the poet turns inward, away from nature and from his priestly concern for others, to examine his own relationship with God. Critics have often noted the likeness of these poems to Job's dialogues, and to the outpourings of Jeremiah and the Psalmists in the Old Testament.

Later come what critics call the 'poems of recovery', the greatest of which is 'That Nature is a Heraclitean Fire and of the Comfort of the Resurrection', an extraordinary reaffirmation of Hopkins' faith in Christ. This poem again uniquely adapts traditional ‡eschatological ideas and imagery to a form which anticipates modern poetry. This experimental sonnet begins with an extravagant description of the natural world, this time borrowing Heraclitus's concept that everything derives from the basic principle of fire and is in a constant state of flux. Hopkins also depicts the tragedy of man as a small element of that fire being drowned 'in an enormous dark' (12) through death. This state of things is reversed, however, by the doctrine of the *resurrection. The transient is replaced by the 'eternal beam', which is Christ, the †light of the world. Hopkins extends the drowning image by describing himself as a foundering ship, and the beacon as a lighthouse.

It happens 'In a flash, at a trumpet crash' (21). Hopkins draws on Christ's teaching that his *second coming will be as unheralded and as sudden as lightning. He is referring also to the Pauline doctrine that believers will be resurrected to the sound of a last trumpet call and transformed into the likeness of Christ (I Corinthians 15:52–3). In the final coda the thought of the *resurrection comes with astonished joyfulness as Hopkins describes how the 'mortal must put on immortality', detritus becoming diamond.

QUESTIONS

1. Where is the ‡sacramentalism of Hopkins' approach to nature reflected also in his view of men and women?
2. What biblical analogues can you find for the 'terrible sonnets' of 1885?

BIBLIOGRAPHY

William Henry Gardner, *Gerard Manley Hopkins (1844–1889): A Study of Poetic Idiosyncrasy in Relation to Poetic Tradition*, 2 vols, London 1944–9. An important study of Hopkins' poems and their influence.

Norman H. Mackenzie, ed., *The Poetical Works of Gerard Manley Hopkins*, Oxford 1990. An accurate and informative, scholarly edition.

The Notebooks and Papers of Gerard Manley Hopkins, 2 vols, 2nd edn, London 1959. Contains Christopher Devlin SJ, ed., *The Sermons and Devotional Writings of Gerard Manley Hopkins*, the standard edition of the sermons.

John Barclay Pick, *Gerard Manley Hopkins: Priest and Poet*, 2nd edn, London 1966. Relates Hopkins' poetry to his ‡Jesuit life and background.

17

EVOLUTION

[*NA2* pp. 1679 f]

The broad concept of evolution was very much in the air during the Victorian period. Consequently the impact of Darwin's particular theory of evolution by natural selection was not entirely the conceptual bombshell that the modern popular imagination pictures it. This is especially so with regard to the belief in the literal truth of the accounts of *creation in the first two chapters of Genesis. No leading church ministers during this period held a literalist interpretation of the Genesis account. The great ‡Evangelical preacher Charles Symeon, for example, made gentle fun of literalist ideas, as did the Evangelical minister and geologist Hugh Miller who held up to ridicule the notion of changes to animals resulting from the *fall of *Adam and Eve. Like the great Protestant theologian of the ‡Reformation, ‡Calvin, they held that the Bible was to be studied for theological, not scientific, knowledge.

This insistence upon a non-literalist reading was equally shared by E.B. Pusey, leader of the ‡Tractarians, and F.D. Maurice and Charles Kingsley of the Christian Socialists, the last a keen amateur geologist. Indeed the leading geologists of the time were ‡Evangelicals like the minister Adam Sedgwick. Their geological studies made it clear that the age of the earth far exceeded the period calculated from the biblical record by Archbishop Ussher as 4004 BC for the date of the *creation. They also suggested the existence of hitherto previously unknown life-forms. This led to support for the notion of phased creation in line with an interpretation of the 'days' of the biblical creation narrative as extended periods.

This notion led some to espouse the 'catastrophe theory'. Gaps in the fossil records made it possible to hypothesise that development occurred within species but not between them, while some environmental catastrophes caused the end of each phase of *creation. This allowed for a process of development within a framework of specific acts of creation.

Others held the 'gap theory', that the accounts in Genesis 1 and Genesis 2 were not complementary but represented two phases of *creation separated by a great time lapse: Genesis 1 was held to be concerned with the phased develop-ment of the earth and Genesis 2 with the much later creation of humankind.

Certain Christians, however, were able to go further in embracing the con-cept of evolution. The ‡Evangelical scholar Patrick Fairbairn, for example, ar-gued that Genesis 1 described a phased *creation in which human life evolved from simpler forms. Earlier, simple forms, he asserted, were 'types' of the later, culminating in the highest point, humankind. Most churchmen, therefore, had minds open to developments in the understanding of human origins by some kind of evolution that allowed for the theological truth of God as creator of all from nothing and of the special place of human beings.

Darwin's *The Origin of Species* thus appeared in a climate open to his gen-eral thesis. What caused difficulties in its reception was his theory regarding the *mechanism* of evolution, natural selection. Natural selection and the associated popularised idea of 'the survival of the fittest' seemed not to require any design-ing, guiding, or purposive mind. There is no absolute need or necessary place for a plan or purpose behind the phases in Darwinian evolution. Evolution oc-curs as the consequence of organisms existing in an environment where they must avoid predators and compete for resources such as food and water. There is no necessity to posit an originator or a guiding vision or purpose behind this evolutionary change. Evolution by natural selection seemed, therefore, to offer a totally materialist understanding of origins and to deny humankind their status as specially created beings. Such a theory seemed, consequently, also to challenge the much-used argument of natural theology that the existence of God could be discerned through the design of the universe.

Darwin refused to commit himself publicly to a stance on these issues whilst his manner of writing at times conferred an apparent purposiveness upon Nature. This seemed to allow for a theistic interpretation of this process since Nature, or Dame Natura, had been understood since the early Middle Ages as the vicegerent of God.

The Christian opposition to Darwinian evolution was focused, therefore, on its theological implications, rather than on the issue of biblical truth; it was also directed towards Darwin's scientific methods. Bishop Samuel Wilber-force, so often derided for his debate with Darwin's proponent, T.H. Huxley, was, in fact, quite competent in his understanding of Darwin. His objections lay equally in the materialist view of *creation and in concern for the absence of scientific evidence in support of the theory. The geologist Adam Sedgwick similarly combined his rejection of the materialist vision with objections to Darwin's non-inductive method and lack of evidence.

In the poet Tennyson we have an example of another, less academic response to Darwinism. For Tennyson, natural selection as 'the survival of the fittest' seemed to suggest a 'Nature, red in tooth and claw', based on predation and destruction. How could such a natural process be the creating means of a †loving God? Previously the situation within wild nature could be seen as a consequence of the *fall of *Adam and Eve, which destroyed the original harmony and peace within *creation. In the light of Darwin, now destruction and predation would need to be understood as chosen by a creator-God. Tennyson's response was, ultimately, to reject Darwinism in its details, whilst maintaining an overall vision of progression in Nature, which eschewed any claim to be scientific (see further the essay on Tennyson).

Yet others accepted that this difficulty was an aspect of that question of evil and suffering that transcended human powers to answer. Those who held science and religion together were able to maintain the position, in the spirit of ‡Calvin's approach to the Bible, that science answers questions regarding the processes of life whilst religion addresses issues of meaning and purpose. Conflict remained for those who considered that science and religion offered competing explanations not only of the origins but also of the meaning of life.

QUESTIONS

1. What approaches to human origins have you noticed in literature of this period?
2. Look at the way in which Browning and Tennyson develop ideas of human progress. To what extent do you think these ideas have links with the theories of evolution outlined here?

BIBLIOGRAPHY

Peter Allan Dale, *In Pursuit of a Scientific Culture: Science, Art, and Society in the Victorian Age*, Madison WI 1989.

Daniel Kohn, ed., *The Darwinian Heritage*, Princeton NJ 1985.

Stephen Prickett, 'Rescuing nature from Darwin: literature and religion in Victorian England', in Franco Marucci and Emma Sdegno, ed., *Athena's Shuttle: Myth, Religion, Ideology From Romanticism to Modernism*, Bologna 2000.

Robert M. Young, *Darwin's Metaphor: Nature's Place in Victorian Culture*, Cambridge 1985.

18

Industrialism

[NA2 pp. 1696 f]

The industrialisation of Britain in the nineteenth century evoked a critical response, not so much because it was viewed as inherently negative, but because of the social conditions to which it gave rise. We must beware of Engels's picture of rural innocence and plenty giving way to urban misery. Other documents of the period, such as Cobbett's *Rural Rides*, give us a stark picture of pre-industrial rural poverty in the early nineteenth century and the misery of the hand-loom weaver. Financially, industrial workers in the nineteenth century may, as Macaulay suggests, have benefited from the rise of the factories. But these gains have to be set against the conditions in which they worked and lived.

Industrialisation led to the break up of established rural communities, with their support networks and the possibility of some basic education for children in Dame schools, and of some help in need from local gentlewomen wherever a landlord accepted responsibility for the welfare of his tenants. The rush to the city led to severe overcrowding in inadequate and unsanitary housing, providing an ideal breeding ground for disease, as we see, for example, in *Bleak House* where Nemo and Joe pass on cholera. We also see it in *North and South* where the working conditions in the mill and the living conditions at home make it impossible for those who have inhaled cotton dust to survive.

In the factories and mills, the drive to maintain production and minimise costs led to absence of concern about working conditions for both adults and children, subject alike to harsh discipline from overseers. Children working in factories from the age of five had no prospect of education or of any other play potentially open to the country child. Young babies were left with minders prepared to dose them with laudanum or gin in order to keep them quiet. After working long hours, little leisure was open to working people other than the gin palaces.

The Christian response was two-fold: political action and missionary activity. In the earlier decades of the century, ‡Evangelicals proved their effectiveness in campaigning against the slave trade. Led by Lord Shaftesbury, attention was then turned to limiting child labour and working hours. We see this concern with children echoed in Elizabeth Barrett Browning's poem 'The Cry of the Children' which might be said to be the poetic war-cry of this battle.

Not all ‡Evangelicals or leading industrialists were behind Shaftesbury. As Dissenters, that is, non-Anglican Protestants, their involvement in public life had been directed towards trade rather than political life. Success in this was seen as a mark of God's favour. Emphasis was therefore upon an individual's endeavour to improve living conditions rather than government legislation. Laissez-faire economics seemed allied to godliness. A popular version of this view, Samuel Smiles's *Self Help* achieved widespread success in the 1860s.

By contrast, the Christian Socialist Movement opposed the alliance of capitalist economics with Christianity. Central to their belief was the unifying principle of brotherhood under Christ: Christ — Son of God, Son of Man — was the elder brother of the human race. Brotherhood, and hence cooperation was therefore at the heart of all human institutions. A system that dehumanised its workers because of an economy based upon competition was therefore seen to be based on a lie.

This did not, however, lead Christian Socialists to support the Chartist Movement. Though much in sympathy with their demands, they saw the Charter as unnecessary. As Charles Kingsley avers in *Alton Locke*, workers already had their charter of equality and freedom in the Christian gospel. It was this charter that he urged them to embrace. The leading figure in the Movement, Frederick Denison Maurice, not only supported the political campaign of preaching and pamphleteering but also became involved in practical initiatives to improve the lives and status of working people, such as the establishment of the Workers' Educational Association and the foundation of Kings College as part of the University of London.

Maurice held to the ideal of the educated worker, rather than to the notion of self-improvement out of the working-class. He wanted society to accept the dignity of work and hence of the worker, remembering that Christ had been the carpenter and that all labour was cooperation with the creating power of God. In this he had much in common with Carlyle's approach to work as found in *Past and Present*, and his views also found eloquent exposition in the novels and fantasy stories of George MacDonald, author of *Lilith* and *The Golden Key*. Both ‡Evangelicals and ‡Tractarians initiated practical responses to the social effects of industrialisation. Evangelicals opened Ragged Schools to provide basic education for adults and children, and missions that offered food, recreation, and education.

In the 1860s, William Booth expressed the attitude of many of his Christian contemporaries in the title of his study of urban poverty, *In Darkest England and the Way Out*. We can see reflections of this same attitude in Dickens's presentation of England in *Hard Times*, where the workers are described as savages in a bestial environment, and of the street urchins in *Bleak House*. The poorly housed, ill fed, and uneducated workers of England's big cities were more benighted and miserable than the African natives who were so much the concern of contemporary missionaries and their English supporters like Mrs Jellyby. They too needed the †light of the Christian gospel and conditions fit for the children of God. The ‡Tractarians equally made the neglected inner cities their priority. Pusey's great sermon 'Our Pharisaism' was a blistering attack on the neglect of the industrial poor who were left, he felt, in deeper ignorance than any African tribe. His question 'Is this a Christian country, or is it Hell?' might easily have been posed by Dickens, who adopted a similar position not only in *Hard Times* but also in the earlier novel *Dombey and Son*, despite the differences between the two writers in attitudes to matters of church practice.

Booth's response to the neglect of the working classes was the establishment of the Salvation Army, offering not only material aid and Christian teaching, but also possibilities of a life that brought some order and some pleasure into lives that lacked both. Dickens was a supporter of this aim, backing the Campaign for Brighter Sundays, to counteract the joyless experience of the ‡Puritan Sunday that allowed neither recreation nor pleasure, an experience he tellingly describes in *Little Dorrit*. This campaign was later continued by the ‡Tractarian Christian Socialist, Stewart Headlam. These enterprises suggest how concern for working people cut across denominational barriers in Victorian society.

QUESTIONS

1. Look up the essay on Elizabeth Barrett Browning's poem 'The Cry of the Children' and its biblical references. How might the insights obtained inform your reading of the entries in this section?

2. Consider the imagery Dickens uses in the extract from *Hard Times* (*NA2* pp. 1711–12). In what ways might your understanding of the background to this imagery enhance your appreciation of his purpose in employing it?

3. How does Maurice's Christian understanding of the dignity of working people compare with the picture given in the entries in this section?

BIBLIOGRAPHY

David J. Bradshaw and Suzanne Ozment, ed., *The Voice of Toil: Nineteenth-century British Writing about Work*, Athens OH 1999.

Patricia E. Johnson, *Hidden Hands: Working-class Women and Victorian Social-problem Fiction*, Athens OH 2001.

Edward Norman, *The Victorian Christian Socialists*, Cambridge 1987.

E.P. Thompson, *The Making of the English Working Class*, London 1980. This covers the earlier period up to the Reform Act of 1838 but is essential for understanding the situation throughout the century.

19

THE WOMAN QUESTION

[NA2 pp. 1719 f]

As in so many other areas, the Victorian period does not offer a uniform Christian response to the debate regarding gender. Whilst many Christians, women as well as men, accepted Sarah Stickney Ellis's view (NA2 pp. 1721–2) that women's nature limited them to the cultivation of the heart and to self-abnegation, others challenged such a stance on religious grounds, or offered a more subtle approach to the issue of gender difference.

Stickney Ellis represents the mingling of two strands in Christian thinking regarding women that develop out of the representation of *Eve in the opening chapters of Genesis. Discussion of Eve by such church ‡Fathers as St Jerome emphasised her weakness and sensuality. It is *Eve, not Adam, who in Genesis 3:1–4 is targeted by the serpent. She is more vulnerable intellectually to the wiles of the serpent and sensually to the appeal of the fruit, it is argued.

One of the consequences of *Adam and Eve's *fall after their ‡sin is the loss of their primal mutuality: henceforward women will be submissive to their husbands (Genesis 3:16). This view is later supported by St Paul's refusal to allow women to speak in the assembly and to have headship over men, as well as his requirement of submission from wives to husbands (I Corinthians 11:1–16; Ephesians 5:21–33). That Adam was made by God first and had a direct relationship with him, and *Eve was then created as his helpmate, seemed to seal the woman's nature as an adjunct to the male. Accordingly the independent woman was regarded as a dangerous and sinful figure; and the female came, in some interpretations, to represent lower or carnal sensual nature needing the control of rational, higher nature identified with the male. We may see some of this even in apparently feminist authors like George Eliot. Rosamund in Middlemarch, for example, is trivial and sensual. She lacks Lydgate's intellectual grasp and his moral integrity. Her name, Rosa Mundi, 'rose of the world' traditionally suggests the attractions of the vanities of the world and again seems to identify the figure of woman with what is sensual and passing.

But this *Adam and Eve account has one other feature. Eve is told she will be saved by childbearing and so the way is prepared for another, potentially more positive, view of women as nurturing mothers, a view culminating in the image of the Virgin †Mary as a mother who was also submissive to the will of God, in her acceptance of becoming the mother of Christ, 'Be it unto me according to thy word' (Luke 1:38). Whatever objections there might have been to Catholic veneration of the Virgin Mary, the widespread and popular iconography of the story of Christmas, of mother and child, was effective in disseminating another version of the submissive woman who enshrines the positive values of the heart.

At first reading, Coventry Patmore's often derided *The Angel in the House* seems to echo Stickney Ellis's sentiments. Closer reading, however, reveals a differing viewpoint and theological stance. Patmore, a Catholic, develops a strand in Catholic and Orthodox thinking that sets women morally above men. His wife is 'the best half of Creation's best'. It is female nature that is found fit to be ennobled by giving birth to the ‡saviour. In the blessed Virgin †Mary, human nature in its female form reaches a height denied to men. All women share in this elevation. Further, precisely because she is capable of motherhood, she is regarded as being closer to divine †love than is the male.

This was a view shared by the fantasy writer, George MacDonald, author of the novels *Phantastes* and *Lilith*, and another great Anglican theologian, Frederick Denison Maurice. Unlike Patmore, who appears to see no role for women outside the home, Maurice and MacDonald were strong supporters of a woman's right to education and to engage in the world. They insisted, however, that the two genders were distinctive and not interchangeable. Maurice, for example, who had given help and support to the establishment of Queen's College, London, for women, did not find the training of women as doctors acceptable, as it breached his understanding of what was inherent in female human nature.

It is against the narrow confines of what is understood as a woman's nature that Florence Nightingale struggles in *Cassandra*. In her remark about marriage (*NA2* p. 1737), she alludes to another version of the *creation story in Genesis. Genesis 1 gives an account of the creation of man and woman as equals in the image of God: 'male and female created he them'. In fact an early translation stated 'male and female created he him' and so it was held to mean that each human being had been originally male and female. In some exegesis this was held to mean that each human being was both male and female, or had both aspects to their being. It is this which was lost in the *fall of *Adam and Eve and marriage was one way in which that original unity was recovered.

Emphasis on this version of Genesis validated women like Florence Nightingale and Harriet Martineau in their pursuit of morally and intellectually challenging occupations in a so-called 'man's world'. Harriet Martineau, the daughter of a ‡Unitarian minister, came from one kind of Protestant tradition that valued freedom of thinking and stressed the essential dignity and equality of all people. In this they were at one with the contemplative branch of Christianity, a tradition that emphasised the dwelling of the Holy Spirit in the depths of Christian and their common identity as images of God. So the first ‡monk, for example, St Antony the Great, could speak of men and women as 'sharing the same intellectual substance', and Gregory of Nazianzen, perhaps the most revered of orthodox theologians, could praise his sister, St Gorgonia, as an equal to men.

Such belief allowed for the emergence of the educated woman, albeit usually within the ‡monastery. Echoes of this tradition can be seen in Thomas More's provision of a classical education for his daughter. Thus the phenomenon of the well-educated Christian woman was not in fact an aberration in the nineteenth century although most Christians would have considered it as such, given the generally constricted nature of their own education. What was new, however, was the demand for participation by such women in public life as authors, scholars, administrators, and teachers, such as we find in *Cassandra*.

We see in Dinah Craike the great potential for charitable work latent in the boredom of middle-class and-upper class female life. This work tended to divert Christian women from demands for professional status: Victorian Christian women busied themselves in charities, often for destitute children and 'fallen' women. Harriet Martineau herself founded a refuge for the latter with the help of Charles Dickens. The dutiful life and influence of the educated and intelligent ‡Tractarian woman often features in the novels of Charlotte Yonge.

Others were inspired by the missionary endeavours of the nineteenth century and gave themselves to fund-raising to support the great missionary societies of the age. Dickens offers a satirical portrait in Mrs Jellyby in *Bleak House*, a woman so consumed with the needs of the 'heathen in Borioboola-ga' that she cannot see the needs beneath her own nose, in her own home and society. Dickens's concern over the blindness of women to the unromantic misery in their own land was shared by the ‡Tractarian Pusey, who complained that when courageous women wished to engage in mission they thought only of overseas mission and ignored great need in England.

Some women were, however, alive to these needs and they were often the Catholic or ‡Tractarian women who joined the burgeoning religious communities in both churches and provided devoted nursing and teaching in the disease-ridden slums of industrialised England. If we approach it from a secular perspective, we can see that these communities provided their members with skills as nurses, teachers, and administrators and offered opportunities for leadership and exercise of authority that would be closed to them in the secular world. Indeed, one of the common complaints against the restoration of female religious communities in the Anglican Church at this time was that women were being removed from the proper control of their fathers and husbands. In the literature of the period a negative view of religious life for women is evident in *Jane Eyre* and in the close of *Hard Times*.

These religious communities were often closely concerned with the other aspect of the woman question raised in the Norton anthology: prostitution. Such communities rarely questioned the social structure that gave rise to prostitution or to which reformed prostitutes must conform. The focus was not so much on the nature and causes of prostitution but on the integration of these women into Victorian society. Thus they may be open to criticism for their moralistic approach that maintained focus on the women's ‡sin. They did, however, at least rescue many women from the disease and violence involved in prostitution and equip them with skills to make a poor, but unexploited, living. The plight of the 'fallen woman' was addressed by Elizabeth Gaskell in *Ruth*, to the outrage of some sections of the Victorian reading public, whilst Dickens's depiction of 'marriage-marketing' in *Dombey and Son* analyses the hypocritical attitudes to the 'fallen woman' in the light of the financial considerations lying behind many respectable marriages.

There were, however, Christian women who did look at this issue through new eyes, seeing its root causes in poverty and the low status of women. Chief among them was Josephine Butler, wife of an Anglican clergyman. Her endeavour to share and understand the lives of the poorest working women led to the improvement of conditions for prostitutes and to an attack on the legal underpinning of dual standards in her society, as well as to the eventual development of the role of the moral welfare worker within the Anglican Church. We can see that throughout the period the social conscience of Christians, particularly of Christian women, prepared them for making common cause with their secular sisters in the growing movement for female emancipation.

QUESTIONS

1. Follow up the biblical references about women and trace their influence in the entries in this section.
2. To what extent is your reading of *The Angel in the House* altered by your awareness of the theological background?
3. Trace the two Christian views of women in *Cassandra*.

BIBLIOGRAPHY

Bonnie S. Anderson and Judith P. Zinsser, *A History of Their Own: Women in Europe from Prehistory to the Present*, 2 vols, Harmondsworth 1988.

Patricia E. Johnson, *Hidden Hands: Working-class Women and Victorian Social-problem Fiction*, Athens OH 2001.

Christine L. Krueger, *The Reader's Repentance: Women Preachers, Women Writers, and Nineteenth-century Social Discourse*, Chicago and London 1992.

Susan Mumm, *Stolen Daughters, Virgin Mothers: Anglican Sisterhoods in Victorian Britain*, London 1999.

20

OSCAR WILDE

[*BAV* pp. 947 f; *NA2* pp. 1747 f; *OA2* pp. 1126 f (*The Importance of Being Earnest*)]

Oscar Wilde is as well known today for his life as for his writing. Indeed, it could well be said that his life was part of his artistic achievement, as he carefully cultivated an image of the aesthete: 'I have put my genius into my life; I have only put my talent into my works.'[1]

The relationship between Wilde's life and Christianity began with a paradox that was typical of him. He and his brother were †baptised as infants into the Church of Ireland. Wilde's father, Sir William, was, in addition to being a prominent surgeon, a convinced Protestant, and aware of the importance of religious orthodoxy in Anglo-Irish Dublin. Two of Wilde's uncles were Church of England clergy. Lady Wilde, however, was a more quixotic figure, and just to be sure of their ‡salvation she may have had her boys baptised as Catholics when Wilde was about four (hence, perhaps, the preoccupation with baptisms in *The Importance of Being Earnest*).[2]

Wilde flirted with Catholicism throughout his life before finally converting on his deathbed. In this he was not alone, as it was the age of Cardinals Newman and Manning, admired Catholic prelates whose influence led to a significant number of conversions. Many in the adult Wilde's circle were Catholics or converts to Catholicism. Robbie Ross — who may have been Wilde's first male lover and who was certainly his lifelong and most loyal friend — was a devout Catholic; and the great love of Wilde's life, Lord Alfred 'Bosie' Douglas, converted some time after Wilde died. John Gray, Wilde's poet friend (whose name inspired the title of *The Picture of Dorian Gray*), became a Catholic priest in an institution that attracted other authors and artists such as Ernest Dowson, Lionel Johnson, and André Raffalovich.

As an undergraduate at Trinity College Dublin, Wilde had several priests as friends. By then, Newman had founded the Catholic University in Dublin,

---

1. Wilde quoted by André Gide (Colm Tóibín, *Love in a Dark Time: Gay Lives from Wilde to Almodóvar*, London 2002, p. 37).

2. Ellmann, *Oscar Wilde*, p. 19. As he lay dying Wilde was conditionally baptised into the Catholic church. As the ‡sacrament of †baptism cannot be given twice, 'conditional baptism' is a form which is used where there is the possibility that the person has already been baptised.

and his rich prose style drew the young Wilde.[3] In Oxford, while Wilde was a student, several of his acquaintances became Catholics, and one close friend, David Hunter-Blair, unsuccessfully tried to convert Wilde who resisted because he said that his father would disinherit him.[4] By 1876, however, Wilde wrote that 'I am more than ever in the toils of the Scarlet Woman' (*Letters*, p. 15).[5] He went several times to hear Cardinal Manning preach, declaring him to be 'more fascinating than ever' (*Letters*, p. 20).

Religion was not absent from Wilde's art at this time. In 'San Miniato', a poem of the early 1870s, Wilde goes to see a Florentine church famous for its religious frescoes. There, he expresses not simply his reverence for Christ, but also worship of the Virgin †Mary, which was more in keeping with Roman or Anglo-Catholicism: 'Mary! Could I but see thy face / Death could not come at all too soon.'[6] In 1877 Wilde was visiting Italy and was in Rome for ‡Easter Sunday. His poem 'Easter Day' (written about the same time as 'E Tenebris') is largely given over to admiration of the pomp surrounding the ‡pope, 'Like some great God, the Holy Lord of Rome'.[7]

Wilde's religious struggles are also reflected in some of his poetry in the anthologies, although not always with his ongoing dalliances with Catholicism. 'Hélas' opposes romantic passion with the teachings of Christianity, 'Mine ancient wisdom, and austere control' (4). The persona of the poem considers that he might once have taken a religious path and 'Struck one clear chord to reach the ears of God' (11), but wonders if this is still possible having 'but touch[ed] the honey of romance' (13).

The poem 'E Tenebris' ('out of darkness', a title that anticipates 'De Profundis', 'out of the depths') follows a fairly standard Christian theme, the doubt and unworthiness of the individual who eventually comes to rest in the peace of Christ. As one might expect, the poem is littered with scriptural allusions (noted in most editions). Its Christ is a very human one, despite initially being at a distance that necessitates his coming down to the poet, his 'wounded hands, the weary human face' (14) unite the suffering poet and his God.

It is human suffering that is the pervasive theme of 'De Profundis', Wilde's long letter to Lord Alfred Douglas, written while he was in Reading gaol. Its title comes from the opening line of Psalm 130: 'Out of the depths have I cried unto

---

3. Ellmann, *Oscar Wilde*, p. 32.

4. Ellmann, *Oscar Wilde*, pp. 51–2.

5. Holland and Hart-Davis, ed., *Complete Letters*; The 'Scarlet Woman' was a reference to a malign figure found in Revelation 17:1–5 and often identified by Protestants with the Roman Catholic Church.

6. *Collins Complete Works*, p. 749.

7. *Collins Complete Works*, p. 771.

thee, O LORD.' Parts of the letter continue the identification between Christ and the author that was found in 'E Tenebris': 'Only one whose life is without stain of any kind can forgive sins', Wilde notes, and 'I must take the burden from you and put it on my own shoulders', just as Jesus shouldered the ‡sins of the world in the carrying of his †cross (*NA2* p. 1805). Wilde stresses Christ's ‡virtue of humility, a virtue that he sees himself as having attained in his incarcerated misery: 'There is only one thing for me now, absolute Humility' (*NA2* p. 1806).

Despite this, Wilde denies that he is conventionally religious: 'Religion does not help me' (*NA2* p. 1807). He takes actual experience ('Whatever is realized is right', *NA2* p. 1808) and spiritualises it: 'There is not a single degradation of the body which I must not try and make into a spiritualizing of the soul' (*NA2* p. 1807). His religion is, therefore, an earthly one, and yet he would retain some of the traditional rituals of Christianity: 'where on an altar, on which no taper burned, a priest, in whose heart peace had no dwelling, might celebrate with unblessed bread and a chalice empty of wine ... agnosticism should have its ritual no less than faith' (*NA2* p. 1807).

Wilde remained attracted to ritual without the accompanying faith throughout the rest of his life. After his release from Reading he travelled in Europe. In 1900 he revisited Rome from where he wrote, 'I do nothing but see the Pope: I have already been blessed many times, once in the private Chapel of the Vatican ... my position is curious: I am not a Catholic: I am simply a violent Papist' (*Letters*, p. 1184). In a self-aware parody of what we would now call 'camp' he notes of the ‡pope that 'Each time he dresses differently; it is most delightful' (*Letters*, p. 1186), while elsewhere, he is disappointed that Leo XIII 'has approved of a dreadful handkerchief, with a portrait of himself in the middle, and basilicas at the corners' (*Letters*, p. 1182).

What can be made of all of this? Summing up the private life of faith of anyone is difficult even given a whole book. Wilde was too much of an outsider, too estranged from the conventions he ridicules in *Earnest* to have remained a member of what he perceived as the bourgeois established church. He remarked to a friend, 'The Catholic Church is for saints and sinners alone. For respectable people the Anglican Church will do.'[8] At the time the Catholic church had just as little sympathy for Wilde's sexuality as any Protestant one did, and Wilde died expressing his outsider status in religious terms as he had lived an outsider in terms of sexual morality.

---

8. Ellmann, *Oscar Wilde*, p. 548.

QUESTIONS

1. Compare Wilde's approach to religion with that of Gerard Manley Hopkins, another poet who converted to Catholicism.
2. Does Classical or Christian reference predominate in Wilde's work?
3. What moral views are put forward by Wilde and how are these related to religion?

BIBLIOGRAPHY

Karl Beckson, 'Oscar Wilde and the religion of art', *Wildean: The Journal of the Oscar Wilde Society* 12 (1998), 25–9.

Richard Ellmann, *Oscar Wilde*, London 1988. Remains the most famous of the biographies of Wilde. It may well be supplemented by reading Wilde's *Letters*.

Hilary Fraser, *Beauty and Belief: Aesthetics and Religion in Victorian Literature*, Cambridge 1986.

Merlin Holland and Rupert Hart-Davis, ed., *The Complete Letters of Oscar Wilde*, London and New York 2000.

The Collins Complete Works of Oscar Wilde. Centenary Edition, Glasgow 1999. This edition is currently the most complete 'Complete Works' available and contains all his poetry and critical prose as well as his more famous plays.

21

GEORGE MACDONALD

[*BACL* pp. 640 f]

Good fantasy writing is, in Coleridge's terms, symbolic: it reveals a transcendent, eternal reality through, and in, the temporal.[1] When thoroughly imagined and expressed, it evokes its own fictive reality, that is, it engages us as *story*, and puts the reader in contact with a reality beyond itself. Images, characters, and plots have their own integrity: we, as readers, suspend disbelief and enter the fictional world. Understood in this light, Christian fantasy writing is the outcome of an imagination that works in ‡sacramental terms, seeing the material world as participant in, and mediator of, the divine.

Never is this more true than of the imagination of the Scottish writer George MacDonald (1824–1905), who is perhaps best known for his children's fantasies *At the Back of the North Wind*, *The Princess and Curdie*, *The Princess and the Goblin*, *The Lost Princess*, and *The Golden Key*.

MacDonald understands the natural world as the created reflection of God. It is, as it were, God's mirror; by looking humbly at it we find his image. It is also, as in the medieval tradition, the vicegerent of God, the created power that bears his imprint and executes his will. Nature is such because it is indwelt by that other created reflection of God, †wisdom. Because of this man can gain natural wisdom from the contemplation of nature and may find instruction in accepting whatever forces he experiences from the natural world. In this sense nature frequently appears specifically as the created reflection of the Holy Spirit. In *At the Back of the North Wind*, for example, North Wind combines the qualities we would associate with both.

As natural beings, humans are also indwelt by †wisdom; at their deepest centre, the heart, natural wisdom speaks of God. Consequently when humans look at the natural world 'deep calleth unto deep' (Psalm 42:7): God's wisdom in the natural world addresses and awakens the wisdom of the heart. Wisdom guides, protects, and reveals to each their identity in God's eyes as images of Christ. The biblical figure of Wisdom is feminine. When she indwells the earth from

---

1. R.J. White, ed., *Coleridge: Lay Sermons*, London 1972, pp. 28–30.

which humans come she is also maternal. This idea is in line with the Orthodox concepts MacDonald imbibed from Jacob Boehme: the eternal Fatherhood of God is mediated temporally in the motherhood of women. This is the source and meaning of the waxing and waning, aged and yet youthful, grandmother figures who guide, instruct, and purge the protagonists of the fantasies.

These figures in the fantasies are not presented as mere abstractions or metaphors. Their characteristics are those of the grandmother; a love more objective than mother-love, a †wisdom and serenity arising from age, a capacity to shock with glimpses of youthful vitality and beauty. This conveys earthly experience whilst also suggesting how such experience also reveals the beauty of God, ever ancient and ever new, the 'Ancient of Days' and the eternal child. Likewise the human fact of possessing, even without knowing, a great-grandmother, speaks of the reality of existence as related beings. Humans cannot exist without the parents from whom they come; neither can they exist without the God from whom they come. To deny either is to reduce humanity to the level of the beasts to which MacDonald constantly likens the forgetful man, as in the Wise Woman's fears that Rosamund would become 'a hideous sort of lizard' in *The Wise Woman* or *The Lost Princess*.

If nature is the *created reflection of God then it finds its high point in human nature, for the human being is the created image of the nature of God. Whenever spiritual life stirs in a person, the end and purpose of their growth is the realisation of identity as a 'Christ-self'. Such an awakening alters the way they perceive others. In their physicality resides the image of Christ, the source of their eternal worth and their claim on others as brothers and sisters. In the short story 'Birth, Dreaming and Death', a village schoolmaster is anxiously awaiting the birth of his child. The night is bitter. He dozes before the fire. A knock on the door. (Is he awake or dreaming?) He finds there an abandoned child whom he takes in and tends:

> But when he had undressed and bathed the little orphan, and having dried him on his knees, set him down to reach for something warm to wrap him in, the boy suddenly looked up in his face, as if revived, and said with a heavenly smile, 'I am the child Jesus.'
>
> 'The child Jesus!' said the dreamer, astonished. 'Thou art like any other child.'
>
> 'No, don't say that,' returned the boy; 'but say, Any other child is like me.'[2]

---

2. George MacDonald, *The Gifts of the Child Christ and Other Tales*, 2 vols, London 1882, II:254.

MacDonald evokes all the realities of caring for the child. Here indeed is a child's body that has been bathed, dried, and warmed. It is in and through this body that Christ is known. We might recall the opening of the first letter of St John: 'That which ... we have heard, which we have seen with our eyes, which we have looked upon, and our hands have handled, of the Word of life ... was manifested, and we have seen it, and bear witness ...' (I John 1:1–2). It is this Good News of God indwelling human flesh which MacDonald's art is intent on conveying.

It is noteworthy that the story just mentioned concerns a dream. In Mac-Donald's view the ‡sacramental nature of human life is far more likely to be perceived through the operation of 'heart, imagination and conscience' than through the 'hireling powers of the intellect'.[3] For him, the imagination is the human capacity to illuminate reality, the faculty that helps us to recognise what is and to appreciate its value. The creative artist does not create at all but gives expression to the primary imaginative act of perception, and the content of any imaginative expression is not produced by the writer's brain but is received by the deepest level of their being. Any true act of the imagination is inherently sacramental since it is giving material embodiment to a divine reality. Where only the brain or the 'hireling intellect' is engaged there can be no true and living imaginative expression, as North Wind tells Diamond in *At the Back of the North Wind*: 'Some of our thoughts are worth nothing because they've got no soul in them. The brain puts them into the mind, not the mind into the brain.'[4]

And where people are out of relationship with God their ability to see is limited to the outer reality, for they can have no true imagination, or what is experienced can be 'dressed' only in the garments of disordered passions. Consequently in the Curdie stories, Curdie sees only a wizened old apple rather than great-great-grandmother when he is in a ‡sinful state and in *At the Back of the North Wind*, North Wind is seen as a ravening wolf by evil characters.

Although MacDonald denies the human origination of thoughts and images, he does not reject the human role in shedding light on them and giving them human dress. God sows seed in the soil of the human spirit: how the seed develops depends upon the nature of the soil and the effectiveness of the 'goblins' and 'miners' of the psyche in producing food for the seed. In the Curdie stories, goblins and miners dig up treasures from the earth. In the †castle of Princess Irene, these treasures enhance her life when all is under the control of spirit. Her life is threatened, however, when the goblins intend to reduce the

---

3. George MacDonald, *Malcolm*, London [no date], p. 32.
4. George MacDonald, *At the Back of the North Wind*, London 1899, p. 213.

whole of life to underground existence, that is, when the life of spirit is totally overwhelmed by the life of the passions derived from the earthly nature.

In the Curdie stories we also find use of a set of biblical images that abound in MacDonald's works, that of the †house/castle/tower/room. A commonplace in medieval literature, the image of the house for the dwelling-place of the ‡soul takes various complex forms in both fantasies and novels. While the †castle or the house speak of the total person, the cottage, the tower, and the hidden room speak of the heart, the spiritual centre where God dwells but where the fool also says 'there is no God' (Psalms 14:1; 53:1). The heart is the place of combat for the soul, the place where compunction, ‡repentance, and ‡purgation occur, the place where conscience speaks. This is the dwelling of the Wise Woman or great-grandmother whom we have already met.

The richly gifted character, like Princess Irene in the Curdie stories, lives in a many-roomed †castle, while the simpler natured Curdie inhabits a cottage. Curdie, one might say, lives more closely to his centre but has fewer treasures to draw into it from his other 'rooms'. Irene, by contrast, has more difficulty in finding her centre amidst the multiplicity of rooms in her palace. The tower is a far less frequented place than the few rooms of Curdie's dwelling but once it is found, guidance, illumination, and self-knowledge are gained.

The imagery of the tower is suggestive of the ‡mystics' concept of 'the high point of the soul' and may also imply the provision of protection. The cottage suggests something much humbler and more vulnerable, the heart as the place of struggle and ‡repentance, as in *The Wise Woman* or *The Lost Princess*. The princess has failed and failed again in her efforts to reform unaided and has reached the stage of accepting her need. She is now more sufficiently aware spiritually to face the †temptations from her wayward passions and heed the advice of the Wise Woman: 'I saw how you rushed into the middle of the ugly creatures; and as they ran from you, so will all kinds of evil things, as long as you keep them outside of you, and do not open the cottage of your heart to let them in.'[5]

Once again this spiritual reality is mediated through mundane imagery. MacDonald uses his art to enable us to appreciate that spiritual combat and ‡purgation take place in our domestic realities, in our homes, rather than in some esoteric spiritual realm divorced from human experience.

---

5. MacDonald, *The Gifts of the Child Christ*, I:260.

QUESTIONS

1. Compare and contrast MacDonald's view of nature with that of any other writer in this volume. In what ways do you find him distinctive?

2. How would you explain MacDonald's view of human imagination and creativity?

BIBLIOGRAPHY

Rolland Hein, *Christian Mythmakers: C.S. Lewis, Madeleine L'Engle, J.R.R. Tolkien, George MacDonald, ...,* Chicago 2002.

Rolland Hein, *The Harmony Within: The Spiritual Vision of George MacDonald,* New York 1999.

Joseph Johnson, *George MacDonald: A Biographical and Critical Appreciation,* London 1906.

Kathryn Lindskoog, *Surprised by C.S. Lewis, George MacDonald, and Dante: An Array of Original Discoveries,* Macon GA 2001.

William Raeper, ed., *The Gold Thread: Essays on George MacDonald,* Edinburgh 1990.

22

FRANCIS THOMPSON, 'THE HOUND OF HEAVEN'

[*BAV* pp. 992 f; *NA2* pp. 1856 f]

Thompson was the son of Catholic converts. Unable to fulfil his vocation to the priesthood, Thompson, like many before him, became a drug addict as a result of medical treatment. He experienced true dereliction, physically and spiritually, living as a vagrant on the banks of the Thames in the closing years of the Victorian age, before experiencing conversion. His poem 'The Hound of Heaven' is, therefore, both an intensely personal account of his own experience and an expression of the relationship between God and every person he has created. This second dimension is effected through Thompson's use of the Bible and of traditional Catholic imagery, especially imagery drawn from the ‡mystics who wrote of the ‡soul's direct contact with God.

Behind this brilliant evocation of the †love affair between God and the ‡soul lies Psalm 139:7, 'Whither shall I go from thy spirit? or whither shall I flee from thy presence?' The emphasis in the poem is on the omnipresence of a loving and all-knowing God. The psalmist we have quoted challenges any tendency to see God as merely a super-being, a God who is simply like a human being, but greater. The psalmist emphasises, rather, that he is the atmosphere, as it were, in which we live.

But the lines we have quoted suggest the possibility of the human ‡soul's desire to escape from the demands of God. Biblically, Thompson would have found this, for example, in the story of Jeremiah, whose determination not to speak the words of †prophecy given him only resulted in greater pain (Jeremiah 20:7–9) and in the story of Jonah, whose attempt to flee his calling as a †prophet takes him through the vicissitudes of being thrown overboard and swallowed by a whale and spewed onto the shore of his God-given destination, until he recognises that he cannot escape from God and from his designs for his life (Jonah 1–2). This understanding of the pursuit is also at the centre of the Song of Songs, where it was sometimes interpreted as the soul seeking the divine †lover (see, for example, Song of Songs 3:1–3). Within the ‡mystical tradition, however, we often find that this pursuer-pursued relationship is reversed. We find, for example, in the *Confessions* of St Augustine, and in the writings of the great Spanish mystic St John of the Cross, an awareness that the reality reverses what is assumed. St Augustine insists that the God he sought outside himself was in fact hidden within him and St John of the Cross asserts that God is the pursuer, the one who is ever seeking relationship, like the sun always sneaking in through any available crack.[1]

We can see that in this poem the ‡soul learns, in reverse, the truth of Jesus' saying 'seek ye first the kingdom of God, and his righteousness; and all these things shall be added unto you' (Matthew 6:33). Evading his pursuer, nothing is given to him, nothing satisfies. He learns the truth on which the ‡mystical tradition insists, that only God suffices, the consistent teaching of, for example, the ‡anchoress Julian of Norwich, and the Carmelite mystics St Teresa of Avila and St John of the Cross. He learns, too, that this 'tremendous lover' is also a jealous one, allowing no rivals for his †love (130–3).

In his allusion to Samson as prisoner of the Philistines pulling down the temple upon himself and upon his enemies, Thompson attributes his own captivity to a desire for satisfactions other than God (for the story of Samson, see Judges 16:23–31). Unlike Samson, however, his desire to destroy his enemy (that is, his †temptations), leads not to death but to eventual new life.

Line 135 suggests the image used by St John of the Cross for the ‡soul in the process of being purified. The fire of divine †love works on the inner being like fire on a log of wood. Just as the fire first chars the wood, making it ugly as the water is driven from it in order for it to be able to catch fire, so the fire of God's love first drives out the soul's ‡sinfulness and imperfection, making it feel ugly to itself, in order for it to be pure enough for divine love to possess it.[2] Thompson, or the persona of the poem, is undergoing the process of purification that alone can lead to full relationship with God.

In lines 171–6, the persona realises that any pleasure, any satisfaction, any †love that he could legitimately seek, lies in God. Before these things can be experienced, all illusions must be abandoned and the stark reality of death and †judgement faced, for lines 152–4 echo Jesus' imagery regarding the day of †judgement (Matthew 13:24–30), and the true status of the human being in confrontation with his *creator must be acknowledged. Firstly, the ‡soul is

---

1. See Kieran Kavanaugh and Otilio Rodriguez, trans., *The Collected Works of St John of the Cross*, Washington DC 1991, 'The Living Flame of Love', stanza 1, para 19 (stanza numbers refer to the commentary on the poem).

2. See Kavanaugh and Rodriguez, trans., *St John of the Cross*, 'The Living Flame of Love', stanza 1, para 15.

reminded that this God against whom he is now complaining is the one who has made all things from nothing (Genesis 1) and this is the one who can make something from the ruins of his life. Secondly, before the creator, the only one who can claim existence without derivation, no created beings can claim to be anything in their own right.

In themselves, human beings are nothing but clay or dust of the earth, totally dependent for human life on the breath of God (as we find in Genesis 2:7). Referring to the fleeing ‡soul as clay also recalls Isaiah's depiction of the creator-created relationship as that between potter and clay (Isaiah 64:8; also Jeremiah 18:4–6). It also takes up Paul's reminder that it is not for the clay to control the potter (Romans 9:21). Thompson brings together, in this stanza, a number of biblical allusions and images that emphasise the nothingness of human beings without God and the plenitude awaiting them when they accept the relationship with their †loving creator for which they were made: all is stored at home. There is no joy apparently lost on earth that will not be found in the vision of God. The poem, therefore, offers us an insight into Thompson's own personal religious struggle, but it also echoes the struggle with God that is at the heart of the Christian ‡mystical tradition.

QUESTIONS

1. What are your immediate impressions on reading this poem?
2. Follow up some of the biblical references and consider the ways in which these may cause you to refine or revise your first impressions.
3. Do you consider it is possible to attain a satisfying reading of this poem without some awareness of Thompson's biblical and Christian framework?

BIBLIOGRAPHY

Paul van Kuykendall Thomson, *Francis Thompson: A Critical Biography*, New York 1961.

John Evangelist Walsh, *Strange Harp, Strange Symphony. The Life of Francis Thompson*, London 1968.

Section 5

THE TWENTIETH CENTURY

1

Overview: The Twentieth Century

The decades around the turn of the century mark both a sea change in literature and a change in the influence of Christianity in British culture. Published in 1903, though completed some twenty years before, Samuel Butler's *The Way of All Flesh* embodies a rejection of times past, questioning the values of Victorian society, and is in part a biting satire of Victorian conceptions of religion through the depiction of a clerical household. In this iconoclastic novel the hero's father, after ordination, becomes cruel and a disciplinarian in his own home — he is the paradigmatic Victorian: humourless, moralising, and oppressive, a pedantic hypocrite; his son Ernest Pontifex is ordained, too, but loses faith in favour of rationalism.

Attacks on Victorian and post-Victorian religion were frequent at this time. George Bernard Shaw, in plays like *Androcles and the Lion* (1913), exposed the gap between faith and practice. In this play Christians are about to be fed to the lions. Ferrovius is a domineering, proud character, though divided and tortured, whose temper gets the better of him. Spintho is a self-pitying, cowardly character, who decides to recant but is eaten by lions anyway. These are contrasted with Lavinia, a humble, sincere woman who turns out to be a free-thinker rather than a Christian. In an appendix added later Shaw relates the play to the circumstances of World War I, in which light it becomes an attack on the church of the day: Ferrovius is typical of the clergy who 'served Mars in the name of Christ' — hypocritical, insincere, and with 'no reasoned convictions'. It is a theme picked up by some of the war poets who attack the church for its complicity with the state in blinkered attitudes to the horrors of war.

Other instances of the assault on Victorian clergy may be seen in writers of the distinctively non-Christian Bloomsbury Group: Lytton Strachey's portrait of an ambitious, scheming Cardinal Manning, leader of the Catholic community in England, in his mocking essays *Eminent Victorians*, or E.M. Forster's satire of Reverend Mr Eager and Reverend Mr Beebe, contrasted with the atheistic rationalist Mr Emerson in *A Room with a View* (1908).

The temper of the early decades of the century was in part moulded by what came before: Victorian doubt, the decadence and ennui of the nineties with its sidelining of moral concerns, and then the ensuing cataclysm of World War I. Religious convictions were weakened as the old values and certainties seemed to disintegrate. The early twentieth century was dominated by modernism, which had its golden age between 1910 and 1925. Writers like T.S. Eliot wrote of a post-war spiritual disillusionment: *The Waste Land* (1922) in particular depicted the desperate absence of faith and the barrenness of post-war society, together with the longing for a renewal and rebirth that remained elusive.

Modernism inherits the epistemological concerns of the Enlightenment: how can we know the world, how can we penetrate reality? In trying to gain a handle on this reality it brings our civilisation and culture into question, smashing the old traditions and beliefs, as reflected in the breakup of traditional literary forms. With the fragmentation comes the search for a new language to express new experiences and feelings. Verse forms, for instance, are often the equivalent of collage in art, in the attempt to construct a literary equation of reality.

For the 'faithless pilgrims' of Conrad's *Heart of Darkness* (1902) reality, especially as reflected in the African landscape, appears chaotic and incomprehensible, even malignant. The inability to locate an objective reality leads, for some, to a belief that there are no absolutes, no universal truth or meaning, only absurdity, chance, and alienation, with a concomitant anguish. The Theatre of the Absurd in the 1950s is an expression of this, though some critics have still linked some works with a spiritual tradition. Samuel Beckett's play *Waiting for Godot* (1954) presents waiting as a predominant characteristic of the human condition. God is absent, though the poet Louis MacNeice perceives in Beckett that 'the absence of God implies the need of God and therefore the presence of at least something spiritual in man'.[1] Martin Esslin sees in *Waiting for Godot* a concern with the hope of ‡salvation and the search for reality, and compares the characters to 'the personifications of virtue and vices in medieval mystery plays'.[2]

With the gradual development of postmodernism the notion of a universal and ultimate reality and of the Christian 'grand narrative' diminish through the rest of the century. There is often now no sense of underlying permanent truth but many coexistent truths and realities that are socially and linguistically conditioned. Meaning has become contextual.

Despite the bleakness from a Christian perspective of the literature of modernism, in the 1930s there are signs of a resurgence of interest in the spiritual

---

1. MacNeice, *Varieties of Parable*, p. 142.
2. MacNeice, *Varieties of Parable*, p. 119, quoting Martin Esslin, *The Theatre of the Absurd*, London 1962. Esslin's treatment of Beckett, the first chapter of his book, 'The search for self', pp. 29–91 of the 3rd edn, 2001, is seminal.

and in Christian ideas of ‡redemption. Eliot in the meditative 'Ash Wednesday' (1930) indicates a gradual turning to faith, couching the desire for rebirth in Christian language. His *Four Quartets* (1945) are outstanding religious meditations on time and history and the timelessness of spirit. His play *Murder in the Cathedral* (1935) is a kind of modern ‡mystery play and *The Cocktail Party* (1949) deals with issues of guilt and redemption.

In the 1940s W.H. Auden also began to develop a concern with religion and increasingly used orthodox Christian beliefs that are explicit or lie in the background of his longer poems and volumes such as *The Quest* (1941), *For the Time Being* (1944), and *The Age of Anxiety* (1947). The poem 'The Sea and the Mirror' presents a reading of Shakespeare's *The Tempest* as Christian ‡allegory. His meditative sequence 'Horae Canonicae' deals directly with Christian themes: the seven church offices give a liturgical structure to this meditation on the unfolding of history with Christ at its centre and ‡redemption a possibility.

Mid-century, a number of Catholic novelists whose faith suffuses their work gain prominence. Of these the greatest is Graham Greene. *Brighton Rock* (1938) is a thriller with guilt and mercy as its themes. *The Power and the Glory* (1940) picks up the same themes through the figure of the unsaintly yet compassionate priest who commits mortal ‡sin. *The Heart of the Matter* (1948) again deals with conscience: Scobie is an isolated figure, a devout Catholic, who struggles to remain faithful to his wife and to honour God. He chooses to ‡damn himself through committing suicide, but out of compassion: he no longer wishes to cause pain for his wife, his mistress, or God.

Evelyn Waugh's Catholic faith becomes prominent in *Brideshead Revisited* (1945) and his later, more serious novels. Of the former, he said its theme is 'the operation of grace' upon its characters. Muriel Spark is another Catholic writer who once stated, against the current of the times, 'I am interested in truth — absolute truth.'[3] In her novels the spiritual dominates, and there are many suggestions of the supernatural under the surface of the world.

William Golding wrote novels in the 1950s that were at odds with the prevailing realism and provincialism of other fiction at the time. His greatest works take ‡free will and inherent evil — †original sin in Christian terms — as principal themes. In *The Lord of the Flies* (1954) boys stranded alone on a Pacific island give free rein to the cruellest instincts that lie beneath a veneer of civilised behaviour. There is much Christian imagery and allusion in this symbolic work. John Wain declares that 'this vision of evil is so black that it can

---

3. Spark, 'The House of Fiction: interviews with seven novelists' (an interview with Frank Kermode) in Malcolm Bradbury, ed., *The Novel Today: Contemporary Writers on Modern Fiction*, new edn, London 1990, p. 142.

only be counterbalanced by a vision of sanctity',[4] which occurs in the person of Simon — spiritual, even ‡mystical, with shades of Moses and Christ. In the Faustian *Pincher Martin* (1965), the anti-hero fights for survival on a rock in the Atlantic, as if in ‡purgatory, making ‡virtues of his endurance and courage, though he refuses to accept the existence of God and his offer of ‡redemption. Both these novels conjure with issues of death, ‡sin, and †judgment, and Louis MacNeice sets Golding's works in a tradition of †parables reaching back to Bunyan's *Pilgrim's Progress*.

The first half of the twentieth century was still conversant with the King James Version of the Bible, and the continued use of its language and imagery is undoubted. In addition to the writers mentioned so far, it may also be found in writers without religious affiliation. The Christian poets rediscovered in the early part of the century — Gerard Manley Hopkins whose work was published for the first time in 1918, and the metaphysical poets who were promoted by T.S. Eliot — had their influence, albeit chiefly a stylistic one (Dylan Thomas, for instance, was influenced by Hopkins technically and by Henry Vaughan in the increasingly religious terms of his later work).

The Christian tradition lives on even in those writers who reject the faith. In the second half of the century the atheistic Jim Crace retells the account of Christ's forty days in the †wilderness in *Quarantine* (1997) but denies his divinity. Margaret Atwood creates a futuristic dystopia, the republic of Gilead, by drawing on ideas from the Old Testament and early ‡Puritan society in *The Handmaid's Tale* (1996). In the semi-autobiographical *Oranges Are Not the Only Fruit* (1985) Jeannette Winterson attacks the restrictiveness of the dissenting religious community in which she was brought up and structures it in eight chapters named after the first eight books of the Bible.

For Christians to write in a culture hostile to 'grand narrative' is not straightforward, but a number of significant figures stand out. One of the foremost religious writers of the later twentieth century was the poet-priest R.S. Thomas who composed very personal works exploring the ‡mystery of a frequently silent God, often in questioning, even angry terms, though displaying compassion and stoicism. Perhaps less anguished by conflicts of personal faith are other Christian poets, such as Elizabeth Jennings who explores spiritual and religious concerns with a deep sensitivity to the suffering of others; Denise Levertov in her later years; Les Murray, who dedicates his volumes, like Bach, 'to the glory of God'; and the Irish poets Patrick Kavanagh and Micheal O'Siadhail. One of the finest Christian novelists of the end of the century is the

---

4. Quoted in MacNeice, *Varieties of Parable*, p.146.

Australian Tim Winton whose works often take a gritty look at the problems of his characters, sometimes with a kind of supernatural realism, as in *Cloudstreet*. The Christian tradition is diminished in influence by the turn of the century but still a force to be reckoned with.

QUESTIONS

1. Louis MacNeice sees traces of a centuries-old †parable tradition in a number of twentieth-century writers. What works would you consider to be in this tradition?
2. Golding's novel *The Lord of the Flies* ends with Ralph weeping 'for the end of innocence, the darkness of man's heart'. How do different writers deal with this theme in a Christian way?

BIBLIOGRAPHY

Boris Ford, ed., *The New Pelican Guide to English Literature*, Harmondsworth 1961, volumes 7 and 8. These volumes contain a large number of helpful essays on individual writers and movements.

George Sutherland Fraser, *The Modern Writer and His World*, rev. edn, Harmondsworth 1964. Provides an overview of 'modernity' in literature, covering the first half of the twentieth century, looking at the novel, drama, poetry, and trends in criticism.

Frederick Louis MacNeice, *Varieties of Parable*, Cambridge 1965. Discusses literary-critical perspectives on †parable and examines the different forms of parable occurring throughout the canon.

Thomas Hardy, *Poems*

[*BAV* pp. 802 f; *NA2* pp. 1916 f; *OA2* pp. 1521 f]

Hardy (1840–1928) was an established novelist before he took to publishing and writing poetry consistently, and he turned to poetry because of the adverse criticism his novels *Tess of the D'Urbervilles* (1891) and *Jude the Obscure* (1896) received. His *Wessex Poems* appeared in 1898, the first of eight collections published between then and 1928.[1] The *Wessex Poems* collection contains many poems that were written earlier, and thus Hardy's poetry ranges from the Victorian period with its questions of faith, the early twentieth century with its focus on war, through to the uneasy equilibrium of the post-war years.

Hardy's particular gift in writing was to explore and capture the unexpected, the accidental, the random, and the improbable. His range of imaginative resources is wide, and he draws on folklore and story, history and current affairs over a long life, nature and religious belief, personal experience of loss and a gift for narrative. Although the emphasis in both his novels and the selection of verse in the anthologies is on the unhappy convergence of otherwise unremarkable human and natural factors, like the 'Titanic' and the iceberg in 'The Convergence of the Twain', there is nevertheless often a delight and hopefulness about his verse. He cheerfully mocks human foibles like the naive guilelessness of the girl, and practised vain acting of the preacher in 'In Church', as well as the pretentious coyness of Amelia and the envy of her interlocutor in 'The Ruined Maid'; and his nostalgia takes a happy turn as he appreciates human warmth and hopes for truth in the folk tradition of 'The Oxen'. He also has a gentle melancholy to set alongside the more urgent pessimism of some of his work: this gentleness appears in 'He Never Expected Much' with its 'neutral-tinted haps' (19), and the earlier (published 1917), delicate appreciation of the natural world and himself in 'Afterwards'.

Hardy was brought up and worked in a society in which the church played a major role. Christianity underpinned the moral and social structures of life. But as Hardy reached maturity, Darwin's new theories and Hardy's own experi-

---

1. See Gibson, *Complete Poems*, pp. xxxv – xxxvi.

ence combined to make him reject Christianity and its view of the world.[2] 'Hap'
and 'The Impercipient' explore different responses to the absence of God and
rational purpose in the world. Hardy toyed with the notion of a deity or deities
who, in the words of King Lear, 'kill us for their sport': Tess's death is the end of
the 'sport' of the 'President of the Immortals';[3] and in 'The Convergence of the
Twain' the ship's fate is decided by 'The Immanent Will' (18) and the 'Spinner
of the Years' (31). In the sonnet 'Hap', Hardy briefly imagines how much more
bearable is the notion of a sadistic deity than reality:

> Steeled by the sense of ire unmerited;
> Half-eased in that a Powerfuller than I
> Had willed and meted me the tears I shed. (6–8)

'But not so': there is no relief in that. 'Crass Casualty' and 'dicing Time' are
the determiners of life: they destroy nature's gifts of joy, obstruct sun and rain,
and withhold blisses with no purpose.

Such a view of life inevitably created a distance between Hardy and the
majority of ordinary people. Hardy's acute perception of the natural world was
an aspect of how he wished to be remembered: 'He was a man who used to notice such things' ('Afterwards', 4); he was also a man of powerful imagination,
who could see beyond appearances. It was, therefore, a 'mystery', one of his
'shortcomings', that he could not see the 'blessed things' that his 'comrades' and
'brethren' saw in the cathedral service of 'The Impercipient'. Again, the poet
toys with the notion that it might be a deliberate thing — '... He who breathes
All's Well to these / Breathes no All's-Well to me' (15–16) — but holds the idea
of his isolation and 'lack' rather than the idea of a malevolent deity. The pity
of it is once more captured in the natural image of the bird 'beshorn of wings'.
And it is in nature, possibly in death, that the poet conceives the resolution of
that separation and the 'disquiet' that clings about them: 'Rest shall we.'

Another 'blessed thing' that Hardy did not understand, but beautifully
describes, is the song of the bird in 'The Darkling Thrush'. A cluster of images
of winter, decay, death, and exhaustion set the scene of the poet's experience in
the first two stanzas. The second two stanzas thrill and swell with the song of
the bird. The bird itself has apparently as much reason as the poet to be dismal:
it was 'an aged thrush, frail, gaunt and small, / In blast-beruffled plume' (21–2).
But the bird and its song can only be described using religious imagery, 'full-
hearted evensong' (evensong is the afternoon service in the Anglican church,

---

2. See the entry 'Darwinism' in Norman Page, ed., *Companion to Hardy*, pp. 81–2.
3. *Tess of the D'Urbervilles*, chapter 59.

often sung by a choir), flinging 'his soul' into his 'carollings', and hinting at 'some blessed Hope whereof he knew'. Here again Hardy is the impercipient, the one who feels the power of, but cannot really enter into, that Hope of which he was 'unaware'.

Hardy's war poems 'Drummer Hodge' (from the Boer War 1899–1902), 'In Time of "The Breaking of Nations"', and 'Channel Firing' (from World War I, 1914–18) gain their impact from the deliberate diversion of attention away from the military horrors. The focus rather is on what is left, what hope can be found. 'Hodge' is a nickname for a rustic, an agricultural labourer: he has been made a drummer and taken from his native soil by war, but by war is reunited with the land, once again becoming part of it. Even the 'foreign constellations' and 'strange stars' become 'His stars eternally'. Hardy finds some kind of hope in the repeated, timeless patterns of life in 'In Time of "The Breaking of Nations"', particularly agricultural life: the harrowing of clods, the smouldering couch-grass, the whispering of a young couple. War is temporary cloud and darkness, a soon-to-be-forgotten episode in an ongoing story. The effect of 'In Time' depends on the understated ordinariness of observed life: clods, an old horse, thin smoke, a maid and her wight. These are real history, real story, as distinct from the 'annals', the artificial record of War. 'Channel Firing', the sound of the 'great guns' firing, is an ironical play on the idiomatic phrase 'a noise loud enough to wake the dead'. God, with unseemly levity and quaint archaism, tells the dead that it is not yet 'Judgement-day', if it ever will happen (9–24), and the ‡Parson sees his preaching as a waste of time. Against this theme of time, past, present, and future, is set the apparent timelessness of 'Stourton Tower, / And Camelot, and starlit Stonehenge': the roaring of the guns disturbs these places but does not touch the heroic, storied, distant past.

These war poems find no hope in conventional religious ideas of Providence or Just War, or the pieties of patriotism, courage, and honour. Instead Hardy looks to organic, ancient, and patterned human life as a defence against the madness of war and the indifference of a puppet God. Sometimes, though, even such hope is not available, and the poet holds on rather to the pain he feels. In 'Neutral Tones' repeated experience of the fact that 'love deceives' brings back to the poet's mind an image of a bleak, dead, joyless landscape and the face with a false smile. The face promises hope but is sterile like the sun 'chidden of God' and 'God-curst'. 'The Voice' was one of a group of poems written by Hardy in 1912–13 after his wife died. Its images of air and sound capture the desolation of loss: the wind can sound like the lost voice but is ungraspable and insubstantial. Regret, yearning, nostalgia and grief are awakened. In the last stanza,

> Thus I; faltering forward,
> Leaves around me falling,
> Wind oozing thin through the thorn from norward,
> And the woman calling (13 – 16)

rhythm and alliteration reinforce the poet's uncertainty: alliteration on *th* in the third line, but lacking from 'norward', together with the repeated present participles (faltering, falling, oozing, calling) and the lack of a main verb, reinforce the insistent sense of loss.

Hardy was unable to find hope in Christianity. He sometimes found it in the enduring nature of humanity, both its vast history and its stoicism in the face of adversity. Sometimes he faced hopelessness and the cruelty of life head on. Sometimes he was able to shrug his shoulders and say, 'Well, World, you have kept faith with me' ('He Never Expected Much', 1).

QUESTIONS

1. What sense of hope do you find in Hardy's poetry?
2. Does Hardy try to make sense of the bizarre coincidences, unpleasant experiences, and unfortunate accidents he records? Choose two or three poems and justify your opinion.
3. What kinds of things does Hardy see as controlling the world in the absence of God?

BIBLIOGRAPHY

James Gibson, ed., *The New Wessex Edition of the Complete Poems of Thomas Hardy*, London 1976. The best edition of the poems.

James Gibson and Trevor Johnson, ed., *Thomas Hardy: Poems. A Selection of Critical Essays*, London 1979: a useful selection of essays.

Michael Millgate, *Thomas Hardy: A Biography*, Oxford 1982.

Norman Page, ed., *Oxford Reader's Companion to Hardy*, Oxford 1999. A treasury of information on all aspects of Hardy's life and work.

F.B. Pinion, *A Commentary on the Poems of Thomas Hardy*, London 1976.

3

Joseph Conrad, *Heart of Darkness*

[*NA2* pp. 1957 f; *OA2* pp. 1613 f]

Conrad was born in Poland and only learned English in his twenties when he was working on English ships as a sailor. *Heart of Darkness*, if not autobiographical, was written out of the author's experience of a journey up the Congo river in 1890. The setting of the story is made to reflect an earlier stage of exploration and exploitation of the African continent, but Conrad knew much of the detail at first hand.

Conrad wrote *Heart of Darkness* in 1899 and published the story in 1902. This dating comes as a surprise because in many ways the portrait of Kurtz anticipates the historical person of Adolf Hitler: the god-like status given to him by his acolytes, his passionate conviction in his ideals, the extraordinary power and persuasiveness of his talk, and the ultimate horror of his vision — 'Exterminate all the brutes!' This suggests that the story might be an exploration of the mystery of evil and how it works in the human ‡soul — a spiritual †journey into human †darkness, as well as a physical journey into the heart of the dark continent of pre-colonial Africa. And the historical parallel of Hitler goes some way to validating Conrad's understanding of human nature in the story.

Conrad sets up a number of oppositions that help us to understand the moral contours of the landscape he presents to us: those that will be mentioned here are †light and †darkness, black and white, abstraction and detail.

The story is told by Marlow as he and his companions wait for a tide in the evening. The light fades as the story progresses and at the end there are 'black clouds' and 'an overcast sky'. This sets the tone for the account that Marlow tells of colonial cruelty and futility. The last words of Marlow, referring to his inability to tell Kurtz's 'Intended' the truth about her beloved, are, 'I could not tell her. It would have been too dark – too dark altogether ...' There is little light in the story, but here there is the suggestion that some glimmer still remains: Marlow's anger at the deception and pity for the deluded woman paradoxically show the triumph of mercy over †judgement, of †light over †darkness.

Another prominent example of the stress on †light and †darkness through-out the work is after the death of Kurtz. When the 'pilgrims' run off to see, Marlow remains eating his dinner and rationalises it thus: 'There was a lamp in there — light, don't you know — and outside it was so beastly, beastly dark.' These are among several hints in the work that point to the classic Christian treatment of the theme of light and darkness, namely the prologue to St John's Gospel.[1] John writes, 'In [Christ] was life; and the life was the light of men. And the light shineth in darkness; and the darkness comprehended it not' (John 1:4–5). Conrad inverts this paradigm and suggests that the light does not com-prehend the darkness. E.M. Forster and F.R. Leavis, followed by many critics, have complained about Conrad's lexical insistence on mystery:

> The same vocabulary, the same adjectival insistence upon inex-pressible and incomprehensible mystery, is applied to the evoca-tion of human profundities and spiritual horrors; to magnifying a thrilled sense of the unspeakable potentialities of the human soul. The actual effect is not to magnify but to muffle.[2]

Undoubtedly this 'insistence' is a habit of Conrad's. But here, it is an essen-tial point that Marlow does not understand the mystery, does not penetrate the †darkness, does not relate to the cruel and bizarre abstractions that surround him: †light and darkness have nothing in common.[3] Even though Marlow is uncomfortable with his aunt's view of his expedition as that of 'an emissary of light, a lower sort of apostle', he retains his humanity, the spark of human decency that allows him to care for both Kurtz and Kurtz's Intended without being tainted by the horrific visions and delusions of the one, or coerced by the blind innocence of the other.

The opposition of white and black is more complex. Conrad makes clear that the imposition of the white man's ideas and conventions on the blacks is nothing short of insanity. The gunship shelling the land, 'firing into a con-tinent', or the ‡pilgrims 'squirting lead into [the] bush' from their rifles are stark images of futility. And when Marlow reaches the Company's station he sees the effects of 'civilisation' in the chain gang and the grove of death. The 'adjectival insistence' here is on blackness: 'black men', 'black rags', 'black shapes', 'black shadows', 'black bones'. The juxtaposition of this horror with

---

1. Other hints are the fact that Marlow says of Kurtz 'He was just a word for me' and the characterisation of Kurtz as 'A voice! a voice!' Marlow also comments that 'the wilderness had found [Kurtz] out early'. In the gospel prologue, Jesus is the Word made flesh; and later John the Baptist says of himself, 'I am the voice of one crying in the wilderness' (John 1:23).

2. F.R. Leavis, *The Great Tradition*, Harmondsworth 1972, pp. 204–5.

3. As St Paul writes, 'what communion hath light with darkness?' (II Corinthians 6:14).

the 'miracle' of the 'white man' who is Company's chief accountant, with his 'high starched collar, white cuffs, a light alpaca jacket, snowy trousers, a clear necktie, and varnished boots' is a veiled commentary on the clash of cultures. Marlow respects the accountant for his 'character' in keeping up appearances, but the man has proved impervious both to the culture around him, and to the cruelty of the imposition of his culture upon another people. By contrast, the cannibals who travel with Marlow on the boat in the earlier part of the story show the kind of 'restraint' or 'some kind of primitive honour' in not looking to eat any of the pilgrims, that Kurtz notably lacked 'in the gratification of his various lusts'.[4]

There are two women devotees of Kurtz in the book: 'the wild and gorgeous apparition' of Kurtz's station, and his Intended. Conrad makes implicit comparisons between them. Both make gestures with their arms: 'Suddenly [the black woman] opened her bared arms and threw them rigid above her head'; and the Intended 'put out her arms as if after a retreating figure, stretching them black and with clasped pale hands ...' Both appear to be reaching out for Kurtz, one with bared black arms, the other clothed in black; both somehow alike in their grief and devotion.[5]

The opposition of abstraction and detail is best illustrated by Marlow's resolute pragmatism. In the mystery of the jungle, with its constant overtones of medieval visions of †hell,[6] he remains both human and practical. He balks at the idea that the blacks he sees can be called 'criminals' or 'enemies' and later 'rebels': 'what thrilled you,' he says, 'was just the thought of their humanity — like yours — the thought of your remote kinship....' He refuses to be swayed by Kurtz's rhetoric. For him reality is the everyday business of repairing the ship's boiler rather than taking sides for or against Kurtz. He prefers kindness to his black steersman to more grandiose schemes of the 'Suppression of Savage Customs'. In the end, though he hates lies, he preserves Kurtz's reputation with a lie, rather than submitting to Kurtz's notion of 'justice' or abstract notions of truth. For Marlow, the †devil is not in the detail, as the saying goes, but in the abstractions that ignore detail. Marlow's faith is the faithfulness that deals with

---

4. A point made by Paul O'Prey, ed., *Joseph Conrad: Heart of Darkness*, Harmondsworth 1983, pp. 17–18.

5. Compare Achebe's view, *NA2* p. 2038, that the black woman 'fulfils a structural requirement of the story: a savage counterpart to the refined, European woman ... The difference in the attitude of the novelist to these two women is conveyed in too many direct and subtle ways to need elaboration.' Undoubtedly the two are treated differently, but Achebe has perhaps missed the fundamental similarities between them: see also Robert Hampson, '*Heart of Darkness* and "the speech that cannot be silenced"', in Childs, ed., *Post-Colonial Theory*, p. 209.

6. One of many examples, Marlow remembers Kurtz 'with the horned shapes stirring at my back, in the glow of fires'.

the smell of dead hippo, rather than the faith that, in Kurtz's ability to 'believe anything', 'electrified large meetings'.

Conrad avoids drawing conclusions from his story. He uses Christian imagery and ideas, especially in the creation of the atmosphere of *Heart of Darkness*, without making any specific theological point.[7] Unless, of course, the need to recognise and respect humanity, whatever bizarre, perverted, or strange shape it may take, is a theological point.

QUESTIONS

1. Patrick Brantlinger, 'Kurtz's "Darkness" and *Heart of Darkness*', in Childs, ed., *Post-Colonial Theory*, p. 197, writes, 'Evil, in short, *is* African in Conrad's story; if it is also European, that is because some white men in the heart of darkness behave like Africans.' Do you agree?
2. What kinds of thing does Conrad portray as virtuous in the novella? How do these things relate to traditional Christian ‡virtues like faith, hope, and †love?
3. What is the 'heart of darkness' in the book?

BIBLIOGRAPHY

Jocelyn Baines, *Joseph Conrad: A Critical Biography*, London 1961. A standard biography.

Peter Childs, ed., *Post-Colonial Theory and English Literature: A Reader*, Edinburgh 1999. Contains four essays on 'Heart of Darkness', with an introduction, all of which address the issues raised by Chinua Achebe, 'An image of Africa', *Research in African Literatures* 9 (1978), 1–15, rpt in *NA2* pp. 2035–40. Achebe argues that Conrad's work is racist.

Owen Knowles and Gene M. Moore, *Oxford Reader's Companion to Conrad*, Oxford 2000. A wide-ranging, encyclopaedic reference work.

Joan E. Steiner, 'Modern Pharisees and false apostles: ironic New Testament parallels in Conrad's "Heart of Darkness"', *Nineteenth-Century Fiction* 37 (1982) 75–96.

---

7. Daphna Erdinast-Vulcan, *Joseph Conrad and the Modern Temper*, Oxford 1991, in a persuasive reading of the novella, pp. 91–108, argues that *Heart of Darkness* has an 'anti-metaphysical thrust', p. 97. This kind of view is taken further by Otto Bohlmann, *Conrad's Existentialism*, Basingstoke 1991 (see, for example, chapter 3).

4

VOICES FROM WORLD WAR I

[*NA2* pp. 2048 f; *OA2* pp. 2050 f (Wilfred Owen, Edward Thomas,
Isaac Rosenberg, David Jones)]

The First World War (1914–18) generated a great deal of verse both good
and bad, expressing a continuum of views from jingoistic propaganda to graphic
portrayals of the horrors of trench warfare. Very often a Christian understanding is entwined with and corresponds to attitudes towards the conflict.

Rupert Brooke wrote his war sonnets at the beginning of the conflict. 'The
Soldier' is typical. In patriotic fashion this poem depicts an *Edenic England,
a pastoral idyll, washed by rivers as paradise was in the book of Genesis, with
a vision of dust returning to dust, the dust of the earth from which *Adam the
first man was made. To Adam God gave the earth in blessing, as the English
landscape is presented as gift here.

In subsequent poets, however, the dust of *Eden gives way to the mud of
†hell. The imagery of hell is commonplace as one might expect. It is found in
Wilfred Owen's grim play on a familiar idiom, 'I have suffered seventh hell',
in a letter to his mother in January 1917, and in his depiction of 'the sorrowful
dark of hell' of the trenches in 'Apologia Pro Poemate Meo' where he asserts,
'I, too, saw God through mud', that is, in the laughter and camaraderie of the
hard-pressed soldiers. In Siegfried Sassoon's 'Glory of Women' the hellishness
is characterised by abandoned corpses trodden in the mud. Sassoon's poem
'The Rear-Guard' describes the tunnels at the Hindenburg Line in terms like a
visitation into Hades, even a †harrowing of hell, comparable to Owen's 'Strange
Meeting', which depicts a confrontation in hell between the poet and an enemy
soldier.

Early poems of the war invoked the consolations of religion, frequently
through prayers. For example W.N. Hodgson's refrain in 'Before Action':

Make me a soldier, Lord.
Make me a man, O Lord.
Help me to die, O Lord.[1]

---

1. Quoted in Spear, *Remembering, We Forget*, p. 100.

Or Evan Morgan's:

> Great God, with tending hand
> Watch o'er our souls.[2]

Rupert Brooke's consolatory and celebratory sonnet 'Peace' begins, 'Now, God be thanked / Who has matched us with His hour', and develops through a Christian understanding of death.[3]

Other poems seem to us intolerably glib, as Charles Hamilton Sorley's:

> Earth that blossomed and was glad
> 'Neath the cross that Christ had,
> Shall rejoice and blossom too
> When the bullet reaches you.[4]

Religious feeling was encouraged by the many wayside shrines in the French countryside, the 'Calvaries', and the imposing churches. However these symbols of Christianity could also induce an angry response, or highlight the mismatch between organised religion and the reality on the ground, as in Owen's 'Anthem for Doomed Youth', which presents an elaborate rejection of the ‡mass for the dead.

The religious assurance of poets in the early years of the conflict began to fade as the realities of war became too challenging for the faith of many. Wilfred Owen expresses some of the paradoxes that faith appeared to engender in a letter home to his mother from a hospital on the Somme in 1917. Of Christ's apparent command to suffer without retaliation he wryly says, 'I think pulpit professionals are ignoring it very skilfully and successfully indeed.... And am I not myself a conscientious objector with a very seared conscience?' He goes on to consider another paradox: Christ says, 'Greater love hath no man than this, that a man lay down his life for his friends' (John 15:13), but he says it equally to Englishman and German, so that 'pure Christianity will not fit in with pure patriotism'.[5]

Siegfried Sassoon's poem '"They"' attacks the glib platitudes of the church. The Bishop speaks of a holy war, a 'just cause'. The enemy is characterised as the 'Anti-Christ'. And in a conventional wartime interpretation of Christianity the soldiers are identified with Christ: he ‡redeems through his †sacrifice and shed blood, and in a comparable way the blood of the fallen purchases a new

---

2. Quoted in Spear, *Remembering, We Forget*, p. 99.
3. Geoffrey Keynes, ed., *The Poetical Works of Rupert Brooke*, London 1946, p. 19.
4. 'All the hills and vales along' in Charles Hamilton Sorley, *Marlborough and Other Poems*, Cambridge 1932.
5. Harold Owen and John Bell, ed., *Wilfred Owen: Collected Letters*, London 1967, p. 461.

beginning for those who survive. As Christ faced death on the †cross, so did they on the battlefields. In the mouth of the Bishop, however, it all sounds facile and ineffectual.

Siegfried Sassoon wrote of his unpublished poem 'Christ and the Soldier': 'I suppose that behind it was the persistent anti-parson mentality — and it *was* difficult to swallow their patriotic pietism, which seemed unreal to many of us front-liners.'[6] The clergy had little idea of the reality of trench warfare and were seen by Sassoon and Owen as complacently hand-in-hand with a nationalistic state that had taken this war too far. When the Bishop in '"They"' says of those who return 'They will not be the same', he means they will have somehow been morally improved by the fight, but the words are heavily ironic as the second stanza indicates, for their bodies are permanently disabled. The church thus is made to appear unthinking and unfeeling. The Bishop takes refuge at the end of the poem behind the pious platitude, 'The ways of God are strange!'

In his poem 'Le Christianisme', Wilfred Owen expresses reservations about the church for failing, in its unworldliness, to embrace the suffering of soldiers, symbolised by the statues of ‡saints packed away for protection in the cellars of a shelled church in Quivières, 'Well out of hearing of our trouble'. The remaining statue of the smiling Virgin, 'halo'd with an old tin hat', seems to be presented as ineffectual and mocking in the face of the †hell of war.

In 'At a Calvary Near the Ancre', Owen again indignantly attacks the church, prompted by a wayside shrine depicting the *crucifixion. He adapts the gospel account so that the 'gentle' Christ is contrasted with the unfeeling priests who stroll by, 'fleshmarked by the Beast', while the soldiers are identified with Christ's anguished disciples. The priests have sold out to the state, ignoring the tenet that 'they who love the greater love / Lay down their life'. It is a scripture that Owen returns to a number of times in his writings, seeing it as the true heart of the Christian faith: 'Greater love hath no man than this, that a man lay down his life for his friends' (John 15:13).

In some poems God himself is portrayed as insensible to human suffering. In 'Greater Love', Owen states 'God seems not to care'. Sassoon, in 'Break of Day', speaks of 'God's blank heart'.

The idea of the Christ-soldier became common. Sassoon uses it in 'The Redeemer' in 1915, identifying the soldier with the suffering Christ, matching physical details such as 'No thorny crown, only a woollen cap' and 'Shouldering his load of planks'. This soldier was 'not uncontent to die / That Lancaster on Lune may stand secure'. Later in the war the notion of †sacrifice for one's

---

6. Quoted in Spear, *Remembering, We Forget.*

country or for a sacred cause was discarded; one died, if anything, for one's comrades.

The Christ-soldier metaphor became overdone and would eventually be thought complacent, though Owen still uses it in a letter to Osbert Sitwell as late as 1918, though with himself cast at least in part in the role of *betrayer:

> For 14 hours yesterday I was at work — teaching Christ to lift his cross by numbers, and how to adjust his crown: I attended his Supper to see that there were no complaints; and inspected his feet that they should be worthy of the nails. I see to it that he is dumb and stands at attention before his accusers. With a piece of silver I buy him everyday, and with maps I make him familiar with the topography of Golgotha.[7]

Another common correlative for suffering was that of *Gethsemane, the 'agony in the garden', where Christ sweated blood the night before his *crucifixion and prayed that the cup of suffering might be taken away. Kipling uses it in his poem 'Gethsemane (1914–18)', where he describes a resting place in Picardy on the way to the front where the locals watched the English soldiers march by:

> And all the time we halted there
> I prayed my cup might pass.
>
> It didn't pass — it didn't pass —
> It didn't pass from me.
> I drank it when we met the gas
> Beyond Gethsemane!

The 'cup' of suffering and death, which is also the communion chalice of wine representing Christ's blood, is found again in Wilfred Owen's 'Spring Offensive' (July, 1918) where, after the soldiers 'carelessly slept' like Christ's disciples in Gethsemane, they charged into battle and 'earth set sudden cups / In thousands for their blood'. Since the consolatory Christian passages from the start of the war the imagery has developed to this potent and disturbing vision.

QUESTIONS

1. Wilfred Owen stated: 'pure Christianity will not fit in with pure patriotism'. Do you find this view reflected in the poetry of the First World War?

---

7. Quoted in Spear, *Remembering, We Forget*, p. 106.

2. To what extent is a religious concept of †sacrifice to be found in the poetry of the time?

BIBLIOGRAPHY

D. J. Enright, 'The Literature of the First World War', in Boris Ford, ed., *From James to Eliot*, The New Pelican Guide to English Literature, volume 7, rev. edn, Harmondsworth 1982, pp. 154–69. An essay focusing on Brooke, Sassoon, and Owen.

Jon Silkin, *Out of Battle: The Poetry of the Great War*, London 1972. Covers all the key figures of World War I poetry. The chapter on Wilfred Owen touches on the spiritual issues.

Hilda D. Spear, *Remembering, We Forget: A Background Study to the Poetry of the First World War*, London 1979. Charts reactions to the war; chapter 5 treats religious responses particularly.

Dennis Welland, *Wilfred Owen: A Critical Study*, rev. edn, London 1978. A useful study of Owen's poetry in context, including the Christian influence in chapters 4 and 5.

WILFRED OWEN

[*NA2* pp. 2066 f; *OA2* pp. 2050 f]

Wilfred Owen is one of the foremost poets of the First World War. Along-side Siegfried Sassoon and others he wrote poetry that exposed the stark realities of war. He believed the truth should be told, and he heavily criticised the jingoistic proponents of war and the 'selective ignorance' of those, including church leaders, who he believed had by their own attitudes been a contributing cause of the war.

Owen was raised by a devoutly ‡Evangelical mother who brought him up to pray and read the Bible daily and who encouraged him to enter the church. His own devoutness is reflected in the sermon topics and Bible quotations he includes in his early letters. Owen left home in 1911 and became assistant to the vicar of Dunsden, near Reading. Here he led a Bible class, became Sunday School Superintendent, sang in the choir, and carried out regular parish duties. He attended the annual Keswick Convention, hearing many Evangelical preachers. It is not surprising therefore, that though he left Dunsden and abandoned his Christian faith in 1913 (he ultimately called it a 'false creed'), his language and imagination are affected by those early years.

His 'Anthem for Doomed Youth' incorporates a bitter and ironic parody of church rites. He catalogues the paraphernalia of a funeral service, translating it item by item into features of the battlefield. The confrontational first line, 'What passing-bells for these who die as cattle?', sets the tone for the poem. The only bells for these youths are the sounds of gunfire; the only prayers are the stutterings of rifles, with something sneering about the way they are said to 'patter'. There are no mourners for these who die in battle; the only choirs are the shrill whining shells overhead. The church rites these men do without are but 'mockeries' to Owen anyway.

The sestet takes on a softer tone. Church candles are paralleled by 'holy glimmers' in the youths' eyes; in a play on words, their pall is the pallor of girls' faces back at home; the tender patience of their loved ones will be their only funeral wreaths. The closing of blinds by those waiting in their home country represents the closing of the eyes of the dead with a gentle finality. This church anthem holds out no hope for the soldiers — they are 'doomed' in this life and in death.

'Apologia Pro Poemate Meo' uses religious imagery in a more benign way. It tells how Owen saw something of God in the soldiers of the trenches and celebrates their comradeship, with barbed implications for non-combatants. He starts with the startling juxtaposition of God and mud — and the smiles and laughter of the men under horrific conditions. He speaks in spiritual terms of man's ability to transcend such circumstances: the spirit sails beyond fear, sickness, guilt. The 'exultation' he observes in the men is religious in its fervour and described in ecclesiastical language: faces 'lift up with passion of obla-tion, / Seraphic for an hour' (15–16), including a hint of Christ's ‡passion and †sacrifice, though at times Owen was to fiercely disparage the soldier-Christ image that was often used by more jingoistic versifiers in the early part of the war. He speaks of 'fellowship' with such men — a word common to the Bible and to ‡Evangelical Christianity, designating strong common bonds. Here the bonds are created by wounds and blood, perhaps with further Christian reso-nance. The poem ends with reference to their existence as 'the sorrowful dark of hell', yet denies that †heaven is anything for them but the 'highway for a shell' overhead.

Though in 'Apolgia' Owen talks of riding free of the 'remorse of murder', in 'Strange Meeting' he confronts the moral issue of what it means to kill some-one not that dissimilar to oneself, and he identifies with the suffering of the lost. The poem is an inversion of the †harrowing of hell: instead of the poet preaching hope or consolation to those who have died, as Christ did between his *crucifixion and *resurrection, the dead in †hell rise up to deliver a ‡homily to him. At the start of the poem the tunnels of the Western Front give way to a vision of Hades where Owen comes face-to-face with the enemy he has killed the day before. His hell is like a scene from the trenches with groaning bodies strewn everywhere, faces scored with torment and hopelessness, but without sound of gun or sight of blood. It is his *alter ego* he meets — the enemy he kills is in part the poet-soldier, Wilfred Owen. The figure describes how they both had hoped, both had hunted 'wildest beauty', but now there is a melancholy acknowledgement of lost potential — this poet could have made people laugh, and more especially weep, but now, he pessimistically avers, the truth must remain untold, the truth about the 'pity of war', and nations will continue in their 'trek from progress', their misguided retreat 'Into vain citadels that are not walled' (33).

The attributes of the poet are listed — courage and †wisdom, the gift to treat ‡mysteries, the mastery to avoid the blindness of the warring world. All these are now lost. The poet can no longer cleanse from bloodguiltiness with the pure, life-giving water of truth. He would have given his whole being to the task. He invokes a Christ-image to convey the kind of agony he would have endured for the cause: 'Foreheads of men have bled where no wounds were' (39). In this context of Christ's agony in the Garden of *Gethsemane, the repeated use of the word 'friend' suggests an element of *Judas-betrayal, particularly reflected in the enemy-friend combination at the start of the final, incomplete stanza.

Each of these poems embodies in different ways and with varying biblical resonance the strong compassion that Owen felt for the soldiers of World War I. It may be that this compassion, as much as the language of the poems, is part of the legacy of Christianity in his work from earlier years.

QUESTIONS

1. Where else do you find images of †hell in Owen's work?
2. Can you trace Owen's compassion in other poems?

BIBLIOGRAPHY

Dominic Hibberd, *Wilfred Owen: A New Biography*, London 2002. An authoritative and perceptive biography.

Dennis Welland, *Wilfred Owen: A Critical Study*, rev. edn, London 1978. A useful study of Owen's poetry in context, including the Christian influence in chapters 4 and 5.

6

WILLIAM BUTLER YEATS

[*BAV* pp. 1020 f (early poems); *NA2* pp. 2085 f; *OA2* pp. 1679 f]

William Butler Yeats was the grandson of a clergyman of the Church of Ireland, the Anglican church in Ireland.[1] By ancestry, he was of Anglo-Irish stock, but his early school days in England reinforced the sense of Irishness that pervades his poetry. Yeats's father, John Butler Yeats, had not inherited his father's faith. He was an agnostic who never went to church but who, in time-honoured tradition, insisted that his children should attend. When the young Willie once refused, his father insisted that he must learn to read instead. His father's reading lesson was apparently such a trial to the boy that he went back to church the next week.

Yeats does seem to have inherited his father's religious doubts and surprised his youthful contemporaries by his interest in Darwin, Huxley, and other thinkers who were considered deeply suspect by the church. He did not, however, share his father's apparently relaxed attitude to religion. His doubt about Christianity was somewhat problematic to him. For some years, he remained an occasional attender at church; but he was increasingly drawn to and fascinated by esoteric theories of religion. In 1890, after having been attached for some time to the Theosophical Society, he was initiated into the Hermetic Order of the Golden Dawn,[2] in which he seems to have viewed the two thousand years of Christianity as one phase, which was on the cusp of being superseded, in a continuing process of religious ‡revelation:

> The darkness drops again; but now I know
> That twenty centuries of stony sleep
> Were vexed to nightmare by a rocking cradle,
> And what rough beast, its hour come round at last,
> Slouches towards Bethlehem to be born? ('The Second Coming',
>   18–22)

---

1. For all biographical detail and much interpretive insight I am indebted to A. Norman Jeffares' still indispensable *W.B. Yeats: Man and Poet*.

2. Harper, *Yeats and the Occult*, p. xv.

Yeats lived in a period when millenarianism was usually an important aspect of speculation in newly emerged and emerging Christian and para-Christian sects. The Darbyite Plymouth Brethren, the Irvingite Catholic Apostolic Church, and others, all took with great seriousness the possibility that the *second coming of Christ was imminent.[3]

Yeats's own take on this religious theme, however, was individual and idiosyncratic, and drew on the remarkable range of his artistic and philosophical reading:

> When the new era comes bringing its stream of irrational force it will, as did Christianity, find its philosophy already impressed on the minority who have, true to phase, turned away at the last gyre from the *Physical Primary*. And it must wake into life, not Durer's, nor Blake's, nor Milton's human form divine — nor yet Nietzsche's superman nor Patmore's catholic, boasting 'a tongue that's dead' — the brood of the Sistine Chapel — but organic groups, *covens* of physical or intellectual kin melted out of the frozen mass.[4]

It is easy to mock this kind of writing, a good deal easier than trying to take it seriously; but there is a body of scholarly opinion on this subject, that also importantly points out that the relationship between Irish folklore and Roman Catholic Irish folk religion is symbiotic rather than oppositional:

> In the Ireland of Yeats's time, the doctrines of the existence of Purgatory and of the 'communion of souls' were of course firmly held. The poor souls in Purgatory might appear, it was believed among the people, to ask the help of the living ... What Chesterton called the 'small arrogant oligarchy' of the living fell into perspective against ... the swarming dead, out of sight, but never out of mind. Yeats, however, was never content with belief in another world: he had always wanted access to it.... After the death of Synge, he turned once again to the techniques ... of spiritualism, mediums and automatic writing.[5]

---

3. For the sake of confusion, it should be pointed out that the Plymouth Brethren, despite their name, actually originated in 1830s Dublin, where J.N. Darby was a Church of Ireland clergyman; and that the Irvingites were, of course, emphatically not Roman Catholic!

4. W.B. Yeats, *A Vision: An Explanation of Life Founded upon the Writings of Giraldus and upon Certain Doctrines Attributed to Kusta Ben Lukam*, London 1925, p. 213. Mercifully, one does not have to be familiar with all the thinkers in the title or the passage cited to understand either the breadth of knowledge or the eccentricity of Yeats in this mode.

5. Harper, *Yeats and the Occult*, p. xvi.

It is possible to question some aspects of this: for while it is certain that Yeats did so turn, and not improbable that this had some relationship to his interest in Irish myth and magic, it is worth recalling that Yeats was not himself a Roman Catholic and that interest in spiritualism in this period was as prevalent in waning Protestant cultures, which had no doctrine of ‡purgatory, as in Catholic ones that did. Spiritualism, like a number of the para-Christian sects already mentioned, flourished well into the twentieth century on the Protestant fringe.

The effects of all this on Yeats's poetic output are not easy to assess, not least because of the breadth of his poetic range and the many other factors in his public and private life. Sometimes, as in 'The Second Coming', ideas from his theological and philosophical speculations find their way explicitly into his poetry to great effect; in other poems, they seem to be more problematic. But that may be just a way of saying that, as with any poet, Yeats wrote some better poems and some worse. At any rate, the spiritual †quest was of vital importance to him from his earliest days, and cannot be ignored in a rounded assessment of either his life or his poetry.

QUESTIONS

1. What part, if any, does Irish folk tradition play in Yeats's spiritual speculations?
2. What effects do Yeats's spiritual speculations have on the merit of the poems in which they have a place?
3. Is there any direct connection between Yeats's millennialism and contemporary conditions in Ireland?

BIBLIOGRAPHY

George Mills Harper, ed., *Yeats and the Occult*, London 1976.
A. Norman Jeffares, *A New Commentary on the Poems of W.B. Yeats*, London 1984.
A. Norman Jeffares, *W.B. Yeats: Man and Poet*, 3rd edn, London 1996.

7

JAMES JOYCE, *ULYSSES*

[*NA2* pp. 2269 f (Proteus and Lestrygonians); *OA2* pp. 1781 f (Nausicaa)]

Joyce, like his fictional counterpart Stephen Daedalus, rejected the Catholicism of his native Ireland and of his mother, living in exile to distance himself from it. What *Ulysses* suggests, in the character of Stephen conveyed in the chapter 'Proteus', is that, regardless of belief or unbelief, the Christian tradition has become part of the emotional and intellectual heritage belonging to the Ireland he wishes to escape and the Europe he desires to embrace. Stephen the young man struggles with the guilt induced by his dying mother's accusation of betrayal because he refuses to compromise his integrity by praying with her after he has rejected their once-shared faith. The religious content of Stephen's stream of consciousness is, therefore, partly the consequence of his guilt. Catholic Christianity and his mother are intertwined.

In his stream of consciousness we become aware, also, of how much Christianity and western culture are intertwined. Stephen's musings range over important Christian figures in the intellectual history of western civilisation: they indicate the shaping influence of Christian faith upon the culture from which his own intellectual formation and aspirations cannot be divorced. Among the figures Stephen muses about are these that follow.

Stephen alludes to St Thomas Aquinas. He was the great systematiser of Catholic doctrine, who harnessed Aristotelian philosophy to the service of theology. Not only was he the authoritative voice of Catholic theology into the twentieth century, but his method of critical enquiry became dominant in western philosophy.

Jacob Boehme was a rather unorthodox Lutheran German ‡mystic, influenced by the teachings of the Catholic philosopher-mystic, Meister Eckhart. Boehme was an important influence in German Romanticism and in Pietism, a form of ‡Evangelical Christianity which emphasised separation from 'the world'.

Joachim of Flore produced influential writings about the coming of the millennium, when Christ would return to establish †heaven on earth. His thought was influential in some Christian quarters well into the nineteenth century, including upon John Wesley, the founder of ‡Methodism.

William of Occam (or Ockham) was an important figure in the development of philosophy and of the scientific approach. He championed the foundation of argument upon observable phenomena against the tradition of beginning from broad generalisations supported by appeal to authorities on the subject. In this way he participated in the shift in thinking characteristic of the Renaissance and of the ‡Reformation.

Duns Scotus was a Franciscan ‡friar and philosopher whose philosophy offered an alternative to the dominant Thomism of St Thomas Aquinas. He was a major liberating philosophical influence on the poet Gerard Manley Hopkins. Pico de Mirandola was a lesser figure but an important example of the creative conjunction between Christianity and ‡neoplatonism in the Renaissance.

As well as these key figures in the western church, Stephen's mind also ranges over important figures from the earlier Christian centuries, such as St Columbanus and St Ambrose. St Columbanus was a sixth-century Irish ‡monk who was responsible for the founding of many ‡monasteries which maintained a tradition of scholarship and learning in Europe.

St Ambrose, Patriarch of Milan, was important not only for his hymnody and contribution to soteriology (the study of Christ as ‡saviour) but even more so for his role in converting St Augustine to Christianity. For good and ill, St Augustine has shaped western philosophy and theology to this day (see the essay 'Christian History and Theology').

We see in Stephen's musings, therefore, that the Christianity he rejects is nonetheless important to the development of the European culture he desires to embrace. Although he wished to escape from the narrowness and philistinism of Catholic Ireland he could not escape from the Catholic Christian roots of the culture to which he aspires. Stephen's Christian background, his intellectual religious preoccupations and his conscious rejection of belief are all evident in his stream of consciousness.

His reflection on birth, rather than staying with the human reality, is deflected to his knowledge of the Jewish ‡Kabbala and the navel-less state of *Eve. But his mind cannot rest there. It quickly moves to Eve as the origin of ‡sin. The notion of conception in sin leads to echoes of Psalm 51, a ‡penitential psalm familiar to Catholics. This notion then turns his thoughts to a reversal of a proposition in the Nicene ‡Creed (the statement of belief recited at every Sunday ‡mass in Catholicism): God the Son was 'begotten not made, consubstantial with the Father'. He then mocks this formula and recalls the defeat of Arius at the Council of Nicea that produced this creed. Arius had affirmed that

Jesus was a divine but created being; he was not 'of one being' with the Father; his defeat established orthodox Christian belief about Christ's divinity.

Memory plus place excite in Stephen images, fantasies, and considerations that continue to express his unwilled engagement with the stuff of Catholicism. His Old Testament reference to the bald Elisha (see II Kings 2:23), used by Joachim of Flore, leads him to the fantasy of a bizarre version of the service of benediction. In this the congregation is blessed by a consecrated host, believed to be no longer unleavened bread but the body of Christ, his 'real presence'; this is held for display in a monstrance. The 'dringdring' marks the bells rung at different stages of the rite, when the monstrance is lifted, moved in the sign of the †cross as a blessing and replaced on the altar. This leads to a reverie on a problem regarding the presence of Christ in the host articulated by William of Occam.

Just as Christians were urged to look for reminders of their faith in the natural world, so Stephen, despite his avowed disbelief, continues the habit. The Pigeonhouse recalls to him the Holy Spirit, symbolised by the dove and the irreverent dialogue he had heard concerning †Mary's explanation to Joseph of her pregnancy. This is a dialogue close in tone, if not in intention, to the stories found in the Protoevangelium, a collection of popular tales about the early life of Christ. In these Joseph is representative of the unbeliever who can think only in grossly natural terms. Joyce shows us a mind in rebellion, distancing itself from its religion through mockery and irreverence yet still in dialogue with it and repeating its patterns.

As in the earlier reverie we see the tension in Stephen between the life of the mind and life as a sensuous, sexual being. The allusion to the virginal conception of Jesus can be seen as the church's rejection of sexuality, hence the perennial need to mock and to express human incredulity which he shares.

The fact that this is a French story reminds Stephen of his time in Paris and of the earthy satisfying of hunger in bodily contact with men equally centred on their basic needs. Even the memory of food in Paris evokes an Old Testament reference to the fleshpots of Egypt. This recalls the longing of the hungry Israelites for the food and security they had known while slaves in Egypt and had lost after their escape into wandering in the †desert (Exodus 16). This suggests the dominance of desire for sensuous gratification, the dominance of the physical.

As his stream of consciousness progresses the scraps of memories of biblical and doctrinal content continue. Recollection of his dying mother's hand and thoughts about forgetting and remembering evoke Psalm 137, the psalm of exiles longing for their homeland and unable to sing on foreign soil, an ironic allusion for Stephen the self-chosen poet-exile.

The following sexual fantasising results in the recollection of the church's attitude to licentious sex, represented by the teaching of St Thomas Aquinas ('Monkwords'). Such condemnation is rejected by Stephen in equating it with the repetitive recitation of the ten Hail †Marys, which forms the basis of the prayer of the rosary ('marybeads'). We have here, once again, an indication of Stephen's internal battle with the formative influences of his Catholic upbringing: the teaching arises in his mind and must be defeated by ridicule. Stephen remains the exile, for whom the homeland, physical, emotional, and intellectual, still exerts its force, however much despised.

QUESTIONS

1. What do the references to such figures as St Thomas Aquinas and William of Occam contribute to this chapter?
2. What do the allusions to the Bible and to Catholic practices tell us about Stephen's mental state?
3. In what ways has your reading of this chapter been affected by your knowledge of the Christian tradition to which Joyce refers?

BIBLIOGRAPHY

Derek Attridge, ed., *The Cambridge Companion to James Joyce*, 2nd edn, Cambridge 2004.

Robert Boyle, *James Joyce's Pauline Vision: A Catholic Exposition*, London 1978.

Clive Hart and David Hayman, ed., *James Joyce's Ulysses: Critical Essays*, Berkeley CA 1974.

R.J. Schork, *Latin and Roman Culture in Joyce*, Gainesville FL 1997.

8

D.H. LAWRENCE

[*NA2* pp. 2313 f; *OA2* pp. 1816 f]

D.H. Lawrence produced a large volume of work in the decades 1910–30. His greatest achievements were the novels *The Rainbow* and *Women in Love*, but he also wrote many poems, plays, essays, short stories, letters, and travel books before he died at the age of forty-four. His work is infused with a religious understanding quite removed from the Congregationalist Christianity of his youth, yet which constantly reinterprets and inverts Christian vocabulary and doctrine to affirm his own vision.

In the poem 'Piano', Lawrence describes the lasting resonance of the hymns he learned as a child. 'In spite of myself', he says, for he had rejected orthodox Christian belief by the age of sixteen, they return him to the 'glamour / Of childish days' (10–11). In the essay 'Hymns in a Man's Life' he asserts that though such hymns may be 'rather bad', and despite his no longer accepting their doctrinal truth, they still induce in him the sense of wonder that he considers to be at the root of 'the religious element inherent in all life'.[1]

The sequence of six poems, *Tortoises*, illustrates how Lawrence applies Christian iconography uniquely to his own thought. In 'Tortoise-Shell' he describes in fine detail the patterning on the baby creature. The poem bursts open ecstatically with 'The Cross, the Cross / Goes deeper in than we know' (1–2). This cross-pattern on the shell of the animal is also there on its upturned belly, appearing to go right the way through it. His essay 'On Being a Man' details how Lawrence associates the †cross with the body: it 'stands for the body, for the dark self which lives in the body'.[2] In Lawrence's terms this is the vital, non-rational, strange self, which 'knows' in a way that originates in the blood, not the mind, instinctively and intuitively, as opposed to the self, which is conscious ego, 'reasonable and sensible and complex and full of good intentions'.[3] In 'Tortoise-Shell' therefore Lawrence illustrates through the cross image how the 'blood' self penetrates our being and our world. The pattern written on the

---

1. James T. Boulton, ed., *Late Essays and Articles*, The Cambridge Edition of the Works of D.H. Lawrence, Cambridge 2004, pp. 128–34.

2. Herbert, ed., *Reflections on the Death of a Porcupine*, p. 216.

3. Herbert, ed., *Reflections on the Death of a Porcupine*, p. 213.

shell is contrasted with the *ten commandments written by God upon stone tablets; Lawrence replaces inanimate stone with 'life-clouded, life-rosy tortoise shell', in accordance with his belief in the life-force permeating *creation.

In 'Tortoise Shout' the †cross image is extended. The primordial shout of the tortoise occurs during coition and represents our being 'crucified into sex'. The sex-act for Lawrence is at its highest an act of the vital, blood self. In 'On Being a Man' he describes it in terms of the conscious-ego self being crucified on the †cross of the 'bodily self'.⁴ So in this poem the cry represents both a 'death-agony' and a 'birth-cry'. It is Christ's loud cry of abandonment on the cross, related in the gospels, from which Lawrence also takes the phrases 'giving up the ghost' and 'torn asunder' (as the veil of the Temple was torn at the *crucifixion and which represents Christ's broken body, John 19:10 and Matthew 17:51). It is also the simultaneous receiving of the Holy Ghost. In the essays in *Reflections on the Death of a Porcupine*, Lawrence perceives the Holy Ghost as mysterious purveyor of the life principle: 'the Holy Ghost hovers among the flames ... and life travels in flame from the unseen to the unseen' and 'the Holy Ghost ... moves us on into the state of blossoming'.⁵ The *crucifixion described by Lawrence marks a breaking out from our self-containedness, our 'single inviolability', into life-driven relatedness through sex, a simultaneous agony and blossoming.

A different manner of adapting Christian symbolism may be seen in the short story *The Horse-Dealer's Daughter*. Here there is an underlying †baptismal image where Mabel Pervin walks into a pool of water in an attempt to take her own life. She sinks below the surface, becomes unconscious, and metaphori-cally enters into death. She is saved by Fergusson at some risk to himself — he already has a heavy cold and cannot swim – who enters the pool to rescue her and restore her to life, not just physical life but an emotional vitalisation. There is a rising to new life — originally Lawrence had called this story 'The Miracle' — and an awakening triggered through the physical touch of another. The result of the encounter is an unexpected blossoming of love, instinctive and non-rational in Fergusson, almost against his will in a painful tearing open of his heart, and for her part described in the biblical language of transfiguration and joy. The opposition of the pool and the graveyard where Fergusson earlier observes Mabel, indicates the contrast of natural, death-into-life forces, with the church that often in Lawrence's work is associated with the conscious, intel-lectual self. The pool, shrouded in dusk, looks forward to the 'hellish flowers' of 'Bavarian Gentians', where the descent into the †darkness of Hades is a descent into life, to the marriage of bride and groom.

---

4. Herbert, ed., *Reflections on the Death of a Porcupine*, p. 216.
5. Herbert, ed., *Reflections on the Death of a Porcupine*, p. 286.

In the essay 'Why the Novel Matters' Lawrence asserts that, contrary to the church's teaching, there should be no division of body and spirit. For him the true self is in the body. He rejects the Pauline description of the body as a 'vessel of clay', a feeble repository for the ‡soul, but asserts the truth of 'man alive', of life itself at work in the body.[6]

Composed not long before his own death, 'The Ship of Death' perhaps unsurprisingly presents Lawrence's version of the doctrine of the *resurrection of the body. In this poem the body rots like a fallen apple and the ‡soul of it is put under great stress. Using the image of the *flood from Genesis, Lawrence declares 'the timid soul / has her footing washed away' (41–2). The ship of death becomes a 'little ark' (38), like Noah's, in which it sets sail towards the oblivion and †darkness of death, perhaps as Mabel Pervin enters the dark pond in *The Horse-Dealer's Daughter*. Eventually, however, †light dawns in the darkness, the waters subside, and the body 'emerges strange and lovely' (98). The 'frail soul steps out, into her house again' (101) with renewed peace.

QUESTIONS

1. Is Lawrence consistent in his refusal to separate body and ‡soul?
2. Are there points at which Lawrence's use of Christian concepts confuses rather than elucidates his meaning?

BIBLIOGRAPHY

Michael Herbert, ed., *Reflections on the Death of a Porcupine*, The Cambridge Edition of the Works of D.H. Lawrence, Cambridge 1988.

Graham Hough, *The Dark Sun: A Study of D.H. Lawrence*, London 1956. A critical study of all the major works, including a chapter on the tales with particular reference to religious meaning and the quarrel with Christianity.

Janice Hubbard Harris, *The Short Fiction of D.H. Lawrence*, New Brunswick NJ 1984. An evaluative study of the short stories and their development. Chapter 5 includes a look at the ritual symbolism of *The Horse Dealer's Daughter*.

Bruce Steele, ed., *England, My England and Other Stories*, The Cambridge Edition of the Works of D.H. Lawrence, Cambridge 1990. An authoritative series. This volume includes *The Horse Dealer's Daughter*.

---

6. Bruce Steele, ed., *Study of Thomas Hardy and Other Essays*, The Cambridge Edition of the Works of D H Lawrence, Cambridge 1985, pp. 193–8: 'so the ... vessel of clay, is just bunk' (p. 193).

9

T.S. ELIOT

THE WASTE LAND

[BACL pp. 688 f; NA2 pp. 2368 f; OA2 pp. 1980 f]

The Waste Land represents a revolution in literature. The poem's fragmented form itself reflects a breakup of consensus and traditional values, particularly following World War I, which shook the foundations of western civilisation. Published in 1922, *The Waste Land* heralded the greatest decade of modernism. With the voice of a †prophet Eliot depicts his civilisation, and the landscape of *The Waste Land* embodies the spiritual sterility and impotence he observes. There is nevertheless a movement forward, of straining after ‡redemption and rebirth, even though such resolution is not achieved within the poem.

The primary image of 'dead land' is developed first in the context of the Book of Common Prayer service for the Burial of the Dead: it is burial ground, the place of death. The life that does stir, does so reluctantly, preferring the oblivion of winter. This is the recurrent environment within which Eliot depicts a modern European civilisation that is morally, spiritually, and emotionally defunct. Images of dryness prevail, despite accounts of rainwater (even the sea here is waste and infertile, a place of death: 'Oed' und leer das Meer') focused in 'dried tubers', 'dry stone', and, recalling the burial liturgy's 'dust to dust', 'a handful of dust'.

The second stanza makes reference to Old Testament †prophecy. The form of address God uses to Ezekiel in his prophecy, 'son of man', is invoked, hard on the heels of another Old Testament term for the Messiah, the Branch, which is merged with Isaiah's characterisation of the Christ to come as 'a root out of a dry ground' (53:2). There is perhaps also a hint of the unwilling prophet Jonah's situation 'where the sun beats, / And the dead tree gives no shelter' (compare Jonah 4:8). The rock that Moses struck to provide water for the Israelites in the †desert (Exodus 17) here remains dry. The redness of the rock recalls the Hebrew word *adam/edom*, which means red, and hence the ground from which *Adam was taken and to which we all return — subject of some wordplay in the initial chapters of Genesis.[1] A sense of sterility and desert †wilderness is

---

1. Classical Hebrew does not supply the vowels in words, and the words *adam* meaning 'man' and *edom* meaning 'red' have the same consonants, d – m; hence the ambiguity.

thus deftly underscored by the biblical connotations in these three sentences. Scriptural analogues are chiefly found in the history of the Israelite people: 'He found him in a desert land, and in the waste howling wilderness' (Deuteronomy 32:10).

The †desert image is further developed in the arid mountain terrain of 'What the Thunder Said'. There are recollections of the poem's opening in 'stony places', dryness, and rock. The initial stanza references *Gethsemane and the agony of Christ, with the party approaching by torchlight to apprehend Christ (John 18:3). There is also the inversion of a biblical phrase in 'He who was living is now dead' underlining the sense of hopelessness and helplessness. A civilisation is slowly dying. This is a threatening, tormenting environment.

Despite the negative impulse in Eliot's exposure of modern civilisation, there are suggestions of hope. The fact that the †quest story, based on the Grail legend, underpins the poem suggests an impulse towards ‡redemption even if that is never to be realised — the Chapel Perilous depicted in the final section is windswept and empty, though that may be illusion, a final test for the questing knight. The rock of 'The Burial of the Dead', although it is inert and dry, provides a positive shade; a place of fear, certainly, but a place where the grim truth may be faced — the narrator invites the reader in to participate in this confrontation with the 'dust' of our civilisation, recalling Isaiah's 'Enter into the rock, and hide thee in the dust' (Isaiah 2:10). There is a sense of moral imperative about doing so.

The beginning of 'What the Thunder Said' alludes to Christ's ‡passion and *crucifixion: *Gethsemane, imprisonment, the palaces of Herod and Pontius Pilate, Christ's death. *Resurrection is not achieved in the poem, but the signs are increasingly forward-looking. The road to *Emmaus is, in fact, a post-resurrection scene from the gospels in which Christ is the third, unrecognised traveller alongside his disciples (Luke 24:13–34), though here the third figure is a more sinister hooded character, suggesting death as much as life.

The parched land and the brewing thunder at last find release in the arrival of rain. The voice of the thunder, like the voice of God, which frequently comes as thunder in the Bible, pronounces words from the Hindu Upanishads, which may as easily be Christian since they translate 'give', 'sympathise', and 'control', asserting a positive moral structure for our civilisation. The narrator is seen fishing, his back turned to the 'arid plain', this time with the suggestion that the sea contains life. One is reminded of another post-resurrection scene in which the disciples fish upon Galilee (John 21). An Old Testament reference to the king Hezekiah, told by the †prophet Isaiah, 'Set thine house in order; for thou shalt die, and not live' (II Kings 20:1) occurs here: 'Shall I at least set my lands in order?' (426) with the unspoken association that Hezekiah reestablished religious law in his kingdom and was blessed with a lengthening of his life.

The Italian seven lines from the end is from Dante's *Purgatorio* and may be translated 'Then he hid in the fire that refines them'. The context in Dante's poem is of one who ‡repents and anticipates †heaven beyond the fires of ‡purgatory. The purifying fire is a common biblical image, contrasting here with the lustful fires of Carthage from which Augustine is delivered in 'The Fire Sermon'.

The final stanza carries on balance more hope than despair. Recalling notions of ‡trinity, the poem ends with the thrice repeated 'falling down' of London Bridge, but also a repetition of the thunder's threefold moral pronouncement, and the final greeting of peace, 'Shantih shantih shantih'.

The lone figure on the sea shore, however, surrounded still by disintegration and collapse, does not present an easy resolution: 'These fragments I have shored against my ruins' (431). The images of death and life in the poem are freighted with ambiguities and all carry multiple associations. Nevertheless there is a struggling towards an answer of some kind, and we as readers are compelled to participate in that struggle as we grapple with the poem.

QUESTIONS

1. Is the subtext of *The Waste Land* Christian, or does Eliot use a Christian vocabulary for secular ends?
2. What is the status of Tiresias, whom Eliot identified as 'the most important personage in the poem, uniting all the rest'? Is he a detached observer, or morally involved?

BIBLIOGRAPHY

Linda Cookson and Bryan Loughrey, ed., *Critical Essays on The Waste Land*, Harlow 1988. A useful collection of essays.

A.D. Moody, *Tracing T.S. Eliot's Spirit: Essays on his Poetry and Thought*, Cambridge 1996. A study of T.S. Eliot's spiritual leanings, with a useful chapter on *The Waste Land*.

Cedric Watts, 'The last 10½ lines of *The Waste Land*', in Cookson and Loughrey, ed., *Critical Essays*: a short essay which finds a search for ‡redemption through religious values in *The Waste Land*.

Robert Wilson, 'Is there hope in *The Waste Land*?' in Cookson and Loughrey, ed., *Critical Essays*. Identifies a positive religious impulse in the poem.

The Complete Poems and Plays [of] T.S. Eliot, London 1969. Comprehensive standard edition.

FOUR QUARTETS

[NA2 pp. 2389 f (Little Gidding); OA2 pp. 2020 f (Little Gidding)]

Eliot completed these four poems, 'Burnt Norton', 'East Coker', 'The Dry Salvages', and 'Little Gidding' between 1935 and 1942. All four are entitled after places of some past or present significance to him, while the later poems are influenced by his experience as a civilian in World War II in London.

Eliot was an Anglo-Catholic, formed in a tradition of disciplined prayer and ‡sacramental life that is evident throughout the poems. He is concerned with contemplative Christianity, that is, with a religious life that seeks full union with God. This brand of Christianity recognises the need for purification if a creature of flesh and blood, living in time, is to be drawn into the life of an all-holy, spiritual God. Eliot's guide in contemplative Christianity was the Carmelite poet and ‡mystic St John of the Cross, whose teaching in *The Ascent of Mount Carmel* pervades all four poems and is paraphrased in sections of 'Burnt Norton' and 'East Coker'.

St John of the Cross's teaching focuses on the consequences for Christians of the †incarnation of Christ. In his becoming a human being, eternity, where God dwells, enters the world of time, where human beings experience their mortal, time-limited existence. This is the primary 'intersection of the timeless with time' (as in 'The Dry Salvages', 4). God, who is pure spirit, pure goodness, pure †love, enters into relationship with his creatures who have a spiritual dimension but experience life though their senses, their minds, and their capacity for memory and imagination. For the fulfilment of their relationship human beings must become pure, like God; this involves recognising that their senses, minds, and memories cannot serve as means of reaching and relating with God.

Such recognition involves undergoing purification of the mind, so that they have a pure faith rather than a mind full of their own ideas about God; of the memory and imagination, so that their hope is in God alone and they do not waste their efforts in vain regrets or wishes about the past and in vain daydreams about the future; of the will, so that they choose and †love God for himself and not for his gifts, rendering them capable of selfless love for others.

This purification is the work of the Holy Spirit (the 'Living Flame of Love', as another of John's works is entitled); this is a painful process whereby the ‡soul of the human is transformed to become like God. The pain consists largely in two experiences: of being in sensory and spiritual †darkness concerning the things of God and in acquiring increasingly painful self-knowledge. The first entails the absence of any religious emotion or moments of sudden insight, for example, that gratify the senses: the inner self must be content to wait on God in darkness. The latter experience brings about the exposure of the self's deepest illusions and self-deceptions and a painful awareness of the difference between the holiness of God and the *fallen state of humankind.

The ideal climate for this work of purification is solitude and silence, that is, withdrawal from the distractions of desires, concepts, or words. It demands detachment from the self, which must learn to seek nothing but God, in order to be able to receive everything from him. The inner self must become still and receptive in order to become a place in which the timeless and time can inter-sect.[2] This place, for St John of the Cross, was first of all the Virgin †Mary. Her detachment from self is evident in her words to the †angel, accepting her role as mother of Christ, 'Be it unto me according to thy word' (Luke 1:38). This is to be the prayer of any contemplative.

This teaching about the necessity of silence highlights the ambivalence about language evident in the writings of St John of the Cross. A consummate poet, he was yet highly conscious of the limitations of human language. Human words cannot adequately express Christ, who is the living Word of God (John 1:1), spoken by God in what is experienced as silence to the human mind.[3]

We can find in this account of St John's teachings all the major themes and allusions of *Four Quartets*. We find in all four a concern for the relationship between time and eternity. Life is wasted by the unpurified memory in seeking meaning and purpose either in a regretted or unfulfilled past or in a desired or feared future. The present moment is avoided, yet it is in this point that the eternal may be experienced. 'Stillness' contrasts with the endless scurrying of the mind and of desires in order to achieve some temporary gratification. It is when this internal scurry and noise is stilled and silenced that the eternal 'now' can be apprehended, the 'still point'. But this is evaded because it brings aware-ness of a reality humans shun and fear. Humankind cannot bear very much reality as Eliot says in 'Burnt Norton', section I.

In 'Burnt Norton' stillness is related to dancing 'at the still point, there the dance is'. This dance is the inner life of the holy ‡Trinity, whose interrelation-ship is called in Greek *perichoresis*, a term linked to dance. To be at the still point is to enter the life of the Godhead where true creative energy is located.

---

2. See *The Ascent of Mount Carmel*, Book 1, chapter 13, paragraph 1, in Kieran Kavanaugh and Otilio Rodriguez, trans., *The Collected Works of St John of the Cross*, Washington DC 1973.

3. Kavanaugh and Rodriguez, trans., *The Ascent of Mount Carmel*, Book 2, chapter 22, paragraph 5.

But Eliot is aware that human beings are *enfleshed*: total and enduring exposure to the life of God is too much for created beings; life in time provides some necessary protection for the unpurified. They must come to the 'still point', not by denying time altogether but by gathering in memories into the present.

In 'East Coker' two experiences of time are contrasted. In section I of the poem Eliot evokes the picture of country folk, married couples, dancing. Their keeping time in the dancing, and in their farming lives, ties them into time as perceived by pagans, cyclical and recurring but having no 'end', both in the sense of ending but also of 'purpose'. Life in time, conceived thus, has no purpose beyond 'Eating and drinking / Dung and death' in endless cycle. Viewed from this perspective, life is an endlessly repeated road to death.

Eliot contrasts this implicitly with Christian time: death is transformed by *resurrection, 'the agony of death and birth' ('East Coker'); this is experienced as purification, in life as well as in and after death. The opening lines of this poem, 'In my end is my beginning', suggest that for the ‡soul under the grace of the resurrection and ready to die to self through the experience of purification, the experience of death will be the beginning of new life, whilst for those living under pagan time, death is implicit in birth: 'In my beginning is my end.'

In 'Dry Salvages' the underlying motif of the †incarnation of Christ is made explicit in section V. Here Eliot contrasts the experience of ‡saints whose whole lives are surrendered to the purification by †love with that of the 'ordinary' Christian. For these there remains the possibility of a fleeting 'touch' of God, a moment out of time and out of 'self'. This is our experience of †incarnation, incomplete and half-understood, a hint of the contemplative experience of time.

'Little Gidding' develops the theme of time and the relative value of human endeavour in the long section that recalls Dante's meeting with people in †hell, ‡purgatory, and paradise in his *Divine Comedy*. Here we have a vision, also, of the contemplative †journey into self-knowledge that leads to a reiteration of the necessity of detachment, of ensuring that we are not rooted in the passing, temporal world.

Eliot's quotation from Julian of Norwich's *Revelations of Divine Love* 'all shall be well' (167 – 8) is a reminder that human history has an end and is therefore only contingent. It has value, however, as the means whereby God fulfils his end or purpose for humankind. Detachment does not mean indifference or failure to value temporal experience at all: it allows its proper valuation and its place in God's purposes. 'Sin is Behovely' (166) equally reminds us that all the negativity, the loss, and the suffering associated with life in time, all that seems to be wasted, has equally been a means whereby God achieves his purposes.

It is here that we see how meditation on the †incarnation becomes also meditation on the death of Jesus. It is through eternity's intersection with time in the incarnation that God becomes in Christ 'the wounded surgeon' who heals human wounds by sharing them and dying a human death ('East Coker'). It is in the death of Christ that humans find their true lives, which are nourished by his gift of himself on the †cross and in the ‡sacrament of the ‡eucharist: 'The dripping blood our only drink, / The bloody flesh our only food' ('East Coker' IV).

Consequently in 'East Coker' the fires caused by the bombers parody the dove that descended upon the apostles in tongues of flame (Acts 2:3), and that is the agent of human purification. Humankind has the choice of living to be destroyed by the fire of its own passions or by the fire of purifying †love which will re-create it. The ultimate prospect the poem offers us is of the triumph, not of the fire of passion, but of the flame of love that will integrate the rose, ancient symbol of human beauty and passion, into the life of the holy ‡Trinity, the crowned knot of fire. The work of the †incarnation will be complete in this ultimate incorporation of purified human capacities into the life of the Godhead.

QUESTIONS

1. What themes of St John of the Cross do you identify in 'Little Gidding'?
2. How would you characterise Eliot's approach to human experience and suffering?
3. To what extent are you persuaded by the optimism of the closing section of 'Little Gidding'?

BIBLIOGRAPHY

Harry Blamires, *Word Unheard: A Guide Through Eliot's 'Four Quartets'*, London 1969.

Denis Donoghue, *Words Alone: The Poet T.S. Eliot*, London 2001.

Edward Lobb, ed., *Words in Time: New Essays on Eliot's Four Quartets*, London 1993.

David A. Moody, ed., *The Cambridge Companion to T.S. Eliot*, Cambridge 1994.

Michael D. Spencer, 'Mysticism in T.S. Eliot's *Four Quartets*', *Studies in Spirituality* 9 (1999), 230–66.

10

SAMUEL BECKETT, *ENDGAME*

[*NA2* pp. 2471 f]

Beckett's relationship to the Christian tradition must be seen as one of antagonism and rejection. Central to his work is a repudiation of the Christian ‡virtue of hope that upholds the belief in the purposive nature of human life and especially of the suffering it entails. In *Endgame*, the Christian idea that the suffering of Christ is ‡redemptive is mocked in the figure of Hamm. His early rhetorical question 'if there be any misery loftier than mine?' echoes the words attributed to Jesus in the Improperia, or reproaches, sung in the Catholic rite on ‡Good Friday (and see also Lamentations 1:12).

Whilst Jesus' suffering has meaning and purpose and suggests a value to life, Hamm's pain has neither meaning or value. In his response of 'Then he's living' to Clov's report on Nagg, 'He's crying', Hamm equates the pain of life with life itself; we cannot find a purpose or meaning within it without engaging in self-deception. Hence his fear, 'we're not beginning to mean something?'

Christian hope hinges on two beliefs: firstly in an abiding providence guiding human life and operating often in emotional and spiritual †darkness; and secondly in the restoration of all things, bringing the end of all tears, at the end of time. The present can be endured through faith in an abiding presence and through hope in final, eternal beatitude. What we find in *Endgame* is that such hope is exposed as false. The characters spend their days either in waiting, not for final glory, but for death and dissolution, or in trying to avoid the pain of existence and the recognition of non-meaning through engaging in reminiscence or fantasy.

Belief in God is just one of these stories told to give an illusion of purpose and hope as we find in the fruitless attempt at prayer and Hamm's comment, 'The bastard! He doesn't exist.' At times the audience, like Hamm, is tempted to the belief that the characters may be 'beginning to mean something' only to realise that this is illusion. The only certainty, the only truth, is the certainty of physical decay, as Hamm reminds Clov. In Beckett we hear echoes of the world-weary tones of the preacher Ecclesiastes taken out of any wider context of belief (see Ecclesiastes 1:1–15).

Behind *Endgame*, however, lie echoes of the earlier parts of another Old Testament book, Job. Job, the just man, is afflicted with countless sufferings by God as part of a challenge to him by the †angel, †Satan, that Job is only righteous because he is prosperous and happy. God accepts the challenge, and Job is afflicted by loss of his wealth, of his loved ones, as well as by a terrible skin disease. In his pain he curses the day he was born, curses the light, and wishes that he had been taken from womb to tomb (Job 3:11).

Here we have the anger at painful existence evident in Hamm and Clov, and, perhaps, one of the significances of the bins in which Nell and Nagg are kept. These suggest both burial urns and wombs as well as implying that ageing flesh is trash. Like Job (Job 3:20–6), Hamm and Clov long for night when it is day and vice versa, both desiring and fearing oblivion. Like him they experience a continual, gratuitous, and inexplicable affliction that calls into question their existence and purpose (see any of Job's complaints, such as those in chapters 8 and 9). Job's cursing of the day he was born is also an implicit cursing of his parents. This too links in with Hamm, whose only term for his father is 'cursed progenitor'. There can be no love for the one responsible for giving the curse of life.

As with Job, too, life is endured as slavery. We see how much Clov is enslaved to the wishes of Hamm, Nagg and Nell are enslaved to both Clov and Hamm, while Hamm himself is enslaved in his dependence on Clov. All are slaves to their suffering existence and to their stratagems in avoiding it.

Beckett offers us a Job-like version of life, but it is Job without his ultimate meeting with God and his restoration. Job's test is short-lived, followed by vindication and renewal. By omitting this Beckett seems to suggest that any such renewal is part of the illusion: the test is all there is. Even envisioning our characters as involved in some kind of purposeful game with a God who tests is an escape into the illusion of purpose and meaning.

This link with the book of Job is also suggested by the title of the play. *Endgame* refers to the game of chess. In one sense what happens between God and Job is a game in which God makes the moves to which Job must respond. In the biblical story it is a game in two ways because in some sense God is playing with Job to test his responses, and secondly, like a game, the testing of Job is limited in time. Beckett challenges us to see this in a different perspective: a game is a game, without any ulterior purpose. We must see their predicament as such a purposeless game, rather than as purposeful test. And the endgame in this form of affliction leads not to vindication and restoration, but to death and decay.

Beckett further parodies Christian hope in his use of the Christian ‡allegorical tradition regarding names, which he twists and deflates. We have seen this tradition at work in the ‡morality play and restoration comedy: the name outlines or implies the nature or moral status of the character. In *Endgame* the names tease us to find meanings but in themselves have none: they expose our need to make his characters 'mean something'. Hamm, for example, has been compared to a ham actor, making bloated rhetoric out of his predicament. The relationship between Hamm and Clov has equally been taken to suggest hammer and nail (*clou* in Beckett's French).[1] This would suggest both their mutual dependence and their capacity to inflict pain on one another. It has also been taken to suggest ham and clove, suggestive of interdependence, and of ultimate non-humanity. Nagg and Nell, similarly, invite us to play and to speculate. None of them yield certain meaning, despite our formation by literary tradition to make them do so.

In *Endgame*, Beckett seeks to undermine all the presuppositions that a Christian culture has offered about the meaning and purpose of time, of suffering, and of human existence.

QUESTIONS

1. What do Nell and Nagg contribute to the presentation of affliction in *Endgame*?
2. To what extent do you consider enslavement an appropriate description of the characters' predicament in the play?
3. What are the functions of the stories and recollections made by the characters?

BIBLIOGRAPHY

Richard Begam, *Samuel Beckett and the End of Modernity*, Stanford CA 1996.

Steven Connor, ed., *Waiting for Godot and Endgame*, Basingstoke 1992: a useful collection of essays.

Charles R. Lyons, 'Beckett's *Endgame*: an anti-myth of creation', *Modern Drama* 7 (1964), 204–9.

Thomas Postlewait, 'Self-performing voices: mind, memory and time in Beckett's drama', *Twentieth-Century Literature* 24 (1978), 473–91.

Christopher Ricks, *Beckett's Dying Words*, Oxford 1993.

---

1. See Martin Esslin, *The Theatre of the Absurd*, 3rd edn, London 2001, p. 82.

11

EDITH SITWELL, 'STILL FALLS THE RAIN'

[NA2 pp. 2527–8]

Edith Sitwell was writing 'Still Falls the Rain' at the time of the first bombing of London in World War II. Writing as a Catholic, she was adapting traditional meditations on the wounds of Christ and applying the concept of Christ's wounds, his suffering, and death, to the suffering and death experienced in the war. An essential tenet of Christianity is that Christ died to save humankind from the eternal death that results from ‡sin: one way of interpreting and expressing this belief is to say that our sins *crucified Christ. In this way, experiences such as war, involving so much sinful destruction and suffering, can be described as a participation in Christ's ‡passion and death, or it can be viewed as Christ being crucified again in his people. This was a not uncommon idea among Catholics of the period. Sitwell uses this idea in the opening stanza, when every year since Christ's coming is seen as a year of sin piercing him: he takes the weight of all man's inhumanity to man and wrongdoing, which the rain of the bombing seems to encompass.

If the bombing takes us to the †cross, it also takes us to the heart of human ‡sin in the betrayal and destruction, not only of human life, but of 'brotherhood' in that life. For Sitwell links *Judas's *betrayal of Jesus with the sin of *Cain, the murderer of his brother Abel (Genesis 4:1–16). Sitwell's message is clear: this war is the destruction of brotherhood just as was Cain's murder of Abel; more than that, it is the betrayal of Christ who is found at the depths of every human being. Linking Cain with the field of blood on which Judas hanged himself (Matthew 27:3–10) reminds us, too, that though Abel's blood spilt by Cain calls for vengeance, the blood of Christ brings pardon and reconciliation, not condemnation (Hebrews 12:24). And so, with this in mind, the poem moves to a plea for mercy, for mercy on the sinful rich man and the beggar since this rain of bombs, like natural rain, affects good and bad alike (Matthew 5:45). In her ironic use of a biblical allusion, which occurs in the context of teaching on mutual, disinterested †love, Sitwell emphasises the absolute absence of such love in this present conflict.

Sitwell intertwines here another biblical *parable, that of the rich man and Lazarus (Luke 16:19–31).[1] The rich man feasts at his table unaware of the poor man languishing at his gate. When they die it is Lazarus who goes to Abraham's bosom and the rich man who is consigned to †hell. When he asks for a warning to be given to his brothers, he is told that a chasm exists between them. As we have seen, Sitwell takes this in the context of Jesus saying that his Father sends the rain on the good and evil alike, that he is no respecter of persons. In this war, Sitwell says, the rich and the poor, the guilty and the innocent, are equally at risk: the rain of bombing falls on rich and poor, good and bad alike. The bombs are no respecter of persons, like God in this alone.

The thought of mercy leads Sitwell to contemplation of the traditional Catholic icon of †love, the Sacred Heart of Jesus. According to St Bonaventure, an early Franciscan ‡friar and theologian, the side of Jesus was wounded so that humans may have access to his loving heart. Similarly, the seventeenth-century nun, St Margaret Mary Alacoque, experienced Christ showing her his wounded heart and telling her 'Behold this heart that has so loved men.' Sitwell takes this idea and deepens it. Christ's heart is wounded with love for humanity by bearing all the wounds it inflicts upon itself and upon all things sentient. Christ's love goes beyond even humanity to embrace the pain of all created things. His heart bears all.

Sitwell continues in her meditation on the wounds of Christ by turning now to the wounded head of Christ, to his crown of thorns, seen as the victor's crown and truly the crown of a king despite the suffering. The quotation of Dr Faustus' vision of the cosmic flow of Christ's mercy in his blood heightens awareness of some kind of victory when one looks beyond immediate suffering. The blood of Jesus is not only his mercy, it is also his life. It is through the flowing blood of Christ that people are ‡redeemed, and therefore to see Christ's blood flowing in the firmament is a reminder that all human life takes place under the life-giving mercy of God, that Christ has ascended into the heavens, and his †love and mercy are victorious there. The bombs may rain down their death and destruction but there is a more powerful, eternal force that abides in the †heavens beyond and above the transient forces of evil.

So Sitwell moves her readers towards hope and assurance: despite the suffering, despite the inhumanity, God's †love endures, his suffering love persists

---

1. The rich man is traditionally called Dives, from Latin *dives* 'a rich man'.

and saves, because all human pain is encompassed by his. Like her Catholic counterpart the artist and writer Caryll Houselander, Sitwell believes 'this war is the Passion', but reminds us that the ‡passion of Christ is ultimately a story of love and restoration, not of horror and destruction. Sitwell succeeds in confronting the pain, despair, and inhumanity of war and in offering a message of hope.

QUESTIONS

1. Examine the structure of the poem and trace the movement through the different wounds of Christ.
2. To what extent do the biblical allusions contribute to the mood and tone of the poem?
3. Would you agree that this is ultimately an optimistic poem? Justify your conclusion.

BIBLIOGRAPHY

James D. Brophy, ed., *Edith Sitwell: The Symbolist Order*, Carbondale IL 1968.

Mark S. Morrisson, 'Edith Sitwell's atomic bomb poems: alchemy and scientific reintegration', *Modernism/Modernity* 9 (2002), 605–33.

12

W.H. Auden, 'Horae Canonicae'

[The 'Horae Canonicae' are not anthologised in the main collections used here, but see *NA2* pp. 2500 f and *OA2* pp. 2091 f for other Auden poems.]

Wystan Hugh Auden (1907–73) is widely celebrated for his politically and socially aware poetry written in the 1930s in companionship with Stephen Spender, Cecil Day-Lewis, and Louis MacNeice (often referred to as Mac Spaunday). In many quarters his later, Christian poetry has been relatively neglected.

Auden came from an Anglo-Catholic background: both his grandfathers were Anglican priests, and his family were believing and devout. Having broken away from his faith in his later teens Auden absorbed two major intellectual influences of his day, Freudianism and Marxism, which made of him a wry critic of the political and social order. The reductionism of Freudianism encouraged a low view of human nature, since so much apparently fine or acceptable behaviour could be attributed to defence mechanisms against the demands of the id, the instinctual driving force of all activity. Marxist theory established a concern for the meaning of history and the shaping power of historical currents. We can see these influences transmuted in his later poetry.

His 're-conversion' to the Anglo-Catholicism of his roots issued out of an encounter with an unashamed capacity for human depravity, which left him questioning the source of his outrage. His Freudian perspective was insufficient as an explanation, but it continued to contribute to an emphasis in his early Christian poetry on utter human ‡sinfulness, which he later considered unbalanced. His newly restored faith also led him to reconsider his approach to history and to human attempts to create a perfect world. Initially the tendency was to deny the value of human activity in the light of the utter transcendence of God: the human †city and the City of God were two antagonistic entities. Auden shifted his perspective here, too, coming to understand the interrelationship between secular and divine time, setting the *crucifixion and *resurrection of Christ at the centre of all time and giving human history its goal or end point in the *second coming of Christ.

Both these new perspectives are evident in his major Christian poem sequence 'Horae Canonicae', written between 1949 and 1954. 'Horae Canonicae' means 'canonical hours', the sevenfold sequence of prayers and psalms that punctuate the day in ‡monastic houses.[1] Auden's poem deals with the day hours. From earliest times these were understood not primarily as means of sanctifying different parts of the day, but as means of setting earthly, secular time within what we might call 'Christ-time', that is time experienced as participation in eternity, in which the critical historical event of Christ's death and *resurrection is an ever-present reality. By living in daily remembrance the worshipper is made a participant in this time. But this is not all. Since in the †incarnation of Christ the eternal entered the world of secular time, the two are now inextricably linked: secular time is a vehicle, as it were, for the eternal purpose, so that its end point will be the fulfilment of everything in the final *second coming of Christ. The hours employ the same understanding of time, then, which is also evident in the ‡mystery plays: human history is salvation history, beginning with *creation through Christ, the Word (as we see in the prologue to St John's Gospel), finding its centre in the ‡salvation wrought by Christ and reaching fulfilment when he establishes the new †heaven and new earth.

'Prime', Auden's first hour, recalls the beginning of Christ's trial before Pilate and his *resurrection appearance to Mary Magdalene. It encompasses, therefore, remembrance of death but also awakening to new life. And so the poem recalls the first waking to life of ‡sinless *Adam before the *fall. Praise for this newness of being is accompanied by awareness of the need to assume responsibility for being a fallen creature whose life, like Adam's, is shaped by his choices. Awakening gives the persona three tasks: to accept his bodily mortality; to accept responsibility for the fallen world; and to die to self in order to live in Christ. From now on in the poem it will be by participating in the history of the victim, whose road to death begins at Prime, that the persona evaluates all human experience.

'Terce' recalls the scourging of Christ, a later *resurrection appearance, and the descent of the Holy Spirit on the disciples giving them the power for their missionary endeavour. It is thus associated with the Spirit of God at work in the world, and by extrapolation with the beginning of the human working day. In this way divine time and secular time intersect. Auden's characters similarly begin their working day, their professions of hangman and judge reminding us that each day takes place within the history of Christ. We are reminded, too,

---

1. The eighth 'hour' is Matins, technically the night office.

that human beings in the secular †city are ignorant and fallible, shadows of the ultimate †judge and dispenser of justice, yet still stumblingly involved in his enterprise. We see, too, *fallen humanity setting about its day in self-obsession caring only for its pleasure or safety. It is this inturning upon the self, the essence of ‡sin, that bred, and breeds, rejection of Christ making people agents every day in the *crucifixion of Christ.

'Sext' recalls the nailing of Christ to the †cross and a *resurrection appearance. Here much is implicit. Auden highlights one kind of dying to self in those who, 'forgetting themselves in a function' (8), are thus responsible for the advance of civilisation, for the establishment of the secular †city against the power of the mob. There is ambivalence here: without these there would be no 'notion of a city' (30) but also 'for this death, / there would be no agents' (31–2). Similarly in section 2 those who wield human authority are those to whom we owe 'basilicas, divas / dictionaries, pastoral verse' (51–2); without these existence would be 'squalid', 'tethered for life to some hut village' (57–8). Yet without them also 'there would be no authority / to command this death' (65–6). There is a dual paradox here. At face value it may seem that the secular city is set squarely in conflict with the †heavenly city. The flowering of human civilisation leads to a structure antagonistic to the things of God. Are we then to see all human values as negated by the divine? Not so, for although this death results from the actions of the secular city, it fulfils the divine purpose and so participates in its own ‡redemption. Whether we know it or not, whether we intend it or not, secular choices and secular time operate within the purposes of God.

'Nones' recalls the time of Christ's death; it is the focal point of the day and of time. This death calls into question the purpose of our activity, making it only a way of passing time until night that foreshadows our death. In this challenge to the human experience of time, bodily time continues undisturbed, reminding people that they are not only conscious subjects, choosing and shaping human history, and unconscious agents in building the †heavenly †city, but also embodied animals, enabled and hampered by a biological rhythm independent of will and choice. It is in this confrontation with death, with emptiness, with mortal enfleshment that the first encounter with 'our Double' (95), our divided selfhood, takes place.

'Vespers' recalls the taking down of Christ from the †cross but, as it is celebrated at nightfall, recalls Christ as the †light of the world, whose *resurrection points to the coming of the *last day when there will only be light (see Revelation 21:23). For Auden the human experience of this light is an unflinching confrontation with oneself, 'in this hour of civil twilight all must wear their own faces'. When the persona describes his Double or anti-type we see that each represents his own parody of the kingdom of God. The persona envisages the good life as a return to *Eden that is all leisure and aesthetic pleasure. His anti-type looks to a future utopia, an earthly New Jerusalem, which is akin to a fascist or Soviet planned society based on enforcement, 'rational virtues', and efficient production. Both dreams are 'ancient fibs'. The grace of this 'secular twilight' is that in this encounter both are forced

> to remember our victim...
>
> on whose immolation ... arcadias, utopias, our dear old bag of a
>   democracy, are alike founded : ...
>
> For without a cement of blood (it must be human, it must be inno-
>   cent) no secular wall will safely stand.

We find Auden asserting once more that no vision of human happiness or perfection, nor even any rough approximation to it, can come to fruition without in some way participating in or deriving from, the reality of ‡salvation in Christ. Whatever succeeds in the secular †city can only do so because Christ has ‡redeemed it.

'Compline' recalls Christ's burial: it sees sleep as a little death, a rehearsal for final death and *resurrection. This involves the experience of sorrow for ‡sin and abandonment into God's hands in acceptance of death and †judgement. So in Auden's poem the three rhythms of secular time, of biological life, and of 'Christ-time' become one. The persona looks back in ‡penitence over the day in which he has made little sense of his life in 'Christ-time': 'I cannot remember / A thing between noon and three' (15–16). But this is accompanied by an intuition that, despite the inadequacy of his mind to grasp the reality of ‡redemption, this is the abiding truth that his heart knows and lends peace to his night:

> maybe
> My heart is confessing her part
> In what happened to us from noon to three,
> That constellations indeed
> Sing of some hilarity beyond
> All liking and happening. (21–6)

The day ends in human muddle, doubt, and uncertainty. It also affirms a hope of eternal life that transcends human inability to grasp, in lines that are theologically very rich. The persona prays

That we, too, may come to the picnic
With nothing to hide, join the dance
As it moves in perichoresis,
Turns about the abiding tree. (61–4)

The picnic is Auden's typically downbeat image of the †wedding feast of the Lamb, the fulfilment of all *creation at the end of time. Perichoresis is the term used to describe the way the three persons of the ‡Trinity relate to one another, and it involves the notion of dance. Ultimate reality, divine †love, is understood as a continual circling of love, an intricate dance. Human beatitude consists in being drawn into this dance of eternal love, which Auden sees as continually celebrating the †cross, the tree of life.

'Lauds' means literally 'praise'. It is the morning-hour of praise and thanksgiving for *creation and re-creation in Christ. So Auden's 'Lauds' begins with cockcrow, the traditional herald of the *resurrection. The muddle and hope of 'Compline' becomes now a song of triumphant praise and assurance. The ‡mass-bell rings to herald the celebration, in concentrated form, of the Christ-event the day will trace, the human version of cockcrow. The new day is God's day, and he will bless the secular and the bodily rhythms of the day since both are renewed by the resurrection. 'The dripping millwheel is again turning' (19), but we know it is turning as a participant in the history of ‡salvation.

QUESTIONS

1. What is the effect of Auden's wry tone in this sequence on your reading of his view of human experience?
2. How would you characterise Auden's view of the secular †city?

BIBLIOGRAPHY

Tom Duggett, 'In solitude, for company: the city in W.H. Auden's "Horae Canonicae"', *English* 54 (2005), 19–27.
Alan Jacobs, 'Auden and the limits of poetry', *First Things* 115 (2001), 26–32. A very useful study, considering the consequences of Auden's faith for his understanding of the poet's vocation.
Arthur Kirsch, *Auden and Christianity*, New Haven, CT 2005. An excellent introduction to Auden's faith expressed in his poetry.
Edward Mendelson, ed., *W.H. Auden: Collected Poems*, London 1991.
Edward Mendelson, *Later Auden*, London 1999. A full, essential study.

13

PHILIP LARKIN, *POEMS*

[*NA2* pp. 2564 f; *OA2* pp. 2173 f]

Philip Larkin, 1922–85, has an established reputation depending on a relatively small output of poems, chiefly published in the collections *The Less Deceived* (1955), *The Whitsun Weddings* (1964), and *High Windows* (1974).[1] Larkin's poetry combines acute observation with a refusal to generalise or resort to abstraction. His language is for the most part concrete and often colloquial; his verse gains much of its power from ordinary scenes vividly evoked, from clear and immediate images, and from unshrinking directness. He was impatient with the Pound and Eliot school of poetry with its allusive and abstract style. Commenting on the 'critical industry' generated by those poets, he remarked, 'to me ... the whole of classical and biblical mythology means very little, and I think that using them today not only fills poems full of dead spots but dodges the writer's duty to be original'.[2] This is a revealing comment: the collocation of 'classical and biblical mythology' associates religion in various forms with the past, as things in which Larkin is not interested, and which have little meaning for him; use of these things, moreover, is inimical to poetic originality. These are attitudes that shape his poetry, assumptions that inform the clear, dry, ironical mind that voices itself in the poems.[3]

Yet religion is a topic to which Larkin returns, especially when he thinks about death. 'Aubade' captures the poet's visceral fear of death: the sense that the one thing permanent, certain, and deliberately unacknowledged is death — a thought at the 'edge of vision', which in the †darkness 'blanks the mind' with its 'glare', and in the †light is 'plain as a wardrobe'. He confidently dismisses religion:

> This is a special way of being afraid
> No trick dispels. Religion used to try,

---

1. See Stephen Regan's 'Introduction', section I, in *Philip Larkin: Contemporary Critical Essays*, pp. 1–6, for a brief review of Larkin's reputation.

2. Larkin talking in an interview: quoted from Terry Whalen, *Philip Larkin and English Poetry*, p. 96.

3. It is important not to identify the personae of the poems too directly with Larkin himself, but that there is a singular consciousness expressing itself is generally agreed.

That vast moth-eaten musical brocade
Created to pretend we never die ... (21–4)

Religion is, by association, a 'trick' of the past: it 'used to try' to dispel fear, but both what it created, its 'musical brocade', and that in the poet's view it *was* created for the very trick of denying death, makes it a delusion. There is also the faintest of allusions to the Book of Common Prayer in the poet's response to the blinding thought of death, in which he rejects remorse: ' — The good not done' (12) echoes the General ‡Confession, 'we have left undone those things which we ought to have done'. Yet religion, with its vast musical brocade, has an artistic richness and substance that the other, universal, delusion — 'the uncaring / Intricate rented world' (46–7) — does not have.

The poet sees religion as being about fear and consolation. The vehicles in 'Ambulances' are like 'confessionals', an image that perfectly captures the mixture: fear of what has happened, and hope that the consequences may be mitigated. In 'High Windows' fear is attributed to older people, apparently oppressed by religion and its structures, people who imagine as 'paradise' a time when there is

No God any more, or sweating in the dark

About hell and that, or having to hide
What you think of the priest. (12–14, Larkin's italics)

By contrast, the religious consolation of 'The Explosion' is only very slightly ironised by being quoted as a voice external to those immediately involved in the mining tragedy:

The dead go on before us, they
Are sitting in God's house in comfort,
We shall see them face to face — (16–18, Larkin's italics)

Indeed, the men going to work 'Through the tall gates standing open' (12) inevitably recalls the image of the 'pearly gates' of †heaven. The poet preserves the integrity of those involved, allows them the specifically religious consolation of life after death and rest from labour for their loved ones, and also their more personal and homely vision of the men 'Larger than life', and the lark's 'eggs unbroken'.

There is generosity of spirit here because Larkin's conviction was that death is the end of everything and that then there is nothing:

this is what we fear — no sight, no sound,
No touch or taste or smell, nothing to think with,

Nothing to love or link with ... ('Aubade', 27–9)

'Nothing' is not always fearful, though: as he thinks of the present, and the past, and the future-in-the-past in 'High Windows', it breaks serene and unbidden on his consciousness:

> Rather than words comes the thought of high windows:
> The sun-comprehending glass,
> And beyond it, the deep blue air, that shows
> Nothing, and is nowhere, and is endless. (17–20)

This 'nothing' is not personal loss, but a kind of transcendence that embraces the more contingent endlessness of the 'slide / To happiness' of the young, as well as the envious regrets of the old.

This idea of transcendence, this nothingness, collides with the clutteredness of the church in 'Church Going'. There is a kind of emptiness about the church in that 'there's nothing going on', but so many things occupy the space: 'matting, seats and stone', books, flowers, brass, organ, font, lectern. There are not only things: there is 'a tense, musty, unignorable silence', echoes that 'snigger', 'Power of some sort', 'ghostly silt' and air in which 'all our compulsions meet, / Are recognised, and robed as destinies' (56–7). All this makes the poet deeply uneasy. His casual blasphemy of thought, of the silence 'Brewed God knows how long', catches him off balance, so he parodies the rituals of church-going to deny it any meaning: taking off his cycle-clips instead of a hat, pronouncing 'Here endeth' to the snigger of the echoes, donating a coin with no value. That prompts the question as to what the church is worth (18, 53), and why he often stops to visit.

The poet has no belief that the church or its rituals mean anything, and is convinced that churches will 'fall completely out of use': the poem's title is, deliberately, 'Church Going'. He wonders what will happen to them when belief dies out: will they become museums or places of superstition? Or, worse, he savagely imagines the visits of 'the ruin-bibber, randy for antique', or the 'Christmas-addict', those who get cheap thrills and sentimental satisfaction from the wreckage of the church and its festivals. The remaining alternative for the last visitor to the church is the poet's 'representative' who comes because 'this cross of ground' once

> held unspilt
> So long and equably what since is found
> Only in separation — marriage, and birth,
> And death, and thoughts of these ... (48–51)

Some vaguely perceived integrity of life and death about the church and its past draws the poet, who imagines that there must be others like himself who are surprised by the hunger 'to be more serious'. And he concludes that the sense that a church is a place 'proper to grow wise in' might only be because 'so many dead lie round'.

Terry Whalen remarks that 'by the time he finishes his investigation he is praising his surroundings with a musing that gives to his agnostic humanism an oddly religious glow' (p. 17). This is an illusion created by Larkin's control of language and development in the poem, and especially in the last stanza. Notable are the inversion and repetition of 'A serious house on serious earth it is' (55), and the use of words that are, if not archaic, at least more common in religious discourse than secular: 'blent', 'robed', 'hunger' in a non-literal sense, even 'wise'. But these are merely disguising the fact that there is no existential difference between those who go to the church because they want to feel 'serious' and the ruin-bibber or Christmas-addict: they all go for personal satisfaction or intimations of the transcendent. The poet suggests that the 'uninformed' one who surprises 'a hunger in himself to be more serious' is superior to those who 'know what rood-lofts were', those who want a 'whiff / Of gown-and-bands and organ pipes and myrrh': but if the church has no meaning this is mere sentiment, and it argues that general ignorance is preferable to particular knowledge. In fact, the poet religiously avoids the question of what the church building is for, though he is anxious to defend it from some non-serious uses.

'Church Going' shows the poet's honesty in trying to articulate what drew him to the church building. It also has a moral: seriousness is better than a tendency to mock or merely to use. But the poet ends as much 'at a loss' as he began: 'If only ...' in the last line suggests a casting around for reasons for his moral.[4] That is perhaps because he has mistaken the 'shell' for the reality, which cannot be understood without some reference to that 'biblical mythology' that Larkin thought meant little. The poem starts with 'nothing' and emptiness, gropes towards seriousness, and ends with the dead. The poet is isolated and sees only from the outside. But it might be that he does not see the reality of

---

4. Several writers see the ending of the poem in a more positive light. Andrew Motion sees it as 'a conclusion in which the fear of death and the loss of religious belief are counteracted by an ineradicable faith in human and individual potential' ('Philip Larkin and symbolism' in Stephen Regan, ed., *Philip Larkin: Contemporary Critical Essays*, p. 33); but seriousness, and even hunger for it, hardly justifies such positive terms. David Lodge ('Philip Larkin: the metonymic muse' in the same collection) remarks on the 'dignity and grandeur of diction' in the last stanza (p. 78), but as the essay above argues, this may be a way of disguising the insubstantial nature of the thought.

the church: those who know it from the inside, religiously as it were, know it as community; know the building as a joyful house on serious earth; know it above all as a place for the coming together of the living and the Living One.

QUESTIONS

1. How successful do you think the conclusion of 'Church Going' is?
2. Do you think Larkin preferred truth or kindness in his poetry (for the collocation, see 'Talking in Bed')? Discuss some examples.

BIBLIOGRAPHY

Andrew Motion, *Philip Larkin: A Writer's Life*, London 1993: a poet's view of the poet.

Stephen Regan, ed., *Philip Larkin: Contemporary Critical Essays*, Basingstoke 1997: a stimulating collection of essays.

Janice Rossen, *Philip Larkin: His Life's Work*, Iowa City 1989, and Terry Whalen, *Philip Larkin and English Poetry*, Basingstoke 1986, are both accessible brief studies of Larkin's poetry.

Anthony Thwaite, *Philip Larkin: Collected Poems*, London 1988, is the standard edition of the verse.

14

EDNA O'BRIEN, *SISTER IMELDA*

[*NA2* pp. 2745 f]

To appreciate this story fully, it is helpful for the reader to have an understanding of the background to the convent boarding-school life Edna O'Brien describes in post-World War II Ireland. In scattered rural areas access to good secondary schools could be difficult, so it was not uncommon for children of secondary school age to study in boarding schools run by religious orders, whose mission was to form their students as committed Catholics rather than to provide a solely secular education.

The origin of these Catholic boarding schools lies in the ‡monastic tradition of taking a few young children into the monastery to be educated and to share the common life there. Most were expected to take on monastic life themselves, while for others it was a preparation for life at court or for an arranged marriage. Until the rapid growth of 'active' communities of religious sisters in the late eighteenth century, the normal way for a Catholic upper- or middle-class girl to receive an education, unless she had a private tutor, was thus to board in a convent of contemplative nuns.

These nuns were bound by 'papal enclosure': that is, they undertook to live entirely within the boundaries of their ‡monastery in order to give themselves without distraction to a life of prayer and worship. Emphasis in this life was upon silence, external and internal; the avoidance of distraction; constant attentiveness to the presence of God; and on austerity intended to prevent desire for any kind of self-gratification interfering with the desire for God. Particular emphasis was also placed upon ‡penitential practices such as ‡fasting and voluntary acts of self-denial as expressions of sorrow for ‡sin, both in the individual nun and in the world. Any seeking after pleasure was to be eschewed.

All this was undertaken within the rhythm of prayer, marking each day and the church's seasons. Each day was shaped by seven 'offices', services of hymns, psalms, Bible readings, and prayer, which punctuated the day and brought the community to church for the longest office in the middle of the night. This night office, called Matins, Nocturns, or Vigils was increasingly seen as a time of prayer for the world, since the darkness of the night suggested the †darkness of ‡sin and despair. We see this in *Sister Imelda*, where the nuns are described as rising in the middle of the night and prostrating themselves in prayer. It is this night office, with its emphasis on prayer for the needs and the sin of the world, to which O'Brien is alluding and which seems so romantic to the more imaginative students.

Such a life required the development and practice of self-control, of detachment from personal desires and tastes. It was also a communal life. In this setting 'particular' friendships could be destructive and disruptive. Favouritism and special, close friendships could give rise to factions and rivalries and envy, which could split communities and undermine leadership. And in a life of chastity and austerity in which the desire for human love is directed towards the †love of God, and the desire for sensual pleasure is continuously denied, too close a friendship with its expressions of affection could easily become unwittingly sexual. The response was generally, therefore, for such friendships to be forbidden, in a way that could often lead to a certain repression in the individual nun and in community relationships, rather than to a family type of non-preferential warmth that was the goal.

Nuns were also regarded as 'brides of Christ', as we again see in *Sister Imelda*. We should not think of this in a sexual sense or imagine that nuns saw themselves as physically brides of Christ. The expression comes from both the Song of Songs, where traditionally this is interpreted as the †love story between the individual ‡soul and Christ, and from the use of the bride image in the letters of St Paul and the book of Revelation where the bride is the church and the groom is Christ (Ephesians 5:21–30; Revelation 21:2).

The nun as 'bride of Christ', therefore, is first of all a sign of human destiny, the church's destiny, to be wedded to Christ, and thus a sign of the fulfilment of relationship between God and humankind. The nun is regarded as a bride, too, because she has responded totally to God's †love for her as we find in the Song of Songs, and has made an exclusive choice of Christ, a choice that excludes the possibility of any other kind of marriage relationship. Being a bride denotes that all personal energies are to be directed towards the growth of relationship with God through Christ. The image is a way of expressing the nun's unavailability for human marriage or for any other kind of human relationship at that level and her total self-gift to God. We can see, however, that for young girls who are discovering their sexuality, this bridal imagery contributes to their fascination with the lives of the nuns with whom they share so much of their lives whilst remaining fundamentally apart from them.

After the ‡Reformation, and especially after the social upheavals of the French Revolution, communities of 'active' sisters developed. These were involved in teaching, nursing, social work, activities that frequently involved the yoking of an essentially ‡monastic pattern of life with the demands of the particular 'mission' of the community. Thus many active teaching communities still lived an essentially cloistered life, rarely leaving their convent, following a monastic rhythm in daily life and maintaining a similar emphasis on silence and austerity.

The schools that such communities provided differed from the boarding convents of the previous age in two major ways. Firstly, there was a new emphasis on professional training and identity for the sisters, who were to be decidedly 'teaching' sisters. This made the life of a sister particularly stressful: at a physical level she was following the demands of the regime of ‡monastic life and at the same time striving to meet professional standards and working to a school timetable. Her training could also, as with Sister Imelda, require time outside the community. This would produce further emotional and spiritual strains, evoking, as it would, memories and habits of another less austere life. This could easily lead to a need for the emotional warmth and comfort of a friendship in a life which offered few legitimate means for its satisfaction. Attachment to a pupil could easily ensue, giving confusing messages to inexperienced adolescents and perhaps also causing similar confusion in the nun, as O'Brien suggests in her portrayal of Sister Imelda.

Secondly, as we have noted, the lives of sisters and pupils were now more distinct. Whilst they shared some of the sisters' worship and withdrawal, the students had separate lives. Girls, therefore, had sufficient seclusion and regimentation to feel resentful or frustrated, as we see in *Sister Imelda*. At the same time, separation from the nuns also enabled a mystique to develop around them, especially in a closed community which offered few channels for adolescent imagination and emotional intensity. O'Brien invites us to ponder upon the easily entangled relationship between sexuality and spirituality, especially in the young.

QUESTIONS

1. Compare and contrast this story with any other on either a theme of teacher-pupil relationships or of first experience of adolescent attachment. In what ways do you find that the context of *Sister Imelda* produces differences in tone and implications?

2. Do you consider it possible to have a full grasp of the characterisation of Sister Imelda without some awareness of the religious background?
3. Consider the ways in which both proximity with, and separation from, the lives of the nuns contributes to the responses of the different students.

BIBLIOGRAPHY

Kiera O'Hara, 'Love objects: love and obsession in the stories of Edna O'Brien', *Studies in Short Fiction* 30 (1993), 317–26.

Jeanette Roberts Schumaker, 'Sacrificial women in short stories by Mary Lavin and Edna O'Brien', *Studies in Short Fiction* 32 (1995), 212–34.

Helen Thompson, 'Uncanny and undomesticated: lesbian desire in Edna O'Brien's *Sister Imelda* and *The High Road*', *Women's Studies* 32 (2003), 21–44.

15

PATRICK KAVANAGH

[Not anthologised]

Patrick Kavanagh was born in 1904 in County Monaghan, a son of 'Catholic Ireland'. His poetry is deeply imbued with a Catholic Christianity that is closely associated with the rhythms of the agricultural life of rural Ireland in the first half of the twentieth century. His poetry is Christian, not because it regularly and explicitly addresses biblical or doctrinal themes, but because there lies at its heart a Christian vision of the way in which a transcendent creator relates with his *creation.

Kavanagh's approach to his Christianity, were he a contemporary poet, would probably be identified by some as 'Celtic' on account of his celebration of earth's relationship with God. While many of the claims for 'Celtic Christianity' are open to question it is nevertheless instructive to set Kavanagh in the context of an Irish Christian culture which found little articulation in the church of his day. In his poem 'March', the trees, along with humankind, are waiting and listening for the coming of the Word of God in human flesh:

> The trees were in suspense,
> Listening with an intense
> Anxiety for the Word
> That in the Beginning stirred
> The dark-branched Tree
> Of Humanity.

This Word is the creating and saving Logos ('Word') of the prologue to St John's Gospel. But the note of yearning also evokes St Paul's vision of the *creation's 'earnest expectation' of the ‡revelation of 'the sons of God', which brings it, as well as human beings, liberation from bondage to decay (Romans 8:19–21). The earth shares in the longings and the destiny of the humanity that is made from that earth. In a similar tone, in the ancient Irish tale of the Voyage of Bran the birds share in humanity's prayer:

> An ancient tree there is with blossoms,
> On which birds call the canonical Hours.

'Tis in harmony it is their wont
To call together every Hour.[1]

It combines praise and thanksgiving for *creation with thankful remembrance and celebration of ‡redemption in the significance accorded to each specific time of prayer. The birds, therefore, laud not only creation in their song but also sing daily hymns of praise for ‡salvation.

Kavanagh represents, then, a Christianity that is close to the earth and understands that, since humankind is made from the earth, that earth participates in the human drama of *fall and ‡redemption. Further, since men and women were made to give praise and thanksgiving to God as creator (Kavanagh's Orthodox forebears would define humankind as ‡eucharistic beings, that is, beings made for thanksgiving), so too, the rest of *creation shares this identity when it expresses its own nature: flowers flowering, birds flying, fish swimming, all give praise and glory to God through their activity. This is a vision that also informs such diverse works as Smart's 'Hymn to David', Hopkins's 'Pied Beauty', the fantasy writing of George MacDonald, and the chorus of the women of Canterbury in Eliot's *Murder in the Cathedral*.

This vision is ‡sacramental: it sees the external created world as participating in, and revealing, an inner eternal, spiritual reality. We see this clearly in these lines from Kavanagh's poem 'The One':

Green, blue, yellow and red —
God is down in the swamps and marshes...

    A primrose, a violet
A violent wild iris — but mostly anonymous performers
Yet an important occasion as the Muse at her toilet
Prepared to inform the local farmers
That beautiful, beautiful, beautiful God
Was breathing His love by a cut-away bog.

The beauty of *creation here does not speak of a distant creator who is remote from his creation like the Unmoved Mover of the philosophers. Here this potentially unlovely bog is beautiful because the beautiful, creating God indwells it, providing its life-force yet not identical with it.

Kavanagh's God, then, is a God of life, a life that embraces the necessary sexuality of his *creation, as we see in the poem 'Miss Universe':

---

1. The 'Hours' are the seven times of prayer which make up the Breviary or Divine Office which is the official worship of Catholic and Orthodox churches.

I learned something of the nature of God's mind,
Not the abstract Creator but He who caresses
The daily and nightly earth ...

There are no recriminations in Heaven. O the sensual throb
Of the explosive body, the tumultuous thighs!

The ‡sacramentality of the earth does not deny all that the term 'earthy' suggests.

For Kavanagh this God of life is essentially, therefore, a God of playfulness, of imagination, as we see in 'A View of God and the Devil' in which God is described as

Experimental
Irresponsible...

... my God who made the grass
And the sun
And stones in streams in April...

Here Kavanagh is close to the spirit of Psalm 108, in which the sea-monsters are made to be God's play-fellows. He emphasises that God takes delight in his *creation and intends to share such pleasure. So in the companion poem 'The Devil' he takes issue with the narrowing of Christianity to a joyless 'severe workfulness', as Dickens expressed it, describing the †devil as 'Solemn / Boring / Conservative / conscious of being uncreative'.

Another, initially more abstract, aspect of Kavanagh's ‡sacramentality is found in 'The Circle'. Starting from this traditional symbol for God as without beginning or end and developing it into the Irish cross which represents the ‡Trinity, Kavanagh quickly relates this to human experience. Human beings come to know God in all their experience of turning and travelling, in the bicycle spoke and the playful tumbling of the acrobat. Then a new note is added; the wheel spokes recall the nails of the †cross, the circle made by the falling axe in the act of execution; within the circle we see the 'tortured face' of Christ; this God whom we meet in the everyday meets us, too, in the human suffering he shared with us.

We see here that Kavanagh's ‡sacramentality derives from the centrality to his Christianity of the †incarnation of Christ. This is particularly evident in the ‡Advent and Christmas poems in which everyday life is seen in the light of the coming of Christ as a child. This emphasis has three particular consequences in Kavanagh's thought.

Firstly, just like the Christ-child, God is to be found most readily in the unspectacular and the ordinary, as we see in 'God in Woman'. Secondly, this ordinariness is not to be equated with pious respectability that conceals refusal of life, as we see in 'Street Corner Christ'. Thirdly, God is experienced most fully in the frailty and failure of life, just as Christ fulfilled himself in the human failure of the †cross, as we see in 'The Gift' and 'From Failure Up'.

Kavanagh's vision, therefore, does not exclude awareness of suffering, ‡sinfulness, and imperfection. Finding God at the root of one's being implies also finding there the conflict between God and self-love that Christ experienced in the gospel accounts of his †temptations. We find this in his longer poem 'Father Mat'. This is a portrait of a good man and priest, 'a part of the place' who finds God in the good earth as well as in his flock. Whilst hearing the ‡confession of their sins his mind is continually drawn away to the beauty beyond the church. His love of the earth becomes the voice of the †Tempter, calling him away from the eternal verities of 'the domestic Virgin and Her Child' towards the 'ecstasy' of Venus.

Similarly a poem like 'The Son of God' shows his acute awareness of the *fallen state of humanity and its need of a †sacrificial ‡saviour. The persona of this poem must face the 'meanness' of his own heart, his reluctance to give himself for others. In the pusillanimous flight from sacrifice he is forced to encounter the truth about the human condition:

> Out beyond Calvary I found myself a house
> And lived there in comfort. But I could hear
> Often on summer evenings from the deserts of the heart
>   Of man the cry for the blood of God's only Son.

The division at the heart of humanity is evident in the ambiguity of this closing line. At his *crucifixion the crowd, humanity, cries for Christ's death, rejecting relationship with God. But 'the cry' can also be the cry of need and longing, an awareness of need of 'the blood of the Lamb' that brings pardon, peace, and reconciliation with God. The 'desert' of the heart, the place in biblical terms of rebellion, of the encounter with one's evil and of meeting with God, needs irrigation by the life-giving blood of Christ if this last meeting is to take place.

We can see in this brief survey of some of Kavanagh's works a Christianity that is rooted in its central doctrines but eschews much of the intellectualisation of faith that reduces it to propositions. His approach is that of the ‡mystic who acknowledges 'We must be nothing, / Nothing that God may make us something', and urges

> Let us lie down again
> Deep in anonymous humility and God
> May find us worthy material for His hand. ('Having Confessed')

At the end of 'Auditors In' the persona reflects:

> I am so glad
> To come accidentally upon
> My self at the end of a tortuous road
> And have learned with surprise that God
> Unworshipped withers to the Futile One.

It is to this realisation that Kavanagh's poetry leads his readers.

QUESTIONS

1. How would you characterise Kavanagh's attitude to nature?
2. How would you describe Kavanagh's God?

BIBLIOGRAPHY

Una Agnew, *The Mystical Imagination of Patrick Kavanagh*, Dublin 1998. An essential critical biography.

The Complete Poems of Patrick Kavanagh with Commentary by Peter Kavanagh, New York 1996. A definitive collection.

Tom Stack, *No Earthly Estate. God and Patrick Kavanagh: An Anthology*, Dublin 2002. An anthology with a very full introductory essay and extensive introductions to individual poems.

Section 6

THE CHRISTIAN TRADITION

1

THE STORY LINE OF THE BIBLE

INTRODUCTION

This essay is about the Christian understanding of the story line of the whole Bible as one coherent narrative of God's dealing with humanity[1]. A number of objections might be made to such a view of the Bible, of which the most obvious would be the view that the New Testament is not continuous with the Hebrew scriptures (the Old Testament).[2] The great majority of writers throughout the history of English literature, however, worked with the Christian view that God has revealed himself supremely in Jesus Christ, as he is described in the New Testament, and that Christ is the fulfilment of the Law, the †Prophets, and the Writings of the Hebrew scriptures;[3] and it is that accepted continuity that is here described. There are, of course, particular places within both the Hebrew scriptures and the New Testament where an alleged internal continuity is questionable on critical grounds: for example in the clear tension in the Hebrew scriptures between Samuel's insistence that a king will be a bad thing for the nation and the subsequent glories of Kings David and Solomon;[4] or in the New Testament, the differing order of events between Luke and the other synoptic gospels.

One matter to keep clear is the difference between the time when a narrative was written and the time it deals with. For example, we might think that the synoptic gospels obviously represent the earliest strand of New Testament

---

1. For the sake of clarity, quotations here are from the New International Version of the Bible. For some sense of the variety of translations used in English literature, see the introductory essays that follow, and especially the essay 'The Bible and Prayer Book' in section 2.

2. We shall also include some consideration of the ‡apocrypha, or deutero-canonical literature: for more information, see the essay on 'The ‡Patristic Period' below.

3. These are the traditional (at least from the second century BC) sub-divisions of the writing of the Old Testament: the Law or Torah, comprising the first five books of the Bible, Genesis to Deuteronomy; the †Prophets, comprising (perhaps surprisingly) Joshua, Judges, the books of Samuel and Kings, Jeremiah, Ezekiel, Isaiah, and the book of the Twelve 'Minor Prophets' (Hosea, Joel, Amos and so on); and the Writings comprising the †wisdom and other books: Ruth, Psalms, Job, Proverbs, Ecclesiastes, Song of Songs, Lamentations, along with the narrative books of Daniel, Esther, Ezra, Nehemiah and Chronicles. See further below.

4. Compare I Samuel 8, for example, with I Kings 10.

tradition, because these narratives deal with the period before Jesus' death. But the New Testament narrative that first reached its full New Testament form was probably Paul's first letter to the Thessalonians, probably some twenty years earlier than the completion of Mark, which is probably the earliest gospel.[5] Similarly in Genesis, the traditions behind the narratives of Abraham and the patriarchs are clearly more ancient, certainly in Jewish terms, than the *Eden narratives earlier in the book.

CREATION TO THE PATRIARCHS

The Bible story line obviously begins with the story of the *creation and of *Adam and Eve. New Testament writers like Paul tend to deal with the Adam and Eve narrative as historical. When Paul writes that 'death reigned from the time of Adam to the time of Moses' (Romans 5:14), he is referring to what he conceives of as a real period of time. In the same verse, he makes clear the view that Adam's ‡sin involves the whole of humanity in the penalty of death. This is a reasonable reading of 'dust you are, and to dust you will return' (Genesis 3:19), though Old Testament scholars are quick to point out that we should not allow Paul's reading of the *fall to cloud a proper scholarly approach to consideration of the narrative. Old Testament scholars tend to point out that this narrative never mentions †Satan, sin, or fall: all these concepts are read into the narrative essentially from Pauline interpretation.[6]

In any case, it may make more sense to speak of a series of *fall narratives, because the ensuing narratives of *Cain and Abel, Noah's *flood, and the tower of Babel all share a sense of trying to explain the problems of human evil and alienation in the context of a *creation in which the delight of the ripe fruit, the love between husband and wife and brother and brother, the towering possibilities of human achievement, and the beauty of the rainbow otherwise suggest a benevolent creator, for relationship with whom humanity has an innate longing.

All this takes us up to the end of Genesis 11. Despite the linking genealogies, it might properly be called prehistory. In Genesis 12 we meet Abraham, the father of the Jewish people. From here to the end of the book of Joshua, we read

---

5. The repetition of 'probably' in sentences like this grates, but it is impossible to avoid in dealing briefly with the results of biblical studies, which are almost never agreed. Of course, there is no suggestion here that the oral and written traditions lying *behind* the synoptics are later than I Thessalonians.

6. We should note though that Paul's is only the fairly standard interpretation of a well-taught Jew: there is no particular reason to suppose that he changed his opinion of Genesis after his conversion.

a kind of organised history. At face value, the narrative suggests that Abraham begat Isaac, who begat Jacob, who begat twelve sons, each of whom is the father of one of the twelve tribes of Israel. The other eleven sons pick on Joseph, his father's favourite, who is sold into Egypt. He prospers there so that, when there is a famine back home, he is in control of the Egyptian granaries from which his bothers have to come to beg for food. Thus Jacob and all his sons and their families come down into Egypt. So ends Genesis.

THE EXODUS AND THE LAW

In *Exodus we find that after a time, these people, now called the Hebrews, become slaves and are oppressed by the Egyptians. Moses, a Hebrew brought up in the court of the Pharaoh, is chosen by God to lead their escape. This is accompanied by several great miracles that afflict the Egyptians, including ultimately a plague that strikes their firstborn children and animals and the drowning of their army in the Red Sea,[7] as they pursue the escaping Hebrews.

After their escape, the Hebrews wander forty years in the †wilderness of the Arabian †desert, led by Moses, during which time they are given the Law, including especially the *ten commandments at Mount Sinai. Their various vicissitudes are the setting for several narratives that resonate for ever after. Manna from †heaven, the golden calf, 'the fiery cloudy pillar',[8] all come from this time. So also do the detailed instruction for making the tabernacle, the place of worship where God is especially present. At the end of the wilderness wandering, Moses dies and command passes to Joshua, who leads the people across the River Jordan into the land of Canaan, which he conquers in a series of battles with local tribes.[9] The wheel thus comes full circle, since the twelve tribes occupy the land which in Genesis 12 was first promised to Abraham.

The great German scholar Martin Noth probably first suggested that what has happened here is that some narratives belonging in common to a number of the Israelite tribes, and some belonging to each, have been worked together into one coherent narrative, which becomes their agreed history when they unite. Some tribes had narratives of a patriarch Abraham, from north of Palestine;

---

7. Probably the Red Sea: the geography is not certain.

8. From William Williams' most famous of Welsh hymns, 'Guide me O thou great Jehovah' (1745), in which the wandering in the †wilderness—'this barren land'—is an extended metaphor for the Christian life.

9. Most famously, of course, 'Joshua fought the battle of Jericho'. All these narratives become source material especially for classic negro spirituals: 'Let my people go' creates a resonance between Hebrew slavery and New World slavery; crossing the Jordan symbolises dying in 'One more river to cross', 'Deep river', 'We are crossing that Jordan river', with Canaan, the Promised Land of †heaven 'on the other side'.

some had narratives of escape from Egyptian slavery in the south; but they now agreed, in the covenant established at Sinai and reaffirmed by Joshua at Shechem at the end of the book Joshua, that they were one people with one God, one worship and one Law. For the intervening books of Leviticus, Numbers, and Deuteronomy lay out in great detail a set of religious and civil laws obviously appropriate to the people's ultimate settlement in Canaan, rather than the nomadic life of the †wilderness in which the narratives of law-giving are set in the texts. Probably most of the books of Law, as we now have them, are from a later part of the tradition than the first settlement in Canaan, though more ancient material may lie behind them.[10]

JUDGES AND KINGS

The next book is Judges, the name for the occasional charismatic figures whom God appoints to lead the Israelites, often militarily against the threat of surrounding tribes: Gideon, Barak, Samson. But these also include †prophetic religious figures like Deborah and Samuel. Samuel, after whom the next two history books are named,[11] is the last and greatest of the Judges. By now, one opposing tribe, the Philistines,[12] have become a powerful enemy, and the people ask Samuel for a king. He anoints first Saul, from the tribe of Benjamin, and later David, of the tribe of Judah. Again, the history looks as if it has been organised from a variety of sources, which paint differing pictures of the relationship between Saul and David. At any rate David eventually becomes the dominant figure and establishes his capital at the Jebusite city of Jerusalem, where he is king of the twelve tribes. The line of David and the pre-eminence of Jerusalem become dominant motifs in Bible history from this point forward. David is succeeded by his son Solomon.

A brief sentence like this last one evokes a host of stories that literary authors would have been familiar with, not least because some of the most vivid narrative writing of the Hebrew scriptures is found in II Samuel and the books

---

10. None of this is to suggest that Abraham, Moses, Joshua, and the rest were not real historical figures: only that the narratives about them have been organised synthetically. The key starting text is Martin Noth, *A History of Pentateuchal Traditions*, 1948, trans. Bernhard W. Anderson, Englewood Cliffs NJ 1972.

11. So that we here pass by the short but vivid book of Ruth, which tells a story of love and loyalty.

12. Philistines have, of course, gained an enduring and entirely unjustified latter-day reputation for being cultural vandals, preferring good tunes and happy endings to high art. On a more serious note, 'Philistine' is etymologically related to Palestine, and the Philistine capital was Gaza, so that the ongoing struggle between Jews and Palestinians over the Gaza strip has ancient and unfortunate antecedents.

of I and II Kings. Solomon was David's son by his favourite wife, Bathsheba, with whom he committed adultery when she was married to Uriah the Hittite, whom David subsequently had killed in battle. David had previously rejected his first wife, Michal, the daughter of Saul, because she was scornful of his excitement when he danced before the Lord in the procession that brought the Ark of the Covenant up to Jerusalem, the procession in which Uzzah was killed because he presumed to touch the ark to steady it — and so on. All this apparently irrelevant detail is mentioned simply because we can be sure that most of the literary authors knew these Hebrew stories as part of their own cultural heritage. Just as they will have known of the Queen of Sheba, celebrated in Handel's *Arrival of the Queen of Sheba*, who came to view Solomon's riches.

Solomon built a temple for the Lord at Jerusalem, the site of which remains the holiest place in Judaism. His was Israel's most grandiose monarchy. He also had a particular reputation for †wisdom — the wisdom of Solomon remains proverbial — and the wisdom literature of the Hebrew scriptures is especially associated with him. Within that tradition would normally be placed the books of Job, Proverbs, Song of Songs, Ecclesiastes, and possibly Psalms. The 150 Psalms are texts for use in the worship of the Temple. Though many are traditionally ascribed to David, the probability is that most of them are later. At any rate, all these texts are associated, with dubious historicity, with Solomon and his Temple.

Solomon was the last of the kings of Israel, in the sense that after him the kingdom divided in two. Here there are echoes of the struggle between David and Saul. Saul was a member of the northern tribe of Benjamin whereas David was a member of the southern tribe of Judah. After Solomon, the kingdom split across this north-south divide, and the books of Kings and Chronicles, with which the history continues, deal alternately with the northern kings of what they now call Israel, and the southern kings of what they now call Judah. This division will remain important well into New Testament times. Jews, by that time, are the people of Judah only, and regard their southern capital Jerusalem as the one true dwelling place of the Lord. They thus despise as ‡heretics the people of the northern kingdom, whose capital and temple had been in Samaria: in other words, the split between Jews and Samaritans starts here.

Returning to the Hebrew scriptures, both Kings and Chronicles assess the kings of northern Israel and southern Judah according to their faithfulness to the one true God, the Lord. There remained a number of other religions available in Palestine, most notably the fertility cult of Baal (or, since there were numerous sites and differences in the cults, the Baals). Some kings were attracted to Baalism, and in the accounts of I and II Kings they are opposed in this by the †prophets of the Lord, especially Elijah and his successor and protégé Elisha. Again the stories are vivid, and tropes from them persist even into our present culture. It was Elijah who was taken up to †heaven in a 'chariot of fire' and to whom God spoke in 'a still small voice'; Elijah who was opposed by the Baalite queen Jezebel, whose name remains an insult.

PROPHETS

Elijah and Elisha were not writing †prophets and not directly attached to the royal court. From this time on, however, there emerge arguably the greatest literary figures of the Hebrew scriptures, the writing prophets. Some, like Isaiah of Jerusalem, were figures of the court: counsellors to particular kings, as Nathan, for example, had earlier been to David. Others, like the northern prophets Amos and Hosea, seem to speak and write from a slightly less central position. Some, like the priestly Jeremiah, were probably associated principally with the Temple. They have essentially two main messages: that the kings and nations should be faithful to the Lord, and that this means true and sincere worship in the Temple and fairness in the administration of the justice system.

Increasingly also, the †prophets predicted that the outcome of unfaithfulness and injustice on the part of kings and people would be the loss of their respective kingdoms to foreign invaders. These prophecies were to come true, which is probably one reason why the writings of those prophets who proved to be right have been preserved in the Hebrew scriptures. Again, the invaders who overran Israel and Judah have come down into our literary heritage. The Assyrians were the first wave.[13] They captured Samaria and most of Judah but not the capital Jerusalem. They were in turn overrun, despite Egyptian support, by the Babylonians under Nebuchadnezzar, who also sacked Jerusalem, taking many of its people captive back to Babylon.

THE EXILE AND RETURN

The period that follows, known as the Exile, seems to have been a particularly fruitful one in creative terms. First, a number of the †prophets do some of their most enduring work in this period; notably Ezekiel and Jeremiah and the prophet whom we usually think of as Deutero-Isaiah, author of Isaiah chapters 40 onwards. Probably the preservation and canonisation of the Hebrew scriptures gains great impetus at this time, both at home and abroad, as the Jews of

---

13. See Byron's 'The Assyrian came down like a wolf on the fold', from 'The Destruction of Sennacherib'.

the widening Diaspora need records of their holy narratives, Law, and teaching. It may be that the first synagogues emerge also. In western art, it becomes archetypally the time when 'by the rivers of Babylon we sat down and wept': the children of Israel 'hung [their] harps on the poplars'[14] not able to 'sing the songs of the LORD while in a foreign land' (Psalm 137).[15] The Exile, though now under the Persian empire succeeding the Babylonians, is also the setting for the stories in the books of Esther and Daniel: the lions' den, the blazing fiery furnace, the moving finger writing at Belshazzar's feast, and 'hanged as high as Haman' all enter our culture from these narratives.

The return from Exile becomes a preoccupying theme for Jewish leaders and †prophets. In Deutero-Isaiah, and so in Handel's *Messiah*, we hear 'The voice of him that crieth in the wilderness, Prepare ye the way of the LORD, make straight in the desert a highway for our God' (Isaiah 40:3, King James Version). Along this highway, Isaiah prophesies, 'a remnant will return' (Isaiah 10:21). The biblical picture of this return is a little confused. The leading figures are Ezra the scribe and Nehemiah the governor, the one a primarily religious figure, the other a politician, whom we meet in the books that bear their names. Nehemiah is apparently responsible for rebuilding the walls of Jerusalem, Ezra for reestablishing the religious Law. But the rebuilding of the Temple seems to take place under the leadership of the later governor Zerubbabel, with particular religious inspiration from the prophets Haggai and Zechariah, whom we find among what is called 'the book of the twelve', the last anthology of religious prophets at the end of the Old Testament, into which the rather untypical stories of Daniel and Jonah also find their way.

Thus, at the end of the Old Testament, Judah and Jerusalem are reestablished, and the Temple rebuilt for worship. Scribal interpretation of the Law is very important, and the local synagogue has become the venue for meeting on the Sabbath and listening to the Law, the Writings, and the †Prophets. Judah had relative freedom and autonomy within the Persian empire. These peaceful times were not to last long. The Persians were soon conquered by Alexander the Great, whose vast empire also covered Egypt to the south of Judah. After Alexander's early death, and the division of his empire, Judah came sometimes under his Seleucid successors from the north, sometimes under his Egyptian successors from the south. The struggle is that of the kings of the north and south in the second part of the book of Daniel. The most vivid episode in this period of Jewish history is the Maccabean revolt, when Jewish priestly leaders

---

14. 'Willows' in the King James version.
15. So also the 'Chorus of the Hebrew Slaves' from Verdi's *Nabucco* (Nebuchadnezzar).

oppose the imposition of Greek customs by Antiochus Epiphanes, including especially the erection of an altar to Zeus within the Temple. The books I and II Maccabees, which record these events, are part of what is called ‡apocryphal literature, part of Christian Roman Catholic and Eastern Orthodox Bibles, but not regarded as authoritative by Jews or Christian Protestants.[16]

ROMAN RULE

Eventually Roman rule replaced the Seleucid dominance over Judah, which mostly becomes the Roman province of Judaea. Slightly different arrangements were made for Judaea over the New Testament period. At the time of the birth of Jesus of Nazareth, the whole kingdom was under Herod the Great, who was a client king of Rome. He is the Herod who is alleged to have had the newborn babies put to death in Bethlehem in Matthew's Gospel. By the time of Jesus' death, Herod the Great had died and his kingdom had been newly divided. Galilee, the northern area that included Jesus' hometown of Nazareth, was under Herod the Great's son, Herod Antipas. Herod Antipas is the Herod who had John the Baptist executed, allegedly at the instigation of his wife's daughter Salome, and to whom the Roman governor Pontius Pilate referred Jesus for examination. Pilate was governor of the southern area that included Jerusalem, and hence referred Jesus to Herod as a courtesy because Jesus came from Herod's area.

HEBREW SCRIPTURES TO NEW TESTAMENT

The historical (as opposed to prehistoric) narratives of the Hebrew scriptures thus cover a period of perhaps 1,200 years, from Abraham to the Seleucid empire. By contrast, the New Testament covers a period of at most 120 years, from the birth of Jesus of Nazareth onwards; and that period is itself sharply divided into two parts: the gospels, Matthew, Mark, Luke, and John, which deal with the life, ministry, death, and *resurrection of Jesus; and the rest, which deal with the first 70 years or so of the Christian church. Moreover, the stories of the birth and early life of Jesus occur in only two of the four gospels: so that it can reasonably be said that in historical terms, the four gospels cover the period of Jesus' public ministry up to his death, which is something less than three years.

---

16. Differing attitudes to them may therefore be expected of different authors within the literature. On the whole, they are not much represented in the canon of later English literature, though they were, for example, much used in Anglo-Saxon Christianity.

THE GOSPELS

In those three years, Jesus is an itinerant preacher, teacher, exorcist, and healer, proclaiming in the synoptics (Matthew, Mark, and Luke) that the kingdom of God is at hand; and in John that he is the embodiment of the kingdom. Motifs and tropes too numerous to mention enter our culture from these narratives: from Jesus' characteristic †parables—the lost sheep, the prodigal son, the good Samaritan, the sower; from his encounters with people—Mary and Martha, Zacchaeus, the woman at the well, the woman taken in adultery; from his miracles of healing—the paralytic, the ten lepers, Jairus's daughter, the man born blind; from his miracles of control over nature—calming the storm, walking on the water, feeding the five thousand; and from his more general teachings—the Beatitudes, the Lord's Prayer, tribute to Caesar, the prohibition of divorce; and much more besides. Even so, the gospels have been called ‡passion narratives with introductions, because of their preoccupation with the last week of Jesus' life: so that Mark, for example, has ten chapters dealing with the two years up to this point and five dealing with the passion. In all the gospels, there follow accounts of the empty tomb and *resurrection appearances. The events of these last days happen in Jerusalem, the capital of Judaea, at the time of Passover.

THE ACTS OF THE APOSTLES

Fifty days after the Passover is the harvest festival of *Pentecost. At that festival, again in Jerusalem, Jesus' disciples resume the public ministry in which they had previously been his coworkers, now claiming explicitly that he is the Messiah and that his *resurrection proves it. This is the first narrative of the church, described in Acts chapter 2. The rest of Acts describes, in a carefully schematised way, the progress of this message, the gospel about Jesus, starting in Jerusalem and ending in Rome: which is to say that Acts represents also the transition from early Christianity being essentially a movement within Judaism to being a new faith for Gentile converts. Acts describes this as a twofold movement: on the one hand the Jewish religious authorities emphatically reject the Christian interpretation of Jesus (whom, after all, they had convicted of blasphemy); on the other hand the Holy Spirit, whom the Christians newly experience in this phase, specifically directs them into the mission to the Gentiles. At the end of Acts, which cannot be later than AD 65, the apostle Paul is greeted in Rome by a Christian congregation that he did not found, and the New Testament also mentions congregations all through Asia Minor and around the Mediterranean seaboard.

THE EPISTLES

The apostles—literally those 'sent out', who founded these congregations that remain the basic model for Christian churches today—needed to keep in touch with the congregations when they moved on to the next place, and they did so by means of epistles, or letters, some of which form the next main body of New Testament literature, from Romans right through to Jude. They are by various authors and almost certainly not all by the people to whom they are attributed, but they give us a vivid and fascinating picture of the new movement as it struggles with its understanding of itself, its relation to Judaism, its theology of Christ, its liturgy, and its ethical practice. These letters have been vital influences in western culture: it is not too far-fetched to suggest that at the time of the ‡Reformation, the map of Europe was divided up according to what the rulers of particular states thought about St Paul's letter to the Romans, which was also the inspiration of St Augustine of Hippo, whose theology dominated the early modern church, and of John Wesley, who revolutionised the church in eighteenth-century England.

REVELATION

The New Testament concludes with the book of ‡Revelation, attributed to John, though probably not the John to whom the gospel of John is attributed. It emerges from the churches in Asia Minor (modern Turkey), and though some of it is given an epistolary framework, it alone in the New Testament is entirely composed of ‡apocalyptic, the literary genre of vivid and fantastic religious imagery, which arose towards the end of the Old Testament period. Here, the apocalyptic expectation has been modified so that Christ, the *Lamb upon the throne, is the centre of the new Jerusalem. The awaited reestablishment of Jerusalem as the focus of God's visible rule has been taken from Judaism and Christianised.

2

THE RELATIONSHIP BETWEEN THE OLD TESTAMENT AND THE NEW TESTAMENT

The writings that Christians call the Old Testament are in fact the Hebrew scriptures, the holy books of Judaism, the religion of the Jews. Students and scholars may indeed prefer to use the term 'Hebrew scriptures', since this avoids giving offence to Jewish readers. For Christians, though, and therefore for the great majority of the authors in the various anthologies of English literature, the Hebrew scriptures are the Old Testament: the first section of the Christian Bible.

In the tradition of the Hebrew scriptures, it was essential to Jewish understanding that the Jews were the chosen people of the one true God, who had made himself known by ‡revelation: to Abraham and his descendants, to Moses, to charismatic leaders like Gideon and Samson, to the kings of the Davidic line, and to the great †prophets like Isaiah and Jeremiah, who challenged injustice and unfaithfulness to God. From the time of Kings David and Solomon onwards, this divine self-revelation was also associated especially with the city of Jerusalem and the Temple there, where the one true God was believed to be especially present. From the eighth century BC onwards, however, the people, and then the city and the Temple itself, were subjected to the power of a succession of foreign empires, of which the latest, in the time of the public ministry of Jesus of Nazareth, was the power of Rome.

One consequence was that Jesus was born into a time of intense religious speculation about the meaning of Jewish chosenness and about the possibility of God's intervention to vindicate himself and his people. This speculation is reflected in the emergence of the literary genre that we call ‡apocalyptic. In the Hebrew scriptures, the second half of the book of Daniel is of this type,[1] as are some of the ‡apocryphal or deutero-canonical books. They all speak in vividly fantastic imagery of God's dramatic intervention into human affairs, and

---

1. Which is why many scholars date it about 150 BC in the time of the Seleucid domination of Israel and Judah—and hence much later than the setting, and possibly the writing, of the stories about Daniel in the first part of the book.

especially into the affairs of the Jewish nation. Eventually, this speculation came to be focused in the expectation of one particular figure, the Messiah, who was expected to be a Jewish leader through whom God would demonstrate his power, vindicate and free the Jewish people, and usher in a time of universal recognition of the one true God. Many scholars believe that Jesus himself stood consciously in this tradition: that he saw himself as †prophesying the coming intervention of God, and that his usual title for himself, 'the son of man', and the central theme of his preaching, the coming 'kingdom of heaven', are both apocalyptic terms.

Whether or not this was so,[2] what is certain is that very soon after his death his followers began to make ‡apocalyptic claims about him, on the basis of their account of his *resurrection. It is important to note that there is no certain reference to the resurrection of the dead in the Hebrew scriptures: on the whole, the only afterlife they predict is in Sheol, a place of shadows with a sense of ghostliness. At the time of Jesus, however, belief in the possibility of a general resurrection at the †last day had become a recognised part of apocalyptic expectation. Jesus then, the Christians claimed (and still claim), was the †prophesied Messiah, and his resurrection proved it.

However, this clearly required a complete reinterpretation of the Messianic expectation. The *resurrection might be claimed as an act that vindicated Jesus himself and authenticated the Messianic claim about him, but it had no direct immediate effect on national politics and was not itself the very public demonstration of God's power that had been expected. Moreover, it was preceded by his very public suffering and vilification at the hands both of the Jewish leaders and the foreign imperial power, both of which were flatly at odds with conventional Messianic understanding and expectation. So the early Christians had to reinterpret the Messianic motif. To make that reinterpretation credible, they had to show that it was compatible with the Hebrew scriptures: that Jesus' kind of Messiahship had been †prophesied all along. The New Testament gives us a fairly clear picture of how they did this.

In literary terms, the most obvious expressions of the relationship between Old and New Testaments are at the beginning of the gospels. John begins 'In the beginning was the word ...'; Mark, 'The beginning of the gospel of Jesus Christ ...' In John, 'the word' soon 'becomes flesh'—that is to say, is †incarnated in the man Jesus of Nazareth—so that in each case there is a clear intention to relate the beginning of this new narrative to the beginning of Genesis, the first book of

---

2. Jesus' self-understanding and the level of his foreknowledge of events are among the most debated topics of study of the synoptic gospels. For this reason, the present essay omits from consideration the several places in the gospels where Jesus speaks about events after his death, including those where he speaks about the status of the Law after him.

the Hebrew scriptures, which begins 'In the beginning God created the heavens and the earth ...' The implication is clear: the God who made the first beginning is making a new beginning with humanity in the person and work of Jesus.

In John, this is explicitly theologised in the first chapter, first in a prologue which identifies Jesus as the †incarnate word, then in a series of encounters in which two motifs stand out: verbs of seeing and looking, and titles of Jesus. John thus invites us to see this Jesus, and that he is the 'Lamb of God' (1:29), 'the man on whom you see the Spirit come down' (1:33), 'God's chosen One' (1:34), 'Rabbi' (1:38), 'Messiah' (1:41), 'the one Moses wrote about in the Law, and about whom the prophets also wrote' (1:45), 'Son of God ... King of Israel' (1:49), 'Son of Man' (1:51). There is here a comprehensive scheme of reference back to the Hebrew scriptures: to the †sacrificial system in the *Lamb of God, to the writings of the Mosaic Law and the †prophets, to the Davidic line of kings of Israel, to the Son of Man in the ‡apocalyptic of Daniel.

Mark similarly moves straight from the claim that Jesus is the Messiah to the claim that this is a fulfilment of the †prophecy of Isaiah. The Messianic claim, as we have seen, arose principally in the intertestamental period, though its interpretation referred back to the Hebrew scriptures, because the Messiah was seen as a new king in the Davidic line. The reference to Isaiah 40 in Mark 1, however, takes us to a series of passages vital to the early Christians' ability to reconfigure the Messianic hope to the shape of the person and work of Jesus of Nazareth. In the later chapters of the book of Isaiah there is an enigmatic figure, the 'Servant of the Lord', clearly heroic, whose suffering is somehow on behalf of the whole Jewish people (many of whose leaders, at the time of writing, were probably in captivity in Babylon). His life is 'a guilt offering' (53:10); 'After the suffering of his soul, he will see the light of life' (53:11).[3] It undoubtedly helped, and still helps, the Christian appropriation of these verses that it is very difficult to understand to whom in Isaiah's[4] time they might refer. Here the Christians found in a book of †prophecy a figure whose ministry to the Jewish people involved suffering and disgrace, and whose potential identification with Jesus of Nazareth was considerably helped by the difficulty of identifying him[5] with any other historical figure. In Acts, the story of the deacon Philip and the

---

3. This translation, which lent itself so easily to interpretation in the light of Jesus' *resurrection, was current in the Septuagint, the pre-Christian Greek version of the Hebrew scriptures which the early Christians probably knew best. It is also found in the Dead Sea Scrolls, which date from about the same time.

4. These passages were probably not written by the †prophet Isaiah of Jerusalem, but by a later prophet writing at the time of the exile in Babylon.

5. Probably 'him', though some scholars suggest that the servant represents the whole Jewish people.

Ethiopian eunuch is probably an authentic reflection of the early church's use of these passages. Philip, speaking to one who has himself known what it is to go under the knife, interprets the lamb silent before the shearer as Christ the *Lamb of God (Acts 8:27–40).

The idea of the ‡redemptive suffering of Jesus was also undoubtedly suggested by the timing of his death. He was *crucified at the time of the feast of Passover, the commemoration of the Hebrew people's escape from plague in Egypt. The Passover involved the sacrifice of a lamb. The Christian appropriation of the idea of sacrifice conflated the Passover lamb with the scapegoat, the animal on whom the Jewish High Priest symbolically laid the ‡sins of the people on the feast of the Day of ‡Atonement. In John 1, as we have seen, the first title of Jesus is on the lips of John the Baptist: 'Look, the Lamb of God, who takes away the sin of the world' (John 1:29). It was this aspect of the work of Jesus that became paramount, reinforced as it soon was by the weekly celebration of the commemorative meal of the Lord's Supper, which was understood to have been instituted at the time of his last Passover by Jesus himself.

The idea of Jesus' being God's new, or second, beginning is expressed throughout the New Testament in several different ways. In Matthew 5, the lengthy teaching of the *sermon on the mount depicts Jesus as a kind of lawgiver analogous to Moses on Mount Sinai. In Romans 5, the idea of Christ as second *Adam, resisting †temptation as Adam did not, is worked out in full into a theology in which Christ is thus capable of remitting the penalty of death to which the ‡sin of Adam doomed humanity. In John 3, the idea of the new beginning is made personal to the individual Christian who must be 'born again' (3:3), and Paul similarly makes clear that every individual participates in this new *creation: 'if anyone is in Christ, he is a new creation: the old has gone, the new has come!' (II Corinthian 5:17).

'The new', of course, was again validated by the narrative of the *resurrection. Here was a man who had really died: if he was alive again, he must be living an entirely new kind of life. The promise of sharing in this life, according to the New Testament, was also guaranteed by a new kind of spiritual experience. Beginning from the account of the day of *Pentecost in Acts 2, the apostles and their followers experience the power of the Holy Spirit. Again, the Spirit of God is a theme taken from the Hebrew scriptures. In the Acts account, Peter is recorded as saying that this is what was †prophesied by the prophet Joel (Acts 2:16), and he quotes a mildly ‡apocalyptic passage from that prophet (Joel 9:28–32). The suggestion of a new activity of the Spirit of God in the apocalyptic age is also found in the book of Ezekiel.

In relation to the Hebrew scriptures, however, the key use that the New Testament makes of the concept of the Holy Spirit is in Paul's dialectic of Law and Spirit in Romans and Galatians. This dialectic is one part of the key theme that this essay must finally consider: what attitude does the New Testament take to the status of the Hebrew scriptures in the new age that its writers claim has dawned in Jesus Christ? And, of course, this attitude, important in New Testament studies, also comes to be the general attitude of the Christian tradition to the Hebrew scriptures for centuries to come.

We have seen already that the New Testament authors took the authority of the Hebrew scriptures for granted. They used the Hebrew scriptures to validate all their claims about Jesus, simply because they were Jews for whom those scriptures were uniquely authoritative. Even while the earliest New Testament books were being written, however, it was clear that the great majority of Jews were not going to accept this reading of their scriptures, and that the new Christian community was going to be one that was predominantly Gentile, because of the extraordinary success of the Gentile mission. The most obvious example is Paul's letter to the Roman church, written some time in the 50s or 60s AD.[6] In his letter, Paul uses two related dialectics to consider the relationship between Judaism and Christianity: Law and Spirit and faith and works.

The dialectic of Law and Spirit is more relevant to our present purpose, since in Jewish thought the idea of Law inevitably connotes the idea of the written law, the Torah, and thus the Hebrew scriptures. What becomes essentially clear is that keeping the whole law is no longer to be a requirement, so that, for example, the new Gentile Christians will not have to change to eating what we now call kosher food. And the work of the Holy Spirit within the individual believer, rather than a detailed knowledge and minute keeping of the Torah, may now be expected to be the fundamental guide of conduct.[7] This move away from the authority of the Torah was decisive: however much Christians claimed, and still claim, to revere the Hebrew scriptures, this attitude to them was clearly and substantially less submissive than could be accepted by orthodox Judaism.

Thus, when the canon of the Christian scriptures came to be formed, the authority and inspiration of the Hebrew scriptures was affirmed by their

---

6. It is in itself extraordinary that there was such a church by that time and that it was clearly not founded by Paul.

7. It is important to realise that, at one level, this was a response to some very practical problems. By what ethical code should the new Gentile Christians live? To what extent did they need to be educated in the very substantial body of the Hebrew scriptures and scribal interpretation of them? How could the Gentile churches be locally autonomous independently of Jewish leadership? And so on.

inclusion as what we now call the Old Testament. Reading the Christ-event in the light of the Hebrew scriptures was still felt to be a vital part of what gave the Christian interpretation of Jesus of Nazareth its validity. In him, God had made a new beginning with humanity: but it was the same God who had made the first beginning, to which the Hebrew scriptures were the essential testimony, and they were to be read along with the New Testament as one unfolding history of God's dealing with his people.

In nearly all subsequent Christian cultures, acceptance of the authority and inspiration of the Old Testament has been considered orthodox, but the process by which the Hebrew scriptures were first used to validate interpretation of the Christ-event still continues, so that there is a tendency not to read these stories on their own terms. Perhaps the most obvious example is the Song of Songs, an erotic poem in the †wisdom tradition, that Christianity reinterprets as relating to the †love of Christ the bridegroom for the church his bride. In some Christian traditions these thoroughgoing ‡typological readings of the Old Testament, whereby every facet of the narrative of the Hebrew scriptures becomes a type or figure of Christ, become almost an independent art form.[8]

As students of literature, we have to take note that nearly all our authors read the Hebrew scriptures through the medium of the Christian tradition, and especially through the medium of how the Hebrew scriptures are treated in the New Testament. For example, they understand Genesis 3 to carry the inevitable implication that 'in Adam all die', whereas this interpretation is not from Genesis 3, but Romans 5 and I Corinthians 15:22. Of course, some Jewish interpretation of the Hebrew scriptures similarly takes liberties with the text that the student of literature might find inauthentic; but a proper respect is due to the continuing tradition of the people to whom these narratives first belonged and continue principally to belong.

QUESTIONS

1. Are Christian readings of the Hebrew scriptures sustainable?
2. Is it possible to speak of the story of the Bible?
3. What place do women play in the main story lines of the Bible?
4. How much do we reliably know about Jesus of Nazareth? How does this picture relate to the Christ of faith—both within the New Testament and in later church tradition?

---

8. One might think particularly of the Plymouth Brethren tradition, in which even the colours and materials of the Tabernacle are interpreted in this way, in a manner akin to some of the more esoteric ‡mystical traditions of interpretation in Judaism itself.

BIBLIOGRAPHY

It is not easy to recommend literature about the Bible to students of English literature. The very large volume of material available contains much that is not academically rigorous. On the other hand, most academic biblical studies material is too specialised. While many authors in the canon of English literature, like Shakespeare and Dickens, had a non-specialist knowledge of the Bible, some, like Herbert and Manley Hopkins, had a relatively specialist knowledge. On the whole, the student of English literature, for all these reasons, is best to use non-specialist material that nonetheless has the weight of some academic understanding behind it. It is this approach that this bibliography tries to adopt. These titles are roughly in order of complexity—from the simplest to the most academic.

David and Pat Alexander, ed., *The Lion Handbook to the Bible*, 3rd edn, Oxford 2002.
John William Drane, *An Introduction to the Bible*, Oxford 1990.
Raymond B. Dillard and Tremper Longman III, *An Introduction to the Old Testament*, Grand Rapids MI 1995.
D.A. Carson, Douglas J. Moo, and Leon Morris, *An Introduction to the New Testament*, Grand Rapids MI 1992.

Students of literature will be particularly interested in those versions of the Bible which were current at the time of authors they are studying. David Daniell's book, *The Bible in English*, is essential, especially with regard to sorting successive editions of translations that may at first sight seem to be the same, but which differ sometimes minimally, sometimes widely. For example the 1599 Geneva Study Bible is widely available on the Internet, but not the 1560 version, which is a more likely source for Shakespeare.

Once you are sure which edition of which version you want to consult, the Internet offers many versions. Mark Goodacre's NTGateway site is an excellent starting point for everything to do with the New Testament on the Web, including a number of versions and URL addresses for further sites. There is a companion Old Testament site in development, but it does not yet offer quite so full a range. Gateway sites are especially important in biblical studies, because of the number of sites that do not offer academic rigour.

David Daniell, *The Bible in English*, New Haven and London 2003.
Lloyd E. Berry, ed., *The Geneva Bible: A Facsimile of the 1560 Edition*, Madison WI 1969.
New Testament Gateway, Old Testament Gateway, <http://www.ntgateway.com>, <http://www.otgateway.com>.

CHRISTIAN HISTORY AND THEOLOGY

The sections below cover the history of the church and theology up to the ‡Reformation. They are merely sketches of complex and important historical developments that pick out some salient features of the thought and characteristics of the periods that are reflected in English literature. After the Reformation these concerns are dealt with in overviews and individual essays (see, for example, the essays on evolution, industrialism, and women in the section 'Romantics and Victorians').

THE PATRISTIC PERIOD

The term ‡*patristic* refers to the period in the history of the Christian church up until the time of the split between the churches of the east and the west in 1032 (usually termed the Great Schism). This period is characterised by the work of the great bishop-theologians who were the ‡Fathers, or sources, of authentic Christian doctrine. The Christian writings that we know as the New Testament were not delivered as a body to the Christian church. Nor did they provide a fully developed and articulated account of all the beliefs introduced with them. It fell to the church of the first ten centuries to determine firstly which of the writings circulating among them were truly inspired by God, and secondly to spell out the implications of the teachings they contained.

This first task was achieved relatively speedily by the bishops who determined the canonical status of the New Testament as we know it today. They selected from the wide variety of documents used in the churches those that had an authentic claim to be derived from apostolic tradition. They rejected as canonical such early documents as the *Didache*, *The Shepherd of Hermas*, and the Epistle of Barnabas, while recognising their Christian authenticity and usefulness. The notion popularised in recent novels[1] that the selection of the New Testament canon was a kind of conspiracy to exclude anything of which the bishops disapproved is merely fiction: works such as the *Didache*, *The Apostolic Constitutions*, and the Epistle of Barnabas, containing teachings about

---

1. Dan Brown's *The Da Vinci Code* among them.

church order, continued to be used and circulated alongside works of a more obviously fictional cast like the infancy gospels, the Protoevangelium of James, and the Gospel of Thomas. Anyone who takes the trouble to read these works for themselves will be able immediately to discern essential differences between the canonical and non-canonical works.

The early church councils also made decisions about the Old Testament, accepting certain books that were later to be rejected by Protestants during the ‡Reformation. These constitute what they called the ‡apocrypha, and what Catholics call the deutero-canonical books; these are the books of Wisdom, Ecclesiasticus, Tobit, Judith, Baruch, I and II Maccabees, together with some additions to the book of Esther and the book of Daniel (including the stories of Bel and the Dragon, and Susanna, the prayer of Azariah, and the Song of the Three Children[2]). These validated books of the Old and New Testaments are referred to as 'the canon of scripture' and their validity as 'canonicity'.

The work of reaching agreement about orthodox doctrine was a much longer and much more divisive process. We can identify the chief tasks as determining the identity of Christ (the task of christology); determining the status of the Holy Spirit (the task of pneumatology) and therefore developing a doctrine of the holy ‡Trinity; determining the way in which Christ ‡redeems humanity (soteriology); determining the nature of humanity and the doctrine of †original sin; and formulating an understanding of the church and its ‡sacraments. Such work involved disputes and often violent conflict between different camps and the calling of councils of bishops to settle them and enunciate orthodox doctrine.

The issues surrounding the nature of Christ centred upon his identity as God and human being. Adoptionists, led by Paul of Samosata, argued that Christ was not born as Son but was adopted by God in his *resurrection. This was condemned. Arius proposed that Christ was a divine but lesser being than God, made by God rather than sharing his substance, that is, his uncreated nature. For some considerable time this became the official faith of the Byzantine empire, resulting in persecution for the few like St Athanasius who opposed Arianism. Arius's doctrine was condemned at the Council of Nicaea in AD 325 at which the basis of the Nicene ‡Creed was produced as an orthodox profession of faith, affirming Christ as 'begotten not made, consubstantial with the Father'.

Some theologians, in an attempt to emphasise the divinity of Christ, argued that his humanity was absorbed by his divinity. Christ was one person with one nature, a divine nature. This was called the Docetic or Monophysite

---

2. The 'three children' are the young men Shadrach, Meshach, and Abednego; the 'Song' is also known as the *Benedicite*, and it is used in the Anglican Book of Common Prayer service of Morning Prayer.

(one nature) ‡heresy, which developed in response to the Council of Nicaea and which persisted in the Coptic Church of Egypt. Reaction to this heresy produced the opposite doctrine identified as Nestorianism, after Nestorius who was responsible for first articulating it. Nestorius so desired to affirm the human nature of Christ that he seemed to be denying the now-orthodox belief that he was one person with two natures, that is, that Christ was fully human and fully divine, his human nature being so united with the divine nature that he constituted one, divine, person. For Nestorius the human nature was more than a vehicle for the divinity of Christ. This was emphasised to the extent that there seemed to be *two* Sons, one human and one divine, so that Christ could be said to be two natures in two persons. Hence †Mary, his mother, could not be called 'God-bearer' (*Theotokos*) without also being entitled 'Man-bearer'. The Nestorian position was condemned at the Council of Chalcedon in 381 in the proclamation of Mary as *Theotokos*. This was understood not as an elevation of Mary but as an affirmation of the two natures of Christ in one person. Many of these issues relating to the person of Christ and the role of Mary form the background to literature such as *The Dream of the Rood* and the lyrics in the medieval period and in much Catholic and Anglo-Catholic work thereafter.

The divinity of the Holy Spirit and the precise meaning of the relationship between Father, Son, and Holy Spirit were also contentious. Key figures in the development of this doctrine were St Augustine in the western church and the Cappadocian ‡Fathers, St Basil, St Gregory Nazianzen, St Gregory of Nyssa, and St John Chrysostom in the east. Their contrasting emphasis on ‡Trinitarian doctrine contributed to the development of a different understanding of the church and its government in the east and west.

Related to christology were the questions of soteriology and †original sin. The eastern ‡Fathers tended to emphasise the need for ‡salvation to be wrought in human flesh. To save humanity God must take upon himself everything human, so that ‡atonement between God and humankind could occur and the power of death be destroyed by God dying a human death. 'What God has not assumed, he has not healed' was an axiom of the proponents of this view. The western Fathers, like St Ambrose of Milan, tended to emphasise †sacrifice to God's justice and Christ's substitution for humankind, in keeping with the Roman legacy of a legal outlook.

Divergent views on soteriology produced divergent doctrines concerning †original sin. In the east, original sin was not understood as an inherited state, as in the west. Rather, it was seen as the loss of the immortality that would have been the destiny of an unfallen *Adam and Eve. It resulted in the damaging or distortion of the image of God in which humanity was created and in its existence in an environment in which ‡sin was easy and goodness difficult. Emphasis was strongly upon the destiny and dignity of humanity as a result of the †incarnation of Christ: through God becoming human, in Christ humanity was to become by God's gift all that God was by nature.

In the west St Augustine was chiefly responsible for delineating the doctrine of †original sin. Although his thinking changed and matured, it tended to stress more strongly the loss of original innocence involved in the *fall. For St Augustine original sin was linked with the corruption of sexuality that affected the state of every human being. Rather than being an inherited environment, original sin was an inherited state of weakened will, darkened understanding, and subjection to concupiscence. The development of his thinking was influenced by the need to counter the teaching of Pelagius, which suggested that human beings were capable of achieving ‡salvation through their own moral effort. This seemed to deny the necessity of ‡redemption of a fallen human nature by Christ. We have here the seeds of the doctrinal arguments that were to emerge at the ‡Reformation.

It was over the nature of church government that conflict emerged between the churches of east and west. The western church had come to acknowledge the primacy of the bishop of Rome as the successor of Peter, whilst the eastern bishops looked more to church councils as ultimate authorities. During his ‡papacy, Pope Leo the Great produced a developed doctrine of the primacy of Peter and his successors over the entire church. After much dispute this was uneasily accepted but opened up a rift between the two churches that culminated in the Great Schism of 1032. The western, Latin, church developed as a centralised body with an increased tendency to systematising and explaining doctrine, which was to culminate in the emergence of ‡scholastic theology. It attempted to elucidate, for example, the precise way in which the bread and wine became the body and blood of Christ during the ‡mass or ‡eucharist, through the doctrine of transubstantiation.

The eastern Greek church continued to develop a theology less concerned to analyse and dissect than to celebrate and participate in the mystery of God. It was to this tradition that Anglicans of the eighteenth and nineteenth centuries often turned for the model of a catholic, that is, universal and non-Protestant, church without the ‡papacy and without the dominance of ‡scholastic theology.

THE MEDIEVAL PERIOD

Theologians of the Middle Ages inherited the hard-won orthodoxy of the ‡patristic period: the major elements of Christian doctrine were already in place and well understood. Europe and most of the world that had historically been subject to the Romans and Greeks were nominally Christian: however, the forces of Islam had already made significant territorial inroads, which the Crusades ultimately failed to bring to a halt. The achievements of the Middle Ages, though they were important at the time and formed the basis for the developments of the ‡Reformation, are thus generally seen more as elaborations of the old (or even as the decay of the primitive purity of the old) than as significantly new and original in themselves. Here, we will briefly consider the Christian developments of the Middle Ages under three headings: the intellectual, the social, and the spiritual.

The most significant intellectual development of the Middle Ages goes under the general term of ‡scholasticism. Until the thirteenth century the philosophy of the western church was predominantly of a ‡neoplatonic cast, mediated through St Augustine and Boethius. It was in this century, however, that the *Physics, Metaphysics*, and *Ethics* of Aristotle became widely available in the west for the first time. Initially these were regarded with suspicion by the church until the great Dominican theologian, St Thomas Aquinas (1224–74), undertook the harmonising of Aristotelian philosophy with Catholic theology. In so doing he established Aristotle as the philosopher of the church and developed a method of dialectical argument and minute analysis. This approach, with its strong emphasis upon human reasoning, was to become the standard approach in the newly developing universities or 'schools', hence its description as 'scholasticism'.

‡Platonists and ‡neoplatonists believed that 'ideas', 'universals', are realities of which concrete particular examples are copies or expressions. These 'ideas' are innate in the human mind. Aristotle, however, argued that it is from the accumulated experience of the particular that we develop the 'idea' or concept. For example, it is because we experience numerous examples of green things that we develop the concept of greenness. Aquinas largely accepted this and taught that there is nothing in the mind that is not first in the senses. This affirmed the value of observable phenomena.

Among later generations of philosophers came those like William of Ockham, or Occam (?1280–1345), who went further in their insistence upon the non-reality of universals. To Occam only observable particulars could be said to exist and universals were merely names for concepts. Their approach is therefore called nominalism from the Latin for names, 'nomines'. This approach gave the impetus to both the empiricism of science and to the ‡Reformation's rejection of authorities other than scripture and reason.

The social developments of the Middle Ages in England had an impact on Christianity. The Norman Conquest of 1066 and its aftermath left the church in the control of the Normans, French-speaking people of the ruling class. By 1087, there are only three ‡abbots in English ‡monasteries with English names; the remainder are French or Continental.

English ‡monasticism before the Conquest was predominantly Benedictine. After the Conquest came a steady influx of new orders from France, some based on reformed Benedictine monasticism such as the Cluniacs and Cistercians, but others were orders of a different kind. These included the ‡mendicant (begging) orders, the Dominicans and Franciscans, whose aim was to minister to the people at large, not to be in isolation from the world. Chaucer's Prologue to *The Canterbury Tales* shows the corruption to which the fourteenth-century orders were susceptible: a French-speaking prioress who cares more about her pet dogs than people, a ‡monk who ignores his monastic rule, ecclesiastical officials like the ‡summoner and ‡pardoner who abuse their positions of power, a ‡friar who can extract money from the poorest but who feels no call to minister to the leper. All these are participating in a ‡pilgrimage that for most has lost its spiritual significance and become a social outing. The presence of the knight, the parson, and the ploughman reminds us, however, that true Christians can be found both among the pilgrims and among different ranks in contemporary society.

The situation depicted by Chaucer may be a literary creation and a rather cynical view of medieval religious life, but it is not markedly at odds with what we know from other sources. In some medieval ideals like that of knighthood, the Christian and secular are also mixed, as we see in Chaucer, *Sir Gawain and the Green Knight*, Malory, and Spenser. So although the discourse of medieval people was shaped by Christianity, a sense of spiritual reality and devotion was not always present, or was merged with other things. One response to this was the growth of reforming tendencies in ‡monasticism, which saw greater asceticism and more rigorous obedience to monastic rules as the way to true spirituality.

These reforming movements were associated with the development of affective spirituality and with the continuance of the Christ-centered mysticism that had blossomed in the 'twelfth-century renaissance' associated with the early Cistercians. Key figures in this development are the 'second founder' of the Cistercisns, St Bernard of Clairvaux, and St Francis of Assisi.

Affective spirituality was based on a new sense of Christ's humanity. In the ‡patristic period, despite the affirmation of the humanity of Christ, emphasis was on his divinity; the worshipper was invited to see through the human flesh of Christ to the God who had taken on humanity without any diminution in his divinity. An icon of the *crucifixion from the ‡patristic period, for example, does not invite or evoke sorrow or compassion for the physical suffering Jesus endured.

After the split between the eastern and western churches, western spirituality took a new turn. A tender love for Christ in his humanity developed. ‡Patristic emphasis on the wounded side of Christ as the source of the ‡sacraments of ‡baptism and ‡eucharist, for example, became an emphasis on the pierced heart of Christ, wounded by his love for *fallen men and women. Meditation on the suffering of Christ was encouraged to stimulate feelings of sorrow and gratitude as well as awareness of Christ's love, so that sorrow for sin, desire to return love for love, and repentance would ensue. Rather than the serene face in an icon of Christ the ruler of all, common in the patristic period, the face that dominates the Middle Ages is the 'Ecce Homo' (behold the man), the face of Christ the Man of Sorrows, shown by Pilate to the crowds after he has been scourged and crowned with thorns. Hence, much of the finest literature of this time reaches out to feel the agony of the ‡saviour as he suffers. At the same time, the development of ideals of chivalry and courtly love enable people to see Jesus as a knight and a spiritual †lover, as in *Ancrene Riwle* and the medieval lyrics. This, combined with continuing discussion of the nature and role of †Mary as ‡saint, mediator, and mother, also leads to affective piety that venerates Mary in her suffering motherhood, and also as the perfect lady, the object of pure courtly love, as once again in the lyrics.[3]

Affective spirituality also gave another flavour to western ‡mysticism. The desire of Christian ‡mystics is for direct, unmediated contact with God, culminating in the union of their will with God's. Devotion to the suffering humanity of Christ stimulated this desire, arousing love and the wish to be united with him in his suffering; this promoted the radical selflessness necessary for mystical union. We can see this affective spirituality at work in the writings of Julian of Norwich and Margery Kempe, whilst that other well-known mystical work of the fourteenth century, *The Cloud of Unknowing*, represents the earlier, ‡patristic approach.

The ‡Reformation can be seen as responding to the problems and opportunities arising in medieval Christianity. It fixed on scripture as the sole authority

---

3. The lyric 'I sing of a maiden / That is makelees' probably reflects the widely accepted notion of the immaculate conception of †Mary. Duns Scotus (1255–1308) popularised the notion, but it was only made official Roman Catholic doctrine in 1854.

for faith and life, and it sought expressions of faith that were real, heartfelt, and open to all. It rejected much of medieval Christianity, but it also borrowed and reframed much.

THE REFORMATION

At the outset of the early modern period, Christianity in western Europe was entirely Roman Catholic. The power and influence of the Roman Catholic church was expressed particularly in the ‡papacy, whereby the authority of the ‡pope in Rome was axiomatic for all western European Christians, including monarchs and other rulers. But at the local level also the authority of the priest was essential for ‡forgiveness: it was he alone, as intermediary between the believer and God, who could pronounce ‡absolution for ‡sins. Of immense power also were the ‡monastic orders, which had been largely responsible for the rapid spread of Christianity in the previous centuries but which had undoubtedly suffered some of the corruptions of power, both at the highest level, where monastic power was a career aspiration for members of the highest classes, and at the lowest, where individual ‡monks (and perhaps to a much lesser extent nuns) were known not to keep their vows of chastity and poverty.

Over the centuries, the power of the ‡papacy in particular had been opposed and sometimes curtailed by various secular political leaders but by the fifteenth century, the wealth, prestige, patronage, and power of the papacy and the ‡monastic orders were still huge. The period we call the ‡Reformation, from the sixteenth century onwards, marks the most radical and far-reaching political and ideological challenge to, and partial overthrow of, Roman Catholic hegemony in western Europe, as well as the permanent emergence of radically different Protestant expressions of Christianity.

It goes without saying that the religious ‡Reformation is also part of wider changes in societies and emerging nation states: the religious ideas that give it impetus are always interacting with other social phenomena, including especially the recovery of classical learning, the beginnings of scientific discovery, rapid growth in dissemination of literary output by printing, relatively stable conditions of trade producing greater prosperity and a much larger class of educated people, and the emergence of the nation state. Fundamentally, however, it still makes most sense to narrate the story of the Reformation, including the English Reformation, from a religious perspective. Such a sentence might seem tautologous, were it not for what David Daniell calls 'a very recent feeling that the field which used to be called The English Reformation had been invaded and made to grow different crops—privatised and fenced off as Early Modern History plc, with whole acres out of bounds'.[4]

Two factors contribute to this feeling. Secular historiography tends to regard relations of economic power within a culture as fundamental to the analysis of that culture. Especially in the pervasive Marxist approach, the accepted ideological systems within the culture are perennially suspect as rationalisations attempting to legitimise and perpetuate the power of the powerful. The ‡Reformation, seen in these terms, is essentially a protest against the abuse of power by the ecclesiastical elite (which it certainly was in part), and less importance is accorded to the specifically ideological, theological, claims made by the protesters in their attempt to throw off the yoke. And on this analysis, the protest movement is then hijacked by rival, secular, power elites (think Henry VIII) for their own political ends (which is again not easy entirely to deny).

On the other hand, there has also more recently emerged a very different reading of what actually happened in English religion at this time. Many of the most influential recent accounts of the English ‡Reformation come from scholars who argue that it was much less pervasively successful and much less popular than had been argued by earlier English historians.[5] In response to all this, Daniell cites with approval what seems a fair question of Patrick Collinson: 'How did one of the most Catholic countries become one of the least?'[6]

It must be remembered, however, that from the time of Henry VIII's establishment of himself as head of the Church of England, refusal to take the oath accepting the sovereign as head of the church could lead to the death of a traitor by being hanged, drawn, and quartered. In Elizabeth I's reign to be a Catholic was to be, *ipso facto*, a traitor. Failure to worship in the newly reformed parishes incurred heavy fines intended to reduce the offender to penury. The possibility, and likely extent, of adopting an outward conformity in such circumstances must therefore be taken into account when considering the success of the Protestantisation of England.

---

4. David Daniell, *The Bible in English*, New Haven and London 2003, p. 128. See also the prize-winning historical study, Eamon Duffy, *The Voices of Morebath: Reformation and Rebellion in an English Village*, New Haven and London 2001; and Duffy's other prize-winning study of pre-Reformation religion in England, which argues that 'late mediaeval Catholicism in England was neither decadent nor decayed, but was a strong and vigorous tradition, and that the Reformation represented a violent rupture from a popular and theologically respectable religious system', *The Stripping of the Altars: Traditional Religion in England c. 1400 – c. 1580*, New Haven and London 1992.

5. Hardly by coincidence, these accounts tend to be by Roman Catholic scholars (who might well respond that the Protestantism of the earlier historians was hardly coincidental either).

6. Daniell, *The Bible in English*, p. 128, citing Patrick Collinson in Nicholas Tyacke, ed., *The Long Reformation in England 1500–1800*, London 1998.

Recent Roman Catholic revision of the account of the English ‡Reformation[7] has at least the merit that it takes the beliefs of non-elite members of society seriously, finding several instances where ordinary people clung to their old faith and practice with some tenacity. It may be legitimately asked whether these historians give sufficient importance to the beliefs of those non-elite members of society who, in extraordinarily large numbers, as Daniell describes, bought Bibles in English so that they themselves could appropriate the meaning of their faith with much less need for the interpolation of clergy and others to instruct them, especially since these purchases were at first always acts of ecclesiastical, and sometimes of political, disobedience. Catholic scholars are quite clearly right, however, in stating that there were strong internal currents pressing for reform within the Roman Catholic church: the voices of early ‡humanists like Erasmus and Thomas More who were loyal Catholics were increasingly powerful.

Whether this movement could have produced sufficient change in the acknowledged abuses of the Roman Catholic church and the ‡monastic orders at this time is open to question; though certainly the ‡Counter-Reformation soon did much to reform some of the abuses of which the ‡Reformers complained. Committed Protestants will tend to respond, however, that neither the ‡humanists nor the Counter-Reformers chose the essential doctrinal targets: that the ‡Reformation was successful because it radically challenged fundamental Roman Catholic doctrines of ‡salvation, which humanism, despite its attack on the methods of ‡scholastic theologians, essentially did not. Any account of the religious content of the Reformation must focus first and foremost on its critique of the whole Roman Catholic scheme of salvation.

The ‡Reformation probably challenged most directly the Roman Catholic idea of ‡purgatory: that after death human ‡souls move immediately neither to †heaven nor †hell, but rather to an intermediate place where they are temporarily punished for their ‡sins on earth, before being allowed into heaven when the purging process is complete. This purging was the spiritualisation of the medical process of purgation, in which a physician might prescribe a purgative, or emetic, medicine to clear the body of unclean humours or vapours, or use fire to burn away infection: the soul was similarly cleansed and purified to be made ready for heaven. The sale of indulgences, whereby the ‡pope authorised ‡pardoners to sell remission from purgatory for money, was barely defensible,

---

7. The recent revision of the history of ‡Reformation can be understood from a comparison between the classic account of Owen Chadwick and those of Christopher Haigh and Diarmaid McCulloch: Owen Chadwick, *The Reformation*, new edn, London 1990; Diarmaid MacCulloch, *The Later Reformation in England 1547–1603*, 2nd edn, Basingstoke 2001; and Christopher Haigh, ed., *The English Reformation Revised*, Cambridge 1987.

even if the money was given to good causes; but, much worse, it was also subject to very widespread abuse. Moreover, it depended on a particular view of the authority of the ‡pope himself, taken from Christ's words to St Peter that whatsoever he loosed on earth would be loosed in †heaven (Matthew 16:19) and asserting the view that the pope was Peter's successor on earth.

Martin Luther, an Augustinian ‡monk and theologian, effectively began the ‡Reformation as a theological movement by challenging this entire scheme of ‡salvation at the point of the sale of indulgences, traditionally starting with his ninety-five theses of 1517 but drawing also on several earlier years of study of the New Testament in particular. With increasing firmness as the controversy grew and the ‡pope vigorously opposed him, Luther argued not only that it was abuse to sell indulgences but also that there was no scriptural authority for the existence of ‡purgatory. And, further, not only could money not buy salvation: neither could any good deeds that one might do in this life achieve it. Arguing from the writings of St Paul, and especially from the Epistle to the Romans, Luther wrote that humankind could be put right with God in one way only: through faith in Christ. Those parts of the Bible that seemed to suggest that one could earn one's way to †heaven, including famously the Epistle of James, Luther discarded, or at least severely downplayed. Scripture was divinely inspired only insofar as it preached Christ and this scheme of salvation and justification by faith alone: *sola fide*. The suggestion that good deeds could save you was exactly what St Paul was explicitly arguing against in Romans when he said that no one could be put right with God by 'works of the law'.

Even more challengingly, at least in institutional terms, Luther also argued that there was no biblical authority for the idea that the ‡pope was St Peter's successor or that he could authoritatively enable people to escape ‡purgatory (even if it existed, which it didn't). Not only that, but the power of the ordinary Roman Catholic priest to ‡absolve people of their ‡sins was denied. The practice by which a priest would hear a person's ‡confession and give absolution involved the church in usurping the function of ‡forgiveness which was God's alone.

In this last point, we can begin to see also how the ‡Reformation seemed to offer people a new freedom in religion. Luther's argument removed the necessity for clerical intermediaries between the believer and God: one ‡confessed one's ‡sins to God; and God ‡forgave them. The clergy, whose corruption was in any case a widespread scandal, need no longer be feared: there would still be a need for learned guides for the believer, but the Christian pastor — who incidentally ought also to be permitted to be married — had essentially a preaching and teaching function. Similarly the celibacy of ‡monks and nuns was a mistake: there was no biblical reason to believe that one was holier if one were unmarried.

It will be seen at once that, for those who wanted to appropriate their own faith both in theology and practice, this system was radically unhierarchical in an entirely new way. Christians with ordinary secular jobs and status might work out their own ‡salvation, might indeed aspire to a new personal holiness that the previous hierarchies had suggested belonged only to clergy, ‡monks, and nuns.

One key factor in this was the availability of the Bible in languages other than Latin, so that the increasing numbers of literate people could read it and, just as importantly, that everyone, including the illiterate, could nonetheless hear it read and understand it.[8] A similar use of the vernacular soon followed in service books. Roman Catholic revisionist historians tend to argue that the Roman Catholic church would soon have given its people the Bible in the vernacular without the intervention of the Reformers; and the Douai-Rheims Roman Catholic version in English soon emerged, probably partly to challenge some of the readings of the ‡Reformed Geneva Bible in particular.

To loyal Catholics like Thomas More, for example, the freedom apparently offered by ‡Reformed religion was illusory. To More, William Tyndale's view that all people might seek the plain meaning of the Bible for themselves was a recipe for chaos: it radically disturbed proper notions of order and authority. People needed to be sure that there was an ultimately authoritative reading of the scriptures and, indeed, an ultimately authoritative guide in matters of Christian faith and practice. Only the authority of the interpretative tradition of the Roman Catholic church and the ultimate authority of the ‡pope offered that security. Like Erasmus, More had been a steady critic of some Roman Catholic practice, especially the working methods of ‡scholastic theologians, and really did want a Roman Catholic church that would change to offer support to Christian men and women as they sought greater understanding of, and personal responsibility for, their faith; but this was anarchy.

Further fuel was added to the fire of religious antagonism by the French theologian John (or Jean) ‡Calvin, whose doctrines were more radical than Luther's. Luther had, for example, retained some aspects of transubstantiation, the idea that the bread and wine of the ‡mass were really changed into the body and blood of Christ. The detail of what Roman Catholics meant by this, and what Luther meant by his partial disagreement with it, is still not entirely agreed upon; but in any case Calvin swept both away by asserting that the mass — now to be renamed the Lord's supper or holy communion — was symbolic only.

---

8. There is a classic collect in the 1662 Prayer Book in which worshippers pray of the scriptures that they may 'hear them read mark learn and inwardly digest them': which might mean either may 'hear them, read, mark, learn and inwardly digest them' or 'hear them read, mark, learn and inwardly digest them'.

The ‡Reformers in fact argued that there were only two ‡sacraments, †baptism and holy communion, and again, they denied the need for a priest to officiate at the latter. In Roman Catholic thinking, the priest offered the ‡mass as a sacrifice; for Protestants, the service was a memorial of the one †sacrifice of Christ on the †cross, eternally effective and not needing to be represented in any form.

If we remember Luther above all for the doctrine of justification by faith alone, we remember ‡Calvin most for the doctrine of election: the idea that God effectively fore-ordains some people for †heaven and some for †hell. The key text for the doctrine of election is John 15:16 (King James Version), 'Ye have not chosen me, but I have chosen you', words addressed by Jesus to his disciples, which at one level are simply the reminder of the facts of the beginning of their itinerant ministry together. Extra theological weight is given to the idea, again, by the teaching of St Paul in Romans 9, for example in verse 18: 'Therefore hath he mercy on whom he will have mercy, and whom he will he hardeneth.' There is not space here for a detailed discussion of the doctrine of election. ‡Calvin's defenders would argue that he expounds the doctrine chiefly to emphasise the grace of God: that whereas Luther emphasised the faith by which one apprehends God's freely offered ‡salvation, what is more important is God's initiative of mercy in the offer, which is an act of his untrammelled will, not a response to human belief.[9] It is that emphasis on the sovereignty of the †love of God which is Calvin's key theme.

‡Calvin's importance for subsequent Protestant thought lies not least in the fact that he was an extensive theological writer and biblical commentator. His writings still show the power of a huge intellect; whereas the key impression one gains from Luther's less systematic and less extensive published work is of the man's passion and urgency. For both men, the power of their doctrine and the success of their challenge to Roman Catholicism inevitably also involved them in changing the polity of both church and state. In England, there has been no large denomination that closely resembles the Lutheran churches of continental Europe: the closest, and that not very close at all, being the Church of England. Calvin's ideas on ecclesiastical organisation are reflected in the churches in the ‡Puritan tradition, especially Congregationalists and Presbyterians, who are now mainly united in the United Reformed Church.

The Church of England goes through many redefinitions in the ‡Reformation and post-Reformation period. It still remains a unique expression of ecclesiastical organisation and ethos, and a unique expression of the church's

---

9. Luther, of course, also held this; but it is the extreme to which ‡Calvin pushes this doctrine of God's sovereign †love which is essential to the election controversy.

relationship to the state, forged principally by the compromise of the early years of the reign of Elizabeth I. The literature of the English Reformation, including Bible translations, Prayer Books, sermons, and ‡homilies, coincides with the explosion of imaginative literature of the same period, especially in poetry and plays. Taking the King James Bible and the complete works of Shakespeare to one's desert island symbolises and reflects the extraordinary influence of the literature of this period on all English literature and culture since. The religious turbulence of the time, both its excitement and its conflict, is reflected in differing degrees in different pieces; but historicism, new or old, undoubtedly needs to continue to take account, and indeed to take more account, of the Reformation background to imaginative English literature than it has done hitherto.

QUESTIONS

1. To what extent have you noticed any of the themes and issues discussed here in any text of the period?
2. How far does changing theology explain or interact with the literary development of English?

BIBLIOGRAPHY

There are many general church histories which will orientate the reader to the development of theology and its influence on literature. The volumes in the Penguin History of Christianity series are reliable and authoritative, for example.

Henry Chadwick, ed., *Not Angels but Anglicans*, Norwich 2000, is a brief and well-illustrated history of Christianity in Britain.

Tim Dowley, ed., *The History of Christianity* (A Lion Handbook), rev. edn, Oxford 1990, and John McManners, ed., *The Oxford Illustrated History of Christianity*, Oxford 1990, take different approaches, but aim to cover the main ideas accessibly.

Philip Hughes, *A History of the Church*, 3 vols, London 1998, is a classic history.

Alister McGrath, *Reformation Thought: An Introduction*, 3rd edn, Oxford 1999: offers a wider introduction to ‡Reformation thought.

The theologies of Luther and ‡Calvin are specialist areas which most English literature students will not need to go into in detail, but the Cambridge Companions edited by Donald K. McKim are reliable guides for the non-specialist: Donald K. McKim, ed., *The Cambridge Companion to John Calvin*, Cambridge 2004, and *The Cambridge Companion to Martin Luther*, Cambridge 2003.

4

Hymnody

Hymnody has always been an important feature of the Christian expression of worship, and in this Christians continue the tradition of ancient Judaism, the hymnal of which was the book of Psalms. Jesus sang hymns with his disciples at the Passover feast (Matthew 26:30; Mark 14:26), and Paul urged his churches to sing 'psalms and hymns and spiritual songs' (Ephesians 5:19; Colossians 3:16) when they met. It is widely thought that the passage of Philippians 2 known as the 'Song of Christ's Humility' (Philippians 2:4–11) was an early Christian hymn. Whether or not this is the case, there can be no doubt that hymns were used in Christian churches from the earliest times.

It is often difficult to place the hymn. Is it specifically literary, or does it aim to embody some other quality or meet some other criterion of use? The earliest-recorded piece of literature in English is Cædmon's so-called 'Hymn', which is not a hymn at all. But it highlights the issue just posed: it praises God, it is didactic, it was widely known, and it is a poem. Many literary works from Old English through to the modern day that are also not hymns share these characteristics. But the hymn, while it usually has these features, is particularly intended for singing in worship and may have no pretensions to literary merit. Some of the extensive corpus of hymns finds a place in the anthologies, but that is usually because the words of hymns reflect the cultural, stylistic, and theological trends of the day. J.R. Watson's *The English Hymn* is a magisterial literary and historical analysis of the hymn, but even here the hymn is still somewhat detached from its musical and functional context.

It would be foolish to attempt a brief account of the impact of the Psalms on English literature and hymnody. More copies of the Psalter than of Gospel books remain from Anglo-Saxon England. The Psalms were glossed and translated into English, paraphrased and set to music, by writers from King Alfred onwards. But alongside the Psalms in early England was a flourishing tradition of Latin hymnody, which was plundered by vernacular writers. *The Dream of the Rood* may have got its fundamental conceit of the †cross as a faithful warrior from the Latin hymn tradition: the cross-hymns of Venantius Fortunatus (530–609), particularly 'Pange lingua' ('Sing, my tongue') and 'Vexilla regis' ('The royal banners') are echoed numerous times in the Anglo-Saxon poem.[1]

In English, at least, the hymn as a literary genre probably begins at the ‡Reformation. There had always been singing in the Christian tradition; and the teaching songs of the Franciscan ‡friars, the chant that accompanied the Gregorian revival, the Christian content of Middle English lyrics, are all important milestones in that tradition. Luther, the father of the ‡Reformation, himself a hymn-writer, contributed much to this tradition and the various English translations of his sixteenth-century hymn 'Ein feste Burg' ('A safe stronghold') can still be heard in twenty-first-century churches. But after the Reformation we begin to see poems in English set to music and used in worship. Several texts from the seventeenth century are indeed still in use to the present day: George Herbert's 'Teach me my God and King'; Bunyan's 'Who would true valour see', and so on. Joseph Addison's gentle and rather pastoral hymns are still popular, such as 'When all thy mercies, O my God / My rising soul surveys'.

The most important English contributors to the tradition of hymnody are, without much doubt, Charles Wesley and Isaac Watts. Watts is slightly the earlier of the two, and a nonconformist by tradition; perhaps his most famous text now would be 'When I survey the wondrous cross' (*BACL* pp. 499–500). Wesley, obviously, is closely associated with the ‡Methodist Revival of the eighteenth and early nineteenth centuries, led above all by his brother John. The sheer volume of Charles Wesley's output is extraordinary: 'Love divine, all loves excelling' (*BACL* pp. 528–9), 'Hark the herald angels sing', 'O for a thousand tongues to sing' would be amongst his most famous works. Methodism, it is said, was born in song: Wesley's hymns were an important part of its appeal to, and success amongst, the new industrial classes.

A measure of the influence of these hymns is the use they are put to in literature. In Blake's *Songs*,[2] for example, he refers to the fact that Jesus

> calls himself a Lamb:
> He is meek and he is mild;
> He became a little child. ('The Lamb', in *Songs of Innocence*)

---

1. J.M. Neale's Victorian translations in *Mediæval Hymns and Sequences*, 3rd edn, London 1867, are still in use, 'Sing, my tongue, the glorious battle' and 'The Royal Banners forward go'. In the former, the †cross is referred to as 'Faithful Cross' and 'Tree of Glory', both expressions used in the vernacular poem. The cross is also spoken of as a *beacen* in the Old English poem, a word meaning (amongst other things) 'banner' or 'standard', the central conceit of the second Latin hymn.

2. Nelson Hilton, 'William Blake, *Songs of Innocence and Experience*', in Duncan Wu, ed., *A Companion to Romanticism*, Oxford 1998, pp. 103–12, makes reference to both the hymn echoes noted.

The echo is from Wesley's 'Gentle Jesus, meek and mild', and particularly the second verse,

> Lamb of God, I look to Thee;
> Thou shalt my Example be;
> Thou art gentle, meek, and mild;
> Thou wast once a little child.[3]

The last of the *Songs of Innocence*, 'On Another's Sorrow', seems to contradict a verse of a famous William Cowper hymn, 'Hark my soul, it is the Lord':

> Can a woman's tender care
> Cease toward the child she bare?
> Yes, she may forgetful be ...

But Blake asserts,

> Can a mother sit and hear
> An infant groan, an infant fear?
> No, no! Never can it be!
> Never, never can it be!

It was perhaps after the Wesleys and the highly successful *Olney Hymns* of Cowper and John Newton (*BACL* pp. 532–8) that the literary impact of hymns waned a little. But at the same time, the popular impact increased. The evangelistic missions of D.L. Moody in the late nineteenth century were hugely dependent on the hymnody especially of Ira D. Sankey and of other nonconformist British and American writers and composers.[4] 'I am so glad that Jesus loves me' and 'Tell me the old, old story' are examples of popular hymns to come out of this movement. They gave strong impetus to the music of many nonconformist denominations and indeed strong impetus to Christian mission generally.

Both ‡Methodism and the more theologically radical later nonconformists specialised also in Sunday schools for children. The tradition of singing in the Sunday schools, when the children attending were at such a formative time in life, created a love of songs, which for many lasted a lifetime. It would not have been uncommon, well towards the end of the twentieth century, to find adults who never in maturity attended church but still sang the religious songs of their nonconformist Sunday school childhood: 'Jesus wants me for a

---

3. John and Charles Wesley, *Hymns and Sacred Poems*, Bristol 1742.

4. Sankey wrote both words and music (so also did Luther); whereas Wesley and Watts, for example, were simply wordsmiths: 'Love divine', interestingly, was probably first sung to the tune of Purcell's 'Fairest Isle'.

sunbeam', 'Jesus loves me, this I know', 'Jesus loves the little children', and so on. The influence of these hymns in the consciousness of traditionally non-conformist communities runs extraordinarily deep. In Glasgow, for example, the football fans still sing 'We're on the road with Ally's army'[5] to the tune of 'Jesus loves the little children' and, in the Protestant blue half of the city, 'Follow, follow, I will follow Rangers' to the tune of Sankey and Moody's 'Follow, follow, I will follow Jesus'. And in Wales, of course, though the tradition is now in decline, this nonconformist culture is expressed by the singing of adult hymns, this time with the original text, at rugby football internationals: above all William Williams' 'Guide me, O Thou great Jehovah' to the Welsh tune 'Cwm Rhondda'—another hymn tune that is widely used, to adapted text, in football grounds across Britain.[6]

The short children's songs were designed to be easily memorable, both in melody and words; but there were also longer hymns for children, still with simple didactic words, but more like adult hymns in length. Perhaps the foremost exponent of this genre was the wife of a Victorian Anglican bishop (in Ireland), Mrs Cecil Frances Alexander,[7] who wrote 'All things bright and beautiful', 'There is a green hill far away', and 'Once in Royal David's city' amongst other hymns. It is notable that her hymns have become part of adult worship repertoire.

The literary merit of hymns is always hard to assess: their popularity in worship is certainly not always dependent on it. Some writers—Herbert, Cowper, and Bunyan for example—are literary figures for other reasons; yet even here, one would not, for example, count 'Teach me, my God and King' amongst Herbert's best works. Herbert and Bunyan were not hymn writers as such. Herbert was writing devotional poetry; Bunyan wrote what became a famous hymn borrowing from a popular genre:

> Who would true Valour see,
>   Let him come hither;
> One here will Constant be,
>   Come Wind, Come Weather...
> No Lyon can him fright,
> He'll with a Gyant Fight ...[8]

---

5. 'Ally' here stands for the name of the latest coach or manager.

6. Though the words are mostly those that Wesley wrote, popular tradition has enshrined the theologically nonsensical 'Bread of heaven / Feed me till I want no more' in the place of 'Feed me now and evermore'.

7. This was her preferred title for herself, and that under which her collected poems were posthumously published in 1896.

8. Roger Sharrock, ed., *John Bunyan: Grace Abounding... and The Pilgrim's Progress*, London 1966, p. 185.

This direct call to courage in the service of a worthy master, in the face of danger and the enemy, is a recognisable genre in British folk-music, though we are here dealing with one of the earliest extant examples. This is a recruiting song, a genre with which we are more familiar from the Napoleonic Wars: 'Over the hills and far away' from Farqhuar's *The Recruiting Officer* and Gay's *Beggar's Opera*, for example.

It is probably best, then, to think of hymn writing as a separate literary craft, with its own distinctive criteria for successful composition. There is little doubt that Charles Wesley—and no doubt at all that Ira D. Sankey—would have preferred to write a hymn that was effective in producing religious conversion than one that was judged to have particular literary merit. Even in this context of specifically religious purpose, however, the pervasive influence of hymnody on literary and wider popular culture from the mid-eighteenth to the mid-twentieth century, is hard to ignore.

QUESTIONS

1. What do you think is the principal appeal of hymns: words, music, or something else?
2. Are hymns literature now in a way they were not when they were written?

BIBLIOGRAPHY

D.H. Lawrence, 'Hymns in a man's life', in James T. Boulton, ed., *Late Essays and Articles*, The Cambridge Edition of the Works of D.H. Lawrence, Cambridge 2004, pp. 128–34. This is an exploration of what the hymn does, and ends, 'Here is the clue to the ordinary Englishman—in the nonconformist hymns' (p. 134).

J.R. Watson, *The English Hymn: A Critical and Historical Study*, Oxford 1999. The most comprehensive work on the topic.

Section 7

GLOSSARY

Glossary of Bible Narratives, Christian Themes, and Christian Terms

The glossary is divided into three parts. The keywords for each of the three parts are prefixed by the appropriate symbol used with the word in the main text of the book: * for a narrative, † for a theme, and ‡ for a Christian term. There is inevitably some element of overlap between the sections.

The first part, with keywords marked * in the main text, deals with straightforward narratives in the Bible, whether these are of actual historical events like the *crucifixion, or stories told by Jesus such as the *parable of the unjust judge. Here the source texts from the Bible are listed and the core elements summarised. More detail will be available in the Bible itself and the reader will find it useful to read the passages there.

The second part, with keywords marked † in the main text, deals with biblical and Christian themes. These themes include people, like †Mary, who appear in Bible narratives in various places, but who also have particular representative or imaginative importance in English literature; they also include theological ideas like †incarnation, and motifs and imagery used in the Bible and literature like the †garden.

The third part, with keywords marked ‡ in the main text, is simply a glossary of terms from theology, Christian history, philosophy, and literature relating to biblical and Christian ideas. Some of these terms, such as ‡Arminianism or ‡equivocation may be unfamiliar, or they may be familiar but used with different senses in modern idiom: ‡Vice, for example, is in common usage, but in relation to historical drama, it has a very particular meaning which is outlined in the gloss.

For the sake of clarity, these symbols are not added to keywords in direct quotations in the main text: this preserves the accuracy of the quotation, but the reader may find reference to keywords in the discussion. Only the first use of the keyword in a paragraph is marked (unless the paragraph is very long, or the word appears in more than one form).

1. * BIBLE NARRATIVES

Adam and Eve | Genesis 2–3

Adam, the first man, was created from the 'dust of the ground'. God put him in the Garden of *Eden to care for it, and gave him dominion over the animals and birds, which Adam named. While Adam slept God created Eve from one of his ribs to be his companion, helper, and wife. In Eden Eve is persuaded by the serpent to eat the fruit of the tree of the knowledge of good and evil even though God had forbidden it, and she encourages Adam to do the same. Because of their disobedience the two are expelled from Eden, though God clothes them first in animal skins. Among their sons were *Cain and Abel.

Adam means 'man' and Eve, the name Adam gives to his wife, means 'living', and becomes 'the mother of all living' (3:20). The *creation of Eve from Adam's rib symbolises the mutual dependence and unity of man and woman in marriage: the two become 'one flesh'.

In literature, Milton elaborates the story of Adam and Eve in *Paradise Lost*; more widely, debates about the nature and roles of the sexes often start from this story.

Annunciation | Luke 1:26–38

The †angel Gabriel gives God's message to †Mary: that she will give birth to a baby, who will be called 'Son of the Most High' and whose 'kingdom will never end' (32–3). Aemilia Lanyer refers to this story in her work.

Ascension | Mark 16:19; Luke 24:51; Acts 1:9

Forty days after his *resurrection, Jesus was taken up into †heaven in a cloud, having blessed his disciples and promised them the gift of the Holy Spirit. He sits 'at the right hand of God', which signifies his power and authority. Herbert refers to the ascension in his poetry.

Betrayal of Christ | Matthew 26:21, 47–9; Mark 14:17, 43–50; Luke 22:21, 47–8; John 13:21–30; 18:2–3

During Jesus' last week in Jerusalem, *Judas arranges with the Jewish leaders to hand Jesus over to them at a convenient time. He is paid 'thirty pieces of silver' for this (Matthew 26:15). After the *last supper, Judas slips out and returns with armed men to capture Jesus. The signal agreed is a kiss of greeting, and when Judas kisses him, Jesus is arrested and ultimately taken for trial and executed.

The name *Judas, the idiom 'thirty pieces of silver', and the notion of betrayal with a kiss are all widely used in literature. See especially poets of World War I.

Cain and Abel | GENESIS 4:1–16

Cain and Abel, the sons of *Adam and Eve, both offer gifts to God; God accepts Abel's gift but not Cain's. In his anger at this, Cain lures Abel into the fields and kills him. He is punished with exile from God's presence, and God puts a mark on him so that nobody will kill him. In literature, Cain is a symbol of deadly strife between those who are closely related: the monster Grendel who eats people in *Beowulf* is descended from Cain, and Frankenstein's monster is likened to Cain. Cain's exile and wandering also make him paradigmatic of those who live long without attachments and suffer punishment, like the Mariner in Coleridge's 'Rime of the Ancient Mariner'.

Cleansing the Temple | MATTHEW 21:12–13; JOHN 2:14–16

On *entering Jerusalem the week before his *crucifixion, Jesus goes to the Temple and angrily upturns the tables of the tradesmen and money changers, driving them out, claiming that they are turning God's house of prayer into 'a den of thieves'. This becomes paradigmatic of righteous anger against injustice.

Creation | GENESIS 1–3

Two accounts are given of creation in the first three chapters of Genesis. The first describes creation as a six-day process. First the creation of †light by the command of God, 'Let there be light'; then follow the earth's atmosphere, dry land and plant life, sun, moon and stars, the birds and sea creatures, land animals, finally culminating in man and woman, created in the image of God. On the seventh day God rests, observing that all he has created is good. The second narrative focuses on the human participants and begins with the creation of Adam from dust and his being given the care of the Garden of *Eden. There God brings the animals to Adam and he gives them names. Finally he makes *Eve out of one of Adam's ribs while he sleeps.

In the †wisdom tradition of the Old Testament and ‡apocrypha, the agent of creation was Wisdom (Job 3:19; Ecclesiasticus 24). The New Testament draws on this tradition in seeing Christ, the Word of God (John 1:1–14), in this role. It also anticipates, as does the Old Testament, a renewed creation to come.

The beauty of creation is widely celebrated in literature; for example Thomson's *The Seasons*, the Romantic poets, and Manley Hopkins. Issues relating to the creation of man feature in *Frankenstein*, and the debates relating to ‡Deism focus in part on creation.

Crucifixion | MATTHEW 27:32–56; MARK 15:16–41; LUKE 23:26–49; JOHN 19:17–37

Jesus was nailed to a †cross at Golgotha, 'the place of the skull', on the hill of Calvary outside the walls of Jerusalem. Two criminals were crucified with him, one of whom railed at him, while the other asked to be remembered when Jesus came into his kingdom. He was ridiculed by the crowd and by the Roman soldiers who offered him sour wine to drink. Most of his disciples deserted him and fled, though his mother was among the few that remained nearby. At three in the afternoon he cried out 'It is finished' and died. He was pierced in the side by a Roman soldier to check that he was dead. His body was taken down and Joseph of Arimathea laid it in a new tomb nearby.

The crucifixion is a powerful image of intense suffering and of innocent death. D.H. Lawrence uses the †cross as an image of extreme bodily feeling in his poems, while the poets of World War I use the crucifixion as an image of the horror and innocent suffering of soldiers. Aphra Behn sees Oroonoko's treatment as like crucifixion.

Eden | GENESIS 2–3

Eden is the †garden which God planted and gave over to the care of Adam. When *Adam and Eve disobey God, they are expelled from the garden and have to work hard to keep themselves. Eden thus symbolises the beauty, fruitfulness, and order of the *creation before the *fall, and the exile from Eden as privation of those things and a lack of connectedness between human beings and the world of work. See also *creation.

Emmaus | LUKE 24:13–35

Luke tells the story of how Christ appeared to two disciples after his *resurrection while they were walking on the road to Emmaus. Christ fell into step beside them and explained the scriptures to them such that they felt their hearts 'strangely warmed' though they did not immediately recognise him. They invited him to share a meal with them, and as he broke bread their eyes were suddenly opened to recognise him, but he immediately disappeared from their sight. The motif of an unrecognised but somehow familiar figure is used by T.S. Eliot in *The Waste Land*.

Entry into Jerusalem | Matthew 21:1–11; John 12:12–16

The church commemorates Jesus' triumphal entry into Jerusalem on Palm Sunday. He rides on a donkey as a king coming in peace, as foretold by the †prophet Zechariah. The crowd welcome him crying their praise and laying palm leaves in the road before him. When their excitement is criticised by the Pharisees, Jesus claims that if the crowd were silent, the very stones would cry out in worship. Aphra Behn alludes to this story in *Oroonoko*.

Eve | See *Adam and Eve

Eve is sometimes seen simply as a mother figure; but for many writers, she is a paradigm of the susceptibility of women to †temptation or represents the persuasive woman who lures men into ‡sin.

Exodus, Egypt, Promised Land | Exodus, Joshua

Exodus is the story of how God led the people of Israel out of slavery in Egypt to freedom. After years of wandering in the †wilderness, they enter and settle in the land he promised them. Moses is the leader of the people under God and gives them the *ten commandments as their basic law.

In the New Testament and more widely, the Exodus is a type of God's ‡redemption of his people fulfilled in Christ. Exodus features in debates about slavery; Egypt often symbolises physical ease, for example, in Joyce's *Ulysses*, whereas reaching the promised land is a goal that demands work and privation.

Fall | Genesis 3

The fall is the term given to the first act of humankind's disobedience against God. *Adam and Eve are forbidden by God to eat fruit from the tree of the knowledge of good and evil in the Garden of *Eden because if they eat it, they will die. However *Eve is †tempted by the serpent who questions God's command and tells her 'you will be like God': she eats, and gives some to Adam. They immediately know themselves to be naked and are ashamed and hide themselves. Thus Adam fell from his original perfection and moral purity, lost his initial close communion with God, and could look forward to a lifetime of toil, ending in death (this is sometimes known as 'the curse'). St Paul teaches that all people participate in the ‡sin and fall of Adam, and reap the consequences of death both spiritual and physical (Romans 5:12–21; I Corinthians 15:21–2).

The fall is a central symbol for loss of innocence in Herbert, Vaughan, Marvell, Milton, Swift, and Pope, for example, but the ‡Exsultet puts it in the positive light of Christ's ‡redemption.

Flood | GENESIS 6–8

Humankind after the *fall increasingly lose touch with God and turn to evil ways. God decides to destroy the earth and humankind with a flood. But one man, Noah, is righteous in God's eyes, and God tells him to build a boat, an ark, to save himself, his family, and the birds and animals. A deluge wipes out all other life, but the floodwaters abate, land reappears, and God makes a covenant with Noah never to destroy the earth with a flood again, and makes the rainbow a sign of this agreement. Poets like Vaughan and Marvell make reference to the cleansing of the flood.

Gethsemane, or the agony in the garden | MATTHEW 26:36–46;
MARK 14:32–42

After the *last supper, Jesus goes with his disciples to the Mount of Olives outside Jerusalem and in the Garden of Gethsemane, an olive grove, he instructs his disciples to pray. He goes apart from them to pray and, deeply anguished, cries out to his Father to release him from his task — 'may this cup be taken from me'. Yet he submits to his Father, 'Yet not as I will but as you will.' In Luke's account, such is Jesus' agony that he sweats drops of blood and an †angel comes to strengthen him (Luke 22:43–4). Three times he returns to his disciples and finds them sleeping, rebuking them with the words 'the spirit is willing but the body [or flesh] is weak'.

Gethsemane is an important image for poets of World War I, especially Kipling and Owen, but T.S. Eliot also alludes to it in *The Waste Land*. For Christian writers, like Herbert, Hopkins, and Elizabeth Barrett Browning, Gethsemane represents their struggle to obey God.

Good Shepherd | JOHN 10:1–18

Drawing on the Old Testament tradition of God being a shepherd to his people (for example in Psalm 23:1; Isaiah 40:11), Jesus refers to himself as the good shepherd who lays down his life for his sheep; the *hireling, he says, runs when he sees dangerous animals approaching the flock. In literature, priests and ministers in the church are 'pastors', that is shepherds, and how they look after their flock, the ordinary folk for whom they are responsible, determines whether they are worthy shepherds or hirelings. This image is much used in Langland, Chaucer, and the Wakefield *Second Shepherds' Play*, but also in Goldsmith's work.

Hireling Shepherd | SEE *GOOD SHEPHERD

Judas | See *Betrayal of Christ

There are slightly different traditions relating to Judas in the Bible, but after he has taken the money to betray Jesus, and done the deed, Judas kills himself in remorse, or dies (Matthew 27:3–10; Acts 1:18–19). The money is used to buy a field called 'Field of Blood'. Judas is a significant image for war poets such as Wilfred Owen and Edith Sitwell.

Lamb of God | JOHN 1:29; REVELATION 5:6, 12

In the Old Testament, the lamb was one of the principal victims in the †sacrifices. John the Baptist sees Jesus as fulfilling this sacrificial and saving role, 'Look, the Lamb of God, who takes away the sin of the world!' In the book of Revelation, the Lamb is at the centre of the throne of †heaven, bearing the marks of his death, but receiving praise and honour for his victory over ‡sin and death. The Lamb is especially significant in the Wakefield *Second Shepherds' Play* and Christopher Smart's 'Jubilate Agno'.

Last supper | MATTHEW 26:17–30; MARK 14:12–26; LUKE 22:7–38; JOHN 13–17; I CORINTHIANS 11:17–33

On the night before he was *crucified, Jesus celebrated the Passover meal with his disciples. At one point he got up to wash the feet of his disciples, to the consternation of Peter. During the meal Jesus hinted that *Judas would *betray him to the authorities, and during the evening Judas slipped out to do just that. Jesus instituted the communion service at this time by saying that the bread of the Passover represented his broken body, while the wine was his blood. In Christian tradition, the last supper is commemorated in the ‡mass for Catholics, the ‡eucharist for Anglicans, and communion for nonconformists. See especially George Herbert's poem 'Love (III)'.

Nativity | MATTHEW 1:18–2:23; LUKE 1:26–2:52

The nativity comprises the stories surrounding Jesus' birth which are found at the beginning of Matthew and Luke. The main stories tell of the appearance to †Mary of the †angel Gabriel foretelling Christ's birth, known as the *annunciation; the birth itself in a stable in Bethlehem; the angels appearing to shepherds outside the town; the worship of the shepherds; and the arrival of three Wise Men from the East bearing gifts for a king, gifts of gold, frankincense, and myrrh. Warned in a dream that King Herod intends to kill the child, Joseph and Mary flee to Egypt.

In literature, the nativity and Christmas are linked especially with hope: see Southwell, Crashaw, Milton. Christmas is also important for other reasons: the festivities prompt the 'beheading game' in *Sir Gawain*, and remind Tennyson of his loss in *In Memoriam*.

Parable of the good Samaritan | LUKE 10:25–37

This story of Jesus tells of a man on a journey who was attacked and robbed. Two religious characters saw him lying by the road and did not help him; but a despised foreigner, a Samaritan, saw him and helped him, even paying for him to stay at an inn until he was better. The parable is told in answer to a man enquiring about what he needs to do to gain eternal life, and wanting to know who his neighbour is so that he can keep the commandment 'Love your neighbour as yourself' (25–9). The man is sure he has done everything he should do to please God. Jesus' story shows that the Samaritan is one whose generosity comes from the heart without calculation. It ignores social barriers. Jews and Samaritans hated each other, and a Jew would have found being told to be like a Samaritan offensive; it is notable that Jesus' questioner does not use the word 'Samaritan' (37). In literature, someone who freely and generously helps someone, particularly someone to whom they owe no obligation, is called 'a good Samaritan'. The image is applied to Jesus in *Piers Plowman*.

Parable of the lost sheep | MATTHEW 18:10–14; LUKE 15:1–7

In this parable, a man with a hundred sheep discovers that he has lost one. He leaves the flock to search for the lost sheep and is overjoyed when he finds it. The parable teaches the value of the individual, the †love of God the shepherd, and the joy in †heaven when anyone ‡repents of ‡sin. The parable is used by Langland and Goldsmith.

Parable of the pearl of great price (or 'the fine pearl') | MATTHEW 13:45

A merchant in pearls finds a superlative one and sells everything he has to buy it. The parable is one of a group in which the teaching is prefaced by the words 'the kingdom of heaven is like …', intended to show how important and valuable being part of that kingdom is: it is 'all or nothing'. Crashaw uses this parable.

Parable of the prodigal son (or 'the lost son') | LUKE 15:11–32

In this parable, a younger son claims his inheritance from his father and leaves home, squandering his money in loose living in a distant country. Ending up in extreme poverty, he decides to return home and to offer himself as a mere servant in his father's house. His father sees him arriving and runs to meet him, embracing him and welcoming him home with unconditional ‡forgiveness. The father kills the 'fatted calf' for a celebratory feast and clothes his son in his best robe. The elder brother is irritated by this since he has remained faithfully at home all the time without reward, and refuses to join in the celebrations for his brother who 'was lost and is found'. The parable presents the essence of the gospel: the forgiving, loving father welcomes the ‡repentant son back home. In the portrait of the elder brother it perhaps takes a swipe at the joylessness of the Pharisees who dismissed 'sinners'. This parable finds echoes in themes of homecoming and welcome for the undeserving in literature. Julian of Norwich uses it, as does *Everyman*, and later Goldsmith also.

Parable of the rich fool who pulled down his barns | Luke 12:16–21

Jesus tells this parable when a man in the crowd asks him to tell his brother he should give him his share of the family inheritance. After delivering a warning against greed, Jesus tells the story of a rich man whose land was so productive that his barns were no longer big enough to contain all his crops. He decided to tear them down and build bigger ones to store the produce. He then sits back, with more than enough to last him for years to come, and tells himself to take life easy and 'eat, drink and be merry'. But he is called a fool, for that night he will die, and someone else will have the benefit of it all. In literature, this parable is associated with being prepared for death, and not relying on wealth: life is uncertain, and particularly in earlier literature, such as *Everyman*, good deeds are regarded as 'treasures in heaven'. Donne also makes use of this parable.

Parable of the rich man and Lazarus | Luke 16:19–31

The beggar Lazarus sits begging at a rich man's gate. He goes hungry and his body is covered with sores, while the rich man indulges himself extravagantly day after day. After his death the position is reversed: Lazarus rests in 'Abraham's bosom' while the rich man burns in †hell. The rich man pleads with Abraham to send Lazarus to him with a sip of water, but Abraham says he cannot due to the great gulf between them. The rich man subsequently asks for Lazarus to return to call on his five brothers to ‡repent so that they might escape similar torment. Abraham refuses, saying they 'have Moses and the prophets'. Even if someone returned to them from the dead — hinting at Christ's *resurrection — they would not change their ways. This ending suggests the parable is directed against those who refuse to respond to the gospel. There are also strong moral lessons to be learned against greed and in favour of giving to the poor.

This parable is widely used in literature: see especially Goldsmith and Sitwell.

Parable of the sheep and goats | MATTHEW 25:31–46

This is one of several †parables told by Jesus concerning his *second coming and the end of the world. It shows how when he returns he will sit in glory upon a throne with the nations gathered before him. He shall separate them like a shepherd dividing sheep from goats, the sheep to his right, the goats to his left. Then he will welcome the 'sheep' into their inheritance in his kingdom and eternal life for, he says, 'I was hungry and you gave me something to eat, thirsty and you gave me something to drink …' — in effect, whenever they helped the poor and needy, it was as if they had helped Christ himself. Those on his left he sends into eternal fire, for they did not serve the needy and so did not serve Christ.

This parable is used in literature as emblematic of the †last judgment in the Wakefield *Second Shepherds' Play*, and Donne, but also in Goldsmith's work in the context of social concern.

Parable of the talents | MATTHEW 25:14–30; AND SEE LUKE 19:11–27

In this parable, a man gives money to his servants when he is going away for a time. When he returns, he finds that some of his servants have used the property well and earned more with it, but one has not but has simply kept the money idle. The productive servants are rewarded, the unproductive one punished. The point of the parable is that everyone has been given gifts, and if they are not used they go to waste. The word 'talent' for a gift or ability is a biblical coinage in English, and thus this parable can be seen to have had a significant influence on literature; but see also Carlyle, who makes specific reference to it.

Parable of the unjust judge (or 'the persistent widow') | LUKE 18:1–8

This is prefaced by 'Jesus told a parable to show [his disciples] that they should always pray and not give up' (1). A wronged widow appeals to a judge who cares for nobody. She is so persistent that eventually the judge grants her justice, so that she will simply leave him alone. Jesus says that God is not like that but will respond to prayer quickly. In literature, the persistence of the widow is more often the focus of allusion than the message that God responds quickly. The nature of the Judge himself is of significance in Bacon's work.

Parable of the wedding feast | MATTHEW 22:1–14 (AND COMPARE
LUKE 14:15–23)

In the parable a man has prepared a great banquet, and sends his servants to tell the invited guests that all is ready. The guests make excuses, so the man sends his servants to collect people wherever they can find them. The thrust of the story is that the 'religious' people for whom the kingdom was prepared do not enjoy it, but the outcasts and ‡sinners who respond to the servants do. In literature this parable links in with others, particularly in its use of feasting as a symbol of the joys of †heaven. See *Everyman* and especially the †wedding feast of the Lamb.

Parable of the wicked tenants | MATTHEW 21:33–41; MARK 12:1–9; LUKE 20:9–19

A landowner cultivates a new vineyard, complete with winepress, walls, and tower, rents it out to tenants, and goes away on a journey. At harvest time he sends servants to take delivery of his produce, but the tenants beat and kill them. He sends a larger group of servants and the same happens to them. Finally he sends his own son, thinking they will treat him with respect. Rather, the tenants kill him too, thinking they can seize the vineyard for themselves. Jesus asks what the owner himself will do when he arrives. The answer comes: he will bring them all to destruction and rent the vineyard out to more responsible growers. The parable picks up an Old Testament image for the Jewish people as God's vineyard, let out to religious leaders; and it predicts the death of Jesus as God's Son at their hands, because he asks them to account for their stewardship and give God his rightful due. See *Ancrene Riwle*.

Parable of the wise and foolish virgins (or 'the ten virgins') | MATTHEW 25:1–13

Another parable of the kingdom of †heaven, this focuses on girls waiting on the bridegroom's arrival. Five of them have prepared themselves, having enough oil for their lamps, but another five run out of oil just at the crucial moment. The latter hurry off to get more oil and miss the party. The teaching here concludes, 'keep watch, because you do not know the day or the hour' when the bridegroom, Christ, will come. Here, once more (as in the *parable of the wedding feast), heaven is seen as a banquet, but the focus of the story is on being prepared for Christ's *second coming. See Langland's *Piers Plowman*.

Parable of the workers in the vineyard | MATTHEW 20:1–16

A parable of the kingdom, this tells the story of a man who hires workers at various stages of the day to work in his vineyard. At the end of the day, he pays them all the same wage. Some complain that they have worked longer than others, but the master responds that he can choose what he does with his money, and he wants to be generous. In God's kingdom, there is no distinction between those who have laboured long and those who come late: 'the last will be first' (16). See Donne.

Pentecost | ACTS 2

Pentecost is the Jewish festival that was being celebrated in Jerusalem when Christ's promise to send the Holy Spirit upon his disciples was fulfilled. One hundred and twenty of them are gathered in secret in an upper room for prayer when the Spirit comes upon them with the sound of a mighty rushing wind and the appearance of tongues of fire over their heads. Filled with the power of God they go out boldly into the streets of the city to praise God and preach to the people. The praise and excitement suggest to some that they are drunk, but the cosmopolitan mix of races that are present in the city are amazed to understand them, each in their own language. Peter preaches a sermon through which 3,000 are converted. For the motif of the coming of the Holy Spirit, see Donne, Herbert, and Auden.

Resurrection | MATTHEW 28:1–15; MARK 16:1–13; LUKE 24:1–12; JOHN 20

On the third day after Jesus' death, early in the morning after the Sabbath, a number of women go to the tomb to anoint Jesus' body, but find the stone rolled away from its entrance and the tomb empty. †Angels appear to them announcing that Christ has risen. Other resurrection narratives include the disciples Peter and John running to the tomb to verify that the body is gone, Mary Magdalene outside the tomb mistaking the risen Christ for a gardener, and Christ's appearance to the disciples in a locked room in Jerusalem later that day and on several other occasions.

Jesus' resurrection is important in Christian poetry, such as Herbert's, and Auden's 'Horae Canonicae'. But the concept of resurrection is a very important literary symbol of hope in a world subject to death and decay.

Second Coming | MATTHEW 24:26–7, 36–44; 26:46; LUKE 21:27; ACTS 1:11; I THESSALONIANS 4:13–5:11; HEBREW 9:28; REVELATION 1:7; 3:11 ETC.

The return of Christ is †prophesied throughout the New Testament. For example, Christ states it will occur during a time of great trial and with cataclysmic signs in the heavens. St Paul speaks of a final trumpet call when the dead are raised to meet Christ in the air. John's ‡apocalyptic vision that ends the New Testament tells of God's †judgement on evildoers, the famed battle of Armageddon, and the glory of a new †heaven and a new earth into which the blessed will enter.

Writers as diverse as the poet of *The Dream of the Rood*, Hopkins and Auden use the story of Christ's return both as a narrative in itself and as a reminder for the need to be spiritually prepared. Others, such as Malory and Yeats, use the idea more loosely.

Sermon on the Mount | MATTHEW 5–7 (AND SEE ALSO THE SIMILAR SERMON ON THE PLAIN, LUKE 6:17–49)

This is a collection of Jesus' core teachings and focuses on the transformed attitudes and actions of those who follow him. The values of his kingdom are entirely different from those espoused by the religious leaders of his day and the world at large.

In literature, the sermon on the mount is a kind of touchstone of Christian behaviour. Many of the most familiar Christian ideas are found here: not only the Beatitudes and the Lord's Prayer, but also expressions that have entered the common idiom — 'salt of the earth', 'jot or tittle', 'an eye for an eye', 'love your enemies', 'do not let your left hand know what your right hand is doing', and many another. The sermon is used extensively in Jonson, Vaughan, Pope, and Goldsmith.

Ten Commandments | EXODUS 20:1–17; DEUTERONOMY 5:6–21

Moses was given these fundamental laws by God for the people when the Israelites were wandering in the desert. The commandments deal with two principal obligations: to honour and worship God properly, and to behave rightly towards others. Christopher Smart uses the biblical ideas, and D.H. Lawrence adapts them.

Woman of Samaria | JOHN 4:1–38

In this story Jesus talks alone with a woman at a well. The woman has had five husbands and is living with another man. She becomes convinced that Jesus is the promised Messiah, and tells all the people of her village, who also believe. Chaucer uses this story to make oblique comment on the Wife of Bath.

2. † CHRISTIAN THEMES

Angels

Angels are pure spirits created before humankind. Biblically they are understood primarily as messengers of God and one of the means God uses to communicate with his people. In the biblical tradition three are named: Raphael in the ‡apocryphal book of Tobit; Gabriel, who announces to the

Virgin †Mary that she will bear the Messiah (the *annunciation, Luke 1:26–38); Michael, who thrusts †Satan down in the book of Revelation (12:9).

Angels attend, help, and minister to people: they tell the shepherds about the birth of the baby Jesus (Luke 2:8–14), one helps Jesus in *Gethsemane (Luke 22:43), and another rescues Peter from prison (Acts 12:7–10). In the *nativity and *resurrection narratives, angels are radiantly beautiful (Matthew 28:3; Luke 2:9, for example). In literature, angels are similarly messengers, guardians, and ministers: see *The Dream of the Rood*, Malory, Spenser, Herbert, Marvell, Addison and Steele, Pope, Blake, Coleridge, and Barrett Browning. The popular notion of an angel, one who is outstandingly kind or (usually a woman) who is particularly beautiful, is also widely found in literature.

Baptism

Baptism denotes both the event in the gospels in which Jesus' identity as God's Son is affirmed, and the rite through which Christians are initiated into Christianity. Jesus was baptised by John the Baptist in the River Jordan, and as Jesus came up out of the water, the Holy Spirit descended upon him in the form of a dove (Matthew 3:13–17; Mark 1:9–11; Luke 3:21–3). In the rest of the New Testament, baptism is the normal sign of ‡repentance and entering into the church, and is associated with the gift of the Holy Spirit (for example Acts 2:38; I Corinthians 12:13). Baptism also symbolises death to ‡sin, burial, and *resurrection to new life for the believer (Romans 6:4; Colossians 2:12). These are all themes that water may allude to in literature: see *King Lear*, Crashaw, Marvell, and Lawrence.

Castle

In literature, the house or castle often represents the ‡soul. The image of the house is used in the biblical tradition, where in the Song of Songs the lover knocks at the door of the loved one's house (5:2–6), and in the book of Revelation, Jesus likewise stands at the door and knocks (3:20). In medieval and later literary tradition, the castle also represents the soul, this time under siege by †temptation and ‡sin. For this motif, see *Ancrene Riwle*, medieval drama, Donne, Browning, Brontë, and MacDonald.

City

Biblically we find both negative and positive images of the city. In Genesis, the city is a place of depravity and ‡sin, as in Sodom and Gomorrah; likewise in the book of Revelation, Babylon (possibly representing the city of

Rome) stands in opposition to God. Positively, the city also represents the earthly dwelling place of God in Jerusalem in the Old Testament and the fulfilment of God's relationship with humanity in the coming of the New Jerusalem, again in the book of Revelation (21:2).

In its negative usage the city becomes an image of the world as shaped by ‡sin, disobedience, and pride, and their consequences. It denotes a superficially alluring but false environment with values in opposition to God's. It is another expression of the concept of 'the world' found frequently in St John's Gospel: those who follow the 'way of the world' are generally drawn to the city where they are †tempted and fall into sin. The city is thus the polar opposite of the innocence of the †garden. The image contributes to the town — country debate which originates in Latin literature, but continues in English. See Goldsmith, Cowper, Blake, and MacDonald.

Cross

The cross is an ambivalent symbol, one of the central paradoxes of Christian theology. It is the means of execution for Jesus and the ultimate symbol of his victory. It is a source of physical torment, but also of spiritual exaltation. The ambivalence is brilliantly exploited by the poet of *The Dream of the Rood*. In the poem, the cross is both beautiful and horrible, both a means of death and a way of life. It is a central symbol in literature, where as well as referring to the cross of Jesus' *crucifixion, it also refers to ‡penitent and self-sacrificial attitudes (Matthew 10:38; Mark 8:34; Luke 9:23): see *The Dream of the Rood*, the medieval lyrics, Spenser, Donne, Herbert, Bunyan, Behn, Wilde, poets of World War I, Lawrence and Kavanagh. See also *crucifixion.

Darkness | See Light.

Desert | See †Wilderness.

Devil(s)

The devil, †Satan, is the leader of the rebellious †angels, changed into devils or demons, who were driven out of †heaven and fell into †hell. In art and literature they are sometimes horned, with tails (see Conrad, for example), and †tempt, trouble, and torment people (see, for example, the ‡Vice and Mephistophilis in *Doctor Faustus*). See †Satan.

Garden

According to Genesis 2, humankind is created to care for a garden, the Garden of *Eden, in which everything they require is provided in abundance.

Harmony is evident between God and Adam who talk to each other freely; Adam is able to share in God's power in naming the animals. Harmony, too, characterises the relationship between human and non-human *creation. Work is not necessary for the production of food, nor do animals prey on one another for food. Equally harmony reigns between *Adam and Eve. God only forbids eating the fruit of the tree of knowledge of good and evil at the centre of the garden. Both innocence and harmony are lost when Adam and Eve disobey God and eat this fruit.

The garden is therefore an image of a lost golden age of harmony and innocence to which people aspire to return. This image is associated in literature with the debate between town and country. See Goldsmith, Cowper, Blake, and MacDonald. See also *Gethsemane.

Harrowing of hell

This is the belief that after Jesus died and before his *resurrection he descended into †hell to set free all those who had been waiting for his coming. The notion is hinted at in the Bible and the ‡creeds. In Ephesians 4:8–9, Christ ascends with captives from the 'lower regions', and in I Peter 3:19 and 4:6, Jesus preaches to the ‡souls in captivity in hell. The reference in the creeds to Christ's descent to 'the dead' or hell was interpreted in this fashion as a heroic expedition to rescue souls from captivity (see *The Dream of the Rood*).

In Christian thinking, since all humankind had been estranged from God as a result of †original sin, no-one could enter †heaven until Christ's death and *resurrection. St Paul taught that all die in Adam and would be made alive in Christ (I Corinthians 15:22). The righteous people who served God by following the Jewish law would be saved by Christ: this belief is expressed in the iconography of the Orthodox church in which the risen Christ is depicted pulling *Adam and Eve out of †hell. See *The Dream of the Rood*, Langland, and poets of World War I, especially Sassoon and Owen.

Heaven

Heaven is the dwelling place of God in glory, where he is praised and his presence is enjoyed by the †angels and by those who have been perfected in †love. The term 'place' is to be understood figuratively. God is spirit and exists in eternity: expressions of time and place are used metaphorically since God is subject to neither. Nevertheless, the joys of heaven are often imaged in very physical terms in literature, both biblical and other—see the †wedding feast of the Lamb, for example.

In some parts of the biblical tradition, Matthew in particular, 'heaven' is a polite alternative for 'God': Matthew's 'kingdom of heaven' equates to Mark's and Luke's 'kingdom of God'. This pattern of usage is found in English literature, too, and it is sometimes difficult to distinguish reference to 'heaven' or 'heavens' from reference to God himself.

To be in heaven is to be permanently in the unveiled presence of God, an experience of supreme bliss. This is sometimes referred to as enjoying the 'beatific vision'. At the end of all things, there will be 'a new heaven and a new earth ... the Holy City, the new Jerusalem' (Revelation 21:1 – 2). Heaven is used very widely throughout English literature both in a loose sense for extreme pleasure, and in its more precise Christian sense as the destiny of those who are saved by Christ.

Hell

Like †heaven, the idea of place in relation to hell must be understood figuratively. It is the dwelling place of the fallen †angels who rebelled against God and of all those who have definitively rejected God. In much Christian thought, to be in hell is to be permanently excluded from the presence of God, in full knowledge of the deprivation of joy such exclusion entails. The Christian imagination has developed an iconography of physical torture and tormenting †devils out of the New Testament references to the fires and pain of hell (see, for example, Matthew 3:12; 18:8; 25:41; Revelation 20:10) as we find, for example, in the paintings of Hieronymus Bosch and in medieval images of the †last judgement. Like heaven, hell is used very widely throughout English literature both in a loose sense for extreme suffering, and in its more precise Christian sense. See also †harrowing of hell.

House | See Castle.

Incarnation

Incarnation means 'becoming or taking on flesh', and it principally refers to the central mystery of Christianity, that in Christ, God became a human being. The biblical material interpreted as pointing to the incarnation is varied: from Isaiah and the Psalms to the gospels and epistles — John 1:14 'The Word became flesh', and Philippians 2:7 'being made in human likeness', are perhaps among the clearest references. The humanity of Jesus is clear from the gospels: he was weary, hungry, thirsty, and suffered on the †cross. His divinity appears in his claims to equality with God and is vindicated by his miracles and *resurrection. The letter to the Hebrews spells out some of the implications of the incarnation: Jesus was 'tempted in every way, just as we are—yet was without sin', so can 'sympathise with our weaknesses' (4:15). The precise nature of the incarnation was much debated in the church, and the ‡creeds represent the doctrines that became accepted as orthodox.

In Christ, God sends his Son to share the human condition and suffer the penalty of human ‡sin. Christ thus both is human and represents humanity in the Godhead. God understands humanity from the inside, not just as creator, but also as one who shares the essential nature of humanity.

The incarnation is a central theme in literature: see the medieval lyrics, Julian of Norwich, *The Second Shepherds' Play*, Donne, Behn, Browning, Eliot, Auden, and Kavanagh.

Journey | See †Quest.

Judgement, judge | See †Last Judgement.

Lamb of sacrifice

In the Old Testament, making a sacrifice, often of a lamb, was a way of repairing one's relationship with God. In particular, the blood of the animal, representing its life, symbolised the seriousness of ‡sin and the fact that sin results in death. Sin is symbolically transferred to the innocent animal that is killed, and the animal's innocence is symbolically attributed to the one making the sacrifice. Thus the sin is dealt with by the real death of an innocent victim being accepted by God as representing another. In the New Testament Jesus is identified by John the Baptist as 'the Lamb of God who takes away the sin of the world' (John 1:29). Jesus becomes the innocent victim, the Lamb who takes the sin of humankind upon himself and dies on their behalf. The biblical book of Hebrews particularly explores the role of †sacrifice in Christianity.

In literature this theme is found in references to taking another's place in relation particularly to suffering and death (see the poets of World War I). It also gives rise to the associations of lambs and innocence with victims and sacrifice: see particularly *The Second Shepherds' Play* and the medieval lyrics, but also the entry on †sacrifice. See also ‡Eucharist.

Last Judgement

Biblically, the last judgement is associated with the end of the world, often referred to as the day of the Lord in the Old Testament (see, for example, Joel 1:15; Amos 5:18–20) and Christ's *second coming in the New. All people will be judged, and the dead await judgement at the last day. There is thus a close relationship between death and judgement (Hebrews 9:27). In various books in the Bible, the judgement is pictured as taking place in a court with God as supreme judge, and all people assembled before him (see, for example, Matthew 25:31–46, the *parable of the sheep and goats, Romans 14:10 and Revelation 20:12). Frequently people are said to be judged according to their deeds (see the references just given), and in early literature such as *Everyman*, the process is depicted rather crudely as balancing an individual's good and bad deeds in an account book or on a set of scales.

The essential features of the last judgement in the Christian tradition are that God's judgement is utterly just and final. It sets all things right, giving punishment and reward where these are due. And it makes an end of injustice, wrong, fear, and inequity: in Revelation 20:14, death and †hell are themselves destroyed.

The theme of judgement is widely used in literature. Sometimes we find a picture similar to the biblical courtroom, as in *The Dream of the Rood* and the ‡mystery plays. Often, the theme of judgement is associated with wicked people getting their come-uppance: some thus welcome it; for others it is a fearful prospect, either because they fear judgement on ‡sin and feel unworthy (see Boswell), or because they know themselves to be wicked (see *Doctor Faustus*).

Light

Generally in biblical and Christian terminology darkness signifies the absence of God and light his presence; light is associated with life, and darkness with death. In the †prophecies of Isaiah, for example, the coming of God to the Israelites is the shining of light upon people who live in the darkness of (spiritual) death (see Isaiah 9:2; 60:1–3).

In the New Testament, light is primarily used in this sense in the writings of St John. The world into which Christ, the Word, is born, lies in darkness, but Christ's coming brings unquenchable light (John 1:4–9). Jesus refers to himself as 'the light of the world' (John 8:12) and gives the commission to his followers to be the same, 'You are the light of the world' (Matthew 5:14).

Darkness signifies godlessness and the desire to avoid God (John 3:19–21). At the end of time, however, all will dwell in the light of the *Lamb of God (Revelation 22:5), and the created lights of Genesis will be replaced by the glory of God himself. For the themes of light and darkness in literature, see, for example, Julian of Norwich, Conrad, Lawrence, Eliot, Beckett, Larkin, and O'Brien.

There is, however, another aspect to night in the New Testament. It is at night that Jesus prays, as in the Garden of *Gethsemane (Luke 22:39–46) and that Nicodemus seeks him (John 3:2). It can therefore also suggest a state of concealment and absence of daytime concerns in which God can be encountered. This apparent paradox is developed in the Christian ‡mystical tradition as a belief that since the light of God is too dazzling to bear, encounter with such light is experienced as darkness: see Vaughan.

Love, *agape*

There are many different kinds of love, and many words for them, both in the biblical tradition and in English. The love of God, for which the Greek word *agape* is used, is central to the Christian tradition. It refers not to merit, desert, or attractiveness in the object, but the nature of the subject: God loves wholly, freely, and without self-interest. God's love is primarily revealed in the gift of his Son (I John 4:10). Christians are commanded to love as God loves: the classic treatment of the theme in the Bible is I Corinthians 13, where the King James Bible (Authorized Version) translates *agape* as 'charity'.

There are many variations on this theme in literature, some of which interact with ideas of romantic love. This is anticipated by the traditional interpretations of the Song of Songs, which see the lover who seeks out the beloved as Christ seeking out the ‡soul, thus making the surface erotic love of the Song symbolic of the spiritual love of Christ for his bride, the church. *Ancrene Riwle* and the medieval lyrics see Christ as the lover-knight who pursues the undeserving beloved. For Blake, Coleridge, Carlyle, and Tennyson among others, love is seen as a power, a principle that maintains the order of the world, or restores it.

Marriage feast of the Lamb | See †wedding feast of the Lamb.

Mary

Mary is the mother of Jesus in the Bible, the one to whom Gabriel revealed God's purpose, who spoke the Magnificat, who ultimately followed her son to Calvary, the place of his death. She is especially venerated in the Roman Catholic tradition, in which it is believed that she was conceived without ‡sin. See also *annunciation: the words of the †angel Gabriel's greeting, 'Hail Mary …' are used as the prayer of that name.

In literature, Mary is both the pure virgin and the suffering mother. As the pure virgin, she represents attractive but unattainable womanhood and contrasts with *Eve, who fell into ‡sin; as the suffering mother, she represents the deep natural human love of a mother at its most vulnerable and in some ways is similar to Eve. The complex web of associations is best illustrated by the medieval lyrics, but see also Spenser, Crashaw, and Wilde for further examples.

Original sin

Original sin refers to the notion that when *Adam and Eve *fell, the whole future human race also fell since they are biologically descended from the original couple and inherit their nature: human nature is tainted. There are many historical variations in the doctrine, but it gives some account of the innate human tendency towards ‡sin and rebellion against God. In the medieval period, it was understood that original sin, re-enacted by each individual act of sin, merited punishment in †hell, and thus original sin is linked with the notion that Christ †harrowed hell and recaptured the ‡souls of the faithful. In several texts, the link with the Easter ‡Exsultet sets original sin in a positive light: see Langland, Julian of Norwich, and Margery Kempe. But the writers of the ‡Reformation and after tend to refer to original sin as 'corruption' and 'depravity' in human nature: see Shakespeare, Donne, Vaughan, Pope, and Carlyle.

Parables

Parables are stories with a metaphorical purpose and were one of Jesus' chief means of teaching in the gospels. There are also parables in the Old Testament such as the story of the ewe lamb told to King David by Nathan, to confront him with the wickedness of his adultery with Bathsheba (II Samuel 12:1–12). In some parables individual elements of the story may also have a particular ‡allegorical significance, such as the elder son in the *parable of the prodigal son, who seems to stand for the Jewish people (Luke 15:11–32). In general, however, biblical parables are not allegorical, and we should not look for point-for-point correspondence between each individual feature and a possible figurative meaning: see 'Bible and Prayerbook' in section 2. For parables in general, and the parabolic style, see *Ancrene Riwle*, Lanyer, Vaughan, Shelley, and Overview: The Twentieth Century. See also individual parables in Bible narratives.

Prophecy, prophet

Biblically, the prophet is one inspired by God with a message for his people. The prophet sometimes enacts the message he has to deliver and, not infrequently, suffers for declaring the unpalatable truth. Most often, prophecy is not about foretelling the future, though that sometimes features in literature: see especially Bede and Malory. The Romantic poets were particularly concerned with the notion of prophecy and their role as prophets, seers who declared an inspired message. See *Ancrene Riwle*, medieval lyrics, Donne, Smart, Barrett Browning, and Eliot.

Quest

The quest in literature has some biblical sources: in the Old Testament the wandering of the Hebrew people in the †wilderness is sometimes understood as a quest for their Promised Land. The Israelites' quest involves †temptation and testing, disobedience and renewal of relationship; it culminates in an affirmation of their identity as the chosen people of God. In the *parable of the prodigal son (Luke 15:11–32), the wastrel's journey is the consequence of ‡sin, testing, and renewal of relationship, culminating in affirmation of his identity as son and not a servant. These provide patterns for stories of the quest for identity and truth that involve experiences of tests withstood or succumbed to, degradation and ‡revelation or affirmation of identity and inheritance: see Spenser, Browning, Yeats, and Eliot. Bunyan's *Pilgrim's Progress* makes links between life, quest, and ‡pilgrimage.

Sacrifice

In St John's Gospel self-sacrifice is presented as the touchstone of †love: to lay one's life down for one's friends is its greatest expression (John 15:14). Similarly, in St Paul's teaching, Christ laid down his life for ‡sinners, as the ultimate act of God's love (Romans 5:6–8). Christ's sacrifice is commemorated in the ‡eucharist or holy communion, and thus features in the poems of the medieval period, Herbert, Crashaw, Smart, and Kavanagh. The theme of dying for others has particular resonance for the war poets, where soldiers are perceived as dying sacrificially so that others can live: see poets of the World War I, Owen. See also the †Lamb of sacrifice.

Satan, the devil

The devil, Satan, is the leader of the rebellious †angels who were driven out of †heaven and fell into †hell. These rebellious angels are identified with the †devils that seek the downfall of human beings, being essentially opposed to goodness. They are mentioned in both Old and New Testaments: see Job 4:18; Isaiah 14:12–15; Matthew 25:41; II Peter 2:4; Jude 6; Revelation 12:7–9. See also the ‡fall of the angels.

In the Old Testament, Satan is an †angel who acts as 'devil's advocate', the opponent, but he only appears a few times (in Job, he casts doubt on

Job's goodness, for example, 1:7 etc.). In the New Testament, Satan is the prince of this world, the opponent of God, the †tempter and tormenter of God's people, the denizen of †hell. Revelation 20:2 puts the ideas of Old and New Testaments together, referring to him as 'the dragon, that old serpent, which is the Devil and Satan'.

Satan is particularly important in Milton, of course; but he also features in Marlowe, Marvell, Bunyan (where he has several different names), Goldsmith, Shelley, and Beckett.

Temptation

*Adam and Eve were tempted by the serpent in the Garden of *Eden and *fell into ‡sin. After his †baptism, Jesus went into the desert, ‡fasted for forty days, and was tempted by the †devil (Matthew 4:1–11; Mark 1:12–13; Luke 4:1–13). Both of these narratives illustrate significant features of temptation in the Christian tradition. At its root, temptation comes from the tempter — †Satan, the devil, the serpent. It can be sensual or spiritual or both — *Eve was drawn by both the attractiveness of the forbidden fruit and the claim that it would make her wise; Jesus was tempted to turn stones into bread because he was hungry and because it would make him popular. John writes of the appeal of the world as 'the lust of the flesh, the lust of the eyes, and the pride of life' (I John 2:16 KJV). And being tempted is not itself sin, but part of being human: Eve at first rejects the blandishments of the tempter, and Jesus rebuffs the tempter altogether — as the writer to the Hebrews puts it, he was 'tempted in every way, just as we are — yet was without sin' (5:15).

In some literature the spiritual world is imagined as one populated by beings who tempt others: the †devil, demons, the serpent, the ‡Vice: see medieval drama and Brontë. Often there is a sexual aspect to temptation: see *Sir Gawain and the Green Knight* and Kavanagh. Other writers see encounter with temptation as spiritual battle: see Barrett Browning and MacDonald.

Wedding feast of the Lamb

This image derives from the book of Revelation 19:7, 9: 'Blessed are they which are called unto the marriage supper of the Lamb.' The wedding feast is the celebration of the union of Christ (the Lamb) and the church (the bride), the final victory of spiritual union and harmony, imaged in very concrete physical terms of feasting. John draws on and combines images from other parts of the biblical tradition: the †Lamb of sacrifice, for example, and Jesus' own teaching in the *parable of the wedding feast. The image is particularly used in reference to the ‡eucharist and †heaven. See *The Second Shepherds' Play*, *Everyman*, Donne, Herbert, and Auden.

Wilderness

The Old Testament Israelites wandered in the wilderness for forty years. During this time their relationship with God was forged through experiences of rebellion and idolatry, ‡repentance, and reaffirmed dedication. Jesus recapitulates the experience of the Israelites when he goes into the desert to ‡fast for forty days (see †temptation). The wilderness is therefore a place of temptation and of encounter with God. In literature, the desert, or wilderness, is frequently the place of testing: see *Ancrene Riwle*, Herbert, Barrett Browning, Conrad, Eliot, Joyce, and Kavanagh. See also *Exodus.

Wisdom

In the biblical tradition wisdom is a divine characteristic. In the Old Testament, wisdom is active in the creating and sustaining of the world (Job 3:19; Psalm 104:24; Jeremiah 51:15; Ecclesiasticus 24). Wisdom is sometimes personified as a beautiful woman, as for example in the book of Proverbs. An important aspect of the biblical tradition is wisdom literature, the proverbial and aphoristic style found in Job, Proverbs, Ecclesiastes, some Psalms, and the books of Wisdom and Ecclesiasticus (Sirach) in the ‡apocrypha. In these books, wisdom is not particularly an intellectual matter but is related to morality and right living; it also deals with more philosophical issues such as the problem of evil (see Job especially). In English literature, Shakespeare can be seen to be concerned with wisdom and its opposite, folly; and writers as diverse as Herbert, Shelley, Carlyle, MacDonald, and Owen deal with wisdom in a wide sense. The inheritors of the style and concerns of wisdom literature include Bacon and Johnson.

Wolf in sheep's clothing

This image derives from Matthew 7:15, 'Beware of false prophets, which come to you in sheep's clothing, but inwardly they are ravening wolves.' In the immediate context, it concerns people who appear to be something they are not, and who deceive anyone who listens to them. The wolf that can be identified as a wolf is less dangerous than the one that is disguised. The image is used with particular force in medieval literature, such as *Piers Plowman* and *The Second Shepherds' Play*, where it ties in with other images relating to sheep and shepherds. But more widely, it can be applied to any false friend, from the ‡Vice in the ‡moralities onwards.

3. ‡ CHRISTIAN TERMS

Abbot

Abbot comes from the Aramaic word 'abba' or father. It is the title given to the head of a ‡monastery that follows the *Benedictine Rule*, historically the main monastic rule in the western church.

Absolution

Absolution means literally 'being freed'. It is the term used to denote the ‡forgiveness of ‡sin in the Catholic and Orthodox ‡sacrament of reconciliation (commonly called 'confession'). It is used to convey the notion that ‡penitents have been set free from the burden of their sins or loosed from bondage to them. In pronouncing the absolution, the priest declares that God forgives the sins that have been properly ‡confessed.

Advent

Advent is from the Latin term *adventus*, meaning 'coming'. It is the season before and culminating in Christmas. Starting at the end of November, it is the traditional beginning of the church's year, and in preparing for Christ's coming as a baby (see *nativity), it also focuses on his *second coming, with reference to ‡eschatological topics.

Allegory

Allegory is a literary term for a story in which each feature, place, or character stands for an idea or a different person. For example, in Bunyan's *Pilgrim's Progress* the main character visits Vanity Fair: this stands for the lure of empty, vain, and ephemeral pleasures, worldly goods, and pastimes that distract the Christian from the pursuit of God and holiness. Everyman and the ‡Vice in the medieval ‡morality plays are typical allegorical figures.

Anchoress, Anchorite

An anchorite is a type of ‡hermit who lives in a cell, with the deliberate intention of being cut off from the world. The three women for whom the *Ancrene Riwle* was written had chosen this form of the devoted life, framed around prayer and self-denial.

Apocalypse and apocalyptic

Apocalyptic is a form of †prophetic writing that speaks in the highly-wrought language of dreams, visions, and ‡revelations usually about the end of all things or the final revelation of God. In the Bible we find forms of apocalyptic writing towards the end of the Gospels of Matthew, Mark, and Luke, when Jesus speaks of the signs of the coming of the end of the world. Apocalyptic in its fullest form is represented by the Old Testament book of Daniel and the New Testament book of Revelation, the latter also known as the 'Apocalypse'. Both of these were written at times of persecution to console and support those who suffered and to assure them of final victory. The language of dreams and visions of things to come enables the writers to speak safely of the present persecution in a code understood by the readers but not by the oppressors.

Apocrypha

Today this refers to two different types of writing. At the ‡Reformation the Protestant churches did not accept some of the Old Testament books, and chapters of books, that had been widely used by the Catholic and Orthodox churches, such as the book of Wisdom, Ecclesiasticus (Sirach), and the historical books of the Maccabees. These remained in use by the Catholic and Orthodox churches, and because of the negative connotations of apocryphal ('secret, hidden', used of the gnostic and more obviously fictional additions to the New Testament canon), became known by them as deutero-canonical ('added to the canon'). Hence it is common to see Bibles entitled 'with Apocrypha', referring to these books.

The term apocryphal is also used for those writings that circulated in the early church but were not accepted as the ‡revealed word of God (commonly called 'the canon of scripture'). These include the Protevangelium of James, a collection of stories about Jesus' early life which was very popular in the Middle Ages, and various Epistles and Acts attributed to apostles named in the canonical gospels such as Andrew or Thomas (but always written much later, and nearly always of a wildly implausible nature).

Arminianism

Jacobus Arminius (1560–1609) was a theologian of the ‡Reformation who reacted against the severity of ‡Calvinist doctrines. In particular, he argued against ‡predestination and believed that Christ died for all and that anyone, by virtue of having ‡free will, could choose to follow Christ.

Atonement

This is one term used to describe the meaning of ‡redemption by Christ. Literally it means 'to make up for' and so suggests that Christ's †sacrifice makes up to God for human ‡sin. It is often linked to the idea that God is perfectly just and so there must be some making good for the offence of human sin.

A second meaning is given it by reading it as at-one-ment: Christ ‡redeems humankind by reconciling them once more with God, making the two 'at one'.

Calvinism

Calvinism refers to the theological views of the ‡Reformation theologian John Calvin (1509–64). Calvin was based for his most productive period in Geneva, his work was continued by many, and his influence is still significant in Protestant Christianity. Calvin is known especially for his doctrine of ‡predestination, that God determines beforehand who will be saved and who ‡damned, and thus that human ‡free will is limited. Like other Reformers, with whom he did not always agree on detail, Calvin championed the idea that the Bible is pre-eminently God's word and the only source of true doctrine, and that people are acceptable to God by faith and through God's grace in Christ.

Catechism

This is a compilation of the official doctrine of a church, often in question-and-answer format. It was used in preparation of catechumens for †baptism and confirmation, and for the teaching of religion in church schools and Sunday Schools.

Confession

Generally this means to admit to ‡sins. Most official church services include a prayer of confession. In the Catholic (both Roman and Anglo-Catholic) and Orthodox churches this also describes the ‡sacrament of reconciliation, or ‡penance, in which the penitent privately confesses sins and receives ‡absolution. It also involves the performance of some form of penance intended to repair the effects of one's sin and strengthen the sinner. In the pre-‡Reformation church some sins attracted public forms of penance.

A second meaning of the term relates to confessing faith, often in times of persecution: in some parts of the church to declare faith is to confess; and those who die as Christians but not necessarily as ‡martyrs are called 'confessors' (Maximus the Confessor, a theologian, and Edward the Confessor, a king of England, are examples).

Counter-Reformation

This was the Catholic church's reformation of itself in response to the Protestant ‡Reformation. It was led by the Council of Trent 1545–63, a meeting of all the Roman Catholic bishops to define their responses to the new

Protestant doctrines. The Council reaffirmed many traditional doctrines of the church and issued the Tridentine ‡Mass, the standard rite in the Catholic church until 1969, and the Roman ‡Catechism, the document outlining basic Catholic teaching.

Creed

The word is from Latin *credo* 'I believe', the first word of most of the official creeds. Creeds are declarations of the core beliefs of Christianity, covering the nature of God and how he has saved believers through Christ. Creeds establish what a given church regards as orthodox belief. The Apostles' Creed is the simplest; the most commonly used in worship is the Nicene Creed, which came out of the Council of Nicaea of AD 325; another more complex and detailed creed is the Athanasian Creed. In more recent times the word has come to mean a more personal assemblage of beliefs.

Damnation

This refers to the belief that the ‡sinner who obdurately rejects God is consigned to †hell and so deprived for all eternity of the presence of God.

Deism

Deism arose largely with the advance of science following the Renaissance. Its fundamental idea was a belief in God as creator of the world, but a denial that God ever intervened in the world. Initially this was a rejection of such things as miracles and ‡revelation, but in due course Deism rejected much of Christian doctrine, and its 'natural religion' is hard to distinguish from rationalism.

Easter

This is the English term used to describe the day on which Jesus rose from the dead; the term 'Easter-event' refers to the sequence of Jesus' suffering, death, *resurrection, and *ascension that brings about ‡salvation.

Equivocation

Equivocation means 'speaking ambiguously', particularly in a situation where the person feels an obligation to speak truth but where unambiguous speech would have dangerous or fatal consequences.

Eschatology

This refers to the end of the world, associated with the *second coming of Christ. The traditional concerns of eschatology are 'the four last things', namely death, †judgement, †heaven, and †hell.

Eucharist

This term means 'thanksgiving' and refers either to the rite of the eucharist or ‡mass, or to the bread and wine consecrated at this rite and known to Roman Catholics as the blessed ‡sacrament. The rite recalls the *last supper when Jesus gave bread and wine to his apostles, saying it was his body and blood, anticipating his †sacrificial death on the following day.

The eucharist is thus understood to recall not only the *last supper but also the †sacrifice of Christ on the †cross and his *resurrection. Following the Jewish understanding of memory the rite is seen as 'making present' these past actions: presence at the rite involved participation in them rather than simply the act of remembrance. The rite also has a future dimension for, as a meal, it anticipates the †wedding feast of the Lamb at the end of time and therefore foreshadows the ultimate union between God and humankind (see Revelation 19:9).

As the blessed ‡sacrament, the eucharist is believed by Roman and Anglo-Catholics and Orthodox Christians to be the 'real presence' of Christ, his body and blood, rather than a symbolic presence to the faith of the worshipper.

Evangelical

From Greek *evangelion* 'good news' or 'gospel', this first of all describes any teaching, message, or way of life directly derived from the gospels or New Testament. It now also refers to one kind of Christianity that rejects the authority of tradition in church teaching and looks solely to the Bible and personal experience of ‡salvation through the †sacrificial death of Christ.

Exsultet

This is the ancient Christian hymn inviting all *creation to rejoice (exult) at the *resurrection of Christ and so at the union of †heaven and earth that it brings about. It is sung to celebrate Christ's resurrection at the Easter Vigil, a ‡mass held either on the Saturday evening preceding Easter Sunday, or in the middle of that night. It is especially notable for the positive acceptance of the bad, †original sin, because it brings about the greater good, the victory of Christ: 'O happy fault, O necessary sin of Adam, that won for us so great a Redeemer!'

Fall of the angels

This is the belief that the *fall of *Adam was not the first fall. Some of the †angels, the attendants of God, rebelled against God and were cast down to †hell, where they became †devils and remain in enmity with God and all things good. Their leader was †Satan or Lucifer, whose pride made him think himself equal to God. The tradition is based on hints found in Isaiah 14:12–15: 'How art thou fallen from heaven, O Lucifer, son of the morning!… For thou hast said in thine heart, I will ascend into heaven … I will be like the most High. Yet thou shalt be brought down to hell …', and the book of Revelation, but also reflects stories circulating in Judaism. The fall of the angels is also mentioned in II Peter 2:4. Milton's *Paradise Lost* describes the fall of the angels and its aftermath.

Fasting

To fast is to go without food (sometimes drink) in order to express sorrow for sin, to purify the ‡soul, or to seek greater inner awareness of God. It may involve total withdrawal from eating or, more commonly, restricting the amount eaten. It should not be confused with abstinence, which is abstaining from eating certain kinds of food, usually meat or animal products.

Fathers

The Fathers are those bishops and theologians who hammered out the essential doctrines and spirituality of the church; in the first eight centuries of the church, they 'fathered' the church's teaching. They include Irenaeus, Athanasius, Gregory of Nazianzen, Gregory of Nyssa, Augustine, Jerome, Gregory the Great, Leo the Great (all of these are referred to as ‡saints, and given the 'St' title). They belonged to the single church existing before the division into Roman Catholic and Orthodox churches in the eleventh century.

Forgiveness

The experience of being received back into friendship with God after ‡repentance and ‡confession (see also ‡absolution). By analogy, when we offer to put aside an offence or hurt done to us, we offer forgiveness.

Free will

Free will is the notion that human beings are free to make choices—they are not programmed or ‡predestined by God to make particular choices or take particular actions; human beings are not puppets manipulated by God. The precise nature of free will was one of the critical questions of the ‡Reformation (see ‡Calvinism, ‡Arminianism).

Friar

A friar is, literally, a brother. He belongs to one of the ‡mendicant orders or begging communities that arose in the thirteenth century. Unlike ‡monks, who remained in one place and were first and foremost dedicated to prayer and worship and often acquired fine churches, friars were committed to poverty and to travelling as preachers; they were therefore more involved in pastoral care of laypeople. They also became important in the development of the European university system. Famous friars are St Francis of Assisi, founder of the Franciscans, and St Dominic, founder of the Order of Preachers (Dominicans).

Good Friday

The day on which Jesus was tried, *crucified, and buried. 'Good' because it was through this terrible process that he brought about ‡salvation for humanity.

Hagiography

Stories of the lives of the ‡saints, emphasising their ‡virtues and the miracles and wonders God produced through them. This was one of the most popular medieval literary genres.

Heresy, heretical

The word has the original meaning of 'choice', and it implies a view not sanctioned by authority or tradition. In Christian terms, it was a belief held to be erroneous by the church: for example, the dualistic belief that matter is evil and spirit good, is the heresy of Manichaeism.

Hermit, eremitical

Hermits live in solitude. They have little or no regular contact with people in order to live in prayer and total devotion to God: this is the eremitical life. Hermits might occasionally venture out to preach or to meet with other hermits. Often they would be sought out by lay people for spiritual guidance. See also ‡anchorite.

Homily

Homilies are addresses to congregations, usually directly related to the biblical readings being used at the service in which the homily is given.

Humanism

In the Renaissance this referred to those scholars who were involved in the restoration of classical learning. They valued human learning and artistic creativity. They can be contrasted with those Christians who held such human activities and the classics in low regard because they derived merely from human nature and were not specifically Christian. Erasmus was a famous humanist.

Jesuit

The Jesuits, the Society of Jesus, were founded in 1540 by Ignatius Loyola as a teaching and missionary movement owing special obedience to the ‡pope. Since the main challenge to Roman Catholicism at the time was ‡Reformation Protestantism, it was inevitable that the Jesuits engaged with the doctrinal issues raised by Reform and came to be seen as the Catholic opposition.

Kabbalism

Kabbala comes from the Jewish word for tradition. It is in origin a ‡mystical and esoteric interpretation of some books of the Old Testament, involving angelology, cosmology, magic, and some aspects of Platonism.

Lollard

Lollards were followers of the early Protestant Wyclif or people who held similar opinions. They protested against corruption in the church in England and demanded the Bible in their own language rather than in Latin. They preached in English, using direct language and straightforward methods of interpretation. This seemed to challenge the church's authority to interpret the Bible by opening it up to personal interpretation.

Martyr

Martyr means 'witness'. In Christian tradition, a martyr is someone who is put to death for their faith.

Mass | See ‡Eucharist

The term comes from the closing words of the Latin mass—*Ite, missa est*, 'Go, you are sent out.'

Mendicant orders | See ‡Friar

As opposed to ‡monks and ‡parsons who live in one place and depend on work and income from lands and other sources, the mendicant orders of the Middle Ages, particularly the Franciscans and Dominicans, were licensed to beg. They were thus free from restrictions that applied to monks and often worked in the growing towns of the later medieval period.

Methodism

Methodism is the name of an original offshoot from Anglicanism. John and Charles Wesley founded and led the movement in the eighteenth century. Their 'method' was to provide for people to be organised into small groups or 'classes', in which they would meet regularly for instruction, counsel, and prayer. Where there was no established church, a chapel could be built with a preacher to teach the people. The movement was initially based within the Church of England, but the Wesleys were concerned with mission, and their methods were not always congenial to the establishment. Eventually the movement split off from the Anglican church, appointed its own ministers, and governed itself through its Conference. The Wesleys were remarkably prolific hymn-writers.

Monasticism

Monasticism is the lifestyle of monks. Monks live either in communities or as ‡hermits. The term derives from *monos* 'one' or 'single'; it means that the monk lives for God alone, as a celibate, single-mindedly devoted to him. In the west most monks live according to the *Rule of St Benedict*, interpreted differently by Carthusians, Cistercians, and the hermits of Camoldoli. The main work of the monk is praise of God in the 'Divine Office', services of psalms and prayers which punctuate the day and night; there is also private prayer and manual work (including, before the printing press, the copying of manuscripts). In medieval times especially, many monks were fine scholars and monasteries provided education for boys entrusted to them as oblates.

Monk | See †Monasticism.

Morality play

A popular play with a message, employing ‡allegory in its story, characters, and settings.

Mystery play

A medieval play dealing with the 'mysteries', the truths of faith, 'making doctrine human'. Mysteries were usually collected and performed in cycles of linked plays representing the whole history of ‡salvation from *creation to the *second coming of Christ at the end of time.

Mysticism, mystic

A mystic has direct, unmediated contact with God, usually as part of a life of prayer and purification. Christian mystical experience is understood as a gift from God, not a state that can be achieved by, for example, meditative techniques. The word mystical is used in a general sense for any religious or quasi-religious experience defying rational explanation.

Neoplatonism

Originating with Plotinus in the third century AD, neoplatonism combines Plato's teaching about the original transcendent Good, the One, with other Greek ideas to develop an understanding of *creation as an emanation from the One down through a hierarchy. The One gives rise to the realm of ideas or intelligence; this realm produces the realm of Soul, and therefore of ‡souls that are all parts of the one Soul. Some of these souls remain purely spiritual, but most sink into bodies, the realm of matter. ‡Salvation entails freeing 'soul' from the body that imprisons it through contemplation first of soul and then of the One, so that the process of descent into matter can be reversed.

Neoplatonism was widely influential in the early Christian world, and there was some debate between it and Christianity, but also some accommodation. Some types of ‡mysticism in which spiritual contemplation of God detaches the ‡soul from the body, may show neoplatonic influence.

Oxford Movement

This movement, also known as Tractarianism, centred around the figures of J.H. Newman, John Keble, and E.B. Pusey in the first half of the nineteenth century. They were particularly concerned to emphasise the more Catholic or High Church traditions of the Church of England against the rationalistic or liberal attitudes common at the time. The leaders of the Oxford Movement interpreted the Book of Common Prayer in the light of the teaching of the church ‡Fathers and sought to restore the dignity and ritual of the church and its ‡sacraments. The 'Tracts for the Times' (whence Tractarianism) were published between 1833 and 1841 and were the main way that the Oxford Movement disseminated their ideas.

Papal, Papacy | See ‡Pope.

Pardoner

In the medieval period, ‡forgiveness of ‡sin was seen as legal rather than theological. Even though sin was forgiven, so that sinners were not excluded from †heaven, their sin was still seen as deserving punishment which would be experienced in ‡purgatory. It was thought possible that the performance of a meritorious deed on earth could achieve a pardon or remission from such punishment. The practice arose of selling such pardons, also known as indulgences, with the funds going to good causes like church-building. It was a system open to corruption. A pardoner was a preacher licensed by the church authorities to sell pardons or indulgences.

Parson

A parson is a parish priest; an ordained minister with full responsibility for pastoral care and rights to perform the church services within his parish. In medieval times, the parson held land and received taxes, 'tithes', from the people.

Passion

From the Latin *passio*, 'suffering', this refers to the suffering of Christ before and during his *crucifixion. The gospels record that he was scourged, crowned with thorns, and made to carry the †cross to the place of execution (this would include the experience of humiliation akin to being in the medieval pillory); he was nailed to the cross, suffered thirst and the mocking of the crowd, before he died.

Patristic | See ‡Fathers

From the Latin *pater* 'father', this refers to the times and writings of the great bishop-theologians of the early church.

Penance, Penitence

Penitence is sorrow for sin; penance is an action taken to express this sorrow and in some way attempt to atone for it (compare giving a present after an argument). Repentance is the more Protestant word from the same root, and it refers to turning away from sin in a determination to change one's life. The penitential psalms were those used in the church to focus on sorrow for sin, for example Psalm 51.

Pilgrim, Pilgrimage

A pilgrimage is a †journey, alone or in company, to pray at a place associated with a holy event or person. The pilgrims of the *Canterbury Tales* are going to the tomb of St Thomas at Canterbury, for example. The purpose is devotional, to seek for help, give thanks, or as an act of ‡penance.

Pope

From the Greek and Latin words meaning 'father'. The bishop of Rome is understood by Roman Catholics to be the successor to St Peter as the visible head of the church on earth. He is head of the college of cardinals with whom he exercises his authority.

Predestination

The belief that God has chosen those whom he intends for ‡salvation. In ‡Calvinism, double predestination refers to the belief that God has foreordained some for †heaven and some for †hell.

Purgatory

Purgatory is, as it were, an ante-chamber to †heaven occupied by those who are insufficiently purified to endure the unmediated presence of God. In medieval times, good deeds, the prayers of the faithful, and the purchase of indulgences were all thought to be effective ways of shortening the time a ‡soul would have to spend in the suffering of purgatory.

Purgatory was conceptualised in penal or legal terms of punishment, and in terms of healing. The penal model considers purgatory as a place where ‡forgiven sinners endure the temporal punishment for ‡sins they have committed. God's mercy forgives them, so they are not ‡damned, but his justice requires this expiation. This view was dominant until the twentieth century in the Catholic church, which inherited the legal outlook of the Romans.

The medical model sees purgatory as a place of purgation or purification: ‡forgiven sinners may still bear moral and spiritual impurities and may not yet be fully selfless: the unmediated presence of God would cause them spiritual pain by exposing to them their lack of holiness. It is therefore a merciful experience of being purified and so rendered fit to be in that presence without suffering. The classic depiction of purgatory is Dante's *Purgatorio*.

Puritan

Puritan is a name given to the powerful extreme Protestant movement in England in the seventeenth century. They opposed all ritual and 'popery' (bishops and vestments, for example) in church, and all frivolity and levity in social life. During Cromwell's Protectorate, they suppressed festivals such as Christmas and closed the theatres, and became widely unpopular. The term is nearly always one of disapprobation in literature: Malvolio in *Twelfth Night* is referred to as a Puritan because he tries to quell Sir Toby's excessive merriment.

Recusant

After the ‡Reformation in Britain all citizens were obliged by law to attend Church of England services. Those Catholics who refused were called recusants, 'refusers'. This made them subject to heavy fines. The law was patchily enforced, but when it was, the fines often led to complete penury for the recusants.

Redemption, Redeemer

Literally redemption means the act of 'buying back' and referred to the freeing of slaves. Through Christ's †sacrifice human beings are redeemed, bought back from slavery to ‡sin and the †devil; Christ is therefore called the redeemer.

Reformation

Reformation usually refers to the period in the early sixteenth century when Protestantism grew up; the great Reformers were Martin Luther and John ‡Calvin. In time, the Reformation gained huge support throughout western Europe and became an alternative to Roman Catholicism. Luther opposed certain doctrines (celibacy of the clergy and ‡purgatory, for example) and practices (selling indulgences, for example) of Catholicism and in arguing against them proposed 'reform' of the church. Ultimately the Reformation became independent in doctrine and organisation, holding the Bible as its authority, and thus rejecting ‡papal authority and much of established tradition.

Repent, Repentance | See ‡Penitence.

Revelation

Revelation usually refers to knowledge given or gained from some other source than the normal processes of thinking. In Christian terms, the preaching of the †prophets is spoken of as revelation: God tells the prophet what he is to say, sometimes something relating to the future that he could not otherwise know. In the New Testament, Jesus is spoken of as the revelation of God, and the book of Revelation, the ‡Apocalypse, describes in vivid images the end of the world and the new order to come.

Sacrament

This is defined as 'an outward sign of inward grace, ordained by Jesus Christ, which effects what it signifies'. That is, a sacrament is an external sign of what God is doing within a person or in the world, in which the external act is not only a sign but is actually the means through which God acts. For example, when babies have water poured over them in †baptism, this is not simply a metaphor for their entering into Jesus' death, and rising into new life, but actually produces this effect in them, making them sharers in his risen life.

Roman Catholics traditionally have seven sacraments: †baptism, confirmation, the ‡eucharist, ordination, marriage, ‡penance, and extreme unction; Protestants have two, baptism and the Lord's supper (communion, eucharist). The adjective sacramental usually now refers to a way of seeing external events as having spiritual meaning.

Saint

Saints are people so holy, so united with God, that it seems that God's power works visibly through them. In Catholic thought, all people who are in †heaven are saints because they are pure and see God face to face. In medieval and later times, saints performed miracles, and after death their relics often had power to heal. Famous saints drew ‡pilgrims to the place of their tombs, and people regarded saints as mediators between them and God, whose prayers could help them in sickness or trouble.

Salvation, Saviour

Salvation is linked to the word for health. It means to be restored to spiritual health and relationship with God and to be saved from the effects and penalties of ‡sin. Jesus' death was the means by which salvation was achieved, and he is therefore the saviour.

Scholasticism

This was the way of doing philosophy and theology from the time of St Thomas Aquinas. It reconciled the philosophy of Aristotle with biblical and ‡patristic theology. See further the section on medieval theology in 'The Christian Tradition' above.

Seven deadly sins

These are the ‡sins traditionally thought to bring death to the ‡soul, opening it up to all other sins. They are: pride, avarice, lust, envy, gluttony, anger, and sloth.

Sin

An action which deliberately rejects or defies God or one's own convictions regarding goodness and right. It breaks the relationship between God and the human being. The act of sin can be physical, mental, or spiritual: for example, pride, the sin of †Satan, is initially a mental and spiritual sin.

Soul

The human being seen as a spiritual entity and not simply as a biological one, a higher animal. The aspect of human beings that makes them able to be in relationship with God. In the Christian tradition the soul is usually understood to be created by God and immortal.

Summoner

The summoner was an officer of an ecclesiastical court, sent to summon people to answer charges.

Tractarianism | See ‡Oxford Movement

Trinity

This is the Christian understanding that God is one substance (unity) in three persons (tri-). The Father, the Son Jesus, and the Holy Spirit are all equally God, though expressing the reality differently. Many images have been ventured to illustrate this doctrine, but it remains a mystery understood only by faith. Trinitarian doctrine was hammered out in the ‡patristic period, and it has since defined orthodox Christianity. Arius was the proponent of a non-Trinitarian view of Jesus in the early period, ‡Unitarians and Mormons do not hold Trinitarian views in the modern era.

In ordinary usage, any three related things or ideas can be called a 'trinity'.

Typology

Typology differs from ‡allegory in that 'types' are real events or things that are held to foreshadow the fuller ‡revelation of Christianity. In Matthew 12:40, Jesus speaks of Jonah being 'three days and three nights in the belly of a huge fish' as a type of his death and burial, being 'three days and three nights in the heart of the earth'. In Christian literature, all kinds of stories and events were interpreted as foreshadowing Christianity: as well as the Servant Songs of Isaiah, Virgil's *Æneid*, for example, was interpreted in this fashion.

Unitarianism

Unitarianism as a movement began in the ‡Reformation period, and it defines itself as not holding the doctrine of the ‡Trinity. Generally speaking, Unitarians hold doctrine of any kind loosely, preferring to allow individuals to come to their own conclusions, and being open particularly to scientific ideas and theories.

Vice, The Vice

Vices are depraved or evil habits. They weaken the ‡soul's love for God and capacity for goodness. The Vice is the character in the ‡morality play who represents the force of habitual evil in human beings. The Vice befriends the central character with the aim of destroying him or her by leading them into moral corruption (see further †wolf in sheep's clothing). The irreverence and ribaldry of the Vice often give rise to broad comedy.

Virtue

Virtue means, literally, a strength or power. Virtues are habits which make the ‡soul strong in terms of its capacity to choose the good and put it into action. Traditionally there are seven virtues just as there are ‡seven deadly sins. The virtues are the three theological virtues of faith, hope, and †love (charity); and the four cardinal virtues of prudence, temperance, fortitude, and justice. Biblically, virtues are listed by St Paul in Galatians 5:22–3 as 'the fruit of the Spirit', namely 'love, joy, peace, longsuffering, gentleness, goodness, faith, meekness, temperance'.

Index